Selected Writings
~ OF ~
# Daniel H. Ludlow

GOSPEL SCHOLARS SERIES

SELECTED WRITINGS
OF
DANIEL H. LUDLOW

DESERET BOOK COMPANY
SALT LAKE CITY, UTAH

© 2000 Daniel H. Ludlow

All rights reserved. No part of this book may be reproduced in any form or by any means without permission in writing from the publisher, Deseret Book Company, P. O. Box 30178, Salt Lake City, Utah 84130. This work is not an official publication of The Church of Jesus Christ of Latter-day Saints. The views expressed herein are the responsibility of the author and do not necessarily represent the position of the Church or of Deseret Book Company.

Deseret Book is a registered trademark of Deseret Book Company.

Library of Congress Cataloging-in-Publication Data

Ludlow, Daniel H.
  [Selections. 2000]
  Selected writings of Daniel H. Ludlow / Daniel H. Ludlow.
    p. cm. – (Gospel scholars series)
  Includes bibliographical references and index.
  ISBN 1-57345-553-9 (hardbound)
    1. Church of Jesus Christ of Latter-day Saints – Doctrines. I. Title. II. Series.
BX8695.L83 A25 2000
230'.9332–dc21
                                                                             00-021966

Printed in the United States of America   72082-6489

10 9 8 7 6 5 4 3 2 1

Contents

STUDYING THE SCRIPTURES
  1 Suggestions on Studying the Scriptures — 3
  2 The Scriptures — 17
  3 How to Get the Most from Your Study of the Old Testament — 25
  4 How to Get the Most from Your Study of the New Testament — 66
  5 How to Get the Most from Your Study of the Book of Mormon — 107
  6 How to Get the Most from Your Study of the Doctrine and Covenants — 134
  7 Bible Dictionary References as Possible Bible Footnotes — 159
  8 The Book of Mormon as a Part of God's System of Witnesses — 179
  9 The Book of Mormon and the Fulness of the Gospel — 186
10 The Book of Mormon, a Modern Scripture — 191
11 Receiving a Testimony of the Book of Mormon — 196

JESUS CHRIST AND HIS ATONEMENT
12 The Old Testament, a Witness for Jesus Christ — 203
13 Jesus Christ, the Beloved Son of God — 213
14 The Greatest Week in History — 236
15 The Greatest Gift — 249
16 The Resurrection — 261

THE PLAN OF PROGRESSION AND ETERNAL LIFE
17 The Plan of Progression and Eternal Life — 279
18 The Pre-earthly Existence of Man — 305
19 Moral Agency — 309
20 Adam and Eve in the Garden of Eden — 322
21 The Purposes of a Mortal Existence — 327

22 The Laws of Justice and Mercy	331
23 The Relationship between Grace and Works	335
24 The First Principles of the Gospel: Faith in Jesus Christ and Repentance	354
25 The Functions and Powers of the Holy Ghost	359
26 Temple Ordinances for the Living and the Dead	364
27 Spiritual and Temporal Death	369
28 The Final Frontier: The Spirit	374
29 The Postmortal Spiritual Existence	396
30 The Three Heavens, or the Three Degrees of Glory	411
31 Eternal Life or Exaltation within the Celestial Kingdom	416
32 Our Divine Destiny—A Third Dimension View	421

PROPHETS OF GOD

33 John, the Beloved Apostle	435
34 Paul—The Man and the Message	451
35 Joseph Smith, the Prophet	487

THE HOUSE OF ISRAEL

36 Joseph Smith's Contributions to an Understanding of Israel	501
37 Of the House of Israel	526
38 The Destiny of the House of Israel	535

SCRIPTURE INDEX	579
SUBJECT INDEX	588

Publisher's Preface

In recent decades, a number of exceptional Latter-day Saint scholars have expanded our understanding of many gospel subjects. Unfortunately, much of what they have written (or given as speeches) has been published for relatively small audiences; in some cases an article or paper has never been published at all. Now Deseret Book is pleased to bring together some of "the best of the best" in the Gospel Scholars Series.

KEY TO SHORTENED REFERENCES

Bible Dictionary
    Bible Dictionary. In the LDS edition of the King James Version of the Bible. Salt Lake City: The Church of Jesus Christ of Latter-day Saints, 1989.

Conference Report
    Official reports of general conference sessions of The Church of Jesus Christ of Latter-day Saints. Salt Lake City, Utah, 1899-present.

Discourses of Brigham Young
    Brigham Young. *Discourses of Brigham Young.* Selected by John A. Widtsoe. Salt Lake City: Deseret Book Co., 1954.

Doctrines of Salvation
    Joseph Fielding Smith. *Doctrines of Salvation.* Compiled by Bruce R. McConkie. 3 vols. Salt Lake City: Bookcraft, 1954–56. (Emphasis in original has not been included in quotations.)

Gospel Doctrine
    Joseph F. Smith. *Gospel Doctrine: Selections from the Sermons and Writings of Joseph F. Smith.* Salt Lake City: Deseret Book Co., 1971.

Gospel Truth
    George Q. Cannon. *Gospel Truth.* Compiled by Jerreld L. Newquist. 2 vols. in one. Salt Lake City: Deseret Book Co., 1974.

History of the Church
    Joseph Smith. *History of The Church of Jesus Christ of Latter-day Saints.* Edited by B. H. Roberts. 7 vols. Salt Lake City: The Church of Jesus Christ of Latter-day Saints, 1932–51.

Journal of Discourses
    Journal of Discourses. 26 vols. London: Latter-day Saints' Book Depot, 1854–86.

Messages of the First Presidency
    Messages of the First Presidency. Compiled by James R. Clark. 6 vols. Salt Lake City: Bookcraft, 1965–75.

Teachings of the Prophet Joseph Smith
    Joseph Smith. *Teachings of the Prophet Joseph Smith.* Selected by Joseph Fielding Smith. Salt Lake City: Deseret Book Co., 1976.

Teachings of Spencer W. Kimball
    Spencer W. Kimball. *Teachings of Spencer W. Kimball.* Edited by Edward L. Kimball. Salt Lake City: Bookcraft, 1982.

Topical Guide
    Topical Guide. In the LDS edition of the King James Version of the Bible. Salt Lake City: The Church of Jesus Christ of Latter-day Saints, 1989.

Studying the Scriptures

Chapter 1

SUGGESTIONS ON STUDYING THE SCRIPTURES

In the April 1976 general conference, President Spencer W. Kimball said, "No father, no son, no mother, no daughter should get so busy that he or she does not have time to study the scriptures."[1]

I do not recall a time in Church history when so much emphasis has been placed by the leaders of the Church on studying the scriptures. President Kimball, who emphasized so much that we should not only lengthen our stride but that we should also quicken our pace, indicated that we should also do this where scripture study is concerned. I think President Kimball was concerned that we do not have a single complete scripture in the Church—not a single one.

None of our scriptures is complete, and there are many scriptures that we do not even have. I think our Heavenly Father would like to give us these scriptures if we would live up to what we already have. But because our Heavenly Father is a loving, kind, merciful Father who is concerned with our welfare and our good, He is not going to give us more scriptures than we are willing to live and to keep—because where much is given, much is expected. If he gives us additional scriptures and we do not read those scriptures or live their teachings, then he brings us under greater condemnation. In 2 Nephi, chapter 28, the Lord has indicated exactly how he works with his children so far as the giving of scriptures is concerned:

"Wo be unto him that shall say: We have received the word of God, and we need no more of the word of God, for we have enough!

"For behold, thus saith the Lord God: I will give unto the children of men line upon line, precept upon precept, here a little and there a little; and blessed are those who hearken unto my precepts, and lend an ear unto my counsel, for they shall learn wisdom; for unto him that receiveth I will give more; and from them that shall say, We have enough, from them shall be taken away even that which they have" (vv. 29–30).

Students of Judaism and Christianity know how literally that prophecy and that statement can be fulfilled. For hundreds of years the Jewish people had their scriptures, the Torah, and they believed in those scriptures and taught them. Then our Heavenly Father decided to give them additional scriptures—the New Testament. Some of those people accepted the New Testament. In fact, nearly all of the early converts to Christianity came out of Judaism, but as a body and as a nation, the Jewish people did not accept the New Testament. The results of that rejection can be seen today. Now, not only do they not have the New Testament, but in essence they do not have the Old Testament either. Once you reject additional words from God, in effect you reject what he has already given. Whereas 2,000 years ago the Jewish people held up a standard—their Old Testament, their Torah—to the world, today those who live in Israel or have visited Israel can verify that the average Israeli is not a religious person so far as the study of the scriptures is concerned. In fact, in Israel the Bible is primarily considered to be a history book and not a book directly from God.

The Christians, of course, did quite well with the New Testament, until our Heavenly Father decided that he would give them additional scriptures. If you read the accounts and writings of Christian ministers in America 140 years ago, you will learn that they were pleading with people to study the scriptures because the scriptures contained the word of God. Two such ministers finally motivated the Prophet Joseph Smith to read the New Testament, which set his soul on fire by these words: "If any of you lack wisdom, let him ask of God, that giveth to all men liberally, and upbraideth not; and it shall be given him" (James 1:5). Those words led to the great inauguration of the dispensation of the fulness of times, but it was primarily a Reverend Green, with his teaching that the New Testament is the word of God, who motivated the Prophet Joseph Smith to seek the help that led to the First Vision.

When our Heavenly Father decided to give the Christian world additional scripture, he brought forth the Book of Mormon. Many in Christianity accepted this book—nearly all of the early converts to Mormonism came out of Christianity. But again, as a body, the Christians did not accept this new scripture, and now their New Testament has been taken away from them. A poll conducted by Dr. George M. Gallup, director of the American Institute of Public Opinion, shows how literally the New Testament has been taken from them. The poll found that the average American over twenty years of age could not name even one of the four Gospels—53 percent could not name one of the books of Matthew, Mark, Luke, or John. That is how literally the New Testament has been taken away from the Christian world.

Therefore, our living prophets and their associates have encouraged the membership of the Church to study the scriptures in hopes that we can prove worthy to receive additional scriptures. You see, our Heavenly Father is not going to give us more scriptures if we do not keep and treasure the scriptures we already have. If he did so, he would bring us under condemnation since we are responsible for all that he has given us that we do not keep.

"For behold, thus saith the Lord God; I will give unto the children of men line upon line, precept upon precept, here a little and there a little; and blessed are those who hearken unto my precepts, and lend an ear unto my counsel, for they shall learn wisdom; for unto him that receiveth I will give more; and from them that shall say, We have enough, from them shall be taken away even that which they have" (2 Nephi 28:30).

When we respond to our Heavenly Father, he gives us more. At any one time, we are responsible for all we have, including that which we do not keep. But any time he gives us more and we do not respond, then he does not give us any more, lest he bring us under greater condemnation by so doing. I think it is significant that in 1977, for the first time this century, additional scriptures were added to the scriptural canon of the Church.

In 1976, President Kimball made a special plea to the membership of the Church to read the scriptures:

"For many years the General Authorities have urged us all with increasing frequency and in a spirit of love to adopt a program of daily gospel study in our homes, both as individuals and as families. . . .

"Nevertheless, we are saddened to learn, as we travel about the stakes and missions of the Church, that there are still many of the Saints who are not reading and pondering the scriptures regularly. . . .

" . . . The prophets of old seem to cry out to us in almost every page of the scriptures, urging us to study the word of the Lord, . . . But we do not always hear, and we might well ask ourselves why. . . .

"Lest the foregoing be lightly passed over, let me pause here to point out a common error in the mind of man—that is, the tendency, when someone speaks of faithfulness or success in one thing or another, to think 'me,' and when someone mentions failure or neglect, to think 'them.' But I ask us all to honestly evaluate our performance in scripture study."[2]

We all have good intentions. I am sure there is not a person in the Church who does not believe we ought to read the scriptures, but we make excuses. Some of us might say, "Well, we have too many scriptures. You know, it would be better if we were Protestant or Catholic because then we would only have two books to read. But as Latter-day Saints we also have the Book of Mormon, the Doctrine and Covenants, and the Pearl of Great Price. We have too many scriptures." Maybe we have convinced the Lord that we have too many scriptures; otherwise, he would give us more. In our hearts, of course, we know that is not true. But in our actions, we prove it is true. We have too many scriptures.

Before President Joseph Fielding Smith became president of the Church, there is a report that he spoke of the importance of the scriptures at a stake conference he attended. During his talk, he asked the membership at that conference, "If the Brethren should publish the sealed portion of the Book of Mormon, how many of you would read the sealed portion?" And virtually every hand went up. Then President Smith asked, "May I see by a show of hands how many of you have read our present Book of Mormon." Very few hands went up. Isn't that interesting? We would all read the sealed portion if it were given to us, but we don't read the scriptures we already have.

Some people say, "Well, it's not a question of having too many scriptures, it's a question of having too little time. There are so many other things to do." And I guess one answer to that could be, "Well, how many fewer hours do you have each day than anyone else? Do you really have fewer than twenty-four hours?" Is it more a matter of priority, maybe, than time? And doesn't our Heavenly Father know how much time we have—not just in each day but in each life? He will judge as to whether we have enough time. I don't think we will determine that. I am sure our Heavenly Father would not be impressed with the excuse that we don't have enough time.

Perhaps we think other things are more important. Again, it's a matter of priority. Certainly other things are more important in certain situations. If you're in a dining room and someone begins choking on some meat, I don't think that is a good time to start reading the scriptures.

Unfortunately, most of us think the best time to read scriptures is some time other than the present. When we are young and busily making friends and associations in school, we don't have time to read the scriptures. We have too many other things to do and to learn. Best wait until we are married and have plenty of free time. But then the children come along, and we think we are even busier than before. Certainly the Lord doesn't expect us to read the scriptures when we're up half the night with the baby. We decide to wait until the children get older—until they no longer wear diapers and can take care of themselves. We'll read the scriptures then.

But the youngsters turn into teenagers and start dating, and again we're up half the night—waiting and worrying. Then, we think we'll have ample time to read and study the scriptures once they leave home. By that time, of course, most of us have difficulty reading and some of us have difficulty concentrating. So we put off reading just a little longer—first for a week, then for a month, then for a year, and finally for a lifetime—all because we do not make scripture reading a priority.

Some people say, "Well, the scriptures were written a long time ago. The Book of Mormon was started 2,600 years ago. Surely there is nothing in the Book of Mormon that can help us today. When I read about those wars and that they used swords and so on when they fought, and today we have atomic bombs and airplanes and so on, I realize there is really nothing I can learn from the Book of Mormon. The scriptures are not relevant today." One way or another, the adversary convinces us that we should not read the scriptures, or he convinces us that we should procrastinate the reading of the scriptures.

We should read them for several reasons. First of all, the Lord himself has commanded us to read the scriptures. "Search the scriptures," the Lord said, "for . . . they are they which testify of me" (John 5:39). Church leaders also encourage us to read the scriptures. Those who have read the scriptures know that they help us solve problems and gain an understanding of the gospel. By reading the scriptures, we learn to appreciate and understand other people. We also gain a testimony and understanding of our Heavenly Father and his divine Son: "This is life eternal, that they might know thee the only true God, and Jesus Christ, whom thou has sent" (John 17:3). How do we know God and about God except in the scriptures? If we don't read the scriptures, how can we possibly obtain a testimony? Just as there are many excuses for not reading the scriptures, so also are there all kinds of reasons we should be reading the scriptures.

Even if we read the scriptures, we may not spend enough meaningful time reading them properly. That is, we tend to read the scriptures as we read a novel—we can pick it up and put it down in a spare moment. It is amazing how often the scriptures and the living prophets exhort us to read and ponder the scriptures regularly. Scripture study is a little different from other types of study. We need to apply our faith, experience, and understanding each time we open the scriptures. We must do this day after day, week after week, year after year. It makes no difference how many times we have read the scriptures. When we reread them, we often see something in them we did not notice before. One reason we may not have noticed certain scriptural teachings in the past is that we may not have faced the problems we face today.

Leaders of the Church have told us why our Heavenly Father does not give us more scripture. President Joseph Fielding Smith said:

"The Lord is withholding from us a great many truths that he would gladly reveal if we were ready to receive them. . . . Until we are prepared to receive the things already given, I fear the Lord will hold from us those other things which one time will be revealed. . . . When we, the members of the Church, reach the point that we are willing to live by all that the Lord has revealed, he will give us more. . . . The Lord is withholding from us great and mighty truths because of the hardness of our hearts. Why should we clamor for more when we will not abide in what we already have?"[3]

Elder Bruce R. McConkie wrote, "When we as a people believe and conform to all of the truths we have received, we shall receive more of the mind and will and voice of the Lord. What we receive and when it comes are in large measure up to us."[4]

As indicated earlier, we do not have a single complete scripture. Certainly the Old Testament is not complete. At least seventeen books referred to in the Old Testament do not appear in that scripture. The New Testament is not a complete book either. Paul refers to other letters that are not found in the New Testament.

We as Latter-day Saints refer to the Book of Mormon as "the stick of Joseph," but at best the Book of Mormon is an abridgment of the book of Joseph. The book of Joseph would be primarily the brass plates of Laban and the large plates of Nephi. Mormon testified on at least two occasions in the Book of Mormon that he did not write one-hundredth part in his record those things that were written on the large plates of Nephi. Even then, approximately two-thirds of the plates—at least according to Orson Pratt—were sealed. The Prophet Joseph Smith did not translate a single word from those portions, so certainly the Book of Mormon is not a complete book.

The Doctrine and Covenants is not a complete book either. Joseph Fielding Smith and others have indicated that there are still many revelations to be included in the Doctrine and Covenants. President Smith said, "Not all of the revelations given to the Prophet Joseph Smith are in the Doctrine and Covenants. . . . The Church has had many other revelations, but we have in the Doctrine and Covenants revelations sufficient to bring to pass our exaltation if we will but heed them. When we, the members of the Church, reach the point that we are willing to live by all that the Lord has revealed, he will give us more that can be placed in the Doctrine and Covenants."[5]

And of course, the Pearl of Great Price is not a complete book. The Brethren have added to the Pearl of Great Price in recent years, but where is the great book of Joseph that rightfully belongs in the Pearl of Great Price? The Prophet Joseph Smith received and translated that book, but it is not published in our present Pearl of Great Price. Students of Church history and readers of the *History of the Church* will recall that in his diary, the Prophet Joseph Smith made several entries concerning his translation of the book of Joseph.

But, to date, the Church has not published the book of Joseph. This is the same Joseph who was sold into Egypt. Joseph prophesied "concerning all his seed," and of Joseph's prophecies, Nephi stated that "there are not many greater" (2 Nephi 4:2). I wonder in what ways we have failed to read and live the scriptures so that the Lord has withheld from us the great prophecies of our great-great-great forefather Joseph.

We do not have a single complete scripture in the Church, and there are many scriptures of which we don't even have a verse. Yet if we were living according to the commandments of our Heavenly Father, we would have these additional scriptures.

So how do we get off dead center so far as scripture study is concerned? We can do several things. First of all, we have to decide that we really are going to improve our scripture study. To increase our likelihood of success, we must involve others in our decision—a spouse or other family member, a roommate, a friend or acquaintance, or several people. If we let others know what our goal is, they can ask us, "How are you coming along?"

Let's assume for a moment that you commit yourself to a minimum daily reading goal of five pages per day. After you make that commitment, you ought to announce it to all your Relief Society sisters or priesthood quorum members. Suggest to these brothers or sisters that when they see you from then on, you want them to ask you, "How are you coming with your reading of five pages of scripture a day?" If you will do that one simple thing, you will start reading the scriptures because it is much easier to read five pages a day than to explain to all your sisters or brothers why you aren't doing it!

Make your reading goal realistic—something you can meet. Don't say, "Well, I am going to read 100 pages a day." Chances are, you are not going to read that much, and after a couple of failures you are going to give up. Your goal doesn't have to be too great to accomplish wonders. Five pages a day, for example, doesn't sound like much. And I doubt that there are very many Latter-day Saints who could not read five pages of scripture a day. But by reading five pages a day, you could read all 531 pages of the Book of Mormon in 107 days—less than four months. At five pages a day, you could read the Doctrine and Covenants (294 pages) in fifty-nine days—less than two months. Nevertheless, most members of the Church have never read the Doctrine and Covenants. You could read the sixty-one pages in the Pearl of Great Price in thirteen days—less than two weeks. Most members haven't read the Pearl of Great Price either. The New Testament published by the Church is 403 pages long. You could read it in eighty-one days if you read five pages a day.

If you add up the 107 days for the Book of Mormon, 59 days for the Doctrine and Covenants, 13 days for the Pearl of Great Price, and 81 days for the New Testament, you have 260 days. In less than nine months, you could read all of the Book of Mormon, Doctrine and Covenants, Pearl of Great Price, and New Testament. The Old Testament would take you a bit longer because of its size. But I don't believe we have too many scriptures or too little time. Such excuses do not justify our not reading the scriptures.

Sometimes emergencies do come up, and on those days you may be absolutely unable to read the scriptures. If you fall behind, simply use Sunday to catch up. Force yourself to keep your minimum commitment. Daily scripture reading is not a great burden, though in your mind it may seem so. What you have got to do is make it a pleasant task—make the scriptures come alive.

Psychologists tell us that we tend to remember about 10 percent of what we read, about 30 percent of what we see, and about 70 percent of what we do. If you want to increase your effectiveness in reading the scriptures from 10 percent to 70 percent, all you have to do is start living the scriptures. Liken the scriptures unto yourself. Place yourself in the position of the original author. Get involved in the story. Moroni saw a vision of all of us, and he says, "Behold, I speak unto you as if ye were present, and yet ye are not. But behold, Jesus Christ hath shown you unto me, and I know your doing" (Mormon 8:35). When you read the writings of Moroni, ask yourself this question: "What did Moroni see that would cause him to put this into the scriptures?" Moroni and other Book of Mormon prophets, including Mormon, Nephi, and Jacob, said that the Lord commanded them what to put in the scriptures. So when you read a page in the Book of Mormon, ask yourself this question: "Why did the Lord command his prophet to put this particular writing in the scriptures?" All of a sudden the scriptures will come alive for you. If you want to go one step further, put yourself in the place of one of the characters. The whole book is transformed when you become involved in it. You see things you are reading from an entirely different perspective once you become involved because you are a participant in this great experience.

As a young boy, I remember President Heber J. Grant talking about putting himself in the place of Nephi and living Nephi's experiences in the Book of Mormon's introductory chapters. I tried that, and it didn't work very well. Nephi was too good a person for me. He was so faithful and thorough in everything he did that he was simply too good for me to relate to. So I decided to relate to Laman. And thankfully, that didn't work out very well either. Finally, I found somebody in the Book of Mormon to whom I could relate in the book's early chapters—Sam. And so I became Sam when I read the Book of Mormon.

I had heard dozens of lectures and sermons on the great example of the faith of Nephi. The scripture that speakers invariably quoted was, "I will go and do the things which the Lord hath commanded, for I know that the Lord giveth no commandments unto the children of men, save he shall prepare a way for them that they may accomplish the thing which he commandeth them" (1 Nephi 3:7). This is a great statement of faith, and it was a thrill to go with my brother Nephi back to the city of Jerusalem to see how the Lord fulfilled his promise in delivering the plates of Laban into our hands and to see our safe return to our father. But Nephi's example of faith that I remember most occurred after we had spent eight years in the wilderness and finally came to the shore of a great sea—Irreantum. It was so great that you couldn't even see to the other side. Our brother Nephi came to us and said that the Lord had commanded him to build a ship so that we could cross that great sea. I guarantee you that I didn't want to get on any ship that Nephi built to cross that great sea. I joined with my brethren in saying, "Our brother is a fool, for he thinketh that he can build a ship" (1 Nephi 17:17).

But then I remember how Nephi likened the scriptures unto us, asking us whether we remembered having read about Moses. He recounted for us the great episodes in the life of Moses written in our scriptures, the brass plates of Laban.

"Now ye know that the children of Israel were in bondage; and . . . ye know that it must needs be a good thing for them, that they should be brought out of bondage. Now ye know that Moses was commanded of the Lord to do that great work; and ye know that by his word the waters of the Red Sea were divided hither and thither, and they passed through on dry ground. But ye know that the Egyptians were drowned in the Red Sea, who were the armies of Pharaoh. And ye also know that they were fed with manna in the wilderness. Yea, and ye also know that Moses, by his word according to the power of God which was in him, smote the rock, and there came forth water, that the children of Israel might quench their thirst" (1 Nephi 17:25–29).

Nephi recounted the miracles of the exodus and likened them to our situation. Then, looking at that great expanse of water, he showed the example of faith I remember most: "If God had commanded me to do all things I could do them. If he should command me that I should say unto this water, be thou earth, it should be earth; and if I should say it, it would be done. And now, if the Lord has such great power, and has wrought so many miracles among the children of men, how is it that he cannot instruct me, that I should build a ship?" (1 Nephi 17:51).

And I thought, "Well, of course, if we really believe that God created the heavens and the earth and all things which in them are, and if God could command the sea to part so the children of Israel could walk across on dry land, and if he could feed people for forty years with manna in the wilderness, why can't he tell my brother Nephi how to build a ship?" All of a sudden I wanted to help him build that ship.

When you live an experience, you seldom forget it. I think this is the lesson Elder Vaughn J. Featherstone was trying to teach the priesthood of the Church during a general conference talk delivered while he was serving as a counselor in the Presiding Bishopric.

"I believe that the scriptures have every dimension of life that we can cleave unto and find a pattern for living, if we will just go back to the scriptures and study them and learn of them," he said. "Let me tell you the greatest experience I believe I have had in all my readings of the scriptures."

Then Elder Featherstone began recounting 3 Nephi 17, in which the resurrected Jesus Christ prayed for the people using language that "cannot be written" (v. 15) and blessed their little children, who were then ministered to by angels.

"'And the multitude did see and hear and bear record . . . and they were in number about two thousand and five hundred [and ONE] souls' who were in that beautiful experience with the Savior," Elder Featherstone said. The record tells us there were 2,500 people present on that occasion, but when Elder Featherstone reads that account there were 2,501 people because he was there also.

"I want you to know I was there. . . . And I promise you that vicariously every single [person] in the Church can read the scriptures and have that same experience with all of the prophets. . . . I so testify and admonish you to read the scriptures, to go back to the sure word of God."[6]

If you want to make the scriptures come alive, all you have to do is liken them unto yourself, place yourself in them, and live them, and you will increase your effectiveness in remembering them from 10 percent to 70 percent.

Next, ponder the scriptures, relate them to everything, and live their principles. I went to the dictionary to see what the word "ponder" means because it is used so many times in the scriptures regarding the reading of the scriptures. Ponder means to meditate on, to think through, to wonder about. Let me give you a few references in the scriptures where the word "ponder" is found.

When the angel appeared to Mary to tell her that she was to be the mother of Christ, Luke 2:19 says, "Mary kept these things, and pondered them in her heart." Nephi, in discussing his writings, says, "I write the things of my soul, . . . For my soul delighteth in the scriptures, and my heart pondereth them . . . and my heart pondereth continually upon the things which I have seen and heard" (1 Nephi 4:15–16). On another occasion, he says, "Behold, my beloved brethren, I suppose that ye ponder somewhat in your hearts concerning that which ye should do after ye have entered in by the way" (2 Nephi 32:1). In the book of Helaman we read, "And it came to pass that Nephi went his way towards his own house, pondering upon the things which the Lord had shown unto him. And it came to pass as he was thus pondering—being much cast down because of the wickedness of the people of the Nephites . . . —and it came to pass as he was thus pondering in his heart, behold, a voice came unto him saying: Blessed art thou, Nephi" (Helaman 10:2–4). During the resurrected Lord's visit to the Nephites, he taught the people for a full day, then made this remarkable and significant statement, "Go ye unto your homes, and ponder upon the things which I have said, and ask of the Father, in my name, that ye may understand, and prepare your minds for the morrow, and I come unto you again" (3 Nephi 17:3).

Ponder the scriptures. Learn to understand them. Prepare your minds for other things. If you do, the scriptures will come alive for you.

A system of marking the scriptures will also help you with your studies. Marking helps you correlate scriptures and learn gospel principles. I use different colors to help me. For example, I usually use a blue pencil for anything that has to do with the house of Israel because the colors on the flag of modern Israel are blue and white. I use green, representing the newness of life, for anything that has to do with the atonement of Jesus Christ. For anything else dealing with Christ, I use yellow, representing the light of the world. If a scripture discusses the priesthood, I use purple. Purple is a kingly color, and it reminds me of a royal priesthood. I use black where the scriptures talk about the devil.

My system may not work for you. The best marking system for you is one that works for you. Some of us mark up our scriptures when we are on missions or during some other early period of our lives, and then we never change them. Perhaps we ought to develop and use a good, meaningful marking system for about five years, then review it to see how it might be improved. Once we have marked our scriptures, we tend to read only the markings rather than everything else. Maybe there is something we ought to learn that we did not see and did not mark the first time through.

I think one of the most significant publishing enterprises of the Church this century is the new Topical Guide appearing after the New Testament in the Church's edition of the Holy Bible. The 598-page Topical Guide features cross-referencing not only to books in the Old Testament and New Testament but to the Church's other scriptures—the Book of Mormon, Doctrine and Covenants, and Pearl of Great Price. Correlating scriptures is not quite as difficult as it once was because the Church has done this for us.

If you want to get the most out of your scripture study, reread the scriptures and study them systematically. Reapply scriptural principles in your life. You are not the same person today you were last year or even last week. Just because you have read the scriptures once does not mean you don't need to go back to them again and again.

Finally, I suggest that you teach the scriptures to others. An excellent way to learn something is to teach it. I can't think of a more enriching assignment in the Church than to be a gospel doctrine teacher. If we as Latter-day Saints really believed that it is important to read and understand the scriptures, every bishop in this Church would have a long list of people who have applied to be the gospel doctrine teacher. If you really want to learn the scriptures, then teach them.

I don't believe that we will ever again have any other manual in the adult curriculum of the Church except the scriptures of the Church. We may see some teacher supplements, study guides, or similar helps, but I believe the manuals of the Church from now on in the adult curriculum are going to be based on the scriptures of the Church. The Brethren are committed to the fact that they want the Latter-day Saints to become acquainted with the scriptures because they realize there is power in living the principles of the scriptures.

I honestly believe that at our final judgment we are going to be held responsible for what we do with the scriptures while we are here on the earth. The scriptures have cost some of the best blood that has ever been on this earth, including "the best blood of the nineteenth century" (D&C 135:6), even that of the Prophet

Joseph Smith. I don't think we are going to get by lightly in regards to the scriptures.

I think we might well be asked a series of questions at the final judgment. The person asking the questions might first of all ask, "Did you have opportunities to read the Book of Mormon while you were on the earth?" If we can honestly answer no, there will be no further questions and no judgment concerning that matter. If we answer yes, however, other questions might follow. As soon as we next answer no, our point of judgment will have arrived.

"Yes, you had opportunities to read the Book of Mormon. Did you read it then? Did you learn the teaching principles contained therein? Did you liken the principles unto yourself? Did you apply these principles in your life? Did you teach these principles to others, including your family?"

If we can honestly answer all these questions yes, then perhaps we will hear the joyful words, "Well done, thou good and faithful servant . . . enter thou into the joy of thy Lord" (Matthew 25:21).

In the talk cited at the outset of this chapter, President Kimball said, "I ask all to begin now to study the scriptures in earnest. . . . And perhaps the easiest and most effective way to do this is to participate in the study program of the Church. . . . It is hoped that all will support this program of scripture study—to give it great emphasis, to see that this well-correlated program of the Church is not diminished by conflicting reading or study assignments. Each of the standard works should be studied intensely in the year it is scheduled for study.

"This month we begin study in the Book of Mormon. . . . We invite you to join in this excellent opportunity, for as the Prophet Joseph Smith said, 'The Book of Mormon [is] the most correct of any book on earth, and the keystone of our religion, and a man [can] get nearer to God by abiding by its precepts than by any other book.' (*History of The Church of Jesus Christ of Latter-day Saints,* 4:461.) You will be blessed and enriched by its contents, for it was written for our day and time—'to the Lamanites, who are a remnant of the house of Israel; and also to Jew and Gentile' (title page)—a fact that is emphasized time and again by its principal authors: Nephi, Mormon, and Moroni. And although we can profit from it in many ways, perhaps learning from it something of history and of war and of peace—still its principal message is the most valuable we can ever receive: that Jesus is the Christ, the Redeemer of the world.

"May we all read the Book of Mormon prayerfully, study it carefully, and receive a testimony of its divinity. For the Savior himself said of it: 'As your Lord and your God liveth it is true.' (D&C 17:6)."[7]

That is my testimony as well. The prophets have admonished us to read not only the Book of Mormon but all the scriptures. May we read them prayerfully, study them carefully, and apply their principles diligently. And by so doing, may we receive a testimony of their divinity.

Notes

From an address delivered during a Brigham Young University Travel Studies Book of Mormon Panama cruise, January 1978.

1. Spencer W. Kimball, "Boys Need Heroes Close By," *Ensign,* May 1976, 47.
2. Spencer W. Kimball, "How Rare a Possession—the Scriptures!" *Ensign,* September 1976, 2, 4.
3. *Doctrines of Salvation,* 3:201–2.
4. Bruce R. McConkie, "A New Commandment: Save Thyself and Thy Kindred!" *Ensign,* August 1976, 11.
5. *Doctrines of Salvation,* 3:202.
6. Vaughn J. Featherstone, in Conference Report, October 1972, 112–13.
7. Spencer W. Kimball, "How Rare a Possession—the Scriptures!" 5.

Chapter 2

THE SCRIPTURES

We will be held accountable at the final judgment for what we do with the scriptures in this life. This is part of our gospel teaching. Statements from latter-day prophets, including Presidents Gordon B. Hinckley, Howard W. Hunter, Ezra Taft Benson, Spencer W. Kimball, Joseph Fielding Smith, and other leaders make this amply clear.

The scriptures have been given to us as a guide, a blueprint of life. We must accept and live according to their teachings if we want promised blessings, or we can reject them and suffer promised consequences.

I thrill to the words of Nephi as he tells us good-bye. Many of us read his words of farewell and get a feeling for what he is saying, but we do not analyze his words. Therefore, we do not really catch their full significance.

"And now, my beloved brethren, and also Jew, and all ye ends of the earth, hearken unto *these words* and believe in Christ; and if ye believe not in these words believe in Christ. And if ye shall believe in Christ ye will believe in these words, for they are the words of Christ . . .

"And if they are not the words of Christ, judge ye—for Christ will show unto you, with power and great glory, that they are his words, at the last day; and you and I shall stand face to face before his bar; and ye shall know that I have been commanded of him to write these things . . .

"And you that will not partake of the goodness of God, and respect *the words of the Jews,* and also *my words,* and *the words which shall proceed forth out of the mouth of the Lamb of God,* behold, I bid you an everlasting farewell, for these words shall condemn you at the last day" (2 Nephi 33:10–11, 14; emphasis added).

For Nephi, writing 600 years before Christ, the phrase "words of the Jews" refers, of course, to portions of the Old Testament found in the plates of Laban. "These words" could also refer to sections of the Old Testament, particularly Isaiah, included in Nephi's two books. "My words" are Nephi's writings in the Book of Mormon. "The words which shall proceed forth out of the mouth of the Lamb of God" surely include the Savior's words in 3 Nephi and in the New Testament, but I also believe they could include the major revelations in the Doctrine and Covenants.

"Behold, I bid you an everlasting farewell, for these words [in the Book of Mormon, the Old Testament, the New Testament, and the Doctrine and Covenants] shall condemn you at the last day. For what I seal on earth, shall be brought against you at the judgment bar; for thus hath the Lord commanded me, and I must obey" (2 Nephi 33:14–15).

These are rather sobering words. We would be wise to read and reread Nephi's farewell. His words serve as a valuable reminder that disrespecting the scriptures leads to condemnation.

I do not know a single place in the scriptures where we are exhorted to read *only*. Rather, we are told to "search [the scriptures] diligently" (Mosiah 1:7) and to "ponder [them] in [our] hearts" (Moroni 10:3). And in our day, the prophets have added the word "daily."

For example, President Hunter has said, "Not only should we study each day, but there should be a regular time set aside when we can concentrate without interference."[1]

President Harold B. Lee said, "Are you continually increasing your testimony by diligent study of the scriptures? Do you have a daily habit of reading the scriptures? If we are not reading the scriptures daily, our testimonies are growing thinner; our spirituality isn't increasing in depth. We . . . must be studying the scriptures and have a daily habit."[2]

And President Hinckley added, "I should like to make a request and offer a challenge to members of the Church throughout the world and to our friends everywhere to read the Book of Mormon. . . . Read as little as one chapter a day each weekday and three chapters each Sunday."[3]

We are dual in nature. We have a physical body that we can all see, but within that physical body is a spirit that gives life to the physical body. When the spirit is not there, the body is not alive. At the time of temporal or physical death, the spirit leaves the physical body. We refer to that as a separation of body and spirit. We understand quite a bit about the physical body. We know we ought to eat certain types of food and that we should eat at regular times.

However, occasions arise when, because of an emergency or something else, we may not get three meals a day, or even one meal a day in certain circumstances. But we understand that if we go for an extended period of time without physical food, the physical body will lose its strength. In fact, if we go too long without food or water, our physical body will die.

What makes us think that our spirit body is less in need of food than our physical body? Our spirit body requires spiritual food in somewhat the same way that our physical body requires physical food. If our spirit body does not receive spiritual food on a regular basis, it becomes weaker and weaker.

We have all had experiences with family members, loved ones, or associates who were once strong in the gospel but who became somewhat indifferent, even going into inactivity or leaving the Church altogether. If you ask them whether they read the scriptures daily, almost without exception they will answer no.

"Well, no, not daily. After I got back from my mission and went back to school and had to find time to study, I sort of got out of the habit. No, I guess I do not read the scriptures every day."

Ask them if they've read them this week.

"Well, no. I really haven't read them this week."

Nor have they read them this month. In all likelihood, they haven't even read them once this year. No wonder they've drifted from the Church.

Our spirits need daily reading and pondering of the scriptures, without exception. And if we make an exception, it ought to be only a one-day exception—just as physical food every day without exception is the ideal. If an emergency arises or if it's fast Sunday, you can survive as long as you have been eating right. Likewise, you can survive a day without spiritual food as long as you've been giving your spirit the right kind of food—the food found in the scriptures.

Elder Henry B. Eyring said, "There are two great keys to inviting the Spirit to guide what words we speak as we feed others. They are the daily study of the scriptures and the power and prayer of faith."[4] That's it. Those are the only two he felt it necessary to list. The Holy Ghost will guide what we say if we study and ponder the scriptures every day.

The words of the scriptures invite the Holy Spirit. The Lord said it this way: "Seek not to declare my word, but first seek to obtain my word, and then shall your tongue be loosed; then, if you desire, you shall have my Spirit and my word, yea, the power of God unto the convincing of men" (D&C 11:21).

I think that applies to more than just missionaries and others trying to lead people into the Church. It also applies to those who are counseling others who are not members of the Church and who are not interested in becoming members of the Church but who have serious personal problems. In those circumstances, as we appeal to God for the right words, he will tell us what to say if we have learned what we should say before the situation arises.

Elder Eyring continues: "With daily study of the scriptures, we can count on this blessing even in casual conversations or in a class when we may be asked by a teacher to respond to a question. We will experience the power the Lord promised: 'Neither take ye thought beforehand what ye shall say; but treasure up in your minds continually the words of life, and it shall be given you in the very hour that portion that shall be meted unto every man' (D&C 84:85).

"We treasure the word of God not only by reading the words of the scriptures but by studying them. We may be nourished more by pondering a few words, allowing the Holy Ghost to make them treasures to us, than to pass quickly and superficially over whole chapters of scripture."[5]

Before the 1970s, we had new manuals nearly every year for the adult curriculum of the Church. In fact, we had new manuals every year for nearly all the major classes in the Church. We had a new manual for the deacons, a new manual for the teachers, and a new manual for the priests. We also had new manuals every year in the gospel doctrine classes and in the Melchizedek Priesthood quorums.

It was not until the early 1970s that Church leaders decided the Latter-day Saints should study the scriptures on a systematic basis. As a result, the Church set up an eight-year study cycle. The first year we studied the book of Genesis and the Pearl of Great Price. The second year we were to study the rest of the Old Testament. The third year was the four gospels; the fourth year the rest of the New Testament. The fifth year was the Book of Mormon through Alma 29; the sixth year the rest of the Book of Mormon. The seventh and eighth years were the Doctrine and Covenants and Church history.

We learned quite a bit from that first cycle, so the second time around we expanded the first year to include the other four books of Moses with Genesis and the Pearl of Great Price. But we never did complete that cycle because in the meantime our missionary work was bringing in approximately 300,000 converts a year. At that rate, we had 1 million new members every three years, or 2 million every six years. Therefore, every seven years we'd have approximately 2.5 million new members who had never studied the Pearl of Great Price and the first part of the Old Testament in a Church class. So the Brethren changed to the four-year cycle we have now—Old Testament, New Testament, Book of Mormon, Doctrine and Covenants and Pearl of Great Price.

The Lord tells us why it is important to study the scriptures, over and over again: "Behold, thus saith the Lord God: I will give unto the children of men line upon line, precept upon precept, here a little and there a little; and blessed are those who hearken unto my precepts, and lend an ear unto my counsel, for they shall learn wisdom; for unto him that receiveth, I will give more." Then comes a sobering thought, "From them that shall say, we have enough, from them shall be taken away even that which they have" (2 Nephi 28:30).

The Jewish people had their Torah, and they held it up to the world, and they believed in it and diligently patterned their lives after it. Then the New Testament came along. In effect, the people said, "We do not need the New Testament. We have the Old Testament." And today it is difficult to find many Jewish people who really believe the Bible to be the word of God. And after hundreds of years the Book of Mormon came forth and they said, "Another Bible? We do not need another Bible. We already have a Bible." Today we're hard-pressed to find many believing Christians who accept the scriptures as the word of God. "From them that shall say, we have enough, from them shall be taken away even that which they have." It may not be literally taken away, but their testimonies of it, their belief in it, will be taken away.

At any one time, we are only held responsible for that part of the scriptures we have but do not keep. Nevertheless, we are denying ourselves of the blessings we could have if we had the portions we do not have.

Therefore, the fact that our scriptures have not been added to in recent years is prima facie evidence that we as a Church are not doing what we should be doing with our scriptures. No wonder President Ezra Taft Benson said, "The whole Church is under condemnation."[6] The Lord, through President Benson, is actually the one who said these words. In the Doctrine and Covenants, the Lord said the whole Church was under condemnation in regard to how they were treating the Book of Mormon (see D&C 84:57). President Benson merely reiterated that statement and reminded us that we remain under condemnation.

The scriptures may be likened to a great treasure house with thousands of rooms. Church members should not think that all they have to do is walk through the hallways of the house in order to glean its treasures. That was one of the reasons behind the eight-year cycle—to give members enough time to really read, study, ponder, and diligently search the scriptures. Too many of us spend too little time in the treasure house. We enter in the front door, run through the hallways, exit the backdoor, and then say, "The prophet said to read it. I've read it." No, I do not think we will find one prophet who says that all we have to do is *read*.

There's a treasure in every room of the treasure house, but all the doors are locked. We need the keys of experience, understanding, faith, and diligence in order to unlock the doors. Only with the right keys can we enter each room, find its treasures, and take them home to bless ourselves and our families.

After we finish, we start over again. And as we return to the first room, we miraculously see treasure we hadn't seen before. Why? Because we have different keys of experience and understanding, faith and diligence. Therefore, we ought to study the scriptures regularly.

Do not say, "I've read it once; I do not need to read it again." You will be proven wrong. I can promise you that if you search the scriptures again, regardless of the book or the number of times you've read it, you will see something in that scripture you did not see before. And what you see this time is something that will help you solve a problem that you are now facing.

I hope there is no teacher in the Church, no LDS chaplain, no one representing the Church who is using any other scriptures than the LDS editions of the scriptures. How unfortunate it would be if we were using the Bible that we used in the Church thirty or forty years ago. The older versions contain virtually no chapter headings. Footnotes were located in the center of the page. There was no Topical Guide. There was no Bible Dictionary. There were few maps.

For awhile, we had all kinds of Bibles in the Church. The Primary had one Bible for the children. The seminary and institutes had one Bible used only in seminaries and institutes. The missionaries had one Bible with missionary references written on it. Then the Brethren decided to come out with the magnificent, absolutely tremendous LDS edition of the King James Version of the Bible. The strength of the King James Version is, in fact, that it is the King James Version—word for word, comma for comma, without a single change. In addition, it contains several excellent helps all the way through, including a tremendous Topical Guide. It contains 3,400 scriptural references under hundreds of major topics associated with the gospel of Jesus Christ.

Most of us have heard of the sealed portion of the Book of Mormon, but have we heard of the sealed portion of the Bible? I could put it more bluntly. Have we read the Bible Dictionary? We all need to take the time to read it; until we do, it will remain unavailable—or sealed—to us.

Decide now to read and study the scriptures. Set aside time every day. Each week read the assigned scriptures in accordance with the Church program of study.

Read and study materials pertaining to the scriptures found in Church publications such as the Church magazines.

Over the years, the *Ensign* magazine has published many articles on the scriptures. Yet when I ask Church members, "Do you remember this?" They say, "No, I didn't know it existed." In October 1979, for example, the *Ensign* ran a major article, "The Church Publishes First LDS Edition of the Bible," emphasizing that doctrinal scholarship is the mission of the new King James Version. Two years later, in October 1981, the *Ensign* ran an article titled "The Church Publishes a New Triple Combination." The article detailed changes and additions to the Book of Mormon, the Doctrine and Covenants, and the Pearl of Great Price.

I believe the Brethren were very disappointed in how Church members were using the new scriptures. When the Brethren visited the stakes, they often noticed that stake presidents, high councilors, and bishops had the old editions. Why? Because they had their old books trained! They felt they didn't need a Topical Guide. They had used their old scriptures so much that if they wanted something on the resurrection they could turn right to it. Why use the new scriptures? The answer, of course, is that the Church published the new scriptures for all members, and the Brethren expected priesthood leaders to set an example.

Therefore, in October 1982 another major article appeared in the *Ensign* on "Using the New LDS Editions of Scripture." In essence, the Brethren said, "We published them and told you about them; now let's use them."

That article was followed by another major article in August 1983: "The Coming Forth of the LDS Editions of Scripture." Church members were told of the many miracles associated with the publication of the new editions of the scriptures.

In October 1983, four years after the Bible was published and two years after the triple combination appeared, the *Ensign* ran another new article: "Discovering the LDS Editions of Scripture." We were still talking about "discovering" the new editions because many members still did not know they existed.

Finally, the First Presidency and Church publications committee put out a video on reading the scriptures. Excerpts from a transcript of this video appeared in the *Ensign* in December 1985. This issue also featured "Feasting Upon the Scriptures," by President Hinckley; "Come, Learn of Me," by Elder Thomas S. Monson, then chairman of the Church publications committee; "Using the New Scriptures," by Elder Boyd K. Packer; and "Come: Hear the Voice of the Lord," by Elder Bruce R. McConkie.

At a general authority training meeting on October 2, 1981, members of the Quorum of the Twelve who formed the publications committee told the leadership of the Church—the First Presidency, the Twelve, the Quorum of the Seventy, the Presiding Bishopric, and so on—that they had to set the example in using the new LDS editions. Elder McConkie told a thrilling story about special scriptures that he had. One scriptural book belonged to President Joseph F. Smith, the sixth prophet. Another had been given to Elder McConkie by his wife-to-be before he set out on his first mission. He mentioned how many thousands of miles it had traveled and how many countries it had visited. Then he said, "These are sacred volumes, and as far as I am concerned there are not any volumes that can compare to them. But they have to go into retirement. They have to go on the shelf. They have to be put in a glass case. My children and grandchildren and great-grandchildren can come and look at them. But as far as studying the gospel and reading the scriptures, I am going to use the new scriptures." And, he said, "If this applies to me, I think it applies to us."

We should be using the new editions of the scriptures ourselves, marking them up, quoting from them, using the teaching aids they contain, and saying to Church members in the stakes and in the military, "Go, and do thou likewise."

That is why I think it is a serious omission if any of us are using editions of the Bible other than the new LDS edition. This is the edition our young men get when they go in the military, and this is the one we can use with non-LDS Christians. They want the King James Version. This is their Bible. We will use their Bible, but we will use the LDS edition's magnificent helps as well.

Notes

Excerpts from a talk given to the LDS Chaplains on 6 October 1997, in their session held in conjunction with the October conference of the Church.

1. Howard W. Hunter, "Reading the Scriptures," *Ensign,* November 1979, 64.
2. Harold B. Lee, regional representatives seminar, 12 December 1970, 10.
3. Gordon B. Hinckley, "'An Angel from on High, the Long, Long Silence Broke,'" *Ensign,* November 1979, 9.
4. Henry B. Eyring, "Feed My Lambs," *Ensign,* November 1997, 83.
5. Ibid., 83–84.
6. Ezra Taft Benson, *A Witness and a Warning* (Salt Lake City: Deseret Book Co., 1988), 75.

Chapter 3

How to Get the Most from Your Study of the Old Testament

I am firmly convinced the Old Testament is one of the greatest books on the face of the earth today. It is indeed the "Book of Books." The Old Testament is the basic scripture for the Jewish people, and—together with the New Testament—is the basic scripture for all Christians. So far as Latter-day Saints are concerned, the Old Testament ranks with the New Testament, the Book of Mormon, the Doctrine and Covenants, and the Pearl of Great Price as an important scripture our Heavenly Father has given for our blessing—and for which we each will be held accountable at our day of judgment.

Many readers already know that the essential meaning of the word *Bible* is *Books,* and as part of the Bible the Old Testament is really made up of a series of books. Some of these books are not closely related to the books that either precede them or follow them. Thus the Old Testament does not always have the consistent flow of story or chronology that might be found in some of the other scriptures.

Also, one of the major purposes of the Old Testament is to lead people to Jesus Christ and to the gospel of Jesus Christ. But the prophecies about Christ and the doctrines of his gospel are so frequently intertwined with the history and daily affairs of the people that the reader might easily become too involved with the history and miss the truly essential teachings. We must take care that that does not happen.

Reasons to Read the Old Testament

We should read the Old Testament consistently and thoroughly for many reasons, including the following:

1. *It is a commandment of God.* The Lord and his prophets have instructed us to read, study, and ponder all of the scriptures available to us. That should be sufficient reason for us to read the Old Testament. When Adam was questioned about why he did a particular thing, he replied simply, "I know not, save the Lord commanded me" (Moses 5:6).

2. *The Old Testament contains many principles of salvation and provides many examples of righteousness.* Stories of faith, devotion, diligence, perseverance, and bravery are in the Old Testament. These, in turn, have inspired and illuminated much of the best literature in the world. The heroic attributes and characteristics of many of these role models—Abraham, Jacob, Joseph, Moses, Elijah, Job, and Daniel, to name a few—are sorely needed in today's world. President Spencer W. Kimball stated: "To know the patriarchs and prophets of the ages past and their faithfulness under stress and temptation and persecution strengthens [us and our] resolves."[1]

3. *Learning and living the principles of righteousness contained in the Old Testament can help us solve many of the problems we face today.* In the scriptures the Lord teaches us correct principles, and then he expects us to use our free agency in living according to these principles so we can receive the blessings associated with such obedience. In the Old Testament, the Lord promised his covenant people that if they lived the principles of righteousness contained in the scriptures, he would (1) bless them with "the rain of your land in his due season," (2) "send grass in the fields for thy cattle," and (3) "prolong your days in the land" (Deuteronomy 11:9, 14–15). Similar blessings await us today.

4. *The Old Testament is a strong witness of the divinity of Jesus Christ.* Indeed, the Old Testament was essentially the only scripture that was available to the Jewish people at the time Jesus Christ was upon the earth and admonished them to "search the scriptures . . . they are they which testify of me" (John 5:39).[2]

Statements of Leaders

Several leaders of the United States have spoken of the worth of the Bible, of which the Old Testament is a vital part. For instance, Abraham Lincoln said, "All the good the Savior gave to the world was communicated through this book. . . .

All things most desirable for man's welfare here and hereafter are to be found portrayed in it."[3]

When President Ronald Reagan proclaimed 1983 to be the Year of the Bible, he encouraged "all citizens, each in his or her own way, to re-examine and rediscover its priceless and timeless message."[4]

Of course, leaders of the Church have also spoken of the Bible's importance. The First Presidency of the Church said: "We commend to all people everywhere the *daily* reading, pondering and heeding of the divine truths of the Holy Bible. . . . When it is read reverently and prayerfully, the Holy Bible becomes a priceless volume, converting the soul to righteousness. . . . As we read the scriptures, we avail ourselves of the better part of the world's literature."[5]

Brigham Young taught: "The doctrines contained in the Bible will lift to a superior condition all who observe them; they will impart to them knowledge, wisdom, charity, fill them with compassion and cause them to feel after the wants of those who are in distress, or in painful or degraded circumstances. They who observe the precepts contained in the Scriptures will be just and true and virtuous and peaceable at home and abroad. Follow out the doctrines of the Bible, and men will make splendid husbands, women excellent wives, and children will be obedient; they will make families happy and the nations wealthy and happy and lifted up above the things of this life."[6]

Wilford Woodruff identified the Bible as "the record of the Jews, given by the inspiration of the Lord through Moses and the ancient Patriarchs and Prophets. . . . It is not in the power of any man . . . to make such a book without the inspiration of the Almighty."[7]

As Latter-day Saints, we are all well acquainted with the statement of the Prophet Joseph Smith that helps explain the statement in the Articles of Faith that "we believe the Bible to be the word of God as far as it is translated correctly" (Articles of Faith 1:8). Joseph Smith said, "I believe the Bible as it read when it came from the pen of the original writers. Ignorant translators, careless transcribers, or designing and corrupt priests have committed many errors."[8] This qualifying statement by the Prophet Joseph Smith should not be interpreted to mean that we do not accept the Bible as inspired scripture from the Lord. Brigham Young explained:

"The Bible is true. It may not all have been translated aright, and many precious things may have been rejected in the compilation and translation of the Bible; but we understand . . . that if all the sayings and doings of the Savior had been written, the world could not contain them. I will say that the world could not understand them. . . . The Bible, *when it is understood,* is one of the simplest books in the world, for, as far as it is translated correctly, it is nothing but truth, and in truth there is no mystery save to the ignorant. The revelations of the Lord to his creatures are adapted to the lowest capacity, and they bring life and salvation to all who are willing to receive them."[9]

THE OLD TESTAMENT IS NOT READ

Despite these and other, similar statements on the importance of the Bible, it has been referred to as the "great unread book." A popular book about the Bible written by Bruce Barton was given the apt title *The Book Nobody Knows*.

Certainly the Old Testament is not given much attention among Christian churches today, with but few exceptions. Many of the Jewish people have also deserted the Old Testament, either through neglect or by a preference for other books containing their oral or written traditions. Even among Latter-day Saints, the Old Testament is perhaps the least read and least understood and appreciated of all our standard works.

Reasons for Not Reading the Old Testament

Why is it that many, if not most, of us have never bothered to read the Old Testament completely through?

One excuse I have heard is that the Old Testament is "simply or primarily a history book about a people who lived a long time ago, with strange customs, in a land that is far away." It is true the Old Testament contains history; but it is not simply or primarily a history book. It is much, much more than that.

Another excuse is that it is "too hard to understand." When questioned further, the person might make such observations as "It is too long," or "The language is too difficult," or "It doesn't seem very relevant today." Although the first two of these excuses might be based on some facts, they are still excuses, and we should recognize them as such. The last excuse isn't at all true if you concentrate on the basic doctrines and gospel teachings in the book. There is such a thing as basic, fundamental truth, and truth is eternal. Thus, the truths contained in the Old Testament apply just as much today as they did when they were given thousands of years ago.

How to Understand the Old Testament

Actually, the Old Testament is not an extremely difficult book to understand. It is a relatively simple book if you understand how and why the book is put together the way it is. Remember the words of Brigham Young: "The Bible, when it is understood, is one of the simplest books in the world, for, as far as it is translated correctly, it is nothing but truth, and in truth there is no mystery save to the ignorant."[10] This statement gives us a clue to understanding the Old Testament: We must read it in the light of the truth the Lord has revealed in the latter days. In doing so, we must study and ponder the book, become acquainted with its makeup and format, and learn its doctrines and teachings.

A statement in the Book of Mormon also gives us a hint as to how we should study the scriptures. In Alma 17:2 we read that the sons of Mosiah "had waxed strong in the knowledge of the truth; for they were men of a sound understanding and they had *searched the scriptures diligently*, that they might know the word of God" (Alma 17:2; emphasis added).

Note again the principle: The scriptures must be *searched diligently*.

Do's and Don'ts

As you approach a study of the Old Testament, I would recommend three do's and three don'ts:

1. *Do* resolve that you are going to read the entire Old Testament, book by book, chapter by chapter, verse by verse. Decide the schedule and pace that is best for you. Some have found it helps to set apart a definite time period each day for studying the scriptures.

2. *Do* determine that your major purpose in studying the Old Testament is to learn the teachings and doctrines that relate (1) to the life, mission, and atonement of Jesus Christ, and (2) to the gospel of Jesus Christ.

3. *Do* use the LDS Edition of the King James Version of the Bible.

Now let's look at three don'ts:

1. *Don't* be too concerned about the pronunciation of names in the Old Testament. These vary from language to language, and even from group to group within a language. Those who speak the "King's English," for example, might not pronounce some of the names the same as those who use "American English," and probably neither group will use the original pronunciation. Isaac does not sound

too much like Yitshak, nor would many people recognize Shlomo as Solomon. Perhaps you have already noted that the LDS Edition of the Bible does not include a pronunciation guide. This should indicate to us that the Brethren might not be too concerned about the pronunciation of biblical names.

2. *Don't* be too concerned about the exact routes of travel of the people in the Bible, nor about their exact places of residence. Having a sense of geography is useful, and it can help in an understanding of the peoples being discussed, but geography usually is not absolutely essential to a correct understanding of the principle or doctrine being discussed.

3. *Don't* restrict your reading of the Old Testament to the time periods you may have set aside each day. Get involved with the teachings of the book so much that you won't want to put it down.

Background to the Old Testament

Religious History of Families

I find it helpful to remember that the Old Testament is essentially a brief review or synopsis of the religious history of a series of families. In order to understand this history, you need to know something about the background of the practices, traditions, beliefs, and customs of that particular family. Also, you need to realize that the people are in a relative state of apostasy during most of the history recorded in this scripture.

The Old Testament begins with the story of the family of Adam; but by the fifth chapter of Genesis—the first book of the Old Testament—we are already reading about the family of Noah, a descendant of Adam; and then we are introduced to the family name-title of Shem, one of the sons of Noah: *Semites.*

By the eleventh chapter of Genesis we are introduced to Abraham—a descendant of Shem who was thus known as a Semite—and soon become acquainted with the name-title of Abraham's family: *Hebrews.*

In chapter 25 of Genesis we read of the birth of Jacob, a grandson of Abraham, and thus a Hebrew. Jacob's name is subsequently changed to Israel, and we note the name-title of his family: *Israelites.*

In chapter 29 of Genesis we read of the birth of Judah, the fourth son of Jacob and thus an Israelite. Subsequently we learn the name-title of Judah's family: *Jews.*

Thus by the time we get through with the very first book in the Old Testament, we have already read of the major early families on the earth, ending with the family of Jacob (Israelites) and the family of Judah (Jews). The remaining thirty-eight books in the Old Testament are primarily concerned with the religious history of these families. And remember, during the time period covered by most of those thirty-eight books, the people are declining into a state of apostasy.

If you understand the relationship between the various families we have mentioned, you understand more than most of the readers of the Old Testament. Many people do not realize that such terms as Semites, Hebrews, Israelites, and Jews are essentially family names. Even fewer people understand the relationship of these families.

A few general statements will help us to see the relationship of these families:
"All Hebrews are Semites, but not all Semites are Hebrews."
"All Israelites are Hebrews, but not all Hebrews are Israelites."
"All Jews are Israelites, but not all Israelites are Jews."

If these terms give you difficulty, let's substitute the first name of the ancient patriarch for the name-title of his particular family: "All descendants of Abraham are also descendants of Shem." The truthfulness of this statement is obvious, for Abraham is a descendant of Shem; thus all of Abraham's descendants would also be descendants of Shem. Now, substituting the important name-titles for the names of the patriarchs, what we have really said is "All Hebrews are Semites."

Shem, of course, had many other family lines in addition to the family line of Abraham. Thus, not all descendants of Shem are descendants of Abraham, or, in other words, "Not all Semites are Hebrews."

We can use the same technique to explain the relationship between the family of Abraham and the family of Jacob:

"All descendants of Jacob are also descendants of Abraham." Again, when you remember that Jacob is Abraham's grandson, it is obvious that the descendants of Jacob would also be descendants of Abraham. Using family name-titles, what we have really said is "All Israelites are Hebrews."

But Abraham had many other grandsons in addition to Jacob; thus not all descendants of Abraham are descendants of Jacob. Or, in other words, "Not all Hebrews are Israelites."

Unfortunately most readers of the Old Testament have not studied this book diligently enough to learn the distinctions between these family names. Yet an understanding of these family relationships is imperative to a correct understanding of the Old Testament and, incidentally, to an understanding of some of the difficult problems in the world today. Perhaps if the people of the world understood these relationships, we could have greater peace in Israel. For example, God promised certain lands in the Near and Middle East to the descendants of Abraham—that is, to the Hebrews, a term that applies to all the descendants of Abraham, which in modern terminology would include both the Arabs and the Jews. However, many Jewish people apply a modern definition of the term *Hebrews;* they apply it only to themselves as Jews rather than to all the peoples to whom the term applied in the Old Testament. Thus, many Jewish people today feel these lands have been promised exclusively to them.

Customs and Practices of the Hebrews

As we study the Old Testament, it is important that we learn and understand the major practices, beliefs, and traditions of these families; such background will give us a greater understanding of many of the stories in the Old Testament. We certainly cannot list all of these customs here, but perhaps we should mention some of the most important ones that were in place by the time of Abraham and thus might be referred to as "manners and customs of the Hebrews."

Patriarchal order. This term indicates that the right to rule or preside over the family belonged to the father and went from father to son.

Law of primogeniture. This custom determined which son should succeed the father as the presiding head of the family. The word *prime* has to do with *first* and the construction *geniture* has to do with *birth*. Thus, everything else being equal, the firstborn son would usually succeed the father as the head of the family.

Law of the birthright or of inheritance. By "right" of his "birth" as a son, the son who succeeded his father as the head of the family was entitled to a double portion of his father's inheritance. Thus, for example, if a father had four sons, upon the death of the father the inheritance would be divided into five portions. Each of the sons—including the birthright son—would receive one of the portions. The birthright son would then receive a second portion to meet such needs as the care of the mother, the care of any unmarried sisters, and so on. The firstborn son had the first right to the birthright blessing, but if he proved to be unworthy, or even less worthy, the birthright could be given to another son. As you may recall, this was the case for several consecutive generations in the Old Testament, beginning with Isaac.

Polygamy. Abraham and some of the other ancient patriarchs practiced polygamy, where they could have more than one wife at the same time. Inasmuch as each of these wives might have her own "firstborn son," the practice was generally followed that the firstborn son of the *first wife* would succeed his father, provided that this son was worthy and qualified.

The wife is included in the family of her husband. When a woman married, she was considered to belong to her husband's family rather than to her father's family. Thus, it was customary for the prospective bridegroom to bring a dowry to the wedding, or, in effect, to reimburse the father for the loss of a daughter at the time of her marriage. This custom of the daughter being associated with the family of her husband after marriage may help explain why the names of daughters are frequently not included in the histories of Hebrew families.

Although we have been able to list only a few of the customs of the Hebrews here, you should already see the importance of learning and understanding these practices so you can more fully understand and appreciate (1) why Abraham, Jacob, and others had more than one wife at the same time; (2) why Isaac, the son of Sarah, became the new head of the family upon the death of Abraham even though Ishmael—Abraham's son through Hagar—was several years older; (3) why Joseph, the eleventh-born son of Jacob but the firstborn of Jacob's second wife, Rachel, became the birthright son when Reuben, the firstborn son of the first wife, Leah, proved to be unworthy.

An understanding of these customs helps you to visualize these people as real people, with real challenges. In other words, an understanding of these customs helps the Old Testament to come alive for you.

Customs and Practices of the Israelites

Now let's look at some other types of practices and customs that largely were developed during the family periods of the Israelites and the Jews.

Dietary restrictions. Many people are surprised to find that the Old Testament contains instructions on the following customs, some of which are still practiced by orthodox Jews today:

1. No flesh was to be eaten from animals unless the animal had a cloven foot *and* chewed its cud (hence, no pork).

2. No flesh taken from the sea was to be eaten unless it had scales.

3. No blood or blood products were to be eaten. Thus no meat was to be consumed unless the animal or fowl had been killed in a certain way, with the blood properly drained.

4. No dairy products and meat products were to be eaten at the same time. Actually this is more a tradition than a religious requirement; it has resulted from an

interpretation of the command in Exodus 23:19: "Thou shalt not seethe a kid [baby goat] in its mother's milk."

To obtain further information on these practices, review such Topical Guide entries as the "Law of Moses," "Blood, Eating of," and "Fish." In the Bible Dictionary, read such items as "Clean and Unclean" and the brief article entitled "Kosher."

Dress and grooming standards. Have you ever wondered where the orthodox Jewish people of today got the idea that men are not to be close shaven on their faces, are not to cut the hair at the corners of the head, and are to wear fringes on their garments? Or why the heads of married women should be shaved, or why women are not to wear things pertaining to a man and vice versa? All of these customs have their roots in the Old Testament, and you can learn more about them by reading the appropriate scriptures listed under such general headings in the Topical Guide as "Israel, Judah, People of" or under such specific headings as "Hair," "Head," "Garment," "Fringe," or "Shave."

Purification procedures. Several chapters in the Old Testament are devoted to special purification rites for women after menstrual periods or giving birth, and for all persons who might have touched a diseased individual or a dead body. For precise information on these procedures, see the article on "Purification" in the Bible Dictionary, and read the appropriate scriptures under the same heading in the Topical Guide.

Sabbath regulations. Laws and regulations concerning the Sabbath day are legion in the Old Testament, and the observance of these laws helped to distinguish the covenant people in the Old Testament from all their neighbors. Note some of their beliefs and teachings concerning the Sabbath:

1. The Sabbath was to be from sundown Friday to sundown Saturday.

2. No work was to be performed on the Sabbath, including no harvesting of food.

3. No fire was to be lit on the Sabbath.

4. Only a certain distance was to be walked on the Sabbath (hence, "a Sabbath day's journey").

Where can you learn the details about these Sabbath regulations? Again, you read the appropriate articles in the Bible Dictionary, such as "Sabbath" and "Sabbath Day's Journey." Also, review the appropriate scriptures under such Topical Guide entries as "Israel, Judah, People of" and "Sabbath."

Religious symbols. Several religious symbols were used by the descendants of Judah in Old Testament times, and some of them are still used by orthodox Jews today. These include the following:

1. The wearing of phylacteries by the men on the forehead and left arm.

2. The use of small containers (called *mezzuzahs*) on the right side of gate posts, doorways, and so forth. These contain the words of selected scriptures.

3. The use of the menorah (seven-stemmed candelabrum) and Sabbath candles.

Again, to obtain additional information on these customs, read the appropriate entries under such headings as "Phylactery" and "Candlestick" in both the Topical Guide and the Bible Dictionary. Although the word *mezzuzah* does not appear in the English editions of the King James Bible, the practice of placing short scriptural quotations in certain places is indicated in Deuteronomy 6:9 and 11:20.

Feasts and festivals. Many chapters in the Old Testament are devoted to the institution and observance of feasts and festivals, including the following: Passover; Yom Kippur (or "Day of Atonement"); Feast of Pentecost (*Shavuot*), also called Feast of Weeks; Feast of the Tabernacles (*Sukkot*); Purim (*Lots*); and Feast of Dedication (*Hanukkah*). Pertinent information on each of these feasts and festivals may be obtained in the excellent Bible Dictionary article entitled "Feasts." Also, appropriate scriptures are listed under the topic "Feast" in the Topical Guide.

Summary of the Background to the Old Testament

This listing of Old Testament practices, customs, beliefs, and traditions could go on much longer. But perhaps I have listed enough of them here to emphasize again why it is necessary to *study diligently* the Old Testament. In some ways it might be considered a difficult book, but if you understand the major family groups in the scripture, and their customs, beliefs, and festivals, you will have come a long way toward a true understanding of the meaning and significance of this holy record. In somewhat the same way, a person studying The Church of Jesus Christ of Latter-day Saints would understand the total picture better if he knew about the exodus from Nauvoo, the trek across the plains, and such doctrines and customs as marriage for time and eternity, the Word of Wisdom, fast Sundays, and the celebration of the 24th of July.

WHY WE USE THE LDS EDITION OF THE KING JAMES VERSION OF THE BIBLE

Why is it so important to use the King James Version of the Bible in our study of the Old Testament? The quick and easy answer is that it is the text used in the latest edition of the Bible published by the Church. But that simply begs another question: Why did the LDS Church in the 1970s elect to use the text of the authorized King James Version in its edition of the Bible, rather than a more recent translation?

Elder Bruce R. McConkie has testified concerning the value of the King James text: "As far as the Bibles of the world are concerned, the King James version is so far ahead of all others that there is little comparison. . . . It is the Bible that came into being to prepare the way for the translation of the Book of Mormon and to set a literary pattern and standard for the revelations in the Doctrine and Covenants. It is the official Bible of the Church."[11]

On another occasion, Elder McConkie wrote: "For nearly four hundred years the King James Version of the Bible has been one of the most stabilizing forces in all Christendom. It has been one of the chief means of preserving the English language as such; but more than this, it has kept right principles before millions of people who have been and are without personal contact with the prophets and witnesses who teach personally the Lord's message of salvation to his earthly children."[12]

While accepting the statements of the Brethren on the value of the King James Version, some members of the Church may still wonder why the text of the Joseph Smith Translation was not used as the basic text for the special LDS edition of the Bible. You may have noted, for example, that in his explanation as to why he selected the King James Version over all the other editions of the Bible published by the world, President Clark indicated he had received his greatest help from what he called the "Inspired Version of Joseph Smith."[13]

So far as I know, Church leaders have never officially explained why they decided to use the King James text in the LDS edition of the Bible. However, it is obvious the following factors were considered in the decision:

1. The authorized King James text has been the basic, standard text for most of the Protestant world since it was first published in the early 1600s. Thus, among other things, when our missionaries quote from this text it is more apt to be recognized and readily accepted by investigators, many of whom come from backgrounds in Protestant churches. Obviously, in the eyes of the investigators it is more effective for the missionary to quote and teach from the investigators' Bible than from a Bible used exclusively by the missionary's Church.

2. The King James text was prepared during an important period of the development of the English language (the Victorian period of literature) when major works in English were being sought and referenced by scholars in the other major languages of the world.

3. The King James text, having been published in 1611, had by the 1970s been

translated into hundreds of different languages, with tens of millions of copies available, and with wide acceptance throughout the world.

4. Key commentaries, reference books, and concordances based on the King James text, which could assist LDS readers in their study of the Bible, are widely available. As an example, the title page of *The Exhaustive Concordance of the Bible* by James Strong indicates that it shows "every word of the text of the common English version of the canonical books, and every occurrence of each word in regular order; . . . also brief dictionaries of the Hebrew and Greek words of the original, with references to the English words." In the "General Preface" of this concordance, the publisher acknowledges that it has used "the text of the English Bible ordinarily in use . . . [as] it is intended to be a permanent standard for purposes of reference."[14]

The Prophet Joseph Smith used the King James text in preparing his "Inspired Version," which was intended to help clarify passages that were awkwardly composed or doctrinally difficult. That the General Authorities had faith and confidence in this Joseph Smith Translation was evidenced when they authorized use of the JST in footnotes in the LDS edition. They also authorized inclusion of a special section entitled "Joseph Smith Translation Excerpts Too Lengthy for Inclusion in Footnotes," which occupies pages 795 through 813 of the appendix of the LDS edition of the Bible. This important instructional aid will be discussed later.

Not only should we use the King James Version of the Bible, but we would do well to use that version as found in the LDS edition of the Bible. I am convinced that the LDS edition of the Bible is the best edition published in modern times. Let's examine the unique elements of this edition, which I believe will make its value apparent.

Title Page

You will note from the title page and the two pages of explanatory introduction that the text of this edition of the Bible is the Authorized King James Version, word for word and comma for comma. This LDS edition was first printed in 1979, and any printing since then should be acceptable.

Contents Page

The page listing the contents provides a list of the thirty-nine books of the Old Testament and the twenty-seven books of the New Testament, in the order in which these books appear in the scriptures. Also, note that the appendix includes the sections headed Topical Guide, Bible Dictionary, Joseph Smith Translation, Gazetteer, and Maps. Each of these sections will be discussed in detail later.

Explanation Concerning Abbreviations

The next page is titled "Explanation Concerning Abbreviations." These abbreviations are "found in footnotes and other study aids" in the LDS edition of the Bible. The abbreviations used in the footnotes include:

GR: An alternate translation from the Greek.

HEB: An alternate translation from the Hebrew.

IE: An explanation of idioms and difficult constructions.

JST: Joseph Smith Translation.

TG: Topical Guide.

OR: Signifies that alternate words follow to clarify the meaning of archaic expressions.

The footnotes identified by these abbreviations are extremely important to a more complete understanding of the Old Testament. In fact, these footnotes are so important that I believe each of them should be marked with a distinctive color, marking both the superscript letter in the text and the abbreviation in the footnote itself. The only exception to this marking might be the TG (or Topical Guide) footnotes, because they are so numerous.

Let me explain this marking system further. You will see that in Genesis chapter one, verse one, the word *created* is preceded by the small superscript letter *c*. You will then note in the footnotes on this page that in chapter one, verse one, the small letter *c* is followed by the abbreviation HEB, with the explanation that in this instance the word *created* could also have been translated as "shaped" or "fashioned." The content of this footnote is so important to an understanding of the first verse of Genesis 1 that I would mark in color both the superscript letter *c* in the text and the abbreviation HEB in the footnote. Then, when I subsequently read the text, the marking on the superscript letter automatically leads me to the appropriate footnote.

Again, I believe all of the footnotes headed by the abbreviations GR, HEB, IE, JST, and OR are so important that each of them should be individually marked with a separate, distinctive color.

As examples, in my copy of the Bible I have marked all of the GR footnotes in green, all of the HEB footnotes in blue, the IE footnotes in yellow, the JST footnotes in red, and the OR footnotes in orange. My selection of these particular colors was entirely personal, and they may not be the best colors for you. I selected the color green for the GR (Greek) footnotes because they both begin with the letters "GR." I used the same principle in selecting orange for the OR footnotes. My reasons for using blue, yellow, and red colors are not quite so obvious. I selected blue for the HEB footnotes because of the blue colors on the modern flag of Israel.

I selected yellow for the IE footnotes since these footnotes clarify idioms and difficult constructions, and yellow seemed to me to signify a new idea. I selected red for the JST footnotes because they are so important, and the color red reminds me to stop and ponder.

Again, select your own colors for your own purposes, but I would strongly urge you to color-mark all these important and significant footnotes.[15]

Cross-References in the Footnotes

As you turn the pages of the Bible, you will see the voluminous cross-references that appear in the footnotes. These cross-references will lead you to appropriate scriptures in all the standard works of the Church, not only to other references in the Old Testament and the New Testament. If you will consistently use these cross-references, you will soon gain an increased appreciation and understanding of the great gospel plan of salvation and exaltation, and of the life, mission, and atonement of Jesus Christ, because these are the common messages of all the standard works.

Understanding and using the cross-references, as well as the other footnotes, are at the very heart and core of anyone's *diligent study* of the Old Testament.

Chapter Headings

All of the chapter headings in the LDS edition of the Bible were prepared initially by a prophet, seer, and revelator serving as a member of the Quorum of the Twelve Apostles. Each heading was then reviewed by three members of the Quorum of the Twelve serving on the scriptures publications committee, and any questions were taken to the Council of the First Presidency and Quorum of the Twelve for a final resolution. This suggests that the chapter and section headings in the LDS editions of the scriptures are the nearest thing to canonized scripture we have in the Church, outside the actual text of the scriptures themselves. I recommend you develop the habit of reading and pondering the chapter headings *before* you read the text of that particular chapter. In fact, I highly recommend that at least once in your life you go through each of the books of scripture, chapter by chapter, reading *only* the chapter headings. This activity will help you develop a feel for the sweep and the grandeur of the scriptures you might not obtain any other way.

In preparation for this discussion, I decided to read all of the chapter headings in the Old Testament without reading the text of each chapter. In one hour and fifteen minutes I had read and marked all of the chapter headings from Genesis through Esther. Then later, in less than one hour, I completed reading the chapter headings of the books Job through Malachi. It was a very worthwhile and enlightening experience. I highly recommend that you do the same.

Just to give you an idea of the importance and significance of the chapter headings, here are the headings for the first three chapters of Genesis:

"Chapter 1—God creates this earth and its heaven and all forms of life in six days—Creative acts of each day set forth—God creates man, both male and female, in his own image—Man given dominion over all things, and commanded to multiply and fill the earth.

"Chapter 2—Creation completed—God rests on the seventh day—Prior spirit creation explained—Adam and Eve placed in Garden of Eden—They are forbidden to eat of the tree of knowledge of good and evil—Adam names every living creature—Adam and Eve are married by the Lord.

"Chapter 3—The Serpent (Lucifer) deceives Eve—She and then Adam partake of the forbidden fruit—Her Seed (Christ) shall bruise the Serpent's head—Role of woman, and of man—Adam and Eve cast out of the Garden of Eden—Adam presides—Eve becomes the mother of all living."

I hope these samples whet your appetite to want to read all the chapter headings. These headings can play an important role in your *diligent study* of the Old Testament.

Appendix

Now let's look together at the major sections in the appendix of the LDS edition of the Bible.

Topical Guide

The official name of the first section of the appendix is "Topical Guide with Selected Concordance and Index." The contents of this section are explained as follows: "This Topical Guide, with selected concordance and index entries, is intended to help the reader find scriptures most often used in gospel classes and study. Because of space limitations, the guide is not intended to be comprehensive. It is also recommended that the reader look up each scripture and examine it in its context, in order to gain a better understanding of it."[16]

Tens of thousands of individual references are listed under the numerous topic headings. Without question, the Topical Guide is the most helpful reference system pertaining to all of the standard works yet published. This system provides us with a highly effective "chain link" referencing system on all the major principles, doctrines, and ordinances of the gospel of Jesus Christ and our Heavenly Father's plan of progression and eternal life.

As you study and use the individual references listed under the various topics, remember to "look up each scripture and examine it in its context, in order to gain a better understanding of it."

As you can imagine, hundreds of people contributed tens of thousands of hours, with the aid of computers, to help prepare the Topical Guide. As Elder Bruce R. McConkie expressed it, "Without the help of the computer, the Topical Guide in the LDS edition of the scriptures could not have been prepared in its thoroughness and accuracy in this century."[17] And all this is now available to us to help us in our *diligent study* of the scriptures.

How can the Topical Guide best serve us in our study? Let me make a couple of suggestions.

Let's assume you want to learn what has been written in the scriptures about the *sacrament*. You will note that this topic is listed on pages 441–42 of the Topical Guide, with appropriate scriptural references. It would not take too long to read all of these scriptural references. Then you might place yourself in the frame of mind of a Gospel Doctrine teacher or a person preparing a talk for sacrament meeting on this subject. Thus, you will want to decide which of these scriptures would be the best one to introduce the subject of "The Sacrament of the Lord's Supper." Let's assume you select Matthew 26:26. You might then write and encircle the number 1 near the reference to Matthew 26:26 in the Topical Guide. If you decide the next important reference you want to quote and discuss on this topic is 3 Nephi 18:7, write and encircle the number 2 next to the reference of 3 Nephi 18:7, and so forth. Thus, in a relatively short time you can develop a priority list of "chain references" on the important ordinance of the sacrament that will be of help to you throughout the remainder of your life.

In time you can develop similar chain reference systems for all the important principles and ordinances of the gospel. Remember, the most difficult task has already been done for you—the identification and listing of all the pertinent scriptures pertaining to particular topics. All you need to do is to read and study the references, select those that are most helpful to you in understanding the topic, and then mark them.

Bible Dictionary

The next major section of the appendix is the Bible Dictionary, consisting of 195 pages of vital information. I believe that the Bible Dictionary in the LDS edition of the Bible is the best Bible dictionary that has ever been published. When a number of scriptural scholars in the Church were assigned to create this dictionary, they first received permission to use the best of what had been printed in other

Bible dictionaries; then they improved on these materials through their understanding of the modern scriptures and their acquaintance with the teachings of the prophets of this dispensation. Unfortunately many members of the Church have not learned how to use this magnificent instructional aid. It is the sealed portion of the Bible!

Perhaps sharing a portion of the preface to the Bible Dictionary might inspire some of us to do more with this important section of the scriptures:

"This dictionary has been designed to provide teachers and students with a concise collection of definitions and explanations of items that are mentioned in or are otherwise associated with the Bible. . . . It is not intended as an official or revealed endorsement by the Church of the doctrinal, historical, cultural, and other matters set forth. Many of the items have been drawn from the best available scholarship of the world and are subject to reevaluation based on new research and discoveries or on new revelation. The topics have been carefully selected and are treated briefly. . . .

"In addition to names of persons and places mentioned in the Bible, there are articles that may be regarded as introductory to the study of scripture, such as *Bible, canon, revelation,* and certain cultural items. A short account is given of each of the books of the Bible. An attempt has been made to deal with a few doctrinal subjects, such as atonement, baptism, Holy Spirit, priesthood, restoration, and resurrection."[18]

As indicated in this preface, scores of entries in the Bible Dictionary should be of great interest to students of the Old Testament, including the "short account" given of each of the books and the identification of the names of many persons and places mentioned in this sacred scripture.

The best, and perhaps the only, way to become acquainted with the contents of the Bible Dictionary is to read all the entries in the dictionary, item-by-item and word-for-word, from "Aaron" through "Zipporah." I'm afraid too many of us wait to use the Bible Dictionary until we feel a definite need for its use, and then we commonly look up only a single topic. Of course, it is better to use the dictionary in this fashion than not to use it at all. But how much better it would be if we would first acquaint ourselves with what is in the dictionary.

For example, I suppose many Gospel Doctrine teachers in the Church have never bothered to read the entry under the "Fall of Adam" heading because they think they already know all they need to know about the fall of Adam. However, I am confident that virtually every member of the Church would have his or her understanding of the Fall expanded by reading what has been provided under that topic. I invite you—indeed, challenge you—to read all the entries in the Bible

Dictionary. They will greatly enhance your understanding of the Bible and of the gospel in general.

Let me share with you a few specific items in the dictionary that will prove of great value and assistance to you.

On pages 622 to 625 of the appendix you will find a series of articles written on the subject of the Bible under such subtitles as "Structure of the Bible," "Preservation of the Text of the Old Testament," "Preservation of the Text of the New Testament," and "Bible, English." This information should prove invaluable to you as you *diligently study* the Old Testament. Additional information on this same general subject is found under the entry "Canon" on pages 630–31.

The Chronological Tables on pages 635 through 645 should also prove indispensable to you. You will find a wealth of information in these tables, including a listing of basic dates and a listing of the kings and prophets of both the kingdom of Judah and the kingdom of Israel. You will also find a great deal of information in these charts under such headings as "Internal History," "External History," "Synchronisms," "Jewish History," "Profane History," "Egypt," "Syria," and "Contemporary Events." Again, these charts have required the combined efforts of many students and scholars of the scriptures, requiring thousands of hours, distilling knowledge that is made available to us in a format that can be easily understood and utilized. You might want to specially mark or tag these tables, as well as the tremendous Harmony of the Gospels charts on pages 684 through 696.

On pages 756 to 759 of the appendix is an extremely interesting entry under the heading "Quotations from the Old Testament found in the New Testament." This worthwhile article is one of the many that might never be discovered even by the serious student of the Bible—unless he or she reads the Bible Dictionary from beginning to end. This valuable list provides us with a listing of all the Old Testament passages that have clearly influenced New Testament writers. These references are all presented in the order of the books of the Old Testament. Thus, you can readily determine that this list includes sixty-four references from Psalms, fifty-five from Isaiah, twenty-six from both Deuteronomy and Exodus, and eighteen from Genesis. If you want to spend some extremely interesting and informative gospel study time, read the passages listed from the Old Testament and then read the corresponding passages from the New Testament.

Joseph Smith Translation

The next major section of the appendix is headed by the descriptive title "Joseph Smith Translation, Excerpts Too Lengthy for Inclusion in Footnotes," found on pages 795 to 813.

Many excerpts from the Joseph Smith Translation are included as footnotes on the pages providing the text of the Bible. However, it was decided that if the footnote from the Joseph Smith Translation would take over nine lines on those pages, it should appear in this special section.

The first reference in this section is Genesis 9:4–6. This does not mean that the Joseph Smith Translation does not make many significant contributions to a correct understanding of the first eight chapters of Genesis. However, if you carefully review those early chapters of Genesis, you will note the numerous cross-references to the books of Moses and Abraham in the Pearl of Great Price. These modern scripture references will provide the student of the Old Testament with invaluable insights into the early chapters of Genesis.

Even then, note the many lengthy contributions of the Joseph Smith Translation in such chapters as Genesis 9, 14, 15, 17, 19, 21, 48, and 50.

Gazetteer

The Gazetteer of the LDS edition of the Bible appears on pages 814 through 827 of the appendix. This list includes the name of every major place or site mentioned in the Bible, with an introductory statement as to how these places can be quickly located in the twenty-two maps that follow.

To help familiarize yourself with the places that pertain primarily to the Old Testament period, you might want to circle those place names in the Gazetteer in one color (perhaps blue). Then you might use another color (perhaps green) for those places primarily associated with the New Testament. The important thing is to use the Gazetteer properly so you can quickly find the location of any places mentioned.

Maps

The twenty-two maps available in the LDS edition of the Bible are among the best biblical maps available. Map number 1 (the physical map of Palestine) can be used to find both Old Testament and New Testament locations. However, maps 2 through 12 are primarily concerned with Old Testament locations, while maps 13 through 22 pertain primarily to the New Testament. As you study the Old Testament, you will want to examine carefully all of the maps of the time period that is most appropriate for each area.

BOOKS OF THE OLD TESTAMENT

Let us now go through each of the books of the Old Testament, one by one, noting particular items pertaining to selected chapters.

The First Book of Moses, Called Genesis

Interestingly enough, I suspect that most people—including Latter-day Saints, other Christians, and Jews—do not know the full correct name of the first book of the Bible. I think if most people were asked to give the full name of the first book of the Bible, they would simply answer "Genesis," or perhaps "The Book of Genesis." The basic meaning of the word Genesis, of course, is "beginning."

However, we see on page 1 of the Bible, the complete name of the first book is The First Book of Moses, Called Genesis. That should pique our interest enough that we might check the exact titles of some of the other early books in the Bible. You will note that the next four books are called, respectively, The Second Book of Moses, Called Exodus; The Third Book of Moses, Called Leviticus; The Fourth Book of Moses, Called Numbers; and The Fifth Book of Moses, Called Deuteronomy. In many languages, these books are simply listed as "The First Book of Moses," "The Second Book of Moses," etc.; the titles of "Genesis," "Exodus," "Leviticus," "Numbers," and "Deuteronomy" are not even listed as part of the titles in those languages.

Because Moses is the author of the first five books in the Bible, these books are often collectively called the *pentateuch,* a Greek word meaning "five books." The Jewish people refer to these five books as the Torah, from a Hebrew word meaning "to cast" or to put forth instruction and God's law.

The chronological chart in the Bible Dictionary indicates that Moses was not born on the earth until approximately 1571 B.C. (Before Christ). However, the same chart indicates the "Fall of Adam" occurred approximately 4,000 years before the birth of Christ. Thus, in order for Moses to provide us with a rather detailed account of the creation in chapter 1 of Genesis, he must either have had written records and oral traditions to draw on, or he must have received the information in revelation from the Lord—or both. Latter-day Saints know one possible source for the information provided by Moses. The first verse from the book of Moses in the Pearl of Great Price[19] indicates that the first part of this record contained "The words of God, which he spake unto Moses at a time when Moses was caught up into an exceedingly high mountain." The information provided in the book of Moses in the Pearl of Great Price largely corresponds to the information in Genesis 1:1 through Genesis 6:13. However, as is readily evident, the account in the book of Moses is much more detailed and explicit than the account in Genesis. Thus, a study of the first six chapters of Genesis should be supplemented by a study of the book of Moses in the Pearl of Great Price.

Also, the cross-reference footnotes in the early chapters of Genesis indicate that chapters 4 and 5 of the book of Abraham in the Pearl of Great Price are concerned with the creation account. These chapters from Abraham thus should be reviewed in conjunction with a study of Genesis chapters 1 and 2.

In reading Genesis, pay special attention to the HEB footnotes, which provide "an alternate translation from the Hebrew." For example, it is of great help to know not only that the word "created" in the first verse of the Bible could also have been translated "shaped" or "fashioned," but that divine activity was always involved. Also, note the possible shade of difference in meaning if the Hebrew word translated "replenish" in Genesis 1:28 had been translated "fill" as it was in verse 22.

Out of the scores of verses I might have selected from Genesis, I have chosen the first part of Genesis 18:14: "Is anything too hard for the Lord?" The answer, of course, is *No*—and that knowledge should give comfort to all of us throughout our lives as we realize that with God's help we can accomplish all our righteous desires.

I urge you to pay special attention to the excerpts from the Joseph Smith Translation that pertain to the book of Genesis, not only those included as footnotes on the pages, but also those included in the section of the appendix titled "Joseph Smith Translation, Excerpts Too Lengthy for Inclusion in Footnotes." The Joseph Smith Translation provides additional vital information on Melchizedek in Genesis chapter 14, on Abraham in chapter 17, and on Joseph in chapters 48 and 50.

The Second Book of Moses, Called Exodus

The word Exodus has the same basic meaning as *departure*. This book is so named, of course, because it details the departure of the Israelites from their bondage in Egypt. This book also shows the beginning of the development of the Israelites as an independent and separate nation or people. The institution of new feasts and festivals, and the building of the tabernacle, all tended to unify and give character to the new nation.

Note the several contributions of the Joseph Smith Translation to this book, particularly the very significant contribution to Exodus 34:1–2.

The verse I have chosen to highlight is Exodus 6:3, which contains the words of God to Moses: "And I appeared unto Abraham, unto Isaac, and unto Jacob, by the name of God Almighty, but by my name *Jehovah* was I not known to them" (emphasis added). Although this verse is subject to at least two major interpretations, many biblical scholars have chosen to believe that the God of the Old Testament was the God we know by the name-title of Elohim, and that God was not known to his people by the name Jehovah. However, we as Latter-day Saints know from other scriptures that the God of the Old Testament is Jesus Christ and that he was known unto his people in the Old Testament by the name *Jehovah*.

Notice the contribution of the Joseph Smith Translation to this matter: "And I appeared unto Abraham, unto Isaac, and unto Jacob. I am the Lord God Almighty; the Lord Jehovah. And was *not* my name known unto them?" (emphasis added).

Joseph Fielding Smith has written: "All revelation since the fall has come through Jesus Christ, who is the Jehovah of the Old Testament."[20] It is evident that *Jehovah* is an important name-title for the God of the Old Testament.

The Third Book of Moses, Called Leviticus

Many readers of the Bible consider this book to be one of the most difficult to understand in the entire Old Testament. A very helpful outline and description of this book is contained on page 724 of the Bible Dictionary under the title "Leviticus." A careful study of this outline would be profitable. Also, be sure to take advantage of the extremely helpful footnotes in this chapter, including the 100 HEB footnotes of "alternate translations from the Hebrew," the 21 OR footnotes providing clarifications of archaic English expressions, and the 20 IE footnotes that provide explanations "of idioms and difficult constructions."

The verse I would like to highlight is Leviticus 19:2, which contains the words of the Lord to Moses: "Speak unto all the congregation of the children of Israel, and say unto them, Ye shall be holy: for I the Lord your God am holy." The terms "I am the Lord" or "I am the Lord your God" appear at least sixteen times in this chapter. These terms not only indicate that the teachings come directly from God, but they also place a "seal of approval" on these admonitions.

The Fourth Book of Moses, Called Numbers

An outline of the major sections of this book is provided in the article titled "Numbers" in the Bible Dictionary. Several key scriptures are interspersed throughout this book. Numbers 21:9 is especially significant when related to 1 Nephi 17:41, Alma 33:18–22, and John 3:14–17. Also, note the Messianic prophecy in Numbers 24:17.

The thought to highlight from the book of Numbers comes from the opening words of Numbers 27:22: "And Moses did as the Lord commanded him." Throughout his life, the great prophet and lawgiver, Moses, demonstrated the importance of obedience; only obedience brings forth the blessings of heaven.

The Fifth Book of Moses, Called Deuteronomy

As we mentioned earlier, the book of Deuteronomy is quoted frequently by the writers of the New Testament. It might also be noted that later writers in the Old

Testament also quoted Deuteronomy, as did Jesus Christ when he answered difficult questions asked by the scribes and the Pharisees.

Particular attention should be given to (1) chapters 4 through 11, which contain some of the great exhortations of Moses to his people, and (2) chapters 29 through 34, which include some of Moses' farewell advice, given shortly before he was taken from the presence of his people. These form the capstone of Moses' prophetic ministry.

I would like to highlight Deuteronomy 10:12: "And now, Israel, what doth the Lord thy God require of thee, but to fear the Lord thy God, to walk in all his ways, and to love him, and to serve the Lord thy God with all thy heart and with all thy soul." This important verse takes on additional significance when you remember that the Hebrew word translated as *fear* has the basic meaning of reverence or awesome respect.

The Book of Joshua

The last sentence in the Bible Dictionary entry on the book of Joshua reads: "The book was regarded by the Jews as the first of the 'former prophets,' but it is more properly a continuation of the first Five Books."

The book of Joshua is primarily an account of the conquest of the land of Canaan by the Israelites under Joshua. It is important to note in the very first chapter that the Lord is speaking to and working through Joshua, and in the last chapter of the book, Joshua acknowledges that the Lord was responsible for all the victories of the Israelites. In the last chapter we read these stirring words from Joshua:

"Now therefore fear the Lord, and serve him in sincerity and in truth: and put away the gods which your fathers served on the other side of the flood, and in Egypt; and serve ye the Lord. And if it seem evil unto you to serve the Lord, choose you this day whom ye will serve . . . but as for me and my house, we will serve the Lord" (Joshua 24:14–15).

Joshua's stirring invitation is as pertinent today as it was at the time it was first given.

The Book of Judges

Moses was known as *the* Prophet among the ancient Israelites; even though some of his successors might also have been prophets, they were known collectively as the judges. The "Book of Judges," together with the small book of Ruth, "contain all the Jewish history that has been preserved to us" in the scriptures "of the times between the death of Joshua and the birth of Samuel."[21] Some of the words in the heading of chapter two set the tone of the entire book: "An angel rebukes Israel for not serving the Lord—A pattern of future events: A new generation arises that forsakes the Lord . . .—The Lord is angry with Israel and ceases to preserve them—He raises up judges to guide and lead them—Canaanites left in land to prove Israel" (that is, to *test* them).

Interesting persons discussed in the book of Judges include Barak, Deborah, Gideon, Jael, Jephthah, and Samson. Each of these is discussed in brief entries under the titles of their names in the Bible Dictionary.

A verse I would like to highlight (Judges 6:13) has special meaning only if I note some of the capitalization: "And Gideon said unto him, Oh my Lord, if the LORD be with us, why then is all this befallen us?" The word *Lord* (with only the first letter capitalized) refers to a messenger and is translated from the Hebrew word *adoni*. The word *LORD* (with all letters capitalized) refers to Jehovah. Such usage is consistent throughout the Old Testament.

The Book of Ruth

This brief book of four chapters is remembered primarily by many (1) because of Ruth's statement of devotion to her mother-in-law, Naomi, and (2) because the book provides critical links in the genealogy of David and thus of the genealogy of Jesus Christ, who was partially a descendant of David.

Surely you remember these words from the book of Ruth: "Intreat me not to leave thee, or to return from following after thee: for whither thou goest, I will go; and where thou lodgest, I will lodge: thy people shall be my people, and thy God my God" (Ruth 1:16).

Such devotion is admirable in any age of the world.

First and Second Samuel

The formal titles of the two books of Samuel are very long: The First Book of Samuel, Otherwise Called the First Book of the Kings, and The Second Book of Samuel, Otherwise Called the Second Book of the Kings. In the Hebrew Bible, these two books are combined into one. These are the first of four consecutive books in the Old Testament dealing with the end of the rule of the judges and the beginning of the reign of the kings over the Israelites. As the titles of the books indicate, the early leading personality during this period of history is Samuel, whose birth, calling as a prophet, and appointment as a judge are reviewed in the first seven chapters of the first book. The heading of chapter eight includes the words: "The Lord consents to give them a king." In a sense, this marks the beginning of the period of the kings among ancient Israel, and Saul, the first king, is mentioned first in chapter 9. Other major personalities introduced in the First Book of Samuel include Jonathan, David, and Goliath.

In 1 Samuel 8:7 we read: "And the Lord said unto Samuel, Hearken unto the voice of the people in all that they say unto thee: for they have not rejected thee, but they have rejected me." When the people reject the prophet of the Lord, they reject the Lord himself.

The Second Book of Samuel begins just after the death of Saul and follows David through the major part of his kingship. It includes the story of Uzzah being smitten for steadying the ark, the dishonorable and sinful acts of David in connection with Bath-sheba and Uriah, and the revolt of David's son Absalom. Nathan is one of the chief prophets of the period. The Messianic statements and prophecies concerning the coming of Christ and David's psalm of praise in chapter 22 comprise some of the spiritual high points of the book. In verse 2 of that chapter we read: "The Lord is my rock, and my fortress, and my deliverer" (2 Samuel 22:2).

Together, these two books cover a period of about 130 years, beginning with the birth of Samuel and ending just before the death of David.

First and Second Kings

Again, the Jews regard our books of First Kings and Second Kings as one book. One Jewish tradition maintains these books were edited by the prophets. The formal titles of these books are The First Book of the Kings, Commonly Called the Third Book of the Kings, and The Second Book of the Kings, Commonly Called the Fourth Book of the Kings.

The entry in the Bible Dictionary states concerning these books: "The books of Kings narrate the history from the rebellion of Adonijah to the final captivity of Judah, including the whole history of the northern kingdom from the separation till its disappearance in 721 B.C. The books were compiled by some unknown writer from a variety of written documents, including the state chronicles."

The First Book of Kings includes an account of the reign of Solomon, including his building and dedicating the temple. Elijah is the major prophet during the latter part of this book, and several of his miraculous accomplishments are listed in chapters 17, 18, and 19.

Do you remember these challenging words from Elijah in 1 Kings 18:21: "And Elijah came unto all the people, and said, How long halt ye between two opinions? if the Lord be God, follow him: but if Baal, then follow him."

The Second Book of Kings begins with the ministry and teachings of Elijah and Elisha. Chapters 1 through 7, and chapter 13:13–21, which tells of the death of Elisha, should be read with great care and much pondering. Chapter 17 tells of the scattering of the ten tribes, and chapters 24 and 25 recount the Babylonian captivity of the kingdom of Judah during the days of King Zedekiah. These chapters should be of particular interest to Latter-day Saints. In 1 Nephi 1:4, we learn that Lehi and his family left Jerusalem "in the commencement of the first year of the reign of Zedekiah, king of Judah."

The words to be highlighted from this book are the words of Elisha to his fearful servant as recorded in 2 Kings 6:16: "Fear not: for they that be with us are more than they that be with them." Truly, one man and God make a majority.

First and Second Chronicles

Formally, these books are called The First Book of the Chronicles and The Second Book of the Chronicles. As you may have already surmised, the two books of Chronicles count as one in the Hebrew canon. Concerning these two books, the Bible Dictionary entry indicates they "give a short history of events from the Creation down to the proclamation of Cyrus allowing the Jews to return to Palestine. . . . The date of composition [of these books] cannot be fixed with certainty."

Actually, the only information in these two books relating to the period of the Creation is a listing of genealogies and family ties from Adam down to the time period being discussed. Most of the events detailed in these books have already been mentioned in First and Second Samuel and First and Second Kings. Verses that might be given special attention in First Chronicles include (1) 1 Chronicles 5:1–2, where additional insight is provided on why Joseph succeeded Reuben as the birthright son of Israel; (2) 1 Chronicles 17:1–15, where dialogue between David and Nathan is provided; and (3) 1 Chronicles 29:29, where the books of "Nathan the prophet" and "Gad the seer" are mentioned. The books of Nathan and Gad are only two of several books that were apparently part of the canonized scriptures at one time, but which do not appear in our present Old Testament. If you are interested in the subject of lost scriptures and in the listing of the books lost from the Bible, read the entry under the title "Lost Books" on pages 725–26 of the Bible Dictionary.

A reference in Second Chronicles that might be pondered is chapter 15, verses 9 and 10. These verses might help explain why the progenitors of Lehi—who was of the blood tribe of Manasseh—left the land of their inheritance and migrated to Jerusalem. Lehi was a descendant of Manasseh, as stated in Alma 10:3; yet Nephi recorded in 1 Nephi 1:4 that his father had dwelt "at Jerusalem in all his days."

Note the exact words of 2 Chronicles 15:9–10: "And he [the Lord] gathered all

Judah and Benjamin, and the strangers with them out of Ephraim and Manasseh, and out of Simeon: for they fell to him out of Israel in abundance, when they saw that the Lord his God was with him. So they gathered themselves together at Jerusalem."

The Lord truly knows the end from the beginning.

Ezra

This section of the Old Testament is known by the designation *Ezra*—not *Book of Ezra,* but simply *Ezra.* It is also worthy of note that the first three verses of Ezra are virtually word-for-word the same as the last two verses of Second Chronicles. Thus, this section or book was clearly intended to be a sequel to First and Second Chronicles.

Although this book is named in honor of the famous priest and scribe called Ezra, the first six chapters of the book describe events that happened sixty to eighty years before Ezra arrived in Jerusalem. These events include King Cyrus of Persia allowing the Jews to go back to Jerusalem to build the temple. The remaining four chapters pertain to the lifetime of Ezra and record his powerful intercessory prayer in behalf of his people, including these words from Ezra 9:9: "We were bondmen; yet our God hath not forsaken us in our bondage, but hath extended mercy unto us."

The Book of Nehemiah

This book is clearly a continuation of Ezra, the two being regarded by the Jews as one book. Little is known about the man Nehemiah except that he was a Jew who held the important position of "cupbearer" to the king of Persia and who received from the king a royal commission authorizing him to rebuild the walls of Jerusalem. The religious position of Nehemiah is not clear; he may have been a Levite or of the tribe of Judah.

Chapter 8 of Nehemiah contains the interesting experience of Ezra "the priest the scribe" (8:9) reading "the law of God distinctly" (8:8) and giving the sense or meaning, while the people stood up in their places.

Nehemiah 9:6 reads: "Thou, even thou, art Lord alone; thou hast made heaven, the heaven of heavens, with all their host, the earth, and all things that are therein, . . . and thou preservest them all."

The Book of Esther

The book of Esther is the second book in the Old Testament bearing the name of a woman, the first being the book of Ruth. The book stands by itself and is not directly connected to any other book in the Bible. Although the existence of God seems to be taken for granted throughout the book, the word or name of God does not appear anywhere in the book. This may help to explain why no fragment of the book of Esther has been found among the Dead Sea Scrolls. As indicated in the Manual of Discipline among the Dead Sea Scrolls, the people of the Qumran community where the scrolls were discovered were under command to preserve any writing with the name of God written thereon. Fragments of all the books of the Old Testament, except Esther, have been found among the scrolls.

The book of Esther provides the background for the institution of the feast of Purim or "the lots." The article under the title "Feasts" in the Bible Dictionary helps us gain an understanding of Purim and of the book of Esther.

An interesting verse in Esther 2:7 provides another name for Esther—Hadassah—which has become the name of the largest women's organization in Judaism today.

The Book of Job

The book of Job is another book that seems to stand by itself in the Old Testament. It contains some of the greatest poetry in the Bible, and its contents have been read, discussed, and pondered by great philosophers throughout the centuries.

Though some sectarian students of the Bible have questioned whether Job actually existed as a separate individual, he is mentioned by name in Ezekiel 14:14, James 5:11, and in Doctrine and Covenants 121:10. Perhaps the most famous single statement by Job is his stirring testimony of the resurrection in Job 19:25–27:

"For I know that my redeemer liveth, and that he shall stand at the latter day upon the earth: And though after my skin worms destroy this body, yet in my flesh shall I see God: Whom I shall see for myself, and mine eyes shall behold."

This statement of the resurrection is one of the strongest in the entire Old Testament.

The Book of Psalms

In the Hebrew canon, the Psalms collectively are referred to by a word which best translates as *praises,* and the titles of some of these praises include another Hebrew word which denotes a composition set to music.

No attempt will be made here to even begin to describe the majesty of some of the profound statements in this book of scripture and in the book of Proverbs that follows it. Suffice it to say that the writers of the New Testament books quote more verses from the book of Psalms than from any other book of the Old

Testament. Indeed, out of a total of 283 direct citations from the Old Testament in the New Testament, 116 have been counted from this one book, many of them referring directly to Jesus Christ.

Notice—and then read and ponder—the Psalms which are headed "A Messianic Psalm" or "Speaking Messianically": 2, 8, 9, 16, 21, 22, 31, 34, 40, 45, 67, 68, 69, 89, 91, 110, 118, and 132. An additional thirty Psalms are also quoted by New Testament writers: 4, 5, 6, 10, 14, 18, 19, 24, 32, 35, 36, 37, 41, 44, 51, 55, 78, 82, 94, 95, 97, 102, 104, 109, 112, 116, 117, 135, 140, and 143.

The Bible Dictionary entry concerning this book includes the following: "No book of the Old Testament is more Christian in its inner sense or more fully attested as such by the use made of it than the Psalms."

Of the scores of verses from the book of Psalms that could have been highlighted, I have selected Psalm 19:1: "The heavens declare the glory of god; and the firmament sheweth his handywork." My commentary on that scripture would be another quotation, from Psalm 14:1: "The fool hath said in his heart, there is no God."

The Proverbs

The Hebrew word which the King James translators translated as *proverb* has variously been rendered as *similitude* or *parable*. However, many of the sayings in this book do not fit neatly under either of these designations.

The various chapters in this book stand by themselves. Indeed, the various proverbs within any single chapter often have little relationship to each other. Special attention might be given to the proverbs in chapter 3, as three of them— from verse 3, verses 11–12, and verse 34—are quoted by New Testament writers.

Although scores of verses could have been highlighted, the thought in Proverbs 3:5 has special meaning for me: "Trust in the Lord with all thine heart; and lean not unto thine own understanding."

This is good advice for all of us, regardless of our station or position in life.

Ecclesiastes or, the Preacher

The Hebrew word that is translated *preacher* in this title essentially means "one who convenes an assembly."

The Bible Dictionary entry on this book should assist you greatly in understanding the flavor of the book. Although many readers of the book consider its message too pessimistic, remember the author is writing from the point of view of the world, where without the truths of the gospel everything is indeed "vain," "empty," and "transitory." Chapters 11 and 12 contain the most spiritual message in the book, including the idea that the only activity of lasting and permanent value comes from obedience to God's commandments. Note particularly the statement in Ecclesiastes 12:7 that at the time of death "the spirit shall return unto God who gave it."

The Song of Solomon

This brief book of eight chapters contains virtually nothing that is edifying so far as the gospel of Jesus Christ is concerned. Perhaps it is sufficient to mention that the book entitled "The Song of Solomon" does not appear in the Joseph Smith Translation of the Bible, and the Prophet Joseph Smith reportedly said: "The Song of Solomon is not inspired writing."[22]

The Book of the Prophet Isaiah

It might be unwise to select any one book of the Old Testament and declare it the most important of them all. However, I must admit that if I were forced to select the Old Testament book I consider to be the most important for the world today, at this time in my life I confess that choice would have to be The Book of the Prophet Isaiah.

Although the Savior was not asked by the Nephites to identify the most important book of their scriptures, it is of interest to note that after the resurrected Jesus Christ quoted Isaiah 54 to the Nephites, he offered the following counsel: "And now, behold, I say unto you, that ye ought to search these things. Yea, a commandment I give unto you that ye search these things diligently; for great are the words of Isaiah.

"For surely he spake as touching all things concerning my people which are of the house of Israel; therefore it must needs be that he must speak also to the Gentiles. And all things that he spake have been and shall be, even according to the words which he spake" (3 Nephi 23:1–3).

My mind cannot conceive of a greater recommendation for reading, studying, and pondering the writings of Isaiah than these words by the resurrected Christ.

As you study Isaiah, pay special attention to those chapters where the chapter headings indicate that the chapter (1) emphasizes the life, mission, and atonement of Jesus Christ, (2) mentions major events that are to precede the second coming of Jesus Christ in the last days, (3) is quoted in the Book of Mormon or in other scriptures, or (4) pertains to the Millennium. After re-reading Isaiah to determine which chapters should be included in which category, I realized that virtually every chapter appeared under one of those headings or another, and several of the chapters were listed under two or more headings.

I am thrilled as I ponder the import of these words of Isaiah: "For unto us a child is born, unto us a son is given: and the government shall be upon his shoulder: and his name shall be called Wonderful, Counsellor, The mighty God, The everlasting Father, The Prince of Peace" (Isaiah 9:6).

These are only a few of the many titles Isaiah used for his Savior and God. The Lord's admonition remains: "Search these things diligently; for great are the words of Isaiah" (3 Nephi 23:1).

The Book of the Prophet Jeremiah

The writings and prophecies of Jeremiah should be of particular interest to Latter-day Saints, as Jeremiah was a contemporary of the prophet Lehi, and some of the writings of Jeremiah are contained on the brass plates of Laban.

Jeremiah lived at a critical time in the history of the kingdom of Judah. He first prophesied of the impending Babylonian captivity and then was an eyewitness of many of the major events associated with it.

Jeremiah's call came directly from the Lord, and Jeremiah 1:4–5 indicates that the call initially came in the pre-earthly existence. Note these words: "Then the word of the Lord came unto me, saying, Before I formed thee in the belly I knew thee; and before thou camest out of the womb I sanctified thee, and I ordained thee a prophet unto the nations."

Note also the frequency with which Jeremiah used either the expression "The Lord said unto me" or "The word of the Lord came unto me saying." One or the other of these expressions is found in half of the verses of the first chapter of Jeremiah. Thus, when we quote this prophet, instead of saying, "According to the prophet Jeremiah," perhaps it would be more correct to say, "According to the Lord as revealed through his prophet Jeremiah."

The entire book of Jeremiah makes for interesting and rather easy reading, but perhaps special attention should be given to those chapters where Jeremiah prophesies concerning the gathering and restoration of Israel in the latter days. These would include chapters 16, 23–25, 30–33, and 50. The miracles associated with this latter-day gathering will be so great that the Lord revealed through his prophet Jeremiah:

"Therefore, behold, the days come, saith the Lord, that it shall no more be said, The Lord liveth, that brought up the children of Israel out of the land of Egypt; but, The Lord liveth, that brought up the children of Israel from the land of the north, and from all the lands whither he had driven them: and I will bring them again into their land that I gave unto their fathers.

"Behold, I will send for many fishers, saith the Lord, and they shall fish them; and after will I send for many hunters, and they shall hunt them from every mountain, and from every hill, and out of the holes of the rocks" (Jeremiah 16:14–16).

Concerning the book of Jeremiah, we might well say, "Great are the words of the Lord which he spake through his prophet Jeremiah."

The Lamentations of Jeremiah

The Bible Dictionary entry concerning this brief book gives us insight into the organizational pattern of the book, as well as much of the import of its message. Unfortunately, much of the beauty of these poems is lost in the translation, as is true with most or all poetic literature.

The Bible Dictionary entry reads in part: "**Lamentations, Book of.** Or, Dirges over the fall of Jerusalem and the nation. Written by Jeremiah. The poems are acrostic, chs. 1, 2, 4 having each 22 verses beginning with the successive letters of the alphabet; ch. 3 has 66 verses, every three beginning each with one letter; ch. 5 is not alphabetical. This beautiful little book is very instructive, e.g., in regard to the scenes in the city, and the feelings of the people, ch. 4; the deep impression made by the destruction of the holy city and temple by Jehovah's own hand (1:21; 2:1–11; 3:42–44); the feeling of sin awakened by it and the deep sense of national humiliation."

Note the yearning of Jeremiah as expressed in the next to last verse of his lamentations: "Turn thou us unto thee, O Lord, and we shall be turned; renew our days as of old" (Lamentations 5:21).

The old days really are better when they were days of righteousness and we are in days of sin.

The Book of the Prophet Ezekiel

The meaning of the name Ezekiel is "God will strengthen." (The *El* portion of a Hebrew name means the word *God*.) It is an appropriate name for this priest of the family of Zadok who was carried captive into Babylon in the days of Nebuchadnezzar and there prophesied for some twenty-two years concerning the future of Israel, both in the immediate future and also in the latter days.

Inasmuch as Ezekiel's prophecies are concerned with two different gatherings (both in the future, from his perspective), care must be taken to determine which of these prophecies are primarily concerned with the latter days. The chapter headings will help somewhat in this determination; you will want to give special attention and consideration to chapters 11, 20, 34–39, and 47–48.

Latter-day Saints will recognize the references to the Bible and the Book of Mormon in this prophecy of Ezekiel:

"The word of the Lord came again unto me, saying, Moreover, thou son of man, take thee one stick, and write upon it, For Judah, and for the children of Israel his companions: then take another stick, and write upon it, For Joseph, the stick of Ephraim, and for all the house of Israel his companions: And join them one to another into one stick; and they shall become one in thine hand.

"And when the children of thy people shall speak unto thee, saying, Wilt thou not shew us what thou meanest by these? Say unto them, Thus saith the Lord God; Behold, I will take the stick of Joseph, which is in the hand of Ephraim, and the tribes of Israel his fellows, and will put them with him, even with the stick of Judah, and make them one stick, and they shall be one in mine hand" (Ezekiel 37:15–19).

I ended this quotation with verse 19, but the remainder of this chapter and the chapters that follow provide vital and interesting information pertaining to the times in which we live. They also provide information that will help us prepare for the second coming of Christ.

The Book of Daniel

Daniel is another prophet whose name ends with the letters El, standing for the word *God*. The full name of DANIEL means "A judge (is) God."

The book of Daniel was written during the period of the exile, as was the book of Ezekiel. Little is known of the hero of the book whose name was Daniel. Nothing at all is known of his parentage, but Daniel 1:3 introduces the possibility that he was of "the king's seed." Daniel is frequently spoken of in modern times as having been a prophet, but the word *prophet* is not used in connection with Daniel in his book. In fact, the only time the word *prophet* appears in the book of Daniel is in Daniel 9:2, and there it refers to Jeremiah.

There is no question, however, as to whether or not Daniel had the spirit of prophecy. His interpretation of dreams and of the writing on the wall of the king's palace—and his visions of the latter days, including the stone cut out of the mountain "without hands" (Daniel 2:34) and the visit of the Son of Man (Christ) with the ancient of days (Adam)—all testify of his spiritual and prophetic powers. Evidently Daniel is one of the relatively few people who have been privileged to see in vision the major events on the earth that will immediately precede the second coming of Jesus Christ.

Fortunately, once you start reading and pondering the book of Daniel it will be hard to put it down. Few books of scripture maintain as high a level of drama and excitement—chapter after chapter after chapter—as the writings of this Hebrew exile. And who can ever forget the thrilling and exciting stories of the fiery furnace and the den of lions?

One insightful quotation from Daniel: "Many shall be purified, and made white, and tried; but the wicked shall do wickedly: and none of the wicked shall understand; but the wise shall understand" (Daniel 12:10).

Brigham Young used similar words in relation to a study of the Bible: "The world could not understand them [the writings of the Bible] . . . and yet it is one of the simplest books in the world."[23]

Hosea

Again we have an example where the name of the book consists only of the name of the major writer: Hosea. You will remember this was also the case with Ezra, and it will be the pattern for all the remaining books of the Old Testament: Joel, Amos, Obadiah, Jonah, Micah, Nahum, Habakkuk, Zephaniah, Haggai, Zechariah, and Malachi.

The Hebrew Old Testament combines all twelve of these books into one, titled "Scroll of the Twelve." The prophets themselves are referred to as the "minor prophets" because of the briefness of their writings.

As indicated in the Bible Dictionary entry on the prophet Hosea, he is "the only prophet of the northern kingdom [kingdom of Israel] who has left written prophecies." However, "the profound thought and pathos of this prophet of the north deeply influenced succeeding writers." Except for Hosea, all the other prophets whose names are listed as titles of books in the Old Testament were sent by the Lord to the citizens of the kingdom of Judah.

New Testament writers were also influenced by Hosea; six quotations from Hosea are included in New Testament books (Hosea 1:10; 2:23; 6:6; 10:8; 11:1; and 13:14)—more than were included from the writings of Joel, Amos, Jonah, and Micah combined.

Perhaps the two best-known statements from Hosea are:

"When Israel was a child, then I loved him, and called my son out of Egypt" (Hosea 11:1, also quoted in Matthew 2:15), and "I will ransom them from the power of the grave; I will redeem them from death: O death, I will be thy plagues; O grave, I will be thy destruction" (Hosea 13:14).

Joel

Although brief in length—only three chapters running a total of 4 1/2 pages—the book of Joel contains significant passages pertaining to the last days. For Latter-day Saints, Joel has the distinction of having been quoted by the Angel Moroni to the Prophet Joseph Smith. Concerning the messages delivered by Moroni on September 21 and 22, 1823, Joseph Smith recorded:

"He . . . quoted the second chapter of Joel, from the twenty-eighth verse to the last. He also said that this was not yet fulfilled, but was soon to be. And he further stated that the fulness of the Gentiles was soon to come in" (Joseph Smith—History 1:41).

The verses from Joel quoted by the Angel Moroni, which he said were soon to be fulfilled, are as follows:

"And it shall come to pass afterward, that I will pour out my spirit upon all flesh; and your sons and your daughters shall prophesy, your old men shall dream dreams, your young men shall see visions: And also upon the servants and upon the handmaids in those days will I pour out my spirit. And I will shew wonders in the heavens and in the earth, blood, and fire, and pillars of smoke. The sun shall be turned into darkness, and the moon into blood, before the great and the terrible day of the Lord come.

"And it shall come to pass, that whosoever shall call on the name of the Lord shall be delivered: for in mount Zion and in Jerusalem shall be deliverance, as the Lord hath said, and in the remnant whom the Lord shall call" (Joel 2:28–32).

The prophecies in the final chapter of Joel—chapter 3—take us right down to the beginning of the Millennium when the Lord shall dwell in Zion.

Amos

Latter-day Saints quote the words of Amos 3:7 almost as frequently as they quote any other single scripture: "Surely the Lord God will do nothing, but he revealeth his secret unto his servants the prophets" (Amos 3:7).

Another statement by Amos used widely by missionaries in the Church is found in Amos 8:11: "Behold, the days come, saith the Lord God, that I will send a famine in the land, not a famine of bread, nor a thirst for water, but of hearing the words of the Lord" (Amos 8:11).

The heading of the last chapter of Amos—chapter nine—indicates that "in the last days [Israel] will be gathered again into their own land, and it shall become productive." Thousands of Latter-day Saint visitors to the modern country of Israel in the past few years can attest to at least a partial fulfillment of this prophecy by Amos.

Obadiah

This is the shortest book in the Old Testament, only one chapter of slightly more than one page. The last verse prophesies of the time when "saviours shall come up on mount Zion."

Jonah

The story of Jonah is one of the best known in the entire Old Testament. Virtually every student of the Bible remembers the account of Jonah being swallowed by a "great fish," in the belly of which he spent three days and three nights. Although some liberal interpreters of the Bible have questioned the authenticity of this story, it is evident that the Savior was aware of the incident, as indicated in his words recorded in Matthew 12:39–40: "An evil and adulterous generation seeketh after a sign; and there shall no sign be given to it, but the sign of the prophet Jonas: For as Jonas was three days and three nights in the whale's belly; so shall the Son of man be three days and three nights in the heart of the earth" (Matthew 12:39–40).

Micah

Every one of the seven chapters of Micah contains a pertinent message for the people on the earth today. His statement on true religion has been quoted by Jewish and Christian preachers throughout the world: "What doth the Lord require of thee, but to do justly, and to love mercy, and to walk humbly with thy God?" (Micah 6:8).

Christians might remember best his prophecy of the birthplace of the Messiah: "But thou, Beth-lehem Ephratah, though thou be little among the thousands of Judah, yet out of thee shall he come forth unto me that is to be ruler in Israel; whose goings forth have been from of old, from everlasting" (Micah 5:2).

Nahum

Only three chapters and less than three pages long, Nahum predicts the great destructions that will occur in the latter days, including the burning of the earth at the Second Coming. The thought at the beginning of Nahum 1:3 is revealing: "The Lord is slow to anger, and great in power."

Habakkuk

This brief book of three chapters reminds us that the just shall live by faith and that patience is necessary to realize the promises of the Lord. Note the message in Habakkuk 2:20: "But the Lord is in his holy temple: let all the earth keep silence before him."

Zephaniah

The word of the Lord through Zephaniah reminds us in three brief chapters that the destruction of the kingdom of Judah anciently was a type and a shadow of the destructions that will occur before the Second Coming. All nations shall assemble to battle, and it will be a day of wrath and of trouble.

A condition to be hoped for is mentioned in Zephaniah 3:9: "For then will I turn to the people a pure language, that they may all call upon the name of the Lord, to serve him with one consent."

Haggai

In the second shortest book of the Old Testament, Haggai speaks of the coming of the Messiah and refers to him as "the desire of all nations" (Haggai 2:7). Then Haggai quotes the words of the Lord concerning the temple: "The glory of this latter house shall be greater than of the former, saith the Lord of hosts: and in this place will I give peace" (Haggai 2:9).

Zechariah

The meaning of the name *Zechariah* is "Jehovah remembers." What an appropriate name for the prophet who has so much to say concerning both the first and the second comings of the Messiah. The book of Zechariah includes more Messianic prophecies per chapter and verse than any other Old Testament book.

The headings of three of the chapters of Zechariah—3, 9, and 11—begin with the words "Zechariah speaks Messianically." Of course, each of these chapters should be read and pondered carefully.

Zechariah 9:9 was quoted by Matthew in the New Testament: "Rejoice greatly, O daughter of Zion; shout, O daughter of Jerusalem: behold, thy King cometh unto thee: he is just, and having salvation; lowly, and riding upon an ass, and upon a colt the foal of an ass" (Zechariah 9:9).

Special attention should also be given to chapters 2, 8, 10, and 12–14, which speak of the gathering of Israel in the last days and of the major events that will occur before the second coming of Christ.

It would be profitable for us to read carefully all the chapters of Zechariah. Jehovah wants us to remember that he remembers.

Malachi

This last book of the Old Testament has been quoted about as widely as any scripture ever recorded. Latter-day Saints pay special attention both to chapter 3, which contains the famous statement on tithing, and chapter 4, which prophesies of the return of Elijah before the coming of the great and dreadful day of the Lord. The Savior quoted these same two chapters to the Nephites in 3 Nephi 24–25, and Moroni quoted and paraphrased portions of both chapters 3 and 4 to the Prophet Joseph Smith on September 21 and 22, 1823.

Then, on April 3, 1836, Elijah appeared in the Kirtland Temple and announced he had returned in fulfillment of the prophecy of Malachi, "To turn the hearts of the fathers to the children, and the children to the fathers, lest the whole earth be smitten with a curse" (Doctrine and Covenants 110:15; compare Malachi 4:6).

Thus, major portions of the writings of Malachi appear in the Bible, in the Book of Mormon, in the Doctrine and Covenants, and in the Pearl of Great Price. Few writers of the Old Testament can claim that distinction.

Testimonies Pertaining to the Old Testament

Near the beginning of this discussion we included testimonies on the value of the Old Testament; as the final area of emphasis in our discussion it seems fitting that we should include two additional prophetic testimonies.

Elder George Q. Cannon has written concerning the Bible: "This book [the Bible] is of priceless worth; its value cannot be estimated by anything that is known among men upon which value is fixed. . . . To the Latter-day Saints it should always be a precious treasure. Beyond any people now upon the face of the earth, they should value it, for the reason that from its pages, from the doctrines set forth by its writers, the epitome of the plan of salvation which is there given unto us, we derive the highest consolation, we obtain the greatest strength. It is, as it were, a constant fountain sending forth streams of living life to satisfy the souls of all who peruse its pages."[24]

This statement by Brother Cannon should answer the charges of those who claim the teachings of the Old Testament are not relevant in today's society. As Latter-day Saints, indeed, as thinking human beings, we should know that human interests, desires, and needs—and the principles that relate to them—have remained relatively constant throughout the centuries. And, unfortunately, the vices, temptations, and evils of the past remain with us today, and we must be warned of them by the voice of the Lord through his ancient prophets as well as through his living prophets, seers, and revelators.

Also, much of the Old Testament was revealed by the Lord to his prophets anciently to provide hope for those then living and to provide instruction and direction for those who would live in the dispensation of the fulness of times with the responsibility to help prepare the world for the second coming of the Messiah. Such writings have great relevance and significance today.

Let me conclude by recalling for you the experience of President Spencer W. Kimball concerning his first reading of the Bible. He wrote: "Let me tell you of one of the goals that I made when I was still but a lad. When I heard a Church leader from Salt Lake City tell us at conference that we should read the scriptures, and I recognized that I had never read the Bible, that very night at the conclusion of that very sermon I walked to my home a block away and climbed up in my little attic room in the top of the house and lighted a little coal-oil lamp that was on the little table, and I read the first chapters of Genesis. A year later I closed the Bible, having read every chapter in that big and glorious book.

"I found that this Bible that I was reading had in it 66 books, and then I was nearly dissuaded when I found that it had in it 1,189 chapters, and then I also found that it had 1,519 pages. It was formidable, but I knew if others did it that I could do it.

"I found that there were certain parts that were hard for a 14-year-old boy to understand. There were some pages that were not especially interesting to me, but when I had read the 66 books and 1,189 chapters and 1,519 pages, I had a glowing satisfaction that I had made a goal and that I had achieved it.

"Now I am not telling you this story to boast; I am merely using this as an example to say that if I could do it by coal-oil light, you can do it by electric light. I have always been glad I read the Bible from cover to cover."[25]

There's a challenge from the Lord through a prophet who has testified during the lifetime of most of us. Will we accept the challenge? Will we *study diligently* the books of the Old Testament? If we do, then I can promise you that we individually can paraphrase the words of President Kimball and say sincerely: "I have always been glad I read the Old Testament from cover to cover."

That is my own testimony; I am grateful we have the Old Testament to read from cover to cover.

My prayer is that we may read it, ponder it, and *study it diligently,* that we may come to a greater understanding and appreciation of our Savior and Redeemer.

Notes

This is a previously unpublished paper, but much of the material was included in the audiotape *How to Get the Most from the Old Testament* (Salt Lake City: Deseret Book Co., 1989), and in a talk presented at the CES Symposium on the Old Testament, Brigham Young University, August 1991.

1. Spencer W. Kimball, *President Kimball Speaks Out* (Salt Lake City: Deseret Book Co., 1981), 96.
2. This concept is discussed at length in chapter 12, "The Old Testament, a Witness for Jesus Christ."
3. Abraham Lincoln, quoted in "President proclaims 1983 Year of Bible," *Church News,* 20 March 1983, 3.
4. Ronald Reagan, quoted in "President proclaims 1983 Year of Bible," *Church News,* 20 March 1983, 3.
5. Spencer W. Kimball, Marion G. Romney, and Gordon B. Hinckley, quoted in "President proclaims 1983 Year of Bible," *Church News,* 20 March 1983, 3; emphasis added.
6. *Discourses of Brigham Young,* 125.
7. Wilford Woodruff, in *Journal of Discourses,* 16:35.
8. *History of the Church,* 6:57.
9. *Discourses of Brigham Young,* 124; emphasis added.
10. *Discourses of Brigham Young,* 124.
11. Bruce R. McConkie, *The Bible, a Sealed Book,* transcript, (Salt Lake City: The Church of Jesus Christ of Latter-day Saints, c. 1984), 4–5.
12. Bruce R. McConkie, *The Promised Messiah* (Salt Lake City: Deseret Book Co., 1978), 89.
13. J. Reuben Clark Jr., *Why the King James Version?* (Salt Lake City: Deseret Book Co., 1979), vii.
14. James Strong, *Exhaustive Concordance of the Bible* (New York: Abingdon Press, 1967), title page.
15. For further discussion on the footnotes in the LDS edition of the Bible, see chapter 4, "How to Get the Most from Your Study of the New Testament."
16. Topical Guide, 1.
17. See Daniel H. Ludlow, "The Old Testament, a Witness for Jesus Christ," in *A Witness of Jesus Christ: The 1989 Sperry Symposium on the Old Testament,* ed. Richard D. Draper (Salt Lake City: Deseret Book Co., 1990), 128.
18. Bible Dictionary, 599.
19. The portion of the Pearl of Great Price called "Selections from the Book of Moses" was "revealed to Joseph Smith the Prophet" between June 1830 and February 1831, and was "an extract from the translation of the Bible" (see the headnote to this book).
20. *Doctrines of Salvation,* 1:27.
21. Bible Dictionary, "Judges, Book of."
22. B. F. Cummings, "The Prophet's Last Letters," *Improvement Era,* 18 (February 1915): 389.
23. *Discourses of Brigham Young,* 124.
24. *Gospel Truth,* 2:248.
25. Spencer W. Kimball, "Planning for a Full and Abundant Life," *Ensign,* May 1974, 88.

Chapter 4

How to Get the Most from Your Study of the New Testament

I consider the New Testament to be one of the greatest of all the scriptures. It is the "Book of Books" so far as an account of the birth, ministry, teachings, atonement, death, and resurrection of Jesus Christ are concerned. And I hasten to add my belief that a knowledge of the atonement of Jesus Christ—and all that the atonement entails—constitutes the most important understanding any person can acquire on this earth. I think it would be fair to state that more people have been led to at least a basic knowledge and testimony of Jesus Christ through the New Testament during the past two millennia than through any other single book. Thus a study of this book deserves our time and best attention.

Why Use the Authorized King James Version?

As we begin, let's consider the question as to why we should use the text of the authorized King James Version of the Bible.[1] The basic reasons why at least one General Authority favored the use of the King James Version are outlined in a 475-page book, *Why the King James Version?*, published in 1956 and written by President J. Reuben Clark Jr., who was then serving as a counselor in the First Presidency. In his book President Clark reviews the origin and the basic contents of many of the major editions of the Bible in existence at that time. In the preface to his book, President Clark writes:

"It should be clearly in mind that *only the New Testament* is considered herein, save for a short discussion of the origin of writing and of modern criticism of the Old Testament. . . .

". . . The author has, in his later years, done some reading in an effort to satisfy himself as to which of the generally used English translations of the New Testament, he might more fully rely upon (judged by his reading) as most accurately recording the words and an account of the works of our Lord and Master, barring the Inspired Version of Joseph Smith. . . . [The] preparation [of the book on the King James Version] has been of greatest value to [the author] personally in helping to confirm and solidify his spiritual instincts regarding the New Testament record and message."[2]

As a result of his extensive research and comprehensive comparison with other editions of the Bible, President Clark became convinced that the King James text was superior to all other English Bibles, and thus used it as the basic New Testament text in his monumental book *Our Lord of the Gospels.*

INSTRUCTIONAL AIDS IN THE LDS EDITION OF THE BIBLE

Not only should we use the King James Version of the Bible, but I believe we should use that version as found in the LDS edition of the Bible. I am convinced that the instructional aids in the LDS edition make it the most important and valuable edition ever published on the earth. I am convinced further that any person who is fully acquainted with the contents of these instructional aids, and who knows how to use them effectively, will understand more about the teachings of the Bible than most so-called scholars who have earned theological degrees in biblical studies but who have not had the benefit of these aids.

Let's consider some of these instructional aids individually, in the order in which they are introduced in the Bible.[3]

"GR" Footnotes

The footnotes labeled "GR" give an alternate translation from the Greek. You know, of course, that we do not have available any of the original books of the Bible—not a single one! All we have are copies of earlier copies of earlier copies—and very few of these "earlier copies" date before about A.D. 900. However, the earliest copies of the New Testament available to us are in the Greek language; thus, we would surely get our "longitude and latitude" better in the New Testament if we could read Greek. Unfortunately most of us do not read Greek, nor do we have the earliest Greek copies readily available to us. But scholars in the Church who are well versed in the Greek language have reviewed these early manuscripts—and the editions based on them—and have provided in the footnotes of the LDS edition some alternate translations that may be more accurate. Thus, in effect, we have in the LDS edition the best of both the Greek and the English New Testaments.

Literally hundreds of contributions from the Greek texts and translations are included as footnotes in the books of the New Testament. If you want to have a thrilling and educational experience, identify and mark each of the hundreds of "GR" footnotes in your New Testament. I promise you that through this single activity your understanding and appreciation of the New Testament will increase greatly. I would suggest you mark them with a colored pencil (perhaps with a green pencil for the "GR" [Greek] footnotes, inasmuch as they both begin with the letters "GR"). In order to identify properly each of these "GR" footnotes, you should mark both the "GR" entry in the footnote *and* the corresponding superscript letter in the text.

As an example, the first "GR" footnote reference in the New Testament is found in Matthew 2:4. You will note that the superscript letter *a* before the word *demanded* in this verse leads us to a "GR" footnote entry, suggesting the alternate wording "inquired." I would suggest you prominently mark both the superscript letter and the footnote reference in green; thus one of these sources will quickly lead you to the other.

Another example on this same page is found in Matthew 2:6, where the superscript letter *d* preceding the word *rule* leads us to a footnote entry for that verse, suggesting the following alternate readings from the Greek: "tend, protect, nurture."

"HEB" Footnotes

The footnotes labeled "HEB" give an alternate translation from the Hebrew. These "HEB" footnotes, of course, are found most frequently in the Old Testament, inasmuch as most of the earliest copies of Old Testament books were written in the Hebrew language. Thus, sometime you might want to mark all the "HEB" footnotes listed in the Old Testament, with their corresponding superscript letters. (Be sure to choose a color different from that you use with the "GR" footnotes.) So far as I have been able to determine, only two "HEB" footnotes appear in the New Testament (Romans 9:29 and Hebrews 2:7), and both of them pertain to verses being quoted from the Old Testament.

"IE" Footnotes

The footnotes labeled "IE" give an explanation of idioms and difficult constructions. The dictionary defines an idiom several ways, including "an expression in the usage of a language that is peculiar to itself either grammatically or in having a meaning that cannot be derived from the conjoined meaning of its elements."[4] That involved definition correctly suggests that an "idiom" is particularly tricky; at first glance it may appear to mean one thing when in actuality it means another.

A good example of an idiom is found in Matthew 22:16, where the King James text reads "neither carest thou for any man." This could more correctly have been translated "you court no man's favor." Another example of an idiom is in Luke 22:66, where the expression "the elders of the people" has reference to "the Sanhedrin." Again, you might want to identify all the "IE" footnotes, together with the superscript letters leading to them, by marking them with a distinctive color.

"JST" Footnotes

The footnotes labeled "JST" give a more correct reading from the Joseph Smith Translation. As we read on the page facing page 1 in the Bible, "Short excerpts are provided in the footnotes; longer excerpts are provided in the Appendix. Italic type in these JST excerpts is used for words not found in the King James Version."[5]

Those who are students of the Book of Mormon will remember that an "angel of the Lord" told the prophet Nephi, nearly six hundred years before the time of Christ, that when the early equivalent of what we call the Bible would come into the control of a particular church, many plain and precious truths would be deleted or changed. The exact words of the angel are recorded as follows:

"Wherefore, these things go forth from the Jews in purity unto the Gentiles, according to the truth which is in God. And after they go forth by the hand of the twelve apostles of the Lamb, from the Jews unto the Gentiles, thou seest the formation of that great and abominable church, which is most abominable above all other churches; for behold, they have taken away from the gospel of the Lamb many parts which are plain and most precious; and also many covenants of the Lord have they taken away. And all this have they done that they might pervert the right ways of the Lord, that they might blind the eyes and harden the hearts of the children of men. Wherefore, thou seest that after the book hath gone forth through the hands of the great and abominable church, that there are many plain and precious things taken away from the book, which is the book of the Lamb of God. And . . . because of the many plain and precious things which have been taken out of the book . . . an exceedingly great many do stumble, yea, insomuch that Satan hath great power over them" (1 Nephi 13:25–29).

A careful reading of 1 Nephi clearly indicates that many "plain and precious" truths of the gospel of the Lamb (Jesus Christ) would be taken from "the book of the Lamb of God" (which would include the New Testament). The excerpts from the Joseph Smith Translation of the Bible which are included in this LDS edition of the scriptures help to restore many of these "plain and precious" truths! Now do you see why the JST footnotes are so valuable? Again, I highly recommend that you distinctly mark every one of them, without exception, perhaps in a bright color such as red; then study and ponder the changes suggested by the JST excerpts until you understand them. If you do this one thing, you will understand more about the New Testament than the biblical scholars who do not have the advantage of these footnotes.

Let's look now at two brief examples of the contribution of the JST footnotes; other examples will be given later when we identify specific scriptures to ponder in the individual books of the New Testament.

1. The King James text of Matthew 4:1–2 reads: "Then was Jesus led up of the Spirit into the wilderness to be tempted of the devil. And when he had fasted forty days and forty nights, he was afterward an hungered."

The Joseph Smith Translation text of these two verses reads: "Then was Jesus led up of the Spirit into the wilderness, to be with God. And when he had fasted forty days and forty nights, and had communed with God, he was afterwards an hungered, and was left to be tempted of the devil."

What an important and significant difference!

2. As a second example of the contribution of the JST excerpts, the King James text of Mark 4:25 reads: "For he that hath, to him shall be given: and he that hath not, from him shall be taken even that which he hath."

The corresponding verse in the JST is: "For he that receiveth, to him shall be given; but he that continueth not to receive, from him shall be taken even that which he hath."

Again, what an important change!

Elder Bruce R. McConkie said concerning the value of the Joseph Smith Translation: "The Joseph Smith Translation, or Inspired Version, is a thousand times over the best Bible now existing on earth. It contains all that the King James Version does, plus pages of additions and corrections and an occasional deletion. It was made by the spirit of revelation, and the changes and additions are the equivalent of the revealed word in the Book of Mormon and the Doctrine and Covenants. For historical and other reasons there have been, among some members of the Church in times past, some prejudice and misunderstanding of the place of the Joseph Smith Translation. I hope this has now all vanished away. The Latter-day

Saint edition of the Bible footnotes many of the major changes made in the Inspired Version and has a seventeen-page section that sets forth excerpts that are too lengthy for inclusion in the footnotes. Reference to this section and to the footnotes themselves will give anyone who has spiritual insight a deep appreciation of the revelatory work of the Prophet Joseph Smith. It is one of the great evidences of his prophetic call."[6]

"OR" Footnotes

The footnotes labeled "OR," which stands for the word *or*, give us alternate words to clarify the meaning of English expressions that have become archaic.

As you are well aware, the meanings of words frequently change. Many of us have witnessed such changes in meanings of words even during our lifetimes. Obviously, many words used by the translators of the King James text in 1611 have changed meanings in the nearly four hundred years that have followed. The "OR" footnotes help us to be aware of these changes.

Again, only two examples from the New Testament:

1. In Mark 6:25 the King James text identifies the object on which the head of John the Baptist was placed as a "charger." The more contemporary word would be "platter."

2. In Luke 2:49 and in many other places of the New Testament, the King James word *wist* (such as in the expression "wist ye not") today would probably be translated as "knew."

If you decide to color mark the "OR" entries, you might want to consider the color orange, which begins with the same letters, "OR."

Scriptural Cross-References

The LDS edition of the Bible provides thousands of cross-references to other scriptures. A glance at the footnotes on almost any page of the Bible will tell us that these scriptural cross references include references to *all* the standard works: the Old Testament, New Testament, Book of Mormon, Doctrine and Covenants, and Pearl of Great Price. The Church has never before published such an extensive cross-referencing system in any edition of the scriptures.

Bible Dictionary

A few of the many individual entries in the Bible Dictionary that should be of great interest to students of the New Testament are: Angels; Anointed One; Atonement; Baptism; Beatitudes; Bishop; Church; Communion; Confirmation; Degrees of Glory; Disciple; Dispensations; Faith; Gentile; Grecians; Holy Ghost; Laying on of hands; Lord's Day; Miracles; Parables; Paradise; Pharisees; Prayer; Repentance; Resurrection; Sadducees; Samaritans; Sanhedrin; Scribe; Son of God; Son of Man; Temple; Temple of Herod; Tetrarch; Transfiguration, Mount of; Wise Men of the East; and Zealots.

Two other major sections of the Bible Dictionary that we should use frequently and repeatedly as we read the New Testament are:

1. *"Harmony of the Gospels" chart.* Beginning on page 684 of the appendix and continuing through page 696 is an extended chart that provides a "Harmony of the Gospels." The headings at the top of these charts provide for a complete chronological listing of all the major events in the life of Jesus Christ as contained in the New Testament, together with the location of the event and the pertinent scriptures from Matthew, Mark, Luke, and John (as well as from Latter-day revelation) pertaining to that particular event. You might use this valuable chart in a variety of ways. As one example, you might glance down the column under the title of a book to note the specific items covered by that particular book. Or, you might select a particular event and then check to see in which books that event is listed. Or, using the listing of the events as your guide, you can read and ponder all the accounts in all of the gospels pertaining to that event; then proceed to the next event.

As you can imagine, the development of these charts required hundreds of hours of dedicated effort.

2. *Quotations from the Old Testament found in the New Testament.* Another valuable instructional aid for students of the New Testament is found on pages 756 through 759, tucked away under the heading "Quotations from the Old Testament found in the New Testament." As the introductory statement to this entry indicates, the list "includes some of the passages in which the New Testament writers have clearly been under the influence of the Old Testament scriptures, without expressly quoting from them." What a valuable resource! Yet I suspect few of us are using it as extensively as we could and should.

In summary, if you want to earn the equivalent of a doctor's degree in biblical studies, just read and ponder and meditate—until you understand—each of the entries of the Bible Dictionary, beginning with the first entry of Aaron (who was a brother of Moses) and continuing through the last entry of Zipporah (who, by the way, was a wife of Moses).

Maps

The appendix concludes with twenty-two maps spread over twenty-four pages. About half of these maps pertain particularly to New Testament times, specifically maps 13 through 22. Maps 14 through 17 are particularly helpful in enabling a person to "follow in the footsteps of Jesus." Map 1 provides the details of the physical area of Palestine.

THE BOOKS AND THE MAJOR GROUPINGS OF THE BOOKS OF THE NEW TESTAMENT

The sequence of the books of the New Testament has varied somewhat over the centuries, but the listing in the authorized King James Version provides for four natural groupings. These groupings are: (1) the first five books, comprising the four Gospels and the book of Acts, all of these being somewhat historical, with the four so-called Gospels emphasizing in particular the birth, life, teachings, death, and resurrection of Jesus Christ, including his ministry and atonement; (2) the fourteen epistles of Paul, arranged in the New Testament essentially according to their length, except for the book of Hebrews, which is placed at the end of his epistles; (3) the seven general epistles, comprising some of the writings of James, Peter, John, and Jude; and (4) the single book of "The Revelation of St. John the Divine."

As you glance through these books, you will note that some of them occupy only about a page or less (such as Philemon, 2 and 3 John, and Jude), while others average over 50 pages (including Matthew, Luke, and Acts). All in all, the 27 books of the New Testament occupy 403 pages in the LDS edition of the Bible, as compared with the 1184 pages that make up the 39 books of the Old Testament.

Let us briefly review each of these major groupings of books in the New Testament.

The Four Gospels and the Book of Acts

The first four books of the New Testament all begin with the words "The Gospel According to," followed respectively by the words "St. Matthew," "St. Mark," "St. Luke," and "St. John." Of course, there is only one gospel, and that gospel is rightfully called the "gospel of Jesus Christ." (The word *gospel* means "good news.") Thus, more accurate, but longer, titles for these books might be "The Gospel of Jesus Christ According to Matthew," and so forth. However, as we study these books carefully we will note that none of the books really attempts to present the fulness of the gospel of Jesus Christ in a systematic manner. Rather, these books consist primarily of the testimonies of the individual authors concerning the good news of the life, ministry, and atonement of Jesus Christ. It is of great interest to me to note that Joseph Smith in the Joseph Smith Translation changed these titles to "The Testimony of St. Matthew," "The Testimony of St. Mark," "The Testimony of St. Luke," and "The Testimony of St. John." These titles in the Joseph Smith Translation reflect more precisely what the books really are: they contain the *testimonies* of these individual brethren of the early church.

It is also interesting to note that the Joseph Smith Translation retains the word *Saint* before the individual names of the authors of these four books. This custom, I suppose, results from the use of this term in the many editions of the New Testament published by the Catholic Church prior to the publication of either the King James or the JST editions. As you know, the Catholic Church has officially elevated some very righteous persons to the status of "sainthood," and all four of these writers have been so named. Of course, we also know that in New Testament times the followers of Jesus Christ were called "Saints," and Matthew, Mark, Luke, and John were all believers in Jesus Christ and were members of his church.

Elder Bruce R. McConkie has written concerning the differences and similarities of the first four books of the New Testament: "The four New Testament gospels . . . present different aspects of our Lord's personality and teachings. It appears that Matthew was directing his gospel to the Jews. He presents Christ as the promised Messiah and Christianity as the fulfilment of Judaism. Mark apparently wrote with the aim of appealing to the Roman or Gentile mind. Luke's gospel presents the Master to the Greeks, to those of culture and refinement. And the gospel of John is the account for the saints; it is pre-eminently the gospel for the Church, for those who understand the scriptures and their symbolisms and who are concerned with spiritual and eternal things. Obviously such varying approaches have the great advantage of presenting the truths of salvation to people of different cultures, backgrounds, and experiences. But the simple fact is that all of the gospel authors wrote by inspiration, and all had the same purposes: 1. To testify of the divine Sonship of our Lord; and 2. To teach the truths of the plan of salvation."[7]

All of the first four books of the New Testament are discussed together on pages 682–83 of the Bible Dictionary under the title "Gospels"; the book by John also has a separate entry on page 715 under the title "John, Gospel of."

The fifth book of the New Testament is named "The Acts of the Apostles," which briefly and aptly describes the essential contents of the book. Perhaps because this book also contains the forty-day ministry of Jesus Christ after his resurrection, together with historical events associated with some of the early leaders of the Church established by Christ, the book of Acts is frequently grouped with the four so-called Gospels.

The Pauline Epistles

As we review the titles of the next fourteen books of the New Testament, you will note that all of them include the name Paul, and most of them begin with the words "The Epistle of Paul the Apostle to the . . ." followed by the name of a group or individual. The first of these books is entitled "The Epistle of Paul the Apostle to the Romans"; followed by "The First . . ." and "The Second Epistle of Paul the Apostle to the Corinthians"; "The Epistle of Paul the Apostle to the Galatians"; then to the "Ephesians"; to the "Philippians"; to the "Colossians"; and "The First . . ." and "The Second Epistle of Paul the Apostle to the Thessalonians"; then "The First . . ." and "The Second Epistle of Paul the Apostle to Timothy." The titles of the next two books do not contain the words "the Apostle," but are simply designated as "The Epistle of Paul to Titus" and "The Epistle of Paul to Philemon"; I have never found a satisfactory explanation as to why the words "the Apostle" are not included in these two titles. The title of the final Pauline epistle, however, includes these two words again: "The Epistle of Paul the Apostle to the Hebrews."

As we discuss each of these books later, we might have time to identify the groups or individuals to whom these epistles were addressed. For now, however, it might be sufficient to indicate that these epistles are all discussed in detail on pages 743–48 of the Bible Dictionary, under the title "Pauline Epistles." You will find in that article that Paul's epistles are frequently divided into four chronological groups, based on the dates when they were written:

1. First and Second Thessalonians—A.D. 50, 51
2. First and Second Corinthians, Galatians, and Romans—A.D. 55, 57
3. Philippians, Colossians, Ephesians, Philemon, and Hebrews—A.D. 60, 62.
4. Titus, and First and Second Timothy—A.D. 64, 65

On occasion, you may want to read Paul's epistles in the chronological order in which he wrote them, rather than in the order in which they appear in the New Testament, which is essentially according to their length. Reading the epistles chronologically may help you understand Paul better and may also help you to see why he said what he did when he said it.

The General Epistles

The titles of the next seven books all contain the word "Epistle," and in five of those titles the word "General" also is included. Thus, as a grouping, these books are known as the "General Epistles"; they are discussed in a very brief article under this title on page 678 of the Bible Dictionary as follows: "They are so named because they are not directed to any one person or specific branch of the Church. The designation is not entirely accurate for 2 and 3 John."

Individually, the "General Epistles" are designated as: "The General Epistle of James," "The First Epistle General of Peter," "The Second Epistle General of Peter," "The First Epistle General of John," "The Second Epistle of John," "The Third Epistle of John," and "The General Epistle of Jude." These books are discussed under their individual titles in the Bible Dictionary.

The Book of Revelation

The last and concluding book of the New Testament is "The Revelation of St. John the Divine." The author of this book is also known by the designations of "John the Beloved," "John the Beloved Disciple" or "John the Apostle." The book is also known as the Apocalypse, from a Greek word meaning *revealed* or *uncovered*. In the Bible Dictionary, on pages 762–63, this book is discussed rather extensively under the title "Revelation of John."

Selected Scriptures to Ponder from Each of the Books of the New Testament

To help us have a better feel for the flavor and content of the New Testament, I have selected examples of "Scriptures to Ponder" from each of the twenty-seven books of the New Testament. Obviously, we can look at only a very limited number of references. However, because each book contains scriptures worthy of careful reading and pondering, at least one example will be discussed from every book, with additional examples from the longer and more critical books.

The Gospel According to St. Matthew[8]

Matthew 5:1–6

"And seeing the multitudes, he went up into a mountain: and when he was set, his disciples came unto him: And he opened his mouth, and taught them, saying, Blessed are the poor in spirit: for theirs is the kingdom of heaven. Blessed are they that mourn: for they shall be comforted. Blessed are the meek: for they shall inherit the earth. Blessed are they which do hunger and thirst after righteousness: for they shall be filled."

This is the beginning of the beatitudes in the Sermon on the Mount.

The Joseph Smith Translation makes a valuable contribution to our understanding of this passage:

"And Jesus, seeing the multitudes, went up into a mountain; and when he was set down, his disciples came unto him; and he opened his mouth, and taught them, saying, Blessed are they who shall believe on me; and again, more blessed are they who shall believe on your words, when ye shall testify that ye have seen me and that I am. Yea, blessed are they who shall believe on your words, and come down into the depth of humility, and be baptized in my name; for they shall be visited with fire and the Holy Ghost, and shall receive a remission of their sins. Yea, blessed are the poor in spirit, who come unto me; for theirs is the kingdom of heaven. And again, blessed are they that mourn; for they shall be comforted. And blessed are the meek; for they shall inherit the earth. And blessed are all they that do hunger and thirst after righteousness; for they shall be filled with the Holy Ghost" (JST, Matthew 5:1–8; see also 3 Nephi 12:1–6).

A careful reading of the beatitudes in the Joseph Smith Translation makes it clear that all of the listed blessings are predicated upon the person's being baptized and receiving the gift of the Holy Ghost. Also, at the beginning of Matthew 6 the Joseph Smith Translation makes it clear that the Savior, at least in this part of the sermon, is speaking only to his disciples, not to the multitude: "And it came to pass that, as Jesus taught his disciples, he said unto them . . . "

Thus it is clear that the following instructions were intended *only* for the apostles: "Therefore I say unto you, Take no thought for your life, what ye shall eat, or what ye shall drink; nor yet for your body, what ye shall put on. Is not the life more than meat, and the body than raiment?" (Matthew 6:25).

Matthew 5:31–32
"It hath been said, Whosoever shall put away his wife, let him give her a writing of divorcement: But I say unto you, That whosoever shall put away his wife, saving for the cause of fornication, causeth her to commit adultery: and whosoever shall marry her that is divorced committeth adultery."

At first glance, this scripture seems to say that anyone who is divorced and then remarries commits adultery, and this is the interpretation placed on it by the Roman Catholic Church. Hundreds of millions of Catholics are guided by this interpretation, and the laws of many countries where Catholics are in the majority have enacted laws forbidding marriage for a divorced person. Catholics recognize the concept of "separate room and board"—wherein a married couple can live apart from each other—but they do not recognize the marriage of divorced people. Thus, many hundreds of thousands of Catholic men and women are living in a "common law" relationship, without benefit of legal marriage. The Savior has suggested that we should "ponder" the scriptures and "search them" diligently. Let's do this by referring to other scriptures with similar wording.

Matthew 19:3–9: "The Pharisees also came unto him, tempting him, and saying unto him, Is it lawful for a man to put away his wife for every cause? And he answered and said unto them, Have ye not read, that he which made them at the beginning made them male and female, and said, For this cause shall a man leave father and mother, and shall cleave to his wife: and they twain shall be one flesh? Wherefore they are no more twain, but one flesh. What therefore God hath joined together, let not man put asunder. They say unto him, Why did Moses then command to give a writing of divorcement, and to put her away? He saith unto them, Moses because of the hardness of your hearts suffered you to put away your wives: but from the beginning it was not so. And I say unto you, Whosoever shall put away his wife, except it be for fornication, and shall marry another, committeth adultery: and whoso married her which is put away doth commit adultery."

Mark 10:2–12 records the same incident in essentially the same words. Note the exact wording of the two key verses at the end, Mark 10:11–12: "And he saith unto them, Whosoever shall put away his wife, and marry another, committeth adultery against her. And if a woman shall put away her husband, and be married to another, she committeth adultery."

Luke 16:18: "Whosoever putteth away his wife, and marrieth another, committeth adultery: and whosoever marrieth her that is put away from her husband committeth adultery."

Remember the suggestion that all the scriptures pertaining to a topic should be considered before a final interpretation. Remember also that at least two of the scriptures mentioned that this law was given to them by Moses. Now let's go back to the writings of Moses and read the exact words of the law.

Deuteronomy 24:1–2: "When a man hath taken a wife, and married her, and it come to pass that she find no favour in his eyes, because he hath found some uncleanness in her: then let him write her a bill of divorcement, and give it in her hand, and send her out of his house. And when she is departed out of his house, she may go and be another man's wife."

This law, given through Moses, makes it absolutely clear that remarriage is possible after a *legal, written bill of divorcement* has been placed in her hands. However, if a husband simply puts his wife away or divorces himself (separates himself) from her without giving the written bill of divorcement, and if she then remarries and has sexual relations with her new partner, of course both of them commit adultery.

In summary, the word *divorce,* standing by itself in the New Testament, is not the legal term; the legal term is *a written bill of divorcement.*

The lives of millions would be blessed if these scriptures were understood correctly. We can see from this example why it is important to read and ponder all of the scriptures pertaining to a particular subject. No wonder the commandment is to ponder the scriptures, not merely to read them.

Matthew 7:23

"And then will I profess unto them, I never knew you: depart from me, ye that work iniquity."

JST: "And then will I say, Ye never knew me; depart from me ye that work iniquity" (JST, Matthew 7:33).

Matthew 13:3–6

"And he spake many things unto them in parables, saying, Behold, a sower went forth to sow; And when he sowed, some seeds fell by the way side, and the fowls came and devoured them up: Some fell upon stony places, where they had not much earth: and forthwith they sprung up, because they had no deepness of earth: And when the sun was up, they were scorched; and because they had no root, they withered away."

As worded in the King James text, the placement of the clause "because they had no deepness of earth" next to "forthwith they sprung up" would seem to suggest that the investigators readily accepted the gospel because they evidently did not have a good understanding of the scriptures, which of course makes little or no sense. However, the Joseph Smith Translation places this key clause after the word "scorched," so that the total idea is expressed as follows: "Some fell upon stony places, where they had not much earth; and forthwith they sprung up; and when the sun was up, they were scorched, because they had no deepness of earth; and because they had no root, they withered away" (JST, Matthew 13:5).

Matthew 16:28

"Verily I say unto you, There be some standing here, which shall not taste of death, till they see the Son of man coming in his kingdom."

Some of the listeners of Jesus misinterpreted this statement, thinking that if some standing there would not taste of death until the second coming of Christ, then the second coming must be during that very generation. Latter-day Saints, however, recognize that this statement pertained to John the Revelator, as is made clear in John 21:20–24, 3 Nephi 28:6–8, and Doctrine and Covenants 7. (See TG, "Translated Beings.")

Matthew 24:1

"And Jesus went out, and departed from the temple: and his disciples came to him for to shew him the buildings of the temple."

JST: "And Jesus went out, and departed from the temple; and his disciples came to him for to hear him, saying, Master, show us concerning the buildings of the temple. . . ."

Matthew 24:28

JST: "And now I show unto you a parable. Behold, wheresoever the carcass is, there will the eagles be gathered together; so likewise shall mine elect be gathered from the four quarters of the earth."

This clarification is also included in the section called "Joseph Smith—Matthew" in the Pearl of Great Price, which is essentially the same as Matthew 24 in the Joseph Smith Translation.

Matthew 24:34

"Verily I say unto you, This generation shall not pass, till all these things be fulfilled."

In context, it is clear that the "generation" mentioned here is the generation in which the preceding signs would be fulfilled, not the generation of those then listening to Jesus.

Matthew 27:50

"Jesus, when he had cried again with a loud voice, yielded up the ghost."

JST: "Jesus when he had cried again with a loud voice, saying, Father, it is finished, thy will is done, yielded up the ghost" (JST, Matthew 27:54).

The Gospel According to St. Mark[9]

Mark 9:43–44

"And if thy hand offend thee, cut it off: it is better for thee to enter into life maimed, than having two hands to go into hell, into the fire that never shall be quenched: Where their worm dieth not, and the fire is not quenched."

See the Joseph Smith Translation of Mark 9:43–48: "It is better for thee, to enter halt into life, than having two feet to be cast into hell; into the fire that never shall be quenched. Therefore, let every man stand or fall, by himself, and not for another; or not trusting another.

"Seek unto my Father, and it shall be done in that very moment what ye shall ask, if ye ask in faith, believing that ye shall receive. And if thine eye which seeth for thee, him that is appointed to watch over thee to show thee light, become a transgressor and offend thee, pluck him out. It is better for thee to enter into the kingdom of God, with one eye, than having two eyes to be cast into hell fire. For it is better that thyself should be saved, than to be cast into hell with thy brother, where their worm dieth not, and where the fire is not quenched."

Mark 14:22–24

"And as they did eat, Jesus took bread, and blessed, and brake it, and gave to them, and said, Take, eat; this is my body. And he took the cup, and when he had given thanks, he gave it to them: and they all drank of it. And he said unto them, this is my blood of the new testament, which is shed for many."

JST: "And as they did eat, Jesus took bread and blessed it, and brake, and gave to them, and said, Take it, and eat. Behold, this is for you to do in remembrance of my body; for as oft as ye do this ye will remember this hour that I was with you. And he took the cup, and when he had given thanks, he gave it to them; and they all drank of it. And he said unto them, this is in remembrance of my blood which is shed for many, and the new testament which I give unto you; for of me ye shall bear record unto all the world. And as oft as ye do this ordinance, ye will remember me in this hour that I was with you and drank with you of this cup, even the last time in my ministry" (JST, Mark 13:20–24).

What a profound difference the Joseph Smith Translation makes. Contrary to what is taught by a major Christian church, we are not partaking of the actual flesh and blood of Jesus Christ when we partake of the emblems of the sacrament, but we partake of these emblems in remembrance of his flesh and blood! (See BD, "Communion.")

The Gospel According to St. Luke[10]

Luke 1:41

"And it came to pass, that, when Elisabeth heard the salutation of Mary, the babe leaped in her womb; and Elisabeth was filled with the Holy Ghost."

Note that the spirit of John the Baptist was evidently in his body in Elizabeth's womb at this time and understood the significance of Mary's announcement.

Luke 2:21–23

"And when eight days were accomplished for the circumcising of the child, his name was called JESUS, which was so named of the angel before he was conceived in the womb. And when the days of her purification according to the law of Moses were accomplished, they brought him to Jerusalem, to present him to the Lord; (As it is written in the law of the Lord, Every male that openeth the womb shall be called holy to the Lord . . .)." (See BD, "Circumcision"; and TG, "Circumcision" and "Purification.")

Luke 2:52

"And Jesus increased in wisdom and stature, and in favour with God and man."

This brief verse of only fourteen words covers eighteen years of the most important life that has ever been lived on this earth—yet it includes the major elements of a person's development: mental, physical, religious, and social.

Luke 6:27–28

"But I say unto you which hear, Love your enemies, do good to them which hate you, Bless them that curse you, and pray for them which despitefully use you."

This verse may describe what Jesus was doing—or thinking—at the time of his trial and scourging.

Luke 10:31–33

"And by chance there came down a certain priest that way: and when he saw him, he passed by on the other side. And likewise a Levite, when he was at the place, came and looked on him, and passed by on the other side. But a certain Samaritan, as he journeyed, came where he was: and when he saw him, he had compassion on him." (See BD, "Priests," "Levi," "Samaritans.")

Luke 11:52

"Woe unto you, lawyers! for ye have taken away the key of knowledge: ye entered not in yourselves, and them that were entering in ye hindered."

JST: "Woe unto you, lawyers! for ye have taken away the key of knowledge, the fulness of the scriptures; ye enter not in yourselves into the kingdom; and those who were entering in, ye hindered."

Luke 17:21

"Neither shall they say, Lo here! or, lo there! for, behold, the kingdom of God is within you."

JST: " . . . For, behold, the kingdom of God has already come unto you."

Luke 22:32

"But I have prayed for thee, that thy faith fail not: and when thou art converted, strengthen thy brethren." (See TG, "Conversion.")

Earlier references indicated that Peter already had a strong testimony of the divinity of Jesus Christ (see Matthew 16:16), but at this period of his life Peter had not been fully converted, that is, his actions were not 100 percent consistent with his knowledge.

Luke 22:44

"And being in an agony he prayed more earnestly: and his sweat was as it were great drops of blood falling down to the ground."

D&C 19:16, 18: "For behold, I, God, have suffered these things for all, that they might not suffer if they would repent . . . Which suffering caused myself, even God, the greatest of all, to tremble because of pain, and to bleed at every pore, and to suffer both body and spirit."

Luke 24:39

"Behold my hands and my feet, that it is I myself: handle me, and see; for a spirit hath not flesh and bones, as ye see me have." (See BD, "Spirit"; and TG, "Spirit" and "Spirits, Disembodied.")

This statement clearly indicates that Jesus believed in spirits and that he understood a basic difference between spirit beings and physical beings.

The Gospel According to St. John[11]

John 1:1

"In the beginning was the Word, and the Word was with God, and the Word was God."

JST: "In the beginning was the gospel preached through the Son. And the gospel was the word, and the word was with the Son, and the Son was with God, and the Son was of God."

John 5:25, 28

"Verily, verily, I say unto you, The hour is coming, and now is, when the dead shall hear the voice of the Son of God: and they that hear shall live. . . . Marvel not at this: for the hour is coming, in the which all that are in the graves shall hear his voice."

The "Vision of the Redemption of the Dead," by Joseph F. Smith, in Doctrine and Covenants 138, provides insightful information on the meaning of this verse.

John 5:31

"If I bear witness of myself, my witness is not true."

JST: "Therefore if I bear witness of myself, yet my witness is true" (JST, John 5:32).

John 8:56

"Your father Abraham rejoiced to see my day: and he saw it, and was glad."
Abraham knew of the gospel of Jesus Christ!

John 10:16

"And other sheep I have, which are not of this fold: them also I must bring, and they shall hear my voice; and there shall be one fold, and one shepherd."

In 3 Nephi 15:13–24 and 3 Nephi 16:1–3, the resurrected Jesus Christ indicates he is going to show himself unto the lost tribes of Israel. The resurrection of Jesus Christ is the proof of his divinity!

John 14:26

"But the Comforter, which is the Holy Ghost, whom the Father will send in my name, he shall teach you all things, and bring all things to your remembrance, whatsoever I have said unto you."

This shows how Matthew, Mark, Luke, and John might have written their accounts many years later and still have written the same thing as one another.

John 19:30–31

"When Jesus therefore had received the vinegar, he said, It is finished: and he bowed his head, and gave up the ghost. The Jews therefore, because it was the preparation, that the bodies should not remain upon the cross on the sabbath day, (for that sabbath day was an high day,) besought Pilate that their legs might be broken, and that they might be taken away."

The LDS edition of the Bible includes the following footnote to verse 31: "Jesus arose on the first day of the week. The previous day was the weekly Sabbath. The day before the Sabbath, being also the day after the Passover meal, could be the 'high' day."

John 20:17

"Jesus saith unto her [Mary Magdalene], Touch me not; for I am not yet ascended to my Father: but go to my brethren, and say unto them, I ascend unto my Father, and your Father; and to my God, and your God.

JST: "Hold me not" (which could also mean "hold back" or "detain me not").

The Acts of the Apostles[12]

Acts 3:20–21

"And he shall send Jesus Christ, which before was preached unto you: Whom the heaven must receive until the times of restitution of all things, which God hath spoken by the mouth of all his holy prophets since the world began." (See BD,

"Restitution; Restoration"; and TG, "Jesus Christ, Second Coming," and "Restoration of the Gospel.")

The word *restitution* could also have been translated as *restoration.*

Acts 13:48

"And when the Gentiles heard this, they were glad, and glorified the word of the Lord: and as many as were ordained to eternal life believed."

JST: "And when the Gentiles heard this, they were glad, and glorified the word of the Lord; and as many as believed were ordained unto eternal life."

Acts 20:35

"I have shewed you all things, how that so labouring ye ought to support the weak, and to remember the words of the Lord Jesus, how he said, It is more blessed to give than to receive."

It is interesting to note that this famous statement is found in the book of Acts, not in one of the Gospels.

The Epistle of Paul the Apostle to the Romans[13]

Romans 5:11

". . . we also joy in God through our Lord Jesus Christ, by whom we have now received the atonement."

The GR footnote indicates that *atonement* means "reconciliation" or "restoration to favor." This is the *only* time the word *atonement* appears in the New Testament. (See BD, "Atonement"; and TG, "Jesus Christ, Atonement Through," and "Redemption.")

Romans 7:15–19

"For that which I do I allow not: for what I would, that do I not; but what I hate, that do I. If then I do that which I would not, I consent unto the law that it is good."

JST: "For that which I am commanded to do, I do; and that which I am commanded not to allow, I allow not. For what I know is not right, I would not do; for that which is sin, I hate. If then I do not that which I would not allow, I consent unto the law, that it is good; and I am not condemned" (JST, Romans 7:15–17).

What a tremendous contribution the Joseph Smith Translation makes to a correct understanding of this verse!

Romans 8:16

"The Spirit itself beareth witness with our spirit, that we are the children of God."

Note that there is a capital "S" in the first "Spirit," referring to the Holy Ghost, and a lowercase "s" in the second "spirit." Each of us has a spirit; it is the life-giving force of our existence. (See TG, "Man, a Spirit Child of Heavenly Father.")

Romans 8:29–30

"For whom he did foreknow, he also did predestinate to be conformed to the image of his Son, that he might be the firstborn among many brethren. Moreover whom he did predestinate, them he also called: and whom he called, them he also justified: and whom he justified, them he also glorified."

These two verses contain the only two times the word *predestinate* is used in all the Bible—although the word *predestinated* is also used twice, in Ephesians 1:5, 11. In all these cases, the Greek word translated *predestinate,* as indicated in the GR footnotes, also has the meaning of "appointed beforehand," or "foreordained." (See TG, "God, Foreknowledge of.")

Romans 11:21, 24

"For if God spared not the natural branches, take heed lest he also spare not thee. . . . For if thou wert cut out of the olive tree which is wild by nature, and wert grafted contrary to nature into a good olive tree: how much more shall these, which be the natural branches, be grafted into their own olive tree?"

(Note: The symbolism of the "natural" and "wild" branches of the olive tree is also included in the allegory of Zenos as recorded in Jacob 5 in the Book of Mormon.)

The First Epistle of Paul the Apostle to the Corinthians[14]

1 Corinthians 2:11

"For what man knoweth the things of a man, save the spirit of man which is in him? even so the things of God knoweth no man, but the Spirit of God."

JST: " . . . even so the things of God knoweth no man, except he has the Spirit of God."

1 Corinthians 10:23–24

"All things are lawful for me, but all things are not expedient: all things are lawful for me, but all things edify not. Let no man seek his own, but every man another's wealth."

JST: "All things are not lawful for me, for all things are not expedient; all things are not lawful, for all things edify not. Let not man seek therefore his own, but every man another's good."

1 Corinthians 14:34–35

"Let your women keep silence in the churches: for it is not permitted unto them to speak; but they are commanded to be under obedience, as also saith the law. And if they will learn any thing, let them ask their husbands at home: for it is a shame for women to speak in the church."

The Joseph Smith Translation replaces "speak" with "rule." (See TG, "Woman.")

1 Corinthians 15:29

"Else what shall they do which are baptized for the dead, if the dead rise not at all? why are they then baptized for the dead?" (See BD, "Baptism"; and TG, "Salvation, for the Dead.")

This statement clearly indicates that Paul and the early Christians had an understanding of the ordinance of baptism for the dead.

1 Corinthians 15:40–42

"There are also celestial bodies, and bodies terrestrial: but the glory of the celestial is one, and the glory of the terrestrial is another. There is one glory of the sun, and another glory of the moon, and another glory of the stars: for one star differeth from another star in glory. So also is the resurrection of the dead. It is sown in corruption; it is raised in incorruption." (See also D&C 76; 88:22–32; BD, "Degrees of Glory"; and TG, "Celestial Glory," "Terrestrial Glory," "Telestial Glory.")

1 Corinthians 15:50

"Now this I say, brethren, that flesh and blood cannot inherit the kingdom of God; neither doth corruption inherit incorruption."

The resurrected Jesus Christ said, "Behold my hands and my feet, that it is I myself: handle me, and see; for a spirit hath not flesh and bones, as ye see me have" (Luke 24:39; see also BD, "Blood" and "Flesh"; and TG, "Flesh and Blood").

Although a resurrected body has "flesh and bones," it does not have "blood." Joseph Smith taught that resurrected beings have "spirit in their bodies, and not blood."[15] President John Taylor also taught this principle: "When the resurrection . . . of man shall be consummated, . . . he [will] still be in the same image, . . . without variation or change in any of his parts or faculties, except the substitution of spirit for blood."[16]

The Second Epistle of Paul the Apostle to the Corinthians

2 Corinthians 11:14

"And no marvel; for Satan himself is transformed into an angel of light."

Doctrine and Covenants 128:20 also tells of an incident where the devil appeared as an angel of light. (See BD, "Devil.")

2 Corinthians 12:2

"I knew a man in Christ above fourteen years ago, (whether in the body, I cannot tell; or whether out of the body, I cannot tell: God knoweth;) such an one caught up to the third heaven."

The GR footnote to this verse reads: "I know a man in Christ who fourteen years ago." (See BD, "Degrees of Glory"; and TG, "Celestial Glory" and "Heaven.")

2 Corinthians 13:1

"This is the third time I am coming to you. In the mouth of two or three witnesses shall every word be established."

The principle of two or three witnesses so that the truth might be established is also mentioned in Deuteronomy 19:15. (See TG, "Witnesses.")

The Epistle of Paul the Apostle to the Galatians[17]

Galatians 1:17–18

"Neither went I up to Jerusalem to them which were apostles before me; but I went into Arabia, and returned again unto Damascus. Then after three years I went up to Jerusalem to see Peter, and abode with him fifteen days."

Galatians 3:6–8

"Even as Abraham believed God, and it was accounted to him for righteousness. Know ye therefore that they which are of faith, the same are the children of Abraham. And the scripture, foreseeing that God would justify the heathen through faith, preached before the gospel unto Abraham, saying, In thee shall all nations be blessed."

The gospel was preached to Abraham, and there is only one gospel: the gospel of Jesus Christ. No wonder some of the Dead Sea Scrolls contained some of the essential teachings of the Gospel of Jesus Christ! (See BD, "Dead Sea Scrolls.")

The Epistle of Paul the Apostle to the Ephesians[18]

Ephesians 1:4–5

"According as he hath chosen us in him before the foundation of the world, that we should be holy and without blame before him in love: Having predestinated us unto the adoption of children by Jesus Christ to himself, according to the good pleasure of his will."

These verses clearly teach of a pre-earthly existence! Also, this is one of only four instances where the word *predestinate* or *predestinated* appears in the Bible.

Ephesians 1:10

"That in the dispensation of the fulness of times he might gather together in one all things in Christ, both which are in heaven, and which are on earth; even in him."

(See BD, "Dispensation"; and TG, "Dispensations," "Israel, Gathering of," "Jesus Christ, Power of," "Last Days," "Restoration of the Gospel.")

Ephesians 2:19–21

"Now therefore ye are no more strangers and foreigners, but fellow citizens with the saints, and of the household of God; and are built upon the foundation of the apostles and prophets, Jesus Christ himself being the chief corner stone; in whom all the building fitly framed together groweth unto an holy temple in the Lord."

This passage indicates the true Church will have "apostles and prophets," with Jesus Christ as the "cornerstone." (See BD, "Church"; and TG, "Cornerstone," "Gentiles," "Strangers.")

Ephesians 4:11–13

"And he gave some, apostles; and some, prophets; and some, evangelists; and some, pastors and teachers; for the perfecting of the saints, for the work of the ministry, for the edifying of the body of Christ: Till we all come in the unity of the faith, and of the knowledge of the Son of God, unto a perfect man, unto the measure of the stature of the fulness of Christ."

These verses indicate some of the purposes of a church organization, as well as some of the offices in the true Church. (See BD, "Church," and "Evangelist"; see also TG, "Apostles," "Church Organization," "Edification," "God, Perfection of," "Man, Potential to Become Like Heavenly Father," "Patriarchs," "Priesthood, History of," "Prophets, Mission of.")

Ephesians 4:26

"Be ye angry, and sin not: let not the sun go down upon your wrath."
JST: "Can ye be angry, and not sin? . . ."

The Epistle of Paul the Apostle to the Philippians[19]

Philippians 3:11

"If by any means I might attain unto the resurrection of the dead."
JST: "If by any means I might attain unto the resurrection of the just."
Everyone attains to the resurrection of the dead.

Philippians 4:8

"Finally, brethren, whatsoever things are true, whatsoever things are honest, whatsoever things are just, whatsoever things are pure, whatsoever things are lovely, whatsoever things are of good report; if there be any virtue, and if there be any praise, think on these things."

This verse is the basis for the wording of Article of Faith 13, "Indeed, we may say that we follow the admonition of Paul. . . ."

The Epistle of Paul the Apostle to the Colossians[20]

Colossians 1:14–16

"In whom we have redemption through his blood, even the forgiveness of sins: Who is the image of the invisible God, the firstborn of every creature: For by him were all things created, that are in heaven, and that are in earth, visible and invisible, whether they be thrones, or dominions, or principalities, or powers: all things were created by him, and for him."

The Joseph Smith Translation version makes no changes in this verse. Of course, God is not literally invisible, but he is "invisible" to sinful man. Also, all things were created by Jesus Christ, the "Firstborn" of every creature. (See BD, "Firstborn"; TG, "Creation," "Firstborn," "God, Body of (Corporeal Nature)," "Jesus Christ, Atonement through," "Jesus Christ, Firstborn," "Redemption," "Remission of Sins.")

The First Epistle of Paul the Apostle to the Thessalonians[21]

1 Thessalonians 4:13–18

"But I would not have you to be ignorant, brethren, concerning them which are asleep, that ye sorrow not, even as others which have no hope. For if we believe that Jesus died and rose again, even so them also which sleep in Jesus will God bring with him. For this we say unto you by the word of the Lord, that we which are alive and remain unto the coming of the Lord shall not prevent them which are asleep. For the Lord himself shall descend from heaven with a shout, with the voice of the archangel, and with the trump of God: and the dead in Christ shall rise first: Then we which are alive and remain shall be caught up together with them in the clouds, to meet the Lord in the air: and so shall we ever be with the Lord. Wherefore comfort one another with these words."

JST: "But I would not have you to be ignorant, brethren, concerning them which are asleep, that ye sorrow not, even as others which have no hope. For if we believe that Jesus died and rose again, even so them also which sleep in Jesus will God bring with him. For this we say unto you by the word of the Lord, that they who are alive at the coming of the Lord, shall not prevent them who remain unto the coming of the Lord, who are asleep. For the Lord himself shall descend from heaven with a shout, with the voice of the archangel, and with the trump of God: and the dead in Christ shall rise first; Then they who are alive, shall be caught up together into the clouds with them who remain, to meet the Lord in the air; and so shall we be ever with the Lord. Wherefore comfort one another with these words."

1 Thessalonians 5:1–6
"But of the times and the seasons, brethren, ye have no need that I write unto you. For yourselves know perfectly that the day of the Lord so cometh as a thief in the night. For when they shall say, Peace and safety; then sudden destruction cometh upon them, as travail upon a woman with child; and they shall not escape. But ye, brethren, are not in darkness, that that day should overtake you as a thief. Ye are all the children of light, and the children of the day: we are not of the night, nor of darkness. Therefore let us not sleep, as do others; but let us watch and be sober."

If Paul were here now, I believe he would give us the same counsel and admonition.

The Second Epistle of Paul the Apostle to the Thessalonians

2 Thessalonians 2:7–9
"For the mystery of iniquity doth already work: only he who now letteth will let, until he be taken out of the way. And then shall that Wicked be revealed, whom the Lord shall consume with the spirit of his mouth, and shall destroy with the brightness of his coming: Even him, whose coming is after the working of Satan with all power and signs and lying wonders."

JST: "For the mystery of iniquity doth already work, and he it is who now worketh, and Christ suffereth him to work, until the time is fulfilled that he shall be taken out of the way. And then shall that wicked one be revealed, whom the Lord shall consume with the spirit of his mouth, and shall destroy with the brightness of his coming. Yea, the Lord, even Jesus, whose coming is not until after there cometh a falling away, by the working of Satan with all power, and signs and lying wonders." (See TG, "Conspiracy," "False Priesthoods," "Jesus Christ, Second Coming," "Secret Combinations.")

The First Epistle of Paul the Apostle to Timothy[22]

1 Timothy 2:13–14
"For Adam was first formed, then Eve. And Adam was not deceived, but the woman being deceived was in the transgression."

It is significant that the word *transgression*, rather than *sin*, is used in describing the Fall. Note also that Adam was not deceived. (See BD, "Fall of Adam"; TG, "Fall of Man," "Man, Physical Creation of," "Transgression.")

1 Timothy 3:2, 12

"A bishop then must be blameless, the husband of one wife, vigilant, sober, of good behaviour, given to hospitality, apt to teach; . . . Let the deacons be the husbands of one wife, ruling their children and their own houses well."

This scripture gives some of the qualifications of a bishop. Also, in the early days of the Church in this dispensation, deacons were primarily mature men. (See BD, "Bishop"; TG, "Bishop," "Deacon," "Priesthood, Qualifying for.")

The Second Epistle of Paul the Apostle to Timothy

2 Timothy 2:8

"Remember that Jesus Christ of the seed of David was raised from the dead according to my gospel."

Of course, it is not "Paul's" gospel. Thus, the Joseph Smith Translation changes the verse from "my gospel" to "the gospel."

2 Timothy 3:16

"All scripture is given by inspiration of God, and is profitable for doctrine, for reproof, for correction, for instruction in righteousness."

JST: "And all Scripture given by inspiration of God, is profitable for doctrine, for reproof, for correction, for instruction in righteousness."

The Epistle of Paul to Titus[23]

Titus 1:15

"Unto the pure all things are pure: but unto them that are defiled and unbelieving is nothing pure; but even their mind and conscience is defiled."

JST: "Unto the pure, let all things be pure. . . . "

Titus 2:14

"Who gave himself for us, that he might redeem us from all iniquity, and purify unto himself a peculiar people, zealous of good works."

Peculiar means "different" or "treasured." (See TG, "Jesus Christ, Atonement through," "Jesus Christ, Redeemer," "Peculiar People," "Redemption," "Zeal.")

The Epistle of Paul to Philemon[24]

Philemon 1:6

"That the communication [GR: participation, fellowship] of thy faith may become effectual [GR: active] by the acknowledging of every good thing which is in you in Christ Jesus."

The Epistle of Paul the Apostle to the Hebrews[25]

Hebrews 1 (heading)

"The Son is in the express image of the person of the Father—Christ is the Only Begotten Son and thus above the angels."

Hebrews 1:6–7

"And again, when he bringeth in the first begotten into the world, he saith, And let all the angels of God worship him. And of the angels he saith, Who maketh his angels spirits, and his ministers a flame of fire."

JST: "And again, when he bringeth in the first-begotten into the world, he saith, And let all the angels of God worship him, who maketh his ministers as a flame of fire. And of the angels he saith, Angels are ministering spirits."

The Joseph Smith Translation clarifies: Angels may already be spirits; Christ does not "make" them spirits. (See BD, "Firstborn"; TG, "Jesus Christ, Firstborn.")

Hebrews 2:6–7

"But one in a certain place testified, saying, What is man, that thou art mindful of him? or the son of man, that thou visitest him? Thou madest him a little lower than the angels; [HEB: "gods"] thou crownedst him with glory and honour, and didst set him over the works of thy hands."

This is a quotation from Psalm 8:5.

Hebrews 5:4

"And no man taketh this honour unto himself, but he that is called of God, as was Aaron."

As we see from this verse, man cannot assume priesthood power, nor does he obtain it through graduation from a divinity school. (See TG, "Priesthood, Authority" and "Priesthood, Qualifying for.")

Hebrews 5:8–10

"Though he were a Son, yet learned he obedience by the things which he suffered; and being made perfect, he became the author of eternal salvation unto all them that obey him; called of God an high priest after the order of Melchisedec."

Christ is also the "Great High Priest"; the office of high priest is an office in the Melchizedek Priesthood. (See BD, "High Priest" and "Melchizedek Priesthood"; TG, "God, Perfection of," "High Priests," "Jesus Christ, Exemplar," "Jesus Christ, Mission of," "Jesus Christ, Temptation of," "Jesus Christ, Types, in Anticipation," "Salvation," "Salvation, Plan of.")

Hebrews 6:1
"Therefore leaving the principles of the doctrine of Christ, let us go on unto perfection. . . ."
JST: "Therefore not leaving the principles of the doctrine of Christ . . . "

Hebrews 7:1–3
"For this Melchisedec, king of Salem, priest of the most high God, who met Abraham returning from the slaughter of the kings, and blessed him; to whom also Abraham gave a tenth part of all; first being by interpretation King of righteousness, and after that also King of Salem, which is, King of peace; without father, without mother, without descent, having neither beginning of days, nor end of life; but made like unto the Son of God; abideth a priest continually."
JST: "For this Melchizedek was ordained a priest after the order of the Son of God, which order was without father, without mother, without descent, having neither beginning of days, nor end of life. And all those who are ordained unto this priesthood are made like unto the Son of God, abiding a priest continually" (JST, Hebrews 7:3).

Hebrews 8:12
"For I will be merciful to their unrighteousness, and their sins and their iniquities will I remember no more."
God can remember, but he will not remember. Therefore, the sins we commit, repent of, and have been forgiven of will not be remembered by God at the day of our judgment.

Hebrews 11:5
"By faith Enoch was translated that he should not see death; and was not found, because God had translated him: for before his translation he had this testimony, that he pleased God."
Enoch and his city were translated, as were Elijah, Moses, John the Beloved, and the three Nephite disciples. (See BD, "Zion"; TG, "Testimony," "Translated Beings," "Zion.")

Hebrews 11:24–26
"By faith Moses, when he was come to years, refused to be called the son of Pharaoh's daughter; choosing rather to suffer affliction with the people of God, than

to enjoy the pleasures of sin for a season; esteeming the reproach of Christ greater riches than the treasures in Egypt: for he had respect unto the recompence of the reward."

Note that Moses knew of the gospel of Jesus Christ!

Hebrews 12:9

"Furthermore we have had fathers of our flesh which corrected us, and we gave them reverence: shall we not much rather be in subjection unto the Father of spirits, and live?"

God the Father is the Father of our spirits. (A few of the TG entries for this verse are "Father," "God," "Heavenly Father," "Man, Antemortal Existence of," "Man, a Spirit Child of Heavenly Father," "Man, Potential to Become Like Heavenly Father," "Reverence," "Spirit Body," "Spirit Creation.")

The General Epistle of James[26]

James 1:5–6

"If any of you lack wisdom, let him ask of God, that giveth to all men liberally, and upbraideth not; and it shall be given him. But let him ask in faith, nothing wavering. For he that wavereth is like a wave of the sea driven with the wind and tossed."

James 2:14, 17, 20, 24, 26

"What doth it profit, my brethren, though a man say he hath faith, and have not works? can faith save him? . . . Even so faith, if it hath not works, is dead, being alone. . . . But wilt thou know, O vain man, that faith without works is dead? . . . Ye see then how that, by works a man is justified, and not by faith only. . . . For as the body without the spirit is dead, so faith without works is dead also." (See JST, James 2:14–21; see also BD, "Faith"; TG, "Faith," "Good Works," "Justification," "Perfection," "Righteousness.")

James 2:19

"Thou believest that there is one God; thou doest well: the devils also believe, and tremble."

James 5:14–15

"Is any sick among you? let him call for the elders of the church; and let them pray over him, anointing him with oil in the name of the Lord: And the prayer of faith shall save the sick, and the Lord shall raise him up; and if he have committed sins, they shall be forgiven him."

Healing is one of the gifts of the Spirit. (See D&C 42:44; 66:9; see also BD,

"Elders"; TG, "Administrations to the Sick," "Anointing," "Elders," "Healing," "Prayer," "Sickness.")

The First Epistle General of Peter[27]

1 Peter 2:9

"But ye are a chosen generation, a royal priesthood, an holy nation, a peculiar people; that ye should shew forth the praises of him who hath called you out of darkness into his marvellous light."

1 Peter 3:18–20

"For Christ also hath once suffered for sins, the just for the unjust, that he might bring us to God, being put to death in the flesh, but quickened by the Spirit: by which also he went and preached unto the spirits in prison; which sometime were disobedient, when once the longsuffering of God waited in the days of Noah, while the ark was a preparing, wherein few, that is, eight souls were saved by water."

This also quoted verbatim in Doctrine and Covenants 138:7–9.

1 Peter 4:6

"For for this cause was the gospel preached also to them that are dead, that they might be judged according to men in the flesh, but live according to God in the spirit."

This verse is quoted verbatim in Doctrine and Covenants 138:10, part of Joseph F. Smith's "Vision of the Redemption of the Dead."

The Second Epistle General of Peter

2 Peter 1:16–19

"For we have not followed cunningly devised fables, when we made known unto you the power and coming of our Lord Jesus Christ, but were eyewitnesses of his majesty. For he received from God the Father honour and glory, when there came such a voice to him from the excellent glory, This is my beloved Son, in whom I am well pleased. And this voice which came from heaven we heard, when we were with him in the holy mount. We have also a more sure word of prophecy; whereunto ye do well that ye take heed, as unto a light that shineth in a dark place, until the day dawn, and the day star arise in your hearts."

This "testimony" of Peter's is similar to the "testimonies" of Matthew, Mark, Luke, and John.

2 Peter 1:20–21

"Knowing this first, that no prophecy of the scripture is of any private interpretation. For the prophecy came not in old time by the will of man: but holy men of God spake as they were moved by the Holy Ghost." (See TG, "Prophecy," "Scriptures, Study.")

2 Peter 3:3–4

"Knowing this first, that there shall come in the last days scoffers, walking after their own lusts, and saying, Where is the promise of his coming? for since the fathers fell asleep, all things continue as they were from the beginning of the creation" (see also JST, 2 Peter 3:3–13).

2 Peter 3:8

"But, beloved, be not ignorant of this one thing, that one day is with the Lord as a thousand years, and a thousand years as one day."

The wording of Abraham 3:4 is "A day unto the Lord . . . being one thousand years according to the time appointed unto that whereon thou standest."

The First Epistle General of John[28]

1 John 2:1–2

"My little children, these things write I unto you, that ye sin not. And if any man sin [JST: "and repent"], we have an advocate with the Father, Jesus Christ the righteous: And he is the propitiation for our sins: and not for ours only, but also for the sins of the whole world."

This is only one of the three times in all the Bible that the word *propitiation* is used; the other instances are found in Romans 3:25 and 1 John 4:10.

1 John 4:12

"No man hath seen God at any time."

JST: "No man hath seen God at any time, except them who believe."

1 John 5:18

"We know that whosoever is born of God sinneth not."

JST: "We know that whosoever is born of God continueth not in sin."

The Second Epistle of John

2 John 1:9

"Whosoever transgresseth, and abideth not in the doctrine of Christ, hath not God. He that abideth in the doctrine of Christ, he hath both the Father and the Son."

Note the wording of 3 Nephi 11:32: "And this is my doctrine, and it is the doctrine which the Father hath given unto me."

The Third Epistle of John

3 John 1:4
"I have no greater joy than to hear that my children walk in truth."

The General Epistle of Jude[29]

Jude 1:6
"And the angels which kept not their first estate, but left their own habitation, he hath reserved in everlasting chains under darkness unto the judgment of the great day."
Compare this scripture with Abraham 3:26: "And they who keep their first estate shall be added upon; and they who keep not their first estate shall not have glory in the same kingdom with those who keep their first estate; and they who keep their second estate shall have glory added upon their heads for ever and ever." (See TG, "Angels," "Death, Spiritual, First," "Devil," "Judgment, the Last," "Man, Antemortal Existence of," "Sons of Perdition," "Spirits, Evil, Unclean.")

Jude 1:9
"Yet Michael the archangel, when contending with the devil he disputed about the body of Moses, durst not bring against him a railing accusation, but said, The Lord rebuke thee." (See BD, "Adam," "Michael"; to identify Adam as Michael, see D&C 27:1; 107:54; 128:21.)

The Revelation of St. John the Divine[30]

Revelation 1:7
"Behold, he cometh with clouds; and every eye shall see him, and they also which pierced him: and all kindreds of the earth shall wail because of him."
This scripture is about the second coming of Christ. Compare this verse to Zechariah 12:10, which reads, "And I will pour upon the house of David, and upon the inhabitants of Jerusalem, the spirit of grace and of supplications: and they shall look upon me whom they have pierced." Compare also the statement of Jesus Christ in Doctrine and Covenants 45:51–53, concerning his appearance on the Mount of Olives as a resurrected being: "And then shall the Jews look upon me and say: What are these wounds in thine hands and in thy feet? Then shall they know

that I am the Lord; for I will say unto them: These wounds are the wounds with which I was wounded in the house of my friends. I am he who was lifted up. I am Jesus that was crucified. I am the Son of God. And then shall they weep because of their iniquities; then shall they lament because they persecuted their king."

Revelation 1:10

"I was in the Spirit on the Lord's day, and heard behind me a great voice, as of a trumpet."

Note that Joseph Smith and Sidney Rigdon were also "in the spirit" when Doctrine and Covenants 76 was received.

The "Lord's day" is Sunday. (See BD, "Lord's Day," "Spirit.")

Revelation 1:18

"I am he that liveth, and was dead; and, behold, I am alive for evermore, Amen; and have the keys of hell and of death."

The resurrection of Jesus Christ is the proof of his divinity. (See BD, "Resurrection.")

Revelation 3:12

"Him that overcometh will I make a pillar in the temple of my God, and he shall go no more out: and I will write upon him the name of my God, and the name of the city of my God, which is new Jerusalem, which cometh down out of heaven from my God: and I will write upon him my new name."

Article of Faith 10 gives further insight into this passage: "We believe in the literal gathering of Israel and in the restoration of the Ten Tribes; that Zion (the New Jerusalem) will be built upon the American continent; that Christ will reign personally upon the earth; and, that the earth will be renewed and receive its paradisiacal glory."

Revelation 4:6

"And before the throne there was a sea of glass like unto crystal: and in the midst of the throne, and round about the throne, were four beasts full of eyes before and behind."

Joseph Smith was very interested in the book of Revelation and asked the Lord about those verses and symbols in which he was most interested. Explanations about some of those verses and symbols are found in Doctrine and Covenants 77 (see D&C 77:1–4).

Revelation 4:10

"The four and twenty elders fall down before him that sat on the throne, and worship him that liveth for ever and ever, and cast their crowns before the throne . . . " (see D&C 77:5).

Revelation 5:1
"And I saw in the right hand of him that sat on the throne a book written within and on the backside, sealed with seven seals" (see D&C 77:6–7).

Revelation 7:1
"And after these things I saw four angels standing on the four corners of the earth, holding the four winds of the earth, that the wind should not blow on the earth, nor on the sea, nor on any tree" (see D&C 77:8).

Revelation 7:2
"And I saw another angel ascending from the east, having the seal of the living God: and he cried with a loud voice to the four angels, to whom it was given to hurt the earth and the sea" (see D&C 77:9–10).

Revelation 7:4
"And I heard the number of them which were sealed: and there were sealed an hundred and forty and four thousand of all the tribes of the children of Israel."
Note that the "seven seals" refers to "seven thousand years" (see D&C 77:11).

Revelation 8:6
"And the seven angels which had the seven trumpets prepared themselves to sound" (see D&C 77:12).

Revelation 9:1
"And the fifth angel sounded, and I saw a star fall from heaven unto the earth: and to him was given the key of the bottomless pit" (see D&C 77:13).

Revelation 10:2, 8–11
"And he had in his hand a little book open: and he set his right foot upon the sea, and his left foot on the earth. . . . And the voice which I heard from heaven spake unto me again, and said, Go and take the little book which is open in the hand of the angel which standeth upon the sea and upon the earth. And I went unto the angel, and said unto him, Give me the little book. And he said unto me, Take it, and eat it up; and it shall make thy belly bitter, but it shall be in thy mouth sweet as honey. And I took the little book out of the angel's hand, and ate it up; and it was in my mouth sweet as honey: and as soon as I had eaten it, my belly was bitter. And he said unto me, Thou must prophesy again before many peoples, and nations, and tongues, and kings" (see D&C 77:14).

Revelation 11:3, 6, 8–12

"And I will give power unto my two witnesses, and they shall prophesy a thousand two hundred and threescore days, clothed in sackcloth. . . . These have power to shut heaven, that it rain not in the days of their prophecy: and have power over waters to turn them to blood, and to smite the earth with all plagues, as often as they will. . . . And their dead bodies shall lie in the street of the great city, which spiritually is called Sodom and Egypt, where also our Lord was crucified. And they of the people and kindreds and tongues and nations shall see their dead bodies three days and an half, and shall not suffer their dead bodies to be put in graves. And they that dwell upon the earth shall rejoice over them, and make merry, and shall send gifts one to another; because these two prophets tormented them that dwelt on the earth. And after three days and an half the Spirit of life from God entered into them, and they stood upon their feet; and great fear fell upon them which saw them. And they heard a great voice from heaven saying unto them, Come up hither. And they ascended up to heaven in a cloud; and their enemies beheld them" (see D&C 77:15).

Revelation 12 (heading)

"John sees the imminent apostasy of the Church—He also sees the war in heaven in the beginning when Satan was cast out—He sees the continuation of that war on earth."

Revelation 12:7–9

"And there was war in heaven: Michael and his angels fought against the dragon; and the dragon fought and his angels, and prevailed not; neither was their place found any more in heaven. And the great dragon was cast out, that old serpent, called the Devil, and Satan, which deceiveth the whole world: he was cast out into the earth, and his angels were cast out with him." (See BD, "Heaven," "War in Heaven"; TG, "Adam," "Angels," "Council in Heaven," "Death, Spiritual, First," "Devil," "Man, Antemortal Existence of," "Rebellion," "War.")

Revelation 14:6–7

"And I saw another angel fly in the midst of heaven, having the everlasting gospel to preach unto them that dwell on the earth, and to every nation, and kindred, and tongue, and people, saying with a loud voice, Fear God, and give glory to him; for the hour of his judgment is come: and worship him that made heaven, and earth, and the sea, and the fountains of waters."

Revelation 19:10

"And I fell at his feet to worship him. And he said unto me, See thou do it not:

I am thy fellowservant, and of thy brethren that have the testimony of Jesus: worship God: for the testimony of Jesus is the spirit of prophecy."

Revelation 20:5–6

"But the rest of the dead lived not again until the thousand years were finished. This is the first resurrection. Blessed and holy is he that hath part in the first resurrection: on such the second death hath no power, but they shall be priests of God and of Christ, and shall reign with him a thousand years." (See BD, "Resurrection," "Spirit"; TG, "Resurrection," "Spirits, Disembodied.")

Revelation 20:7

"And when the thousand years are expired, Satan shall be loosed out of his prison." (See BD, "Devil.")

Revelation 22:7

"Behold, I come quickly: blessed is he that keepeth the sayings of the prophecy of this book."

Revelation 22:8–9, 13

"And I John saw these things, and heard them. And when I had heard and seen, I fell down to worship before the feet of the angel which shewed me these things. Then saith he unto me, See thou do it not: for I am thy fellowservant, and of thy brethren the prophets, and of them which keep the sayings of this book: worship God. . . . I am Alpha and Omega, the beginning and the end, the first and the last."

Revelation 22:18–19

"For I testify unto every man that heareth the words of the prophecy of this book, If any man shall add unto these things, God shall add unto him the plagues that are written in this book: And if any man shall take away from the words of the book of this prophecy, God shall take away his part out of the book of life, and out of the holy city, and from the things which are written in this book."

"This book" does not refer to the Bible; it does not even refer to the New Testament; it refers *only* to this book of Revelation.

Revelation 22:20

"He which testifieth these things saith, Surely I come quickly. Amen. Even so, come, Lord Jesus."

It is entirely fitting that the last words in the New Testament are directed toward the second coming of the Savior—the greatest event which is yet to occur in the history of this earth. One of the major purposes of the restoration of the gospel and of the Church is to help prepare a people to be worthy to live with Jesus Christ when he comes. Therefore, if we are living as we should, we could also echo the words of John: "Even so, come, Lord Jesus."

TESTIMONIES OF CHURCH LEADERS AND OTHERS ON THE VALUE OF THE NEW TESTAMENT

The fifth and final section of this presentation will include statements from Church and other leaders pertaining to the value and importance of the New Testament. 2 Corinthians 13:1 reads: "In the mouth of two or three witnesses shall every word be established." Similar wording in the Old Testament is in Deuteronomy 19:15. In keeping with this principle of multiple witnesses, I will include testimonies of others.

George Q. Cannon
Speaking of the Bible, including the New Testament: "This book is of priceless worth; its value cannot be estimated by anything that is known among men upon which value is fixed. . . . To the Latter-day Saints it should always be a precious treasure. . . . It is, as it were, a constant fountain sending forth streams of living life to satisfy the souls of all who peruse its pages."[31]

Ezra Taft Benson
"I love the Bible, both the Old and New Testaments. It is a source of great truth. It teaches us about the life and ministry of the Master."[32]

Joseph Smith
"We were now individually members of, and acknowledged of God, 'The Church of Jesus Christ,' organized in accordance with commandments and revelations given by Him to ourselves in these last days, as well as according to the order of the Church as recorded in the New Testament."[33]

Brigham Young
"We believe the New Testament. . . . We give great credit to the Apostles, translators, and the fathers that have preserved and handed down the Bible to us. . . . In this they have certainly bequeathed a great blessing to the world."[34]

"The Bible, *when it is understood,* is one of the simplest books in the world, for, as far as it is translated correctly, it is nothing but truth, and in truth there is no mystery save to the ignorant. The revelations of the Lord to his creatures are adapted to the lowest capacity, and they bring life and salvation to all who are willing to receive them."[35]

"In all my teachings, I have taught the Gospel from the Old and New Testaments. I found therein every doctrine, and the proof of every doctrine, the Latter-day Saints believe in, as far as I know. . . . There may be some doctrines about which little is said in the Bible, but they are all couched therein, and I believe the doctrines because they are true, and I have taught them because they are calculated to save the children of men."[36]

"The doctrines contained in the Bible will lift to a superior condition all who observe them."[37]

First Presidency:
Spencer W. Kimball, Marion G. Romney, and Gordon B. Hinckley

"We commend to all people everywhere the daily reading, pondering and heeding of the divine truths of the Holy Bible. . . . When it is read reverently and prayerfully, the Holy Bible becomes a priceless volume, converting the soul to righteousness. . . . As we read the scriptures, we avail ourselves of the better part of the world's literature."[38]

Joseph F. Smith

"I do not believe that any upright, honest man or woman, possessing common intelligence, can read the Gospels of the New Testament and the testimonies therein given of the Savior, without intuitively feeling that he was what he professed to be. . . . The Spirit of the Lord bears witness in unmistakable language that burns with conviction."[39]

Bruce R. McConkie

"Now, let us speak particularly of these wondrous books that we call the four gospels. They contain hidden and unknown treasures. We haven't caught the vision and come to realize what we can get out of the gospels. Would it surprise you if I suggested that there is more knowledge in the four gospels, more revealed truth relative to the nature and kind of being that God our Father is, than in all the rest of holy writ combined? All we need to do is learn how to get that knowledge out. We need guidance. We need the Spirit of the Lord to direct us as we study."[40]

Near the beginning of this presentation, I made two statements I repeat here for emphasis and by way of conclusion:

1. The New Testament is the "Book of Books" so far as an account of the birth, ministry, teachings, atonement, death, and resurrection of Jesus Christ are concerned.

2. I firmly believe that an appreciation and knowledge of the atonement of Jesus Christ—and all that the atonement entails—constitute the most important understanding any person can acquire on this earth.

My prayer is that each one of us might follow the admonition of Elder McConkie to seek the Spirit of the Lord to direct us as we study the New Testament. That we might read it, ponder it, understand and love it, and learn to live its teachings is the prayer I ask for all of us.

Notes

This is a previously unpublished paper.

1. For further discussion on this question, see chapter 3, "How to Get the Most from Your Study of the Old Testament."
2. J. Reuben Clark Jr., *Why the King James Version?* (Salt Lake City: Deseret Book Co., 1956), v–vii.
3. For a more complete discussion on the instructional aids found in the LDS edition of the Bible, including a treatment on the Topical Guide, see chapter 3, "How to Get the Most from Your Study of the Old Testament."
4. *Merriam-Webster's Collegiate Dictionary,* 10th ed. (Springfield, Mass.: Merriam-Webster, Inc., 1993), "idiom."
5. See the interesting and helpful discussion in the Bible Dictionary, "Joseph Smith Translation," 717.
6. Bruce R. McConkie, *The Bible, a Sealed Book,* transcript, (Salt Lake City: The Church of Jesus Christ of Latter-day Saints, c. 1984), 5.
7. Bruce R. McConkie, *Mormon Doctrine,* 2d ed. (Salt Lake City: Bookcraft, 1966), 336.
8. For additional information on Matthew, see Bible Dictionary, "Matthew," 729 (for Matthew as a person); "Gospels," 682–83 (which includes the Gospel of Matthew).
9. For additional information on Mark, see Bible Dictionary, "Mark," 728 (for Mark as a person); "Gospels," 682–83 (which includes the Gospel of Mark).
10. For additional information on Luke, see Bible Dictionary, "Luke," 726 (for Luke as a person); "Gospels," 682–83 (which includes the Gospel of Luke).
11. For additional information on John, see Bible Dictionary, "John," 715 (for John as a person); "John, Gospel of," 725–26; "Gospels," 682–83 (which includes the Gospel of John).
12. For additional information on Acts, see Bible Dictionary, "Acts of the Apostles," 603–4; "Apostle," 612.
13. For additional information on Paul and his epistle to the Romans, see Bible Dictionary, "Paul," 742–43; "Pauline Epistles," 745; "Roman Empire," 763–64; "Rome," 764.
14. For additional information on Paul's epistles to the Corinthians, see Bible Dictionary, "Pauline Epistles," 743–44; "Corinth," 650.
15. *Teachings of the Prophet Joseph Smith,* 200.
16. John Taylor, *Mediation and Atonement* (Salt Lake City: Deseret News Co., 1975), 166.
17. For additional information on Paul's epistle to the Galatians, see Bible Dictionary, "Pauline Epistles," 744–45; "Galatia," 767–77.
18. For additional information on Paul's epistle to the Ephesians, see Bible Dictionary, "Pauline Epistles," 746; "Ephesus," 665–66.
19. For additional information on Paul's epistle to the Philippians, see Bible Dictionary, "Pauline Epistles," 745–46; "Philippi," 750.

20. For additional information on Paul's epistle to the Colossians, see Bible Dictionary, "Pauline Epistles," 746; "Colosse," 648.
21. For additional information on Paul's epistles to the Thessalonians, see Bible Dictionary, "Pauline Epistles," 743; "Thessalonica," 785.
22. For additional information on Paul's epistles to Timothy, see Bible Dictionary, "Pauline Epistles," 747; "Timothy," 785.
23. For additional information on Paul's epistle to Titus, see Bible Dictionary, "Pauline Epistles," 747; "Titus," 785–86.
24. For additional information on Paul's epistle to Philemon, see Bible Dictionary, "Pauline Epistles," 746; "Philemon," 750.
25. For additional information on Paul's epistle to the Hebrews, see Bible Dictionary, "Pauline Epistles," 746–47.
26. For additional information on James and his epistle, see Bible Dictionary, "James," 709 (for James as a person); "James, Epistle of," 709–10.
27. For additional information on Peter and his epistles, see Bible Dictionary, "Peter," 749 (for Peter as a person); "Peter, Epistles of," 749–50.
28. For additional information on John and his epistles, see Bible Dictionary, "John," 715 (for John as a person); "John, Epistles of," 715.
29. For additional information on Jude and his epistle, see Bible Dictionary, "Jude," 719 (for Jude as a person); "Jude, Epistle of," 719.
30. For additional information on John and his revelation, see Bible Dictionary, "John," 715 (for John as a person); "Revelation of John," 762–63.
31. *Gospel Truth,* 2:248.
32. Ezra Taft Benson, *A Witness and a Warning* (Salt Lake City: Deseret Book Co., 1988), 23.
33. *History of the Church,* 1:79. This statement was made on the occasion of the organization of the Church on 6 April 1830.
34. Brigham Young, in *Journal of Discourses,* 1:242.
35. *Discourses of Brigham Young,* 124; emphasis added.
36. Brigham Young, in *Journal of Discourses,* 16:73–74.
37. *Discourses of Brigham Young,* 125.
38. Spencer W. Kimball, Marion G. Romney, and Gordon B. Hinckley, quoted in "President proclaims 1983 Year of Bible," *Church News,* 20 March 1983, 3.
39. Joseph F. Smith, in *Journal of Discourses,* 19:261.
40. Bruce R. McConkie, "Drink from the Fountain," *Ensign,* April 1975, 70.

Chapter 5

How to Get the Most from Your Study of the Book of Mormon

I believe that every person in the Church who can learn to read should do so. And I believe that every person who can read, should read the Book of Mormon and the other scriptures of the Church. And they should read them again and again.

The scriptures are the "will . . . mind . . . word . . . [and] voice of the Lord" (D&C 68:4) to all of the people who live on the earth.

Unfortunately, an overwhelming majority of people on earth have not read any book of scripture completely, and I'm afraid that is also true of most Latter-day Saints regarding the Book of Mormon and the other scriptures.

Perhaps one reason some members have not read the Bible is that they may feel it was written by peoples who lived thousands of years ago in areas thousands of miles away, and that its messages pertain only to the peoples of those times. These members do not realize that the truths and principles of the scriptures are eternal. They apply to all peoples of all times in all places, including each of us, here and now. In fact, the Book of Mormon was written explicitly for our time, for us.

Perhaps another reason many people have not read the scriptures is because they think the scriptures are "too difficult" to read. True, the Bible has been translated from earlier languages and is written in the vocabulary and idioms of the English language of over 300 years ago. However, this is not true of the Book of Mormon. Also, recent editions of the scriptures provide numerous footnotes, cross references, explanatory notes, alternate readings, guides, and dictionary entries to help us understand the scriptures more fully.

We should not read the Book of Mormon or any other scriptures casually as we might read a newspaper, a popular magazine, or a novel. We are counseled to search the scriptures diligently (see Alma 17:2), to ponder them in our hearts (see Moroni 10:3), and to liken them unto ourselves (see 1 Nephi 19:23–24).

The time, effort, thought, and meditation required of this type of reading are well worth it because an understanding and application of the scriptures will help us become better and happier persons. Personal improvement and happiness are two of the many promises given to those who read, hear, study, and live the word of God. The scriptures are indeed "the power of God unto salvation" as declared by the Lord himself (D&C 68:4).

During my more than six decades on the earth, I have read many of the "best sellers" and significant books written by the scholars of the world. I can say in all honesty and sincerity that if I had to choose between having either the scriptures of the Church or having all the other books ever published on this earth, there is absolutely no question as to which I would choose. I would select the scriptures.

The Lord has emphasized from the beginning the importance of reading the scriptures. Our latter-day prophets have reiterated this plea. In the April 1983 general conference, President Gordon B. Hinckley mentioned the request of the Brethren "that all Saints everywhere begin a *daily reading of those scriptures* that provide the account of the life of Christ." He said the presiding officers of the Church hoped that "each family [would] read [each day] from the four Gospels and Third Nephi, the actual scriptures and teachings of the Savior."[1]

President Ezra Taft Benson emphasized that our daily scripture study should include the Book of Mormon: "Unless we read the Book of Mormon and give heed to its teachings, the Lord has stated in section 84 of the Doctrine and Covenants that the whole Church is under condemnation: 'And this condemnation resteth upon the children of Zion, even all' (D&C 84:56). . . . Now we not only need to *say* more about the Book of Mormon, but we need to *do* more with it. . . . The Book of Mormon has not been, nor is it yet, the center of our personal study, family teaching, preaching, and missionary work. Of this we must repent. . . . As President Marion G. Romney [said,] 'I counsel you, my beloved brothers and sisters and friends everywhere, to make reading in the Book of Mormon a few minutes each day a lifelong practice.'"[2]

In keeping with these admonitions, I share a few ideas as to how we all might get the most out of our study of the Book of Mormon. Many of these suggestions would apply to reading the other scriptures as well, but for this discussion I will relate them only to the Book of Mormon. I will discuss these ideas under several major headings:

1. What the Book of Mormon is and is not.
2. The author of the Book of Mormon.
3. The plates of the Book of Mormon.
4. The engravers of the plates from which our present Book of Mormon was translated.
5. The prophets of the Book of Mormon.
6. The peoples of the Book of Mormon.
7. The purposes of the Book of Mormon.
8. General do's and don'ts in studying the Book of Mormon.
9. Hints and helps in reading the Book of Mormon.
10. My testimony of the Book of Mormon.

Note that I used the term "our present Book of Mormon." I am convinced that some day we will have available to us a much larger and more extensive record of the ancient inhabitants of the land we now call the Americas. It may not even be called the Book of Mormon; rather, it may simply be known as the "Record of the Nephites" or some similar title.

I am equally convinced, however, that this expanded record will not be made available to us until we have read our present Book of Mormon again and again, and have learned to apply its principles in our lives. As our prophets have frequently reminded us, the Book of Mormon is not on trial, but we are on trial as to what we do with this sacred volume of scripture.

What the Book of Mormon Is and Is Not

The Book of Mormon is largely a condensed religious record of three major groups of people who lived in the lands we now call the Americas beginning over 2,000 years before the birth of Jesus Christ and continuing until about 421 A.D. A major portion of the book is concerned with the religious record of the descendants of a colony of people who left Jerusalem about 600 B.C. under the leadership of a prophet named Lehi. It contains many of their religious beliefs, principles, and practices. It records the exact words of many of their prophets. It tells of the appearance and teachings of the resurrected Jesus Christ to them shortly after his ascension into heaven (see 3 Nephi 10:18).

The Book of Mormon is *not* a geography book of ancient America, nor is it a secular history of the peoples who lived in the Americas in ancient times, although it does provide limited information on their types of government, modes of transportation, and agricultural practices. Some of their wars are described in detail, perhaps partially because one of the major engravers of the record was a great military leader himself, in addition to being a religious leader and historian.

Also, the Book of Mormon does *not* purport to tell all the story of all the peoples who lived in all these lands during all this time period. It clearly contains only a severely abridged account of a minority group during part of their history in perhaps a relatively small geographical area. We should remember that the last date in the Book of Mormon is over 1,000 years before the coming of Columbus to the Americas. Therefore, the Book of Mormon does NOT tell us what happened during that 1,000 years, nor does it tell us of any additional peoples who may have been discovered during that time or who may have come from foreign lands to the Americas.

The Author of the Book of Mormon

Usually when a book is printed, the name of the author is listed prominently on its cover. This, however, was not the case when the Book of Mormon was first published. As a result, many people not acquainted with the book have unfortunately assumed that Mormon is its author. Although Mormon did write and abridge much of what is in our present Book of Mormon, he is not its author. Nor is Joseph Smith its author, although the term "author and proprietor" was listed by his name in the first edition of 1830 in order to comply with the copyright laws of New York. In subsequent editions, Joseph Smith is rightfully identified as the translator.

As we will see later, many persons engraved and wrote on the plates from which we get the Book of Mormon, and many prophets and others are quoted extensively. But if any one person qualifies to be referred to as the "author" of the Book of Mormon, that person is Jesus Christ. The subtitle of the Book of Mormon, "Another Testament of Jesus Christ," is entirely fitting. As we will also see later, virtually all of those who wrote the accounts comprising our present Book of Mormon were specifically directed in their efforts by Jesus Christ himself. Also, the major message of the book centers on Christ. As Nephi, the first major writer in our present Book of Mormon, has declared:

"Behold I say unto you, that as these things are true, and as the Lord God liveth, there is none other name given under heaven save it be this Jesus Christ, of which I have spoken, whereby man can be saved. Wherefore, for this cause hath the Lord God promised unto me that these things which I write shall be kept and preserved, and handed down . . . from generation to generation as long as the earth shall stand; and they shall go according to the will and pleasure of God; and the nations who shall possess them shall be judged of them according to the words which are written.

"For we labor diligently to write, to persuade our children, and also our brethren, to believe in Christ, and to be reconciled to God; for we know that it is by grace that we are saved, after all we can do. . . . we believe in Christ . . . we talk of Christ, we rejoice in Christ, we preach of Christ, we prophesy of Christ, and we write according to our prophecies, that our children may know of what source they may look for a remission of their sins" (2 Nephi 25:20–26).

"And now, my beloved brethren, and also Jew, and all ye ends of the earth, hearken unto these words and believe in Christ; and if ye believe not in these words believe in Christ. And if ye shall believe in Christ ye will believe in these words, for they are the words of Christ, and he hath given them unto me; and they teach all men that they should do good. And if they are not the words of Christ, judge ye—for Christ will show unto you, with power and great glory, that they are his words, at the last day; and you and I shall stand face to face before his bar; and ye shall know that I have been commanded of him to write these things, notwithstanding my weakness" (2 Nephi 33:10–11).

The other major writers of the Book of Mormon also testify that they wrote only those things they were commanded to write by Christ. Thus, Jesus Christ might correctly be identified as the author of this book. In modern times the resurrected Jesus Christ has testified concerning his acceptance of the Book of Mormon: "As your Lord and your God liveth it is true" (D&C 17:6).

THE PLATES OF THE BOOK OF MORMON

Although the various peoples of the Book of Mormon kept many different types of records, we need to understand the origin and history of only five major sets of plates associated either directly or indirectly with our present Book of Mormon in order to understand the essential makeup of the book. Only two of these sets of plates—the small plates of Nephi and the plates of Mormon—were given to the Prophet Joseph Smith and translated by him. The five major sets of plates, in chronological sequence, are: the plates of Ether, the brass plates of Laban, the large plates of Nephi, the small plates of Nephi, and the plates of Mormon.

The Plates of Ether

Our present Book of Mormon refers to the "twenty and four plates . . . which is called the Book of Ether" (Ether 1:2). These plates cover more than 2,000 years of history of a numerous people. All that we have of these plates in our present Book of Mormon is the relatively brief abridgment and summary in the Book of Ether of the people we refer to as Jaredites—thirty-one pages in our current edition. So far as we know, Joseph Smith never had the plates of Ether in his possession.

The Brass Plates of Laban

In referring to these plates as "the brass plates of Laban," I realize I am using a modern term that is frequently used by members of the Church. However, the present Book of Mormon does not refer to these plates a single time in precisely this same word order; rather, these plates are referred to as "the plates of brass" (1 Nephi 3:12, 24; 4:16, 24, 38; 5:10, 14; 2 Nephi 5:12). This word order might be awkward for us in modern English, but it would be 100 percent consistent with both ancient and modern Hebrew usage. Such usage in the translation by Joseph Smith is one of thousands of indications that the Book of Mormon is precisely what it claims to be: a translation from an ancient text prepared in the Hebrew pattern of thought.

The plates of brass were written in Egyptian as indicated in Mosiah 1:4, which mentions that Lehi could read the engravings on these plates because he had "been taught in the language of the Egyptians." These plates are primarily concerned with the descendants of Joseph, who was sold into Egypt. Therefore, in a sense the plates of brass might be considered as part of the "stick of Joseph" or the "stick of Ephraim" mentioned in the Old Testament and in other scriptures (see Ezekiel 37:16–19).

Lehi's sons obtained the plates of brass when they left Jerusalem approximately 600 years before the time of Christ. The plates of brass contained "the five books of Moses" (1 Nephi 5:11) and many other books found in our present Old Testament, including the book of Isaiah. However, the plates of brass were more complete and more comprehensive than our Old Testament. Nephi, who was personally acquainted with the contents of the brass plates and who saw our present Old Testament in vision, said that "many plain and precious things" (1 Nephi 13:20) had been taken from the earlier records before they appeared in our present Bible. The teachings of many additional prophets were also found on the brass plates, including the words of Ezias, Neum, Zenos, and Zenock.

Joseph Smith did not translate directly from the plates of brass, and we have no evidence that he ever had them in his possession. We have in our present Book of Mormon only those portions of the brass plates that were quoted by the engravers of the two sets of plates given to Joseph Smith: the small plates of Nephi and the plates of Mormon.

The Large Plates of Nephi

These plates, started shortly after Lehi left Jerusalem, contained both a religious and a secular history of the members of the Lehite colony and of their descendants. These plates contained a series of books that were named after the authors who wrote on the plates. Evidently, Lehi was the earliest writer on these plates, although the engraver of the record might have been Nephi, who then named the book in honor of his father. The large plates of Nephi essentially covered the history of the Lehite people—more commonly know as the Nephites—from approximately 600 years before Christ to approximately 400 years after Christ. Mormon abridged these plates in the fourth century A.D. We have parts of Mormon's abridgment in our present Book of Mormon. However, the unabridged large plates of Nephi contain many items not found in our present Book of Mormon, including "a full account of the history of [Nephi's] people" (1 Nephi 9:2; see also 2 Nephi 4:14; Jacob 1:2–3), the genealogy of Lehi (1 Nephi 19:2), and the "more part" of the teachings of the resurrected Jesus Christ to the Nephite nation (3 Nephi 26:7). Again, we have no indication that Joseph Smith ever had the large plates of Nephi in his possession, or that he ever translated directly from them.

The Small Plates of Nephi

These plates were started approximately 570 B.C. and contain primarily a religious history of the Lehite colony for the first 470 years of its existence (1 Nephi 6:3, 5; 9:4; 19:2–6; 2 Nephi 5:29–32; Jacob 1:4). Some of the religious teachings of the plates of brass were copied onto these plates (2 Nephi 4:15). A translation of these plates comprises the first 143 pages of the present edition of the Book of Mormon, including the books of 1 Nephi (pages 1–53), 2 Nephi (pages 53–117), Jacob (pages 117–35), Enos (pages 136–38), Jarom (pages 138–40), and Omni (pages 140–43). The small plates of Nephi contain the "first person" account of the various writers on these plates. In other words, these plates have not been abridged. The Prophet Joseph Smith was given the small plates of Nephi. He had them in his possession; he translated directly from them.

The Plates of Mormon

The Plates of Mormon were the plates delivered to the Prophet Joseph Smith by Moroni on September 22, 1827. Essentially these plates contain (1) an abridgment by Mormon of the books on the large plates of Nephi, (2) first-person accounts by Mormon, including the section titled "The Words of Mormon," (3) personal accounts of Moroni, and (4) Moroni's abridgment of the plates of Ether. A portion of the plates of Mormon were sealed and have not yet been translated. We are not certain of the exact contents of this sealed portion. However, Moroni evidently was the major writer of the sealed portion (see Ether 4:5).

The following books in our present Book of Mormon come from the plates of Mormon, which are largely an abridgment of the large plates of Nephi (pages 145–468): Mosiah, Alma, Helaman, 3 Nephi, and 4 Nephi. Mormon wrote Mormon 1–7 (Moroni wrote Mormon 8–9). The plates of Mormon also contain Moroni's abridgement of the plates of Ether and Moroni's own writings in the book of Moroni, which include one discourse and two letters by Mormon (Moroni 7–9).

The Engravers of the Plates

These plates contain the words of many different persons. However, when we remember that our present Book of Mormon consists only of (1) the small plates of Nephi and (2) portions of the plates of Mormon that contain the abridgments and writings of Mormon and Moroni, then we can immediately see that there were relatively few engravers on the plates received by the Prophet Joseph Smith. Indeed, these engravers number only eleven.

Nine engravers contributed to the small plates of Nephi:

1. Nephi, who provides the information in 1 Nephi and 2 Nephi.

2. Jacob, the brother of Nephi, who provides the information in the seven chapters of the book that bears his name.

3. Enos, who engraved the book that bears his name.

4. Jarom, who engraved the two-page record that bears his name.

5. Omni, who is responsible for the first three verses of the book that bears his name.

6. Amaron, who engraved verses 4–8 of the book of Omni.

7. Chemish, who has the distinction of engraving only one verse in the Book of Mormon, Omni 1:9.

8. Abinadom, the son of Chemish, who engraved twice as much as his father, the two verses comprising Omni 1:10–11.

9. Amaleki, the son of Abinadom, who engraved verses 12–30 of the book of Omni.

The two engravers of the plates of Mormon—the other set of plates received by the Prophet Joseph Smith—are the father and son combination of Mormon and Moroni.

1. Mormon engraved the information contained in the following sections of the Book of Mormon: Words of Mormon (pages 143–45), Book of Mosiah (pages 145–207), Book of Alma (pages 207–368), Book of Helaman (pages 368–406), 3 Nephi (pages 406–64), 4 Nephi (pages 465–68), and the first seven chapters of the "smaller" Book of Mormon within the Book of Mormon (pages 469–81).

The smaller Book of Mormon is primarily an abridgment by Mormon on his own plates of Mormon of a much longer record he had earlier written on the large plates of Nephi. In other words, Mormon was one of the original writers on the large plates of Nephi—together with Mosiah, Alma, Helaman, and others. After Mormon had written his extensive record on the large plates of Nephi, he was commanded by the Lord to prepare the plates of Mormon and to include on them an abridgment of all the books on the large plates of Nephi. Mormon also abridged his own record, which constitutes the "smaller" Book of Mormon on pages 468–81 of the 1981 edition.

2. Moroni was the second engraver on the plates of Mormon. As mentioned earlier, Moroni wrote Mormon 8–9, abridged the Book of Ether, and produced the Book of Moroni.

Except for the relatively brief contributions of Enos, Jarom, Omni, Amaron, Chemish, Abinadom, and Amaleki, which comprise less than eight pages of our present text, all of the records included in our present Book of Mormon were engraved by four persons: Nephi, Jacob, Mormon, and Moroni. To understand and appreciate the Book of Mormon, we should know something about these four major engravers. They had several significant and remarkable characteristics and experiences in common:

1. *The four engravers were all personal witnesses of the Lord Jesus Christ during the time they lived in mortality on the earth.* Nephi and his brother Jacob, who lived approximately 500 to 600 years before Christ, were personal witnesses of Jesus Christ before his earthly birth. He visited and talked with them (2 Nephi 11:3). Mormon and Moroni, who lived from approximately 310 to 421 after the birth of Christ, were personal witnesses of the resurrected Jesus Christ. The Savior visited and spoke with them (Mormon 1:15; Ether 12:22–23, 38–39).

These four engravers or writers or editors or compilers were tutored by the Savior as to what they should write. They were strong witnesses of his divinity. Is it any wonder that their writings are identified as "Another Testament of Jesus Christ"?

2. *The four engravers were visited and tutored by angels or translated beings.* Nephi and Jacob were both tutored by angels sent directly from the presence of the Lord as recorded in 1 Nephi 11 and 2 Nephi 10. Mormon and Moroni were tutored by translated beings who had been caught up to heaven in the presence of the Lord, including the three Nephite disciples, as indicated in 3 Nephi 28:26 and Mormon 8:11.

3. *The four engravers all had visions of us—or our times and our challenges—and they wrote especially for us to help us solve our problems* (see 2 Nephi 6, 25, 26; Jacob 4; Mormon 8, 9; Moroni 1). These engravers did not write for their contemporaries; they wrote for us. There is not even a hint that any of these writers received as much as one *senine* in royalty payments for the publication of their records. Indeed, their records were not even published during their lifetimes.

Think of the possible implications of this truth—both as to what was included in the Book of Mormon and as to how we should read the Book of Mormon. Note, for example, the words of Moroni as he first started his engravings on the plates of Mormon: "Behold, the Lord hath shown unto me great and marvelous things concerning that which must shortly come, at that day when these things shall come forth among you. Behold, I speak unto you as if ye were present, and yet ye are not. But behold, Jesus Christ hath shown you unto me, and I know your doing" (Mormon 8:34–35).

Moroni is directly responsible for the materials on pages 481–531 of our present Book of Mormon. If you want a thrill and a meaningful insight into the Book of Mormon, just read or reread any one of those fifty pages. Then close the book, close your eyes, and ask yourself these questions: "What did the great prophet Moroni see in his vision of us and of our day that would prompt him to write this particular incident from the many teachings that were available to him in the voluminous records he had at his disposal?" "What principle or truth is Moroni trying to teach me and my generation that will help us to solve our problems?"

If you will do this as you read the Book of Mormon, the book will come alive for you to such an extent that you will have difficulty putting it down. Do you remember the testimony of Parley P. Pratt as he read the Book of Mormon in this manner? He wrote:

"I read all day; eating was a burden, I had no desire for food; sleep was a burden when the night came, for I preferred reading to sleep. As I read, the spirit of the Lord was upon me, and I knew and comprehended that the book was true, as plainly and manifestly as a man comprehends and knows that he exists. . . . I esteemed the Book, or the information contained in it, more than all the riches of the world."³

Apply the same principle as you read the pages engraved by Mormon, Nephi, or Jacob. When you read a page or a chapter from the engravings of Mormon, close the book, close your eyes, and then ask yourself: "What is there of such importance in this story that the prophet Mormon—who had a vision of me and my day, and who had such voluminous records at his disposal that he couldn't even record 'a hundredth part' of the total—would decide to include it in his abridged engravings?"

The Book of Mormon was written for us by prophets who had had visions of our day. In many ways, it is the most modern and timely of all our scriptures.

4. *The four engravers were faithful in being guided by the Lord as to what they should write; they wrote only those things commanded by him.* On several occasions they indicated, in essence, that they "intended to have written more," or were about to write on a particular subject but stopped because "the Lord forbade." Notice, for example, the words of Mormon of such an experience: "And now there cannot be written in this book even a hundredth part of the things which Jesus did truly teach unto the people; But behold the plates of Nephi do contain the more part of the things which he taught the people. And these things have I written, which are a lesser part of the things which he taught the people; and I have written them to the intent that they may be brought again unto this people, from the Gentiles, according to the words which Jesus hath spoken.

"And when they shall have received this, which is expedient that they should have first, to try their faith, and if it shall so be that they shall believe these things then shall the greater things be made manifest unto them. And if it so be that they will not believe these things, then shall the greater things be withheld from them, unto their condemnation. Behold, I was about to write them, all which were engraven upon the plates of Nephi, but the Lord forbade it, saying: I will try the faith of my people.

"Therefore I, Mormon, do write the things which have been commanded me of the Lord. And now I, Mormon, make an end of my sayings, and proceed to write the things which have been commanded me" (3 Nephi 26:6–12).

On other occasions the engravers indicated that they wrote on a particular subject, or related a particular incident, because the Lord had commanded them to do so (see 3 Nephi 23:7–14).

5. *The four engravers all bore strong testimonies of the divinity of Jesus Christ.* Their testimonies appear on almost every page of their writings. Refer, for example,

to the hundreds of scriptures listed on pages 175–85 in the index of the Book of Mormon under the numerous titles headed by the words "Jesus Christ." When all of their testimonies are combined, it is evident that we have an almost irrefutable testimony that Jesus Christ is indeed the divine Son of God, the Savior and Redeemer of the world. No wonder one of the major purposes of the Book of Mormon as listed on the title page is to convince "the Jew and Gentile that JESUS is the CHRIST, the ETERNAL GOD, manifesting himself unto all nations."

6. *The four engravers all warned us that we will be held accountable for what we do with what they have written.* Nephi cautions us in the last chapter engraved by him: "And now, my beloved brethren, and also Jew, and all ye ends of the earth, hearken unto these words and believe in Christ; and if ye believe not in these words believe in Christ. And if ye shall believe in Christ ye will believe in these words, for they are the words of Christ, and he hath given them unto me; and they teach all men that they should do good. And if they are not the words of Christ, judge ye—for Christ will show unto you, with power and great glory, that they are his words, at the last day; and you and I shall stand face to face before his bar; and ye shall know that I have been commanded of him to write these things, notwithstanding my weakness.

"And I pray the Father in the name of Christ that many of us, if not all, may be saved in his kingdom at that great and last day.

"And now, my beloved brethren, all those who are of the house of Israel, and all ye ends of the earth, I speak unto you as the voice of one crying from the dust: Farewell until that great day shall come.

"And you that will not partake of the goodness of God, and respect the words of the Jews [the Old Testament], and also my words [the Book of Mormon], and the words which shall proceed forth out of the mouth of the Lamb of God [the New Testament], behold, I bid you an everlasting farewell, for these words shall condemn you at the last day. For what I seal on earth, shall be brought against you at the judgment bar; for thus hath the Lord commanded me, and I must obey. Amen" (2 Nephi 33:10–15).

Jacob informs us that we will also meet him at the judgment seat of God. Note these words of caution: "O then, my beloved brethren, repent ye, and enter in at the strait gate, and continue in the way which is narrow, until ye shall obtain eternal life. O be wise; what can I say more? Finally, I bid you farewell, until I shall meet you before the pleasing bar of God, which bar striketh the wicked with awful dread and fear. Amen" (Jacob 6:11–13).

Mormon provided the following caution: "And these things doth the Spirit manifest unto me; therefore I write unto you all. And for this cause I write unto you, that ye may know that ye must all stand before the judgment-seat of Christ, yea, every soul who belongs to the whole human family of Adam; and ye must stand to be judged of your works, whether they be good or evil; . . . and I would that I could persuade all ye ends of the earth to repent and prepare to stand before the judgment-seat of Christ" (Mormon 3:20, 21–22).

And finally Moroni adds his solemn warning: "And now I speak unto all the ends of the earth. . . . I exhort you to remember these things; for the time speedily cometh that ye shall know that I lie not, for ye shall see me at the bar of God; and the Lord God will say unto you: Did I not declare my words unto you, which were written by this man, like as one crying from the dead, yea, even as one speaking out of the dust? . . . And God shall show unto you, that that which I have written is true" (Moroni 10:24, 27, 29).

The Prophets of the Book of Mormon

In addition to the four engravers, many additional persons mentioned in the Book of Mormon might qualify for the title of "prophet." Just the Lehite portion of the record might well include the following persons, listed alphabetically:

Abinadi; Alma the elder; Alma the younger; Benjamin; Enos; Gidgiddoni; Helaman, the son of Alma; Helaman, the son of Helaman; Lehi, the father of Nephi; Lehi, the son of Helaman; Nephi, the son of Lehi; Nephi, the son of Helaman; Nephi, the son of Nephi, who was the son of Helaman; Nephi, after whom 4 Nephi is named; and Samuel the Lamanite.

Other great religious leaders and teachers of righteousness might also be included, such as Aaron; Ammon; Amulek; Himni; Jarom; Joseph, the son of Lehi; Lachoneus; Moroni, the righteous Nephite military commander; Mosiah; Omner; and Shiblon.

Even with this partial list, we should be aware that the number of prophets among the Lehite people in the lands of the Americas seem to exceed the number of prophets among the Kingdom of Judah during the same period of time. In making such a comparison, however, we should remember two salient facts: (1) our present Old Testament is incomplete, and many "plain and precious truths," including the words of many prophets, have been deleted; (2) our present Book of Mormon contains only a partial account of what was originally written of these prophets; the "sealed portion" of the plates of Mormon may include the names and teachings of many additional prophets.

Other prophets could be mentioned from the Jaredite account, including the brother of Jared. Still other prophets are quoted who belong to the period covered by the plates of brass, such as the prophets Ezias, Neum, Zenos, and Zenock.

The words of all of these prophets were engraved on the plates for us by engravers who were themselves prophets. Thus, for example, when the prophet Mormon quotes from the prophet Abinadi, whose writings are included in the records of the prophet Alma, we in a sense have a second or even third witness of these testimonies when they are included in this sacred scripture.

The Peoples of the Book of Mormon

Although many different peoples are identified in the Book of Mormon, I mention only a few of the major groups. The words Lamanite and Lamanites are used more frequently than any other name designating a particular people, appearing over 700 times in our present Book of Mormon. During the first 600 years or so of the history of the descendants of Lehi and his colony, the term Lamanite is used to refer to a descendant of Laman or, in a more general sense, as a descendant of those who remained with Laman during the great division of about 570 B.C. This usage continued to the time of Christ.

Then, for approximately 200 years (from about 34 A.D. to 231 A.D.), there were no "manner of -ites" among the people (4 Nephi 1:17). Finally, as the record indicates, "in the two hundred and thirty and first year, there was a great division among the people . . . and . . . they who rejected the gospel were called Lamanites. . . . And they were taught to hate the children of God, even as the Lamanites were taught to hate the children of Nephi from the beginning" (4 Nephi 1:35, 38–39).

The term Lamanite had a different meaning at the close of the Book of Mormon than it had near the beginning. We should keep this distinction in mind when we use the term Lamanite in our day to refer to the descendants of those mentioned at the close of the Book of Mormon.

The words Nephite and Nephites are the second most frequently used terms to designate a family group, appearing nearly 400 times in our present Book of Mormon. These terms refer to the descendants of Nephi and to the descendants of those who joined with Nephi in approximately 570 B.C. or who believed in the basic teachings of Nephi. Following the great division in 231 A.D., "there arose a people who were called the Nephites, and they were true believers in Christ" (4 Nephi 1:36).

The other family names coming from the original family of Lehi are the terms

Lemuelites (found five times), Jacobites (listed four times), and Josephites (also listed four times). The word Samite does not appear a single time, nor is the term "the people of Sam" ever used. Perhaps the reason is provided in 2 Nephi 4:11:

"And after [Lehi] had made an end of speaking unto them, he spake unto Sam, saying: Blessed art thou, and thy seed; for thou shalt inherit the land like unto thy brother Nephi. And thy seed shall be numbered with his seed; and thou shalt be even like unto thy brother, and thy seed like unto his seed; and thou shalt be blessed in all thy days" (2 Nephi 4:11).

Two other terms are used quite extensively by members of the Church to refer to other major groupings of the Book of Mormon, but interestingly enough these terms are not used extensively within the Book of Mormon. For example, the word Jaredite appears only twice in the Book of Mormon (in Moroni 9:23 and in the introductory statement of the Book of Ether), and the term "people of Jared" is used only twice (in Moroni 1:1 and on the Book of Mormon title page). Perhaps it would be more accurate and consistent to use the term "people of Jared" as Moroni does in the title page of the Book of Mormon.

Some Book of Mormon readers might be surprised to learn that the words Mulekite and Mulekites do not appear a single time in the Book of Mormon. Indeed, the word Mulek appears only seventeen times: thirteen times to refer to a city, one time to refer to the land northward, and only three times to refer to a specific person (see Mosiah 25:2; Helaman 6:10; and Helaman 8:21).

However, the term "people of Zarahemla" is used fourteen times to refer to the people we often call Mulekites. Perhaps we should start using the term "people of Zarahemla" instead of the word "Mulekites" in referring to those people who left Jerusalem just a few years after the people of Lehi had departed from that city.

Such usage might keep us from saying that Mulek, the son of Zedekiah, was the leader of the colony at the time it left Jerusalem. Such a claim is not made within the Book of Mormon, and it is very unlikely that Mulek was the leader. Mulek is not mentioned in the Bible. However, we know from the Bible that Zedekiah, the vassal king of Judah and the father of Mulek, was only thirty-two years old when he was taken captive by the Babylonians at the time the city of Jerusalem was destroyed. Although Zedekiah's son Mulek was not taken captive to Babylon, he obviously was very young and probably was not the leader of the small colony of people that fled from Jerusalem to escape the Babylonians. Later, they were led by the Lord to the lands we now know of as the Americas. More than likely the young boy Mulek was taken by the colony to preserve his life and also to preserve the seed of Zedekiah.

The Book of Mormon also includes other names of peoples ending in the suffix "ite"; these designate groups were named after a particular powerful leader or after a noted progenitor. The names of the groups beginning with the letter A include Amalekites (eighteen times), Amalickiahites (four times), Amlicites (twenty-seven times), Ammonihahites (one time), Ammonites (two times), and Amulonites (seven times). Also, the term "Anti-Nephi-Lehies" is briefly used to describe the "people of Ammon."

Also, some groups were identified by particular characteristics, such as the "Gadianton robbers."

However, the major groups of people to keep in mind as you read the record are (1) the Lamanites, (2) the Nephites, (3) the people of Zarahemla (sometimes erroneously called the Mulekites), and (4) the people of Jared, sometimes called Jaredites.

The Purposes of the Book of Mormon

What is the purpose of the Book of Mormon? When asked that question, many Latter-day Saints respond by quoting from the title page of the Book of Mormon: "to the convincing of the Jew and Gentile that Jesus is the Christ." This is just one of the major purposes of the Book of Mormon; there are several other very important purposes:

1. *To be a witness or testament of the divinity of Jesus Christ, and to bring to the Jews the testimony of the Nephites that Jesus is the Christ.*

We often use the word "witness" to identify this purpose of the Book of Mormon, but I am convinced that the word "testament" is a stronger and more comprehensive word. I was living in Australia several years ago when the Brethren decided on the subtitle for the Book of Mormon, "Another Testament of Jesus Christ." I immediately went to the National Library in Perth, Australia, obtained the largest dictionary I could find, and traced the etymology of the word testament. I found that the current word came from middle English, which, in turn, came from late Latin, and then from an earlier Latin word that essentially means *covenant*. The Latin word is *testari*, which means "to be a witness." Then I found this intriguing explanation:

"TESTAMENT (Middle English from Late Latin from Latin)

"LL (Late Latin) *testamentum*—COVENANT. Translation of Greek *diatheke*, or covenant.

"L (Latin) last will from *testari*, to be a witness, make, a will . . . both from a prehistoric Italic compound, whose first and second constituents respectively are akin to L (Latin) *tres* three and L (Latin) *stare* to stand: from the witness standing by as a third party in a litigation—more at THREE, STAND."

All of us are acquainted with the principle taught by our Heavenly Father that in the mouth of two or three witnesses every truth will be established (see Deuteronomy 17:6, 2 Corinthians 13:1). I am convinced that the wording "Another Testament" was divinely inspired. In the roots of the word testament, we have the concepts of three, witness, testimony, and covenant.

2. *To fulfill biblical prophecy and to be a witness or another testament of the Bible.*

Several biblical prophecies and statements—from both the Old Testament and New Testament—that pertain directly to the Book of Mormon or to the peoples of the Book of Mormon are listed in the Topical Guide under the heading "Book of Mormon" and in the Bible Dictionary under "Ephraim, Stick of" in the LDS edition of the Holy Bible.

Concerning the purpose of the Book of Mormon as another testament of the Bible, note these explanatory words of Mormon as to one of the reasons he prepared and wrote on the plates of Mormon:

"Therefore repent, and be baptized in the name of Jesus, and lay hold upon the gospel of Christ, which shall be set before you, not only in this record but also in the record which shall come unto the Gentiles from the Jews, which record shall come from the Gentiles unto you. For behold, this is written for the intent that ye may believe that; and if ye believe that ye will believe this also" (Mormon 7:8–9).

Note again the emphasis by Mormon: "This [the Book of Mormon] is written for the intent that ye may believe that [the Bible]; and if ye believe that [the Bible] ye will believe this [the Book of Mormon] also."

These statements indicate that the Book of Mormon is indeed a witness for the Bible, and that the Bible is also a witness for the Book of Mormon.

Moroni, the last engraver on the plates of Mormon, also indicated the prophesied connection between these two volumes of scripture. I suspect Moroni 10:4 is the most frequently quoted single verse in the entire Book of Mormon. I am also convinced that it cannot be fully understood out of the context of the verse that precedes it and the verse that follows it. Note carefully the words of all three of these verses:

"Behold, I would exhort you that when ye shall read these things, if it be wisdom in God that ye should read them, that ye would remember how merciful the

Lord hath been unto the children of men, from the creation of Adam even down until the time that ye shall receive these things, and ponder it in your hearts.

"And when ye shall receive these things, I would exhort you that ye would ask God, the Eternal Father, in the name of Christ, if these things are not true; and if ye shall ask with a sincere heart, with real intent, having faith in Christ, he will manifest the truth of it unto you, by the power of the Holy Ghost.

"And by the power of the Holy Ghost ye may know the truth of all things" (Moroni 10:3–5).

Although "Bible" and "Book of Mormon" do not appear in these words by Moroni—these titles were not in use in the days of Moroni—a careful reading indicates that Moroni is saying in essence that you must accept the truthfulness of both these books if you study and ponder them in sincerity and truth. You cannot accept the truthfulness of one without accepting the other.

Notice the exhortation in verse 3 that after you read "these things" (the records of the Book of Mormon), you should remember "how merciful the Lord hath been unto the children of men, from the creation of Adam . . . and ponder it [the way God has dealt with the children of men] in your hearts." In which of these two scriptures—the Bible or the Book of Mormon—do we read of the "creation of Adam"? The answer, of course, is the Bible. This information is not in the Book of Mormon. Indeed, this same Moroni, when he started his abridgment of the record of Ether, stated: "And as I suppose that the first part of this record, which speaks concerning the creation of the world, and also of Adam . . . is had among the Jews—Therefore I do not write those things which transpired from the days of Adam" (Ether 1:3–4).

Therefore in verse 3, Moroni is telling us we must read the Bible and ponder it in our hearts. Then, in verse 4, Moroni says that when we are ready to receive "these things"—including both the Bible and the Book of Mormon—we should "ask God, the Eternal Father, in the name of Christ, if these things [the Bible and the Book of Mormon] are not true; and if ye shall ask with a sincere heart, with real intent, having faith in Christ, he will manifest the truth of it [the Book of Mormon] unto you, by the power of the Holy Ghost."

And then the clinching statement: "And by the power of the Holy Ghost ye may know the truth of all things."

These testimonies are similar to the one given by President Brigham Young concerning this topic: "No man can say that this book (laying his hand on the Bible) is true . . . and at the same time say, that the Book of Mormon is untrue. . . . There is not that person on the face of the earth who has had the privilege of learning the

Gospel of Jesus Christ from these two books, that can say that one is true, and the other is false. No Latter-day Saint, no man or woman, can say the Book of Mormon is true, and at the same time say that the Bible is untrue. If one be true, both are."[4]

3. *To convince the Lamanites that they are of the house of Israel.*

As the Book of Mormon title page states: "To show unto the remnant of the House of Israel what great things the Lord hath done for their fathers; and that they may know the covenants of the Lord, that they are not cast off forever."[5]

The Book of Mormon offers a knowledge of the Savior unto the remnants of the House of Israel through the testimony of the Nephites. This purpose of the Book of Mormon is concerned with the workings of the Lord with various groups within the House of Israel. Note the numerous references listed under the following topics in the Book of Mormon index: "Israel"; "Israel, Gathering Of"; "Israel, Scattering Of"; and "Israel, Ten Lost Tribes Of."

4. *To restore to the knowledge of mankind many plain and precious truths concerning the gospel of Jesus Christ.*

You might want to review the index and prepare a list of all the headings pertaining to the basic principles, doctrines, and ordinances of the gospel of Jesus Christ. Then note the numerous references from the Book of Mormon pertaining to these topics. The Book of Mormon has made many contributions on such vital subjects as the atonement of Jesus Christ, baptism, becoming sons and daughters of Christ, being born again, the birth of Jesus, the devil, faith, the fall of Adam, final judgment, freedom, God, Israel, the Holy Ghost and Holy Spirit, and hope.

In addition, the Book of Mormon has contributed to our knowledge and understanding of Jesus Christ (as Jehovah, Messiah, Savior, Redeemer), joy and happiness, laws of mercy and justice, life after death, ministering of angels, miracles, priestcraft, prophets, redemption, resurrection, sanctification, scriptures, secret combinations, seers, service to fellowmen, status of little children who die without baptism, traditions, translated beings, and the tree of life.

5. *To convince mankind that every person must be judged of his works; to test the faith of this generation; to help the faithful.*

The twenty related headings listed under "Judgment" in the index should indicate something about the importance of the Book of Mormon on these subjects.

6. *To help the people of this generation solve their problems; to provide mankind with secrets of national survival; to prepare the faithful for the Second Coming of Jesus Christ and the millennial reign.*

The Book of Mormon offers many major messages for our time. Following is only a partial list of those messages that seem to have a modern application. In other words, the Book of Mormon provides information on these subjects that should help us solve serious problems and challenges we now face. Some of these pertain primarily to members of the Church, but most of them pertain to all mankind.

1. The principle of moral agency. This is critical to our political, economic, and social life. See 2 Nephi 2:11, 15–16, 26–27; 10:23; 26:27; Mosiah 2:33; 5:8; 18:28; 23:13; Alma 3:26–27; 12:31; 13:3; 29:4–5; 41:3–7; 58:40–41; 61:9, 21; Helaman 14:30–31.

2. Dealing with unbelievers within the Church. The story of Korihor in Alma 30:37–53 is a good example. See also Alma 1:1–25; 2; 11:21–46; 12:1–9; 14:26–29; 15:1–12; 31–35.

3. The preparation of a people for the Second Coming of Jesus Christ and the millennial reign. The seven pages of the Book of Omni (361 B.C. to 130 B.C.) and the four pages of 4 Nephi (36 A.D. to 321 A.D.) cover 516 years—half the time period of the Lehite record. But the 261 pages of Mosiah, Alma, and Helaman cover only 130 years (130 B.C. to 1 B.C.). Why? See also Helaman 14–16 and 3 Nephi 1–11.

4. The nature and purpose of translated beings. The experience of the three Nephite disciples helps us understand Elijah, Moses, and John the Revelator. The Book of Mormon indeed offers "inspired commentary" on the Bible. See Alma 45:18–19; 3 Nephi 28:1–12; 36–40; Ether 15:34.

5. The proper uses of wealth. See 2 Nephi 26:30; Jacob 2:12–14; 17–19; Mosiah 4:16, 26.

6. America is a choice land to the righteous. See 1 Nephi 2:19–20; 13:30; 2 Nephi 1:1–12, 20; 10:19; Alma 36:30; 37:13; Ether 1:38–43; 2:7–12, 15; 9:20; 10:28; 13:2.

7. The principles of national survival, including the importance of the spirit of discernment. See Alma 43:23–24; Mosiah 10:10–11; Alma 2:30–38; 37:13; 56:46–56; 3 Nephi 4:8–15; Mormon 2:14–15; 3:2, 7–8; Ether 2:7–12; 9:20; Moroni 9:20.

8. Advice and principles concerning different types of government. For examples on monarchy, the reign of judges, and other government types, see Mosiah 2:9–19; 11:1–15; 23:7–8; 29:1–44; Helaman 5:1–2; 3 Nephi 7:1–3; Ether 6:22–30.

9. What causes war? The Book of Mormon examines cycles of righteousness, blessings, prosperity, pride, selfishness (class distinction, persecution, hatred), war, punishment, humility, and repentance. See 1 Nephi 14:15–17; 22:13–14, 17; Alma 16:9–10; 50:21; Mormon 4:11–12; Ether 13–15.

10. Is war justified? See 1 Nephi 14:15–17; 22:13–14; Alma 16:9–10; 43:46–47; 48:14; 50:21; 3 Nephi 3:20–21; Mormon 4:11–12; Ether 13–15).

11. Does God always protect the righteous in time of war or threatened destruction?

12. The reality of the devil and some of the methods he uses.

13. The importance of keeping a sacred oath or of keeping one's word.

14. Why we should be humble without being compelled to be humble. See Alma 31 for Alma's experience with the Zoramites.

15. Warnings against indifference and procrastination.

16. Warnings against pride.

17. Warnings against the dangers of following false traditions.

18. Warnings against the teachings of agnostics, atheists, and unbelievers. See the stories of Korihor (Alma 30), Nehor (Alma 1–2), and Sherem (Jacob 7).

19. Warnings against hypocrisy and idols.

20. Warnings against unchastity.

21. Warnings against priestcraft. " He commandeth that there shall be no priestcrafts; for, behold, priestcrafts are that men preach and set themselves up for a light unto the world, that they may get gain and praise of the world; but they seek not the welfare of Zion" (2 Nephi 26:29).

22. Warnings against the evils and dangers of secret combinations. Such warnings can be found in several books: 2 Nephi 9:9; 26:22; Alma; Helaman; 3 Nephi; 4 Nephi; Mormon; Ether 8–9, 11, 13, 14. The warnings found in the Book of Ether may be why Moroni included this book.

23. Warnings against the corrupting powers of heavy taxation. See the example of wicked king Noah in Mosiah 11.

24. The importance of serving our fellowmen.

General Do's And Don'ts

Although the Book of Mormon was written by writers who lived hundreds of years ago, in many ways it is as timely as today's newspapers and magazines. One reason the Book of Mormon is so timely is that it was written by men who saw in vision the conditions of our day; therefore, they were able to write about today's problems even though they lived centuries ago. The following scriptures from the Book of Mormon clearly indicate that the four major writers of the sacred Nephite scripture knew a great deal about us and the problems of our time:

Nephi: 1 Nephi 9:1–6; 10–16 (especially 13:30–42 and 14:1–30); 2 Nephi 26:16–33; 27–33).
Jacob: 2 Nephi 6:8–15.
Mormon: Words of Mormon 1:1–9; Mormon 5:8–24; 7:1–10.
Moroni: Mormon 8:12–41; 9:1–37; Ether 4:1, 6; 12:38–39.

Here are some do's and don'ts that may help you in your serious study of the Book of Mormon:

Do's

Do become so well acquainted with the four major engravers and the two sets of plates translated by Joseph Smith that you can identify with the writers and their plates. You will then more easily and effectively "liken the scriptures" unto yourself.

Do learn all the names of the books of the Book of Mormon in the order in which they appear so you can easily locate the books and find references in them. The Book of Mormon contains only fifteen books (as compared with sixty-six books in the Bible—thirty-nine in the Old Testament and twenty-seven in the New Testament): 1 Nephi, 2 Nephi, Jacob, Enos, Jarom, Omni, Words of Mormon, Mosiah, Alma, Helaman, 3 Nephi, 4 Nephi, Mormon, Ether, and Moroni.

Do develop a personal, meaningful, workable, marking system. Use different colored pencils. You remember about 70 percent of what you do but only about 10 percent of what you read.

Do remember that this book is essentially a record of a group of Israelites; thus, relate what you know concerning the history, manner, customs, traditions, and language of the Israelites to the story of the descendants of Lehi and his colony.

One idea concerning the "language of the Israelites"—Hebrew—will help you understand many otherwise difficult grammatical constructions in the Book of Mormon. In Hebrew, the noun usually precedes any adjective or descriptive word pertaining to it. The Israelite says "morning good" rather than "good morning." Now note these examples taken only from the opening chapters of 1 Nephi: "altar of stones" (1 Nephi 2:5), "river of water" (1 Nephi 2:6), "waters of the river" (1 Nephi 2:9), "valley of Lemuel" (1 Nephi 2:14), "plates of brass" (1 Nephi 3:12).

Another interesting custom of the Israelites is that once a woman is married, she is considered to be part of her husband's family. She is usually not mentioned in her father's record. In the family record of Lehi, covering nearly 1,000 years and 500 pages, only three women belonging to these peoples are mentioned by name: Sariah, Abish, and Isabel (contrast with Joseph Smith–History 1:4).

Do become acquainted with the doctrinal teachings of the Book of Mormon. It contains the "fulness of the gospel" of salvation. In other words, it contains instructions on everything you need to know and do in order to return to the presence of God. As Joseph Smith said, "A man would get nearer to God by abiding by its precepts, than by any other book."[5]

Do pray about what you have read.

Do bear your testimony concerning its truthfulness.

Don'ts

Don't claim that the Book of Mormon is primarily a history book, or a book on archaeology or geography, or a book that tells everything about all the peoples who lived in all the lands of the Americas before the coming of Columbus. Limit your claims and purposes of the book to those of the original writers and engravers.

Don't become too concerned about the exact location of the various cities and lands mentioned in the Book of Mormon. You might want to become oriented to the general location of three or four of the major lands as described in the book—such as the lands of Nephi, Zarahemla, and Bountiful—but do not become so preoccupied with their exact location in relationship to current lands and cities that it diverts your attention from the major religious messages of the Book of Mormon.

Don't worry about trying to "prove" the Book of Mormon to others. The Book of Mormon contains its own proofs, which prove (1) the truthfulness of its teachings concerning the divinity of Jesus Christ and (2) the principles and ordinances of the gospel of Jesus Christ. As President Benson mentioned during the 1987 April general conference:

"We are not required to prove that the Book of Mormon is true or is an authentic record through external evidences—though there are many. It never has been the case, nor is it so now, that the studies of the learned will prove the Book of Mormon true or false. The origin, preparation, translation, and verification of the truth of the Book of Mormon have all been retained in the hands of the Lord, and the Lord makes no mistakes. You can be assured of that.

"God has built in His own proof system of the Book of Mormon as found in Moroni, chapter 10, and in the testimonies of the Three and the Eight Witnesses and in various sections of the Doctrine and Covenants.

"We each need to get our own testimony of the Book of Mormon through the Holy Ghost. Then our testimony, coupled with the Book of Mormon, should be shared with others so that they, too, can know through the Holy Ghost of its truthfulness."[6]

Don't let critics or opponents of the Book of Mormon bother you with their challenges to "prove" the authenticity of the book. Remember the story of Korihor in Alma 30. The burden of proof is upon the critics, and they simply cannot prove the Book of Mormon is not true just as Korihor could not prove that God does not exist. "Ye receive no witness until after the trial of your faith" (Ether 12:6).

Don't let differences in the pronunciation of the names in the Book of Mormon by different people bother you. Many of these names are of Hebrew origin, and others, such as most of the names in the Book of Ether, come from an even earlier culture. Undoubtedly, at best, we are not pronouncing these names correctly according to their original pronunciation.

Don't become unduly concerned about the changes that have been made in the various editions and printings of the Book of Mormon. The 1981 edition is the most accurate of all, and is faithful to the printer's manuscript and to what we have of the dictated (or original) manuscript. No major doctrinal errors or changes have been made in any of the editions.

Don't let criticisms of the Book of Mormon by anti-LDS critics bother you even for one second, whether such criticisms are concerned with the critics' interpretation of the doctrines of the book or with any lack of so-called "archaeological evidences" that they may think they perceive. Invariably, their criticisms are without substance; they are a smoke screen to serve as a weak excuse and defense for their not having paid the price of reading the Book of Mormon and praying about its truthfulness.

To quote a parable by Hugh Nibley on Book of Mormon criticism may be helpful:

"A young man once long ago claimed he had found a large diamond in his field as he was ploughing. He put the stone on display to the public free of charge, and everyone took sides. A psychologist showed, by citing some famous case studies, that the young man was suffering from a well-known form of delusion. An historian showed that other men have also claimed to have found diamonds in fields and been deceived. A geologist proved that there were no diamonds in the area but only quartz: the young man had been fooled by a quartz. When asked to inspect the stone itself, the geologist declined with a weary, tolerant smile and a kindly shake of the head. An English professor showed that the young man in describing his stone used the very same language that others had used in describing uncut diamonds: he was, therefore, simply speaking the common language of his time. A sociologist showed that only three out of 177 florists' assistants in four major cities believed the stone was genuine. A clergyman wrote a book to show that it was not the young man but someone else who had found the stone.

"Finally an indigent jeweler named Snite pointed out that since the stone was still available for examination the answer to the question of whether it was a diamond or not had absolutely nothing to do with who found it, or whether the finder was honest or sane, or who believed him, or whether he would know a diamond from a brick, or whether diamonds had ever been found in fields, or whether people had ever been fooled by quartz or glass, but was to be answered simply and solely by putting the stone to certain well-known tests for diamonds. Experts on diamonds were called in. Some of them declared it genuine. The others made nervous jokes about it and declared that they could not very well jeopardize their dignity and reputations by appearing to take the thing too seriously. To hide the bad impression thus made, someone came out with the theory that the stone was really a synthetic diamond, very skillfully made, but a fake just the same. The objection to this is that the production of a good synthetic diamond [157] years ago would have been an even more remarkable feat than the finding of a real one."[7]

This story has many morals. The Book of Mormon is a spiritual diamond. Our challenge to the critics should be to apply the spiritual tests to see whether it is a real genuine diamond; in other words, the critics should read it, compare its teachings with those of the Bible, and pray about it.

Specific Hints and Helps

Now for some specific hints and helps as you read and ponder the Book of Mormon:

1. Use the 1981 edition or a later edition.
2. Read the chapter headings.
3. Use the footnotes and the cross references, and use the helps in the Bible, including the Topical Guide and the Bible Dictionary.
4. Become acquainted with the Index.
5. Pay special attention to sections that begin or end with the following expressions:

"And thus it is. Amen" (1 Nephi 14:30) and "And thus we see" (1 Nephi 16:29; 17:3). Nephi, Jacob, Mormon, and Moroni use these expressions to reinforce a major point they have just made.

Of course, these suggestions are useless unless we read and reread the Book of Mormon. Here are a few ideas that might help you in your resolve to make study of the Book of Mormon a lifetime pursuit and to make this study more effective. Just start where you are.

1. Develop a desire to read the scriptures.

2. Hope that the scriptures are true, that they are the word of the Lord (see Hebrews 11:1; Alma 32:21).

3. Decide to read the scriptures.

4. Commit to a definite minimum schedule—daily, weekly, and monthly.

5. Read a little from the scriptures each day.

6. Involve others in your decision.

7. Liken the scriptures unto yourself (see 1 Nephi 19:22–23). Remember Nephi's words: "And it came to pass that I, Nephi, said unto my father: I will go and do the things which the Lord hath commanded, for I know that the Lord giveth no commandments unto the children of men, save he shall prepare a way for them that they may accomplish the thing which he commandeth them" (1 Nephi 3:7).

"And I said unto them: If God had commanded me to do all things I could do them. If he should command me that I should say unto this water, be thou earth, it should be earth; and if I should say it, it would be done. And now, if the Lord has such great power, and has wrought so many miracles among the children of men, how is it that he cannot instruct me, that I should build a ship?" (1 Nephi 17:50–51).

8. Place yourself in the position of the original author (see Mormon 8:34–35).

President Brigham Young asked, "Do you read the Scriptures, my brethren and sisters, as though you were writing them a thousand, two thousand, or five thousand years ago? Do you read them as though you stood in the place of the men who wrote them? If you do not, . . . it is your privilege to do so."[8]

9. Ask yourself why the Lord had his prophets include specific teachings found in the Book of Mormon (see 3 Nephi 16:6–12).

10. Ponder the scriptures (see 2 Nephi 4:15–16; 3 Nephi 17:3; Moroni 10:3–5).

11. Learn the principles and their relationships to each other.

12. Relate the principles in the scriptures to everything else, including the teachings of the living prophets (see 2 Nephi 11:8).

13. Live the principles of the scriptures. Reading without living is like a glass eye—all for show and nothing for use.

14. Study systematically and correlate with other scriptures.

15. Develop a meaningful marking system.

16. Teach the scriptures to others, including your family.

17. Reread the scriptures.

18. Reapply the principles in your life—you are a different person from when you last read the scriptures.

19. Prepare to meet the Savior.

Notes

This is a previously unpublished paper.

1. Gordon B. Hinckley, in "One Chapter a Day," *Church News,* 10 April 1983, 24.
2. Ezra Taft Benson, in Conference Report, April 1986, 4–5.
3. *Autobiography of Parley P. Pratt,* ed. Parley P. Pratt [Jr.] (Salt Lake City: Deseret Book Co., 1985), 20, 22.
4. Brigham Young, in *Journal of Discourses,* 1:38.
5. *Teachings of the Prophet Joseph Smith,* 194.
6. Ezra Taft Benson, "The Book of Mormon and the Doctrine and Covenants," *Ensign,* May 1987, 83–84.
7. Hugh Nibley, *Lehi in the Desert and The World of the Jaredites* (Salt Lake City: Deseret Book Co. and FARMS, 1988), 121–22.
8. Brigham Young, in *Journal of Discourses,* 7:333.

Chapter 6

HOW TO GET THE MOST FROM YOUR STUDY OF THE DOCTRINE AND COVENANTS

The Doctrine and Covenants is one of the most important books on earth. Of this book, President Joseph Fielding Smith said, "In my judgment there is no book on earth yet come to man as important as the book known as the Doctrine and Covenants."[1]

This agrees with the appraisal of President Wilford Woodruff, who said, "I consider that the Doctrine and Covenants, our Testament, contains a code of the most solemn, the most Godlike proclamations ever made to the human family."[2]

I add my testimony of the value of the Doctrine and Covenants to those of the Brethren. I know it is one of the five most important books on earth—joined by the Old Testament, the New Testament, the Book of Mormon, and the Pearl of Great Price.

WHAT IS THE DOCTRINE AND COVENANTS?

Primarily, the Doctrine and Covenants is a book of revelations. Most of the sections contain direct revelations from God to his prophets (primarily Joseph Smith), but other sections contain information derived from revelations, such as answers to scriptural questions (sections 77 and 113), items of instruction (sections 130 and 131), letters (sections 127 and 128), inspired translation of earlier scripture (section 7), and prayers, including the dedicatory prayer for the Kirtland Temple (sections 13, 65, and 109).

Both the preface (section 1) and the appendix (section 133) were received by revelation, although they were given for a specific purpose. Other sections are almost pure prophecy (sections 87 and 121), while others include the minutes of a high council meeting (section 102), a declaration of belief concerning government (section 134), historical information on the martyrdom of Joseph Smith and his brother Hyrum (section 135), and instructions concerning the organization of the Saints for migration to the West (section 136). The Doctrine and Covenants also contains two official declarations. "Official Declaration—1" (the Manifesto) concerns the cessation of polygamy, and "Official Declaration—2" discusses the priesthood being given to all worthy male members. Both declarations were also received by revelation given to the prophet at that time and then individually approved by the Quorum of the Twelve Apostles and later by the membership of the Church.

Have any sections been added to the Doctrine and Covenants since the death of the Prophet Joseph Smith except for sections 135, 136, 137, and 138, and the first and second Official Declarations? Yes. Sections 2, 13, 77, 85, 87, 103, 105, and 108 through 132 were not published in the 1835 edition (some of them had not even been received by that time) but were published in later editions after being accepted by the Church as canonized scripture.

What Is the Relationship of Our Present Doctrine and Covenants to the Publication Called *A Book of Commandments*?

A brief history of *A Book of Commandments* is necessary to answer this question. Soon after Joseph Smith received some of the early revelations, members of the Church or other inquiring individuals were naturally interested in knowing exactly what the revelations said. Often the revelations were written down and circulated, even if they were given primarily for the benefit of a particular person or group of people. The revelations were treated much the same way as patriarchal blessings might be recorded and distributed today, even though they are for the personal benefit and instruction of the person receiving the blessing.

In time, copies of several of the revelations were in circulation, and, as would be normal, some persons started to make a collection of these revelations. Missionaries traveling away from the headquarters of the Church particularly were interested in having complete and correct copies of these revelations, particularly if the revelations could assist them in their missionary efforts.

Because of a growing interest in and demand for the revelations, the matter of their possible publication received special attention at a conference of the Church held during November 1831. A specific request was made of the Lord, and sections 1 and 133 were received during the conference as a result. After a vote by the members at the conference, the Church proceeded with the publication of sixty-five of the revelations in a book to be titled *A Book of Commandments.*

At this special conference at Hiram, Ohio, on November 1, 1831, just nineteen months after the organization of the Church, the Lord gave a revelation to the Prophet Joseph Smith that the Lord said was to serve as "my preface unto the book of my commandments" (D&C 1:6). The *History of the Church* contains the following account from the *Far West Record:*

During the afternoon of November 1, "Brother Joseph Smith, Jun., said that inasmuch as the Lord has bestowed a great blessing upon us in giving commandments and revelations, he asked the conference what testimony they were willing to attach to these commandments which would shortly be sent to the world. A number of the brethren arose and said that they were willing to testify to the world that they knew that they were of the Lord."

During the second day's proceedings, "The revelation of last evening read by the moderator [this was Oliver Cowdery]. The brethren then arose in turn and bore witness to the truth of the Book of Commandments; after which Brother Joseph Smith, Jun., arose and expressed his feelings and gratitude concerning the commandments and preface received yesterday."[3]

Oliver Cowdery and John Whitmer were given the responsibility of taking the selected sixty-five revelations to Jackson County, Missouri, where they were to be printed by the W. W. Phelps and Company printing press. Initially ten thousand copies were to be printed; this was later changed to three thousand copies.

A number of copies of all sixty-five chapters had been printed—but none bound into books—when, on July 20, 1833, a mob destroyed the press and most of the printed chapters. The book, however, was subsequently published but was never made widely available. The title page stated: "A Book of Commandments for the Government of the Church of Christ, organized According to Law, on the 6th of April, 1830. Published by W. W. Phelps & Co., 1833."

This was the forerunner of the book now known as the Doctrine and Covenants.

What Is the Significance of the Words *Doctrine* and *Covenants*?

Smith and Sjodahl briefly explained the meaning of these words in their *Doctrine and Covenants Commentary:*

"The doctrine of the Lord is that, 'Whosoever repenteth and cometh unto me, the same is [of] my church.'" The term *covenant,* meanwhile, "signifies the settled arrangement between God and man, whereby the eternal Father undertakes to save His children. This arrangement is also called His 'oath,' His 'counsel,' and His 'promise' (Psalm 89:3, 4; Hebrews 6:13–20)."[4]

The *Institute Self-Instruction Course* on the Doctrine and Covenants adds:

"DOCTRINE: Gospel teachings or positions which have such general acceptance as to be considered settled and therefore authoritative; statements of the fundamental revealed message of salvation through Jesus Christ; gospel truths; the system of principles, rules, and laws under which the Church operates.

"The instructional aspect of the gospel through which one may come to know God and eternal truths respecting the purpose of life and the means of salvation.

"COVENANTS: The revealed terms and conditions upon which a person may qualify himself to receive promised blessings from God through entering into agreements to be obedient; a binding contract or mutual promise between God and man; the revealed conditional promises of the Lord.

"The operational or practical side of living the gospel by those who have faith in God's promises and are willing to agree to live his way in order to achieve the promised blessings."[5]

WHAT IS THE RELATIONSHIP OF THE PRESENT EDITION OF THE DOCTRINE AND COVENANTS TO ALL THE EARLIER MAJOR ENGLISH EDITIONS?

Usually only six major editions are listed in English: 1833, 1835, 1844, 1876, 1921, and 1981, but sometimes the 1879 edition is also listed because that edition used footnotes for the first time. Here is a rundown on the various English-language editions:

1. 1833 edition—published under the title *A Book of Commandments;* consisted of sixty-five chapters.

2. 1835 edition—consisted of 102 sections and seven Lectures on Faith. The sections of the current edition that were published in the 1835 edition include sections 1, 3–12, 14–76, 78–84, 86, 88–102, 104, 106–107, 133–134.

3. 1844 edition—consisted of 111 sections and the Lectures on Faith.

4. 1876 edition—consisted of 136 sections and the Lectures on Faith. This edition included this statement: "First issued, as divided into chapters and verses, by Orson Pratt." Concerning the revelations in this edition, Elder Joseph F. Smith of

the Quorum of the Twelve proposed the following at the October 1880 general conference: "I move that we receive and accept the revelations contained in these books, as revelations from God to the Church of Jesus Christ of Latter Saints, and to all the world."[6] The motion was accepted unanimously.

5. 1879 edition—consisted of 136 sections and the Lectures on Faith. This was the first edition "issued with footnotes."

6. 1921 edition—consisted of 136 sections and the first Official Declaration but did not include the Lectures on Faith. "First published in double-column pages, with new section headings, revised footnote references, and index."

7. 1981 edition—This is the latest edition, although some printings have been published since 1981. This edition is noted for its revised and expanded section headings, a great increase in the number of footnote references, a greatly expanded and enlarged index, and the addition of two new sections (137 and 138) and Official Declaration—2.

What Is the Relationship of the Doctrine and Covenants to the Other Canonized Scriptures of the Church?

In answering this question, we might also provide answers to such questions as "Who is the author of the Doctrine and Covenants" and "Why is a study of the Doctrine and Covenants so important today?"

The Doctrine and Covenants is unique among the standard works of the Church. It was revealed in this dispensation and is intended almost entirely for people who will live on the earth during this dispensation.

The Old Testament was revealed to prophets in ancient times primarily to prepare the people of those days for the first coming of the Savior. Gospel principles in the Old Testament, of course, are beneficial and instructive for all people of all ages.

The New Testament was written as a witness and testimony of the divinity of Jesus Christ, and as such it is important for all people of all times. The latter part of the New Testament, however, consists of letters and other instructions concerned primarily with the branches and members of the Church in the meridian of time.

The Book of Mormon was written and compiled by prophets in ancient times but is primarily intended for people of this dispensation as an additional witness of the Bible and of the divinity of Jesus Christ.

The Pearl of Great Price contains writings and teachings of ancient prophets as well as the history and testimony of Joseph Smith and doctrinal instructions by other prophets of this dispensation.

More than any other canonized scriptures, the Doctrine and Covenants has largely been revealed to and written by the prophets of this dispensation for the instruction and edification of the people of this time.

THE DOCTRINE AND COVENANTS AND THE BOOK OF MORMON

Many of us are aware of the emphasis placed by President Ezra Taft Benson on reading the Book of Mormon. Fewer of us, however, are aware of the strong emphasis he has placed on reading, pondering, and living the teachings of the Doctrine and Covenants. For example, President Benson made the following statements concerning the Doctrine and Covenants in the 1986 October general conference of the Church:

"I would like to speak particularly about the Book of Mormon and the Doctrine and Covenants. . . .

"Each of these two books of modern scripture contains a powerful proclamation to the world. The Book of Mormon title page declares its purpose is threefold: to show what great things the Lord has done, to teach of the covenants of the Lord, and to convince both Jew and Gentile that Jesus is the Christ.

"Section 1 of the Doctrine and Covenants is the Lord's preface to the book. The Doctrine and Covenants is the only book in the world that has a preface written by the Lord himself. In that preface He declares to the world that His voice is unto all men (see v. 2), that the coming of the Lord is nigh (see v. 12), and that the truths found in the Doctrine and Covenants will all be fulfilled (see vs. 37–38).

"Each of these two great latter-day scriptures bears powerful and eloquent witness of the Lord Jesus Christ. Virtually every page of both the Doctrine and Covenants and the Book of Mormon teaches about the Master—His great love for His children and His atoning sacrifice—and teaches us how to live so that we can return to Him and our Heavenly Father.

"Each of these two great latter-day books of scripture contains the knowledge and the power to help us live better lives in a time of great wickedness and evil. Those who carefully and prayerfully search the pages of these books will find comfort, counsel, guidance, and the quiet power to improve their lives."

President Benson then quoted President Joseph Fielding Smith concerning the revelations in the Doctrine and Covenants: "'If we will put them into practice, if we will keep the commandments of the Lord, we will know the truth and there shall be no weapon formed against us that shall prosper. There shall be no false doctrines, no teaching of men that will deceive us. . . . If we will search these revelations then we will be fortified against errors and we will be made strong' (in Conference Report, Oct. 1931, p. 17)."

Then President Benson provides us with an inspired interpretation of Moses 7:61: "Many years before the coming of the Savior to this earth, the prophet Enoch saw the latter days. He observed the great wickedness that would prevail on the earth at this time and foretold the 'great tribulations' that would result from such wickedness; but in the midst of what was otherwise a very gloomy prophecy, the Lord promised, 'But my people will I preserve' (Moses 7:61). How would He do so? Note what the Lord Himself promised He would do to preserve His people. He said:

"'And *righteousness will I send down out of heaven;* and *truth will I send forth out of the earth,* to bear testimony of mine Only Begotten; . . . and *righteousness and truth* will I cause to sweep the earth as with a flood, to gather out mine elect from the four quarters of the earth, unto a place which I shall prepare' (Moses 7:62; italics added)."

President Benson continues: "The Lord promised, therefore, that righteousness would come from heaven and truth out of the earth. We have seen the marvelous fulfillment of that prophecy in our generation. The Book of Mormon has come forth out of the earth, filled with truth, serving as the very 'keystone of our religion.' . . . God has also sent down righteousness from heaven. The Father Himself appeared with His Son to the Prophet Joseph Smith. The angel Moroni, John the Baptist, Peter, James, and numerous other angels were directed by heaven to restore the necessary powers to the kingdom. Further, the Prophet Joseph Smith received revelation after revelation from the heavens during those first critical years of the Church's growth. These revelations have been preserved for us in the Doctrine and Covenants.

"These two great works of scripture, then, become a major tool in the Lord's hand for preserving His people in the latter days. . . . The Doctrine and Covenants is a glorious book of scripture given directly to our generation. It contains the will of the Lord for us in these last days that precede the second coming of Christ. It contains many truths and doctrines not fully revealed in other scripture. Like the Book of Mormon, it will strengthen those who carefully and prayerfully study from its pages."[7]

The Book of Mormon and the Doctrine and Covenants were again on the mind of President Benson during the April 1987 general conference of the Church: "The Book of Mormon and the Doctrine and Covenants testify of each other. You cannot believe one and not the other.... The Doctrine and Covenants is the binding link between the Book of Mormon and the continuing work of the Restoration through the Prophet Joseph Smith and his successors.

"In the Doctrine and Covenants we learn of temple work, eternal families, the degrees of glory, Church organization, and many other great truths of the Restoration.... The Book of Mormon brings men to Christ. The Doctrine and Covenants brings men to Christ's kingdom, even The Church of Jesus Christ of Latter-day Saints, 'the only true and living church upon the face of the whole earth' (v. 30). I know that.

"The Book of Mormon is the 'keystone' of our religion, and the Doctrine and Covenants is the capstone, with continuing latter-day revelation. The Lord has placed His stamp of approval on both the keystone and the capstone....

"God bless us all to use all the scriptures, but in particular the instrument He designed to bring us to Christ—the Book of Mormon, the keystone of our religion—along with its companion volume, the capstone, the Doctrine and Covenants, the instrument to bring us to Christ's kingdom, The Church of Jesus Christ of Latter-day Saints....

"I promise you that as you more diligently study modern revelation on gospel subjects, your power to teach and preach will be magnified."[8]

Reasons for Reading the Doctrine and Covenants and the Book of Mormon

One reason we should read the Book of Mormon is that Jesus Christ is its author. The word author means "to bring about" or "to be responsible for." Sometimes Joseph Smith is thought of as the author of the Book of Mormon, and he was even listed in the first edition of the Book of Mormon as the author and proprietor. However, this wording was simply to meet the requirement of the copyright law in effect at that time. Joseph Smith's contribution to the Book of Mormon was tremendous, but he was its translator, not its author.

Nor was Mormon its author, although he provided us with 338 pages of the present 531 pages in the Book of Mormon. However, he mentioned that most of his writings were really abridgements or condensations of much more voluminous records. Also, Mormon did not write a single word in the books of 1 Nephi, 2 Nephi, Jacob, Enos, Jarom, and Omni. Nor did he write the last 50 pages in our present Book of Mormon; these are primarily the words of Moroni, although he did include a few items written by his father. Mormon, therefore, could not be listed as the author of the entire book. Nor could Nephi, who engraved the first 117 pages; nor could Jacob, who engraved the next 19 pages; nor could Moroni, who provided us with the last 50 pages. If only one person could be listed as the author of the Book of Mormon, that person would need to be Jesus Christ.

The same thing is also true concerning the Doctrine and Covenants. In fact, even a much higher percentage of the Doctrine and Covenants came directly from the Lord himself.

All revelations come from the Lord. The apostle Peter said that prophecy "came not in old time by the will of man: but holy men of God spake as they were moved by the Holy Ghost" (2 Peter 1:21). The same might also be said of revelation. When a person reads the revelations of the Doctrine and Covenants, he is literally reading the mind and will of the Lord as given through his prophets.

Concerning this principle, Elder John A. Widtsoe has written: "The Giver of all the revelations is Jesus Christ. The God spoken of in the Doctrine and Covenants is Jesus of Nazareth. Apparently the Father does not speak in them. He speaks through his Son. It is a fundamental doctrine of Mormonism that God the Father has commissioned his Son Jesus Christ to do certain work. He is the one that looks after the affairs of this earth, and all things pertaining to the Church are done by him. God the Father has appeared very few times upon the earth, at the beginning of the dispensations. He appeared in the Garden of Eden. He spoke out of heaven at the time of the Savior's baptism. He appeared in the grove to the Prophet Joseph Smith."[9]

Do we really believe this truth, that Jesus Christ is the actual author of the Doctrine and Covenants? If so, we will not have any difficulty reading and pondering this sacred scripture.

As mentioned in chapter 5, except for the 7½ pages comprising the small books of Enos, Jarom, and Omni, the remainder of the Book of Mormon was written or engraved by Nephi (117 pages), Jacob (19 pages), Mormon (338 pages), or Moroni (50 pages). Chapter 5 also outlined some of the major characteristics of these persons. As you review these major characteristics, attributes, and experiences, reflect on how many of these also apply to Joseph Smith and therefore also have application to the Doctrine and Covenants:

1. They were personal witnesses of the Lord Jesus Christ during the time they lived upon the earth.

2. They were visited and tutored by angels or translated beings.

3. They were directed by Jesus Christ as to what they should put in their records.

4. They had visions of our day, and they provided material especially for us.

All of these reasons for reading the Book of Mormon also apply to reading the Doctrine and Covenants. Joseph Smith was a personal witness of Jesus Christ. He was tutored by angels. He was directed by Jesus Christ as to what he should include in the Doctrine and Covenants.

Obviously the Doctrine and Covenants was written for us in our day. Indeed, it was revealed in our day; for English-speaking members of the Church, it was revealed in their native tongue. The Doctrine and Covenants is not translated so far as English is concerned.

How to Get the Most from Our Study of the Doctrine and Covenants

The following suggestions will help us get the most out of our study of the Doctrine and Covenants:

1. *Use the latest edition—one published at least since 1981—and become acquainted with its many learning, teaching, and studying aids.*

The latest edition includes new and enlarged section headings, more voluminous footnotes and cross-references, and an extensive index that provides a list of the major scriptures for hundreds of gospel topics.

Editions of the Doctrine and Covenants published since 1981 feature:

a. *Title page.* Note the statement, "With some additions by his successors in the presidency of the Church."

b. *"Explanatory Introduction"* (three pages), including the "Testimony of the Twelve Apostles to the Truth of the Book of Doctrine and Covenants."

At a general assembly held in Kirtland, Ohio, in August 1835, further consideration was given to the publication of some of the revelations received by Joseph Smith. Many persons bore individual testimonies that they knew the revelations were true and represented the mind and will of the Lord. W. W. Phelps then read a written testimony of the Twelve, which follows:

"*The Testimony of the Witnesses to the Book of the Lord's Commandments, which commandments He gave to His Church through Joseph Smith, Jun., who was appointed by the voice of the Church for this purpose:*

"We, therefore, feel willing to bear testimony to all the world of mankind, to every creature upon the face of the earth, that the Lord has borne record to our souls, through the Holy Ghost shed forth upon us, that these commandments were given by inspiration of God, and are profitable for all men and are verily true.

"We give this testimony unto the world, the Lord being our helper; and it is through the grace of God the Father, and His Son, Jesus Christ, that we are permitted to have this privilege of bearing this testimony unto the world, in the which we rejoice exceedingly, praying the Lord always that the children of men may be profited thereby."

"The names of the Twelve were:

Thomas B. Marsh	Orson Hyde	William Smith
David W. Patten	Wm. E. McLellin	Orson Pratt
Brigham Young	Parley P. Pratt	John F. Boynton
Heber C. Kimball	Luke S. Johnson	Lyman E. Johnson"

This testimony has been included in every copy of the Doctrine and Covenants ever published. In the 1835 edition, the testimony was published on page 256 as part of the minutes of the general assembly of August 17, 1835, without the printed names of the individual members of the Quorum of the Twelve.

Subsequently, it was decided to publish the testimony on a separate page near the front of the volume, and to add the names of the Twelve "in the order in which they stood in the quorum."[10]

c. *"Chronological Order of Contents"* (two pages). Note the location of the section entries and the date of the revelation or event.

d. *Section headings or headnotes.* Headings have been greatly enlarged and are more complete. For example, the heading to section 78 explains that this section no longer contains the "code names" originally used to protect the identity of individuals named in this revelation.

e. *Section summaries or subheadings.* These additions are very helpful, especially on longer sections.

f. *Footnotes and cross-references.* The footnotes have been greatly increased and offer thorough cross-referencing to the other standard works.

g. *Sections 137 and 138.* These sections were officially added to the Doctrine and Covenants after first appearing as supplements to the Pearl of Great Price.

h. *Official Declaration—1.* This declaration contains excerpts from three addresses by President Wilford Woodruff.

i. *Official Declaration—2.* This declaration appeared for the first time in the 1981 edition and includes a letter signed by the First Presidency and read in general conference by President N. Eldon Tanner.

j. *Four new maps.* These maps are of the New England area, New York–Ohio area, Missouri-Illinois area, and the United States in 1847.

k. *Index to the triple combination.* The index was expanded to 416 pages.

2. *Develop a meaningful marking and cross-referencing system for the Doctrine and Covenants.*

An effective marking and cross-referencing system will help you become more involved with the scriptures. Make certain any marking system you develop is relevant and has meaning for you.

3. *Relate the things you learn in the Doctrine and Covenants to similar teachings in the other scriptures.*

Another valuable contribution of the Doctrine and Covenants is that it serves as an inspired commentary on some of the other scriptures. Note, for example, how much more we know about the following topics because of the contributions of the Doctrine and Covenants:

a. Isaiah—section 113.

b. Malachi and Elijah—sections 2 and 110:13–16.

c. John, the beloved disciple (John 21)—section 7.

d. Preaching the gospel to the dead (1 Peter 3:18–20; 4:6)—section 138.

e. Book of Revelation—section 77.

f. The Apocrypha—section 91.

g. The parable of the wheat and tares (Matthew 13:24–30)—sections 86:1–11 and 101:65–67.

h. The parable of the ten virgins (Matthew 25:1–13)—sections 45:56–59 and 63:54.

i. Husbands, wives, little children ("as an explanation of 1 Corinthians 7:14")—section 74.

j. Degrees of glory (John 5:29)—section 76.

4. *Liken the scriptures unto yourself.*

One of the most valuable suggestions I could give concerning your study of the Doctrine and Covenants is that you liken each of the pertinent revelations to yourself.

Let me share with you a suggestion I received from Elder Rex D. Pinegar concerning this principle while I was serving as a mission president in Australia. Elder Pinegar suggested that whenever you found a scripture containing a great truth directed to an individual you cross out the name of the individual and write in your own name. As an example, in Doctrine and Covenants 8:1, cross out the name "Oliver Cowdery"; then write in your own name and reread verses 1–5, applying the principles that pertain to your own salvation.

Let's review a few other sections to see how this principle might work:
Section:
3, especially verses 9–10 (write in your name for "Joseph").
8, especially verses 1–3.
23, especially verses 1 and 6 (write in your name for "Oliver" in verse 1 and for "Joseph Knight" in verse 6).
30, especially verses 1–2 (write in your name for "David").
39, especially verses 7–8 (write in your name for "James").
50, especially verses 13–14, 17 (write in your name at the beginning of verse 13).
64, especially verses 8–10, 32–33 (write in your name at the beginning of verse 8).

5. *Ask for assistance from the Holy Ghost in understanding these revelations and principles.*

Things of the Spirit are known only by the power of the Spirit. Many spiritual truths in the Doctrine and Covenants can only be fully understood and appreciated through the promptings and guidance of the Holy Spirit. Of course, the guiding influence of the Spirit should be earnestly sought whenever we read any of the scriptures or study any of the principles or ordinances of the gospel.

6. *Learn the principles of life contained in this book of scripture and live them.*

This is perhaps the most important suggestion of all—and perhaps the most difficult to apply. The Doctrine and Covenants is similar to the other scriptures in that it is like a great treasure house with many rooms. Each room contains a precious treasure that can help you in your personal life. However, all of the rooms are locked, and you can unlock them only with the keys of experience and understanding. You should not read the Doctrine and Covenants the way you read novels, magazines, or newspapers; rather, you should ponder and meditate upon each section and, in some instances, on almost each verse.

THE TEACHINGS OF THE DOCTRINE AND COVENANTS

One essential key to use in our study is to become well acquainted with some of the major teachings in the Doctrine and Covenants, especially with verses that make a primary contribution to our understanding of particular principles, ordinances, policies, or practices.

The "Grandest" Principle of the Gospel

While doing research on a different topic, I discovered a very interesting article that appeared in an old *Contributor* magazine in August 1895. A letter addressed to readers indicated that "the Young Men's and Young Ladies' M.I.A. of the Twentieth Ward" had invited people to respond to the following question: "What, in your opinion, constitutes the grandest principle, or the most attractive feature of the Gospel?"

The issue published several answers. For example, Brother Henry W. Naisbitt wrote: "I respectfully submit that the grandest principle revealed in this dispensation was that of the personality of Deity, in connection with the old yet ever essential Fatherhood of God."

Brother George Reynolds then indicated: "What feature of the Gospel is most attractive to us individually depends largely on our own peculiar mental makeup. We view things from our particular standpoint, and from that standpoint judge them. To me there is no principle of the Gospel more attractive than that which assures me, I am a son of God literally and truly, with all the possibilities within my reach of becoming like my great Father; and that all mankind are like me, His children, his sons and daughters."

Brother T. B. Lewis suggested: "I consider marriage for time and eternity the grandest principle, or the most attractive feature of the Gospel."

Brother David McKenzie provided another answer: "The principle of Love stands pre-eminent. . . . Surely love must be the 'most attractive feature,' although it may not technically be called a 'principle of the Gospel.'"

George G. Bywater included several of these ideas in his answer: "In accordance with this postulate, the grandest principle or the most attractive feature of the Gospel must be sought for in man as the crowning work of the Creator. Love is the crowning attribute of God and man."

Brother Thomas Hull made similar expressions: "As I reflect upon the many grand principles thereof, there opens up before my vision, the glorious prospect of man's destiny, his likeness of God, eternal progression, endless lives, and there whispers to my soul, in tones of softest, sweetest melody, the voice of God, in constant and immediate revelation, guiding ever in the way of life. The principle of eternal covenants rises before me, binding us to eternity."[11]

Interestingly enough, if we analyze these "grandest" principles of the gospel, we will note that in each instance the Doctrine and Covenants contributes more to our understanding concerning these principles than any of the other scriptures. In most instances the Doctrine and Covenants contributes more than all of the other scriptures combined.

Let's review again the "grandest" principles listed by the respondents:

1. The literal fatherhood of God (and thus the brotherhood and sisterhood of us all).
2. The plan of eternal progression and eventual godhood.
3. The reality of pre-earthly and postmortal existence.
4. Relationship of laws and blessings (and punishments).
5. The nature of an "opposition in all things."
6. Vital necessity of agency.
7. Love.

These grand principles are essentially the same truths we need to know and implement in our lives in order to achieve eternal life—the greatest gift of God to man. Before we can fully understand or appreciate the blessings of eternal life, we must understand these truths:

1. Nature of God.
2. Mission and atonement of Jesus Christ.
3. Concept of "eternity to eternity."
4. Purposes of a mortal existence.
5. Principles and ordinances of the gospel leading to the celestial kingdom.
6. Principles and ordinances of the gospel leading to eternal life in the presence of God.

Doctrinal Differences between Christian Groups

Another technique I use to determine the value of the teachings in the Doctrine and Covenants is to consider the important areas of doctrinal differences between and among the various Christian groups. Reflect in your mind on the contributions of the Doctrine and Covenants to the varied Christian beliefs related to each of these areas:

1. Nature of God and the Godhead.
2. Relationship of Jesus Christ to God the Father.
3. Nature of man (purpose of existence).
4. Baptism by water (authority, method, necessity, words of baptismal prayer).
5. Baptism of Holy Ghost (confirmation).
6. Sacrament of the Lord's Supper (purpose of emblems).
7. Extent and nature of Christ's atonement.
8. Scriptures (place or purpose, extent, literalness, and interpretation of).
9. Priesthood authority.
10. Organization and government of the Church.
11. Revelation and prophecy (nature and purpose of).

List of Important Items from the Topical Guide

In reviewing all 3,495 items in the Topical Guide of the LDS edition of the Bible, I made an alphabetical list of those topics on which the Doctrine and Covenants makes a significant contribution—usually a contribution that equals the contribution of all the other scriptures. Then I prepared a similar alphabetical list from the Index in the triple combination through the letter "c" to illustrate the tremendous contribution of the Doctrine and Covenants. I include here only a few selected topics from both of the extensive lists I generated. Again, reflect upon some of the great contributions the Doctrine and Covenants makes in these areas. Also, you might want to complete on your own "Items from the Index" list from "D" through "Z" in order to develop your own appreciation of the contribution of the Doctrine and Covenants.

Items Pertaining to the Gospel of Jesus Christ and the Kingdom of God on Earth and in Heaven that Are Emphasized in the Doctrine and Covenants

Items from the Topical Guide	Items from the Index
A	*A*
Abraham Covenant	Abraham
Accountability	Abrahamic Covenant
Adam	Abundance
Administrations, Sick	Acceptable
Adulterer, Adultery	Agency, Agent
Agency	Angel
Angels, Ministering of	Angels, Ministering of
Apostasy	Anointing, Anoint
Apostles	Apostasy
	Apostle
	Accountability, Age of
	Accountable
	Act
	Ask
	Authority
B	*B*
Baptism for the Dead	Baptism, Baptize
Bishop	Baptism for the Dead
	Beginning
	Bishop
	Bless, Blessing
	Body, Bodies

C
Celestial Glory
Church
Covenants

C
Celestial glory
Chasten, Chastisement
Church of Firstborn
Church of God
Commandments of God
Common Consent
Confirm
Consecration, Law of
Contrite
Council
Counsel
Counselor
Court
Covenant
Creation, Create
Crown

Significant Topics—and Related Sections in the Doctrine and Covenants

Following are possible topics and verses from the Doctrine and Covenants to emphasize and enlarge upon. I provide here only a few examples, encouraging you to prepare a similar, more detailed list of your own.

A
Aaronic Priesthood: 13

B
Baptism: 20:37; 71–74; 33:11–12
Baptism for the Dead: 127; 128; 137; 138:33; 1 Corinthians 15:29

C
Called, Chosen: 121:34–40
Church, one True: 1:30

D
Death: 42:45–47
Degrees of Glory: 76
    In the Resurrection: 88:15–32 (especially 25–28)

E
Eternal (and Endless) Punishment: 19:6–12

G
Gethsemane Experience: 19:16–18
God Seen Only by those Who Have Been Quickened: 67:11–13
God's Voice or Servants' Voice—the same: 1:38; 18:33–36; 68:4 (will, mind, word, voice, power)

H
Holy Ghost (Godhead): 130:22

I
Instruction Items: 129; 130; 131; 137 (One-Verse Sermons: 6:7; 11:21)

K
Kingdom of God and Heaven: 65:6

L
Last Days: 45, 133
Law: 88:34–38

M
Marriage: 49:15–17
Millennium: 29:7–11

N
New Jerusalem: 84:1–4

O
Official Declarations 1 and 2 (Principle of Continuous Revelation)

P
Parables—Explanation of Earlier: 101
Postmortal Spirit World: 138
Prayer "that is expedient for you": 88:64
Pre-earthly Existence: 93:29–38
Priesthood: 107
  Duties of: 20:38
  History of: 84:6
Principles of Life: 88:117–126
Prophets: 117:4, 6

R
Repentance and Forgiveness: 58:42–43
Reproving: 121:41–43

S
Sacrament—of the Lord's Supper: 20:75–79; 27:1–2
Sons of Perdition: 76:31–47
Soul of Man—Worth of: 88:15–16
Spirit World: 138

T
Testimony of Jesus Christ: 76:22–24
Thoughts: 6:16 (33:1); 9:9; 33:1; 88:109

V
Voice of God: 18:33–36

W
War in Heaven: 29:36
Word of Wisdom: 89
Worth of Souls: 18:15–16

Z
Zion: 105:5–6

IMPORTANCE OF ALL THE SCRIPTURES

Scripture might be defined as the will, mind, word, or voice of God revealed to man (see D&C 68:4). In this sense, scripture could be spoken or written. However, some scripture has been written down and accepted as official canon by members of the Church. As such, it is part of the scriptures or standard works of the Church.

Several latter-day prophets, seers, and revelators have testified of the importance of the scriptures:

Elder Boyd K. Packer said: "If [you] are acquainted with the revelations, there is no question—personal or social or political or occupational—that need go unanswered. Therein is contained the fulness of the everlasting gospel. Therein we find principles of truth that will resolve every confusion and every problem and every dilemma that will face the human family or any individual in it."[12]

Elder Bruce R. McConkie said: "I think that people who study the scriptures get a dimension to their life that nobody else gets and that can't be gained in any way except by studying the scriptures. There's an increase in faith and a desire to do what's right and a feeling of inspiration and understanding that comes to people who study the gospel—meaning particularly the standard works—and who ponder the principles, that can't come in any other way."[13]

President Harold B. Lee said: "I say that we need to teach our people to find their answers in the scriptures. If only each of us would be wise enough to say that we aren't able to answer any question unless we can find a doctrinal answer in the scriptures! And if we hear someone teaching something that is contrary to what is in the scriptures, each of us may know whether the things spoken are false—it is as simple as that. But the unfortunate thing is that so many of us are not reading the scriptures. We do not know what is in them, and therefore we speculate about the things that we ought to have found in the scriptures themselves. I think that therein is one of our biggest dangers of today."[14]

President Lee also said: "Are you . . . continually increasing your testimony by diligent study of the scriptures? Do you have a daily habit of reading the scriptures? If we're not reading the scriptures daily, our testimonies are growing thinner, our spirituality isn't increasing in depth. We, ourselves, must be studying the scriptures and have a daily habit."[15]

President Spencer W. Kimball said: "I find that when I get casual in my relationships with divinity and when it seems that no divine ear is listening and no divine voice is speaking, that I am far, far away. If I immerse myself in the scriptures the distance narrows and the spirituality returns."[16]

A study of the scriptures will help us feel closer to God. An understanding of the scriptures will bring additional power and blessings into our lives.

Why Is the Principle of Continuous Revelation So Basic to All the Teachings and Claims of the Church?

The principle of continuous revelation is basic not only to the Doctrine and Covenants but also to the very existence of the Church. We proclaim to the world in the ninth Article of Faith:

"We believe all that God has revealed, all that He does now reveal, and we believe that He will yet reveal many great and important things pertaining to the Kingdom of God." In ancient times, the Lord said through his prophet Amos, "Surely the Lord God will do nothing, but he revealeth his secret unto his servants the prophets" (Amos 3:7). And in the New Testament we read that Jesus Christ is "the same yesterday, and to day, and for ever" (Hebrews 13:8).

Inspired prophets of this dispensation have indicated that the "rock" upon which the Church at the time of Christ was built was really "the rock of revelation" (as described in Matthew 16:18). As stated again and again, revelation is the lifeblood of the Church.

In his inspiring talk in the April 1977 general conference titled "Revelation: The Word of the Lord to His Prophets," President Spencer W. Kimball made the following essential points:

"Of all things, that for which we should be most grateful today is that the heavens are indeed open and that the restored church of Jesus Christ is founded upon the rock of revelation. Continuous revelation is indeed the very lifeblood of the gospel of the living Lord and Savior, Jesus Christ. . . .

"The foreverness of this kingdom and the revelations which it brought into existence are absolute realities. Never again will the sun [of revelation] go down; never again will all men prove totally unworthy of communication with their Maker. Never again will God be hidden from his children on the earth. Revelation is here to remain. . . .

" . . . Again we testify to the world that revelation continues and that the vaults and files of the Church contain these revelations which come month to month and day to day. We testify also that there is, since 1830 when The Church of Jesus Christ of Latter-day Saints was organized, and will continue to be, so long as time shall last, a prophet, recognized of God and his people, who will continue to interpret the mind and will of the Lord. . . .

" . . . I say, in the deepest of humility, but also by the power and force of a burning testimony in my soul, that from the prophet of the Restoration to the prophet of our own year, the communication line is unbroken, the authority is continuous, and light, brilliant and penetrating, continues to shine. The sound of the voice of the Lord is a continuous melody and a thunderous appeal. For nearly a century and a half there has been no interruption.

"Man never needs to stand alone. Every faithful person may have the inspiration for his own limited kingdom. But the Lord definitely calls prophets today and reveals his secrets unto them as he did yesterday, he does today, and will do tomorrow: that is the way it is."[17]

Additional statements on the need for continuous revelation have been given by prophets, seers, and revelators of this dispensation. The need for ongoing revelation may appear to be at variance with an emphasis on reading the scriptures, but it is not.

Wilford Woodruff: "I will refer to a certain meeting I attended in the town of Kirtland in my early days. . . . Some remarks were made . . . with regard to the living oracles and with regard to the written word of God. . . . A leading man in the church . . . talked upon the subject, and said: 'You have got the word of God before you here in the Bible, Book of Mormon, and Doctrine and Covenants; you have the written word of God, and you who give revelations should give revelations according to those books, as what is written in those books is the word of God. We should confine ourselves to them.'

"When he concluded, Brother Joseph turned to Brother Brigham Young and said, 'Brother Brigham, I want you to take the stand and tell us your views with regard to the written oracles and the written word of God.' Brother Brigham took the stand, and he took the Bible, and laid it down; he took the Book of Mormon, and laid it down; and he took the Book of Doctrine and Covenants, and laid it down before him, and he said: 'There is the written word of God to us, concerning the work of God from the beginning of the world, almost, to our day. And now,' said he, *'when compared with the living oracles those books are nothing to me;* those books do not convey the word of God direct to us now, as do the words of a Prophet or a man bearing the Holy Priesthood in our day and generation. *I would rather have the living oracles than all the writing in the books.'* That was the course he pursued. When he was through, Brother Joseph said to the congregation, *'Brother Brigham has told you the word of the Lord, and he has told you the truth.'*

" . . . The Bible is all right, the Book of Mormon is all right, the Doctrine and Covenants is all right, and they proclaim the work of God and the word of God in the earth in this day and generation until the coming of the Son of Man; but the Holy Priesthood is not confined particularly to those books, that is, *it did not cease when those books were made.*"[18]

John Taylor: "Those books [the scriptures] are good for example, precedent, and investigation, and for developing certain laws and principles; but they do not, they cannot touch every case required to be adjudicated and set in order; we require a living tree—a living fountain—living intelligence, proceeding from the living priesthood in heaven, through the living priesthood on earth."[19]

George Q. Cannon: "As Latter-day Saints, we need constantly the guidance of Jehovah. We have the Bible, the Book of Mormon and the Book of Doctrine and Covenants; but all these books, without the living oracles and a constant stream of revelation from the Lord, would not lead any people into the Celestial Kingdom of God."[20]

More Revelations in the Future

Not a single one of our present scriptures is complete, including our present Doctrine and Covenants. It is my firm belief that if we as Latter-day Saints learn the principles and doctrines of the Doctrine and Covenants and live them in our lives, the Lord will instruct his prophets to include more of his revelations in this sacred scripture.

Concerning this principle, President Joseph Fielding Smith has stated: "Not all of the revelations given to the Prophet Joseph Smith are in the Doctrine and Covenants. He made a selection for this book by revelation. The Church has had many other revelations, but we have in the Doctrine and Covenants revelations sufficient to bring to pass our exaltation if we will but heed them. When we, the members of the Church, reach the point that we are willing to live by all that the Lord has revealed, he will give us more that can be placed in the Doctrine and Covenants. The Lord is withholding from us great and mighty truths because of the hardness of our hearts. Why should we clamor for more when we will not abide in what we already have? We are led by revelation today just as much as they were anciently."[21]

Elder Bruce R. McConkie has also written concerning this principle:

"The last word has not been spoken on any subject. Streams of living water shall yet flow from the Eternal Spring who is the source of all truth. There are more things we do not know about the doctrines of salvation than there are things we do know.

"When we as a people believe and conform to all of the truths we have received, we shall receive more of the mind and will and voice of the Lord. What we receive and when it comes are in large measure up to us. The Lord has many things he wants to tell us, but so far we have not attained that unity and spiritual stature which will enable us to pull down knowledge from heaven upon us.

"We praise God because he has seen fit to give to us what we have received, including these two revelations on salvation for the dead [sections 137 and 138], and pray that we may believe and obey with that faith and devotion which will cause the Lord to give us more of his eternal word. The more we know, the more scripture we receive, the more we have in our standard works, the greater is our chance of gaining eternal life in our Father's kingdom. We can never live a law until it is revealed to us. Can any of us know too much? Can we receive too much revelation? Can we add too much to our holy writ?

"What a wondrous thing it is to worship a God who still speaks, whose voice is still heard, whose words are without end!"[22]

In a later talk to regional representatives, Elder McConkie suggested seven steps to follow if we expect to receive further canonized scriptures from the Lord:

"May I suggest for you and your families and all those with whom you labor in the kingdom, the following:

"1. Study the scriptures daily. Drink directly from Holy Writ. Learn the word as it is found in the scriptures.

"2. Mark a new set of the Standard Works. Learn to use the footnotes and teaching aids in our new editions of the scriptures. Pay particular attention to the inspired changes made by the Prophet Joseph Smith in the Bible. Be sure any quotations you make include the new textual corrections.

"3. Apply what you learn to your life and to your administrative assignments in the Church. Act and live as the scriptures decree.

"4. Use the scriptures in all your sermons and teaching. Rely upon the scriptures. Quote the scriptures. Believe the scriptures. Choose your illustrations from them.

"5. Ponder the revealed word in your hearts. Pray about its deep and hidden meanings. Let the things of eternity be your constant meditation.

"6. Expound the scriptures. Explain their meanings. Let others know what you know. Raise your voice in testimony.

"7. Get others to go and do likewise with reference to all these things."[23]

Summary

Wouldn't it be wonderful if we were a generation that would truly "receive" and live our present scriptures so that we could receive even more of the word of God? All of our blessings are predicated upon obedience to laws, and the gospel laws are found in the scriptures.

If we had in the scriptures the "greater" truths and laws that are currently being withheld from us—and if we could then live these greater truths—we could receive even greater blessings from our Heavenly Father.

Notes

From a previously unpublished paper.

1. *Doctrines of Salvation,* 3:198.
2. Wilford Woodruff, in *Journal of Discourses,* 22:146.
3. *History of the Church,* 1:222.
4. Hyrum M. Smith and Janne M. Sjodahl, *Doctrine and Covenants Commentary* (Salt Lake City: Deseret Book Co., 1978), 59, 4.

5. *Institute Self-Instruction Course* (Salt Lake City: The Church of Jesus Christ of Latter-day Saints), 51.
6. Joseph F. Smith, "Fiftieth Semi-annual Conference," *Millennial Star,* 42 (15 November 1880): 724.
7. Ezra Taft Benson, "The Gift of Modern Revelation," *Ensign,* November 1986, 79–80.
8. Ezra Taft Benson, "The Book of Mormon and the Doctrine and Covenants," *Ensign,* May 1987, 83, 85.
9. John A. Widtsoe, *The Message of the Doctrine and Covenants* (Salt Lake City: Bookcraft, 1969), 8–9.
10. *History of the Church,* 2:245.
11. "The Grandest Principle of the Gospel," in *The Contributor,* 16 August 1895, 610–14.
12. Boyd K. Packer, "Teach the Scriptures," address to religious educators of the Church Educational System, 14 October 1977, 5.
13. Bruce R. McConkie, "Spare time's rare to Apostle," *Church News,* 24 January 1976, 4.
14. Harold B. Lee, "Find the Answers in the Scriptures," *Ensign,* December 1972, 3.
15. Harold B. Lee, regional representatives seminar, 12 December 1970, 10.
16. *Teachings of Spencer W. Kimball,* 135.
17. Spencer W. Kimball, "Revelation: The Word of the Lord to His Prophets," *Ensign,* May 1977, 76–78.
18. Wilford Woodruff, in Conference Report, October 1897, 22–23; emphasis added.
19. John Taylor, "On Priesthood," *Millennial Star,* 9 (1 November 1847): 323.
20. *Gospel Truth,* 1:323.
21. *Doctrines of Salvation,* 3:202.
22. Bruce R. McConkie, "A New Commandment: Save Thyself and Thy Kindred!" *Ensign,* August 1976, 11.
23. Bruce R. McConkie, "Holy Writ: Published Anew," address delivered at regional representatives' seminar, Salt Lake City, Utah, 2 April 1982, 3–4.

Chapter 7

BIBLE DICTIONARY REFERENCES AS POSSIBLE BIBLE FOOTNOTES

There are very few BD (Bible Dictionary) footnotes in the present editions of the scriptures. Yet the information in the entries of the Bible Dictionary add a great deal to the understanding of both the Old Testament and the New Testament. In fact, it has been suggested that if the serious student of the Bible would become fully acquainted with the contents of all the entries in the Bible Dictionary, it would be the equivalent of a Ph.D. in biblical studies.

This list of proposed BD "footnotes" has been prepared to assist and encourage the reader of the Bible to become acquainted with the marvelous contents of the Bible aid known as the Bible Dictionary. The list suggests exact scriptural references where you might write in BD entries in your Bible, either in the margin or at the bottom of the page, with some type of notation (perhaps a superscript letter) in the text at the appropriate place. For instance, you might go to Genesis 1:1 (see the list below), mark some kind of superscript in the verse, mark a corresponding letter or symbol in the margin or at the bottom of your page, and then write "BD: God" next to that symbol. The word *God* refers you to an article by that title in the Bible Dictionary.

OLD TESTAMENT

For a discussion on the Old Testament as a whole: BD: Bible, p. 622; Canon, p. 630; Chronology, p. 635; Chronological Table, p. 635; Codex, p. 647; Dead Sea Scrolls, p. 654; Joseph Smith Translation, p. 717; Judah, Stick of, p. 719;

Pentateuch, p. 748; Quotations from the Old Testament found in the New Testament, p. 756; Septuagint, p. 771; Torah, p. 786; Vulgate, p. 787.

Genesis
(For a discussion on the book of Genesis as a whole: BD, p. 678)
1:1 God
1:24 Animals
2:8 Eden
2:11 Gold
2:12 Bdellium
2:13 Ethiopia; Gihon
2:21 Eve
3:6 Fall of Adam
4:1 Cain
4:2 Agriculture
4:4 Abel
4:21 Harp
4:26 Enos; Prayer
5:8 Seth
5:18 Enoch
5:21 Methusaleh
5:29 Noah
5:32 Ham; Japheth; Shem
6:4 Giants
6:9 Noah
6:14 Ark; Gopher Wood
6:15 Cubit
8:4 Ararat
8:20 Altar
9:3 Flesh
9:13 Rainbow
9:22 Canaan
10:2 Magog
10:4 Chittim
10:10 Babylon or Babel; Assyria (& Babylonia); Shinar, Plain of
10:11 Rehoboth
10:15 Heth; Hittites; Sidon
10:16 Gergashites
10:17 Hivites
10:18 Canaanites
10:19 Gaza; Gerar; Zeboim
10:22 Aram; Syria
10:24 Eber
10:25 Peleg
10:28 Sheba
10:29 Havilah
11:24 Terah
11:27 Haran
11:27 Lot
11:28 Ur
11:29 Sarah
12:8 Ai and Hai
12:15 Pharoah
14:1 Chedorlaomer
14:3 Siddim, Vale of
14:5 Emims; Rephaim
14:13 Hebrew; Mamre
14:18 Melchizedek
14:20 Tithe
15:2 Eliezer
15:12 Dreams
16:1 Hagar
16:11 Ishmael
17:5 Names of Persons
17:9 Abraham
17:12 Circumcision
19:24 Gomorrah
19:37 Moab
19:38 Ammon

20:2 Abimelech
21:3 Isaac
21:31 Beersheba
22:2 Moriah
22:14 Jehovah-jireh
22:23 Bethuel; Rebekah
23:2 Kirjath-arba
23:9 Machpelah
24:10 Mesopotamia
24:29 Laban
24:65 Veil
25:1 Keturah
25:2 Midian
25:26 Jacob
25:30 Edom
25:33 Esau
25:34 Birthright
27:1 Blindness
27:28 Dew
28:19 Luz
29:6 Rachel
29:29 Bilhah
29:30 Leah
29:32 Reuben
29:33 Simeon
29:34 Levi
29:35 Judah
30:8 Naphtali
30:11 Gad
30:13 Asher
30:18 Issachar
30:20 Zebulun
30:21 Dinah
30:24 Joseph
31:47 Galeed
31:54 High Places
32:3 Edom

32:28 Israel
32:30 Peniel
33:18 Shechem
33:20 El-elohe-Israel
35:7 El-bethel
35:18 Benjamin, Benoni
35:19 Bethlehem
36:35 Hadad
37:17 Dothan
37:36 Potiphar
38:6 Tamar
41:45 Asenath; On; Poti-pherah; Zaphnath-paaneah
41:51 Manasseh
41:52 Ephraim
43:33 Firstborn
46:11 Kohath
47:11 Rameses
48:7 Padan
49:10 Shiloh
49:19 Gad
49:31 Rebekah
50:2 Embalming

Exodus
(For a discussion on the book of Exodus as a whole: BD, p. 668)
1:11 Pithom; Raamses
2:15 Midianites
2:20 Hospitality
2:21 Zipporah
3:1 Jethro
3:2 Burning Bush
4:4 Rod
4:6 Leprosy
5:3 Sacrifices
6:3 Jehovah
6:20 Jochebed

6:23 Abihu; Eleazar; Ithamar
9:31 Barley
9:32 Rye
12:8 Bitter herbs
12:22 Hyssop
13:1 Phylacteries
13:4 Abib; see also Calendar
13:11 Firstborn; see also Birthright
13:19 Joseph
14:7 Chariot
15:20 Dancing; Music
15:22 Wilderness of the Exodus
16:1 Sin
16:15 Manna
16:22 Omer
16:29 Sabbath Day's Journey
17:1 Rephidim
17:10 Hur
17:15 Jehovah-nissi
20:8 Sabbath
20:12 Family
20:13 Murder
22:5 Usury
23:14 Feasts
24:9 Elders
24:13 Joshua
25:10 Ark of the Covenant
25:22 Mercy Seat
25:30 Shewbread
25:31 Candlestick
26:7 Tabernacle
28:6 Ephod
28:11 Engraving
28:17 Carbuncle
28:18 Emerald
28:20 Beryl; Jasper
28:39 Embroidery

29:6 High Priest
29:38 Daily Service
30:7 Incense
30:24 Cassia
30:34 Stacte
31:6 Aholiab
32:4 Calves
34:28 Commandments, The Ten
34:29 Law of Moses
40:15 Priests

Leviticus
(For a discussion on the book of
    Leviticus as a whole: BD, p. 724)
1:14 Dove
8:8 Urim and Thummim
10:1 Abihu; Nadab
11:4 Camel
11:5 Clean and Unclean; Kosher
11:6 Hare
11:7 Swine
11:9 Fish
11:18 Gier Eagle
11:19 Bat
11:44 Holiness
13:10 Quick
16:12 Censer
16:21 Scapegoat
17:10 Blood
19:9 Gleanings
19:18 Revenge
19:27 Beard
19:28 Cutting the Flesh
19:31 Divination
20:10 Adultery
22:9 Firstfruits
23:10–14 Wave Offering
23:27 Atonement

25:4 Sabbatical year
25:11 Jubilee
27:16 Weights and Measures
27:26 Vows

Numbers
(For a discussion on the book of Numbers as a whole: BD, p. 739)
1:1 Sinai
3:19 Amram
9:14 Stranger
10:10 New Moon
11:26 Eldad and Medad
11:29 Prophet
13:6 Caleb
13:21 Zin
13:28 Tell el-Amarna Letters
13:33 Anak (Anakim)
15:38 Hem of Garment
19:9 Purification
20:1 Kadesh
20:13 Meribah
20:22 Hor
20:22 Aaron
21:9 Serpent, Brazen
21:13 Amon
21:14 Lost Books
21:15 Ar
21:16 Fiery Serpents
21:20 Pisgah
21:26 Sihon
21:33 Edrei
22:5 Balaam
24:6 Aloes
25:7 Phinehas
26:59 Miriam
27:12 Abarim
31:8 Balaam

33:35 Ezion-gaber
33:38 Aaron
33:47 Abarim
34:5 Egypt, River of
34:6 Great Sea
34:11 Chinnereth
35:6 Cities of Refuge

Deuteronomy
(For a discussion on the book of Deuteronomy as a whole: BD, p. 656)
1:4 Bashan
2:5 Seir
2:8 Elath
3:11 Og
4:48 Sion
6:8 Frontlets
8:8 Vine
8:9 Minues
11:26 Ebal, Mount
11:30 Gilgal
12:22 Hart
14:1 Disfigurement
14:2 Peculiar
16:4 Leaven
18:10 Molech
19:5 Helve
19:19 Punishments
19:21 Retaliation
21:17 Inheritance
23:18 Dog
24:1 Divorce
25:5 Levirate Marriage
25:14 Ephah
27:15 Amen
28:27 Emerods
29:23 Brimstone

32:20 Froward
32:33 Asp; Dragon
32:49 Nebo
33:17 Ephraim
34:5 Moses

Joshua
(For a discussion on the book of
  Joshua as a whole: BD, p. 718)
1:4 Euphrates
2:1 Rahab; Shittim
3:8 Jordan River
3:10 Perizzites; Girgashites
4:19 Gilgal
6:11 Gideon
6:17 Accursed
7:1 Achan
8:30 Ebal, Mount
10:1 Adoni-zedek
10:12 Ajalon
10:13 Jasher
11:9 Horse
11:6 Hough
11:22 Gath
13:6 Hill Country
14:15 Arba
15:3 Adar
15:7 Addummim
15:25 Kerioth
15:31 Ziklag
15:45 Ekron
15:55 Carmel
15:62 En-gedi
17:11 Bethshan or Bethshean; Endor
17:16 Jezreel
18:1 Shiloah
18:25 Ramah
19:28 Zidon

19:29 Tyre
19:37 Edrei
19:40 Dan
20:7 Galilee
24:2 Nahor

Judges
(For a discussion on the book of
  Judges as a whole: BD, p. 719)
1:18 Ashkelon
1:31 Accho
2:13 Ashtaroth
3:15 Ehud
4:4 Deborah
4:5 Esdraelon
4:6 Barak
4:7 Kishon
5:14 Amalek
5:19 Megiddo; Armageddon
5:24 Jael
6:24 Jehovah-shalom
6:32 Jerubbaal
9:5 Jotham
9:7 Gerizim
10:17 Mizpeh
11:1 Jephthah
12:6 Shibboleth
13:24 Samson
15:9 Lehi
16:4 Delilah
16:11 Occupy
16:23 Dagon
18:21 Carriage
19:10 Jebus
21:8 Jabesh

Ruth
(For a discussion on the book of Ruth
  as a whole: BD, p. 764)

1:2 Naomi
1:20 Shaddai (Almighty)
2:1 Boaz
4:1 Gate
4:11 Ephratah
4:17 Jesse; Obed

1 Samuel
(For a discussion on the book of 1
 Samuel as a whole: BD, p. 769)
1:2 Hannah
1:20 Samuel
3:20 Prophet
6:21 Kirjath-jearim
7:1 Abinadab
7:12 Ebenezer
9:2 Saul
9:9 Seer
10:1 Anoint
10:2 Rachel
10:8 Gilgal
10:11 School of Prophets
10:22 Stuff
11:1 Covenant
12:9 Sisera
13:18 Beth-horon
13:20 Coulter
14:49 Michal
14:50 Abner; Ahimaaz; Ahinoarn
15:6 Kenites
15:8 Agag
16:8 Abinadab
16:13 David
17:1 Azekah
17:2 Elah, Valley of
17:4 Giants
17:7 Weaving
17:23 Goliath

17:40 Sling
17:54 Jerusalem
19:13 Teraphim
21:1 Ahimelech
21:10 Achish; Gath
22:5 Gad
22:20 Abiathar
23:18 Covenant
25:1 Samuel
25:3 Abigail (wife of Nabal)
28:4 Gilboa
28:7 En-dor
31:2 Abinadab
31:4 Saul

2 Samuel
(For a discussion on the book of 2
 Samuel as a whole: BD, p. 769)
2:23 Asahel
3:3 Absalom
3:4 Adonijah
3:27 Abner
4:4 Mephibosheth
5:1 Hebron
5:11 Hiram
5:14 Nathan; Solomon
6:6 Uzzah
8:6 Syria
8:13 Salt, Valley of
8:16 Recorder
8:17 Scribe; Zadok
8:18 Benaiah
11:12 Bathsheba
11:21 Jerubbesheth
13:5 Meat
15:12 Ahithophel
15:23 Kidron
15:24 Abiathar

15:27 Ahimaaz
16:5 Shimei
16:15 Ahithophel
17:25 Amasa
18:6 Ephraim, Wood of
18:9 Absalom
20:10 Amasa
20:24 Adoniram (Adoram)
23:6 Belial
23:24 Asahel
23:30 Benaiah

1 Kings
(For a discussion on the book of 1
   Kings as a whole: BD, p. 721)
1:5 Adonijah
1:33 Gihon
2:26 Eli
2:28 Joab
4:24 Tiphsah
6:9 Cedar
7:21 Jachin
7:24 Knop
7:33 Felloes
7:46 Succoth
8:1 Zion
8:1 Ark of the Covenant
8:2 Ethanim
9:15 Megiddo
10:22 Commerce
11:5 Milcom
11:7 Chemosh
11:26 Jeroboam
11:5 Milcom
11:29 Ahijah
11:40 Shishak
12:22 Shemaiah
12:28 Idol

14:21 Rehoboam
15:8 Asa
15:16 Baasha
15:18 Ben-hadad
15:24 Jehoshaphat
16:6 Baasha
16:16 Omri
16:24 Samaria
16:30 Ahab
16:31 Baal; Jezebel
16:32 Elijah
16:34 Hiel; Jericho
18:40 Kishon
19:15 Hazael
19:16 Elisha
22:50 Jehoram

2 Kings
(For a discussion on the book of 2
   Kings as a whole: BD, p. 721)
2:25 Carmel
3:4 Mesha
5:1 Naaman
5:3 Leprosy
5:12 Damascus
6:25 Cab
8:25 Ahaziah
8:26 Athaliah
8:28 Ramoth-gilead
9:21 Naboth
10:12 Shearing House
11:2 Joash
11:2 Jehoshabeath
11:16 Athaliah
12:2 Jehoiada
12:21 Amaziah
13:20 Elisha
14:13 Ephraim, Gate of

14:19 Amaziah
14:21 Azariah or Uzziah
14:29 Zachariah
15:10 Shallum
15:25 Pekah
15:29 Tiglath-pileser
15:37 Rezin
16:1 Ahaz
16:6 Jew
17:3 Shalmaneser
17:6 Halah
17:24 Cuth, Cuthah; Sepharvaim
17:30 Succoth-benoth
17:31 Adrammelech; Idol
18:1 Hezekiah
18:13 Captivities of the Israelites: Sennacherib
18:18 Eliakim
19:23 Fir
19:36 Nineveh
19:37 Adrammelech; Nisroch
20:12 Merodach-baladan
20:18 Eunuch
20:20 Hezekiah's Tunnel
22:1 Josiah
22:14 College
23:10 Topheth
23:11 Chamberlain
23:29 Necho
23:34 Eliakim
25:9 Temple of Solomon
25:27 Evil-merodach

1 Chronicles
(For a discussion on the book of 1 Chronicles as a whole: BD, p. 635)
1:1 Enos; Genealogy
1:3 Lamech
1:10 Nimrod
1:23 Ophir
1:35 Reuel
2:3 Onan
2:16 Abigail (sister of David)
3:1 Ahinoam; Daniel
4:43 Amalekites
5:1 Ephraim
5:18 Buckler
5:26 Captivities of the Israelites
6:39 Asaph
6:71 Golan
10:10 Dagon
15:24 Obed-edom
16:39 Gibeon

2 Chronicles
(For a discussion on the book of 2 Chronicles as a whole: BD, p. 635)
2:8 Almug
2:16 Joppa
4:6 Laver
6:2 Temple of Solomon
8:4 Hamath
10:18 Adoniram (Hadoram)
20:35 Ahaziah
26:15 Engines of War
28:3 Hinnom, valley of
35:13 Sod
35:22 Esdraelon; Megiddo
36:21 Sabbatical year

Ezra
(For a discussion on the book of Ezra as a whole: BD, p. 669)
1:8 Zerubbabel
2:63 Tirshatha
2:70 Levites
3:10 Temple of Zerubbabel

4:2 Esarhaddon
4:5 Darius
4:6 Ahasuerus
4:7 Artaxerxes
4:9 Apharsachites, -sathchites, -sites; Dehavites; Dinaites
5:1 Haggai
6:1 Scroll

Nehemiah
(For a discussion on the book of Nehemiah as a whole: BD, p. 738)
1:1 Shushan
2:1 Nisan
2:10 Sanballot
3:1 Hananeel
7:63 Habaiah
7:65 Urim and Thummim
9:2 Prayer
11:30 Lachish
11:32 Nob
12:4 Zechariah
12:22 Darius
13:28 Temple on Mount Gerizim

Esther
(For a discussion on the book of Esther as a whole: BD, p. 667)
1:9 Vashti
2:12 Myrrh
2:16 Tebeth
3:1 Haman
3:7 Adar
8:9 Sivan
9:26 Purim

Job
(For a discussion on the book of Job as a whole: BD, p. 713)

9:9 Pleiades
10:21 Darkness
16:13 Gall
17:6 Tabret
19:27 Reins
21:12 Organ
23:12 Convince
26:6 Abaddon
30:4 Mallows
32:2 Elihu
38:12 Dayspring
33:18 Pit
40:15 Behemoth

Psalms
(For a discussion on the book of Psalms as a whole: BD, pp. 754–55)
4:2 Leasing
11:4 Heaven
12:2 Vanity
16:10 Sheol
18:30 Buckler
19:1 Firmament
23:4 Rod
37:14 Conversation
67:2 Health
74:14 Leviathan
74:19 Dove
89:12 Hermon
104:18 Coney
110:4 Melchizedek Priesthood
118:25 Hosanna
146:1 Hallelujah
150:3 Psaltery

Proverbs
(For a discussion on the book of Proverbs as a whole: BD, p. 754)
8:27 Compass

12:22 Abomination
13:24 Rod
16:33 Lots, casting of
22:29 Mean
23:34 Ship, Shipping

Ecclesiastes
(For a discussion on the book of
  Ecclesiastes as a whole: BD, p. 659)
1:2 Vanity
12:5 Almond Tree

The Song of Solomon
(For a discussion on The Song of
  Solomon as a whole: BD, p. 766;
  also see "Canticles," p. 631)
1:12 Spikenard
2:1 Sharon
2:12 Turtle
7:13 Mandrake

Isaiah
(For a discussion on the book of Isaiah
  as a whole: BD, p. 707)
1:1 Jotham
1:25 Refiner
2:6 Replenish
2:16 Tarshish
3:18 Caul; Tire
3:22 Wimple
6:2 Seraphim
6:13 Teil
7:14 Immanuel
11:8 Cockatrice
11:11 Pathros
14:12 Devil; Lucifer
14:23 Bittern
20:1 Sargon
20:6 Isles
28:27 Cummin

29:1 Ariel
33:21 Galley
38:21 Medicine
46:1 Bel; Nebo
49:12 Sinim, Land of
58:8 Health
59:17 Breastplate
60:6 Dromedary
62:4 Beulah
62:4 Hephzibah
66:3 Swine

Jeremiah
(For a discussion on the book of
  Jeremiah as a whole: BD, p. 711)
1:3 Jehoiakim
6:20 Frankincense
7:31 Gehenna; Idol
8:22 Balm
23:6 Zedekiah
27:9 Sorcerer
29:21 Ahab
32:12 Baruch
33:17 Wanted
36:2 Writing
39:3 Nergal-sharezer
46:2 Carchemish; Nebuchadnezzar
46:4 Brigandine
48:11 Lees
48:33 Music
50:29 Holy One of Israel

Lamentations
(For a discussion on the book of
  Lamentations as a whole: BD,
  p. 722)
2:19 Watches
3:15 Wormwood
4:21 Uz

Ezekiel
(For a discussion on the book of
   Ezekiel as a whole: BD, p. 668)
1:1 Chebar
1:2 Jehoiachin
2:6 Scorpion
8:14 Tammuz
8:16 Gabriel
22:26 Holiness
26:9 Engines of War
27:14 Mule
35:15 Idumea
37:16 Ephraim, Stick of; Judah, Stick of
38:2 Gog
45:14 Cor
48:35 Jehovah-Shammah

Daniel
(For a discussion on the book of Daniel
   as a whole: BD, p. 653)
1:3 Daniel
1:7 Belteshazzar
1:12 Pulse
1:21 Cyrus
2:4 Syriack
2:27 Soothsayer
3:5 Dulcimer
3:6 Hour
3:20 Abednego
5:1 Belshazzar
5:25 Mene mene tekel upharsin
5:31 Darius
7:9 Fire
9:1 Ahasuerus
9:25 Messiah

Hosea
(For a discussion on the book of Hosea
   as a whole: BD, p. 705)
1:6 Lo-ruhamah
1:9 Lo-ammi
9:6 Noph
13:8 Caul

Joel
(For a discussion on the book of Joel
   as a whole: BD, p. 714)
1:4 Cankerworm
3:2 Jehoshaphat, Valley of
3:4 Palestine
3:8 Sabeans

Amos
(For a discussion on the book of Amos
   as a whole: BD, p. 607)
1:6 Gaza
1:8 Ashdod
1:14 Rabbah
2:11 Nazarite
4:1 Kine
4:6 Cleanness of Teeth
6:12 Hemlock
9:7 Philistines

Obadiah
(For a discussion on the book of
   Obadiah as a whole: BD, p. 739)
1:3 Selah
1:20 Zarephath

Jonah
(For a discussion on the book of Jonah
   as a whole: BD, p. 716)
4:6 Gourd

Micah
(For a discussion on the book of Micah
   as a whole: BD, p. 731)
5:14 Grove

Nahum

(For a discussion on the book of
  Nahum as a whole: BD, p. 736)
3:8 No
3:19 Bruit

Habakkuk

(For a discussion on the book of
  Habakkuk as a whole: BD, p. 697)
3:3 Paran

Zephaniah

(For a discussion on the book of
  Zephaniah as a whole: BD, p. 791)
3:9 Writing

Haggai

(For a discussion on the book of
  Haggai as a whole: BD, p. 698)

Zechariah

(For a discussion on the book of
  Zechariah as a whole: BD, pp.
  791–92)
1:7 Sebat; Calendar
8:5 Games
8:19 Fasts
9:10 River
9:13 Greece; Javan
10:11 Nile
12:11 Rimmon
14:4 Olives, Mount of

Malachi

(For a discussion on the book of
  Malachi as a whole: BD, p. 728)
1:11 Meat (Meal) Offering
3:2 Fullers
3:8 Tithe
4:4 Horeb

New Testament

For a discussion on the New Testament as a whole: BD: Bible, p. 622; Canon, p. 630; Epistles, p. 666; General Epistles, p. 678; Gospels, p. 682; Harmony of the Gospels, p. 684; Joseph Smith Translation, p. 717; Parables, p. 740; Quotations from the Old Testament found in the New Testament, p. 756.

Matthew

(For a discussion on the book of
  Matthew as a whole: BD, p. 729;
  also "Gospels," p. 682)
1:1 Christ; Names of Christ
1:9 Ezekias
1:16 Joseph
1:18 Mary
1:20 Dreams
2:1 Bethlehem; Wise Men of the East
2:11 Frankincense; House
2:14 Egypt
2:22 Archelaus
2:23 Nazarene
3:1 Pilate
3:2 Kingdom of Heaven
3:4 Locusts
3:6 Confession

3:8 Meet
3:11 Fire
3:13 Jordan River
4:5 Pinnacle of the Temple
4:18 Fish
4:21 James
4:25 Decapolis
5:1 Sermon on the Mount
5:3 Beatitudes
6:1 Almsgiving
6:9 Lord's Prayer
6:24 Mammon
8:2 Leper
8:28 Gergesenes
9:11 Publicans
9:15 Fasts
10:3 Thaddaeus
10:4 Judas
10:5 Samaritan
10:10 Scrip
10:32 Confession
11:21 Chorazin
12:24 Beelzebub
12:31 Blasphemy
13:21 By and by
13:25 Tares
13:55 Brethren of the Lord
14:1 Herod
14:3 Salome
14:6 Herodias
14:8 Charger
14:10 John the Baptist
15:2 Elders
15:5 Corban
16:13 Caesarea Philippi
16:14 Jeremias
16:17 Bar-jona

16:18 Church
16:27 Angels
17:2 Transfiguration, Mount of
17:5 Shechinah
19:3 Divorce
21:5 Sion
21:15 Scribe
21:19 Presently
22:17 Caesar
23:5 Hem of Garment; Phylacteries
23:14 Damnation
23:15 Proselytes
23:23 Anise
23:25 Zacharias
24:3 Coming of Jesus Christ
24:5 Christs, false
24:15 Abomination of Desolation
26:15 Piece of Silver
26:36 Gethsemane
27:2 Pilate
27:3 Potter's Field
27:16 Barabbas
27:27 Praetoriurn
27:32 Cyrene
27:43 Son of God
27:46 Eli
27:53 Resurrection
27:57 Arimathaea

Mark
(For a discussion on the book of Mark as a whole: BD, p. 728; also "Gospels," p. 682; "Parables," p. 740)
1:6 Camel's hair
1:19 Zebedee
1:20 John (Apostle)
1:30 Anon

Bible Dictionary References as Possible Bible Footnotes • *173*

2:14 Alphaeus; Matthew
2:18 Disciple
2:22 Bottles
3:6 Herodians
3:17 Boanerges
3:18 Bartholomew
4:34 Parables
5:1 Gadara
5:22 Jairus
6:3 Joses
6:5 Miracles
6:17 Machaerus (prison)
6:53 Gennesareth, land of
7:26 Syrophenician
7:34 Ephphatha
7:35 Miracles
8:10 Dalmanutha
9:5 Rabbi
9:42 Millstone
9:43 Hell
10:46 Bartimaeus
11:12 Fig Tree
14:36 Abba
14:51 Clothing
15:22 Golgotha
15:34 Eloi; Eli
16:19 Ascension

Luke
(For a discussion on the book of Luke as a whole: BD, p. 726; also "Gospels," p. 682; "Parables," p. 740)
1:3 Theophilus
1:5 Elisabeth; Zacharias
1:17 Elias
1:26 Annunciation; Gabriel; Nazareth
2:1 Augustus

2:2 Cyrenius
2:4 Judaea
2:21 Jesus
2:36 Anna
3:1 Abilene; Tetrarch; Trachonitis
3:8 Genealogy
3:17 Fan
3:27 Joanna
3:30 Juda
3:38 Adam
4:25 Elias; Elijah
4:26 Sarepta
4:27 Eliseus
4:31 Capernaum
4:41 Son of God
5:21 Blasphemy
5:33 Fasts
6:13 Apostle
6:15 Zelotes
7:11 Nain
7:38 Furniture
8:2 Mary Magdalene
10:34 Anoint
10:38 Martha
11:37 Pharisees
11:44 Burial
12:59 Money
13:4 Siloam
13:14 Synagogue
13:19 Mustard
15:16 Husks
16:22 Abraham's Bosom
18:24 Money
19:2 Zacchaeus
19:20 Pound
19:29 Bethphage
22:4 Captain of the Temple

23:33 Calvary; Crucifixion
23:43 Paradise
24:13 Emmaus
24:18 Cleopas

John
(For a discussion on the book of John as a whole: BD, p. 715; also "Miracles," p. 732; "Parables," p. 740)
1:4 Light of Christ
1:5 Darkness
1:26 John the Baptist
1:28 Bethabara
1:32 Dove, Sign of
1:40 Andrew; Peter
1:42 Cephas; Jona
1:44 Bethsaida.; Philip
1:45 Nathanael
2:1 Cana of Galilee
2:11 Miracles
3:1 Nicodemus
3:5 Baptism
3:23 Aenon; Salim
4:5 Sychar
4:6 Jacob's well
5:4 Bethesda
6:1 Tiberias, Sea of
6:23 Tiberias
7:1 Sanhedrin
7:39 Holy Ghost
8:20 Temple of Herod
9:39 Blindness
10:23 Solomon's Porch
11:1 Bethany; Lazarus
11:16 Didymus; Thomas
11:49 Caiaphas
11:54 Ephraim

12:3 Mary
12:20 Greece
13:2 Lord's Supper
14:2 Degrees of Glory
14:16 Comforter
18:1 Cedron
18:13 Annas
18:28 Judgment hall
19:25 Cleophas
19:38 Joseph (of Arimathaea)
20:16 Rabboni
20:17 Heaven

Acts
(For a discussion on the book of Acts as a whole: BD, p. 603)
1:2 Peter
1:9 Cloud
1:19 Aceldarna
1:23 Barsabas, Matthias
1:23 Joseph
2:9 Cappadocia; Elam; Parthians
2:10 Libya
2:29 Patriarch
2:38 Repentance
3:2 Temple of Herod
3:10 Beautiful Gate
3:19 Conversion
3:21 Dispensations
3:21 Restitution
4:1 Sadducees
4:36 Barnabas
5:1 Ananias
5:21 Senate
5:34 Gamaliel; Sanhedrin
6:1 Grecians; Hellenists
6:5 Antioch; Nicholas; Stephen
6:9 Cilicia; Libertinas

7:36 Red Sea
7:56 Son of Man
7:60 Stephen
8:17 Confirmation
8:27 Eunuch
8:30 Esaias
8:36 Baptism
8:40 Ashdod
9:5 Goads
9:10 Ananias
9:11 Tarsus
9:33 Aeneas
9:36 Dorcas
10:1 Centurian; Cornelius
10:38 Anointed (one)
11:26 Christians
11:28 Agabus; Claudius
12:4 Easter; Quatemion
12:12 Mark
12:20 Herod
13:4 Cyprus
13:6 Bar-jesus
13:7 Deputy
13:9 Paul
13:11 Blindness
13:51 Iconium
14:6 Lycaonia
14:12 Jupiter; Mercurius
14:13 Gate
15:18 Knowledge
15:22 Barsabas
16:1 Eunice
16:6 Galatia
16:7 Mysia
16:8 Troas
16:9 Macedonia
16:12 Colony

16:14 Thyatira
16:16 Divination
16:38 Roman Empire
17:1 Thessalonica
17:15 Athens
17:18 Epicureans; Stoics
17:19 Areopagus
17:34 Areopagite
18:1 Corinth
18:2 Aquila
18:12 Achaia; Gallio
18:27 Epistles
18:28 Convince
19:13 Exorcist
19:22 Erastus
19:24 Demetrius; Diana
19:29 Gaius
19:31 Games
19:35 Ephesus
20:9 Eutychus
21:7 Accho; Ptolemais
21:31 Claudius
22:3 Scribe
23:2 Ananias
23:23 Caesarea
23:24 Felix
23:31 Antipatris
24:24 Drusilla
24:27 Festus
25:13 Agrippa
27:1 Augustus
27:12 Crete
27:14 Euroclydon
27:17 Helps
27:34 Health
28:11 Castor and Pollux
28:15 Appi Forum

Romans
(For a discussion on the book of
  Romans as a whole: BD, "Pauline
  Epistles," pp. 743–44, 745)
1:13 Let
1:14 Barbarian
2:15 Conscience
7:2 Marriage
7:5 Flesh
8:15 Abba
9:11 Election
11:13 Gentile
11:17 Olive tree
16:3 Priscilla
16:10 Aristobulus
16:21 Jason
16:23 Erastus

1 Corinthians
(For a discussion on the book of 1
  Corinthians as a whole: BD,
  "Pauline Epistles," pp. 743–44)
1:11 Chloe
8:1 Charity
10:16 Communion
15:22 Atonement
15:41 Degrees of Glory
16:22 Anathema; Maran-atha

2 Corinthians
(For a discussion on the book of 2
  Corinthians as a whole: BD,
  "Pauline Epistles," pp. 743–44)
1:22 Earnest
11:32 Aretas

Galatians
(For a discussion on the book of
  Galatians as a whole: BD, "Pauline
  Epistles," pp. 743–46)
1:19 Apostle
1:21 Syria
2:9 James
3:29 Seed of Abraham

Ephesians
(For a discussion on the book of
  Ephesians as a whole: BD, "Pauline
  Epistles," pp. 743, 745–46)
1:7 Redemption
1:9 Mystery
6:1 Family

Philippians
(For a discussion on the book of
  Philippians as a whole: BD,
  "Pauline Epistles," pp. 743, 745–46)
1:1 Ministry; Philippi; Saint
3:2 Dog
4:3 Book of Life; Clement
4:6 Prayer
4:13 Grace

Colossians
(For a discussion on the book of
  Colossians as a whole: BD,
  "Pauline Epistles," pp. 743, 746)
1:2 Colosse
2:18 Angels
3:11 Scythian
3:16 Hymns
4:9 Onesimus; Philemon
4:13 Hierapolis
4:14 Luke
4:16 Laodicea

1 Thessalonians
(For a discussion on the book of 1
  Thessalonians as a whole: BD,
  "Pauline Epistles," p. 743)

4:15 Prevent
5:15 Revenge

2 Thessalonians
(For a discussion on the book of 2 Thessalonians as a whole: BD, "Pauline Epistles," p. 743)
1:1 Silas
2:1 Parousia

1 Timothy
(For a discussion on the book of 1 Timothy as a whole: BD, "Pastoral Epistles," p. 742; "Pauline Epistles," pp. 743, 747)
2:12 Suffer(ed)
3:1 Bishop

2 Timothy
(For a discussion on the book of 2 Timothy as a whole: BD, "Pastoral Epistles," p. 742; "Pauline Epistles," pp. 743, 747–48)
1:5 Timothy
1:17 Rome
3:3 Incontinency
3:8 Jannes
3:11 Antioch
3:15 Scripture
4:5 Evangelist
4:10 Dalmatia
4:19 Prisca
4:21 Linus

Titus
(For a discussion on the book of Titus as a whole: BD, "Pastoral Epistles," p. 742; "Pauline Epistles," pp. 743, 747)
1:4 Titus

1:8 Hospitality
3:5 Regeneration
3:13 Apollos

Philemon
(For a discussion on the book of Philemon as a whole: BD, "Pauline Epistles," pp. 743, 745, 746)
1:24 Aristarchus

Hebrews
(For a discussion on the book of Hebrews as a whole: BD, "Pauline Epistles," pp. 743, 746–47)
1:4 Angels
4:8 Jesus
7:1 Salem
9:5 Cherubim
9:9 Symbolism
9:22 Blood
10:10 Atonement
11:1 Faith
11:4 Abel
11:5 Enoch
13:10 Altar

James
(For a discussion on the book of James as a whole: BD, p. 709)
1:1 Dispersion
1:13 Tempt
1:23 Glass
2:26 Death
3:6 Gehenna
3:13 Conversation

1 Peter
(For a discussion on the book of 1 Peter as a whole: BD, p. 749)
1:1 Pontus

1:19 Lamb of God
2:25 Bishop
5:1 Elders

2 Peter
(For a discussion on the book of 2
   Peter as a whole: BD, p. 749)
1:5 Knowledge
1:19 Daystar

1 John
(For a discussion on the book of
   1 John as a whole: BD, p. 715)
2:1 Advocate; Paraclete
2:18 Antichrist

2 John
(For a discussion on the book of
   2 John as a whole: BD, p. 715)
1:7 Antichrist

3 John
(For a discussion on the book of
   3 John as a whole: BD, p. 715)
1:9 Diotrephes

Jude
(For a discussion on the book of Jude
   as a whole: BD, p. 719)
1:9 Michael
1:11 Korah

Revelation
(For a discussion on the book of
   Revelation as a whole: BD, p. 762)
1:8 Alpha; Omega
1:9 Patmos
1:10 Lord's day
1:11 Asia; Ephesus
2:6 Nicolaitans
2:13 Martyr
2:23 Reins
3:14 Amen; Jesus
3:18 Anoint
4:6 Glass
9:11 Abaddon; Apollyon
12:3 Dragon
12:7 War in Heaven
14:3 Music
14:4 Devil
14:8 Babylon
17:6 Admiration
18:12 Thyine wood
19:1 Alleluia
19:10 Prophet
19:20 Fire
20:5 Resurrection
20:8 Gog
21:19 Chalcedony
21:20 Chrysolite

Note
This is a previously unpublished paper.

Chapter 8

THE BOOK OF MORMON AS A PART OF GOD'S SYSTEM OF WITNESSES

One of the major purposes of our existence upon this earth is to learn to walk by faith. To help us realize this purpose, the Lord removed our memory of the premortal existence, allowing us to truly learn to develop our powers of faith in him here in this life. God does not let our faith go unanswered, however. He has promised that certain *evidences* or *witnesses* will "follow them that believe" (Mark 16:17–18). Therefore, we can know our faith in him is not in vain, and thus we can be encouraged to further develop our faith.

The Book of Mormon plays a unique role in God's system of witnesses because it testifies to man of the actuality of God and also of the truthfulness of his work upon the earth. However, the Book of Mormon is not the only witness provided by God. One of the prophets has stated, "*In the mouth of two or three witnesses shall every word be established*" (2 Corinthians 13:1; emphasis added).

MEMBERS OF THE GODHEAD TESTIFY OF EACH OTHER

The three members of the Godhead apparently follow this same law of witnessing or testifying of each other. In fact, in the New Testament the Savior testifies of the Father and his work so frequently, and indicates so often that he and the Father are *one,* that traditional Christianity has come to believe that God the Father and Jesus Christ the Son are one in substance as well as in other areas. That such is not the case was made absolutely clear by the first vision of Joseph Smith.

The members of the Godhead are, however, *one* in many respects (goals, purposes, ideals), and they are also *one in testimony*. Note the significance of the following statement of the resurrected Jesus Christ concerning this matter:

"I say unto you, that the Father, and the Son, and the Holy Ghost are one; and I am in the Father, and the Father in me, and the Father and I are one . . . *and I bear record of the Father, and the Father beareth record of me . . . and whoso believeth in me believeth in the Father also;* and unto him will the Father bear record of me, for he will visit him with fire and with the Holy Ghost. And thus will the Father bear record of me, and the Holy Ghost will bear record unto him of the Father and me; for the Father, and I, and the Holy Ghost are one" (3 Nephi 11:27, 32, 35–36; emphasis added).

Here the Savior makes two very important points: (1) the three members of the Godhead are *one* in the sense that they testify or witness of each other, and (2) if we accept or believe in any one of the members of the Godhead, we must accept or believe in the others, for they all testify of each other.

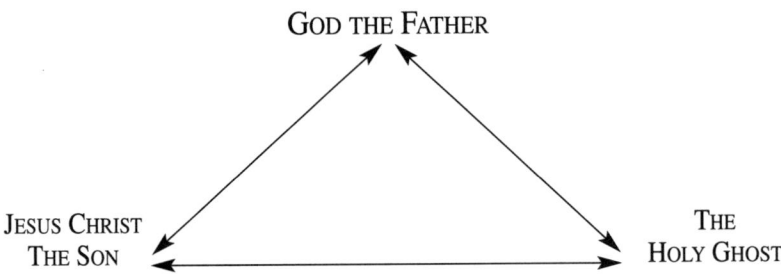

The three members of the Godhead testify and witness of each other: "I bear record of the Father, and the Father beareth record of me, and the Holy Ghost beareth record of the Father and me . . . and whoso believeth in me believeth in the Father also" (3 Nephi 11:32, 35).

The Scriptures Testify of Each Other and of the Members of the Godhead

The same divine law of witnesses applies also to the holy scriptures. The Holy Bible is one witness to the divinity of Jesus Christ, but where are the second and third witnesses? We Latter-day Saints believe the Book of Mormon to be a second witness (the "American" witness) to the divine mission of the Savior, and we believe the third great witness is yet to come forth. The Lord taught of the existence of three scriptural witnesses in these words:

"For behold, I shall speak unto the Jews and they shall write it; and I shall also speak unto the Nephites and they shall write it; and I shall also speak unto the other tribes of the house of Israel, which I have led away, and they shall write it; . . . And it shall come to pass that the Jews shall have the words of the Nephites, and the Nephites shall have the words of the Jews; and the Nephites and the Jews shall have the words of the lost tribes of Israel; and the lost tribes of Israel shall have the words of the Nephites and the Jews . . . and my word . . . shall be gathered in one" (2 Nephi 29:12–14).

We will have three great scriptural witnesses brought forth by the Lord. The relationship of these records to each other is also made clear in the Book of Mormon. In his farewell address, Mormon made the following statement to the Lamanites of this dispensation: "Therefore repent, and be baptized in the name of Jesus, and lay hold upon the gospel of Christ, which shall be set before you, not only in this record [the Book of Mormon] but also in the record which shall come unto the Gentiles from the Jews, which record [the Bible] shall come from the Gentiles unto you. For behold, this [the Book of Mormon] is *written for the intent that ye may believe that* [the Bible]*; and if ye believe that* [the Bible] *ye will believe this* [the Book of Mormon] *also*" (Mormon 7:8–9; emphasis added).

Here Mormon says that one of the major purposes of the coming forth of the Book of Mormon is to testify of the Bible, and he also states that if we honestly accept one of these scriptures, we will accept the other, for the two scriptures testify of each other. This is also the testimony of President Brigham Young:

"No man can say that this book (laying his hand on the Bible) is true . . . and at the same time say, that the Book of Mormon is untrue. . . . There is not that person on the face of the earth who has had the privilege of learning the Gospel of Jesus Christ from these two books, that can say that one is true, and the other is false. No Latter-day Saint, no man or woman, can say the Book of Mormon is true, and at the same time say that the Bible is untrue. If one be true, both are."[1]

In addition to testifying of other scriptures, the Book of Mormon also testifies of the divinity of Jesus Christ. Nephi, the first major historian in the Book of Mormon, made this comment concerning the relationship between the teachings of Christ and the Book of Mormon: "And now, my beloved brethren, and also Jew, and all ye ends of the earth, hearken unto these words [the Book of Mormon] and believe in Christ; and if ye believe not in these words believe in Christ. And if ye shall believe in Christ ye will believe in these words [the Book of Mormon], for they are the words of Christ" (2 Nephi 33:10).

According to the testimonies of the great Book of Mormon prophets Mormon and Nephi, if we accept the Book of Mormon, we must also accept both the Bible and the divinity of the Savior, for the Book of Mormon testifies of these things. In like manner, if we accept either the Bible or the divinity of the Savior, we will also accept the Book of Mormon.

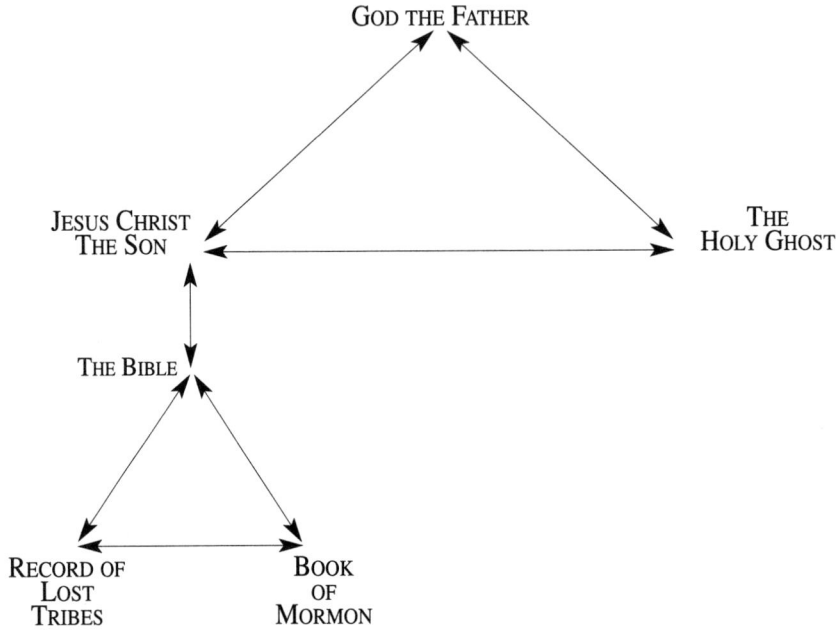

The Book of Mormon is written for the intent that we may believe the Bible; if we believe the Bible, we will also believe the Book of Mormon (Mormon 7:9). If we hearken unto the words of the Book of Mormon, we will believe in Christ; if we believe in Christ, we will also believe in the Book of Mormon (2 Nephi 33:10).

Special Witnesses to the Book of Mormon

The Lord has even provided us with a series of witnesses to the scriptures themselves. In relationship to the Book of Mormon, at least three groups of human witnesses were promised by the Lord and have been provided (2 Nephi 11:3; 2 Nephi 27:12–14; Ether 5:2–4; and D&C 5:11–15). First of all, we have the life and testimony of the Prophet Joseph Smith as a witness that the Book of Mormon is true. The Prophet declared that the record was given to him by an angel sent from God and that he translated the record by the gift and power of God (see JS—H 1:30–54, 59, 67). Joseph Smith sealed this testimony with his life.

Second, we have the testimonies of the three special witnesses—Oliver Cowdery, David Whitmer, and Martin Harris. These men testified that the Book of Mormon had "been translated by the gift and power of God, for his voice hath declared it unto us; wherefore we know of a surety that the work is true." They also claimed they had "seen the engravings . . . upon the plates . . . they have been shown unto us by the power of God, and not of man. . . . And we declare that an angel of God came down from heaven, and he brought and laid before our eyes, that we beheld and saw the plates, and the engravings thereon" ("The Testimony of Three Witnesses" in the front of the Book of Mormon). None of these three special witnesses ever denied his testimony of the things he had both seen and heard.

Then we have the testimonies of the eight special witnesses. They said Joseph Smith showed them the plates and that they handled them with their own hands and saw the engravings thereon: "And this we bear record with words of soberness . . . that the said Smith has got the plates of which we have spoken" ("The Testimony of Eight Witnesses" in the front of the Book of Mormon). Again, none of these men ever denied his testimony.

These groups of special witnesses not only testify of each other, but they also serve as witnesses to the claims of Joseph Smith regarding the truthfulness of the Book of Mormon. If we accept the testimony of any of these groups of human witnesses, we must accept the Book of Mormon and the Bible and also the divinity of Jesus Christ. (See figure on the following page.)

If we accept the testimony of any of the human witnesses, we must also accept the prophetic calling of Joseph Smith, the Book of Mormon, the Bible, and the divinity of Jesus Christ.

The Holy Ghost Testifies of the Truth of these Things

In addition to the testimony of other people and of the scriptures, however, the Lord has promised us a "more sure witness" of the truth of these things. This more sure witness is the Holy Ghost. Paul tells us that no man knoweth of the things of God except by the Spirit of God (1 Corinthians 2:11), and in 1 John 5:6 we read: "It is the Spirit that beareth witness, because the Spirit is truth."

The best and most effective way to discover truth in the spiritual and religious realm is to ask God. As the Savior said, "Ask, and it shall be given you" (Matthew 7:7), and as James added, "let him ask in faith, nothing wavering" (James 1:6).

The last writer in the Book of Mormon gives us a specific formula by which

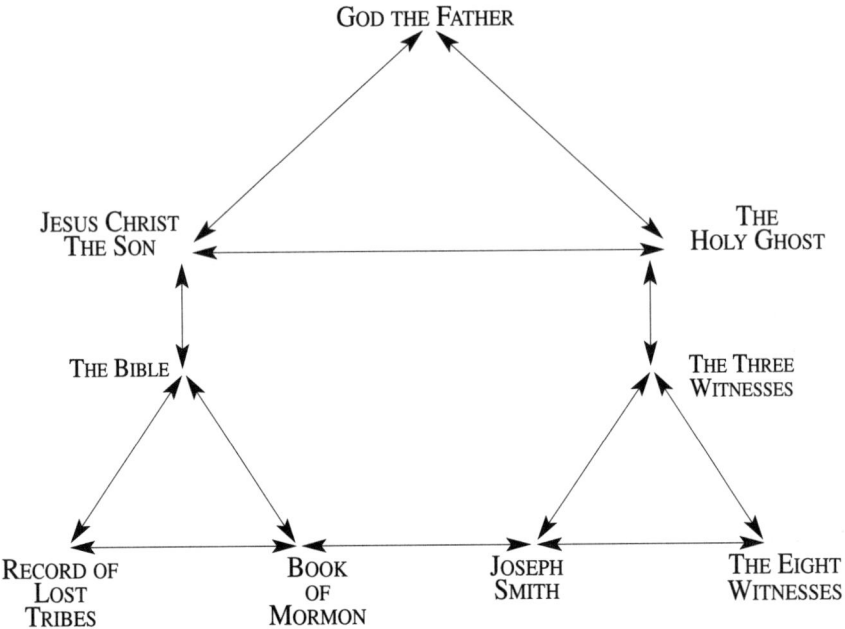

we can arrive at a knowledge of the truth of spiritual things, including the knowledge of whether the Book of Mormon is true:

"Behold, I would exhort you that when ye shall read these things, if it be wisdom in God that ye should read them, that ye would remember how merciful the Lord hath been unto the children of men, from the creation of Adam even down until the time that ye shall receive these things, and ponder it in your hearts.

"And when ye shall receive these things, I would exhort you that ye would ask God, the Eternal Father, in the name of Christ, if these things are not true; and if ye shall ask with a sincere heart, with real intent, having faith in Christ, he will manifest the truth of it unto you, by the power of the Holy Ghost.

"And *by the power of the Holy Ghost ye may know the truth of all things*" (Moroni 10:3–5; emphasis added).

Surely God the Father has provided us with ample witnesses in our day that the work of this dispensation is true. He has borne his testimony to us through his prophets and his divine Son. He has sent angels again to the earth with the glad tidings of the gospel. He has provided scriptural and human witnesses to his great work. He has promised us the witness of his emissary, the Holy Ghost, if we are sincere and faithful. As the prophet Moroni stated: "All this shall stand as a testimony against the world at the last day" (Ether 5:4).

It now behooves us to examine honestly and sincerely these witnesses and their testimonies. If we do, the Lord has promised us we will not find them wanting.

Notes

This material was initially published as Appendix A in *A Companion to Your Study of the Book of Mormon* (Salt Lake City: Deseret Book Co., 1976), 342–48.

1. Brigham Young, in *Journal of Discourses,* 1:38.

Chapter 9

THE BOOK OF MORMON AND THE FULNESS OF THE GOSPEL

Question: Why do we say that the Book of Mormon contains "the fulness of the gospel" (D&C 20:9) when it doesn't contain some of the basic teachings of the Church? Why doesn't it include such doctrines as the three degrees of glory, marriage for eternity, premortal existence of spirits, and baptism for the dead?

Response: Jesus Christ himself defined the word *gospel* to the Nephites: "Behold I have given unto you my gospel, and this is the gospel which I have given unto you—that I came into the world to do the will of my Father, because my Father sent me." The Savior then reviewed for the Nephites the facts of the Atonement, including the need to repent, be baptized, receive the Holy Ghost, and endure to the end (3 Nephi 27:13–22).

Gospel means "good news"—the good news that Jesus Christ has made it possible for us to return to the presence of our Heavenly Father. Through the Savior's perfect, sinless life and his suffering in Gethsemane and on the cross, Jesus Christ atoned for the original transgression of Adam and Eve and made it possible for us to be redeemed from spiritual death, which is the consequence of sin. Also through his atonement, including his crucifixion and resurrection, he has saved us from the permanent effects of physical death.

In addition to these aspects of the Atonement, which apply to all mankind, the "good news" also includes things we must do in order to re-enter God's presence. Peter mentioned some of these principles when he and other apostles were asked on the day of Pentecost, "Men and brethren, what shall we do?" His reply was "Repent, and be baptized every one of you in the name of Jesus Christ for the remission of sins, and ye shall receive the gift of the Holy Ghost" (Acts 2:37–38).

Peter's answer parallels our fourth article of faith: "We believe that the first principles and ordinances of the Gospel are: first, Faith in the Lord Jesus Christ; second, Repentance; third, Baptism by immersion for the remission of sins; fourth, Laying on of hands for the gift of the Holy Ghost."

One of the best summary statements of the gospel was given by the Savior to the Nephites: "And no unclean thing can enter into his kingdom; therefore nothing entereth into his rest save it be those who have washed their garments in my blood, because of their faith, and the repentance of all their sins, and their faithfulness unto the end.

"Now this is the commandment: Repent, all ye ends of the earth, and come unto me and be baptized in my name, that ye may be sanctified by the reception of the Holy Ghost, that ye may stand spotless before me at the last day.

"Verily, verily, I say unto you, this is my gospel; and ye know the things that ye must do in my church; for the works which ye have seen me do that shall ye also do" (3 Nephi 27:19–21).

The essentials of the "fulness of the gospel" are contained in this one brief statement from the Book of Mormon, although they are also discussed in greater detail throughout this sacred scripture. In these verses, the Book of Mormon clearly emphasizes and explains the doctrine of the Atonement and the basic principles and ordinances of the gospel. (See the many references to these topics in the index of the Book of Mormon.) If these are observed, a person may regain the presence of God in the celestial kingdom. Thus, the Book of Mormon can appropriately be said to contain the fulness of the gospel—the "good news"—even though it might not discuss all the ordinances necessary for exaltation.

Now let's look at the second part of the question—why the Book of Mormon doesn't contain information on all the doctrines of the Church.

An effective author has an audience and a purpose in mind as he prepares his material. Thus, it is important to understand the purpose of the authors of the Book of Mormon in order to understand why it contains what it does and why it doesn't contain other information.

The four major writers (engravers and/or compilers) of the Book of Mormon are Nephi (117 pages), Jacob (19 pages), Mormon (338 pages), and Moroni (50 pages). All four of these authors were personal witnesses of Jesus Christ. Nephi and Jacob were visited by the premortal Jesus Christ (2 Nephi 11:2–3), and Mormon and Moroni were visited by the resurrected Jesus Christ (Mormon 1:15; Ether 12:39). Moroni also provides us with the testimony of the brother of Jared concerning the premortal Christ (Ether 3:9–16). Thus, the writings of these four brethren constitute a strong witness for the divinity of Christ.

All four of these authors indicate that the major purpose of their writings is to lead people to Christ. Some of them also indicate that they intend their writings to serve as a second witness of the teachings of the Bible (the "record of the Jews"). At no time do any of them indicate that they will include all the teachings and ordinances of the gospel. In fact, they frequently mention they will include only those things that are necessary to a belief in Christ or those things they have been inspired or commanded to write (1 Nephi 19:2; 2 Nephi 28:2; 31:1; 32:7; Jacob 1:17–19; 3 Nephi 26:12; 30:1; Mormon 5:9–13; 8:1; Ether 8:20; 13:13).

As brief examples, note the following statements of these four authors concerning their knowledge of Christ:

Nephi: "We labor diligently to write, to persuade our children, and also our brethren, to believe in Christ. . . . We talk of Christ, we rejoice in Christ, we preach of Christ, we prophesy of Christ, and we write according to our prophecies, that our children may know to what source they may look for a remission of their sins" (2 Nephi 25:23, 26).

Jacob: "For this intent have we written these things, that they [the readers] may know that we knew of Christ, and we had a hope of his glory many hundred years before his coming; and not only we ourselves had a hope of his glory, but also all the holy prophets which were before us" (Jacob 4:4).

Mormon: "Know ye that ye must come to the knowledge of your fathers, and repent of all your sins and iniquities, and believe in Jesus Christ, that he is the Son of God. . . . Therefore repent, and be baptized in the name of Jesus, and lay hold upon the gospel of Christ, which shall be set before you, not only in this record but also in the record which shall come unto the Gentiles from the Jews, which record shall come from the Gentiles unto you. For behold, this [the Book of Mormon] is written for the intent that ye may believe that [the Bible]; and if ye believe that ye will believe this also; and if ye believe this ye will know concerning your fathers, and also the marvelous works which were wrought by the power of God among them" (Mormon 7:5, 8–9).

Moroni: "I exhort you to remember these things; . . . for ye shall see me at the bar of God; and the Lord God will say unto you: Did I not declare my words unto you, which were written by this man? . . . Yea, come unto Christ, and be perfected in him. . . . And again, if ye by the grace of God are perfect in Christ, and deny not his power, then are ye sanctified in Christ by the grace of God, through the shedding of the blood of Christ, which is in the covenant of the Father unto the remission of your sins, that ye become holy, without spot" (Moroni 10:27, 32–33).

These four writers also understood that their writings would come forth in the last days during a period of unbelief, when the true Church had been taken from the earth (2 Nephi 25:3–23; 26:16–24; Jacob 4:4, 13–16; Mormon 8:25–35; Moroni 10:24–34). Thus, their stated purpose was to help lead us to Christ and to the true Church, rather than to provide all the teachings and ordinances of the gospel that we might receive after becoming members of the Church.

Explaining some of the procedures he followed during the abridgment of the plates, Mormon indicated that it wasn't possible to record everything: "I cannot write the hundredth part of the things of my people" (Words of Mormon 1:5). However, he and the other major writers of the plates were faithful to their express mission of testifying of Jesus Christ.

The Lord has indicated that he works with his children by providing them information "line upon line, precept upon precept, here a little and there a little" (2 Nephi 28:30). Thus, even on April 6, 1830, when the Church was restored in this dispensation, many of the ordinances we now have were not available to the early Church members. For example, the revelations providing much of the information on the topics mentioned in the question were not received until later:

1. A wealth of information on the three degrees of glory is contained in Doctrine and Covenants 76, which was not received until February 16, 1832.

2. Major teachings and instructions pertaining to marriage for eternity date from May 1843 (D&C 131) and July 1843 (D&C 132).

3. Teachings pertaining to the premortal existence of spirits were not given by the Prophet Joseph Smith until well after the establishment of the Church. Some of his most significant statements on this subject were made at the April conference of the Church in 1844.[1]

4. Instructions on baptism for the dead are found primarily in Doctrine and Covenants 124 (January 1841) and sections 127 and 128 (September 1842).

When Jesus Christ was on the earth, he also experienced the gospel "line upon line": "He received not of the fulness at first, but continued from grace to grace, until he received a fulness; and thus he was called the Son of God, because he received not of the fulness at the first" (D&C 93:13–14).

Concerning this principle of learning line upon line and precept upon precept, the Lord has said: "I give unto you these sayings that you may understand and know how to worship, and know what you worship, that you may come unto the Father in my name, and in due time receive of his fulness. . . . And no man receiveth a fulness unless he keepeth his commandments" (D&C 93:19, 27).

These principles are consistent with the concept of a living prophet who is entitled to receive the mind and will of the Lord by the power of the Holy Ghost for the members of the true Church (D&C 68:4). This idea is also expressed in our ninth article of faith: "We believe all that God has revealed, all that He does now reveal, and we believe that He will yet reveal many great and important things pertaining to the Kingdom of God."

These teachings and doctrines are in accord with the statement of the Prophet Joseph Smith that the principles of the gospel are "according to the Holy Scriptures, and the Book of Mormon; and the only way that man can enter into the celestial kingdom."[2] The fulness of the gospel as contained in the Book of Mormon means that it contains those instructions a person needs to observe in order to be worthy to enter the presence of God in the celestial kingdom.

Notes

From "I Have a Question," *Ensign*, September 1985, 17–19.

1. See *Teachings of the Prophet Joseph Smith*, 342–62.
2. *Teachings of the Prophet Joseph Smith*, 16.

Chapter 10

THE BOOK OF MORMON, A MODERN SCRIPTURE

Some people are surprised when they discover there are other scriptures in addition to the Bible. In fact, when the Book of Mormon was translated by Joseph Smith and was first published in 1830, many people said, in essence, "A new Bible? We have a Bible, and there cannot be another Bible."

Fortunately, during the past 130 years there has been a change in this thinking. Many reputable Bible scholars now readily admit that the Bible is not a closed book; indeed, there are at least sixteen books mentioned in the Bible that do not even appear in our present versions. Thus we know that the Bible in and of itself is not complete. Also, a little serious thinking should help us realize there might well be other scriptures in addition to the Bible. Why should God speak only to one nation? He himself has said that he is not a respecter of persons and is unchangeable—the same yesterday, today, and tomorrow. Surely, then, if he spoke to one nation in former times and taught them his gospel, he has done the same thing for other nations and can and will do the same thing for us if we are worthy.

Isaiah stated that the Lord teaches his people "line upon line and precept upon precept" (Isaiah 28:10). His statement indicates that revelation never ceases and the scriptures are never closed so long as the people are righteous and keep God's commandments which have been revealed to them. Paul also indicates there could be more than one scripture. In his second letter to the Corinthians, he states, "In the mouth of two or three witnesses shall every word be established" (2 Corinthians 13:1). The Bible is one witness to the divinity of Christ, but where are the additional witnesses?

I believe the Old Testament prophet Ezekiel knew of one of these additional witnesses. In chapter 37 of his book, he states, "The word of the Lord came again unto me, saying, Moreover, thou son of man, take thee one stick, and write upon it, For Judah, and for the children of Israel his companions: then take another stick, and write upon it, For Joseph, the stick of Ephraim, and for all the house of Israel his companions: and join them one to another into one stick; and they shall become one in thine hand. And when the children of thy people shall speak unto thee, saying, Wilt thou not shew us what thou meanest by these? Say unto them, Thus saith the Lord God; behold, I will take the stick of Joseph, which is in the hand of Ephraim, and the tribes of Israel his fellows, and will put them with him, even with the stick of Judah, and make them one stick, and they shall be one in mine hand" (Ezekiel 37:15–19).

When we recall that in ancient times it was the custom to write on parchment and roll it on a stick, it becomes very evident that the Lord is talking here of two separate records. One of these records is to be of Judah and those of the house of Israel who are connected with him; this, of course, is the Bible. The other record is to be of Joseph and those of the house of Israel who are with him. But where is there any record of the descendants of Joseph? Certainly that record is not the Bible, for the Bible does not tell the story of the descendants of Joseph. Also, Ezekiel distinctly states that the records of Judah and Joseph are to be separate from each other; otherwise how could they be put together and become one in the hand of the Lord?

The Book of Mormon fulfills all the requirements for this additional scripture. In the first place, it reveals the gospel "line upon line, precept upon precept" and thus helps establish the previous word of the Lord. One of its major purposes is to serve as another witness to the divinity of Christ. Also, the Book of Mormon is primarily a record of the descendants of Joseph.

Although it is not possible to consider in detail the multitudinous claims and teachings of the Book of Mormon, let us look briefly at some of its major teachings. The Book of Mormon might be called the "American Scripture," for it tells of three major groups of people who came to the continent of North and South America before the time of Christ.

The first of these groups came here during the worldwide dispersion of the people at the time of the tower of Babel. Concerning this dispersion, we read in the book of Genesis, "So the Lord scattered them abroad from thence upon the face of all the earth" (Genesis 11:8).

The people who came to this continent at that time were led by a man called Jared; thus, they are called Jaredites in the Book of Mormon. The Jaredites lived here for about two thousand years and built one of the great civilizations of all time, but this great nation was virtually destroyed in a great civil war sometime between 600 B.C. and 200 B.C. The records of the Jaredites were preserved, however, and later came into the possession of the second group of people who came to this continent.

That second group came from Jerusalem about 600 B.C. during the reign of Zedekiah, king of Judah. The great prophet of that day was Jeremiah, but the Bible states there were also other prophets at that time. One of those prophets was named Lehi, and the Book of Mormon tells how Lehi was warned by the Lord to flee out of Jerusalem because of the impending destruction of that city by Babylonia. Lehi gathered together his family and the family of a man called Ishmael, and they traveled for eight years in a south-southeast direction, until they finally arrived at the shores of a great sea, evidently the Sea of Arabia. There they built a ship, and after traveling for eight years, they were finally led by the Lord to the shores of this continent, which was their promised land. Soon after their arrival here, the group divided into two factions: the more righteous group was led by Nephi, the son of Lehi, and they became the white-skinned Nephites of the Book of Mormon; the more wicked group followed after Laman, another of the sons of Lehi, and in time the Lamanites became a dark and a loathsome people because they disobeyed the commandments of God.

After nearly one thousand years these two factions met in a great war, and the Nephite nation was virtually destroyed. The Lamanites survived the war but broke up into small tribes later; they were discovered in this condition by Columbus and were given the name of "Indians." Thus the Book of Mormon teaches that the American Indians are largely of the house of Israel.

The third group of people mentioned in the Book of Mormon arrived here shortly before 580 B.C. and also came from Jerusalem. One of the infant sons of King Zedekiah, called Mulek, was with this group, and so they were called the Mulekites. Sometime after arriving in the promised land, the Mulekites joined with the Nephites; these two groups then intermarried and became one.

About A.D. 34—which was nearly 350 years before the combined Mulekite-Nephite nation was destroyed—an event of tremendous importance happened. The resurrected Christ appeared to that people and taught them his gospel. The Savior had previously prophesied of that visit while he lived in mortality on the eastern continent. Perhaps you recall the statement of Christ in the book of John when He said, "And other sheep I have which are not of this fold: them also I must bring, and they shall hear my voice; and there shall be one fold, and one shepherd" (John 10:16).

Who were these additional people to be visited by the Savior? Some have said that they were the Gentiles around Palestine; however, there is no record whatsoever that the Savior ever preached to the Gentiles while he lived upon the earth. In fact, in Matthew 15:24, he very clearly stated, "I am not sent but unto the lost sheep of the house of Israel."

The Savior fulfilled his promise of visiting his other sheep when he appeared as a resurrected being to the righteous people on this continent. His gospel teachings in the Book of Mormon are both clear and comprehensive, and because they have come to us through only one translation, they are very easy to understand.

Someone has said that if a person should discover a manuscript containing fifty words of Jesus Christ in addition to those in the New Testament, such a discovery would be the most important find of the past nineteen hundred years. In the Book of Mormon we find not only fifty additional words of Christ but fifty times fifty—and many more. No wonder this book is held in such high esteem by those who have read it that it has now been published in most of the major languages of the world and continues to sell at the rate of tens of thousands of copies per year. The Book of Mormon restores many of the plain and precious truths of the gospel of Christ, which had been partially lost through the many translations of the Bible.

You might be interested in the testimony of a Christian minister on this point. He writes: "I have been a minister . . . for 37 years. I have built up a library of the greatest books in the world, costing me more than $12,000. But I have found here in the Book of Mormon a library more valuable than all the collections of books in the world because it is the word of God."[1]

But, you might ask, how can one be certain the Book of Mormon is truly the word of God? In the book of John, the Savior said: "My doctrine is not mine, but his that sent me. If any man will do his will, he shall know of the doctrine, whether it be of God, or whether I speak of myself" (John 7:16–17). Thus, if we want to know whether the gospel is true, we should live the gospel and then Christ will manifest the truth of it unto us. He has given us a similar promise in connection with the Book of Mormon. In the last chapter of this modern scripture, we read this unique statement: "And when ye shall receive these things, I would exhort you that ye would ask God, the Eternal Father, in the name of Christ, if these things are not true; and if ye shall ask with a sincere heart, with real intent, having faith in Christ, he will manifest the truth of it unto you, by the power of the Holy Ghost. And by the power of the Holy Ghost ye may know the truth of all things" (Moroni 10:4–5).

I, together with tens of thousands of others, have put this promise to the test and have found it to be true. If one reads the Book of Mormon with a sincere heart and with real intent and then asks God in the name of Christ if this book is not true, God reveals the truth of it unto him by the power of the Holy Ghost.

What a wonderful promise and assurance! God does not ask us to accept his scriptures blindly. He gives us witnesses to the truthfulness of his scriptures, and then these scriptures testify to us of the divinity of Christ. Thus we can all come to a knowledge of the truth.

I have a strong testimony of the truthfulness of the gospel of Christ, and I should like to bear that testimony to you. I know that God lives and that we are his children. I know that Jesus is the Christ, the Savior and Redeemer of the world, the eldest Son of God in the Spirit and the Only Begotten Son of God in the flesh. I know that Joseph Smith was a prophet of God, foreordained to restore the fulness of the gospel in this dispensation. I know the Bible is the word of God, and I also know the Book of Mormon is the word of God. These truths have been made manifest unto me by the power of the Holy Ghost, and I am as sure of them as I am that I exist. They have brought joy and peace into my life, and I pray they might also bring peace and happiness into your life.

Notes

From an address delivered over KSL Radio, Salt Lake City, 2 February 1958.

1. LeGrand Richards, *A Marvelous Work and a Wonder,* rev. ed. (Salt Lake City: Deseret Book, 1988), 79.

Chapter 11

RECEIVING A TESTIMONY OF THE BOOK OF MORMON

Question: A friend of mine says he has prayed about the Book of Mormon but has not received a testimony of its truthfulness. Shouldn't Moroni's promise always work?

Response: To understand the promise found in Moroni 10:4, a person should read and ponder the verses immediately before and after. In the first edition of the Book of Mormon (1830), all of Moroni chapter 10 was written as one paragraph.

Let us examine carefully and individually verses 1–5:

Verse 1: "Now I, Moroni, write somewhat as seemeth me good; and I write unto my brethren, the Lamanites; and I would that they should know that more than four hundred and twenty years have passed away since the sign was given of the coming of Christ."

Although Moroni is addressing himself specifically to "the Lamanites," these words, as well as all of the words in the Book of Mormon, apply also to the Jews and the Gentiles (see title page).

Verse 2: "And I seal up these records, after I have spoken a few words by way of exhortation unto you."

The words *these records* referred to the records upon which Moroni was then writing (the plates of Mormon), which were later received by Joseph Smith and translated as the Book of Mormon.

Verse 3: "Behold, I would exhort you that when ye shall read these things, if it be wisdom in God that ye should read them, that ye would remember how merciful the Lord hath been unto the children of men, from the creation of Adam even down until the time that ye shall receive these things, and ponder it in your hearts."

Too frequently this verse is not quoted in connection with verse four and, when quoted, is often misinterpreted. However, it is a key verse to understanding the full promise of Moroni 10:1–5. When analyzed thoroughly, this verse indicates that the honest seeker after truth must do two things:

1. Read the Book of Mormon. The words *these things* in verse three refer back to the words *these records* in verse two—the records from which our present Book of Mormon was translated.

2. "Ponder" the dealings of God with men as recorded in the Book of Mormon, and then compare them with the dealings of God with men as recorded in the Bible. Although the word Bible is not found in this verse, Moroni indicates that the person should "remember how merciful the Lord hath been unto the children of men, *from the creation of Adam* even down until the time that ye shall receive these things" (emphasis added). The Bible provides a story of the Creation and the history of events from that time forward. However, the account of the Creation and subsequent happenings are not contained in the Book of Mormon. In fact, Moroni had earlier acknowledged that the Book of Mormon would not include this information. In explaining his abridgement of the book of Ether, Moroni wrote:

"And now I, Moroni . . . take mine account from the twenty and four plates which were found by the people of Limhi, which is called the Book of Ether. And as I suppose that the first part of this record, which speaks concerning the creation of the world, and also of Adam, and an account from that time even to the great tower, and whatsoever things transpired among the children of men until that time, is had among the Jews—*therefore I do not write those things which transpired from the days of Adam until that time*" (Ether 1:1–4; emphasis added).

Thus, if a sincere person hasn't gained a testimony of the Book of Mormon after reading it, he should—as Moroni seems to suggest here—read the Bible as well, pondering in his heart both scriptural accounts of God's dealings with his children.

Verse 4: "And when ye shall receive these things, I would exhort you that ye would ask God, the Eternal Father, in the name of Christ, if these things are not true; and if ye shall ask with a sincere heart, with real intent, having faith in Christ, he will manifest the truth of it unto you, by the power of the Holy Ghost."

Note that the word *read* is not even included in this verse; rather, the verb is *receive*. In other words, after the person has (1) read the Book of Mormon and (2) pondered the dealings of God with the peoples of the Book of Mormon and the Bible, he must then put himself in a frame of mind where he would be willing to "receive" or "accept" all these things. Then he must ask "with a sincere heart, with real intent, having faith in Christ." Sincere pondering of the scriptures helps put a person into an appropriate frame of mind to ask for—and receive—divine guidance.

The things we should be in a position to receive (accept) may refer not only to the Book of Mormon, but also to everything mentioned in verses two and three. Similarly, the word *it* near the end of verse four ("he will manifest the truth of it unto you") may refer to the process of God's dealing with men, as well as to the Book of Mormon itself. In either case, if a person receives "the truth of it," he will believe in (accept) the Book of Mormon.

Verse 5: "And by the power of the Holy Ghost ye may know the truth of all things."

This verse indicates that the principles contained in the formula for learning truth as explained in verses one through four can also be applied to areas other than learning the truth of the Book of Mormon.

As to whether this promise is Moroni's or the Lord's, Doctrine and Covenants 68:4 reads: "And whatsoever they [the Lord's chosen servants] shall speak when moved upon by the Holy Ghost shall be scripture, shall be the will of the Lord, shall be the mind of the Lord, shall be the word of the Lord, shall be the voice of the Lord, and the power of God unto salvation."

When Moroni "speaks" or writes by the power of the Holy Ghost, his writings represent the "will . . . , mind . . . , word . . . , [and] voice of the Lord." Thus it is appropriate to say this promise comes from the Lord through the writings of Moroni.

When a person follows this divine formula, the results are certain: He will gain a testimony of the Book of Mormon. God cannot and does not lie, and his promises made through his prophets are sure. Therefore, any person who claims to have followed the various requirements but says he has not gained a testimony should check to see which step he has not followed faithfully or completely:

1. He should read and ponder the Book of Mormon—all of it.
2. He should remember the methods God has used in working with the peoples of both the Book of Mormon and the Bible—and ponder these things in his heart.
3. He should put himself in a frame of mind where he would be willing to accept (receive) all of "these things"—the Book of Mormon, the Bible, and the way God works with men.
4. "With a sincere heart, with real intent, having faith in Christ," he should ask God, the Eternal Father, in the name of Jesus Christ "if these things are not true."
5. He should be able to recognize the promptings and feelings which will be

evidences to him of the truth of "these things" (including the Book of Mormon) as they are made manifest unto him "by the power of the Holy Ghost."

Note

From "I Have a Question," *Ensign,* March 1986, 50–51.

Jesus Christ and His Atonement

Chapter 12

THE OLD TESTAMENT, A WITNESS FOR JESUS CHRIST

Although the Old Testament as a witness for Jesus Christ will certainly be the main thrust of this chapter, the Old Testament is also a witness for other things in other areas. For example, the Old Testament is also a witness for the gospel plan of progression and salvation and a witness for the other scriptures, especially for the Book of Mormon. In other words, the Old Testament is a key part of God's system of witnesses.

In Deuteronomy 19:15 we read, "At the mouth of two witnesses, or at the mouth of three witnesses" shall matters "be established." Matthew 18:16 states, "In the mouth of two or three witnesses every word may be established." And in 2 Corinthians 13:1 we read, "In the mouth of two or three witnesses shall every word be established." As we hope to demonstrate in this discussion, the Old Testament is a very important witness in establishing the words and the truths of our Heavenly Father.

"EVERY DOCTRINE"

A statement by Brigham Young on the value of the Bible in learning the truths of the gospel has had a great influence on me: "In all my teachings, I have taught the Gospel from the Old and New Testaments. I found therein every doctrine, and the proof of every doctrine, the Latter-day Saints believe in, as far as I know, therefore I do not refer to the Book of Mormon as often as I otherwise should. There may be some doctrines about which little is said in the Bible, but they are all couched therein, and I believe the doctrines because they are true, and I have taught them because they are calculated to save the children of men."[1]

Let me repeat a key sentence from this statement by Brigham Young: "I found therein [in the Bible] every doctrine and the proof of every doctrine the Latter-day Saints believe in, as far as I know."

I love the Book of Mormon, and I love to teach the doctrines of the gospel from the Book of Mormon. But after reading this statement from Brigham Young, I decided to put the statement to a test. I reread the Book of Mormon, noting and recording every basic, essential doctrine of the gospel that was mentioned in that glorious scripture. Then I reread the Bible, and placed appropriate references from the Bible next to the doctrines I had listed from the Book of Mormon. There was at least one biblical reference for each doctrine from the Book of Mormon, without exception. I challenge you to try that same exercise. Not only will it help you in reading these two books again, but you will obtain a greater knowledge of the gospel and a greater appreciation of the Bible.

THE SCRIPTURES TESTIFY OF JESUS CHRIST

A statement in the Book of Mormon gives us a hint about how we should study the scriptures. In Alma 17:2 we read that the sons of Mosiah "had waxed strong in the knowledge of the truth; for they were men of a sound understanding and they had *searched the scriptures diligently,* that they might know the word of God" (Alma 17:2; emphasis added). The principle, then, is this: The scriptures must be searched diligently.

The reason why the scriptures should be searched diligently is given in a statement by the Savior in John 5:39: "They are they which testify of me." The requirement is clear: We should search the scriptures diligently so we might have a stronger testimony of Jesus Christ.

The Old Testament includes many statements and prophecies of Jesus Christ as the great Jehovah of the Old Testament, prophecies concerning the life, mission, and atonement of Jesus Christ on the earth as recorded in the New Testament, prophecies relating to events on the earth immediately preceding his second coming, and still other prophecies relating to his millennial reign as King of kings and Lord of lords. The strength of multiple witnesses in the Old Testament of the total mission of Jesus Christ can prove to be a weakness, however, if the reader does not recognize which prophecies were fulfilled during Old Testament times, which were fulfilled during the New Testament period, which are being fulfilled at the present time, and which are still to be fulfilled in the future.

For example, one reason the Jewish people as a nation did not accept Jesus Christ as the Messiah at his first coming was that they felt some of the prophecies pertaining to his second coming should have been fulfilled at that time. Some felt he should have led the Israelites to victory over the Romans and established at his first advent his great millennial reign of peace and righteousness. No wonder Peter warned us: "No prophecy of the scripture is of any private interpretation. For the prophecy came not in old time by the will of man: but holy men of God spake as they were moved by the Holy Ghost" (2 Peter 1:20–21).

Thus, one reason we should search the Old Testament diligently is so we can truly understand it. Then, and only then, will it become "one of the simplest books in the world," as Brigham Young told us.

THE OLD TESTAMENT TESTIFIES OF JESUS CHRIST

The Old Testament contains the essential things the world needs to know to gain a testimony of Jesus Christ and of his gospel. A serious, diligent study of the Old Testament will reveal the many essential doctrines the prophets of ancient Judah knew about the birth, life, and atonement of the Messiah, the Anointed One, whom we know by the name-title Jesus Christ. I will mention very briefly a few of these essential doctrines, together with at least one key scriptural reference pertaining to each. I also suggest some titles from the Topical Guide and the Bible Dictionary that you might review for additional information and insight.

1. The Messiah would be born of a virgin (Isaiah 7:14; see also TG, "Jesus Christ, Birth of"; BD, "Christ, Names of").

2. The Messiah would be born in Bethlehem of Judea (Micah 5:2; see also TG, "Jesus Christ, Messiah" and "Jesus Christ, Prophecies about"; BD, "Bethlehem" and "Messiah").

3. The Messiah would be reared in the tribal lands assigned to Zebulun and Naphtali, which includes Nazareth and the Galilee (Isaiah 9:1–2; see also TG, "Jesus Christ, Messiah" and "Jesus Christ, Prophecies about"; BD, "Galilee," "Messiah," "Naphtali," "Nazareth," and "Zebulun").

4. The Messiah would have power over the physical elements of the earth, including the physical body. Thus, he could heal the sick, cause the blind to see, and so forth (Isaiah 42:5–7; see also TG, "Jesus Christ, Mission of" and "Jesus Christ, Power of"; BD, "Messiah").

5. The Messiah would bear the sin of the world and the iniquities and transgressions of many (Isaiah 50:6; 53:4–6; see also TG, "Iniquity," "Jesus Christ, Atonement through," "Jesus Christ, Savior," "Sin," and "Transgress, Transgression"; and BD, "Christ, Names of" and "Messiah").

6. The Messiah would be "lifted up on a tree" (crucified) and have his hands and feet "pierced" (Psalm 22:16; Zechariah 12:10; 13:6; see also TG, "Jesus Christ, Crucifixion of" and "Jesus Christ, Death of"; BD, "Crucifixion").

7. The Messiah would be resurrected from the dead and provide resurrection for all mankind (Job 19:25; Isaiah 25:8; 26:19; 53:12; Ezekiel 37:12; Hosea 13:14; see also TG, "Jesus Christ, Resurrection" and "Resurrection"; BD, "Death," "Messiah," and "Resurrection"). The Old Testament teachings on the resurrection of the Messiah are particularly important, since the resurrection of Jesus Christ is the proof of his divinity.

In addition to these essential teachings associated directly with the atonement of Jesus Christ, the Old Testament includes many other interesting and confirming prophecies about his life on earth. Again, I shall mention briefly only a few, with one or more related scriptures:

1. The Messiah would be of the loins of David; indeed, the title "Son of David" would be one of his sacred titles (2 Samuel 7:13; Psalms 89:4; 132:17; Isaiah 9:7; 11:1; Jeremiah 23:5; 33:15).

2. The Messiah would come forth out of Egypt (Hosea 11:1).

3. The Messiah would ride into Jerusalem on the foal of an ass (Zechariah 9:9).

4. The Messiah would be betrayed for thirty pieces of silver (Zechariah 11:12–13).

5. The Messiah would be with the wicked in his death (Isaiah 53:9).

6. The Messiah would be with the rich in his grave (Isaiah 53:9).

7. The Messiah would be called by many titles, including the sacred title "Son of Man," meaning "Son of Man of Holiness" or "Son of God."

If the readers of the Old Testament realized the multitudinous titles in that scripture that refer to Jesus Christ, I feel confident they would have a greater understanding and appreciation of the teachings of the Old Testament on the life, mission, and atonement of Jesus Christ. Many of these titles are listed in the Bible Dictionary under "Christ, Names of." In just this brief passage from Isaiah 54:5—"for thy Maker is thine husband; the Lord of hosts is his name; and thy Redeemer the Holy One of Israel; the God of the whole earth shall he be called"—Isaiah included at least five titles referring to Jesus Christ. Notice additional titles for Jesus Christ in just a few other samples of the writings of Isaiah:

"Behold, a virgin shall conceive, and bear a son, and shall call his name Immanuel," meaning "With us is God" (Isaiah 7:14).

"For unto us a child is born, unto us a son is given: and the government shall be upon his shoulder: and his name shall be called Wonderful, Counsellor, The mighty God, The everlasting Father, The Prince of Peace" (Isaiah 9:6).

"Behold, God is my salvation; . . . the Lord Jehovah is my strength and my song" (Isaiah 12:2).

"Thus saith the Lord, your redeemer, the Holy One of Israel; . . . I am the Lord, your Holy One, the creator of Israel, your King" (Isaiah 43:14–15).

"Thus saith the Lord the King of Israel, and his redeemer the Lord of hosts: I am the first, and I am the last; and beside me there is no God" (Isaiah 44:6).

"All flesh shall know that I the Lord am thy Saviour and thy Redeemer, the mighty One of Jacob" (Isaiah 49:26).

The Topical Guide has more headings beginning with the words "Jesus Christ" than any other. These headings are all followed by scores of separate references pertaining to that particular topic. Many of these headings include a word or a term that might also be used as a title for Jesus Christ: Jesus Christ, Advocate; . . . Creator; . . . Davidic Descent of; . . . Exemplar; . . . Firstborn; . . . Good Shepherd; . . . Head of the Church; . . . Jehovah; . . . Judge; . . . King; . . . Lamb of God; . . . Light of the World; . . . Lord; . . . Mediator; . . . Messenger of the Covenant; . . . Messiah; . . . Only Begotten Son; . . . Redeemer; . . . Rock; . . . Savior; and . . . Son of Man.

I hope these examples convince you that the Old Testament contains many teachings related to the important doctrine that Jesus Christ is the Messiah, the Anointed One. Every time we read one of the titles that refer to him we should think of him. Truly, these scriptures testify of him.

The Old Testament Teaches the Gospel of Jesus Christ

In preparing for this discussion, I decided to identify and list every chapter heading in the Old Testament that contained information related to the gospel—the "good news"—of Jesus Christ: his life, mission, or atonement. I was amazed and delighted at the number of chapters I listed. Granted, I sometimes had to make a judgment call about whether or not to list a particular chapter, but usually the chapter heading was so detailed there was no question. In addition, I identified every chapter heading that makes a direct reference to Jesus Christ, including such key words or phrases as "Christ," "Messiah," "Son of God," "speaking Messianically," "Second Coming," or "Millennium." In the list below, I have put an asterisk after the chapter number if the chapter heading includes one of these key words or phrases. I did not include an asterisk if the chapter heading used "Jehovah" or "I AM," even though we as Latter-day Saints know these terms also apply to Jesus Christ.

Here is a list of the chapters, arranged by book:

Genesis 1–2, 3*, 4, 6–9, 12–14, 16–17, 21–22, 24–28, 32–33, 35, 48, 49*, JST 50). (Summary: 26 of 50; 2 asterisks.)

Exodus 3, 4, 6, 12–13, 18–20, 24, 27–35, 39–40. (Summary: 20 of 40.)

Leviticus 1, 4–11, 16–17, 19–23, 25–27. (Summary: 19 of 27.)

Numbers 3, 6–11, 14–15, 18, 21, 24*, 27–29. (Summary: 15 of 36; 1 asterisk.)

Deuteronomy 4–11, 13–17, 18*, 26–30, 32–33. (Summary: 21 of 34; 1 asterisk.)

Joshua 1, 5, 24. (Summary: 3 of 24.)

Judges 2, 10. (Summary: 2 of 21.)

Ruth 4. (Summary: 1 of 4.)

1 Samuel 3, 8–10, 16. (Summary: 5 of 31.)

2 Samuel 7*, 22–24. (Summary: 4 of 24; 1 asterisk.)

1 Kings 3, 6–8, 17–19. (Summary: 7 of 22.)

2 Kings 2, 4, 13, 18, 23. (Summary: 5 of 25.)

1 Chronicles 13, 17, 28. (Summary: 3 of 29.)

2 Chronicles 4–8, 15, 29–30, 34–35. (Summary: 10 of 36.)

Ezra 2, 6, 9. (Summary: 3 of 10.)

Nehemiah 7–8, 10, 13. (Summary: 4 of 13.)

Esther 0. (Summary: 0 of 10.)

Job 1–2, 4, 12–14, 19*, 38, 42. (Summary: 9 of 42; 1 asterisk.)

Psalms 1, 2*, 3–7, 8*, 9*, 11, 13–15, 16*, 17–20, 21*, 22*, 23–25, 27–30, 31*, 33, 34*, 36–37, 40*, 44, 45*, 46–49, 50*, 53, 59, 62, 67*, 68*, 69*, 72*, 73, 76, 78–87, 89*, 90, 91*, 92–94, 97*, 102–7, 108*, 110*, 111–13, 115–17, 118*, 119, 121, 123–30, 132*, 134–36, 138–39, 144–50. (Summary: 104 of 150; 22 asterisks.)

Proverbs 1–4, 8–9, 14, 29. (Summary: 8 of 31.)

Ecclesiastes 2, 3, 7–9, 11–12. (Summary: 7 of 12.)

Song of Solomon 0. (Summary: 0 of 8.)

Isaiah 1, 2*, 3, 4*, 5, 6*, 7*, 8*, 9*, 10*, 11*, 12*, 13*, 14*, 16*, 17–18, 22*, 24*, 25–27, 28*, 29–31, 32*, 33*, 34*, 35, 40*, 41, 42*, 43–44, 45*, 46, 48, 49*,

50*, 51*, 52*, 53*, 54*, 55–58, 59*, 60*, 61*, 62*, 63*, 64*, 65*, 66*. (Summary: 56 of 66; 35 asterisks.)

Jeremiah 1–2, 3*, 4–11, 13–18, 22, 23*, 25*, 30*, 31*, 32, 33*, 50. (Summary: 25 of 52; 6 asterisks.)

Lamentations 3–4. (Summary: 2 of 5.)

Ezekiel 1–4, 8–10, 11*, 12–14, 16*, 17*, 18, 20*, 28, 33, 34*, 36*, 37*, 38*, 39–48. (Summary: 31 of 48; 8 asterisks.)

Daniel 2, 3*, 4–6, 7*, 8*, 9*, 10*, 11*, 12*. (Summary: 11 of 12; 7 asterisks.)

Hosea 2*, 3*, 12–13, 14*. (Summary: 5 of 14; 3 asterisks.)

Joel 2*, 3*. (Summary: 2 of 3; 2 asterisks.)

Amos 3–8, 9*. (Summary: 7 of 9; 1 asterisk.)

Obadiah 1. (Summary: 1 of 1.)

Jonah 1, 4. (Summary: 2 of 4.)

Micah 2–3, 4*, 5*, 6, 7*. (Summary: 6 of 7; 3 asterisks.)

Nalium 1*, 2*. (Summary: 2 of 3; 2 asterisks.)

Habakkuk 2. (Summary: 1 of 3.)

Zephaniah 1*, 2, 3*. (Summary: 3 of 3; 2 asterisks.)

Haggai 1, 2*. (Summary: 2 of 2; 1 asterisk.)

Zechariah 1, 2*, 3*, 5, 6*, 7, 8*, 9*, 10, 11*, 12*, 13*, 14*. (Summary: 13 of 14; 9 asterisks.)

Malachi 1–2, 3*, 4*. (Summary: 4 of 4; 2 asterisks.)

Summary of all the chapters in the 39 books of the Old Testament:

Total number of chapters: 929.

Number of chapters referring to the life, mission, or atonement of Jesus Christ: 449 (or 48%).

Number of chapters identified by an asterisk (indicating that the chapter heading contains a key word or phrase pertaining specifically to Jesus Christ): 108 (12% of total, or 24% of those pertaining to Jesus Christ).

What a clear demonstration that the Old Testament is something more than history! It is indeed a strong witness for Jesus Christ.

As impressive as these figures are, however, we must not suppose that if a chapter does not include a reference to the life, mission, or atonement of Jesus Christ we need not read, study, and ponder that chapter. Hundreds of important principles and teachings are contained in many of the other chapters. For example, 2 Kings 1, 5, 6, 7, and 17 are not in the list; yet powerful messages are contained in all of those chapters.

To get an idea of the significance and detail of the chapter headings, let's read those for the first three chapters of Genesis:

"Chapter 1: God creates this earth and its heaven and all forms of life in six days—Creative acts of each day set forth—God creates man, both male and female, in his own image—Man given dominion over all things, and commanded to multiply and fill the earth."

"Chapter 2: Creation completed—God rests on the seventh day—Prior spirit creation explained—Adam and Eve placed in Garden of Eden—They are forbidden to eat of the tree of knowledge of good and evil—Adam names every living creature—Adam and Eve are married by the Lord."

"Chapter 3: The Serpent (Lucifer) deceives Eve—She and then Adam partake of the forbidden fruit—Her Seed (Christ) shall bruise the Serpent's head—Role of woman, and of man—Adam and Eve cast out of the Garden of Eden—Adam presides—Eve becomes the mother of all living."

I hope these samples whet your appetite to read all the chapter headings in the scriptures.

The Old Testament As a Witness for Other Scriptures

In addition to serving as a witness for Jesus Christ and for some of the basic doctrines and principles of the gospel of Jesus Christ, the Old Testament also serves as a witness for the other scriptures. The statement by Amos that "surely the Lord God will do nothing, but he revealeth his secret unto his servants the prophets" (Amos 3:7), and the statement by God himself that he is an unchangeable God, the same yesterday, today, and tomorrow, both suggest the possibility that he has given other scriptures.

The Old Testament supports the basic claims of the New Testament, as indicated by the many Old Testament statements quoted by New Testament writers. In addition, the Old Testament serves as a witness of the Book of Mormon, as indicated in Ezekiel 37, and of both the Book of Mormon and the Doctrine and Covenants, as indicated in Psalm 85: "Truth shall spring out of the earth; and righteousness shall look down from heaven" (Psalm 85:11; see also Moses 7:62). President Ezra Taft Benson's inspired interpretation of this expression is that it refers to the Book of Mormon ("Truth will I send forth out of the earth") and to the revelations of the last days, including those that have "been preserved for us in the Doctrine and Covenants."[2]

Two of the major engravers of the sets of plates from which we get the Book of Mormon—Nephi on the Small Plates, and Mormon on the Plates of Mormon—have also testified of the role of the Old Testament as a scriptural witness.

In the last chapter Nephi engraved, he warned: "And you that will not partake of the goodness of God, and respect the words of the Jews [the Old Testament], and also my words [the Book of Mormon], and the words which shall proceed forth out of the mouth of the Lamb of God [including the New Testament], behold, I bid you an everlasting farewell, for these words shall condemn you at the last day. For what I seal on earth, shall be brought against you at the judgment bar; for thus hath the Lord commanded me, and I must obey. Amen" (2 Nephi 33:14–15).

The last chapter engraved by Mormon on his plates includes these words: "Therefore repent, and be baptized in the name of Jesus, and lay hold upon the gospel of Christ, which shall be set before you, not only in this record [the Book of Mormon] but also in the record which shall come unto the Gentiles from the Jews, which record [the Bible] shall come from the Gentiles unto you. For behold, this [the Book of Mormon] is written for the intent that ye may believe that [the Bible]; and if ye believe that [the Bible] ye will believe this [the Book of Mormon] also" (Mormon 7:8–9).

Although Moroni's famous challenge in the last chapter he engraved on the plates of Mormon is usually interpreted to pertain primarily to the Book of Mormon, a careful reading of his words indicates the Bible is also involved. Let's review his words in Moroni 10:3: "Behold, I would exhort you that when ye shall read these things [from the plates of Mormon], if it be wisdom in God that ye should read them, that ye would remember how merciful the Lord hath been unto the children of men, from the creation of Adam even down until the time that ye shall receive these things, and ponder it in your hearts."

Let's consider those words for a moment to make certain we understand what Moroni is asking us to do. It is obvious that he is asking us to read the Book of Mormon, but isn't it equally obvious that he is asking us to read the Bible? Notice again his counsel that we "would remember how merciful the Lord hath been unto the children of men, from the creation of Adam even down until the time that ye shall receive these things." Where do we read about the Creation and about events from the time of the Creation? They are found in the Bible; they are not found in the Book of Mormon. In fact, this same Moroni, when he started his abridgment of the plates of Ether, recorded: "And as I suppose that the first part of this record, which speaks concerning the creation of the world, and also of Adam, and an account from that time . . . is had among the Jews—Therefore I do not write those things which transpired from the days of Adam" (Ether 1:3–4).

No wonder Brigham Young testified of these two powerful scriptural witnesses: "No man can say that this book (laying his hand on the Bible) is true . . . and at the same time say, that the Book of Mormon is untrue. . . . There is not that person on the face of the earth who has had the privilege of learning the Gospel of Jesus Christ from these two books, that can say that one is true, and the other is false. . . . If one be true, both are."[3]

And that is my testimony. Both the Bible and the Book of Mormon are true because they teach the same things, and they both teach that Jesus Christ is the Divine Son of God, the Savior and Redeemer of the world. I testify further that the Old Testament is an important part of the biblical testimony of the Messiah, the Anointed One. The Old Testament is a witness for Jesus Christ. Of these things I bear witness in the name of Jesus Christ.

Notes

From *A Witness of Jesus Christ,* 1989 Sperry Symposium on the Old Testament, edited by Richard D. Draper (Salt Lake City, Utah: Deseret Book Company, 1990).

1. Brigham Young, in *Journal of Discourses,* 16:73–74.
2. Ezra Taft Benson, in Conference Report, October 1986, 102.
3. Brigham Young, in *Journal of Discourses,* 1:38.

Chapter 13

JESUS CHRIST, THE BELOVED SON OF GOD

Jesus Christ is the "beloved Son" of God (Matthew 3:17), and I humbly and gratefully bear the following witness concerning him.

HE IS OUR ELDER BROTHER

He is the Firstborn Son of God in the spirit, and thus is the Elder Brother of us all, as we are also the sons and daughters of God in the spirit. In our pre-earthly existence we knew him as our Elder Brother, a position and title he shall hold forever. He was "in the beginning with the Father" (D&C 93:21) and was known as the "Great I Am" in the pre-earthly councils of the Gods (D&C 29:1; Exodus 3:14). He is separate and distinct from both the spirit body and physical body of his Heavenly Father, but is one with his Father in witness, testimony, truth, doctrine, power, ideals, and goals (see 3 Nephi 11:27–36). As it is the work and glory of the Father, it is also the work and glory of his Beloved Son "to bring to pass the immortality and eternal life of man" (Moses 1:39).

HE IS THE FOREORDAINED SAVIOR AND REDEEMER

In the pre-earthly councils when the great plan of progression and eternal life was presented to us by his and our Heavenly Father, our Elder Brother lovingly and voluntarily offered to become our Redeemer and Savior in this physical, earthly existence. He agreed then to take upon himself the suffering that normally would come upon us whenever we disobey divine law, upon the condition that we would repent and stop breaking the law.

He also agreed to offer his life to save us from the permanent effects of physical death. When his offer was gratefully accepted by those of us who agreed then to participate in the glorious plan, he became known as the one "Chosen from the beginning" (Moses 4:2) and was the foreordained one from before the "foundation of the world" (1 Peter 1:20).

He Is Alpha and Omega

He is the "Amen, the faithful and true witness, the beginning of the creation of God" (Revelation 3:14). He is "Alpha and Omega, the beginning and the ending . . . the first and the last" (Revelation 1:8, 11).

He Is the Great I AM

One of his sacred names or titles by which he was known in the pre-earthly councils was the Great I Am. He has revealed this term in several places in the scriptures.

When he directed Moses to tell the children of Israel that the God of their fathers had sent him (Moses) to deliver them from bondage, Moses inquired what he might say if the Israelites asked, "What is his name?" (Exodus 3:13). The Savior replied, "I AM THAT I AM: . . . Thus shalt thou say unto the children of Israel, I AM hath sent me unto you" (Exodus 3:14; capitalization in original).

On January 2, 1831, the Savior used the following descriptive terms in revealing his mind and will to his prophet on the earth, Joseph Smith:

"Thus saith the Lord your God, even Jesus Christ, the Great I Am, Alpha and Omega, the beginning and the end, the same which looked upon the wide expanse of eternity, and all the seraphic hosts of heaven, before the world was made;

"The same which knoweth all things, for all things are present before mine eyes;

"I am the same which spake, and the world was made, and all things came by me" (D&C 38:1–3).

He Is the Creator of Earth and Heavens

Under the direction of our Heavenly Father, the beloved Son of God organized out of the eternal elements of already existing planets the earth of a terrestrial order containing the Garden of Eden.[1] He thus became the great and supreme Creator of the heavens and the earth and all things which in them are (see 2 Nephi 9:5; Alma 30:44). It is by and through him that our Heavenly Father made the world and all things (see Hebrews 1:2; 1 Corinthians 8:6).

It is he "which spake, and the world was made" (see D&C 38:3). "He is in the sun, and the light of the sun . . . As also he is in the moon, and is the light of the moon, and . . . the light of the stars, and the power thereof by which they were made" (D&C 88:7–9).

By his power, earths have been brought into existence, given their revolutions and times and seasons. By this same power, earths go into a higher state of existence.[2]

He Is the Author of Salvation

When the earth fell to its telestial state through the disobedience of Adam and Eve, angels were sent under his direction to teach Adam and Eve the saving principles of his gospel, providing the means by which they might again regain the presence of our Heavenly Father, this time with physical bodies of celestial glory. All "angels and authorities and powers [are] subject unto him" (1 Peter 3:22).

By the unchangeable priesthood authority which was after the Order of the Son of God and which bore his divine name (see Hebrews 7:24; D&C 107:3), sacred ordinances, including baptism by immersion for the remission of sins, started to be performed on the earth. It was in anticipation of his coming that the ancients offered sacrifice, for he was foreordained from before the foundations of the world to be the "Lamb of God" (John 1:29) without spot or blemish to be slain as a great and infinite sacrifice in the meridian of time.

It was from his mouth that the commandment to repent went forth "in a firm decree . . . that it should be in the world, until the end thereof" (Moses 5:15, 59).

He is the "author and finisher of our faith" (Hebrews 12:2), and both he and his gospel are the "same yesterday, and to day, and for ever" (Hebrews 13:8).

He Is Our Advocate and Mediator with Our Heavenly Father

In order to protect us from the full and eternal demands of the law of justice, he became our righteous "advocate with the Father" (1 John 2:1; D&C 29:5), "the mediator of the new testament . . . and . . . of the new covenant" (Hebrews 9:15; 12:24), the one "great Mediator" (2 Nephi 2:27–28) "between God and men" (1 Timothy 2:5). Through his mediation and atonement, men can be made perfect (see D&C 76:69).

As he himself has said, "no man cometh unto the Father, but by me" (John 14:6).

He Is the Anointed One of the Old Testament

He was, and is, the "God of Abraham . . . Isaac, and . . . Jacob" (Exodus 3:15), the "Mighty One of Israel" (1 Nephi 22:12).

He is the "Almighty God" (Revelation 1:8; Jacob 2:10) who spoke with Moses on Mount Sinai, and with all his ancient prophets (see 3 Nephi 15:4–5).

Isaiah used several titles and descriptive phrases in prophesying of the earthly birth and mission of the Savior:

"Behold, a virgin shall conceive, and bear a son, and shall call his name Immanuel [meaning 'With us is God']" (Isaiah 7:14).

"For unto us a child is born, unto us a son is given: and the government shall be upon his shoulder: and his name shall be called Wonderful, Counsellor, The mighty God, The everlasting Father, The Prince of Peace" (Isaiah 9:6).

"Behold, God is my salvation . . . the Lord JEHOVAH is my strength and my song; he also is become my salvation. Therefore with joy shall ye draw water out of the wells of salvation" (Isaiah 12:2–3).

"For thy Maker is thine husband; the Lord of Hosts is his name; and thy Redeemer the Holy One of Israel; The God of the whole earth shall he be called" (Isaiah 54:5).

He Is the Jehovah of the Old Testament

During most of the Old Testament period he was known by the name-title Jehovah, together with other descriptive terms.

It was he who was rejected by Cain, the first murderer, who rebelliously said, "Who is the Lord that I should know him?" (Moses 5:16).

It was he who spoke to Enoch face to face as one man speaketh with another, introducing himself as the "Messiah, the King of Zion, the Rock of Heaven, . . . the Son of Man" (Moses 7:53–54).

It was he who commanded Noah to preach repentance to his generation and then to build the ark in order to escape the destruction of the flood (see Genesis 6:13–22).

It was he who said to Abraham: "I am the Lord thy God. . . . I stretch my hand over the sea, and it obeys my voice; I cause the wind and the fire to be my chariot; I say to the mountains—Depart hence—and behold, they are taken away by a whirlwind, in an instant, suddenly. My name is Jehovah, and I know the end from the beginning; therefore my hand shall be over thee" (Abraham 2:7–8).

It was he who appeared to Moses on Sinai and on sundry occasions, giving Moses the laws and priesthood the people were willing to accept. Later he said concerning the law he had given to Moses, "I am he that gave the law, and I am he who covenanted with my people Israel" (3 Nephi 15:5).

He Is the God of Abraham, Isaac, and Jacob, and of All Israel

His relationship to the prophets and leaders of ancient Israel is constantly affirmed. Frequently as a term of introduction he identified himself as the "God of Abraham, the God of Isaac, and the God of Jacob" (Exodus 3:6, 15–16).

Other terms by which he was identified are the "son of Abraham" (Matthew 1:1), the "mighty One of Jacob" (Isaiah 60:16), the "Lion of the tribe of Judah" (Revelation 5:5), the "stem" and "root of Jesse" (Isaiah 11:1; Romans 15:12).

He is the "consolation of Israel" (Luke 2:25), the "Star out of Jacob" (Numbers 24:17) who is "the brightness of his [God's] glory" (Hebrews 1:3), the "bright and morning star" (Revelation 22:16), the "hope of glory" (Colossians 1:27), the prophesied "Shiloh" (Genesis 49:10), the Bridegroom who is yet to claim fully his bride (see Revelation 19:7–9).

He is the spiritual "Rock of Israel" (2 Samuel 23:3; 1 Corinthians 10:4), our "fortress" against the fiery slings and darts of the adversary (Psalm 18:2), the sure foundation upon which all of us can build our homes of faith to be safe and secure from the winds and storms of life. "There is . . . [no] rock like our God" (1 Samuel 2:2).

He is the "King of the Jews" (Matthew 27:11, 37; Mark 15:2) who was rejected by his own, the "rock of offense to both the houses of Israel" (Isaiah 8:14), the "stone of Israel" (Genesis 49:24), which the builders rejected and "set at naught" (Acts 4:11), but which is become the "head stone" (Psalm 118:22) and the "chief corner stone" (Ephesians 2:20), the "living stone, disallowed indeed of men, but chosen of God, and precious" (1 Peter 2:4). He is "the Deliverer" (Romans 11:26) and "Governor" who will eventually rule over Israel (Matthew 2:6).

Numerous references tie him to King David. He is the "Branch of righteousness . . . unto David" (Jeremiah 33:15), the "root and offspring of David" (Revelation 22:16) and the "horn of David [who is] to bud" (Psalm 132:17), the "son of David" (Matthew 1:1) born in the city of David's birth (see Micah 5:2), who is "holy . . . true . . . [and] hath the key of David" (Revelation 3:7).

He is the "messenger of the covenant" (Malachi 3:1; 3 Nephi 24:1) and the "messenger of salvation" (D&C 93:8) to all those who will live on the earth. He is the "minister of the sanctuary, and of the true tabernacle" (Hebrews 8:2). He was chosen for these positions by our Heavenly Father when the Father said, "I will send the first" (Abraham 3:27).

He Is the Only Begotten Son of God in the Flesh

Luke's account of the conception and birth of the long-awaited Holy One of Israel, "the true Messiah" (2 Nephi 1:10), is as follows:

"The angel Gabriel was sent from God . . . to a virgin [named] Mary . . . and said . . . Fear not, Mary: for thou hast found favour with God. And, behold, thou shalt conceive in thy womb, and bring forth a son, and shalt call his name Jesus. He shall be great, and shall be called the Son of the Highest. . . . The Holy Ghost shall come upon thee, and the power of the Highest shall overshadow thee: therefore . . . that holy thing which shall be born of thee shall be called the Son of God" (Luke 1:26–27, 30–32, 35).

He was and is the "only begotten" of the Father in the flesh (John 1:14, 18; 3:16).

He is actually, literally, physically, biologically the Son of God, who was sent into the world (see 1 John 4:9) and who manifested himself among men (see D&C 76:23).

He Is the Word of God Made Flesh

He is the "Word of life" (1 John 1:1) and "The Word of God" (Revelation 19:13) who was with God, who was God, and who "made flesh [his] tabernacle and dwelt among the sons of men" (D&C 93:4; see also John 1:1, 14).

The Apostle John bears the following witness concerning the relationship between our Heavenly Father, the Son of our Heavenly Father, and the gospel of his Son:

"In the beginning was the gospel preached through the Son. And the gospel was the word, and the word was with the Son, and the Son was with God, and the Son was of God.

"The same was in the beginning with God.

"All things were made by him; and without him was not anything made which was made.

"In him was the gospel, and the gospel was the life, and the life was the light of men;

"And the light shineth in the world, and the world perceiveth it not" (JST, John 1:1–5).

He Is the Holy Child of Bethlehem

New titles for the Jehovah of the Old Testament could then appropriately be used. He is the "Holy Child" (Moroni 8:3) of Bethlehem, the "son of Mary" (Mark 6:3), the Seed of the woman who should bruise the serpent's head (see Genesis 3:15).

He is also God's "holy child Jesus" (Acts 4:27), the "Son of the Blessed" (Mark 14:61) and "Son of the Highest" (Luke 1:32). In his physical body he is "the image of God" (2 Corinthians 4:4) and "the express image of [God's] person" (Hebrews 1:3).

He Is the Prophet of Nazareth

He is God's own Son called forth from Egypt (see Hosea 11:1; Matthew 2:15).

He was inspired to dwell in the cities of Nazareth and Capernaum, in the lands of Zebulun and Naphtali, where Isaiah had prophesied that the people there who were sitting in darkness would see a great light, even Jesus Christ and the light of his gospel (see Matthew 4:13–16; Isaiah 9:1–2). He is the Nazarene, reared in the lands of Zebulun and Naphtali, as foretold both by Isaiah and an unnamed prophet quoted by Matthew (see Matthew 2:23).

He is the boy of Nazareth and of the temple who wanted to be about his Father's business (see Luke 2:49).

He is the "prophet of Nazareth" (Matthew 21:11) who was not without honor save in his own country (see John 4:44), "the carpenter" (Mark 6:3) whose hands and teachings have helped to fashion the lives of many.

He Is the Lord of the Earth

The title Lord is used numerous times in the scriptures to refer to him. Often this term is used in connection with other titles. Thus he is the
"Lord Jesus" (Luke 24:3);
"Lord Jesus Christ" (Mosiah 3:12);
"Lord God" (2 Nephi 1:5);
"Lord God Almighty" (2 Nephi 9:46);
"Lord God Omnipotent" (Mosiah 3:21); and
"Lord Jehovah" (2 Nephi 22:2).
He is also the
"Lord Our Righteousness" (Jeremiah 23:6);
"Lord of glory" (James 2:1);
"Lord from heaven" (1 Corinthians 15:47);
"Lord . . . of the sabbath" (Mark 2:28); and
"Lord of all" (Acts 10:36).

He Is the Prince of Peace, a Teacher of Righteousness

He is "our peace" (Ephesians 2:14), the "Founder" (Mosiah 15:18) and the "Prince of Peace" (Isaiah 9:6). Only through following his example and living his gospel can we find the "peace of God, which passeth all understanding" (Philippians 4:7).

He is the "Good Master" who is the giver of eternal life (Mark 10:17), the sower of the good seed (see Matthew 13:3–9) who allows the wheat and the tares to grow together.

He is the "teacher come from God" (John 3:2) who taught as he had been taught by his Father (see John 8:28). He has "given us an understanding, that we may know him that is true" (1 John 5:20).

He Is the Healing Physician

He is the great "physician" (Matthew 9:12) who came to heal those who were spiritually and physically sick. He cured "all manner of sickness and . . . disease" (Matthew 4:23), and "cast out many devils" (Mark 1:34).

He opened the eyes of him who had been blind from birth (see John 9:1–7) and "unstopped the ears of the deaf" (3 Nephi 26:15). At his command, lepers were cleansed (see Matthew 8:2–4), the lame took up their beds and walked (see John 5:1–9), and even the dead were brought back to life again (see Matthew 9:24–26; John 11:8–53).

To those burdened with anxiety and sin, he counseled: "Be born again" (John 3:3), "Keep the commandments" (Matthew 19:17), "Go, and sin no more" (John 8:11).

He is the "author of eternal salvation" (Hebrews 5:9) and "captain of [man's] salvation" (Hebrews 2:10). He is "able to save them to the uttermost" (Hebrews 7:25).

He Is the God of Miracles

He is the "God of miracles" (2 Nephi 27:23); the elements of the earth, which he organized, quickly and gladly obey this "God of nature" (1 Nephi 19:12).

At his word, water turned into wine (see John 2:7–9). He blessed and brake a few loaves and fishes, and thousands were fed (see Matthew 14:15–21; 15:32–38). He walked upon the waters which he had created (see Matthew 14:25–27). At his command, the winds ceased, and the waves became peaceful and still (see Luke 8:24). We exclaim with his disciples: "What manner of man is this! for . . . even the winds and water . . . obey him" (Matthew 8:27).

He Is the Good and True and Great Shepherd Who Is Known by His Sheep

He is the "good," the "great," and the "true shepherd" (John 10:11; Hebrews 13:20; Helaman 15:13) who gave his life for his sheep (see John 10:11, 15). He knows and "numbereth his sheep, and they know him" (1 Nephi 22:25).

He seeks his other sheep and desires to gather them together that they might hear his voice and follow it and become one fold with him as their one Shepherd (see John 10:14–16; Alma 5:57). He can then "feed his flock" (Isaiah 40:11) and, acting as the "door of the sheep" (John 10:7), can protect them from the ravening wolves of deceit and hypocrisy.

He Is the Lord of the Vineyard

He is the "lord of the vineyard" (Mark 12:9), the "true vine" (1 Nephi 15:15), who "saw that his fruit was good" (Jacob 5:75).

As he himself taught, "I am the true vine, and my Father is the husbandman. Every branch in me that beareth not fruit he taketh away: and every branch that beareth fruit, he purgeth it [that is, purifies it], that it may bring forth more fruit" (John 15:1–2).

Through partaking of the fruits of the gospel of the True Vine, we can enjoy the fruits of eternal life.

He Is the Bread of Life

He is the "bread of life" (John 6:35, 48–51), the "true bread from heaven," (John 6:32) and the living manna, which provides sustenance throughout eternity.

How fitting that he who was born in a city whose name means "the house of bread" [Bethlehem] was himself the true Bread of Heaven.

In answer to the observation of the people that "our fathers did eat manna in the desert; as it is written, He gave them bread from heaven to eat" (John 6:31), he taught:

"Verily, verily, I say unto you, Moses gave you not that bread from heaven; but my Father giveth you the true bread from heaven.

"For the bread of God is he which cometh down from heaven, and giveth life unto the world.

" . . . I am the bread of life: he that cometh to me shall never hunger" (John 6:32–33, 35).

He and His Gospel Provide the Living Water

He is the source of the living water, which quenches the thirst of those who seek him; whosoever partakes of his water shall not thirst again (see John 4:10–14).

His teachings to the woman of Samaria at Jacob's well are instructive:

"There cometh a woman of Samaria to draw water: Jesus saith unto her, Give me to drink. . . .

"Then saith the woman of Samaria unto him, How is it that thou, being a Jew, askest drink of me, which am a woman of Samaria? for the Jews have no dealings with the Samaritans.

"Jesus answered and said unto her, If thou knewest the gift of God, and who it is that saith to thee, Give me to drink; thou wouldest have asked of him, and he would have given thee living water.

"The woman saith unto him, Sir, thou hast nothing to draw with, and the well is deep: from whence then hast thou that living water? . . .

"Jesus answered and said unto her, Whosoever drinketh of this water shall thirst again:

"But whosoever drinketh of the water that I shall give him shall never thirst; but the water that I shall give him shall be in him a well of water springing up into everlasting life" (John 4:7, 9–11, 13–14).

HE IS THE LIGHT, LIFE, AND TRUTH OF THE WORLD

He is the "light, and the life, and the truth of the world" (Ether 4:12), the "true Light, which lighteth every man" (John 1:9), an "everlasting light" (Isaiah 60:19) "which shineth in darkness" (D&C 6:21) illuminating those who sit there, including the Gentiles (see Luke 2:32).

He is the "great light" (Isaiah 9:2) which we should all hold up (see 3 Nephi 18:24) to lighten the whole world. If we "walk in the light of the Lord" (Isaiah 2:5), he "will be a light unto [us] forever" (2 Nephi 10:14).

HE IS THE PERFECT EXEMPLAR, THE SINLESS ONE

He is the example of the perfect life, the one who knew and did no sin (see 2 Corinthians 5:21; 1 Peter 2:22) but who is able to succor them that are tempted (see Hebrews 2:18).

He learned "obedience by the things which he suffered" (Hebrews 5:8) and then counseled:

"Follow me" (Matthew 4:19);

"I am the way" (John 14:6);

"Do as I have done" (John 13:15);

"Be perfect even as I" (3 Nephi 12:48);

"That which ye have seen me do even that shall ye do" (3 Nephi 27:21);

"What manner of men ought ye to be? . . . even as I am" (3 Nephi 27:27).

Truly he has left us "an example, that [we] should follow his steps" (1 Peter 2:21).

Because of his perfect life, he is the Sinless One, "holy, harmless, undefiled" (Hebrews 7:26). The term *Holy* rightfully precedes other titles:

"Holy Child" (Moroni 8:3);

"Holy God" (2 Nephi 9:39);

"Holy Messiah" (2 Nephi 2:6);

"Holy One" (2 Nephi 2:10);

"Holy One of Israel" (1 Nephi 19:14; Isaiah 1:4);

"Holy One of Jacob" (2 Nephi 27:34);

"Holy One of God" (Mark 1:24).

HE IS THE HEAD OF HIS CHURCH, WHICH IS BUILT UPON HIS GOSPEL

He is the head and foundation of his true and living church (see Colossians 1:18; 1 Corinthians 3:11; Ephesians 5:23; D&C 1:30). His church should contain the words "The Church of Jesus Christ" if it has been established by him and is built upon his gospel (see 3 Nephi 27:8).

He is the "captain of [man's] salvation" (Hebrews 2:10).

HE IS THE PROMISED SAVIOR AND REDEEMER

In the Garden of Gethsemane, on Calvary and in the tomb, he became the Savior and "Redeemer of Israel" (1 Nephi 21:7) and of the world (see 1 Nephi 10:4–6) and of all mankind.

In Gethsemane he sweat great drops of blood in his infinite agony (see D&C 19:16–20) as he fulfilled his promise to us in the pre-earthly councils by atoning for the fall of Adam and Eve unconditionally and for our sins upon the condition of our repentance. There, he who "came into the world to save sinners" (1 Timothy 1:15) gave himself for us and our sins (see Galatians 1:4; Titus 2:14) and "obtained eternal redemption for us" (Hebrews 9:12). He sanctified "the people with his own blood" (Hebrews 13:12) and cleansed from all sin those who have fellowship with him (see 1 John 1:7).

At Calvary and in the tomb he exercised the power given him at conception by his Immortal Father, bursting the chains of physical death not only for himself but for all mankind. Indeed, "as in Adam all die, even so in Christ shall all be made alive" (1 Corinthians 15:22). "Greater love hath no man than this, that a man lay down his life for his friends" (John 15:13).

Each time we partake of the sacramental emblems, we should remember his saviorship and his redeemership: the bread in remembrance of his earthly body and resurrected flesh when he atoned for the physical death; the liquid in remembrance of the blood he shed in Gethsemane when he atoned for spiritual death.

Many scriptures pertain to his roles as Savior and Redeemer. He is the "mediator between God and men" (1 Timothy 2:5), the "mediator of a better covenant" (Hebrews 8:6), and the "mediator of the new covenant" (JST, Hebrews 9:15).

It is he who "came into the world to save sinners" (1 Timothy 1:15), to "make intercession" (Hebrews 7:25), to give himself for us "that he might redeem us from all iniquity, and purify unto himself a peculiar people, zealous of good works" (Titus 2:14).

He Is the Anointed One of the New Testament

Finally in the meridian of time the words of the prophets were fulfilled, and the Anointed One of Jewish hope and expectation called "the Messiah" (Daniel 9:25–26) in the Old Testament became the Anointed One of Christian belief and practice called "the Christ" in the New Testament (John 1:41).

His names and titles are variously combined:
"Christ Jesus" (Alma 5:44);
"Christ of God" (Luke 9:20);
"Christ the Son" (Alma 11:44);
"the Lord's Christ" (Luke 2:26).

His full name and title, "Jesus Christ," is the only name whereby salvation and exaltation come (2 Nephi 25:20).

He Is the Lamb of God

He is the "Lamb of God" (1 Nephi 10:10) "without blemish and without spot" (1 Peter 1:19) who "offered himself without spot" (Hebrews 9:14) as a sacrifice for "the sin of the world" (John 1:29) and as "an offering . . . to God for a sweet-smelling savour" (Ephesians 5:2).

He was "brought as a lamb to the slaughter" (Isaiah 53:7), and through the shedding of his blood he has provided redemption (see Ephesians 1:7) that we may be cleansed (see Mormon 9:6) and our robes become white (see Revelation 7:14).

He "hath borne our griefs, and carried our sorrows" (Isaiah 53:4). He has saved his people (see Matthew 1:21) and made "propitiation for our sins: and . . . the sins of the whole world" (1 John 2:2).

"Worthy is the Lamb that was slain" (Revelation 5:12). He hath "perfected for ever them that are sanctified" (Hebrews 10:14).

He Is the First Fruits of the Resurrection

He is the "resurrection, and the life" (John 11:25), the "forerunner" (Hebrews 6:20), the "firstborn from the dead" (Colossians 1:18), the "firstfruits of them that slept" (1 Corinthians 15:20).

He who died and tasted death for every man (see 1 Thessalonians 4:14; Hebrews 2:9) was "raised from the dead" (2 Timothy 2:8) for himself and for every man. As Paul declared, "For as in Adam all die, even so in Christ shall all be made alive" (1 Corinthians 15:22).

Although he "made his grave with the wicked, and with the rich in his death" (Isaiah 53:9), now "he is risen" (Matthew 28:6) with a resurrected body of "flesh and bones" (Luke 24:39), breaking the "bands of this temporal death" (Alma 11:42; see also 22:14), and thus "swallow[ing] up death in victory" (Isaiah 25:8) and "gain[ing] the victory over the grave" (Mormon 7:5).

"Hell must deliver up its captive spirits, and the grave must deliver up its captive bodies, and the bodies and the spirits of men will be restored one to the other; and it is by the power of the resurrection of the Holy One of Israel" (2 Nephi 9:12).

O grave, where is thy victory? O death, where is thy sting? (See 1 Corinthians 15:55.)

HE IS THE ONE WHO OFFERED AN INFINITE ATONEMENT

In anticipation of the false teachings of those who would attempt to limit the extent of his atonement so far as original sin is concerned, wrongly teaching that infants would need to be baptized to remove original sin, Jesus Christ reiterated and emphasized:

"Listen to the words of Christ, your Redeemer, your Lord and your God. Behold, I came into the world not to call the righteous but sinners to repentance; the whole need no physician, but they that are sick; wherefore, *little children are whole, for they are not capable of committing sin; wherefore the curse of Adam is taken from them in me,* that it hath no power over them" (Moroni 8:8; emphasis added).

Mormon, a Book of Mormon prophet, has also written concerning the infinite nature of the Atonement as it removes the responsibility of original sin from all mankind:

"Little children cannot repent; wherefore, it is awful wickedness to deny the pure mercies of God unto them, for they are all alive in him because of his mercy.

"And *he that saith that little children need baptism denieth the mercies of Christ, and setteth at nought the atonement of him and the power of his redemption.*

"... I speak it boldly; God hath commanded me" (Moroni 8:19–21; emphasis added).

Amulek, a Book of Mormon prophet, testified concerning the infinite atonement of Jesus Christ:

"For it is expedient that there should be a great and last sacrifice; ... an infinite and eternal sacrifice.... There can be nothing which is short of an infinite atonement which will suffice for the sins of the world.... And behold, this is the whole meaning of the law [of Moses], every whit pointing to that great and last sacrifice; and that great and last sacrifice will be *the Son of God,* yea, infinite and eternal" (Alma 34:10, 12, 14; emphasis added).

HE IS THE HEAD OF HIS CHURCH AND KINGDOM IN THE LATTER DAYS

In our own day and time, our Heavenly Father and his Divine Son continue their work to bring to pass the eternal life of all mankind. In the spring of 1820 the iron ceiling of heaven shattered, and the long, dark night of apostasy ceased. The personal appearance of both our Heavenly Father and his Son Jesus Christ to the boy prophet Joseph Smith signaled the dawn of the dispensation of the fulness of times, prophesied by the prophets of the Old Testament and by the apostles of the New Testament (see Acts 3:21; Ephesians 1:10).

Again came the reassuring and reconfirming approbation of our Heavenly Father: "This is My Beloved Son. Hear Him!" (Joseph Smith—History 1:17).

Again the voice of the Savior was heard on the earth, this time rebuking the hypocrisy of those who drew near unto him with their lips and honored him with their mouths, but whose hearts were far removed from him because they taught "for doctrines the commandments of men" (Joseph Smith—History 1:19).

An angelic messenger was sent to reveal an additional scripture with the announced purpose of convincing "Jew and Gentile that JESUS is the CHRIST, the ETERNAL GOD, manifesting himself unto all nations" (Title Page of the Book of Mormon).

Additional angelic messengers including John the Baptist, Peter, James, and John the Beloved, were sent to restore, by the laying on of hands, lost priesthood authority and keys.

On April 6, 1830, Jesus Christ re-established his church and kingdom upon the earth (see D&C 21:3). Following an eternal principle that if he establishes a church and if it is founded on his gospel, then it should be called by his name, he thus designated the title of his church for this new dispensation as "The Church of Jesus Christ of Latter-day Saints" (D&C 115:3–4), indicating that it is "the only true and living church upon the face of the whole earth" (D&C 1:30).

Since that historic day, Jesus Christ, the source of all truth, has continued to reveal to his living modern prophets those principles and ordinances that are necessary to the restitution or restoration of all things prophesied by Peter, Paul, and other ancient prophets and apostles (see Acts 3:21; Ephesians 1:10).

The Savior has already appeared several times in this dispensation, including his appearance in the spring of 1820 (see Joseph Smith—History 1:17). On April 3, 1836, his manifestation in the Kirtland Temple was followed by the appearances of several resurrected Old Testament prophets:

Moses, the great lawgiver of Israel, who restored "the keys of the gathering of Israel from the four parts of the earth";

Elias, who "committed the dispensation of the gospel of Abraham, saying that in us and our seed all generations after us should be blessed"; and

Elijah, who announced that he came in fulfillment of the prophecy of Malachi that he [Elijah] should return to the earth "before the great and dreadful day of the Lord . . . to turn the hearts of the fathers to the children, and the children to the fathers" (see D&C 110:11–15).

At that occasion, the Savior announced that the fame of his house (the Kirtland Temple) would spread to foreign lands and that this would be the beginning of "the blessing which shall be poured out upon the heads of my people" (D&C 110:10).

The Savior has promised that he will continue to appear to his chosen leaders and people.

He will appear to the earthly leaders of his kingdom at Adam-Ondi-Ahman, where Adam, the Ancient of Days, will also be in attendance (see Daniel 7:9–14; D&C 107:53; 116:1).

He will appear to the Jewish people on the Mount of Olives as prophesied in the book of Zechariah in the Old Testament (14:4), the book of Acts in the New Testament (1:11), and in his modern scripture, the Doctrine and Covenants (D&C 45:48–53). At that time the words of the two witnesses who appeared in white on the occasion of his ascension into heaven will be fulfilled, for "this same Jesus, which is taken up . . . into heaven, shall so come in like manner" again to the earth (Acts 1:11).

Also at that time the words of the ancient prophet Isaiah shall be fulfilled, for a nation of converted believers shall "be born at once" (Isaiah 66:8). The Jews shall finally recognize and receive their long-awaited Messiah. As he himself has stated:

"And then shall the Jews look upon me and say: What are these wounds in thine hands and in thy feet?

"Then shall they know that I am the *Lord;* for I will say unto them: These wounds are the wounds with which I was wounded in the house of my friends. I am he who was lifted up. I am *Jesus* that was crucified. I am the *Son of God.*

"And then shall they weep because of their iniquities; then shall they lament because they persecuted *their king*" (D&C 45:51–53; emphasis added; see also Zechariah 13:6).

Then Jesus Christ, the Messiah, the King of the Jews who are converted, will lead *converted* Israel to victory over all their enemies. He is "the Deliverer" who shall "come out of Sion" (Romans 11:26), the great everlasting king of Israel and of the whole earth (see Malachi 1:14; Psalm 47:7; Jeremiah 10:10).

The Savior will also appear at the time of his second coming to fulfill the prophecies of his ancient prophets and apostles.

He Is King of Kings

He is the "King of kings" (1 Timothy 6:15; Revelation 17:14) who will return to the earth in the last days, "crowned with glory and honour" (Hebrews 2:9), cleansing the earth from all iniquity.

He shall claim his right to reign (see D&C 58:22), both politically and religiously, shall establish fully his kingdom of peace and righteousness, and shall "reign personally upon the earth" for a thousand years (Article of Faith 10). His dominion shall be everlasting, and "his kingdom . . . shall not be destroyed" (Daniel 7:14).

He is the "King of Zion" (Moses 7:53) and of his saints; his ways are "just and true" (Revelation 15:3).

He is the "heavenly King" whom we should all thank (Mosiah 2:19), before whom "every knee should bow . . . and . . . every tongue should confess" (Philippians 2:10–11).

"Let the dead speak forth anthems of eternal praise to the King Immanuel" (D&C 128:22).

"Let the mountains shout for joy, and all ye valleys cry aloud; and all ye seas and dry lands tell the wonders of your Eternal King!" (D&C 128:23). "Behold [his] glory" (Alma 5:50).

From Zion, the New Jerusalem on the American continent, the "King of glory" (Psalm 24:10) shall send "forth his law" (Isaiah 2:3; see also Articles of Faith 1:10).

He Is Lord of Lords

He is the "Lord of lords" (1 Timothy 6:15; Revelation 17:14).

He is also the merciful and faithful Apostle and High Priest forever after the order of Melchizedek (see Hebrews 2:17; 3:1; 5:6; Psalm 110:4) who presides over his church.

His coming in power and great glory shall fulfill the prayer "Thy kingdom come. Thy will be done in earth, as it is in heaven" (Matthew 6:10).

From old Jerusalem, which shall become a holy city at his presence, he shall send forth his word to all the faithful Saints (see Isaiah 2:3). May we be among that blessed number!

He Is the Righteous Judge of the Whole Earth

He will exercise his right as the righteous judge of the whole earth (see 2 Timothy 4:8; Genesis 18:25; Moses 6:57) who "shall execute judgment" (Jeremiah 23:5). He is the "Holy One" (Acts 3:14) and the "Just One" (Acts 7:52), "ordained of God" (Acts 10:42) to be the "Eternal Judge" (Moroni 10:34). For judgment he came into the world (see John 9:39).

He is a God of justice, law, and order, a God of mercy, kindness, and love. His "judgment is true" (John 8:16) and righteous.

Into his hands all judgment has been committed (see John 5:22). By and through him all will be judged of their thoughts, words, and deeds (see Mosiah 4:30; Alma 12:14), whether done in secret (Romans 2:15) or in public.

He shall "bring every work into judgment" (Ecclesiastes 12:14); and all, both the "righteous and the wicked" (Ecclesiastes 3:17), will stand "before the judgment-seat" (2 Nephi 9:15) to meet him "face to face" (2 Nephi 33:11).

He is the "Judge of quick and dead" (Acts 10:42), the "keeper of the gate" who "employeth no servant there" (2 Nephi 9:41).

He has the "keys of hell and of death" (Revelation 1:18) and points out the strait and narrow path leading to eternal life (see Matthew 7:14) which is the "greatest of all the gifts of God" (D&C 14:7).

Only through accepting his holy name and obeying the principles of his saving gospel can we regain the presence of his and our Heavenly Father. Truly his name is the only name under heaven whereby salvation and exaltation come (2 Nephi 25:20).

He Is the Father, the Very Eternal Father of Heaven and of Earth

A few of the meanings of his dual titles, Father and Son, become evident with a careful reading of the scriptures.

He is rightfully referred to as the "Father" (Jacob 7:22) because he *is* the Father by divine investiture of authority: he is the only legal heir of our Heavenly Father upon the earth; he represents, speaks for, and acts for and in behalf of his and our Heavenly Father.

He is the "Father of heaven" (1 Nephi 22:9) and "of earth" (Helaman 14:12) because he created or organized this earth and its heavens (see 3 Nephi 9:15).

He is the Father of those who accept his gospel and become "his sons, and his daughters" spiritually (Mosiah 5:7) because it is through his atonement that the gospel was made efficacious upon the earth.

He is the Father of our resurrected bodies (see John 11:25) because it was through the gift of his life that the immortality of all mankind has been assured.

The Father "gave [him] of his fulness" (D&C 93:4), and he has "received all power, both in heaven and on earth" (D&C 93:17).

He Is the Divine and Eternal Son of His Father

He is rightfully referred to as the Son in many senses. He is the Son because he is the Firstborn Son of God in the spirit. He is also the Son because he is the Only Begotten Son of God in the flesh. *These two sacred titles belong uniquely and forever to him.*

He is also the Son because he seeks and does the will of his Father, submitting his desires to that of his Divine Parent. He said, "The Father hath sent me" (John 5:36) and "My doctrine is not mine, but his that sent me" (John 7:16).

His sonship titles include:

"Son of Righteousness" (Ether 9:22);
"Son of the living God" (Matthew 16:16);
"Son of the most high God" (Mark 5:7);
"Son of the everlasting God" (1 Nephi 11:32).

As a Son he is one with the Father (see John 10:30). He sits on the right hand of God (see Hebrews 1:3) and is "heir of all things" (Hebrews 1:2). As we are also children of God in the spirit, we are also heirs of God and joint-heirs with Christ, if only we are faithful so we might be glorified together with him (see Romans 8:14–17).

Because he is from eternity to eternity—that is, from pre-earthly spirit world to postmortal spirit world and the resurrection—his titles are frequently prefaced by such words as *eternal, everlasting* and *endless:*

"Eternal Father" (Mosiah 15:4);
"Eternal God" (1 Nephi 12:18);
"Eternal Head" (Helaman 13:38);
"Eternal Judge" (Moroni 10:34);
"Everlasting Father" (Isaiah 9:6);
"Everlasting God" (1 Nephi 15:15);
"Endless" (D&C 19:4).

He Is the Son of Man

His sacred title "Son of Man" means Son of Man of Holiness—"Man of Holiness" being a title that pertains to our Heavenly Father (Moses 6:57). This title is used repeatedly in testimony of his divine sonship (see Matthew 12:8, 32; 16:13, 27; John 3:13–14).

He Is Distinct in Spirit Body and Physical Body but One in Testimony with the Other Members of the Godhead

Throughout the scriptures, Jesus Christ and his prophets and apostles emphasize the Savior's oneness with our Father in Heaven and the Holy Ghost, the other members of the Godhead.

"And no man hath seen God at any time, except he hath borne record of the Son; for except it is through him no man can be saved" (JST, John 1:19).

"Behold, I am Jesus Christ the Son of God. I created the heavens and the earth, and all things that in them are. I was with the Father from the beginning. I am in the Father, and the Father in me; and in me hath the Father glorified his name" (3 Nephi 9:15).

"For behold, verily I say unto you, that the Father, and the Son, and the Holy Ghost are one; and I am in the Father, and the Father in me, and the Father and I are one. . . . And this is my doctrine, and it is the doctrine which the Father hath given unto me; and I bear record of the Father, and the Father beareth record of me, and the Holy Ghost beareth record of the Father and me. . . . And thus will the Father bear record of me, and the Holy Ghost will bear record unto [man] of the Father and me; for the Father, and I, and the Holy Ghost are one" (3 Nephi 11:27, 32, 36).

"And the Father and I are one. I am in the Father and the Father in me; and inasmuch as ye have received me, ye are in me and I in you" (D&C 50:43).

He Is One Who Testifies of Himself and Receives the Testimonies of Others

He refers to himself by different titles when he speaks with his prophet Isaiah:
"Thus saith the Lord, your redeemer, the Holy One of Israel . . . I am the Lord, your Holy One, the creator of Israel, your King" (Isaiah 43:14–15).

"Thus saith the Lord the King of Israel, and his redeemer the Lord of hosts; I am the first, and I am the last; and beside me there is no God" (Isaiah 44:6).

"All flesh shall know that I the Lord am thy Saviour and thy Redeemer, the mighty One of Jacob" (Isaiah 49:26).

We reaffirm the testimonies of those who recognized his divinity on the earth:

The fisherman Andrew said to his brother Peter, "We have found the Messias, which is, being interpreted, the Christ" (John 1:41).

Peter testified, "Thou art the Christ, the Son of the living God" (Matthew 16:16); and "We believe and are sure that thou art that Christ, the Son of the living God" (John 6:69).

John the Baptist declared, "And I saw, and bare record that this is the Son of God" (John 1:34; see also D&C 93:11–17).

Nathaniel, speaking to Jesus, said, "Rabbi, thou art the Son of God; thou art the King of Israel" (John 1:49).

The Samaritans who testified of him at Jacob's well said, "We . . . know that this is indeed the Christ, the Saviour of the world" (John 4:42).

We even recognize the insight of the evil spirits who were convinced of his divinity although not converted to his teachings:

One evil spirit said in the synagogue at Capernaum, "I know thee who thou art; the Holy One of God" (Luke 4:34).

Another called out of the tomb, "Jesus, thou Son of the most high God" (Mark 5:7).

And still another evil spirit who, at Jesus' bidding, came out of the sick, said, "Thou art Christ the Son of God" (Luke 4:41).

He Is the Beloved Son of God Forever

Our Father in Heaven has used the title Beloved Son on several occasions to designate the relationship between him and his divine Son. At the time of the baptism of Jesus Christ, our Heavenly Father spoke from the heavens, saying, "This is my beloved Son, in whom I am well pleased. Hear ye him" (JST, Matthew 3:46; see also Matthew 3:17).

On the Mount of Transfiguration, when Peter, James, and John were with the Savior, a voice came out of the cloud that overshadowed them, saying, "This is my beloved Son, in whom I am well pleased; hear ye him" (Matthew 17:5; see also Luke 9:35).

And in the spring of 1820, on the American continent, our Heavenly Father inaugurated the great dispensation of the fulness of times as he appeared with his Son Jesus Christ to the boy prophet Joseph Smith and announced, pointing to the Savior, "This is My Beloved Son. Hear Him!" (Joseph Smith—History 1:17).

That we might hear him, believe him, and follow him should be the fervent prayer of all those who have taken his name upon us.

Of all these things I bear witness concerning Jesus Christ, the Beloved Son of God.

Notes

Initially prepared as an Easter message in the *Church News,* 29 March 1980, 8–10, 13.

1. See Joseph Smith, *Discourses of the Prophet Joseph Smith,* ed. Alma P. Burton (Salt Lake City: Deseret Book Co., 1977), 126.
2. See Brigham Young, as quoted in Daniel H. Ludlow, ed., *Latter-day Prophets Speak* (Salt Lake City: Bookcraft, 1988), 183.

Chapter 14

THE GREATEST WEEK IN HISTORY

When the history of this world is finally written up with an eternal perspective, many events will vie as being worthy to be included. However, because of their significance to every person who has ever lived on this earth or who will ever live on it, the events of the last week of the Savior's life—from the Sunday morning of his triumphal entry into the city of Jerusalem to the Sunday morning of the resurrection—will undoubtedly be acclaimed as the greatest week in history. Without the events of that week, particularly those that took place in the Garden of Gethsemane and at the time of the resurrection, everything else is virtually meaningless.

Obviously an article such as this could barely list, let alone discuss, all the week's events that are recorded in the scriptures. Thus, the article will discuss in some detail only one or two events from each day, and it will mention only briefly some of the others.

THE FIRST DAY (SUNDAY)

Sunday has been the first day of the week since the time of creation. On this particular Sunday, the first day of the greatest week in history, the Savior left the small village of Bethany, where he had spent the Sabbath with his friends Mary, Martha, and Lazarus, and ascended the slopes leading toward Jerusalem, less than three miles away.

Near the village of Bethphage, he dispatched some of his disciples to obtain a small donkey for him so he could enter Jerusalem seated on the donkey; this act would not only fulfill the prophecies but would also indicate that he came in peace.

Matthew records that "a very great multitude" had come out to greet the

Master, spreading their garments and the branches of trees before him and crying, "Hosanna to the Son of David: Blessed is he that cometh in the name of the Lord; Hosanna in the highest" (Matthew 21:8–9).

All of these acts were symbols of respect, and the use of the title "Son of David" indicated that the multitude accepted the Savior as the long-awaited Messiah, for this was the sacred title reserved for the Messiah.

And why shouldn't the common believing people be ready to accept Jesus Christ as the Messiah? Did he not fulfill the words of their prophets? Was he not a descendant of Judah through the loins of David, just as their prophets had said? Had he not been born of a virgin named Mary in the city of Bethlehem?

Had he not come forth out of Egypt, been reared in Nazareth, proven his mastery over the elements of the earth and the human body by changing the water to wine, by stilling the wind, by calming the waves, by causing the lame to walk, the blind to see, and the deaf to hear, and by bringing the very dead back to life again—all as part of the "mighty miracles" the prophets had said he would perform? And here he was, seated on the foal of an ass, entering into the holy city of Jerusalem just as their prophet Zechariah had foretold.

No wonder the common people followed him in great multitudes, greeting him as the Messiah, the "Son of David." Evidently many of the people expected him to now go into the city and fulfill some of the other prophecies stated about him, including his taking possession of the armies of Israel and leading them to victory over their enemies and then establishing a reign of peace and justice and righteousness upon the earth. He had fulfilled the words of the prophets with his past deeds; surely he would now fulfill the remainder of their words.

As history and the prophets have indicated, the tragic mistake made by the believing Jews at that time was that they expected the Savior to do at his first coming some of the things that he was to do at his second coming. Jacob, the Book of Mormon prophet, had stated hundreds of years before the birth of the Savior that the Jews would deny the Messiah when he came, because they were "looking beyond the mark" (Jacob 4:14).

It was not until later in the week, after the Savior had made such statements as "Render . . . unto Caesar the things which are Caesar's" (Matthew 22:21) and "My kingdom is not of this world" (John 18:36) that the people were to change their cries from "Hosanna to the Son of David" to "Crucify him!" It was not until later in the week that the believers among the common people felt he had betrayed them; therefore they agreed to betray him. On that first Palm Sunday, the cries were still "Hosanna to the Son of David."

These cries were also heard across the valley from the Mount of Olives on the temple mount, where the Pharisees and some of the jealous religious and secular leaders were assembled. Their consternation at this adulation being given the Savior was so great that they exclaimed, "The world is gone after him" (John 12:19).

When the Savior came nearer to Jerusalem, he wept over the city as he contemplated the future destruction that would come upon its inhabitants. His soul continued to be troubled after he had entered Jerusalem; there he prayed, "Father, save me from this hour: but for this cause came I unto this hour." A voice answered him from heaven, causing some of the people to exclaim that it thundered, while others replied, "An angel spake to him" (John 12:27, 29).

Then the Savior gave his discourse on the children of light, reminding the people that the light would be with them only "yet a little while" and admonishing them: "While ye have light, believe in the light, that ye may be the children of light" (John 12:35–36). And when "the eventide was come, he went out unto Bethany with the twelve" (Mark 11:11).

The Second Day (Monday)

Early on the second day, Monday, the Savior returned again to Jerusalem from Bethany. Matthew records the trip as follows:

"Now in the morning as he returned into the city, he hungered. And when he saw a fig tree in the way, he came to it, and found nothing thereon, but leaves only, and said unto it, Let no fruit grow on thee henceforward, for ever. And presently the fig tree withered away. And when the disciples saw it, they marvelled, saying, How soon is the fig tree withered away!" (Matthew 21:18–20).

This incident of the blighting of the fig tree has been difficult for many people to understand because it is so different from the other miracles of the Savior. Before, he had brought relief to the suffering and had largely used his powers for beneficial purposes and blessings; indeed, he had brought the dead back to life again. But here, he appears to have rendered a final judgment and caused death. However, the disciples undoubtedly learned a great lesson from this incident. Among other things, they surely recognized now that the Savior had power to cause death as well as to give life; thus, they realized it would be possible for him to voluntarily give his life as he had said. They had cause to remember this lesson before the week was out.

Another possible lesson learned by the disciples from this incident is that neither they nor anyone else should pretend to be something they really are not. The leafy fig tree pretended to have fruit, for the leaf and the fruit of the fig normally develop together. However, this leafy fig tree was deceptively barren.

Elder James E. Talmage has suggested that the tree was blighted not because it was fruitless (so were the other fig trees at this time of the year, late March or early April), but because it was deceptively barren and represented "a type of human hypocrisy."[1]

Another event that possibly happened on this second day of the week was the cleansing of the temple. Some students of the Gospels have placed this incident on Sunday, the first day, because of the context of Matthew 21:12 and Luke 19:45. However, others have interpreted Mark 11:11, 15 as meaning that the event took place on Monday.

Regardless of the exact day, it was three years to the week from the time the Savior had driven the money changers from the temple on an earlier date. On that occasion, he had accused them of making his *"Father's house* an house of merchandise" (John 2:16; emphasis added). On this occasion, now that he had openly avowed himself to be the Messiah, the Savior referred to the temple as "my house" when he quoted the scripture: "My house shall be called the house of prayer; but ye have made it a den of thieves" (Matthew 21:13). Before the week was over, the Savior would say to the rebellious residents of Jerusalem concerning the temple, "Behold, *your house* is left unto you desolate" (Matthew 23:38; emphasis added). The shift in the words showing possession is both interesting and significant.

The apostate religious leaders were outraged at this treatment by the Savior, and "the chief priests and the scribes and the chief of the people sought to destroy him." However, the common people "were very attentive to hear him" (Luke 19:47–48).

The chief priests and the scribes were further displeased when they saw the Savior healing the blind and the lame who came to him in the temple; and they were incensed when they heard the children crying in the temple, "Hosanna to the Son of David."

Matthew records the end of the incident as follows: And the chief priests and the scribes "said unto him, Hearest thou what these say? And Jesus saith unto them, Yea; have ye never read, Out of the mouth of babes and sucklings thou hast perfected praise? And he left them, and went out of the city into Bethany; and he lodged there" (Matthew 21:6–17).

The Third and Fourth Days
(Tuesday and Wednesday)

The events of Tuesday and Wednesday will be considered together, not only because many of the events are related but also because it is not always evident from the scriptures exactly which events happened on which days.

The record is clear, however, that after the events of Sunday and Monday, when the common people had demonstrated their love and interest in the Messiah, both the secular and religious leaders felt threatened by his possible leadership and determined they would challenge him and hopefully discredit him in the eyes of the people. Thus, they had spent their time devising barbed questions with which they hoped to discredit him.

When the Savior arrived at the temple mount, the first group to come forth with their question was a delegation representing the hierarchy of the temple. They remembered only too vividly how he had cast out the moneychangers and had accused them of making "his" house a den of thieves. Therefore, they accosted him with their carefully prepared question: "By what authority doest thou these things? and who gave thee this authority?" (Matthew 21:23).

The Savior countered with a question of his own: "I also will ask you one thing, which if ye tell me, I in like wise will tell you by what authority I do these things. The baptism of John, whence was it? from heaven, or of men?" (Matthew 21:24–25).

It is of interest to note that the members of the delegation did not consider answering him with what they really believed; rather, they considered their answer in light of how the people might respond, for "they reasoned with themselves, saying, If we shall say, From heaven; he will say unto us, Why did ye not then believe him? But if we shall say, Of men; we fear the people; for all hold John as a prophet. And they answered Jesus, and said, We cannot tell. And he said unto them, Neither tell I you by what authority I do these things" (Matthew 21:25–27).

The Savior then turned questioner, and with the challenging introduction of "What think ye," he gave his last three parables to a public audience: the parable of the Two Sons, the parable of the Wicked Husbandmen, and the parable of the Royal Marriage Feast (see Matthew 21:28–46; 22:1–14).

The next group to attempt to ridicule the Master were the Herodians, those who supported the rulership of Herod and the Roman leaders and who sought to bring down any possible new religious leadership. Their barbed question was, "What thinkest thou? Is it lawful to give tribute unto Caesar, or not?

"But Jesus perceived their wickedness, and said, Why tempt ye me, ye hypocrites? Shew me the tribute money. And they brought unto him a penny. And he saith unto them, Whose is this image and superscription?

"They say unto him, Caesar's. Then saith he unto them, Render therefore unto Caesar the things which are Caesar's; and unto God the things that are God's" (Matthew 22:17–21).

The Sadducees were the next group to attempt to trick the Savior; they were of that faction of Judaism who were the avowed opponents of the Pharisees and who disagreed with them on many religious questions, including the resurrection. On this occasion the Sadducees asked the Master a question based on the extremely unlikely situation of a woman who had been married to, and then widowed by, seven consecutive brothers. Their query was, "in the resurrection whose wife shall she be of the seven?" (Matthew 22:28).

The Savior, sensing that the real question was not whose wife she would be, but whether or not there was indeed a resurrection, answered their direct question but briefly, pointing out that eternal marriage relationships were determined by the power of the priesthood here upon this earth; thus, "they neither marry, nor are given in marriage" in the resurrection.

Then the Master dealt with the real substance of the question: "But as touching the resurrection of the dead, have ye not read that which was spoken unto you by God, saying, I am the God of Abraham, and the God of Isaac, and the God of Jacob? God is not the God of the dead, but of the living" (Matthew 22:30–32).

The honest in heart who were present quickly recognized the unassailable logic used by the Savior: Abraham, Isaac, and Jacob had all died many years before— yet God still said he was their God and that he was God only of the living. Therefore, Abraham, Isaac, and Jacob must still be living! Certain of the scribes who were present exclaimed, "Master, thou hast well said." The logic silenced the Sadducees, "and after that they durst not ask him any question at all" (Luke 20:39–40).

The final group, the Pharisees, were ready with their question, however, which was put to the Master by one of their number, a lawyer: "Master, which is the great commandment in the law?" (Matthew 22:36), or, as Mark phrased it, "Which is the first commandment of all?" (Mark 12:28).

The Savior's answer, however, was definite and unequivocal. He replied in almost the same words as Moses used with the children of Israel, which words

Moses had commanded the Israelites to teach diligently to their children: "Thou shalt love the Lord thy God with all thy heart, and with all thy soul, and with all thy mind. This is the first and great commandment. And the second is like unto it, Thou shalt love thy neighbour as thyself" (Matthew 22:37–39).

After answering the Pharisees, the Savior turned questioner and asked them: "What think ye of Christ? whose son is he?" Their prompt reply was, "The Son of David.

"He saith unto them, How then doth David in spirit call him Lord. . . . If David then call him Lord, how is he his son?

"And no man was able to answer him a word, neither durst any man from that day forth ask him any more questions" (Matthew 22:42–46).

The Savior then turned to the disciples and taught them, in the hearing of the multitude, of the false teachings and practices of the scribes and the Pharisees. He frequently used the word *hypocrite* in referring to the self-assumed teachers, and he concluded his denunciation by referring to them as "serpents" and a "generation of vipers" (Matthew 23:33).

The Savior then lamented over Jerusalem, reminding the people of the many prophets who had been sent to them, and yet how frequently the people had rejected these prophets. He also pronounced the destruction that was yet to come upon the people and upon the city, stating concerning the temple, "there shall not be left here one stone upon another" (Matthew 24:2).

Next, the Savior went to the Mount of Olives, where the disciples met with him privately and asked him to explain his prophecies concerning the destruction of Jerusalem and the subsequent events that were to follow until the end of the world. The teachings of the Savior on this subject occupy three chapters in the Gospels (Matthew 24, Mark 13, and Luke 21).

However, to make the teachings even more clear and plain, the Savior revealed them to the Prophet Joseph Smith in this dispensation, and they are printed in Joseph Smith–Matthew, chapter 1, in the Pearl of Great Price. The Savior specifically stated, "I speak these things unto you for the elect's sake" (verse 23). Thus, every person who has elected and determined to follow the Savior and his teachings should carefully review these inspired teachings.

After answering the specific points raised by his disciples, the Savior concluded his teachings to them that day by giving the last three parables that are recorded in the New Testament: the parable of the Ten Virgins, the parable of the Entrusted Talents, and the parable of the Inevitable Judgment.

The Savior then returned to Bethany to spend the night and to prepare for the trying ordeal that was ahead.

THE FIFTH AND SIXTH DAYS (THURSDAY AND FRIDAY)

The scriptures give very few details of the events during the early part of Thursday, the fifth day. The indications are that sometime during the day Judas Iscariot had plotted with the "chief priests and the Pharisees" to betray the Christ and deliver him into their hands. Also, the Savior had given instructions to his disciples as to where the feast of the Passover was to be observed by them that evening.

Several significant events took place at the time of the Passover meal, which was held in the "guestchamber . . . a large upper room" of one of the "goodmen" in the city of Jerusalem (Mark 14:14–15). Here it was revealed that Judas Iscariot should be the one who was to betray the Savior. Here the sacrament of the Lord's Supper was instituted. Here the Savior washed the feet of the disciples and asked them to continue to perform this ordinance.

After Judas left the gathering, the Savior gave a new commandment to the remaining disciples in these words: "That ye love one another; as I have loved you, that ye also love one another" (John 13:34). It was also on this occasion that he counseled Peter, "When thou art converted, strengthen thy brethren" (Luke 22:32).

The Savior reminded his disciples that he was soon to leave them, yet he would not leave them comfortless but would send them the "other Comforter," the Holy Ghost. He explained that the Holy Ghost shall "bring all things to your remembrance, whatsoever I have said unto you" (John 14:26).

Then the Savior uttered the superb allegory of the vine and the branches, wherein he said, "I am the true vine, and my Father is the husbandman. . . . I am the vine, ye are the branches: He that abideth in me, and I in him, the same bringeth forth much fruit" (John 15:1, 5).

This was followed by the "high priestly" prayer of the Savior in which he said: "Father, the hour is come; glorify thy Son, that thy Son also may glorify thee: as thou hast given him power over all flesh, that he should give eternal life to as many as thou hast given him. And this is life eternal, that they might know thee the only true God, and Jesus Christ, whom thou hast sent" (John 17:1–3).

The Savior's statement "the hour is come" was soon followed by his leaving the upper room and proceeding to the Mount of Olives and to the Garden of Gethsemane, where occurred one of the most important and transcendent events in the history of the world. It was here that he atoned for the original transgressions of Adam and Eve, and it was here that he took upon himself the sins of all mankind upon the condition of repentance of their sins.

The events in the Garden of Gethsemane and what happened in the next three days were so important that the Savior exclaimed, "for this cause came I unto this hour" (John 12:27).

Upon leaving the Garden of Gethsemane, the Savior met Judas and "the chief priests, and captains of the temple, and the elders" who had come to take him to trial (Luke 22:52).

The events of the remainder of that night and the chief events of the next day (Friday) are listed by the writers of the four Gospels. These events include the appearance and illegal trial before the high priest (Caiaphas) and the Sanhedrin, where he was first charged with sedition (disturbing the peace) but was then accused of blasphemy (falsely assuming the power of God), which was the most serious charge in Jewish law.

When he was asked directly, "Tell us whether thou be the Christ, the Son of God" (Matthew 26:63), his answer was clear and definite, "I am" (Mark 14:62). The apostate high priest cried out, "He hath spoken blasphemy; what further need have we of witnesses? . . . He is guilty of death" (Matthew 26:65–66).

Thus one of the greatest ironies in history occurred, for Jesus, the divine Son of God, the one person who could not have been guilty of falsely assuming the power of God, was found guilty of blasphemy! Also, the only person since the fall of Adam who had power over physical death was condemned to die! However, the power to pronounce and carry out capital punishment independently had been taken away from the Jewish council by Roman decree; thus the leaders of the Sanhedrin had him delivered to Pilate so an official decree of death could be issued.

The Savior was thus brought to trial before Pontius Pilate, the procurator of Judea who lived in Caesarea but who happened to be in Jerusalem for the Jewish feasts. There, Pilate came outside to hear their charges. The charge was now changed to that of high treason, the most serious offense in the Roman law. To back their charge of treason against the Savior, the members of the Sanhedrin falsely claimed the Savior had forbidden the people to give tribute to Caesar (his actual words were, "Render unto Caesar the things which are Caesar's"—Matthew 22:21), and they also accused him of making himself a king (Luke 23:2). When Pilate asked the Savior directly, "Art thou the king of the Jews?" (Luke 23:3), the Savior answered, "My kingdom is not of this world" (John 18:36).

Thus finding no fault in him, Pilate was about to let the Savior go free when one of the priests claimed that Jesus had been teaching treason "beginning from Galilee to this place" (Luke 23:5).

As soon as Pilate was reminded that Jesus was a Galilean, he sent the Savior to be tried by Herod, the vassal ruler of the province of Galilee, who was also in Jerusalem for the Passover season. However, when the Savior refused to answer any of the questions put to him by Herod, he was taken again before Pilate by the members of the Sanhedrin, who were determined to have a death sentence pronounced against him.

Pilate could still find no fault in the Savior and so declared, saying, "I will . . . chastise him, and release him" (Luke 23:16). Pilate also reminded the Jews that it was the custom during the Passover season to release one of the prisoners from prison; he told them that he was willing to invoke this precedence for the release of Jesus. However, the people cried, "Release . . . Barabbas" (Luke 23:18); thus, a murderer and one guilty of sedition was released, while the innocent man was retained.

When Pilate finally asked the people what they wanted him to do with Jesus, their awful cry was, "Crucify him, crucify him" (Luke 23:21).

Pilate's reply was that he found no fault in the man and that he washed his hands of his blood. And then came the awful condemnatory cry, "His blood be on us, and on our children" (Matthew 27:25). Even then, Pilate was about to let the Savior go with just a scourging and a chastisement, when a person cried out the barb, "If thou let this man go, thou art not Caesar's friend; whosoever maketh himself a king speaketh against Caesar" (John 19:12). This taunt proved to be too much for Pilate, who had received what power he had from Caesar.

Thus Pilate finally agreed to the crucifixion and turned Jesus over to his soldiers to be scourged.

Then followed the torturous walk to Golgotha, where the tired physical body of the Savior was given the assistance of Simon of Cyrene in carrying the cross.

Pilate had earlier ordered that the words "JESUS OF NAZARETH THE KING OF THE JEWS" should be inscribed on the cross in Hebrew, Greek, and Latin characters. When the Jewish leaders tried to get him to change the inscription from "The King of the Jews" to "he said, I am King of the Jews," Pilate replied: "What I have written I have written" (John 19:21–22).

It was about the third hour (9:00 A.M.) of the sixth day (Friday) when the Savior was nailed to the cross. Despite the pain of the nailing, the Savior later could still look upon the Roman soldiers and say, "Father, forgive them; for they know not what they do" (Luke 23:34).

About noon a great earthquake occurred, which among other things rent the veil of the temple. The light of the sun was also obscured, and "there was a darkness over all the earth until the ninth hour" (Luke 23:44).

It was about three in the afternoon when the Savior cried out, "My God, my God, why hast thou forsaken me?" (Matthew 27:46). Then he said, "It is finished" (John 19:30), and "Father, into thy hands I commend my spirit" (Luke 23:46).

Thus, the one who had been given power over death by his Father voluntarily gave up his life so that physical death could be conquered and all of us might live eternally.

According to religious law, it was not proper to leave a body unburied on the Sabbath day. Therefore, as sundown approached, the followers of the Savior took his body from the cross and quickly and incompletely prepared it for burial. The body was then laid in the tomb offered by one of his disciples, Joseph of Arimathaea.

And thus ended Friday, the sixth day, perhaps the darkest day in the history of the world.

The Seventh Day (Saturday)

The New Testament is practically silent concerning the events of the seventh day while the body of the Savior lay in the tomb. The most extensive account in the four Gospels is the terse statement by Luke that they "rested the sabbath day according to the commandment" (Luke 23:56).

Later, however, Peter mentioned some of the happenings of that seventh day: "For Christ also hath once suffered for sins, the just for the unjust, that he might bring us to God, being put to death in the flesh, but quickened by the Spirit: by which also he went and preached unto the spirits in prison; . . . for for this cause was the gospel preached also to them that are dead, that they might be judged according to men in the flesh, but live according to God in the spirit" (1 Peter 3:18–19; 4:6).

While the Savior was still on the cross, he had hinted concerning some of his actions in the immediate future, for he had promised the repentant thief, "To day shalt thou be with me in paradise" (Luke 23:43). Earlier in his ministry the Savior had prophesied concerning his activities in the postmortal spirit world: "Verily, verily, I say unto you, The hour is coming, and now is, when the dead shall hear the voice of the Son of God: and they that hear shall live. For as the Father hath life in himself; so hath he given to the Son to have life in himself; and hath given him authority to execute judgment also, because he is the Son of man" (John 5:25–28).

The Lord revealed to Joseph F. Smith, the sixth president of the Church in this dispensation, what actually occurred on that momentous day, which from an eternal perspective may be one of the most important days of all time (D&C 138).

The Book of Mormon also tells us of some of the activities of Jesus on this seventh day when his body lay in the tomb in Jerusalem. It was on this day that the Savior spoke out of the darkness to the Nephite survivors on the American continent. He did not appear to them on that occasion, but he spoke to them and, among other things, said:

"Behold, I am Jesus Christ the Son of God. I created the heavens and the earth, and all things that in them are. I was with the Father from the beginning. I am in the Father, and the Father in me; and in me hath the Father glorified his name. I came unto my own, and my own received me not. And the scriptures concerning my coming are fulfilled. And as many as have received me, to them have I given to become the sons of God; and even so will I to as many as shall believe on my name, for behold, by me redemption cometh" (3 Nephi 9:13–17).

Among many peoples on the earth the seventh day was a day of physical darkness, but it was only the brief darkness of the night that was to precede the most glorious dawn in history.

The Eighth Day (Sunday)

Although the resurrection occurred on the eighth day, according to the actual time that had elapsed it had not yet been a full week since Jesus had left Bethany the previous Sunday to go to Jerusalem.

John records that "it was yet dark" on "the first day of the week" (John 20:1) when Mary Magdalene and "the other Mary" came to the tomb of the Savior with their sweet spices to anoint his body. However, they found the tomb empty, and an angel soon explained to them why the body of the Savior was not therein: "Fear not ye: for I know that ye seek Jesus, which was crucified. He is not here: for he is risen, as he said. Come, see the place where the Lord lay. And go quickly, and tell his disciples that he is risen from the dead" (Matthew 28:5–7).

And so the darkness and the despair of Friday were changed into the light and joy of the day when the Savior was resurrected from the dead, breaking forever the bands of physical death and guaranteeing every person life after death. What event in all history is there to compare with this?

Before the day was ended, many witnesses could testify of the literalness of the resurrection, not only because of the appearances of the resurrected Christ but also because of the appearances of other resurrected beings, for Matthew records that "many bodies of the saints which slept arose, and came out of the graves after his resurrection, and went into the holy city, and appeared unto many" (Matthew 27:52–53).

The peoples of the Book of Mormon also had these additional witnesses, for just as Samuel the Lamanite had prophesied, after the resurrection of the Savior on the eastern continent many bodies of the saints in the Americas also "did arise and appear unto many and did minister unto them" (3 Nephi 23:11).

Within the next few weeks, the resurrected Christ appeared several times, including appearances to Mary Magdalene, to the other women, to the two disciples on the way to Emmaus, to Peter, to ten of the apostles on the day of his resurrection, to the eleven apostles (including Thomas) a week after his resurrection, to seven of the disciples on the shore of the Sea of Tiberias, to the eleven apostles on a mountain in Galilee, to more than five hundred brethren at one time, and to the apostles at the time of his ascension into heaven. The Book of Mormon tells of additional appearances of the resurrected Christ, including one appearance to twenty-five hundred persons and later appearances to even larger groups.

The resurrection of Jesus Christ is one of the most carefully documented events in history, as it should rightfully be, for it was the crowning event in the most important week in the history of the world.

The apostle John listed the following reason for including in his Gospel the major events of the last week in the earthly life of the Savior: "These are written, that ye might believe that Jesus is the Christ, the Son of God; and that believing ye might have life through his name" (John 20:31).

Notes

From *Ensign,* April 1972, 34–46.

1. James E. Talmage, *Jesus the Christ* (Salt Lake City: Deseret Book, 1983), 490.

Chapter 15

THE GREATEST GIFT

A recent word-association survey, in which people were asked to name the first thing or person that came to mind when they heard the word *Christmas*, revealed that the thing mentioned most frequently was the word *gift*, and the person mentioned most frequently was Jesus Christ. Other things mentioned frequently included toys, cards, and trees; other personalities mentioned included Santa Claus. From this survey reported in the national press, it seems apparent that the giving of gifts has become a traditional feature of Christmas.

In considering the topic of this chapter, "The Greatest Gift," perhaps we can determine the real significance of Christmas by comparing the possible relationships between the thing (that is, the gift) and the person (Jesus Christ) mentioned most frequently in the word association survey mentioned above.

THE GIFT

According to *Webster's Third International Dictionary,* the word *gift* means "the act, right, or power of giving or conferring; that which is *given* or *bestowed;* anything which is voluntarily transferred by one person to another without compensation. Synonyms: donation, present, benefaction, gratuity, boon."

A gift is something *given,* something "presented as a gift or bestowed without compensation."

The dictionary defines *greatest* as the "superlative of *Great.* Much more than ordinary or average; much higher in some quality or degree; of most importance;

highest in its class; main; chief. Synonyms: excellent, immense, majestic, grand, eminent, noble, powerful."

When we combine all of these elements, we see that at least three essentials are necessary for a gift given by one person to another to be considered "the greatest gift":

1. The *giver* must have the full right, power, authority, and means to give the gift.

2. The *gift* (which can be an object, opportunity, or privilege) must be transferred voluntarily and must be of intrinsic value or worth, capable of changing the status, outlook, or position of the person to whom it is offered.

3. The *receiver* must accept or receive the gift; a gift proffered but not accepted is not a gift.

The offering and receiving of a gift are very similar to the making of a covenant: two parties are involved, and something of value or worth is promised and transferred.

Thus, the greatest gift any one could give to another would be the gift that would require the most right, power, authority, or means of the donor to give and that would be of most value and would have the greatest impact or influence on the receiver over the longest period of time possible.

Jesus Christ: "In the Beginning"

In considering the tremendous contribution of Jesus Christ to the giving of gifts, we need to start with an explanation of our relationship to him and to our Heavenly Father. Jesus said, "I came to do the will of him who sent me" (John 6:38–40), and "This is life eternal: that they might know thee, the only true God, and Jesus Christ whom thou hast sent" (John 17:3). Both of these great Beings have given us very significant gifts. In order to understand the magnitude of their gifts, we need to know our situation when the gifts were offered, our condition now as a result of their offer, and our possible potential position if we accept the gifts.

Thus, I would like to start at the very beginning of our relationship with our Heavenly Father and with Jesus Christ. However, I am not certain of the time that is implicit in the statement "In the beginning" regarding our relationship with them. We do know from the scriptures and from modern prophets, however, that immediately before the creation or organization of this earth in its present form, we lived with our Heavenly Father and his sons and daughters. Thus we all learned to call him Father and to refer to each other as brother and sister. Jesus Christ was our Elder Brother as the Firstborn Son of God in the spirit (see Colossians 1:15).

The scriptures do not state exactly what gifts our Heavenly Father had bestowed upon us to enable us to progress to that point of our existence. But our Heavenly Father certainly was at least partly responsible for the gift of our spiritual bodies in that pre-earthly existence.

We know much more from the scriptures, from the temple endowment, and from modern prophets concerning the new gifts our Heavenly Father made possible to us as his sons and daughters, including his greatest gift: eternal life—the same quality and kind of life he enjoys. No wonder the sons and daughters of God shouted for joy when that great gift was offered in the great council in heaven (see Job 38:7).

The plan of progression and gift of eternal life offered by our Father in Heaven involved many other gifts, including the opportunity of gaining a physical body, the opportunity to obey physical laws and to enjoy the blessings of such obedience, the opportunity to choose, and the privilege of agency. Such proferred opportunities and potential blessings could enable us to achieve our maximum destiny; the only major limiting factor would be ourselves.

As our Heavenly Father offered these gifts to us, I feel confident he explained carefully and in detail each gift with all of its ramifications and potential. Surely he must have explained the nature of law—that every law has opposite and equal consequence. Thus, in the mortal realm, when laws are obeyed (which constitutes righteousness), the consequence is a blessing that causes joy and happiness; when a law is disobeyed (which constitutes wickedness), the consequence is a punishment that causes misery and unhappiness.

He may have explained the necessity of placing a veil of forgetfulness over our minds so we could exercise true freedom of choice in our new physical existence. He may also have explained the possibility of spiritual death (the consequence of our sin or disobedience to law) and the inevitability of physical death (the eventual separation of our spiritual and physical bodies).

Perhaps it was at this point in the great council that our Elder Brother (whose names and titles include Jehovah and Jesus Christ) indicated his full acceptance of the plan by saying, "Father, thy will be done, and the glory be thine forever" (Moses 4:2). Jesus then offered two major gifts to his Heavenly Father and to us. He offered to help us overcome spiritual death by promising to suffer for our sins if we would stop sinning—that is, if we would repent or stop breaking the law. He also offered to conquer physical death by providing for our resurrection. Jesus would be *able* to do these things for us because (1) he would live a sinless life on the earth and thus would have power over all law, having broken no law, and (2) he would have power to live forever in his physical body and yet would have the capacity to die, as his physical body would be fathered by our Eternal Father in Heaven and yet mothered by a mortal mother. Jesus was *willing* to do these things because of his great love for us and his concern for our welfare.

At some point in the great council, some of our brothers and sisters questioned whether or not they wanted to accept the proffered plan and its associated gifts, for sometimes receiving gifts requires commitment and dedication on the part of the receiver. They evidently either lacked confidence in themselves to keep the commandments leading toward eternal life, lacked trust in the plan of our Heavenly Father, or lacked faith in the ability or willingness of Jesus Christ to atone for both spiritual and physical death and thus bring us "at one" with God again.

These doubters had a leader whose names and titles include Lucifer, Satan, and the devil. He sought to destroy the plan of progression by denying the agency of man. Thus we read in the scriptures:

"Satan rebelled against me, and sought to destroy the agency of man, which I, the Lord God, had given him. . . . And he became Satan, yea, even the devil, the father of all lies, to deceive and to blind men, and to lead them captive at his will, even as many as would not hearken unto my voice" (Moses 4:1, 3–4).

You know the essentials of the remainder of the story. A war was fought in heaven. It was not a war of bloodshed resulting in physical casualties, but a war involving ideologies and faithfulness, resulting in spiritual casualties. Each of us who have lived on the earth accepted the offered gifts and entered into covenants with our Heavenly Father and with Jesus Christ, who was our Advocate and Mediator with the Father. However, one third of the host of heaven decided not to accept the plan; they rejected the proffered gift and withdrew themselves from the plan that would enable them to progress toward eternal life. Through open rebellion against our Heavenly Father, they became sinful and were cast out of heaven and out of his presence.

Adam and Eve

The great plan started to be implemented. A physical earth was organized out of existing matter. Physical bodies were prepared to receive the spiritual bodies of Adam and Eve, and they became "living souls" with a veil of forgetfulness over their minds.

Our Heavenly Father then gave them the opportunity to choose by giving them laws, by telling them what they should do and should not do. He also explained the consequences of their choices. For example, the Father instructed Adam and Eve to "be fruitful, and multiply, and replenish the earth" and promised them that they would "have joy and rejoicing in [their] posterity" (Moses 2:27).

"But of the tree of the knowledge of good and evil, thou shalt not eat of it, nevertheless, thou mayest choose for thyself, for it is given unto thee; but, remember that I forbid it, for in the day thou eatest thereof thou shalt surely die" (Moses 3:17).

In this last verse of scripture, our Heavenly Father states a law, indicates its consequences, and reiterates the principle of agency.

Lucifer wanted desperately to introduce sin into the world. He tried to get Adam to break one of the laws, and later persuaded Eve to disobey a commandment of God by partaking of the fruit of the tree of knowledge of good and evil. When Adam also partook of this fruit, he and Eve became subject to the consequence of disobeying that law: physical death. They also suffered spiritual death because of their disobedience: they were cast out of the presence of God. Adam and Eve became subject to both physical death and spiritual death, as did their posterity.

The Birth of the Savior

Finally, much later in the earth's history, the time came for the promised earthly birth of Jesus. If Jesus had not been born as covenanted, or if he had failed to keep the promises made to us in the great pre-earthly council, we could not be delivered from the permanent effects of both physical and spiritual death. As one prophet has exclaimed:

"It is expedient that an atonement should be made; for according to the great plan of the Eternal God there must be an atonement made, or else all mankind must unavoidably perish; yea, . . . all are fallen and are lost, and must perish except it be through the atonement which it is expedient should be made" (Alma 34:9).

No wonder the birth of the promised Atoner was announced by an angel sent from the presence of God. Gabriel said to Mary:

"Fear not, Mary: for thou hast found favour with God. And, behold, thou shalt conceive in thy womb, and bring forth a son and shall call his name Jesus. He shall be great, and shall be called the Son of the Highest . . . and of his kingdom there shall be no end" (Luke 1:30–33).

No wonder even choirs of heavenly hosts burst into praise when Jesus Christ was born on the earth as promised. Luke records the announcement of this momentous event in these well-known words:

"And she brought forth her firstborn son. . . .

"And there were in the same country shepherds abiding in the field, keeping watch over their flock by night. And, lo, the angel of the Lord came upon them, and the glory of the Lord shone round about them: and they were sore afraid. And the angel said unto them, Fear not: for, behold, I bring you good tidings of great joy, which shall be to all people. For unto you is born this day in the city of David a Saviour, which is Christ the Lord. And this shall be a sign unto you; Ye shall find the babe wrapped in swaddling clothes, lying in a manger.

"And suddenly there was with the angel a multitude of heavenly hosts praising God, and saying, Glory to God in the highest, and on earth peace, good will toward men" (Luke 2:7–14).

Because Jesus Christ was the literal "son of the Highest" in the flesh, he was *able* to overcome physical death. He was *able* to overcome spiritual death by withstanding the temptations of Satan; he did not succumb to any of them. He also lived a sinless life. Thus he gained power over all law, including the power to apply the law of mercy and to satisfy the demands of the law of justice.

The critical question then became whether he was *willing* to save us from spiritual death by suffering for our sins and whether he was *willing* to save us from a permanent physical death by voluntarily allowing his mortal life to be taken and thus provide for our resurrection. His birth, which we celebrate on December 25 each year with the rest of the Christian world, would have become virtually meaningless without his atonement.

The Atonement of Jesus Christ

The "good news" or gospel of Jesus Christ is that because of his love for us, Jesus Christ did indeed atone for our sins and did indeed provide for our resurrection, becoming the Savior and Redeemer of all mankind.

Many of the covenants made with us in the pre-earthly existence were fulfilled in the Garden of Gethsemane, on the cross, and at the tomb when Jesus was resurrected. We must know for ourselves that these covenants were kept. We must have implicit faith, "nothing wavering" (James 1:6), in the reality of the atonement so we will be "firm and steadfast" (1 Nephi 2:10) in our determination to keep our part of the covenants and receive the promised gifts.

In this life we probably never will come to a full understanding of exactly how these great covenants were and will be fulfilled.

Jesus Christ has offered us a brief insight into his suffering in the Garden of Gethsemane:

"Behold, I, God, have suffered these things for all, that they might not suffer if they would repent; But if they would not repent they must suffer even as I; which suffering caused myself, even God, the greatest of all, to tremble because of pain, and to bleed at every pore, and to suffer both body and spirit—and would that I might not drink the bitter cup, and shrink—nevertheless, glory be to the Father, and I partook and finished my preparations unto the children of men" (D&C 19:16–19).

We have an illuminating statement of his experience on the cross in Matthew and Mark:

"And when the sixth hour was come, there was darkness over the whole land until the ninth hour. And at the ninth hour Jesus cried with a loud voice saying, Eloi, Eloi, lama sabachthani? which is being interpreted, My God, my God, why hast thou forsaken me?" (Mark 15:33–34; see also Matthew 27:45–46).

The combined testimonies of Luke and John continue the account to the climax of the Savior's crucifixion on the cross:

"And when Jesus had cried with a loud voice, he said, Father, into thy hands I commend my spirit" (Luke 23:46).

"Jesus . . . said, It is finished: and he bowed his head, and gave up the ghost" (John 19:30).

A few professed ministers of religion have greatly misunderstood some of these scriptures. The expression "It is finished" was not one of despair and discouragement; it was a triumphant exclamation of accomplishment: "It is finished! I have completed the work thou sent me forth to do! I have overcome the devil and the world! I have finished my preparations unto the children of men!"

No wonder the Father allowed the Son to suffer in Gethsemane despite the petition "O my Father, if it be possible, let this cup pass from me" (Matthew 26:39). How gratefully the Father must have heard the additional words: "Nevertheless not as I will, but as thou wilt" (Matthew 26:39).

The full impact and meaning of the Savior's question "My God, why hast thou forsaken me?" can be understood when we remember the covenants made in the great pre-earthly council.

The Father withdrew his Spirit from the Son at the moment of great testing on the cross so that when the victory came—as it most assuredly would come—it would be the Son's victory. In effect, it appears our Father was saying, "Greater love hath no Father for his Son than this—he wants his Son to be faithful to his covenants, and to share in the honor, power, and glory of the Father."

A Book of Mormon prophet had the opportunity to see the relationship of these events even before they occurred on the earth. When Nephi desired to know the meaning of the various elements seen by his father, Lehi, in the "tree of life" vision, an angel was sent to tutor him. Nephi recorded:

"I saw the heavens open; and an angel came down and stood before me; and he said unto me: Nephi, what beholdest thou? And I said unto him: A virgin, most beautiful and fair above all other virgins.

"And he said unto me: Knowest thou the condescension of God? And I said unto him: I know that he loveth his children; nevertheless, I do not know the meaning of all things.

"And he said unto me: Behold, the virgin whom thou seest is the mother of the Son of God, after the manner of the flesh. . . . And I looked and beheld the virgin again, bearing a child in her arms.

"And the angel said unto me: Behold the Lamb of God, yea, even the Son of the Eternal Father! Knowest thou the meaning of the tree which thy father saw? And I answered him, saying: Yea, it is the love of God . . . ; wherefore, it is the most desirable above all things. And he spake unto me, saying: Yea, and the most joyous to the soul. . . .

"And it came to pass that the angel spake unto me again, saying: Look! And I looked and beheld the Lamb of God, that he was taken by the people; yea, the Son of the everlasting God was judged of the world; and I saw and bear record. And I, Nephi, saw that he was lifted up upon the cross and slain for the sins of the world" (1 Nephi 11:14–24, 31–33).

These scriptural explanations are most impressive and beautiful:

The precious tree of life, whose delicious fruit is desirable above all other fruit, represents the *love of God.*

The greatest example on earth of the love of God and of the condescension of God is the life, mission, and atonement of his Son. God so loved his Son—and his other children—that he allowed his Beloved Son to suffer "both body and spirit," "to bleed at every pore," "to be lifted up on a cross and crucified" so the covenants of the Father and the Son with us would be kept!

Blessed forever be the holy names of the Father and the Son! What a tremendous sacrifice the offering of their gifts required!

Our Heavenly Father has offered to us the greatest gift he can offer: the opportunity to receive and inherit eternal life. Inherent within this gift are the gift of a physical body, the gift of agency, the gift of his Only Begotten Son. As the scriptures record, "God so loved the world that he *gave* his only begotten Son" (John 3:16).

Jesus Christ has offered the Father and us the greatest gift he can offer: his sinless life, his perfect example, his atonement.

The Gift We Give

A critical question remains: What is the greatest gift we can give to our Heavenly Father and to our Elder Brother Jesus Christ for their inestimable gifts to us?

We know we can never, ever fully repay. Neither individually nor collectively can we reciprocate in kind. We have neither the right, power, authority, nor the means to offer them immortality and eternal life—gifts they already possess.

We do not have the right nor ability to "bestow upon them" any gifts of wealth, or honor, or power, or position. What treasure could we possibly give to them? They created the heavens and earth and "all things which in them are" (3 Nephi 9:15). Anything we have—*anything*—has already come to us as a gift from them. In reality they own it; we do not. We cannot *give* something we do not fully possess.

What gifts could we even think to offer Gods who are omnipresent in influence and power, and who are omniscient and omnipotent?

Returning to our definition of *gift,* anything we offer obviously must rest upon the exercise of our agency to do it. They cannot and will not force us to do things against our will. Even if we were so forced, it would not be a *gift* from us, for by definition a gift is something voluntarily bestowed by the donor.

What, then, can we give?

We can honor them, revere, adore, respect, worship, and love them.

We can show our appreciation for what they have given to us by being worthy to receive and by accepting the gifts they have already offered. We do this by keeping all previous commitments with them, including those made at baptism, or when partaking of the sacrament, or in accepting a Church calling, or when receiving sacred ordinances in the temple.

We can show our appreciation for their gifts and sacrifices by repenting of our sins. We do not show love and appreciation to them if we continue to break the laws they have given to us.

In modern times, the Lord has reviewed the first and second great commandments, on which all other laws are based:

"Thou shalt love the Lord thy God with all thy heart, with all thy might, mind, and strength; and in the name of Jesus Christ thou shalt serve him. Thou shalt love thy neighbor as thyself" (D&C 59:5–6).

He has also declared in thirteen words the principle of how we can show our love for him:

"If thou lovest me thou shalt serve me and keep all my commandments" (D&C 42:29).

Jesus Christ has indicated several ways in which we might serve him:

"Then shall the King say unto them on his right hand, Come ye blessed of my Father, inherit the kingdom prepared for you from the foundation of the world: For I was an hungered, and ye gave me meat: I was thirsty, and ye gave me drink: I was a stranger, and ye took me in: naked, and ye clothed me: I was sick, and ye visited me: I was in prison, and ye came unto me.

"Then shall the righteous answer him, saying; Lord, when saw we thee an hungered, and fed thee? or thirsty, and gave thee drink? When saw we thee a stranger, and took thee in? or naked, and clothed thee? Or when saw we thee sick or in prison, and came unto thee?

"And the King shall answer and say unto them, Verily I say unto you, Inasmuch as ye have done it unto one of the least of these my brethren, ye have done it unto me. . . . And these [who so do] shall go . . . unto life eternal" (Matthew 25:34–40, 46).

A significant teaching of the resurrected Jesus Christ on love and service has been preserved in the writings of the apostle John:

"Jesus saith to Simon Peter, Simon . . . lovest thou me more than these? He saith unto him, Yea, Lord; thou knowest that I love thee. He saith unto him, Feed my lambs.

"He saith to him again the second time, Simon . . . , lovest thou me? He saith unto him, Yea, Lord: thou knowest that I love thee. He saith unto him, Feed my sheep.

"He saith unto him the third time, Simon . . . , lovest thou me? Peter was grieved because he said unto him the third time, Lovest thou me? and he said unto him, Lord, thou knowest all things; thou knowest that I love thee. Jesus saith unto him, Feed my sheep" (John 21:15–17).

As impressive as these verses are in the English, they have additional meaning in the Greek text, which is the earliest version of the New Testament now available to us. In the Greek New Testament, the Lord uses different words for the term translated only as *love* in the English. Also, in the Greek he uses different expressions for the term translated in the English only as *feed*.

Thus, these verses state two principles in unmistakable plainness: (1) those who truly love the Lord express that love through service and (2) our service should increase in quality and quantity as we increase in love toward him.

We love by serving, feeding, nurturing, protecting, safeguarding the sheep of the Master Shepherd—which includes all of us.

However, even if we should serve him with 100 percent devotion and endure to the very end of physical life, we still would not be able to repay fully for the gifts we have received.

King Benjamin reminds us:

"I tell you these things that ye may learn wisdom; that ye may learn that when ye are in the service of your fellow beings ye are only in the service of your God. . . .

"I say unto you, my brethren, that if you should render all the thanks and praise which your whole soul has power to possess, to that God who has created you, and has kept and preserved you. . . . If you should serve him who has created you from the beginning, and is preserving you from day to day, by lending you breath, that ye may live and move and do according to your own will, and even supporting you from one moment to another—I say, if ye should serve him with all your whole souls yet ye would be unprofitable servants.

"And behold, all that he requires of you is to keep his commandments; and he has promised you that if ye would keep his commandments ye should prosper in the land; and he never doth vary from that which he hath said; therefore, if ye do keep his commandments he doth bless you and prosper you.

"And now, in the first place, he hath created you, and granted unto you your lives, for which ye are indebted unto him. And secondly, he doth require that ye should do as he hath commanded you; for which if ye do, he doth immediately bless you; and therefore he hath paid you. And ye are still indebted unto him, and are, and will be, forever and ever; therefore, of what have ye to boast?" (Mosiah 2:17, 20–24).

Even though we cannot fully repay, even though we may often feel inadequate and unworthy in our efforts, the "greatest gift" we can give to Heavenly Father and his Son Jesus Christ is still *ourselves*. Our earlier definition and explanation stipulated that the true value of a gift is largely determined by the "right, power, and authority" of the person to give the gift. What do we individually have the most "right, power, and authority" over? *Ourselves*.

Our actions, *our* words, *our* thoughts—all are determined almost exclusively by ourselves. These are gifts we can give that cannot be given by anyone else. But we must give them voluntarily. We must *desire* and *want* to do according to our Father's will, above anything else.

In light of this, several scriptures take on new meanings:

"Seek ye first the kingdom of God, and his righteousness; and all these things shall be added unto you" (Matthew 6:33).

"It is not meet that I should command in all things; for he that is compelled in all things, the same is a slothful and not a wise servant; wherefore he receiveth no reward. Verily I say, men should be anxiously engaged in a good cause, and do many things of their own free will, and bring to pass much righteousness" (D&C 58:26–27).

"He who seeketh to save his life shall lose it; and he who loseth his life for my sake shall find it" (JST, Matthew 10:34).

During the holidays, we frequently wish each other a merry Christmas and a happy New Year.

The degree to which we will have a truly joyous holiday season will depend largely upon the extent to which we are able to give ourselves as gifts in service to others. It truly is "more blessed to give than to receive" (Acts 20:35).

And, in all our giving, may we remember to give sincere thanks to those special two who have given so much to us—and who have promised to give us so much more when we have learned to accept worthily what they already have offered.

For I testify, with the apostle John, that "God so loved the world, that he gave his only begotten Son, that whosoever believeth in him should not perish, but have everlasting life" (John 3:16). May we find the eternal life we seek! I also testify that Jesus Christ so loved us, his friends, that he laid down his life for us—and greater love hath no man than this (see John 15:13).

May we show our love and appreciation to them by keeping their commandments and by serving them through serving others.

Note

Christmas message prepared for a sacrament meeting in the Eighteenth Ward, Salt Lake Emigration Stake, December 1983.

Chapter 16

THE RESURRECTION

In speaking of the atonement of Jesus Christ, of which the resurrection is one of the most important aspects, Elder Bruce R. McConkie has written: "Nothing in the entire plan of salvation compares in any way in importance with that most transcendent of all events, the atoning sacrifice of our Lord. It is the most important single thing that has ever occurred in the entire history of created things; it is the rock foundation upon which the gospel and all other things rest."[1]

President Ezra Taft Benson has borne his testimony concerning the resurrection, and in so doing has provided a measure by which we might determine the relative importance of an event: "The greatest events of history are those which affect the greatest number for the longest periods. By this standard, no event could be more important to individuals or nations than the resurrection of the Master. The eventual resurrection of every soul who has lived and died on earth is a scriptural certainty. And surely there is no event for which one should make more careful preparation.

"Nothing is more absolutely universal than the resurrection. . . . No other single influence has had so great an impact on this earth as the life of Jesus the Christ."[2]

Another important witness of the importance of the resurrection is Jacob, the early Book of Mormon prophet who was the son of Lehi. Jacob has left his inspired words on what would have been our eternal state if it were not for the resurrection:

"For as death hath passed upon all men, to fulfill the merciful plan of the great Creator, there must needs be a power of resurrection. . . . For behold, if the flesh should rise no more our spirits must become subject to . . . the devil . . . and we become devils, angels to a devil, to be shut out from the presence of our God, and to remain with the father of lies, in misery, like unto himself" (2 Nephi 9:6, 8–9).

This sobering truth is also verified by the prophet Abinadi: "Were it not for the atonement, which God himself shall make for the sins and iniquities of his people, . . . they must unavoidably perish" (Mosiah 13:28).

Thus, "in the mouth of two or three witnesses," as is required by the scriptures, the Atonement—including what happened in Gethsemane and at the time of the resurrection—has been proclaimed to be the most important event in the history of mankind. It will vitally and eternally affect every person who has been born on this earth or who will ever live on this earth. My mind cannot conceive of greater events than those associated with the Atonement.

I am also convinced that the resurrection of Jesus Christ is one of the most important events because it is the proof of his divinity. If Jesus Christ is indeed resurrected from the dead and has provided the resurrection for all of us, then he has power over death, which in turn proves he has the power of God, and is indeed the Son of God as he so proclaimed.

As is befitting its importance, the resurrection of Jesus Christ is one of the most carefully documented events in history. Appropriate references are found in all the scriptures pertaining to this event and to its consequences in our own lives. Some of the most important of these scriptures are indexed in the Topical Guide of the LDS Edition of the Bible under such headings as "Resurrection," "Celestial Glory," "Terrestrial Glory," and "Telestial Glory." Also insightful articles are included in the Bible Dictionary under the headings "Resurrection" and "Degrees of Glory." I urge and encourage you to read and ponder these materials. Pray about them. Organize and prepare talks and lesson materials from them. Following these suggestions will help you get these scriptures riveted in your minds.

However, in the main, we will not be discussing these scriptural references in this chapter, as important and vital as they are. They are readily available to you; study and ponder them on your own. Rather, here we will rely primarily on the inspired statements of the prophets, seers, and revelators of this dispensation. Some of these statements are not readily available in the published writings of these brethren; thus they will be included here for your convenience and reference.

In considering how I might best present this topic, I have concluded that I should cover as many aspects of the subject as possible, even though some of them may be touched upon only lightly.

Many Latter-day Saints already know a great deal about the resurrection; they have read and pondered the appropriate scriptures, they have observed the teachings

The Resurrection • 263

of the leaders of the Church in this dispensation, they have prayed about the matter—and through these means they have gained considerable knowledge and strong testimonies of the resurrection.

However, I am persuaded that many members of the Church are still struggling to understand the various ramifications of the resurrection and to obtain a firm and strong testimony of it.

Thus, I have decided to use a "question and answer" approach here. These are the twenty-two questions we will consider, in the order that we will discuss them:

1. What is the resurrection?
2. To whom does the resurrection apply?
3. Is the resurrection infinite?
4. Does this mean that every spirit that has had a physical body must be resurrected, whether it is the spirit of a person or the spirit of an animal, a fish, an insect, or a plant?
5. By what power or means is the resurrection accomplished?
6. What is the role of Jesus Christ so far as the resurrection is concerned?
7. What is the role of our individual spirits in regard to our own resurrection?
8. Was anyone resurrected before the resurrection of Jesus Christ?
9. When did the first "general" resurrection occur?
10. Has there been a general resurrection since the resurrection of Jesus Christ?
11. Can a righteous person who has passed through the experience of temporal death be resurrected *now* if it is in keeping with the plan and purpose of our Heavenly Father for that person?
12. What is meant by the terms "first resurrection" and "second resurrection"?
13. What is the shape, form, or frame of the body when it is resurrected from the dead?
14. What is the state or condition of the body when it is resurrected from the dead?
15. What are the orders or degrees of the physical matter comprising resurrected bodies?
16. What are the attributes or characteristics of people who inherit each of these different degrees?
17. Who or what determines the order or degree of the resurrected body an individual receives?
18. Does an individual person who is now on this earth have agency as to whether or not he or she will be resurrected from the dead?

19. Does an individual who is now on this earth have agency as to the degree or order of resurrected body he or she will receive in the resurrection?

20. Might the resurrection be considered a type of judgment?

21. Is the resurrection the same as the "final judgment"?

22. What is the testimony of our living prophet, Gordon B. Hinckley, on the subject of the resurrection?

Some Answers

Now let's consider each of these questions, one at a time, and provide some answers.

1. What is the resurrection?

The resurrection is the reuniting of the spirit with its physical body. Resurrection is one of the unconditional features of the atonement of Jesus Christ. It is also the crowning aspect, and one of the concluding aspects, of the second estate.

Elder Hyrum M. Smith of the Quorum of the Twelve provided the following brief explanation:

"Death is the dissolution of the body, and the resurrection is the reanimation of the body; yea the actual and literal reuniting of the Spirit with the body."[3]

2. To whom does the resurrection apply?

The resurrection applies to every person who has ever lived or will ever live on this earth, without exception. Even those who become sons of perdition in the flesh will be resurrected (see 1 Corinthians 15:22; Alma 11:44).

President Joseph F. Smith, the sixth president of the Church in this dispensation, has stated: "Every creature that is born in the image of God will be resurrected from the dead. . . . Just as sure as we go down into the grave, through the transgression of our first parents, by whom death came into the world, so sure will we be resurrected from the dead by the power of Jesus Christ. It matters not whether we have done well or ill, whether we have been intelligent or ignorant, or whether we have been bondsmen or slaves or freemen, all men will be raised from the dead."[4]

3. Is the resurrection infinite?

Yes. The scriptures and the teachings of the prophets, seers, and revelators are very clear on this matter.

Jacob mentions the need for an infinite atonement in the book of 2 Nephi: "It must needs be an infinite atonement—save it should be an infinite atonement this corruption could not put on incorruption" (2 Nephi 9:7).

Amulek testifies in the book of Alma, "There can be nothing which is short of an infinite atonement which will suffice for the sins of the world" (Alma 34:12).

4. Does this mean that every spirit that has had a physical body must be resurrected, whether it is the spirit of a person or the spirit of an animal, a fish, an insect, or a plant?

Yes. The resurrection even applies to the earth itself (see D&C 88:17–18, 25–26) and to everything that has ever lived on this earth. Some leaders of the Church have suggested that the resurrection of Jesus Christ also applies to everything that has ever lived on any of the earths created by Jesus Christ.

Joseph Fielding Smith stated: "The Savior is not going to save only mankind. Everything God has created must be restored, . . . everything the Lord has created. . . . Everything that has life [was] created in the image of its spirit, and is a living soul, and therefore entitled to the resurrection."[5]

The Lord states in section 29 of the Doctrine and Covenants that

"all things shall become new, even the heaven and the earth, and all the fulness thereof, both men and beasts, the fowls of the air, and the fishes of the sea . . . for it is the workmanship of mine hand" (D&C 29:24–25).

Elder Bruce R. McConkie has taught: "Just as the creative [power] and [the] redemptive powers of Christ extend to the earth and all things thereon, as also to the infinite expanse of worlds in immensity, so the power of the resurrection is universal in scope. Man, the earth, and all life thereon will come forth in the resurrection. And the resurrection applies to and is going on in other worlds and other galaxies."[6]

5. By what power or means is the resurrection accomplished?

By the power of God the Father and of his Son Jesus Christ.

In 1 Corinthians 6:14 we read: "And God hath both raised up the Lord, and will also raise us up by his own power."

President John Taylor made this clear in his book *Mediation and Atonement:*

"The Son hath life inherent in Himself, even as the Father hath life in Himself, He having received this power from the Father. Also, . . . He had power in Himself to lay down this body, and also to take it up again; and in this respect He differed from others. . . . Hence . . . He . . . becomes the means of the resurrection of all men from the dead."⁷

6. What is the role of Jesus Christ so far as the resurrection is concerned?

Jesus Christ, as the Only Begotten Son of God in the flesh, inherited power over physical death. And as the Son of mortal Mary, he had the capacity to die.

Jesus declared: "Therefore doth my Father love me, because I lay down my life, that I might take it again.

"No man taketh it from me, but I lay it down of myself. I have power to lay it down, and I have power to take it again. This commandment have I received of my Father" (John 10:17–18).

7. What is the role of our individual spirits in regard to our own resurrections?

Our spirits will be empowered by the gift of Jesus Christ to help bring forth our bodies out of the grave.

Note the following statements from some of the presidents of the Church in this dispensation. First let me quote two statements by President Joseph F. Smith:

"[As] Jesus, the Only Begotten of the Father . . . had power to lay down his life and take it up again, . . . we too, in his name and through his redeeming blood, will have power in due time to resurrect these our bodies after they shall have been committed to the earth."⁸

"What is the body without the spirit? It is lifeless clay. What is it that affects this lifeless clay? It is the spirit, [and the spirit] will redeem these tabernacles and bring them forth out of the graves."⁹

The following is an observation by President Spencer W. Kimball: "There will be a literal resurrection, when this live and conscious spirit will return . . . to take up its reconstructed and resurrected body."¹⁰

According to Brigham Young, the resurrection is an ordinance of the priesthood, which by definition is the power to act in the name of Jesus Christ. Thus another person who has already been resurrected will give us the power that will enable us to be resurrected. Note these words of Brigham Young:

"Some person holding the keys of the resurrection, having previously passed through that ordeal, will be delegated to resurrect our bodies, and our spirits will be there and prepared to enter into their bodies."¹¹

8. Was anyone resurrected before the resurrection of Jesus Christ?

No. Jesus Christ is the "firstfruits" of the resurrection; he then made it possible for others subsequently to be resurrected. No one was resurrected before Jesus Christ.

In 1 Corinthians 15:19–23 we read:

"If in this life only we have hope in Christ, we are of all men most miserable.

"But now is Christ risen from the dead, and become the firstfruits of them that slept.

"For since by man came death, by man came also the resurrection of the dead.

"For as in Adam all die, even so in Christ shall all be made alive.

"But every man in his own order: Christ the firstfruits."

President Brigham Young said: "Jesus is the first begotten from the dead. . . . He is the Master of the resurrection—the first flesh that lived here after receiving the glory of the resurrection."[12]

9. When did the first "general" resurrection occur?

The first general resurrection was at the time Jesus Christ was resurrected.

Evidence that there was a general resurrection immediately after the resurrection of Jesus Christ is made clear in two of our scriptures.

In the book of Matthew in the New Testament we read:

"And the graves were opened; and many bodies of the saints which slept arose, And came out of the graves after his resurrection, and went into the holy city, and appeared unto many" (Matthew 27:52–53).

A second witness of this general resurrection is also contained in the Book of Mormon. Approximately forty years before the resurrection of Jesus Christ, the prophet Samuel the Lamanite had prophesied: "And many graves shall be opened, and shall yield up many of their dead; and many saints shall appear unto many" (Helaman 13:25).

So important was this additional witness of this first general resurrection that when the resurrected Jesus Christ visited with his disciples on the western continent soon after his resurrection, he commanded them to include the fulfillment of this prophecy in their records. Note these words in 3 Nephi:

"Verily I say unto you, I commanded my servant Samuel, the Lamanite, that he should testify unto this people, that at the day that the Father should glorify his name in me that there were many saints who should arise from the dead, and should appear unto many, and should minister unto them. And he said unto them: Was it not so?

"And his disciples answered him and said: Yea, Lord, Samuel did prophesy according to thy words, and they were all fulfilled.

"And Jesus said unto them: How be it that ye have not written this thing, that many saints did arise and appear unto many and did minister unto them?

"And it came to pass that Nephi remembered that this thing had not been written.

"And it came to pass that Jesus commanded that it should be written; therefore it was written according as he commanded" (3 Nephi 23:9–13).

10. Has there been a general resurrection since the resurrection of Jesus Christ?

No. The next general resurrection will be at the time of the second coming of Jesus Christ.

Concerning this next general resurrection, President Joseph Fielding Smith has written: "The Lord has promised that at the time of his Second Advent the graves will be opened, and the just shall come forth to reign with him on the earth for a thousand years."[13]

11. Can a righteous person who has passed through the experience of temporal death be resurrected *now* if it is in keeping with the plan and purpose of our Heavenly Father for that person?

Yes, if it is necessary for a specific person who died after the resurrection of Jesus Christ to be resurrected in order to perform a mission here on earth requiring a physical body, that person might be resurrected.

Elder Bruce R. McConkie has written: "We have no knowledge that the resurrection is going on now or that any persons have been resurrected since the day in which Christ came forth excepting Peter, James, and Moroni, all of whom had special labors to perform in this day which necessitated tangible resurrected bodies."[14]

12. What is meant by the terms "first resurrection" and "second resurrection"?

The term "first resurrection" refers to the resurrection of the righteous or just. If a person is resurrected at the first opportunity he has to be resurrected after his death, then he comes forth in the morning of his first resurrection.

The term "second resurrection" refers to the resurrection of the wicked or unjust.

In section 76 of the Doctrine and Covenants, the Lord gave the following explanation of John 5:29:

"Speaking of the resurrection of the dead [they] shall come forth; they who have done good, in the resurrection of the just; and they who have done evil, in the resurrection of the unjust" (D&C 76:16–17).

Later in that section, in verses 64–65, the Lord speaks of the resurrection of the righteous:

"These are they who shall *have part* in the first resurrection.

"These are they who shall *come forth* in the resurrection of the just" (D&C 76:64–65; emphasis added).

13. What is the shape, form, or frame of the body when it is resurrected from the dead?

The physical body will be restored to its proper and perfect form or frame (see Alma 11:42–45; 40:23; 41:4), regardless of what might have happened to the physical body at the time of death or after the time of death.

Amulek taught: "The spirit and the body shall be reunited again in its perfect form; both limb and joint shall be restored to its proper frame. . . . Now, this restoration shall come to all . . . ; and even there shall not so much as a hair of their heads be lost; but every thing shall be restored to its perfect frame" (Alma 11:43–44).

14. What is the state or condition of the body when it is resurrected from the dead?

The physical body will come forth from the grave as it is laid down, except that the blood will be replaced by spirit. Immediately after the resurrection, the physical body of an infant or child begins to grow further and the physical body of all resurrected beings begins to develop toward its perfect condition.

The Prophet Joseph Smith made this very clear in his teachings:

"As concerning the resurrection, I will merely say that all men will come from the grave as they lie down, whether old or young; there will not be 'added unto their stature one cubit,' neither taken from it, . . . having spirit in their bodies, and not blood."[15]

This same concept was clearly taught by President John Taylor: "When the resurrection . . . of man shall be consummated, . . . he [will] still be in the same image, and have the same likeness, without variation or change in any of his parts or faculties, except the substitution of spirit for blood."[16]

I must confess that when I first came to understand that the body comes forth from the grave as it is laid down with all its physical imperfections, it bothered me somewhat. I knew that eventually the resurrected body would be perfect, but from some of the funeral sermons I had heard, I had falsely assumed that the body would be perfect *when* it first came out of the grave.

But I must also confess that after studying the inspired teachings of the modern prophets on this subject, and after applying logic and reason, I have now reached the point that I rejoice when I realize my body will come forth from the grave with its imperfections, for *then* after the resurrection my spirit can help my physical body overcome these defects and deformities. If I lay down a body with scars and imperfections, and yet resurrect a perfect body, who or what has been tampering with my physical body while it has been in the grave and while my spirit has been away from it in the postmortal spirit world?

I have truly now reached a point where I can rejoice in the following words of President Joseph F. Smith:

"What a glorious thought it is, to me at least, . . . that those from whom we have to part here, we will meet again and see as they are. We will meet the same identical being . . . the same form and likeness, . . . even to the wounds in the flesh. Not that a person will always be marred by scars, wounds, deformities, defects or infirmities, for these will be removed in their course, in their proper time, according to the merciful providence of God."[17]

Now other inspired statements of the Brethren concerning the resurrection have taken on additional meaning for me.

From President Joseph F. Smith: "The child that was buried in its infancy will come up in the form of the child that it was when it was laid down; then it will begin to develop. From the day of the resurrection, the body will develop until it reaches the full measure of the stature of its spirit, whether it be male or female."[18]

From President Joseph Fielding Smith: "The mortal body will not grow in the grave, for that is contrary to nature. So each body will come forth the same stature as when laid in the earth. Children will rise as they were laid away, but after the resurrection their bodies will grow to the full stature of their spirits. Deformities will be erased."[19]

15. What are the orders or degrees of the physical matter comprising resurrected bodies?

There are at least three orders of glory, and at least one order not of glory:
1. Celestial glory.
2. Terrestrial glory.
3. Telestial glory.
4. An order "without glory."
However, there may be many degrees within each of these orders. As an example, we know from section 131 of the Doctrine and Covenants that there are

three heavens or degrees within the celestial kingdom. It is not known precisely how many other degrees there are in the other "orders" or "kingdoms."

The Savior taught: "In my Father's house are many mansions: if it were not so, I would have told you. I go to prepare a place for you" (John 14:2).

Elder James E. Talmage explained: "The three kingdoms of widely differing glories are organized on an orderly plan of gradation. . . . The telestial kingdom comprises several subdivisions; this is also the case . . . with the celestial; and, by analogy, we conclude that a similar condition prevails in the terrestrial. Thus the innumerable degrees of merit amongst mankind are provided for in an infinity of graded glories."[20]

16. What are the attributes or characteristics of people who inherit each of these different degrees?

Doctrine and Covenants 76 supplies us with most of the answers:

1. Celestial glory: "They are they who received the testimony of Jesus, and believed on his name and were baptized after the manner of his burial, . . . that by keeping the commandments they might be washed and cleansed from all their sins, and receive the Holy Spirit. . . . These are they who shall have part in the first resurrection. These are they who shall come forth in the resurrection of the just" (D&C 76:51–52, 64–65).

2. Terrestrial glory: "These are they who died without law; . . . the spirits of men kept in prison, . . . who received not the testimony of Jesus in the flesh, but afterwards received it. These are they who are honorable men of the earth . . . who are not valiant in the testimony of Jesus" (D&C 76:72–75, 79).

3. Telestial glory: "These are they who received not the gospel of Christ . . . [but] who deny not the Holy Spirit. These are they who are thrust down to hell [and] . . . who shall not be redeemed from the devil until the last resurrection. . . . These are they who are liars, and sorcerers, and adulterers, and whoremongers, and whosoever loves and makes a lie" (D&C 76:82–85, 103).

4. Those "without glory": These are they "who know my power, and have been made partakers thereof, . . . [who] deny the truth and defy my power—they are they who are the sons of perdition, of whom I say that it had been better for them never to have been born; . . . concerning whom I have said there is no forgiveness in this world nor in the world to come" (D&C 76:31–32, 34–37).

17. Who or what determines the order or degree of the resurrected body an individual receives?

This is largely determined by the individual himself or herself: What laws has the individual obeyed? Over what laws does he or she have power? (see D&C 88:2–4, 15–31).

President Wilford Woodruff stated: "If a man cannot abide a celestial law, he cannot receive a celestial glory, if a man cannot abide a terrestrial law he cannot receive a terrestrial glory; and if he cannot abide a telestial law he cannot receive a telestial glory, but will have to dwell in a kingdom which is not a kingdom of glory. This is according to the revelations of God to us."[21]

President Joseph F. Smith added: "When we come forth out of the grave, . . . our spirits shall enter into [our physical bodies] again, and they shall become living souls. . . . And then those who have . . . been subject and obedient to the celestial law will . . . be quickened by the celestial glory. And those who have . . . been subject and obedient to the terrestrial law will . . . be quickened by the terrestrial glory. And those who have . . . been subject and obedient to the telestial law, will . . . be quickened by a telestial glory."[22]

Elder George Q. Cannon asked a pertinent question and then answered it: "Why is it that there are these differences? Is it because God has chosen some of us for the telestial glory, some of us for the terrestrial glory, and some of us for the celestial glory? No, there is no such predestination as this. We are all born with our free agency; with the power within ourselves, aided by the blessing of God, to attain unto the highest glory. How shall we attain unto the highest glory? There is only one way, and that is by observing the highest laws. . . . The man or woman who expects to attain to the highest glory without obeying these laws, deceives himself or herself. It cannot be done." [23]

Concerning resurrected celestial bodies, Elder Melvin J. Ballard wrote: "Those who come forth in the celestial glory with celestial bodies have a body that is more refined. It is different. The very fibre and texture of the celestial body is more pure and holy than a telestial or terrestrial body, and a celestial body alone can endure celestial glory."[24]

18. Does an individual person who is now on this earth have agency as to whether or not he or she will be resurrected from the dead?

No. The resurrection is an unconditional aspect of the Atonement. All will be resurrected without exception.

Elder James E. Talmage explained that the gospel "affirms . . . that a Redeemer was provided before the world was . . . [and] that general salvation, in the sense of redemption from the effects of the fall [including the resurrection], comes to all without their seeking it."[25]

19. Does an individual who is now on this earth have agency as to the degree or order of resurrected body he or she will receive in the resurrection?

Absolutely yes. The individual definitely has agency to decide which laws he or she will obey and thus will determine which order of resurrected physical body he or she will receive.

Elder Bruce R. McConkie indicated: "By one degree of obedience or another, all men, in this life, develop either celestial, terrestrial, or telestial bodies (or in the case of those destined to be sons of perdition, bodies of a baser sort)."[26]

20. Might the resurrection be considered a type of judgment?

Yes. As indicated in the answer to question 15, at the time of the resurrection, each will come forth with a body that is particular to one of the degrees of glory or one without glory. Thus, the resurrection might be considered a type of judgment.

21. Is the resurrection the same as the "final judgment"?

No. The "final judgment" of a person takes place sometime after the resurrection of that person. The final judgment is also a vital part of our Heavenly Father's glorious plan of progression and eternal life.

22. What is the testimony of our living prophet, Gordon B. Hinckley, on the subject of the resurrection?

President Hinckley penned the following lines some years ago while seated in the funeral service of a friend:

> What is this thing that men call death,
> This quiet passing in the night?
> 'Tis not the end, but genesis
> Of better worlds and greater light.
>
> O God, touch Thou my aching heart,
> And calm my troubled, haunting fears.
> Let hope and faith, transcendent, pure,
> Give strength and peace beyond my tears.

There is no death, but only change
With recompense for victory won;
The gift of Him who loved all men,
The Son of God, the Holy One.[27]

And now, another brief testimony from President Hinckley:

"None of us fully understands the Atonement. I think it is beyond the comprehension of any man, but we know something of it, and we know that as a result of it all will be resurrected from the grave, and that those who walk in obedience to His commandments will be given the opportunity of going on to eternal exaltation. Nothing can compare with that. All of us are going to die someday, but that won't be the end. We'll go on living because Christ broke the bands of death for each of us."[28]

SUMMARY AND TESTIMONY

These words of our living prophet form part of my testimony concerning the subject of the Atonement and the resurrection. We may know only a portion of what there is to know about these subjects. But we know enough to understand that the Atonement is an essential part of the great plan of progression and eternal life that our Heavenly Father has made available to us. And we know enough to realize that the resurrection is made possible for us (1) through the Father's gift of his Son, and (2) through the Son's gift of his life.

Therefore, my prayer for each of us is that we might show our appreciation unto our Father and unto our Savior for these gifts by striving diligently to serve them and to keep their commandments.

Notes

From a talk given at the BYU Campus Education Week, 16 August 1999.

1. Bruce R. McConkie, *Mormon Doctrine*, 2d ed. (Salt Lake City: Bookcraft, 1966), 60.
2. Ezra Taft Benson, *So Shall Ye Reap*, comp. Reed A. Benson (Salt Lake City: Deseret Book Co., 1960), 4, 6.
3. Hyrum M. Smith, in Conference Report, April 1917, 31.
4. Joseph F. Smith, "Discourse by President Joseph F. Smith," *Millennial Star*, 58 (12 March 1896): 162.
5. Joseph Fielding Smith, *Seek Ye Earnestly* (Salt Lake City: Deseret Book Co., 1970), 280.
6. McConkie, *Mormon Doctrine*, 642.
7. John Taylor, *Mediation and Atonement* (Salt Lake City: Deseret News Co., 1882), 146.
8. Joseph F. Smith, in *Journal of Discourses*, 18:277.
9. Joseph F. Smith, in *Journal of Discourses*, 25:250.
10. *Teachings of Spencer W. Kimball*, 46.

11. Brigham Young, in *Journal of Discourses,* 9:139.
12. Brigham Young, in *Journal of Discourses,* 8:260.
13. *Doctrines of Salvation,* 2:295.
14. McConkie, *Mormon Doctrine,* 639.
15. *Teachings of the Prophet Joseph Smith,* 199–200.
16. John Taylor, *Mediation and Atonement,* 166.
17. *Gospel Doctrine,* 23.
18. Ibid., 24.
19. Joseph Fielding Smith, *Church History and Modern Revelation,* 2 vols. (Salt Lake City: The Church of Jesus Christ of Latter-day Saints, 1953), 2:110.
20. James E. Talmage, *The House of the Lord,* rev. ed. (Salt Lake City: Deseret Book Co., 1976), 83.
21. Wilford Woodruff, in *Journal of Discourses,* 12:278.
22. *Gospel Doctrine,* 450–51.
23. George Q. Cannon, in Conference Report, April 1900, 54.
24. Melvin J. Ballard, in *Sermons and Missionary Services of Melvin J. Ballard,* comp. Bryant S. Hinckley (Salt Lake City: Deseret Book Co., 1949), 256.
25. James E. Talmage, *Jesus the Christ* (Salt Lake City: Deseret Book Co., 1983), 29.
26. Bruce R. McConkie, *Doctrinal New Testament Commentary,* 3 vols. (Salt Lake City: Bookcraft, 1965–73), 1:196.
27. Gordon B. Hinckley, *Teachings of Gordon B. Hinckley* (Salt Lake City: Deseret Book Co., 1997), 552.
28. Ibid., 554.

The Plan of Progression and Eternal Life

Chapter 17

THE PLAN OF PROGRESSION AND ETERNAL LIFE

This chapter consists of eight outlines giving basic resources and asking fundamental questions about the various aspects of our Father's plan for his children. Those who study these materials carefully will develop a much deeper understanding and appreciation for this wonderful plan and its meaning in our lives.

OUTLINE 1: THE PRE-EARTHLY EXISTENCE OF THE SPIRIT

Topical Guide: "Man, a Spirit Child of Heavenly Father," 305; "Man, Antemortal Existence of," 305; "Spirit Body," 493.

Index to Triple Combination: "Premortal Existence," 274; "Spirit World," 346.

Articles in *Jesus Christ and His Gospel*[1]: "Council in Heaven," 83; "First Estate," 168; "Intelligences," 249–51; "Origin of Man," 374–76; "Pre-Existence (Pre-Earthly Existence)," 396; Premortal Life," 396–400; "Spirit Body," 441–42; "The Origin of Man," 477–83.

Pages in *Latter-day Prophets Speak*[2]: 3–10

Selected Questions for Discussion

By what means on this earth do we learn about the pre-earthly existence? The scriptures, the word of the Lord to his prophets (including his current prophets), the temple endowment, personal revelation, the inspiration that has come to others, and so forth.

What are some of the things we know about our pre-earthly existence? Joseph Smith: "Intelligence is eternal and exists upon a self-existent principle."[3]

Joseph Smith: "The spirit of man is not a created being; it existed from eternity, and will exist to eternity."[4]

Joseph F. Smith: "A spirit born of God is an immortal being."[5]

What do we know about our existence as an intelligence ("pure" intelligence)? Very little, except that it is eternal in nature and can neither be created nor destroyed (see Abraham 3:21–23).

Joseph Smith: "The mind or the intelligence which man possesses is co-equal [co-eternal] with God himself.... I am dwelling on the immortality of the spirit of man. Is it logical to say that the intelligence of spirits is immortal, and yet that it had a beginning? The intelligence of spirits had no beginning, neither will it have an end.... There never was a time when there were not spirits; for they are co-equal [co-eternal] with our Father in heaven.... Intelligence is eternal and exists upon a self-existent principle. It is a spirit from age to age, and there is no creation about it."[6]

What do we know about our existence as spirit children of our Heavenly Father ("organized intelligence" or "personages of spirit")? Quite a bit, especially from latter-day scriptures and teachings. (Note the significance of Abraham 3:22.)

Joseph F. Smith and First Presidency: "The doctrine of the pre-existence,—revealed so plainly, particularly in latter days, pours a wonderful flood of light upon the otherwise mysterious problem of man's origin. It shows that man, as a spirit, was begotten and born of heavenly parents, and reared to maturity in the eternal mansions of the Father, prior to coming upon the earth in a temporal body to undergo an experience in mortality. It teaches that all men existed in the spirit before any man existed in the flesh, and that all who have inhabited the earth since Adam have taken bodies and become souls in like manner."[7]

What elements are included in the term "the spirit of man"? Intelligence and personage of spirit.

Joseph Fielding Smith: "There is something called intelligence which always existed. It is the real eternal part of man, which was not created or made. This intelligence combined with the spirit constitutes a spiritual identity or individual. The spirit of man, then, is a combination of the intelligence and the spirit which is an entity begotten of God."[8]

"The Lord had shown unto me . . . the intelligences that were organized before the world was" (Abraham 3:22).

What is the relationship of God the Father to the spirits of everyone who has ever lived on this earth or who will ever live on this earth? He is "the God of the spirits of all flesh" (Numbers 16:22). "We are the children of God" (Romans 8:16).

Joseph F. Smith and First Presidency: "All people who come to this earth and are born in mortality had a pre-existent, spiritual personality as the sons or daughters of the Eternal Father."[9]

What is meant by the term first estate*?* The pre-earthly existence (see Jude 1:6).

What were some of the major purposes of the great Council in Heaven? To present, explain, and discuss the plan of progression and eternal life; to vote on this plan.

Who were some of the major personalities involved in the discussions and decisions in the great pre-earthly council? "Man of Holiness" (God the Father), "the great I AM" (Jesus Christ), "Michael" (Adam), "Lucifer" (the devil, Satan).

What were some of the major issues underlying the "war in heaven"? The role of agency and of faith; the necessity of a "veil of forgetfulness"; whether the great I AM [Jesus Christ] would be *able* to atone; whether Jesus Christ would be *willing* to atone; the selfish desire of Lucifer to put his throne above the throne of God (see 2 Nephi 24:12–14).

What were some of the consequences of the war in heaven? Those who voted against the plan (Lucifer and his followers) were not allowed to participate in the plan of having physical bodies, and so forth.

Did we have agency in that stage of our pre-earthly existence when we existed as organized intelligences (as personages of spirit, as spirit children of our Heavenly Father)? Definitely yes. Otherwise we would not have had freedom to vote on whether or not we would accept the plan of our Heavenly Father.

What is the difference between "agency" and "moral agency"? "Agency" is essentially the freedom of choice; a person has "moral agency" when and to the extent that he or she knows the consequences of the choice before the agency is exercised.

What is usually meant by the term "free agency"? Simply "agency" or "freedom of choice."

What is the stated goal ("work and glory") of our Heavenly Father in regard to his children? "To bring to pass the immortality and eternal life of man" (Moses 1:39).

Why is it important that we learn as much about our pre-earthly existence as our Heavenly Father feels he should give to us (a) as individuals, (b) as a Church, and (c) as all mankind? If we know where we came from and our potential, then we are more likely to understand and appreciate why we are here on this physical earth and what we might become in the future.

Does an individual on this earth now have agency or freedom of choice as to whether he or she will participate in a pre-earthly existence? No, that agency was "used up" when the vote was taken at the grand council.

Does an individual on this earth now have agency or freedom of choice as to whether he or she will participate in a physical, mortal existence on this earth? Obviously no.

OUTLINE 2: PURPOSES OF A MORTAL, PHYSICAL EXPERIENCE

Topical Guide: "Probation, Probationary," 393; "Test, Try, Prove," 522.

Index to Triple Combination: "Commandments of God," 54–56; "Mortal, Mortality," 232.

Articles in *Jesus Christ and His Gospel*: "Birth," 41–42; "Commandments," 69–71; "Fall of Adam," 163–66; "Mankind," 347–49; "Mortality," 358–59; "Obedience," 366–68; "Physical Body," 381–83; "Purpose of Earth Life," 402–8; "Second Estate," 435–36; "Worlds," 470–71.

Pages in *Latter-day Prophets Speak*: 11–25.

Selected Questions for Discussion

What does the word create *mean in regard to the creation of the earth?* Footnote 1c for Genesis 1:1 in the LDS edition of the Bible gives this answer: "Shaped, fashioned, created; always divine activity; see Abr. 4:1, organized, formed."

Was the earth created spiritually before it was created physically (naturally)? Yes. "I, the Lord God, created all things . . . spiritually, before they were naturally upon the face of the earth" (Moses 3:5).

Who were some of the major personalities involved in the "spiritual" and the "physical" creations of the earth? God the Father, Jesus Christ (the Son), Michael (Adam).

When this earth was first created, what was its "order" or "degree" of physical matter? Paradisiacal, meaning terrestrial.

What are some of the major purposes of our coming to live on this physical earth?

1. *To obtain a physical body.* Joseph Smith: "We came to this earth that we might have a [physical] body and present it pure before God in the celestial kingdom."[10]

Brigham Young: "Our mortal bodies are all important to us; without them we never can be glorified in the eternities that will be."[11]

John Taylor: "The object of man's taking a body is, that through the redemption of Jesus Christ both soul and body may be exalted in the eternal world, when the earth shall be celestial, and obtain a higher exaltation than he could be capable of doing without a body."[12]

Joseph F. Smith: "We have come to sojourn in the flesh, to obtain tabernacles for our immortal spirits."[13]

Joseph F. Smith: "It is absolutely necessary that we should come to the earth and take upon us tabernacles; because if we did not have tabernacles we could not be like God, or like Jesus Christ."[14]

2. *To be tried, tested, proven; to gain a knowledge of good and evil.* "We will prove them herewith, to see if they will do all things whatsoever the Lord their God shall command them" (Abraham 3:25). "For a trial of their faith" (D&C 105:19).

Brigham Young: "There is not, has not been, and never can be any method, scheme, or plan devised by any being in this world for intelligence to eternally exist and obtain an exaltation, without knowing the good and the evil—without tasting the bitter and the sweet."[15]

Lorenzo Snow: "We are here that we may be educated in a school of suffering and of fiery trials, which school was necessary for Jesus our Elder Brother, who, the scriptures tell us, was made perfect through suffering. It is necessary we suffer in all things, that we may be qualified and worthy to rule and govern all things, even as our Father in heaven and His Eldest Son, Jesus."[16]

Brigham Young: "If man could have been made perfect, in his double capacity of body and spirit, without passing through the ordeals of mortality, there would have been no necessity of our coming into this state of trial and suffering. Could the Lord have glorified His children in spirit, without a body like his own, he no doubt would have done so."[17]

3. *To give our spirits the opportunity to learn to obey physical laws (and thus to receive the blessings predicated upon such obedience).* Joseph F. Smith: "Man is a dual being, composed of the spirit which gives life, force, intelligence and capacity to man, and the body which is the tenement of the spirit and is suited to

its form, adapted to its necessities, and acts in harmony with and to its utmost capacity yields obedience to the will of the spirit. The two combined constitute the soul. The body is dependent upon the spirit, and the spirit during its natural occupancy of the body is subject to the laws which apply to and govern it in the mortal state."[18]

James E. Talmage: "The purpose of our mortal probation is that of education, training, trial, and test, whereby we demonstrate whether we will obey the commandments of the Lord our God and so lay hold on the boundless opportunities of advancement in the eternal worlds."[19]

4. *To help in the preparation of other physical bodies so other spirits can experience an earthly existence.* John Taylor: "We came here . . . and took bodies . . . to propagate our species."[20]

5. *To help family members (both descendants and progenitors) and others (friends, neighbors, associates, all mankind) learn and obey those laws and commandments that will enable them to return to live with our Heavenly Father forever.* Brigham Young: "All intelligent beings who are crowned with crowns of glory, immortality, and eternal lives must pass through every ordeal appointed for intelligent beings to pass through, to gain their glory and exaltation."[21]

Why is a "veil of forgetfulness" at the time of our physical birth necessary for the mortal experience? It is necessary in order for us to truly exercise faith.

Brigham Young: "It has . . . been decreed by the Almighty that spirits, upon taking bodies, shall forget all they had known previously, or they could not have a day of trial."[22]

How important is our mortal physical experience? It is a necessary and important part of the plan of eternal progression.

Joseph Fielding Smith: "This life is the most vital period in our eternal existence."[23]

Bruce R. McConkie: "In a very real and literal sense the life that we are now living is the final examination for that infinite period of preparation that we had in the premortal life. Now if we do not respond as we ought to respond . . . then in effect we are throwing away all of the preparation that we made in the premortal life. . . . Now this life is not only the final examination for the life, the eternity, that went before, but this mortal probation is an entrance examination to determine the sphere, and the place, and the kingdom and the reward that we will have in the mansions ahead. . . . In a very real and definite sense, that singles out this mortal probation as the most important part of all eternity."[24]

In the pre-earthly existence, did we have agency or freedom of choice as to whether or not we wanted to participate in the great plan of physical life on a physical earth? Absolutely yes.

Does an individual on this earth now have choice or agency as to whether he or she will participate in the great plan of physical life on a physical earth? Obviously, no.

Outline 3: Physical (or Temporal) Death

Topical Guide: "Death," 89–90.
Bible Dictionary: "Death," 655.
Index to Triple Combination: "Death, Physical," 73–74.
Articles in *Jesus Christ and His Gospel:* "Afterlife," 5–6; "Death and Dying," 96–101.
Pages in *Latter-day Prophets Speak:* 48–49.

Selected Questions for Discussion

What is death? A separation.

What is "physical death"? The separation of the spirit from the physical body.

Brigham Young: "What is commonly called death does not destroy the body, it only causes a separation of spirit and body."[25]

Joseph F. Smith: "That which we call death is merely the slumber and rest of this mortal clay, and that only for a little season, while the spirit, the life, has gone to enjoy again the presence and society of those from whence it came, and to whom it is joy again to return."[26]

Orson F. Whitney: "The change called death is but a temporary separation of the spirit from the body. . . . None of our dear departed ones are dead. They have but gone before. This so-called death, when properly understood, is simply a going back home."[27]

Boyd K. Packer: "Mortal death is no more an ending than birth was a beginning."[28]

Why is the term temporal death *often used in the Book of Mormon in place of physical death?* Physical death (separation of the spirit and the physical body) is "temporary." "And we see that death comes upon mankind, yea, . . . the temporal death" (Alma 12:24).

Why is death necessary? Death is the natural consequence of the Fall of Adam.

"By reason of transgression cometh the fall, which fall bringeth death" (Moses 6:59).

Bruce R. McConkie: "Our scriptures say: 'Death hath passed upon all men, to fulfil the merciful plan of the great Creator.' (2 Ne. 9:6.) Where the true Saints are concerned there is no sorrow in death except that which attends a temporary separation from loved ones. Birth and death are both essential steps in the unfolding drama of eternity.

"We shouted for joy at the privilege of becoming mortal because without the tests of mortality there could be no eternal life. We now sing praises to the great Redeemer for the privilege of passing from this life because without death and the resurrection we could not be raised in immortal glory and gain eternal life. . . .

"Now, we do not seek death, though it is part of the merciful plan of the great Creator. Rather, we rejoice in life."[29]

Should we mourn for those who die? Yes. However, for the righteous who die we should mourn only because we are temporarily separated from them.

Joseph Smith: "The Lord takes many away, even in infancy, that they may escape the envy of man, and the sorrows and evils of this present world; they were too pure, too lovely, to live on earth; therefore, if rightly considered, instead of mourning we have reason to rejoice as they are delivered from evil, and we shall soon have them again."[30]

Spencer W. Kimball: "In death do we grieve for the one who passes on, or is it self-pity? To doubt the wisdom and justice of the passing of a loved one is to place a limitation on the term of life. It is to say that it is more important to continue to live here than to go into other fields. Do we grieve when our son is graduated from the local high school and is sent away from home to a university of higher learning? Do we grieve inconsolably when our son is called away from our daily embrace to distant lands to preach the gospel? To continue to grieve without faith and understanding and trust when a son goes into another world is to question the long-range program of God, life eternal with all its opportunities and blessings."[31]

Spencer W. Kimball: "If we say that early death is a calamity, disaster, or tragedy, would it not be saying that mortality is preferable to earlier entrance into the spirit world and to eventual salvation and exaltation? If mortality be the perfect state, then death would be frustration, but the gospel teaches us there is no tragedy in death, but only in sin. '. . . blessed are the dead that die in the Lord. . . . ' (D&C 63:49.)"[32]

Who must die? Everyone. "As in Adam all die" (1 Corinthians 15:22).

Did Jesus Christ have power over death? Could he have lived forever? Yes, to both questions; however, he had to die in order to bring about the resurrection of all mankind, who "must needs die" (see 2 Samuel 14:14).

What power enabled Jesus Christ to overcome death (to bring about the resurrection)? The power he received as the "Only Begotten Son of God" in the flesh. The father of the physical body of Jesus Christ was our (and his) immortal Father in Heaven. "For as the Father hath life in himself; so hath he given to the Son to have life in himself" (John 5:26).

Are both death and the resurrection infinite? Yes. Every living thing possesses a spirit that must be separated at least temporarily from its physical body, which is death. Likewise, the spirit of every living thing must eventually be rejoined with its physical body, which is resurrection.

What is the difference between a translated being and a resurrected being? A resurrected being has already gone through the processes of both death and resurrection.

Do translated beings need to die? Yes. Joseph Fielding Smith: "Translated beings are still mortal and will have to pass through the experience of death, or the separation of the spirit and the body, although this will be instantaneous"[33] (see also 3 Nephi 28:17, 36–40).

What is meant by the term spiritual death*?* The spirit is separated from God.

Can the spirit die? No. The spirit is eternal. The spiritual death referred to in the scriptures pertains to the relationship of the spirit to the Spirit of our Heavenly Father. However, the spirit cannot be destroyed or annihilated.

What did the Savior mean when he said, "Whosoever . . . believeth in me shall never die" (John 11:26)? He was referring primarily to spiritual death; however, in the preceding verse he referred also to the power of the resurrection: "I am the resurrection, and the life: he that believeth in me, though he were dead, yet shall he live."

What is meant by the statement that the righteous "shall not taste of death"? Their death shall not be bitter. "Those that die in me shall not taste of death, for it shall be sweet unto them; And they that die not in me, wo unto them, for their death is bitter" (D&C 42:46–47).

Does an individual on this earth now have choice or agency as to whether he or she will die a physical death? No.

Does that mean we are predestined to die? That depends on your definition of predestination. In the pre-earthly existence, we had agency or freedom of choice as to whether or not we would come upon this physical earth and take upon ourselves mortal bodies; however, we "used up" that agency in the pre-earthly existence.

Thus, now we *must* die. Those people who do not believe in (or understand) our pre-earthly existence would probably say we are predestined to die. But the fact is that at one time we had agency in whether or not we would die.

OUTLINE 4: THE POSTMORTAL SPIRIT WORLD

Topical Guide: "Spirits in Prison," 494.
Bible Dictionary: "Paradise," 742.
Index to Triple Combination: "Spirit World," 346.
Articles in *Jesus Christ and His Gospel:* "Spirit Prison," 443–44; "Spirit World," 446–49.
Pages in *Latter-day Prophets Speak:* 26–35.

Selected Questions for Discussion

Who goes into the postmortal spirit world upon death? "Now, concerning the state of the soul between death and the resurrection—Behold, it has been made known unto me by an angel, that the spirits of all men, as soon as they are departed from this mortal body, . . . whether they be good or evil, are taken home to that God who gave them life" (Alma 40:11).

Brigham Young: "It reads that the spirit goes to God who gave it. Let me render this Scripture a little plainer; when the spirits leave their bodies they are in the presence of our Father and God, [in the sense that] they are prepared then to see, hear and understand spiritual things. But where is the spirit world? It is incorporated within this celestial system. Can you see it with your natural eyes? No. Can you see spirits in this room? No. Suppose the Lord should touch your eyes that you might see, could you then see the spirits? Yes, as plainly as you now see bodies, as did the servant of Elijah [2 Kings 6:17]. If the Lord would permit it, and it was His will that it should be done, you could see the spirits that have departed from this world as plainly as you now see bodies with your natural eyes."[34]

If we can be permitted to see and visit with those in the postmortal spirit world, can they also be permitted to see and visit with us? Yes.

Joseph F. Smith: "Those who have passed beyond, can see more clearly through the veil back here to us than it is possible for us to see to them from our sphere of action. . . . We live in their presence, they see us, they are solicitous for our welfare, they love us now more than ever. For now they see the dangers that beset us; . . . their desire for our well being, must be greater than that which we feel for ourselves."[35]

Joseph F. Smith: "Our fathers and mothers, brothers, sisters and friends who have passed away from this earth, having been faithful, and worthy to enjoy these rights and privileges, may have a mission given them to visit relatives and friends upon the earth again, bringing from the divine Presence messages of love, of warning, of reproof and instruction to those whom they had learned to love in the flesh."[36]

Charles A. Callis: "Death does not congeal the lips of those who go before us; they are not far from us and they help us more than we know."[37]

Is the postmortal spirit world the same as the pre-earthly spirit world? No.

Where is the postmortal spirit world? It is on this earth.

Brigham Young: "When you lay down this tabernacle, where are you going? Into the spiritual world. . . . Where is the spirit world? It is right here. Do the good and evil spirits go together? Yes, they do. Do they both inhabit one kingdom? Yes, they do. . . . Do they go beyond the boundaries of the organized earth? No, they do not."[38]

Brigham Young: "The spirit world . . . is on this earth."[39]

Parley P. Pratt: "The [postmortal] spirit world is not the heaven where Jesus Christ [and] his Father . . . dwell. . . . As to its location, it is here on the very planet where we were born; or, in other words, the earth."[40]

What are the major divisions in the postmortal spirit world?

1. *Paradise.* Who qualifies to go to paradise? What are some of the conditions in paradise? What are some of the major activities of people in paradise? See Luke 23:43; Alma 40:12; D&C 77:2; 138:16, 36.

2. *Spirit "prison."* Who goes to the spirit prison? What are some of the major activities there? What enables a person to leave the spirit prison? For answers, see especially 1 Peter 3:19; 4:16; Alma 40:13–14; D&C 76:73; 138:28–29, 57; Moses 7:38, 57.

Brigham Young: "Suppose . . . that a man is evil in his heart—wholly given up to wickedness, and in that condition dies, his spirit will enter the spirit-world intent upon evil."[41]

What can we do here in this life to help people leave the spirit prison? Search out the vital statistics concerning their lives here upon earth, and then act as vicarious proxies in doing their temple work for them.

Brigham Young: "You may ask if they are baptized there [in the postmortal spirit world]? No. Can they have hands laid upon them for the gift of the Holy

Ghost? No. None of the outward ordinances that pertain to the flesh are administered there, but the light, glory, and power of the Holy Ghost are enjoyed."[42]

Is the veil of forgetfulness (the "veil of mortality") automatically removed at the time of death when the person enters the postmortal spirit world? No. However, Jesus Christ and perhaps some other righteous persons have been so faithful and diligent in this life that the veil of forgetfulness has been removed from them while they were still living on earth.

By what means or power is the veil of forgetfulness removed? By the power of the individual's spirit, working in conjunction with the Spirit of our Heavenly Father. (See D&C 8:1–4 and the accompanying footnote references for these verses.)

What are some of the major conditions or characteristics in the postmortal spirit world? The spirit body is perfect. Spirits know each other. Spirits have the ability to travel in time and space.

Brigham Young: "The brightness and glory of the next apartment is inexpressible. . . . They move with ease and like lightning. If we want to visit Jerusalem, or this, that, or the other place—and I presume we will be permitted if we desire—there we are, looking at its streets. If we want to behold Jerusalem as it was in the days of the Savior; or if we want to see the Garden of Eden as it was when created, there we are, and we see it as it existed spiritually, for it was created first spiritually and then temporally, and spiritually it still remains. . . . Here, we are continually troubled with ills and ailments of various kinds . . . , but in the spirit world we are free from all this."[43]

Parley P. Pratt: "[The postmortal spirit world] is an intermediate state, a probation, a place of preparation, improvement, instruction, or education, where spirits are chastened and improved, and where, if found worthy, they may be taught a knowledge of the gospel."[44]

How long will a person remain in the postmortal spirit world? From his or her death until his or her resurrection. For some, it will be a long time (as an example, Cain will spend thousands of years there); for others, it will be only the "twinkling of an eye" (as examples, translated beings and the righteous upon the earth at the Second Coming and during the Millennium).

What analogies might be used to help a person understand more about the conditions and characteristics of the postmortal spirit world? The different "frequencies" involved in sight and in hearing. Radio. Television. Internet systems. Information highway. As an example, hundreds of sounds now surround us, but we cannot hear them by ourselves—these sounds are on a frequency our ears cannot hear. However, a radio can change the frequencies of these sounds into frequencies our ears can hear.

Does an individual on this earth now have choice or agency as to whether he or she will eventually go to the postmortal spirit world? No.

OUTLINE 5: THE RESURRECTION

Topical Guide: "Resurrection," 426–27.
Bible Dictionary: "Resurrection," 761.
Index to Triple Combination: "Resurrection," 302–3.
Articles in *Jesus Christ and His Gospel*: "Immortality," 242–44; "Immortality and Eternal Life," 244–45; "Resurrection of Jesus Christ," 272–73; "Resurrection," 417–20.
Pages in *Latter-day Prophets Speak*: 36–49.

Selected Questions for Discussion

What is resurrection? Resurrection is the reuniting of the spirit with its physical body. Resurrection is one of the unconditional aspects of the Atonement of Jesus Christ.

John Taylor: "In the resurrection, both body and spirit will . . . be reunited."[45]

Hyrum M. Smith: "Death is the dissolution of the body, and the resurrection is the reanimation of the body; yea the actual and literal reuniting of the Spirit with the body."[46]

Who is resurrected? All will be resurrected, without exception. Even sons of perdition in the flesh will be resurrected (see 1 Corinthians 15:22; Alma 11:44).

Joseph F. Smith: "Every creature that is born in the image of God will be resurrected from the dead. . . . Just as sure as we go down into the grave, through the transgression of our first parents, by whom death came into the world, so sure will we be resurrected from the dead by the power of Jesus Christ. It matters not whether we have done well or ill, whether we have been intelligent or ignorant, or whether we have been bondsmen or slaves or freemen, all men will be raised from the dead."[47]

Is the resurrection "infinite"? Yes.

Does this mean that every spirit that has had a "body" must be resurrected, whether it is the spirit of a person, or the spirit of an animal, of a plant, of a fish, or even of an insect? Yes. The resurrection applies to the earth itself (see D&C

88:17–18, 25–26) and to everything that has ever lived on this earth. Some leaders of the Church have suggested that the resurrection might also apply to everything that has ever lived on any of the earths created by Jesus Christ.

Must every person be resurrected? Yes.

Is there a literal resurrection of a physical body? Yes.

Joseph Fielding Smith: "The Savior is not going to save only mankind. Everything God has created must be restored, . . . everything the Lord has created. . . . Everything that has life [was] created in the image of its spirit, and is a living soul, and therefore entitled to the resurrection."[48]

By what power or means is the resurrection accomplished?

1. *By the power of God the Father and of Jesus Christ the Son.* John Taylor: "The Son hath life inherent in Himself, even as the Father hath life in Himself, He having received this power from the Father. Also, . . . He had power in Himself . . . to lay down this body, and also to take it up again; and in this respect He differed from others. . . . Hence . . . He . . . becomes the means of the resurrection of all men from the dead"[49] (see also 1 Corinthians 6:14).

2. *By the power of our own spirit.* Joseph F. Smith: "Jesus, the Only Begotten of the Father, . . . had power to lay down his life and take it up again, and if we keep inviolate the covenants of the Gospel, remaining faithful and true to the end, we too, in his name and through his redeeming blood, will have power in due time to resurrect these our bodies after they shall have been committed to the earth."[50]

Joseph F. Smith: "What is the body without the spirit? It is lifeless clay. What is it that affects this lifeless clay? It is the spirit, [and the spirit] will redeem these tabernacles and bring them forth out of the graves."[51]

Spencer W. Kimball: "There will be a literal resurrection, when this live and conscious spirit will return . . . to take up its reconstructed and resurrected body."[52]

Was anyone resurrected before the resurrection of Jesus Christ? No. No one was resurrected before Jesus Christ; he is the "firstfruits" of the resurrection (1 Corinthians 15:20) and made it possible for others subsequently to be resurrected.

What is the "first resurrection"? The resurrection of the righteous or the just. If a person is resurrected at the first opportunity he has to be resurrected after his death, then he comes forth in the morning of the first resurrection.

What is the "second resurrection"? The resurrection of the wicked or unjust.

Has there been a general resurrection since the resurrection at the time of Christ? No. The first general resurrection was at the time Jesus Christ was resurrected; the next general resurrection will be at the time of the second coming of Jesus Christ. However, if it is necessary for a specific person to be resurrected in order to perform a mission here on earth (such as the angel Moroni) that person might be resurrected.

What is the status (shape, form, frame) of the body when it is resurrected from the dead? The physical body will be restored to its proper and perfect form or frame (see Alma 11:43–45; 40:23; 41:4), regardless of what may have happened to the physical body at the time of death or after the time of death.

What is the state *or* condition *of the body when it is resurrected?* The physical body will come forth from the grave as it is laid down. Then, immediately after the resurrection, the body will begin to grow and develop (for children) and to be restored to its perfect condition (for the aged and infirm).

Joseph Smith: "All men will come from the grave as they lie down."[53]

John Taylor: "When the resurrection . . . of man shall be consummated, . . . he [will] still be in the same image, and have the same likeness, without variation or change in any of his parts or faculties, except the substitution of spirit for blood."[54]

Joseph F. Smith: "What a glorious thought it is, to me at least, . . . that those from whom we have to part here, we will meet again and see as they are. We will meet the same identical being . . . , even to the wounds in the flesh. Not that a person will always be marred by scars, wounds, deformities, defects or infirmities, for these will be removed in their course, in their proper time, according to the merciful providence of God."[55]

Joseph Fielding Smith: "The mortal body will not grow in the grave, for that is contrary to nature. . . . After the resurrection . . . deformities will be erased."[56]

Are these the same conditions for the resurrection of the bodies of children? Yes.

Joseph F. Smith: "The child that was buried in its infancy will come up in the form of the child that it was when it was laid down; then it will begin to develop. From the day of the resurrection, the body will develop."[57]

Joseph Fielding Smith: "Children will rise as they were laid away, but after the resurrection their bodies will grow to the full stature of their spirits."[58]

Is the resurrection a type of judgment? Yes. At the time of the resurrection, you will come forth with a body of a particular "order" of matter. Thus, this is a type or degree of judgment.

Is it the "final" judgment? No.

Does an individual on this earth now have choice or agency as to whether he or she will be resurrected from the dead? No.

Outline 6: The Three Degrees of Glory

Topical Guide: "Celestial Glory," 54; "Telestial Glory," 518; "Terrestrial Glory," 522.
Bible Dictionary: "Degrees of Glory," 655.
Index to Triple Combination: "Celestial Glory," 44; "Telestial Glory," 361–62; "Terrestrial," 364.
Articles in *Jesus Christ and His Gospel:* "Celestial Kingdom," 56; "Degrees of Glory," 101–4; "Telestial Kingdom," 451–52; "Terrestrial Kingdom," 454–55.
Pages in *Latter-day Prophets Speak:* 61–70.

Selected Questions for Discussion

What are the "orders" or "degrees" of the physical matter comprising resurrected bodies? What are the attributes or characteristics of people who inherit each of these different "degrees"?

1. *Celestial glory.* They who "come forth in the resurrection of the just," "received the testimony of Jesus," "were baptized . . . in his name . . . that by keeping the commandments they might be washed and cleansed from all their sins, and receive the Holy Spirit by the laying on of hands of him who is ordained and sealed unto this power," and "overcome all things" (D&C 76:50–60). These people might be characterized as being "thee oriented."

2. *Terrestrial glory.* They "who died without law," "the spirits of men kept in prison," "who received not the testimony of Jesus in the flesh, but afterwards received it," "who are honorable men of the earth," "who are not valiant in the testimony of Jesus" (D&C 76:71–79). These people might be characterized as being "we oriented."

3. *Telestial glory.* They "who received not the gospel of Christ, neither the testimony of Jesus," "who deny not the Holy Spirit," "who are thrust down to hell," "who shall not be redeemed from the devil until the last resurrection," "who will not be gathered with the saints, . . . and received into the cloud," "who are liars, and sorcerers, and adulterers, and whoremongers, and whosoever loves and makes a lie." "And . . . where God and Christ dwell they cannot come, worlds without end" (D&C 76:81–88, 98–112). These people might be characterized as being "me oriented."

4. *Bodies "without glory."* They who "are the sons of perdition, of whom I say that it had been better for them never to have been born." They "deny the truth and defy my power— . . . concerning whom I have said there is no forgiveness in this

world nor in the world to come—Having . . . crucified [the Only Begotten Son of the Father] unto themselves." These are "the only ones on whom the second death shall have any power" (compare D&C 76:31–39).

How many "heavens" or "degrees" are found within each of the orders of the resurrection? There are three heavens or degrees within the celestial kingdom. It is not known precisely how many there are in the other "orders." "In my Father's house are many mansions: if it were not so, I would have told you. I go to prepare a place for you" (John 14:2).

James E. Talmage: "The three kingdoms of widely differing glories are organized on an orderly plan of gradation. . . . The telestial kingdom comprises several subdivisions; this is also the case . . . with the celestial; and, by analogy, we conclude that a similar condition prevails in the terrestrial. Thus the innumerable degrees of merit amongst mankind are provided for in an infinity of graded glories."[59]

What determines the "order" or "degree" of resurrected body an individual will receive? This is largely determined by the individual himself or herself (see D&C 88:2–4, 15–31). What laws has the individual obeyed? Over what laws does he or she have power?

Wilford Woodruff: "If a man cannot abide a celestial law, he cannot receive a celestial glory, if a man cannot abide a terrestrial law he cannot receive a terrestrial glory; and if he cannot abide a telestial law he cannot receive a telestial glory, but will have to dwell in a kingdom which is not a kingdom of glory. This is according to the revelations of God to us."[60]

Joseph F. Smith: "When we come forth out of the grave, . . . our spirits shall enter into [our physical bodies] again, and they shall become living souls. . . . And then those who have . . . been subject and obedient to the celestial law will . . . be quickened by the celestial glory. And those who have . . . been subject and obedient to the terrestrial law will . . . be quickened by the terrestrial glory. And those who have . . . been subject and obedient to the telestial law, will . . . be quickened by a telestial glory."[61]

George Q. Cannon: "Why is it that there are these differences? Is it because God has chosen some of us for the telestial glory, some of us for the terrestrial glory, and some of us for the celestial glory? No, there is no such predestination as this. We are all born with our free agency; with the power within ourselves, aided by the blessing of God, to attain unto the highest glory. How shall we attain unto the highest glory? There is only one way, and that is by observing the highest laws. . . . The man or woman who expects to attain to the highest glory without obeying these laws, deceives himself or herself. It cannot be done."[62]

Melvin J. Ballard: "Those who come forth in the celestial glory with celestial bodies have a body that is more refined. It is different. The very fibre and texture of the celestial body is more pure and holy than a telestial or terrestrial body, and a celestial body alone can endure celestial glory."[63]

What should be the goal of every person on the earth so far as a degree of glory in the hereafter is concerned? To inherit the highest degree within the celestial kingdom.

Wilford Woodruff: "Celestial glory is worth all we possess; if it calls for every dollar we own and our lives into the bargain, if we obtain an entrance into the celestial kingdom of God it will amply repay us."[64]

What does the individual need to do in order to inherit the celestial kingdom? Become sanctified, pure, spotless (see 3 Nephi 27:19–27). Technically, baptism is not a prerequisite for the celestial kingdom; for example, "all children who die before they arrive at the years of accountability [and thus before baptism] are saved in the celestial kingdom of heaven" (D&C 137:10). However, for all those who have committed sin, baptism of both water and the spirit are necessary for them to be sanctified; thus "Except a man be born of water and of the Spirit, he cannot enter into the kingdom of God" (John 3:5).

What does the individual need to do in order to inherit the highest degree *of the celestial kingdom?* Become sanctified and obey all of the laws and commandments of our Heavenly Father, including the law of the "new and everlasting covenant of marriage."

What about those who do not marry in this life? Everyone will have the opportunity to marry if he or she wishes, if not in this life, then in the life hereafter.

What role does the gospel of Jesus Christ play in regard to the celestial kingdom? The gospel of Jesus Christ contains the principles and ordinances that must be learned and followed in order for each of us to enter the presence of God the Father with a resurrected body of celestial matter.

George Albert Smith: "The gospel has been restored in these latter days to prepare men for the celestial kingdom."[65]

Can a person progress from one kingdom of glory to another in the hereafter? The scriptures indicate some restrictions pertaining to progression from some of the kingdoms to other kingdoms.

Melvin J. Ballard: "So far as the telestial group is concerned . . . 'Where God and Christ dwell they cannot come, worlds without end' [D&C 76:112]. I take it upon the same basis, the same argument likewise applies to the terrestrial world."[66]

Spencer W. Kimball: "After a person has been assigned to his place in the kingdom, . . . he will never advance from his assigned glory to another glory. . . . That is why we must make our decisions early in life and why it is imperative that such decisions be right."[67]

Does an individual on this earth now have choice or agency as to whether or not he or she will receive some "order" or "degree" of physical body at the time of his or her resurrection? No. However, the individual definitely has agency to decide which laws he or she will obey and thus which order of resurrected body he or she will receive.

OUTLINE 7: THE FINAL JUDGMENT

Topical Guide: "Jesus Christ, Judge," 248; "Judgment," 262–63; "Judgment, the Last," 263.
Index to Triple Combination: "Judgment," 189–90.
Articles in *Jesus Christ and His Gospel*: "Judgment," 311–14; "Judgment Day, Final," 314–17.
Pages in *Latter-day Prophets Speak*: 50–60.

Selected Questions for Discussion
Who will be judged at the final judgment? Everyone will be judged—"we shall all stand before the judgment seat of Christ" (Romans 14:10).
Joseph F. Smith: "Every man will have to render an account of his stewardship, and every one will be held responsible for his own works, whether good or evil."[68]
When does the "final judgment" occur for an individual in relationship to that individual's resurrection? After the resurrection. "When all men shall have passed from this first death unto life, . . . they must appear before the judgment-seat of the Holy One of Israel; and then cometh the judgment" (2 Nephi 9:15).
Of what will each individual be judged at the final judgment? His or her thoughts, words, and deeds (see Alma 12:14–15). "For our words will condemn us, yea, all our works will condemn us; . . . and our thoughts will also condemn us" (Alma 12:14). "For God shall bring every work into judgment, with every secret thing, whether it be good, or whether it be evil" (Ecclesiastes 12:14). "For all thy doings thou shalt be brought into judgment" (1 Nephi 10:20). "I say unto you, That every idle word that men shall speak, they shall give account thereof in the day of judgment" (Matthew 12:36).

Brigham Young: "Each and every intelligent being will be judged according to the deeds done in the body, according to his works, faith, desires, and honesty or dishonesty before God; every *trait* of his character will receive its just merit or demerit, and he will be judged according to the law of heaven."[69]

Brigham Young: "We shall be judged according to the deeds done in the body and according to the thoughts and intents of the heart."[70]

John Taylor: "For every word and every secret thought we shall have to give an account in the day when accounts have to be rendered before God."[71]

Under whose direction will the final judgment take place? Who is the judge of the "quick" and the "dead"? Jesus Christ is ordained of God to be Judge both of the living and of the dead. "I will execute judgment: I am the LORD" (Ecclesiastes 12:12). "The Lord shall judge the ends of the earth" (1 Samuel 2:10). "Every man's judgment cometh from the Lord" (Proverbs 29:26). "The Father judgeth no man, but hath committed all judgment unto the Son" (John 5:22). "I, the Lord, will judge all men according to their works, according to the desire of their hearts" (D&C 137:9).

What words characterize the nature and process of the final judgment? "The judgments of the Lord are true and righteous altogether" (Psalm 19:9). "The judgment of God is according to truth" (Romans 2:2). "He shall execute judgment in righteousness" (1 Nephi 22:21; see also John 8:16; Moses 6:57).

Spencer W. Kimball: "The Lord will judge with the same measurements meted out by us. If we are harsh, we should not expect other than harshness. If we are merciful with those who injure us, he will be merciful with us in our errors. If we are unforgiving, he will leave us weltering in our own sins."[72]

Will the final judgment be very similar to the judgments of the world? If not, how will it differ? No. A person's status at the final judgment will be determined largely by the individual himself or herself, but will be confirmed by two or more "witnesses" serving as "judges." People after their judgment see as they are seen, know as they are known, and understand their condition as God understands it; thus everyone leaves the judgment bar knowing that God's judgment is fair and true.

John Taylor: "My understanding of the [final judgment] is, that God has made each man a register within himself, and each man can read his own register. . . . Now, if you are in possession of a spirit or intellectuality of that kind, whereby you are enabled to read your own acts, do you not think that that being who has placed that spirit and intelligence within you holds the keys of that intelligence, and can read it whenever he pleases? Is not that philosophical, reasonable, and scriptural? I think it is. . . . Well, then, upon this principle we can readily perceive how the Lord will bring into judgment the actions of men when he shall call them forth at the last day. . . . Then the secret thoughts of all men are revealed before Him with whom we have to do; we cannot hide them; it would be in vain for a man to say then, I did not do so-and-so; the command would be, Unravel and read the record which he has made of himself, and let it testify in relation to these things. . . . If a man has acted fraudulently against his neighbor—has committed murder, or adultery, or any thing else, and wants to cover it up, that record will stare him in the face, he tells the story himself, and bears witness against himself. It is written that Jesus will judge not after the sight of the eye, or after the hearing of the ear, but with righteousness shall he judge the poor, and reprove with equity the meek of the earth. It is not because somebody has seen things, or heard anything by which a man will be judged and condemned, but it is because that record that is written by the man himself in the tablets of his own mind—that record that cannot lie—will in that day be unfolded before God and angels, and those who shall sit as judges."[73]

John Taylor: "If I had time to enter into this subject alone I could show you upon scientific principles that man himself is a self-registering machine, his eyes, his ears, his nose, the touch, the taste, and all the various senses of the body, are so many media whereby man lays up for himself a record . . . ; and when the time comes for that record to be unfolded . . . all things, we are told, are naked and open before him with whom we have to do."[74]

Spencer W. Kimball: "Men's deeds and thoughts must be recorded in heaven, and recording angels will not fail to make complete recordings of our thoughts and actions. . . . There will be no omissions in the heavenly records, and they will all be available at the day of judgment. . . . At that day we may be sure that we shall receive fair judgment. The judges will have the facts as they may be played back from our own records, and our voices and the pictures of our acts and the recordings of our thoughts will testify against and for us."[75]

Can a person truly forget anything he has ever seen or said or done? Joseph F. Smith: "In reality a man cannot forget anything. He may have a lapse of memory; he may not be able to recall at the moment a thing that he knows, or words that he has spoken; . . . but let God Almighty touch the mainspring of the memory, and awaken recollection, and you will find then that you have not even forgotten a single idle word that you have spoken."[76]

If a person has fully repented of a sin and has been forgiven, can he remember his sin? Yes. If the person could not remember the sin once he had repented, what would prevent him from committing the sin again?

Can *God remember the sin of a repentant sinner?* Yes. If the person can remember, but God cannot remember, then would this not make the person greater than God in this respect?

Does God remember the sin of a repentant sinner? No, he does not remember. It is not that he cannot remember the sins that have been repented of, but he himself has stated that he will not remember them: "I, even I, am he that blotteth out thy transgressions for mine own sake, and will not remember thy sins" (Isaiah 43:25). "For I will forgive their iniquity, and I will remember their sin no more" (Jeremiah 31:34). "And their sins and iniquities will I remember no more" (Hebrews 10:17).

Does an individual on this earth now have choice or agency as to whether he or she will be judged at the final judgment? No.

OUTLINE 8: EXALTATION AND ETERNAL LIFE (GODHOOD)

Topical Guide: "Earth, Purpose of," 115–16; "Eternal Life," 125–26; "Exaltation," 128–29; "Family, Eternal," 138; "God, Eternal Nature of," 173–74; "Jesus Christ, Mission of," 250–51; "Man, Potential to Become like Heavenly Father," 307.

Index to Triple Combination: "Celestial Glory," 44; "Continue, Continuation," 61; "Eternal Life," 98; "Exaltation," 100; "Immortality, Immortal," 161–62; "Salvation," 314–15.

Articles in *Jesus Christ and His Gospel:* "Endless and Eternal," 146–47; "Eternal Life," 151–53; "Eternal Lives, Eternal Increase," 153–54; "Eternal Progression," 154–56; "Exaltation," 159; "Godhood," 205–9; "Heirs," 226–28; "Immortality and Eternal Life," 244–45; "Plan of Salvation, Plan of Redemption," 383–89.

Pages in *Latter-day Prophets Speak:* 71–79.

Selected Questions for Discussion

What is meant by the word exaltation? Exaltation is to be saved in the highest degree of the celestial kingdom with the power of eternal increase. Bruce R. McConkie: "Exaltation consists in the continuation of the family unit in eternity. Exaltation is eternal life, the kind of life which God lives. Those who obtain it . . . [have] a continuation of the seeds forever . . . ; that is, they have spirit children in the resurrection, in relation to which offspring they stand in the same position that God our Father stands to us."[77]

What is meant by the term eternal life? Eternal life is to have the power of eternal increase; sometimes this gift is referred to as "eternal lives" (see D&C 132:24, 55).

Joseph Fielding Smith: "Eternal life is the same kind of life possessed by the Father and the Son with the power of eternal increase."[78]

What differences are there, if any, between these two terms? The two words mean essentially the same; both of them have to do with the power of becoming as God is.

What differences are there, if any, between the terms immortality *and* eternal life*?* Immortality has to do with the resurrection. Eternal life has to do with exaltation in the highest degree of the celestial kingdom.

In what sense or degree should we be concerned with our individual "eternal life"? Marion G. Romney: "The supreme objective of men who understand God, their relationship to him, and his designs for them is to gain eternal life. This is as it should be, for eternal life ' . . . is the greatest of all the gifts of God' (D&C 14:7). To bring men to eternal life is God's 'work and glory.' To this end he conceives, brings into being, directs and uses all his creations (Moses 1:38–39)."[79]

What are some of the attributes that characterize eternal life (eternal lives)?

1. *Immortality, with a resurrected celestial body of flesh and bones.*

2. *Being in the highest degree of the celestial kingdom, in the presence of God our Heavenly Father.*

3. *Having the power of eternal increase (eternal lives).* "This is eternal lives—to know the only wise and true God, and Jesus Christ, whom he hath sent" (D&C 132:24).

4. *Becoming perfect.* "I would that ye should be perfect even as I, or your Father who is in heaven is perfect" (3 Nephi 12:48).

5. *Being a "joint-heir" with Jesus Christ in participating in and enjoying the type of life that God himself enjoys.* "The Spirit itself beareth witness with our spirit, that we are the children of God: and if children, then heirs; heirs of God, and joint-heirs with Christ . . . that we may be also glorified together" (Romans 8:16–17).

Lorenzo Snow: "We believe that we are the offspring of our Father in heaven. . . . There is the nature of deity in the composition of our spiritual organization; in our spiritual birth our Father transmitted to us the capabilities, powers and faculties which he himself possessed, as much so as the child . . . possesses, although in an undeveloped state, the faculties, powers and susceptibilities of its parent."[80]

6. *Godhood.* "Then shall they be gods, because they have no end . . . they have all power, and the angels are subject unto them" (D&C 132:20).

Joseph Smith: "You have got to learn how to be Gods yourselves, ... the same as all Gods have done before you, namely, by going from one small degree to another, and from a small capacity to a great one; from grace to grace, from exaltation to exaltation."[81]

Lorenzo Snow: "As man now is, God once was; As God now is, man may be."[82]

John Taylor: "Man ... is a God in embryo and will live and progress throughout the eternal ages, if obedient to the laws of the Godhead, as the Gods progress throughout the eternal ages."[83]

Brigham Young: "Man is made an agent to himself before his God; he is organized for the express purpose, that he may become like his master.... [W]hen we have [proven ourselves] and been faithful with all things He puts into our possession ... [we will become] capable of creating worlds on worlds, and becoming Gods."[84]

Can men and women, as gods and goddesses, organize and populate new worlds? Yes.

Brigham Young: "I expect, if ... faithful, ... that [we] shall see the time ... that we shall know how to prepare to organize an earth like this—know how to people that earth, how to redeem it, how to sanctify it, and how to glorify it, with those who live upon it who hearken to our counsels.... I am on the way, and so are you, and every faithful servant of God.... This is a key for you. The faithful will become Gods."[85]

Is eternal progression a law of heaven? Yes.

Wilford Woodruff: "If there was a point where man in his progression could not proceed any further, the very idea would throw a gloom over every intelligent and reflecting mind."[86]

Does an individual now have choice or agency as to whether he or she will receive or inherit exaltation or eternal life? Absolutely *yes.*

Concluding Thoughts

Bruce R. McConkie: "The last word has not been spoken on any subject. Streams of living water shall yet flow from the Eternal Spring who is the source of all truth. There are more things we do not know about the doctrines of salvation than there are things we do know."[87]

Brigham Young: "Could we live to the age of Methuselah ... and spend our lives in searching after the principles of eternal life, we would find ... that we had been but children . . . just commencing to learn the things which pertains to the eternities of the Gods."[88]

Notes

These outlines were prepared to help guide discussions in Education Week programs throughout the Church.

1. Daniel H. Ludlow, ed., *Jesus Christ and His Gospel: Selections from the Encyclopedia of Mormonism* (New York: Macmillan Publishing Co., 1992; Salt Lake City: Deseret Book Co., 1994).
2. Daniel H. Ludlow, ed., *Latter-day Prophets Speak* (Salt Lake City: Bookcraft, 1948).
3. *Teachings of the Prophet Joseph Smith*, 354.
4. *History of the Church*, 3:387.
5. *Gospel Doctrine*, 12.
6. *Teachings of the Prophet Joseph Smith*, 353–54.
7. Joseph F. Smith, John R. Winder, and Anthon H. Lund, in *Messages of the First Presidency*, 4:205.
8. Joseph Fielding Smith, *The Progress of Man* (Salt Lake City: Deseret Book Co., 1964), 11.
9. *Gospel Doctrine*, 12.
10. *Teachings of the Prophet Joseph Smith*, 181.
11. Brigham Young, in *Journal of Discourses*, 9:286.
12. John Taylor, "Extract from a work by Elder John Taylor about to be published in France," *Millennial Star*, 13 (15 March 1851): 81.
13. Joseph F. Smith, in *Journal of Discourses*, 19:259.
14. Joseph F. Smith, in *Journal of Discourses*, 25:58.
15. Brigham Young, in *Journal of Discourses*, 7:237.
16. Lorenzo Snow, "Address to the Saints in Great Britain," *Millennial Star*, 13 (15 March 1851): 363.
17. Brigham Young, in *Journal of Discourses*, 11:43.
18. Joseph F. Smith, in *Journal of Discourses*, 23:169.
19. James E. Talmage, *The Vitality of Mormonism* (Salt Lake City: Deseret Book Co., 1948), 238.
20. John Taylor, "Extract from a work by Elder John Taylor about to be published in France," *Millennial Star*, 13 (15 March 1851): 81.
21. Brigham Young, in *Journal of Discourses*, 8:150.
22. Brigham Young, in *Journal of Discourses*, 6:333.
23. *Doctrines of Salvation*, 1:69.
24. Bruce R. McConkie, *Report of the Brisbane Australia Area Conference*, Feb.–Mar. 1976, 15.
25. Brigham Young, in *Journal of Discourses*, 3:276.
26. Joseph F. Smith, in *Journal of Discourses*, 19:263.
27. Orson F. Whitney, "We Walk by Faith," *Improvement Era*, 19 (May 1916): 608–9.
28. Boyd K. Packer, in Conference Report, October 1975, 147.
29. Bruce R. McConkie, in Conference Report, October 1976, 158–59.
30. *History of the Church*, 4:553.
31. *Teachings of Spencer W. Kimball*, 41.
32. Spencer W. Kimball, *Faith Precedes the Miracle* (Salt Lake City: Deseret Book Co., 1972), 101.
33. Joseph Fielding Smith, *Answers to Gospel Questions*, 5 vols. (Salt Lake City: Deseret Book Co., 1957–66), 1:165.
34. Brigham Young, in *Journal of Discourses*, 3:368.
35. Joseph F. Smith, in *Messages of the First Presidency*, 5:6–7.
36. Joseph F. Smith, in *Journal of Discourses*, 22:351.
37. Charles A. Callis, in Conference Report, October 1939, 20.
38. Brigham Young, in *Journal of Discourses*, 3:369.
39. Brigham Young, in *Journal of Discourses*, 3:372.

40. Parley P. Pratt, *Key to the Science of Theology* (Salt Lake City: Deseret Book Co., 1965), 126.
41. Brigham Young, in *Journal of Discourses,* 7:333.
42. Brigham Young, in *Journal of Discourses,* 2:138.
43. Brigham Young, in *Journal of Discourses,* 14:231.
44. Pratt, *Key to the Science of Theology,* 126.
45. John Taylor, *The Government of God* (Liverpool, England: S. W. Richards, 1852), 27.
46. Hyrum M. Smith, in Conference Report, April 1917, 31.
47. Joseph F. Smith, "Discourse by President Joseph F. Smith," *Millennial Star,* 58 (12 March 1896): 162.
48. Joseph Fielding Smith, *Seek Ye Earnestly* (Salt Lake City: Deseret Book Co., 1970), 280.
49. John Taylor, *Mediation and Atonement* (Salt Lake City: Deseret News Co., 1882), 146–47.
50. Joseph F. Smith, in *Journal of Discourses,* 18:277.
51. Joseph F. Smith, in *Journal of Discourses,* 25:250.
52. *Teachings of Spencer W. Kimball,* 46.
53. *Teachings of the Prophet Joseph Smith,* 199.
54. Taylor, *Mediation and Atonement,* 166.
55. *Gospel Doctrine,* 23.
56. Joseph Fielding Smith, *Church History and Modern Revelation,* 2 vols. (Salt Lake City: The Church of Jesus Christ of Latter-day Saints, 1953), 2:301.
57. *Gospel Doctrine,* 24.
58. Smith, *Church History and Modern Revelation,* 2:301.
59. James E. Talmage, *The House of the Lord,* rev. ed. (Salt Lake City: Deseret Book Co., 1976), 83.
60. Wilford Woodruff, in *Journal of Discourses,* 12:278.
61. *Gospel Doctrine,* 450–51.
62. George Q. Cannon, in Conference Report, April 1900, 54.
63. Melvin J. Ballard, *Sermons and Missionary Services of Melvin J. Ballard,* comp. Bryant S. Hinckley (Salt Lake City: Deseret Book Co., 1949), 256.
64. Wilford Woodruff, in *Journal of Discourses,* 17:250.
65. George Albert Smith, in Conference Report, October 1926, 103.
66. Ballard, *Sermons and Missionary Services of Melvin J. Ballard,* 255.
67. Spencer W. Kimball, *The Miracle of Forgiveness* (Salt Lake City: Bookcraft, 1988), 243–44.
68. Joseph F. Smith, in *Journal of Discourses,* 24:78.
69. Brigham Young, in *Journal of Discourses,* 8:154.
70. Brigham Young, in *Journal of Discourses,* 14:99.
71. John Taylor, in *Journal of Discourses,* 24:232.
72. Kimball, *The Miracle of Forgiveness,* 267.
73. John Taylor, in *Journal of Discourses,* 11:77–79.
74. John Taylor, in *Journal of Discourses,* 26:31.
75. Kimball, *The Miracle of Forgiveness,* 109.
76. *Gospel Doctrine,* 311.
77. Bruce R. McConkie, *Mormon Doctrine,* 2d ed. (Salt Lake City: Bookcraft, 1966), 257.
78. Joseph Fielding Smith, *The Way to Perfection* (Salt Lake City: Deseret Book Co., 1966), 331.
79. Marion G. Romney, in Conference Report, October 1965, 20.
80. Lorenzo Snow, in *Journal of Discourses,* 14:300, 302.
81. *Teachings of the Prophet Joseph Smith,* 346.
82. Lorenzo Snow, in Eliza R. Snow, *Biography and Family Record of Lorenzo Snow* (Salt Lake City: Deseret News Press, 1884), 467.
83. John Taylor, in *Journal of Discourses,* 23:65.
84. Brigham Young, in *Journal of Discourses,* 3:93.
85. Brigham Young, in *Journal of Discourses,* 6:274–75.
86. Wilford Woodruff, in *Journal of Discourses,* 6:120.
87. Bruce R. McConkie, "A New Commandment: Save Thyself and Thy Kindred!" *Ensign,* August 1976, 11.
88. Brigham Young, in *Journal of Discourses,* 3:202–3.

Chapter 1 8

THE PRE-EARTHLY EXISTENCE OF MAN

We have two words in the English language to designate time relationships that have always seemed a little misleading and self-contradictory to me. One of these words—"prehistoric"—is used to denote something very old. I think most of us would agree that the term doesn't really mean what it says when it is broken down into its component parts. That is, it does not refer to a period before history, but to a period before some arbitrary point within history, such as before written history.

The other word that appears to me to be somewhat misleading is used in connection with the soul or the spirit of man. That word is "pre-existence." I suspect that when we use this word we are really thinking of a pre-earthly existence, not of an existence of man before he actually existed, which, of course, would be a contradiction of terms.

Therefore, in discussing the subject of an earlier existence of man, I should like to use the term "pre-earthly existence" rather than the traditional term of "pre-existence." With this as background, let us turn directly to the problem itself: Did we or did we not exist as individuals before we were born on this earth, and, if so, what was the nature of that existence and where did we live?"

All of the major philosophies and religions of the world have attempted to find an answer to this important question, but Christianity, as it is taught in both the Old Testament and the New Testament, offers the most complete and satisfactory answer of all. Although the teachings of the prophets as they are recorded in the present versions of the ancient scripture are not always as clear as many people would like them to be, I believe the prophets very clearly and definitely taught a pre-earthly existence. Modern prophets have added greatly to our knowledge of this earlier life.

First, I should like to outline the teachings of the prophets on the subject of the pre-earthly existence of man. Then I will examine together some of the statements in the Bible that support and clarify these teachings.

Joseph Smith, the prophet of the restoration of the gospel in this dispensation, taught that every person who has lived or who ever will live on this earth had a pre-earthly existence—first, as an individual entity called an "ego" or an "intelligence," and later as a spirit child of God clothed with a spiritual body. The Prophet said:

"The mind or the intelligence which man possesses is co-equal with God himself. . . . I am dwelling on the immortality of the spirit of man. Is it logical to say that the intelligence of spirits is immortal, and yet that it had a beginning? The intelligence of spirits had no beginning, neither will it have an end. That is good logic. That which has a beginning may have an end. There never was a time when there were not spirits; for they are co-equal [coeternal] with our Father in heaven. . . . Intelligence is eternal and exists upon a self-existent principle. It is a spirit from age to age, and there is no creation about it."[1]

At the same time he made this statement, Joseph Smith also maintained that all matter existed in an elementary state from eternity and that it can neither be created nor destroyed, although it can be changed in nature or condition. This truth has since been verified by the researches of science.

The scriptures are not too clear on the exact status of the spirit before it became what the scriptures refer to as an "organized intelligence." However, the scriptures do indicate that sometime in the past this ego, spirit, or intelligence—in other words, the part of your being with which you are now doing your thinking—was clothed with a spiritual body by God. From this time forth we rightfully began to refer to God as our Father. This was our first birth, and through it all we became sons and daughters unto God. Thus, we are all truly brothers and sisters, for we are spiritually all sons and daughters of God.

The spiritual body that we had in the pre-earthly existence, however, was not a body of flesh and bones such as we now have. Rather, it was composed of spiritual matter—matter much more refined, elastic, and pure than the bodies we now have. This truth was taught to us by the Savior. Do you remember the account of the first appearance of the resurrected Christ to the eleven apostles? The apostles were gathered together in a room, and when the resurrected Savior appeared to them, "They were terrified and affrighted, and supposed that they had seen a spirit. And he said unto them: Why are ye troubled? and why do thoughts arise in your hearts? Behold my hands and my feet, that it is I myself; handle me, and see; for a spirit hath not flesh and bones, as ye see me have" (Luke 24:37–39).

In this brief statement, the Savior acknowledges two very important things: First, spirits do exist, and second, spirits do not have bodies of flesh and bones. Many of the earlier prophets were acquainted with the doctrine that we had an existence before this life as spiritual sons and daughters unto God. In Hebrews 12:9 Paul states: "Furthermore, we have had fathers of our flesh which corrected us, and we gave them reverence: shall we not much rather be in subjection unto the Father of spirits and live?" Here Paul clearly states that we all have a Father of our spirits.

In Numbers 16 and 17 Moses refers to the "God of the spirits of all flesh." In Ecclesiastes 12:7 we read that the spirit will return unto God who gave it. How could a spirit return to God unless it had once been in the presence of God? Also, God told Jeremiah that he was chosen as a prophet in the spirit world before he ever came here upon this earth. In chapter one of his book, Jeremiah tells us, "Then the word of the Lord came unto me, saying: Before I formed thee in the belly I knew thee; and before thou camest forth out of the womb I sanctified thee, and I ordained thee a prophet unto the nations" (Jeremiah 1:4–5).

Job also understood this doctrine. He was asked by the Lord: "Where wast thou when I laid the foundations of the earth? . . . when the morning stars sang together, and all the sons of God shouted for joy?" (Job 38:4, 7). Notice in these verses that the sons of God existed before the earth existed in its present form. Also, notice the plurality of the term "sons."

Another indication that we all lived before we came upon this earth is found in Deuteronomy 32:8: "The most High divided to the nations their inheritance, when he separated the sons of Adam, he set the bounds of the people according to the number of the children of Israel." How could God have known the number of the children of Israel before they ever appeared on the earth unless they existed somewhere else at that time. This idea is substantiated further in Acts 17:26. Here we read that the Lord "hath made of one blood all nations of men for to dwell on all the face of the earth, and hath determined the times before appointed, and the bounds of their habitation." Apparently, God knew every person who was going to come to the earth before they were born here. Paul summarizes these ideas in his epistle to the Romans: "The Spirit itself beareth witness with our spirit, that we are the children of God" (Romans 8:16).

Perhaps the most striking scriptures of all on the doctrine of a pre-earthly existence, however, come from the teachings of the Savior in the New Testament. For example, you may recall this story as recorded in the Gospel of John: "And as Jesus passed by, he saw a man which was blind from birth. And his disciples asked him, saying, Master, who did sin, this man, or his parents, that he was born blind? Jesus answered, Neither hath this man sinned, nor his parents: but that the works of God should be made manifest in him" (John 9:1–3).

Notice the definite implication of a pre-earthly existence in both the question and the answer. If there were no such earlier life, the easiest and most obvious answer of the Savior would have been: "There is no existence before birth; therefore this man could not have sinned before he was born." However, the Savior made no such statement. Instead, he confirmed the belief of his disciples in an existence before birth by acknowledging that it was possible to commit sins before birth, but that this was not the case in the instance of this particular man.

On other instances, the Savior also taught that we are all sons and daughters of God. Did he not teach us to pray to "our Father which art in heaven" (Luke 11:2)? Notice the use of the pronoun "our." Also, when the Savior appeared to Mary Magdalene on the morning of his resurrection, he said to her: "Go to my brethren, and say unto them, I ascend unto my Father, and your Father" (John 20:17). It is obvious that Jesus Christ is saying here that God is our Father in a sense that God is also his Father. That is, God is the Father of all of us as spirit children. This is exemplified in scriptures that refer to Jesus Christ as the "firstborn" (D&C 93:21–22; Colossians 1:15). If Jesus Christ were the only son of God in the spirit, why would the scriptures use the adjective "first"?

Of course, the scriptures make it clear that Jesus has another father-son relationship with God that the rest of us do not have. God is the father of the Savior's physical body as well as of his spirit body. Jesus is the "firstborn" in the spirit but the "only begotten" in the flesh.

What a wonderful message the gospel has for us concerning our pre-earthly existence. We are all truly brothers and sisters—all sons and daughters of divine parentage. This knowledge should help us understand one of the major purposes of life on this earth: to learn to walk by faith in an existence out of the presence of God where a veil is drawn over our eyes concerning our previous life with God. This enables us to gain a testimony of God through faith rather than by sight. The knowledge of a pre-earthly life should help us in our endeavors to love our neighbors as ourselves, and to love God our Father with all our heart, mind, might, and strength. It is indeed one of the greatest truths to be revealed to man.

Notes

From an address delivered over KSL Radio, Salt Lake City, Utah, 3 November 1957.

1. *Teachings of the Prophet Joseph Smith*, 353–54.

Chapter 19

MORAL AGENCY

The subject I should like to examine in this chapter is basic to the gospel of Jesus Christ, and yet I am not going to discuss faith or repentance or the Atonement. But faith, repentance, the Atonement, and all the other principles, ordinances, and doctrines of the gospel are based on this principle; indeed, they would be virtually inoperative and unable to exist without the principle of moral agency.

Concerning the principle of agency, President David O. McKay has written: "Next to the bestowal of life itself, the right to direct that life is God's greatest gift to man. . . . Freedom of choice is more to be treasured than any possession earth can give. It is inherent in the spirit of man. It is a divine gift to every normal being. . . . Everyone has this most precious of all life's endowments—the gift of free agency—man's inherited and inalienable right."[1]

AGENCY IN THE PRE-EARTHLY EXISTENCE

In discussing this topic with you, I would like to begin at the beginning, but so far as I can tell, there never was a beginning so far as the exercising of agency is concerned. According to the Prophet Joseph Smith, our minds or intelligences—those parts of our being with which we think and make choices and determine actions—have always existed. Concerning this the Prophet said:

"The mind or the intelligence which man possesses is co-equal with God himself. . . .

" . . . The intelligence of spirits had no beginning, neither will it have an end.

... There never was a time when there were not spirits; for they are co-equal [co-eternal] with our Father in heaven. ...

" ... Intelligence is eternal and exists upon a self-existent principle. It is a spirit from age to age, and there is no creation about it."[2]

Thus the capacity of choice, which is a most essential element in agency, has evidently always been part of our being.

In the process of time each of our intelligences was clothed with a spiritual body by heavenly parents, and we became personages of spirit with spirit bodies of eyes and ears and hands and feet. All of us on this earth had the same Father of our spirit bodies, and because he lives in heaven we have been rightfully taught to refer to him as "our Father in Heaven."

Our spirit bodies were capable of tremendous accomplishments, but they also had some serious limitations. There were some laws that they could not obey, and therefore there were some blessings not available to them. Thus, our Heavenly Father called us into a grand council in heaven where he proposed a plan that would give us further opportunities of growth and development by giving us further opportunities of choice. There the importance of moral agency and its four necessary and essential conditions were explained to us. First, we must have the opportunity of choice—that is, the operation of law. Second, there must be the possibility of the existence of opposites—good and evil, virtue and vice. These two make possible the third element, freedom of choice—that is, agency. Then finally, we must have knowledge of the law and its consequences. All four of these conditions are necessary in order to accomplish the progression which would enable us to become as our Father in Heaven, which was the main purpose of this new earth plan that he proposed.

When we lived with our Father in Heaven we did not need to exercise faith in his existence. We knew that he was, because we saw him; we walked and talked with him. We knew he existed and were convinced of his existence, but we were not necessarily converted to him and to his great principles, because our knowledge of him had come from external sources with virtually no effort on our part. So that we would come to a knowledge of him in and of ourselves, our Heavenly Father proposed that when we came to this earth through the process of birth, a veil of forgetfulness would be placed over our minds so that we would not remember our pre-earthly existence with him. Only then could the choices that we made here upon this earth truly come from within us. Our Father in Heaven then promised us that while we were here on the earth he would give us law and would provide the possibility of opposites, would give us agency, and would send angels and prophets to teach us and give us scriptures so we could learn the laws and why we should keep them. Thus, he promised us the necessary conditions on this earth so that we could become morally free before him.

The nature of law was also explained in that pre-earthly council—that each law has consequences, opposite and equal. Whenever a law is kept or obeyed, the consequence is a blessing which results in joy or happiness. Whenever a law is broken or disobeyed, the consequence is a punishment, which results in misery or unhappiness. This simple and perhaps overgeneralized explanation of the law of justice portrays how order is accomplished, for in the payment of the law of either obedience or disobedience, the law is brought back into a state of balance and thus order prevails. The law of justice then always requires a payment.

But another law also operates in the moral realm—the law of mercy, which in no way robs or violates the law of justice but which makes possible the vicarious payment of broken law. For example, the law of mercy permits the disobedience of a person to be atoned for, or paid for, by the obedience of the Redeemer, providing that the person who disobeyed the law will cease being disobedient—in other words, providing that person repents and stops breaking the law.

The great plan of salvation and exaltation was then explained to us: why the possibility of opposition must exist upon the earth and how it would occur through the fall of man, how the law of justice would require a payment for the broken law, and how the law of mercy would make the Atonement possible. The explanation of these things was later revealed to the prophet Lehi, and he taught them to his family in these words:

"For it must needs be, that there is an opposition in all things. If not so . . . righteousness could not be brought to pass, neither wickedness, neither holiness nor misery, neither good nor bad. . . .

" . . . There is a God, and he hath created all things, both the heavens and the earth, and all things that in them are, both things to act and things to be acted upon.

"And to bring about his eternal purposes . . . the Lord God gave unto man that he should act for himself. Wherefore, man could not act for himself save it should be that he was enticed by the one or the other. . . .

"And the Messiah cometh in the fulness of time, that he may redeem the children of men from the fall. And because that they are redeemed from the fall they have become free forever, knowing good from evil; to act for themselves and not to be acted upon, save it be by the punishment of the law. . . .

"Wherefore, men are free according to the flesh; and all things are given them which are expedient unto man. And they are free to choose liberty and eternal life, through the great Mediator of all men, or to choose captivity and death" (2 Nephi 2:11, 14–16, 26–27).

It was then explained in this great pre-earthly council that as we would come to the earth the Spirit of Christ would be placed within each of us and another member of the Godhead, the Holy Ghost, would be empowered to witness, reveal, and testify to our spirits. Then, even though we had a veil of mortality over our minds, the Holy Ghost would be able to bring all things to our remembrance if we would listen to the words of the prophets, would read the words of the scriptures, and would respond to the Spirit of Christ that is within each of us by praying to our Father in Heaven. This time, however, the knowledge would come to us by an act of will on our part. We would have internalized it; it would have become part of our very being, and therefore no one throughout all eternity could take this knowledge away from us unless we, by an act of will, would allow this knowledge to be taken away.

Now there were other purposes, of course, for the earth life. We came here also to receive physical bodies capable of procreation. But the God-given power to have children would not be placed in our physical bodies until we had arrived at an age of accountability and had matured in experience so we could exercise our agency in using these powers in righteousness.

It was soon evident when this great plan was presented to us that, because of the Atonement and the principle of agency, this earth life could become a great testing and proving period where, if we proved faithful to all the laws given to us by our Heavenly Father, we would become even as he is and share with him his power and glory. Perhaps it was when we realized this that the "sons of God shouted for joy," as recorded in the book of Job (Job 38:7).

Lucifer's Plan to Deny Agency

There were some, however, in that pre-earthly council who did not shout for joy. They either lacked faith in our Heavenly Father, in the Savior, or in the gospel plan; or they lacked faith in their own ability or willingness to keep the law that would be given to them. Thus they actively opposed the plan of our Heavenly Father. Their leader was called Lucifer, "the son of the morning"; he is also known as the devil or Satan.

Lucifer not only opposed the plan of our Heavenly Father but he sought to amend and change the terms of salvation by denying men their agency and by dethroning our Heavenly Father. The exact words of Lucifer's boast are contained in the book of Moses: "I will redeem all mankind, that one soul shall not be lost, and surely I will do it; wherefore give me thine honor" (Moses 4:1).

We do not know all of the details of Lucifer's amended plan, but we do know from revelation that he "sought to destroy the agency of man" (Moses 4:3). This could be accomplished in many ways, including denying us either the opportunity of choice or the freedom of choice. In either case, not "one soul" would have been lost. It is sin that causes a soul to be lost, but how can a person sin if he does not have the opportunity to sin? That is, how can a person disobey a law if he does not have a law?

Lucifer's plan appealed to some, but it did not appeal to any of us who are here. We saw that under his plan we would lose the challenge of growth and progression. We did not want to live in a world where we would be on the same plane forever. We had enough faith in our Heavenly Father and in his plan, in Jesus Christ, and in ourselves that we wanted to live in a world where there would be opportunities for further development. At the same time, I am sure we realized that if we were not faithful to these laws and opportunities, we might even be worse off than we had been before.

Thus there was a great war in heaven, and a key issue in that war was whether or not man was to be a moral agent while upon the earth. A vote was taken. (By the way, that in itself indicates that we had our agency there; in a sense Lucifer exercised his agency in an attempt to deny us the right to exercise our agency.) Two-thirds of those present voted for the plan of our Heavenly Father; one-third voted against the plan and did not participate in it.

Freedom in the Garden of Eden

So the plan was put into operation. A physical earth was created or organized. Physical bodies were prepared for Adam and Eve. Their spirit bodies were placed in those physical bodies, and they became living souls. Then our Heavenly Father started to keep the promises that he had made to us by giving them the opportunity of choice. He did this by giving them law, by telling them what they should do and what they should not do: "Partake of the fruit of the tree of life." "Multiply." "Do not partake of the fruit of the tree of knowledge of good and evil." Through his selection of the laws, he also gave them the possibility of opposites. Next he explained the consequences of those laws: "Partake of the fruit of the tree of life, and ye shall live forever" (Genesis 3:23). "Multiply, and you shall have joy and rejoicing in your posterity" (Genesis 1:28). "Partake of the fruit of the tree of knowledge of good and evil, and you shall surely die" (Genesis 3:3; Abraham 5:13). Then our Heavenly Father did one other thing: he explained the consequences of their choices and also explained that they would have the freedom to choose under this great earth plan. Notice how all three of these elements are present in one verse in the book of Moses:

"But of the tree of the knowledge of good and evil, thou shalt not eat of it, nevertheless, thou mayest choose for thyself, for it is given unto thee; but, remember that I forbid it, for in the day thou eatest thereof thou shalt surely die" (Moses 3:17).

Well, you know the rest of that story. Lucifer and his followers were cast out of heaven. In order to make all of us subject to him, thus enabling him to put his throne above the throne of God, he needed to accomplish two things: first of all, to get sin into the world, and then to keep Jesus Christ from atoning for that sin.

Therefore, Lucifer tried to get Adam to disobey one of the laws. When he was unsuccessful in this, he concentrated on Eve and finally enticed her to partake of the fruit of the tree of knowledge of good and evil. Eve then persuaded Adam to partake of that same fruit. Although Adam and Eve had great intellect and powers of reason in the Garden of Eden, they were without experience; although they had the opportunity of choice and the freedom of choice in the Garden of Eden, yet they were not morally free because they did not fully understand the consequences of their choice. Oh, they heard the words of our Heavenly Father, "In the day thou eatest thereof thou shalt surely die," but what was death to Adam and Eve? The veil of forgetfulness had already been placed over their minds—they had never seen death nor experienced it; they could not understand it. And because they did not fully comprehend the consequences of what they did, their disobedience of the law is referred to as a transgression, not as a sin, and consequently comes under the unconditional part of the atonement of Jesus Christ.

As a result of those transgressions, two deaths were introduced into the earth: physical death, which eventually resulted from their partaking of that particular fruit; and spiritual death, which resulted from their disobeying our Heavenly Father. Thus misery and suffering, which are the consequences of broken law, entered into the world.

The Atonement of Christ

Now let us skip four thousand years of history and come to the birth of Christ—a very important period so far as all mankind is concerned. Indeed, the prophet Jacob in the Book of Mormon said that if Jesus Christ did not atone, then all mankind must unavoidably perish and we would all "become devils, angels to a devil, to be shut out from the presence of our God, and to remain with the father of lies, in misery, like unto himself" (2 Nephi 9:9). The plan was that Jesus Christ would be born into this earth as the Only Begotten Son of God in the flesh and would have power over the physical death. The plan also required that Jesus Christ would be sinless while he lived upon the earth so that he would have power over all the laws and would be able to atone for the spiritual death introduced by the fall of Adam and Eve.

Lucifer knew these two essential and necessary characteristics that Christ must possess. He may have known this because of his pre-earthly experience; if not, then surely he knew it because of the words of the prophets of God here upon the earth. Therefore, when the Savior was born, Lucifer tried in every way that he could think of to keep Jesus Christ from achieving his great divine destiny. He tried to get Jesus Christ to deny his divine sonship, but the Savior replied, "I came into the world to do the will of my Father." He tried to get Jesus Christ to break one of the laws, for he knew that if he could get the Savior to break only one law—to commit only one sin—then the Savior would not have power over all of the laws and therefore could not atone for the sins of all mankind.

But Jesus completely resisted the enticements of Lucifer; Jesus did not disobey any laws, and so he is referred to in the scriptures as the Sinless One. Jesus Christ was thus able to atone for both the physical death and the spiritual death. He was able to atone for the physical death because of the power that he had inherited from the Father as the Only Begotten Son of God in the flesh; he was *able* to atone for the spiritual death because he was sinless.

The next crucial question was "Would he be *willing* to atone for those deaths? Would he be willing to endure the intense suffering and pain that would be required to pay for the sins of all mankind? Would he be willing to submit to the chains of physical death and thereby voluntarily break the bands or the chains of physical death for all mankind?" The New Testament records the drama of the experiences of the Savior in Gethsemane, at Golgotha, and at the tomb, where he fully atoned for the two deaths, conquering both the grave and hell and thus becoming the great Savior and Redeemer of all mankind. In remembrance of the two aspects of his atonement, we have been commanded that when we partake of the sacrament we partake of two emblems—bread in remembrance of the body of Christ, which he gave as a ransom for all; and a liquid in remembrance of the blood of Christ, which he shed for the remission of our sins (see JST, Matthew 26:22–25).

As a result of the atonement of Jesus Christ, we are all freed from the bondage of the original transgression of Adam and Eve, as well as being freed from all those transgressions we committed before we arrived at the age of accountability. As the Savior himself has said, "I, the Lord God, make you free, therefore ye are free indeed; and the law also maketh you free" (D&C 98:8). Therefore, because of the Atonement, the extent of our individual agency today is in direct proportion to the number and kind of laws we know and keep. Likewise, the loss of our agency today can be measured in direct proportion to the number and kind of laws we disobey. Perfect freedom is made possible to us through the Atonement, but it can come only through perfect obedience to the law.

The atonement of Jesus Christ also meant that Lucifer could not obtain his goal. He cannot win all of us. He cannot win Christ; Christ is already beyond his power. He cannot win those who have already lived on the earth obedient to the laws of our Heavenly Father and who have now been resurrected.

Efforts to Limit Human Freedom

But Lucifer is trying to run up as high a score as he can, and he does this by trying to keep us individually from achieving the great divine purposes for which we came here upon this earth, including the exercise of our agency. He can do it by denying us any one of the four essential qualities of moral agency.

He can do it by denying us the opportunity of choice, and he tries to do this through certain types of governments (such as dictatorships), through the lack of governments (anarchy), and so on.

He tries to do this by destroying, in our minds at least, the idea that there is a necessity of opposition, and therefore he tries to teach us, "There is no sin. It mattereth not what a man does; whatsoever a man does; It's not sin. Eat, drink, and be merry, for tomorrow we die" (see 2 Nephi 28:8; Alma 30:17). Thus he destroys the role of opposition in our lives, or at least he attempts to do so.

He can also do it by destroying our freedom of choice. He does this by enticing us to give up our right of agency to other persons or to other institutions and allow them to make our choices for us, resulting in the evil that presidents of the Church have talked about in communism and socialism and other orders of this type.

He also does it by trying to encourage us not to come to a knowledge of our Heavenly Father by not listening to the prophets, by not studying the scriptures, and therefore by not knowing the consequences of our choices. He seeks to seduce us by saying, in effect, "The scriptures are irrelevant today. They were written a long time ago. Don't pay any attention to them," and "There are no such things as prophets upon the earth; they ceased at the time of Christ." Or he says that the heavens are sealed; there is no revelation today. He even says that God is dead!

Thus in one way or another he tries to entice us to become like him and to become subject to the misery and unhappiness that he now participates in. To achieve his devilish aims, Lucifer can and does work through many means: business entities, governments on all levels, military forces, educational institutions, secret combinations of all kinds, and even families, teachers, and churches. Wherever and whenever you find a person or an institution that seeks to destroy the agency of man, there you will find the influence of Lucifer.

President Henry D. Moyle addressed this subject in these words: "All we have to do is . . . examine any movement that may be brought into our midst . . . , and if it . . . attempt[s] to deprive us in the slightest respect of our free agency, we should avoid it as we would avoid immorality or anything else that is vicious. . . . Free agency is as necessary for our eternal salvation as is our virtue. And . . . as we guard our virtue with our lives, so should we guard our free agency."[3]

President Marion G. Romney, when he was a member of the Council of the Twelve, gave this advice:

"One of the fundamental doctrines of revealed truth is that . . . God endowed men with free agency (Moses 7:32). The preservation of this free agency is more important than the preservation of life itself. . . . Everything which militates against man's enjoyment of this endowment persuades not to believe in Christ, for He is the author of free agency.

"Now the world today is in the throes of a great social and political revolution. In almost every department of society laws and practices are being daily proposed and adopted which greatly alter the course of our lives. Indeed, some of them are literally shaking the foundations of our political and social institutions. If you would know truth from error in this bitterly contested arena, apply Mormon's test to these innovations [as recorded in Moroni 7:16–18]. Do they facilitate or restrict the exercise of man's divine endowment of agency? Tested by this standard, most of them will fall quickly into their proper category as between good and evil."[4]

As an example of how sin can put us into bondage, let us consider for a moment the Word of Wisdom, because this is a physical law that we can see and understand rather readily. The Lord has said tobacco is not good for man—that is the law. We have our agency either to obey or to disobey the law. If we obey the law and do not smoke cigarettes, we enjoy better health than we would if we disobeyed the law. Also, by keeping the law we still have our agency as to whether or not we will continue to keep the law. However, as soon as we disobey the law—in this case, when we become addicted to nicotine—we not only suffer the penalty of poorer health, but we also practically lose our agency in that matter. The broken law has a claim over us; we have become slaves to the drug; and the broken law will continue to have a claim over us until we stop breaking the law—that is, until we repent. And essentially the same principle is involved in all of the laws given to us by our Heavenly Father.

Scriptural References to Freedom

Now let's consider some scriptures pertaining to the principle of agency:

"If ye continue in my word, then are ye my disciples indeed; and ye shall know the truth, and the truth shall make you free" (John 8:31–32).

"Though he were a Son, yet learned he obedience by the things which he suffered; and being made perfect, he became the author of eternal salvation unto all them that obey him" (Hebrews 5:8–9).

"Stand fast therefore in the liberty wherewith Christ hath made us free, and be not entangled again with the yoke of bondage" (Galatians 5:1).

"Men should be anxiously engaged in a good cause, and do many things of their own free will, and bring to pass much righteousness; for the power is in them, wherein they are agents unto themselves. And inasmuch as men do good they shall in nowise lose their reward" (D&C 58:27–28).

"And it must needs be that the devil should tempt the children of men, or they could not be agents unto themselves; for if they never should have bitter they could not know the sweet" (D&C 29:39).

"Whosoever perisheth, perisheth unto himself; and whosoever doeth iniquity, doeth it unto himself; for behold, ye are free; ye are permitted to act for yourselves; for behold, God hath given unto you a knowledge and he hath made you free.

"He hath given unto you that ye might know good from evil, and he hath given unto you that ye might choose life or death; and ye can do good and be restored unto that which is good, or have that which is good restored unto you; or ye can do evil, and have that which is evil restored unto you" (Helaman 14:30–31).

"Be not deceived; God is not mocked; for whatsoever a man soweth, that shall he also reap" (Galatians 6:7).

"To him that knoweth to do good, and doeth it not, to him it is sin" (James 4:17).

"The wages of sin is death; but the gift of God is eternal life through Jesus Christ our Lord" (Romans 6:23).

"This is life eternal, that they might know thee the only true God, and Jesus Christ, whom thou hast sent" (John 17:3).

Freedom Necessary for the Gospel to Flourish

An atmosphere of freedom is necessary for the teaching and accepting of the gospel of Jesus Christ. The missionaries and the message of the restored gospel have been received by the nations of the earth in almost the same proportion as those nations have accepted the principles of freedom. So intertwined are the principles of the gospel and the principles of agency that they have become almost as one. This characteristic has been pointed out by President John Taylor in these words:

"Besides the preaching of the Gospel, we have another mission, namely, the perpetuation of the free agency of man and the maintenance of liberty, freedom, and the rights of man. . . . We have a right to liberty—that was a right that God gave to all men; and if there has been oppression, fraud or tyranny in the earth, it has been the result of the wickedness and corruptions of men and has always been opposed to God and the principles of truth."[5]

Now, if what we have been discussing here is true, we as Latter-day Saints should be the most free of any people on the face of this earth. We have all the opportunities of choice that other people do—and more, because we have the additional laws and principles of the restored gospel. We have all the possibilities of opposites shared by other people and more, because of the differences between the brightness of the noonday sun of the restored gospel as compared with the moonlight of Protestant and Catholic Christianity and the darkness of skepticism, agnosticism, and atheism. We have all the freedom of choice enjoyed by other people and more, because we have modern scriptures and living prophets to guide us day by day. Thus if we as Latter-day Saints are not the most free people on the face of the earth, then we should be, because we have to the greatest extent the necessary components of moral agency.

At an American Independence Day celebration, Elder Richard L. Evans said:

"May we take a moment from some of the side issues and from some of the irrelevant celebration and clear our thoughts and humble our hearts and get down on our knees and simply, fervently, thank God for freedom—and then get on our feet with a firm resolve to preserve it against all who secretly or openly would set it aside.

"Thank God for freedom—and for the Founding Fathers who reaffirmed to a new nation, an eternal timeless truth: that the right of choice—that the free agency of man—is a God-given inalienable right, and is essential to the peace and growth and progress and salvation of the very soul. This truth has been challenged again and again, and will yet be challenged again and again. It was challenged in the heavens before time began, by the brilliant but rebellious Lucifer. There was war in heaven—for freedom. And anyone who seeks to enslave men in any sense, in mind, in spirit, in thought—anyone who seeks to enslave the minds, the hearts, the spirits of men—is essentially in league with Satan himself, for 'where the spirit of the Lord is, there is liberty' (2 Corinthians 3:17).

"Thank God for the Constitution of our country, which was brought into being 'by the hands of wise men whom [the Lord God] raised up unto this very purpose' (D&C 101:80). Thank God for the promise that in this choice land, men 'shall be free from bondage, and from captivity, and from all other nations under heaven, if they will but serve' God (Ether 2:12).

"Thank God for the right of choice, for the right to become whatever we can become in a free and provident land that, despite its imperfections, has proved to be more efficient for progress and human happiness than any society founded on the false philosophies that would seek to enslave the minds and souls of men.

"God grant that we may repent wherever we have departed from the principles of freedom—that we may preserve the right to fail and the incentive to succeed, and live, as did the Founding Fathers, knowing that there are no acceptable substitutes for freedom."[6]

We teach our children that when they pray they should thank their Heavenly Father for the blessings that he has given to them. I hope that in our daily private and family prayers we will always thank our Heavenly Father for the great blessing that he has given us on this earth—the gift of moral agency—and also for the right and opportunity to exercise this gift as members of his church and kingdom and as citizens of this country.

I bear my personal witness to the fact that our Heavenly Father and his divine Son, Jesus Christ, are the fountainhead of all truth and freedom. By following their teachings we can be free indeed and can find the joy and happiness that "surpasseth all understanding."

Notes

Excerpts from a devotional talk given at Brigham Young University and published in *Brigham Young University Speeches of the Year,* 2 July 1974, 309–22.

1. David O. McKay, "Free Agency . . . the Gift Divine," *Improvement Era,* 65 (February 1962): 86.
2. *Teachings of the Prophet Joseph Smith,* 353–54.

3. Henry D. Moyle, in Conference Report, October 1947, 46.
4. Marion G. Romney, "Your Quest for Truth," *Speeches of the Year* (Provo, Utah: Brigham Young University Press, 30 May 1957), 10, 11.
5. John Taylor, in *Journal of Discourses,* 23:63.
6. Richard L. Evans, *From the Crossroads* (New York: Harper & Brothers, 1955), 45.

Chapter 20

ADAM AND EVE IN THE GARDEN OF EDEN

One of the most mentioned but least understood events in the history of the world is the story of Adam and Eve in the Garden of Eden. Many of the conflicting sermons delivered on this subject clearly indicate the great diversity of belief within Christianity concerning the necessity of the Fall of Adam and the role of Adam in the gospel plan of salvation. Adam is frequently portrayed as the villain of humanity—the anti-Christ responsible for all of the pains, diseases, ills, sorrows, wars, and troubles of mankind. By others, Adam is portrayed as the unwitting tool of a capricious God—an instrument for God who, at best, served merely in starting the human race. I do not believe the scriptures warrant these harsh views of Adam and the Fall. In fact, the scriptures indicate that Adam was one of the greatest men who ever lived on the earth and that his Fall was necessary in the plan of God.

In order to understand the role of Adam and the necessity of his Fall in the gospel of Jesus Christ, it is necessary to return to the idea of our pre-earthly existence. The gospel of Christ teaches that everyone of us who has lived or who ever will live on this earth existed as a spirit son or daughter of God before we were born. These spirit bodies given to us by God had many desirable attributes, but as bodies of spirit they also had limitations. For example, they were apparently denied the powers of procreation and thus were not able to increase. As God wanted his children to partake of the same privileges and blessings he enjoyed, he called a great council in heaven and presented a plan whereby we might leave his presence and come down upon an earth to learn to walk by faith, gain experience, and obtain bodies of flesh and bones that would have the power of procreation.

All of us were present at that great council and heard the plan presented by God. After the plan had been presented, the firstborn son of God in the spirit, whose name was Jehovah (or Jesus Christ), spoke in favor of the plan. However, another of the spirit sons of God, named Lucifer, opposed the plan and led an active resistance against it. A great conflict raged in heaven over the merits of the plan. Another of the sons of God, called Michael, came to the support of, and was instrumental in defending, the plan of God. After some time, the proposal of God was accepted. Lucifer and his followers, however, refused to accept the plan of the atonement of Jesus Christ, which would enable men to return to God's presence with physical bodies. Because of their rebellion, Lucifer and his followers were denied the privilege of obtaining these earthly bodies.

Several biblical writers have written of this war in heaven and of the part Michael and Lucifer played in it. John tells us: "And there was war in heaven; Michael and his angels fought against the dragon; and the dragon fought and his angels, and prevailed not; neither was their place found anymore in heaven. And the great dragon was cast out, that old serpent, called the devil, and Satan, which deceiveth the whole world; he was cast out into the earth, and his angels were cast out with him" (Revelation 12:7–9). Peter writes of the "angels that sinned" who were cast out (2 Peter 2:4), and in Jude we read of the "angels which kept not their first estate" (Jude 6). Isaiah was also familiar with the war in heaven. He wrote: "How art thou fallen from heaven, O Lucifer, son of the morning! how art thou cut down to the ground, which didst weaken the nations! For thou hast said in thine heart, I will ascend into heaven, I will exalt my throne above the stars of God" (Isaiah 14:12–13).

When Lucifer and his followers were cast out, the great plan of God was put into operation. First, as indicated in Moses 3:5, there was a spirit creation. Then the earth and everything that was placed on it was created physically. An account of this creation is given in the first two chapters of Genesis.

In the physical creation, God prepared a garden "eastward in Eden" (Genesis 2:8) and a physical body for man. Then the spirit of man was placed in the body, or as the scriptures put it, God "breathed into his nostrils the breath of life; and man became a living soul" (Genesis 2:7). According to the teachings of the Prophet Joseph Smith, the spirit that was put into this body of the first man was the spirit of Michael the Archangel, who became known on the earth as Adam or, as Daniel called him, the Ancient of Days. Thus, the Adam of this world is in reality the Michael of the pre-earthly existence who helped defend the plan of God in the great war in heaven as spoken of by John the Revelator. He was one of God's chosen leaders before he ever came to the earth.

After Adam became a living soul on the earth, a female helpmate was given to him, and he called her Eve. God then placed Adam and Eve in the garden he had prepared for them, and he gave certain commandments to them. First, he commanded them to multiply and replenish the earth, and subdue it. It is evident that this commandment referred to a future time and did not apply to Adam and Eve when they were in the Garden of Eden. This is evident from the fact that they did not have the knowledge necessary to use the power of procreation at that time; also, the earth was not then in need of "being subdued" by Adam, as it was spontaneously producing fruits and flowers and all the necessities of life.

The second commandment given to Adam and Eve, however, could be either obeyed or disobeyed by them at that time. This commandment of the Lord is recorded in the book of Moses: "Of every tree of the garden thou mayest freely eat, but of the tree of the knowledge of good and evil, thou shalt not eat of it, nevertheless, thou mayest choose for thyself, for it is given unto thee; but, remember that I forbid it, for in the day thou eatest thereof thou shalt surely die" (Moses 3:16–17).

This commandment introduced the possibility for a world of opposition—of good and evil—to come into being. Until that time, apparently, the Garden of Eden was not a world of opposition; in the absence of a knowledge of good and evil, the Garden of Eden was a world of complete innocence. This fact is brought out clearly by the Book of Mormon prophet Lehi. He states: "And now, behold, if Adam had not transgressed he would not have fallen, but he would have remained in the Garden of Eden. And all things which were created must have remained in the same state in which they were after they were created; and they must have remained forever, and had no end. And they *would* have had no children; wherefore they would have remained in a state of innocence, having no joy, for they knew no misery; doing no good, for they knew no sin" (2 Nephi 2:22–23; emphasis added).

Thus the status of Adam and Eve when they were in the Garden of Eden might be summarized as follows:

1. They were in a state of innocence; they did not know the difference between good and evil.
2. They would not have had children.
3. They were in the presence of God.
4. They were not subject to temporal death; they were not mortal.

Adam and Eve continued to live in the Garden of Eden in this condition until Lucifer, the personage of spirit who had opposed the plan of God in the great council of heaven, spoke through the serpent and tempted Eve to partake of the forbidden fruit. When Eve resisted the temptation, saying that God had forbidden the partaking of it upon the penalty of death, Lucifer replied: "Ye shall not surely die; For

God doth know that in the day ye eat thereof, then your eyes shall be opened, and ye shall be as gods, knowing good and evil" (Moses 4:10–11).

After she partook of the fruit, Eve realized that because of her transgression she would be cast out of the Garden of Eden. With deep concern, she asked Adam to partake of the fruit, and Adam, seeing that he could not multiply and replenish the earth without his helpmate, decided to partake of the fruit. Then Adam and Eve suffered the penalty of the law they had broken—they suffered spiritual death or, in other words, were cast out of the presence of God; also, the seeds of physical death became part of their physical bodies.

After Adam and Eve were driven from the Garden of Eden, the Lord sent an angel to teach them the gospel. They were told that they were suffering from the consequences of sin, and in this condition they could not regain the presence of God. However, they were promised that if they would truly and humbly repent of their sins and thenceforth keep all the commandments of God, they could be forgiven through the atonement that was to be wrought by Jesus Christ and could thus return to God's presence. Also, they were assured that the Savior would bring to pass the resurrection of their bodies after their temporal death. When Adam and Eve heard these truths of the gospel, they were glad. In the book of Moses, Adam is recorded as saying, "Blessed be the name of God, for because of my transgression my eyes are opened, and in this life I shall have joy, and again in the flesh I shall see God. And Eve, his wife, heard all these things and was glad, saying: Were it not for our transgression, we never should have had seed, and never should have known good and evil, and the joy of our redemption, and the eternal life which God giveth unto all the obedient" (Moses 5:10–11).

Once the gospel was taught to Adam and Eve, they rejoiced because of their Fall, because they could then multiply and replenish the earth, and because upon obedience to the principles and ordinances of the gospel they could regain God's presence.

The good news of the gospel for all of us concerning the Fall is that it did take place. Because of the Fall of Adam, we were able to be born upon this earth, and through the atonement of Jesus Christ we can return to God and experience the joy of eternal life. The prophet Lehi summarized this idea in a very brief sentence: "Adam fell that men might be; and men are, that they might have joy" (2 Nephi 2:25).

In summary of the status of Adam and Eve after the Fall, we find that they had a knowledge of good and evil, that they could have children, that they had suffered spiritual death (were cast out of God's presence), and that they had introduced the seeds of temporal death into their bodies and had thus become mortal.

When viewed in connection with the atonement of Jesus Christ, the Fall of Adam takes on an entirely new light. Instead of thwarting the plan of God, it was the means by which God made it possible for Adam and Eve to have children and therefore for us to come to this earth. It was the means by which God made it possible for us to live in a world of opposition—of good and evil—where we could obtain valuable experience learning to walk by faith out of his presence. It was also the means ordained of God to accomplish his work and glory in connection with this earth: "to bring to pass the immortality and eternal life of man" (Moses 1:39).

Note

From an address delivered over KSL Radio, Salt Lake City, Utah, 10 November 1957.

Chapter 21

THE PURPOSES OF A MORTAL EXISTENCE

"What is man, that thou art mindful of him? and the son of man, that thou visitest him? For thou hast made him a little lower than the angels, and hast crowned him with glory and honour" (Psalms 8:4–5).

This question from the book of Psalms had undoubtedly been asked before it was written, and it certainly has been asked many times since that day. "What is man?" Often this question is asked in connection with another question: "What is the purpose of our mortal existence on this earth?"

The prophets and the scriptures teach that the "ego," the "intelligence," or the "I am" part of man—the part with which we do our thinking—has always existed. This portion of our being operates on a self-existent principle and can neither be created nor destroyed; it is coequal (that is, coeternal) with God.

Somewhere in the past, however, this "ego" or "intelligence" of ours was clothed with a spirit body by an act of God. We all became sons and daughters of God, for he spiritually begot us. These spirit bodies enabled us to do many things we could not do before, but as bodies of spirit they had limitations and apparently did not have the power of increase.

Because of his great love for us, God called all of his spirit sons and daughters together in a great council in heaven and there presented a proposal whereby we could take upon ourselves bodies of flesh and bones that would have the power of increase. This existence was to take place on an earth out of the presence of God. It was also decided that at the time of our birth upon this earth, the memory of our pre-earthly existence would be taken from us. This would enable us to have another worthwhile and valuable experience—to develop our spiritual powers by learning to walk by faith.

It was further proposed that this earth life be in a world of opposition—of good and evil—where we could have our moral agency and could choose for ourselves the way we wanted to go. The experience on earth would thus be a testing place for us or, as the scriptures call it, a "probationary state" (Alma 12:24)—a place where we could prove what we could do by ourselves outside God's presence.

When this plan was presented in the great council of heaven, it was apparently received with mixed feelings. Some of the spirits, headed by Lucifer, thought they could detect a flaw in the plan of God. They maintained that all of us would undoubtedly sin inasmuch as the proposed world was to be a place of both good and evil where we could exercise our agency. In this sinful condition, they said, we could never re-enter the presence of God, as no unclean or evil thing can dwell there. These spirits opposed the plan of God.

Other spirits, headed by Jehovah, the firstborn Son of God in the spirit, defended the plan of God. They pointed out that his plan included vicarious payment for the sins of mankind upon conditions of repentance—provided someone could be found who would be *willing* and *able* to pay for those sins. Such a person would have to be the son of God in the flesh—as well as in the spirit—so that he would be able to endure suffering for the sins of man and would have power over death in order to bring to pass the resurrection. Jehovah offered himself as the sacrifice to save us from death and redeem us from the consequences of our sins if we would repent.

Lucifer and his followers, however, did not believe that Jehovah could be given this much power—they denied the power of God upon which the atonement of Christ is based. When the earth plan was finally carried out, God—knowing that Lucifer and his followers would not accept the atonement of Christ—did not allow them to obtain bodies of flesh and bones and to participate in the great earth experience.

For the other spirits, however, the great plan was carried forth. The earth was organized in a natural, physical condition, and physical bodies were prepared for the father and mother of mankind—Adam and Eve. Their spirits were placed in these bodies and they became living souls.

To introduce the possibility of a world of law, commandments were given to Adam and Eve. When they transgressed one of these commandments, they were driven out of the garden; sin entered into the world and it became a world of opposition—a world of both good and evil. At this time, a veil was drawn over their eyes so they could not remember their pre-earthly life. God then caused that angels should be sent to Adam and Eve to teach them the principles upon which they could regain the presence of God. These basic principles or fundamental truths were based on the atonement of Christ; thus they are frequently referred to as the gospel of Jesus Christ.

One purpose of this mortal, earthly existence was to obtain bodies of flesh and bones that would have the power of increase. In our mortal state we were to be the union of a pre-earthly spirit with a body composed of earthly, physical elements. This union is referred to in the scriptures as making up a soul: "And the spirit and the body are the soul of man. And the resurrection from the dead is the redemption of the soul" (D&C 88:15). This resurrection—or the permanent possession of our physical bodies after death—was to be provided for us by the resurrection, which was to be wrought by Jesus Christ.

In order to assure the fulfillment of this purpose of obtaining physical bodies, God gave us a commandment to multiply and replenish the earth. The importance of this commandment is immediately evident because the other sons and daughters of God will be privileged to come here to obtain bodies of flesh and bones only if we keep this commandment.

A second purpose of this mortal existence was to gain experience in a world of opposition or, as the Book of Mormon prophet Lehi stated, to "have joy" (2 Nephi 2:25). This joy spoken of by Lehi is not to be used as a synonym for pleasure. Rather, it is used in the scripture to indicate the feeling that comes to one who has experienced the laws of opposition—who knows the bitter but now tastes the sweet, who has suffered pain and anguish but now enjoys comfort and peace. Such experience or joy is possible only in a world of good and evil—a world of opposition. In explaining this principle to one of his sons, Lehi said: "For it must needs be, that there is opposition in all things. If not so, . . . righteousness could not be brought to pass, neither wickedness, neither holiness nor misery, neither good nor bad" (2 Nephi 2:11). Later in his discussion, Lehi explains the conditions that prevailed in the Garden of Eden with Adam and Eve, and he concludes: "Wherefore, they would have remained in a state of innocence, having no joy, for they knew no misery; doing no good, for they knew no sin. But behold, all things have been done in the wisdom of him who knoweth all things. Adam fell that men might be; and men are that they might have joy" (2 Nephi 2:23–25).

A third purpose of mortality was to develop the powers of moral agency given to us by God—to see if we would choose the good rather than the evil. This purpose is outlined clearly in the book of Abraham in the Pearl of Great Price: "And we will prove them herewith, to see if they will do all things whatsoever the Lord their God shall command them, and they who keep their first estate (that is, our pre-earthly state) shall be added upon, and they who keep not their first estate shall not have glory in the same kingdom with those who keep their first estate; and they who keep their second estate (that is, our earthly existence) shall have glory added upon their heads for ever and ever" (Abraham 3:25–26). Clearly, this life is a testing place whereby we can prove to God whether we are willing to keep all his commandments.

A fourth purpose of this earthly existence is to learn to develop the powers of faith that are within us. When we were living as spirit children in the presence of God, we walked by sight. We did not have to exercise faith in God's existence, for we knew he existed. However, the veil of mortality takes away our former knowledge and gives us the opportunity to come to this knowledge again through faith. This knowledge can become more deeply implanted in our hearts and minds than ever before. In his first letter to the Corinthian saints, Paul compared our present knowledge in mortality to that which we will possess after this life. He stated: "For now we see through a glass darkly; but then face to face; now I know in part; but then shall I know even as also I am known" (1 Corinthians 13:12).

When viewed in relationship to what went before and what is going to come after, this earthly or mortal existence of ours takes on new and important significance. We are not organisms that merely happened to develop or evolve from lower orders of existence. We are not creatures who have been placed here on earth and then deserted by the God who created us. We are not—as one of the characters of Shakespeare said—"a poor player that struts and frets his hour upon the stage and then is heard no more."[1]

Rather, we are spiritually begotten sons and daughters of God, going through perhaps the most critical period of our entire existence. We have waited for millennia for the opportunity of this experience—and the consequences of the acts performed here will be felt by us during the eternities to come. Now that we have obtained the blessings of an earthly existence, we should strive to keep all the commandments of God so that we will be worthy of the immortality we have already received and of the eternal life—or the power of eternal joy and increase—that is promised to those who prove faithful here. Only through such obedience can we experience joy in this life and eternal happiness in the life to come.

Notes

From an address delivered over KSL Radio, Salt Lake City, Utah, 17 November 1957.

1. William Shakespeare, *Macbeth*, 5.5.28–29.

Chapter 22

THE LAWS OF JUSTICE AND MERCY

Although there are great differences of opinion among the teachers of Christianity concerning the personality and the nature of God, there is relatively little disagreement to the fact that God is a God of order and thus a God of law. Perhaps this unanimity comes from the clearness of the teachings of the scriptures on this point.

In a modern scripture, the Lord has stated, "Behold, mine house is a house of order, . . . and not a house of confusion" (D&C 132:8).

Elsewhere, the Lord said, "Verily I say unto you, that which is governed by law is also preserved by law and perfected and sanctified by the same. . . . All kingdoms have a law given . . . and unto every law there are certain bounds also and conditions. All beings who abide not in those conditions are not justified" (D&C 88:34, 37–39).

Of course, we as mortal beings understand relatively few of the laws of God, but as he teaches us more of his gospel we become better acquainted with him and his works. Also, science is helping us to understand some of the laws of God as they pertain to the physical world. However, those laws that pertain to the moral and spiritual realm are often not clearly understood by man—yet they are probably even more important to our eternal welfare than are some of the physical laws we are coming to understand. For example, there are laws associated with the gospel that every person must keep before he can regain the presence of God. Jesus Christ referred to some of these laws in John 3:5 when he said, "Except a man be born of water and of the Spirit, he cannot enter into the kingdom of God."

In fact, the scriptures teach that every blessing received by man comes as a result of obedience to law. In the Doctrine and Covenants we read: "There is a law, irrevocably decreed in heaven before the foundations of this world, upon which all blessings are predicated. And when we obtain any blessing from God, it is by obedience to that law upon which it is predicated" (D&C 130:20, 21).

Some laws of God, however, work in relationship to other laws and help to keep them in a state of balance or order. This discussion is primarily concerned with two of these laws—the law of justice and the law of mercy. Although complete definitions of these laws are not available from scripture, we do know some of the major functions of the laws. The law of justice, for example, operates on the principle that for every *transgressed law,* a payment—a suffering or a punishment—must be made. Likewise, for every *obeyed law,* a payment—a reward or blessing—must be made. The law of justice, working in relation with other laws, helps to keep order or balance, and makes possible a world of opposition—good and evil, happiness and sorrow, pleasure and pain, joy and misery. The first of each of these pairs of attributes—good, happiness, pleasure, and joy—are the result of obedience to law. The second of each of these pairs of attributes—evil, sorrow, pain, and misery are the result of disobedience or transgression of law. According to the law of justice, these blessings *must come* with obedience and these punishments *must be inflicted* with disobedience.

When we sin (knowingly transgress the law), we must be punished; when we obey (observe the law), we must be blessed. This is only just—and it is based on the law of justice. Inasmuch as God is just, when we commit a sin and will not repent, *God must allow the law to inflict upon us the punishment* associated with that law, *regardless of how much he might love us as individuals.* Otherwise God would become unjust and a respecter of persons. Likewise, when we are righteous and keep the law, God must bless us because of our obedience. God stated this fact in these words: "I the Lord am bound when ye do what I say, but when ye do not what I say, ye have no promise" (D&C 82:10). In addition to being a just God, however, God is also a merciful being who believes in the law of mercy. This law does *not* make invalid any of the claims of justice, but it works in relationship with the law of justice.

The law of mercy might be stated somewhat as follows: Yes, it is true that there must be a penalty or punishment attached to every transgression of law according to the law of justice; however, the person who breaks the law does not necessarily have to make full payment of the transgressed law *if someone else can be found who is* willing *and* able *to make suitable payment for him and if the transgressor is willing to accept the condition of payment.* Thus the law of mercy does not in any way deny the claims of justice, but it does make possible the *vicarious* payment of some of those claims.

Perhaps an analogy of how these laws might work in a situation outside the gospel would help us to understand how these laws operate within the gospel. Care must be taken, however, not to carry the implications of the analogy too far. For example, we have banking laws concerning checking accounts which state that a person must not write a check for more money than he has in his account. Let us assume that you have $400 in your account, but you write a check for $1,000. You have thus transgressed a banking law, and *according to the law of justice* a penalty must be inflicted that at least amounts to the payment of the $600 overdraft in order to bring things back into balance. However, the bank is not too concerned whether you or someone else makes the payment so long as it receives the $600 and is able to balance its books. Let us further assume that you find someone—perhaps your father or a friend—who is both able and willing to advance you the money to pay the bank. According to the law of mercy, this vicarious payment for and in your behalf could be made by someone else if he is willing and able to do so and if you are willing to accept his conditions of payment. The law of justice has thus received all of its demands, for full payment has been made. The law of mercy—upon specified conditions—has enabled someone other than the person who transgressed the law to make the payment.

Every scripture that refers to the atonement of Christ or to any doctrine based on the Atonement—for example, the doctrine of repentance—is concerned with the laws of justice and mercy. In a sense, the Atonement was necessary because of the law of justice and was possible because of the law of mercy. In another sense, the law of mercy was made active on this earth by the atonement of Christ.

One of the clearest scriptures concerning the laws of justice and mercy is found in the Book of Mormon, wherein the prophet Alma explains to his son Corianton the functions and relationships of these two laws:

"And now, my son, I perceive there is somewhat more which doth worry your mind, which ye cannot understand—which is concerning the justice of God in the punishment of the sinner; for ye do try to suppose that it is injustice that the sinner should be consigned to a state of misery. Now, my son, I will explain this thing unto thee" (Alma 42:1–2).

Alma then explained to Corianton the plan of salvation as determined before the foundation of the world. He told the story of Adam and Eve in the Garden of Eden, how they had been given commandments, had transgressed a law of God, and had been cast out of the presence of God. Then God caused that the gospel should be taught to Adam and Eve, and he granted unto them a probationary time to repent of their sins. He promised them that they could be saved and redeemed from their fall if they would accept the atonement of Jesus Christ that was to be wrought for them and if they would repent of their sins. Now let us return to the words of Alma:

"Therefore, according to justice, the plan of redemption could not be brought about, only on conditions of repentance of men in this probationary state, . . . for except it were for these conditions, mercy could not take effect except it would destroy the work of justice. Now the work of justice could not be destroyed; if so, God would cease to be God.

"And thus we see that all mankind were fallen, and they were in the grasp of justice; yea, the justice of God, which consigned them forever to be cut off from his presence. And now, the plan of mercy could not be brought about except an atonement should be made; therefore God himself atoneth for the sins of the world, to bring about the plan of mercy, to appease the demands of justice, that God might be a perfect, just God, and a merciful God also.

"And mercy claimeth the penitent, and mercy cometh because of the atonement; and the atonement bringeth to pass the resurrection of the dead; and the resurrection of the dead bringeth back men into the presence of God; and thus they are restored into his presence, to be judged according to their works, according to the law and justice. For behold, justice exerciseth all his demands, and also mercy claimeth all which is her own; and thus, none but the truly penitent are saved. What, do ye suppose that mercy can rob justice? I say unto you, Nay; not one whit. If so, God would cease to be God. And thus God bringeth about his great and eternal purposes, which were prepared from the foundation of the world" (Alma 42:13–15, 23–26).

At first glance it might appear to us as it did to Corianton—that we would be better off if there were no law of justice. This is not the case. Without the law of justice there would be disorder, confusion, and partiality—both on earth and in heaven. But the law of justice tempered by the law of mercy makes possible a world of progression, a place where there can be opposition and true joy.

These two laws are incomplete in and of themselves. However, when they work in relationship to each other and to the other laws of God, they form the basis of the gospel plan of salvation, which provides for a world of order and progression, of fairness and equality to all.

Note

From an address delivered over KSL Radio, Salt Lake City, Utah, 24 November 1957.

Chapter 23

THE RELATIONSHIP BETWEEN GRACE AND WORKS

The topic of grace and works has the possibility of eternal consequences. It is timely and worthy of our attention and interest. It is fundamental to many other teachings of the gospel and thus is worthy of our study, research, and pondering.

In searching for materials on this subject, I checked under the entry "grace" in the index to Church periodicals for 1961–83. I was dumbfounded to find just five articles listed. Three were from the *Church News*. The fourth article, a general conference talk by Elder Mark E. Petersen titled "We Believe in Being Honest,"[1] was not related directly to the topic of grace and works. The fifth article, the only one in Church periodicals in twenty-three years to specifically address the topic, was very good. Written by Gerald N. Lund, it was titled "Salvation: By Grace or by Works?"[2] I commend it highly.

In doing further research, I discovered the text of a masterful discourse, "What Think Ye of Salvation by Grace?" by Elder Bruce R. McConkie, given at a Brigham Young University devotional on January 10, 1984.[3] I urge you to read and ponder the entire talk.

In his talk, Elder McConkie referred to the teaching of salvation by grace and faith alone as the second great heresy of "a now fallen and decadent Christianity." He identified the first and chief heresy as the false doctrine introduced by Catholic Christianity that God is "no longer a personal Father, no longer a personage of tabernacle, [but] an incomprehensible three-in-one spirit essence that filled the immensity of space."[4]

He described the second heresy as "the doctrine that we are justified by faith alone, without the works of the law. It is the doctrine that we are saved by grace alone, without works. It is the doctrine that we may be born again simply by confessing the Lord Jesus with our lips while we continue to live in our sins."[5] Elder McConkie referred to this false teaching as "one of the great religious phenomena of the ages, one that is now sweeping through Protestant Christianity."[6]

Those of us who have been in the front lines of missionary service in recent years know how extensively the Protestants are using this heresy against the true Church. Some of the first challenges against the Church in this dispensation concerned the reality of the First Vision and whether the Book of Mormon could actually be the word of God. Later the attack was against the practice of polygamy and, still later, the denial of priesthood privileges to blacks. More recently the attacks have centered on the place of women in the Church—specifically, the position of the Church on the Equal Rights Amendment and the question of giving the priesthood to women.

Certainly one of the major charges apostate Christianity and some of the groups of ex-Mormons bring against the true Church today is that neither the Church nor its members are Christian. The supposed evidence brought against us is that we must not believe in the atonement of Jesus Christ because we do not believe man is saved by grace alone; rather, we say that works are also necessary.

Hundreds of statements against the doctrinal position of the Church on this subject could be produced, but maybe a summary of one letter will suffice. Understand that its author is bitterly opposed to the message of the Restoration. Statements such as "Mormonism is not of God" and "The only instances in which the Book of Mormon is right are those where it borrows phrases from the Bible, God's word" indicate how the author feels.

The parts of this letter that caught my eye, however, are those that imply that we are unchristian. For example, "The Book of Mormon and all of Mormonism denies the gospel message that 'it is by grace that you have been saved, through faith; not by anything of your own, but by a gift from God; not by anything that you have done, so that nobody can claim the credit.'" This, of course, is from Ephesians 2:8–9 in the Jerusalem Bible. The author continues: "Good works are not prerequisite to salvation but rather are the result of our being saved: 'For we are his [God's] workmanship, created in Christ Jesus for good works, which God prepared beforehand, that we should walk in them.'" This appears to be a paraphrase of Ephesians 2:10. Finally, the author cites Romans 11:6 in the Revised Standard Version by stating: "Paul makes it clear that salvation cannot be on the basis of both grace and works. It is an either/or situation: 'But if it is by grace, it is no longer on the basis of works; otherwise grace would no longer be grace.'"

This letter pinpoints the problem inherent in our topic as viewed by our Protestant friends. In using the word *problem,* I am well aware of statements by present leaders that we don't have problems in the Church; rather, we have challenges and opportunities. Therefore, the word *problem* is not used to reflect our understanding of the topic. I really believe that any member of the Church who has read the scriptures, especially the new editions with their accompanying chapter headings and footnotes, and who has attended meetings and classes and listened attentively should not have any serious problem with the subject of grace and works. Those outside the Church, however, think we have a problem with this subject, and it is from their viewpoint that I use the word *problem.* Actually, it is their problem, not ours.

Definition of Terms

An understanding of the meanings and implications of the major terms in my title is critical to this discussion. I can think of few topics to which an understanding of the terms would be more important.

Relationship. The word *relationship* is defined only briefly in the dictionary: "the state or character of being related or interrelated: a connection by way of relation."[7] A statement under the word *relation* seems to be relevant: "an aspect or quality (as resemblance, direction, difference) that can be predicated only of two or more things taken together: something perceived or discovered by observing or thinking about two or more things at the same time."[8]

Grace. The unabridged dictionary devotes eleven column inches to a definition of *grace.* This long definition includes "beneficence or generosity shown by God to man . . . ; disposition to kindness, favor, clemency, or compassion: benign goodwill . . . ; the favor shown or the portion allotted by fortune or Providence."[9]

I also went to *Strong's Exhaustive Concordance* to obtain help on the meaning of the word *grace* as used in both the Old Testament and the New Testament. I discovered that this English word is used 37 times in the Old Testament and 130 times in the New Testament (King James Version). Of the 130 usages in the New Testament, 107 are from the writings of Paul. The word *grace* appears only 4 times in the Gospels and is used 19 additional times by authors other than Paul.

The primary root of the Hebrew word defined as grace is *chânan* (khaw-nan´), which means "to bend or stoop in kindness to an inferior; to favor, bestow"; to "have (shew) mercy (on, upon)."[10]

The primary root of the Greek word translated as *grace* in the New Testament is *chairo* (khah´ee-ro), which means "to be 'cheer'ful, i.e., calmly happy or well-off." Other definitions for this Greek word are "the divine influence upon the heart," "grace (-ious)" manner or act; "benefit, favour, gift, . . . pleasure, thank (-s, -worthy)."[11]

Note that all three of these definitions—English, Hebrew, and Greek—include the idea that grace is a gift from God to man. Hence, in order to have a true concept of grace, we must have a true concept of God.

Works. The word *works* is, of course, the "plural of work," and *Webster's Unabridged Dictionary* devotes eight column inches to definitions of the word *work*. For purposes of brevity, I have paraphrased some of these definitions: to bring to pass; to fashion or create by expending labor or exertion upon; to set or keep in motion, operation, or activity; to cause to toil or labor; to pay with labor or service; to get oneself into or out of a condition or position by gradual stages.

When we apply the dictionary definitions of *work* to the principles and ordinances of the gospel, it is readily apparent that all ordinances would be considered works because they require the action of one who is ordained.

Basic Scriptures

Let us refer briefly to some of the major scriptures from the New Testament on this subject. Many of these references have been interpreted by some to be contradictory to the official position of the Church.

Acts 15:11: This passage is not changed in the Joseph Smith Translation: "But we believe that through the grace of the Lord Jesus Christ we shall be saved."

Romans 3:23–24, 27–28: "For all have sinned, and come short of the glory of God; Being justified freely by his grace through the redemption that is in Christ Jesus. . . . Where is boasting then? It is excluded. By what law? of works? Nay: but by the law of faith. Therefore we conclude that a man is justified by faith without the deeds of the law."

Compare that passage in the King James Version with the same passage in the Joseph Smith Translation: "For all have sinned, and come short of the glory of God; Therefore being justified only by his grace through the redemption that is in Christ Jesus. . . . Where is boasting then? It is excluded. By what law? of works? Nay; but by the law of faith. Therefore we conclude that a man is justified by faith alone without the deeds of the law."

Romans 4:2–5: "For if Abraham were justified by works, he hath whereof to glory, but not before God. For what saith the scripture? Abraham believed God, and it was counted unto him for righteousness. Now to him that worketh is the reward not reckoned of grace, but of debt. But to him that worketh not, but believeth on him that justifieth the ungodly, his faith is counted for righteousness."

Compare those verses in the King James Version with the same verses in the Joseph Smith Translation: "For if Abraham were justified by the law of works, he hath to glory in himself; but not of God. For what saith the Scripture? Abraham believed God, and it was counted unto him for righteousness. Now to him who is justified by the law of works, is the reward reckoned, not of grace, but of debt. But to him that seeketh not to be justified by the law of works, but believeth on him who justifieth not the ungodly, his faith is counted for righteousness."

Romans 4:13–16: "For the promise, that he should be the heir of the world, was not to Abraham, or to his seed, through the law, but through the righteousness of faith. For if they which are of the law be heirs, faith is made void, and the promise made of none effect: Because the law worketh wrath: for where no law is, there is no transgression. Therefore it is of faith, that it might be by grace; to the end the promise might be sure to all the seed, not to that only which is of the law, but to that also which is of the faith of Abraham; who is the father of us all."

Compare that passage in the King James Version with the same passage in the Joseph Smith Translation: "For the promise, that he should be the heir of the world, was not to Abraham, or to his seed, through the law, but through the righteousness of faith. For if they which are of the law be heirs, faith is made void, and the promise made of none effect. Because the law worketh wrath: for where no law is, there is no transgression. Therefore ye are justified of faith and works, through grace, to the end the promise might be sure to all the seed; not to them only who are of the law, but to them also who are of the faith of Abraham; who is the father of us all."

Romans 11:5–6: "Even so then at this present time also there is a remnant according to the election of grace. And if by grace, then is it no more of works: otherwise grace is no more grace. But if it be of works, then is it no more grace: otherwise work is no more work" (no changes in the Joseph Smith Translation).

Galatians 2:16: "Knowing that a man is not justified by the works of the law, but by the faith of Jesus Christ, even we have believed in Jesus Christ, that we might be justified by the faith of Christ, and not by the works of the law: for by the works of the law shall no flesh be justified" (no changes in the Joseph Smith Translation).

Galatians 5:4: "Christ is become of no effect unto you, whosoever of you are justified by the law; ye are fallen from grace" (no changes in the Joseph Smith Translation).

Ephesians 2:4–10: "But God, who is rich in mercy, for his great love wherewith he loved us, Even when we were dead in sins, hath quickened us together with Christ, (by grace ye are saved;) And hath raised us up together, and made us sit together in heavenly places in Christ Jesus: That in the ages to come he might shew the exceeding riches of his grace in his kindness toward us through Christ Jesus.

"For by grace are ye saved through faith; and that not of yourselves: it is the gift of God. Not of works, lest any man should boast. For we are his workmanship, created in Christ Jesus unto good works, which God hath before ordained that we should walk in them" (no changes except in verse 8 in the Joseph Smith Translation).

Ephesians 4:5–8: "One Lord, one faith, one baptism, One God and Father of all, who is above all, and through all, and in you all. But unto every one of us is given grace according to the measure of the gift of Christ. Wherefore he saith, When he ascended up on high, he led captivity captive, and gave gifts unto men" (no changes in the Joseph Smith Translation).

James 2:14–20: "What doth it profit, my brethren, though a man say he hath faith, and have not works? can faith save him? If a brother or sister be naked, and destitute of daily food, And one of you say unto them, Depart in peace, be ye warmed and filled; notwithstanding ye give them not those things which are needful to the body; what doth it profit?

"Even so faith, if it hath not works, is dead, being alone. Yea, a man may say, Thou hast faith, and I have works: shew me thy faith without thy works, and I will shew thee my faith by my works. Thou believest that there is one God; thou doest well: the devils also believe, and tremble. But wilt thou know, O vain man, that faith without works is dead?"

Compare that passage in the King James Version with the same passage in the Joseph Smith Translation. The correction is primarily a change in organization:

"What profit is it, my brethren, for a man to say he hath faith, and hath not works? can faith save him? Yea, a man may say, I will show thee I have faith without works; but I say, Show me thy faith without works, and I will show thee my faith by my works. For if a brother or sister be naked and destitute, and one of you say, Depart in peace, be warmed and filled; notwithstanding he give not those things which are needful to the body; what profit is your faith unto such?

"Even so faith, if it have not works is dead, being alone. Therefore wilt thou know, O vain man, that faith without works is dead and cannot save you? Thou believest there is one God; thou doest well; the devils also believe, and tremble; thou hast made thyself like unto them, not being justified" (James 2:14–19).

After reviewing all the pertinent scriptures on this subject in the New Testament in the King James Version and after carefully comparing them with the primary Greek words from which they were translated, with the Joseph Smith Translation, and with the teachings of modern prophets, I am convinced that the problem is neither with the translation nor with the wording of the scriptures. I am also convinced that Paul and all the other authors of New Testament books understood the doctrine of grace and works completely and spoke from a true gospel perspective as well as from the perspective of the old covenant.

Part of the problem is the failure of some persons to read all the scriptures pertaining to the subject. They select only those references that agree with their particular philosophy, and then they conveniently ignore others that shed additional light on the subject.

Another problem is in the interpretation. Here Peter's warning is appropriate: "Knowing this first, that no prophecy of the scripture is of any private interpretation. For the prophecy came not in old time by the will of man: but holy men of God spake as they were moved by the Holy Ghost" (2 Peter 1:20–21).

Still another problem concerns the definition and meaning of such basic terms as *grace, faith, works, saved,* and *salvation.* We need to clarify these terms with our friends in other Christian churches and then be certain we use them precisely and correctly. We should be more precise, for example, than some of us have been over the controversy about which day of the week is the correct Sabbath day. One particular Christian group has indicated that we should worship on the Sabbath day, which they say is Saturday. Too many of us argue that Saturday is not the Sabbath day, whereas we should be pointing out that Saturday is not the day of Christian worship. We should know, however, that the word *Sabbath* comes from the same Hebrew root as the word *seventh.* Saturday is the seventh day; therefore, it is the Sabbath day. Sunday is not the Sabbath (the seventh) day. Rather, Sunday is the first day of the week; it is the "Lord's day" and the day on which Christians worship. Although the terms *Sabbath* and *Lord's day* are used correctly in the pamphlet prepared by the Church on that subject, some of us as members do not use the terms precisely. Let us not be guilty of such carelessness in regard to the terms associated with our subject of grace and works.

The extent of the problem, however, goes beyond mere definition of words. It is concerned with such questions as the following:

1. Is there a God? If so, what kind of being is he? Is he an invisible spirit, without body, parts, or passions? or is he a loving, kind, merciful Father in Heaven?

2. Are others associated with God in a group known as the Godhead? If so, are they simply different manifestations of the one God as proposed in the Trinitarian creeds? Or are they separate individuals, distinct from each other, with different functions, as explained by believers in tritheism?

3. Exactly what were the consequences of the fall of Adam and Eve? Was the Fall necessary? Are we born in original sin? That is, do we as descendants of Adam and Eve individually carry responsibility for their fall?

4. Was Jesus Christ the divine Son of God? If so, does that mean he is simply God made incarnate among men, or was he actually, literally, physically, biologically the Son of God in the flesh?

5. Did Jesus Christ accomplish the Atonement? If so, what does that mean? Did the Atonement pertain only to the physical death introduced by the fall of Adam and Eve, and is the resurrection universal? Or did the Atonement also pertain to spiritual death, and to the original transgression of Adam and Eve? If the atonement of Jesus Christ has been fully accomplished, is there anything man can or should do to be saved in the kingdom of God? Or does the Atonement of Jesus Christ guarantee that all believers in him will automatically be saved in his presence in a fulness of joy?

Also, does the Atonement apply only to those who have lived on the earth after the time of Christ and to those who had the privilege of hearing the gospel while they lived upon the earth? Or does the Atonement apply also to those who lived before the birth of the Savior? What about those who have never had an opportunity to hear the gospel, whether they lived before or after the birth of Jesus Christ?

The answers to these questions are essential to an understanding of the nature of man and the potential of mankind. They are also essential to an understanding of our topic of grace and works. Here is my understanding of the answers to these questions as taught by the Church:

1. Yes, there is a God. He is a resurrected God of glory, with a glorified body of flesh and bone. He is literally the father of our spirits; and because he dwells in the heavens, we rightfully refer to him as "Our Father which art in heaven" (Matthew 6:9). He loves and cares for us as a good, loving, kind, merciful father would.

2. Yes, others are associated with him in a special quorum known as the Godhead. One other member is the firstborn Son of God in the Spirit, our elder brother, whom we know by his earthly name and title, Jesus Christ. Another member is the Holy Ghost, a personage of spirit, whose functions include testifying that Jesus Christ is the divine Son of God.

3. The fall of Adam and Eve introduced both physical death and spiritual death into the world. As indicated in the dictionary at the end of the Latter-day Saint edition of the King James Version of the Bible, the Fall "was a necessary step in the progress of man, and provisions for a Savior had been made even before the fall had occurred. Jesus Christ came to atone for the fall of Adam and also for man's individual sins."[12] Because of the atonement of Jesus Christ, we are not born in original sin.

4. Yes, Jesus Christ was actually, literally, physically, biologically the Son of God in the flesh, the Only Begotten of the Father in this sense.

5. Yes, Jesus Christ has completed the Atonement. Because he was the Only Begotten Son of God in the flesh, he inherited power over death from his immortal Father and was able to atone unconditionally for the physical death introduced by the fall of Adam and Eve and provide for the resurrection of all mankind. Because he lived a sinless life upon the earth, Christ was able, by assuming full responsibility for the original transgression of Adam and Eve, to atone unconditionally for the spiritual death of mankind introduced by their fall. Adam and Eve, however, were still responsible for any sins they committed after they obtained a knowledge of good and evil, just as we are responsible for our own sins after we arrive at the age of accountability. The atonement of Jesus Christ has made it possible for us to receive a full remission of our sins, but such forgiveness is conditional upon our observing and keeping the first principles and ordinances of the gospel. Thus, there are still some things that man can and must do before he can enter into the kingdom of God, and there are some additional things man can and must do before he can enjoy a fulness of joy in the presence of God.

Furthermore, both the unconditional and the conditional aspects of the Atonement pertain to all mankind, without exception, whether the person lived on the earth before or after the time of Christ, and whether the person had opportunity to hear the gospel while living upon the earth. Herein lies the importance of teaching the gospel to those in the postmortal spirit world, as indicated in 1 Peter 3–4, and the importance of performing vicarious ordinances for those who have died without the opportunity of hearing and accepting the gospel, as indicated in 1 Corinthians 15:29, where Paul mentions baptism for the dead.

Now that we have reviewed these essential questions and answers, it is easy to see that the fundamental question before us is not "Are we saved by grace?" The answer to that question is a definite, firm, everlasting yes. Rather, the question is "Are we saved by grace *alone*?" The answer to that question is an equally definite no.

Elder Bruce R. McConkie has answered the question "Does salvation come by grace?" in these words:

"It surely does, without any question, in all its parts, types, kinds, and degrees.

"We are saved by grace . . . ; it is a gift of God. . . .

"In his goodness and grace the great God ordained and established the plan of salvation. No works on our part were required.

"In his goodness and grace he created this earth and all that is on it, with man as the crowning creature of his creating. . . . No works on our part were required.

"In his goodness and grace he provided for the Fall of man, thus bringing mortality and death and a probationary estate into being—without all of which there would be no immortality and eternal life. And again no works on our part were required.

"In his goodness and grace—and this above all—he gave his Only Begotten Son to ransom man and all life from the temporal and spiritual death brought into the world by the Fall of Adam.

"He sent his Son to redeem mankind, to atone for the sins of the world, 'to bring to pass the immortality and eternal life of man' (Moses 1:39). And again all this comes to us as a free gift and without works.

"There is nothing any man could do to create himself. This was the work of the Lord God.

"Nor did we have any part in the Fall of man, without which there could be no salvation. The Lord provided the way, and Adam and Eve put the system into operation.

"And finally, there neither has been, nor is, nor ever can be any way nor means by which man alone can, by any power he possesses, redeem himself."[13]

It is true that the atonement of Jesus Christ has several unconditional aspects, requiring neither effort nor works on our part. These include (1) the resurrection of all mankind and (2) the removal of responsibility for original sin. These gifts come to us as an act of grace, of pure love, on the part of our Heavenly Father and his Son, Jesus Christ.

But it is also true that the Atonement contains conditional aspects. For example, entrance into the kingdom of God is conditional upon our being baptized of the water and of the Spirit, as taught so clearly by the Savior in John 3:3–5. The enjoyment of a fulness of joy in the presence of our Heavenly Father and of Jesus Christ—that is, the achievement of eternal life—is conditional upon our keeping all of the commandments upon which this blessing is predicated and upon our enduring and remaining faithful to the end. That works are also required on our part to inherit eternal life is clearly and plainly taught in other places in the scriptures. Note the following statements from the New Testament:

Acts 16:30–33: The jailer said, "Sirs, what must I do to be saved? And they said, Believe on the Lord Jesus Christ, and thou shalt be saved, and thy house. And they spake unto him the word of the Lord, and to all that were in his house. And he took them the same hour of the night, and washed their stripes; and was baptized, he and all his, straightway."

I listed this reference first because it is a classic example of how too many people quote one part of a scripture but ignore other verses that pertain to the same subject.

Matthew 5:48: "Be ye therefore perfect, even as your Father which is in heaven is perfect."

Matthew 7:21, 24, 26: "Not every one that saith unto me, Lord, Lord, shall enter into the kingdom of heaven; but he that doeth the will of my Father which is in heaven. . . . Therefore whosoever heareth these sayings of mine, and doeth them, I will liken him unto a wise man, which built his house upon a rock. . . . And every one that heareth these sayings of mine, and doeth them not, shall be likened unto a foolish man, which built his house upon the sand."

Mark 1:15: "The time is fulfilled, and the kingdom of God is at hand: repent ye, and believe the gospel."

Mark 16:16: "He that believeth and is baptized shall be saved; but he that believeth not shall be damned" (this verse was not changed in the Joseph Smith Translation).

Luke 6:46: "And why call ye me, Lord, Lord, and do not the things which I say?"

Luke 8:21: "And he answered and said unto them, My mother and my brethren are these which hear the word of God, and do it."

John 7:17: "If any man will do his will, he shall know of the doctrine, whether it be of God, or whether I speak of myself."

Acts 2:37–38: "Now when they heard this, they were pricked in their heart, and said unto Peter and to the rest of the apostles, Men and brethren, what shall we do? Then Peter said unto them, Repent, and be baptized every one of you in the name of

Jesus Christ for the remission of sins, and ye shall receive the gift of the Holy Ghost."

Romans 10:9–10: "If thou shalt confess with thy mouth the Lord Jesus, and shalt believe in thine heart that God hath raised him from the dead, thou shalt be saved. For with the heart man believeth unto righteousness; and with the mouth confession is made unto salvation" (no changes in the Joseph Smith Translation).

James 4:17: "Therefore to him that knoweth to do good, and doeth it not, to him it is sin."

Revelation 22:14: "Blessed are they that do his commandments, that they may have right to the tree of life."

ADDITIONAL IDEAS ON THE TOPIC OF GRACE AND WORKS

If I had the opportunity, I would enlarge the topic of grace and works to include the word *faith* and the relationship among grace, faith, and works. I might even be tempted to include the word *justification*. Many of Paul's writings include elements of faith and justification in his explanation of salvation. Concerning this relationship, Gerald N. Lund has written: "Remember that Paul said we are justified *through* and *by* faith (see Gal. 2:16; Rom. 3:28), which is the first principle of the gospel. In other words, faith is the principle that activates the power of the Atonement in our lives, and we are put back into a proper relationship with God (justification) as faith activates that power. There are marvelous implications in this concept, and perhaps [an] analogy can help us see more clearly the role faith and works play in achieving salvation:

"We are like a powerhouse on a mighty river. The powerhouse has no power residing in itself; the potential power rests in the energy of the river. When that source of power flows through the generators of the power plant, power is transferred from the river to the power plant and sent out into the homes (lives) of others. So it is with faith. The power to achieve justification does not reside in man. Man requires the power of the atonement of Christ flowing into him. If no power is being generated, one does not—indeed, cannot—turn the generators by hand (justification by works); but rather, an effort is made to remove those things which have blocked the power from flowing into the generators (working righteousness as a result of faith). With this background then, one can understand why the scriptures clearly stress that faith *includes* works (see James 2:17–26); that is, obedience, commitment, and repentance—these are the works of faith that open up the channels so that the power of the atoning sacrifice of Christ can flow into us, redeem us from sin, and bring us back into the presence of God. Disobedience and wickedness dam those channels. (How literal is the word *damnation*!) The righteous works in themselves do not save us. The atoning power of God saves us. But our righteous works, activated by our faith in the Savior, are the condition for the operation of that power. Thus, each of us has something to say about whether he will be able to seek the gift and power of the Atonement in his behalf."[14]

If we examined the problems of understanding the relationship between grace and works from the viewpoint of explaining to others the place of original sin in the plan of salvation, perhaps we could see more clearly the major components in the relationship between grace and works.

Several years ago I was privileged to serve as dean in the College of Religious Instruction at Brigham Young University. During that time, one of our more able and forceful faculty members used to dramatize the importance of the Atonement by emphasizing what would have happened if the Atonement had not occurred. He used to begin his discussion somewhat as follows:

"If there is no atonement of Jesus Christ, *we are all born in original sin. Thus, the Catholics are right* from their viewpoint when they teach about original sin, for they do not fully believe in the Atonement."

He emphasized the various elements of this statement as I have emphasized them here and, unfortunately, some of his students heard (or remembered) only those elements he had emphasized: "We are all born in original sin. Thus, the Catholics are right." Also, unfortunately, many confused students wrote letters to dismayed parents, who inquired of concerned General Authorities, who called a responsible President Ernest L. Wilkinson, who contacted a wondering Dean Ludlow, who met with a worried faculty member to find out what was actually said.

You may question the methodology or the emphasis of the faculty member—especially in a 7 A.M. class when half the students were still sleepy—but when you objectively and dispassionately examine his teachings, isn't he right? In substance, if it were not for the Atonement, wouldn't we all be born in (or with the consequences of) original sin? In substance, did not the atonement of Jesus Christ either remove these consequences fully or make it possible for us to remove them through our actions? If these two statements are true, then do not the rules of logic and reason lead to the conclusion that if you believe in original sin, you do not believe in the atonement of Jesus Christ? Isn't this essentially what the Lord is teaching us through his prophet Mormon, as explained in Mormon's inspired letter to his son Moroni:

"Listen to the words of Christ, your Redeemer, your Lord and your God.

Behold, I came into the world not to call the righteous but sinners to repentance; the whole need no physician, but they that are sick; wherefore, little children are whole, for they are not capable of committing sin; wherefore the curse of Adam is taken from them in me, that it hath no power over them....

"And after this manner did the Holy Ghost manifest the word of God unto me; wherefore . . . I know that it is solemn mockery before God, that ye should baptize little children.... Little children are alive in Christ, even from the foundation of the world.... Little children cannot repent; wherefore, it is awful wickedness to deny the pure mercies of God unto them, for they are all alive in him because of his mercy.

"And *he that saith that little children need baptism denieth the mercies of Christ, and setteth at naught the atonement of him and the power of his redemption.* Wo unto such, for they are in danger of death, hell, and an endless torment. I speak it boldly; God hath commanded me" (Moroni 8:8–9, 12, 19–21; emphasis added).

Do not these words really indicate that if you believe in the necessity of infant baptism to remove the effects of original sin, you do not believe in the full atonement of Jesus Christ? I will now use the technique of my faculty friend to put over a major point concerning the relationship between the Atonement and our subject of grace and works:

If salvation consists only of the resurrection from physical death and if the atonement of Jesus Christ is not concerned with redemption from spiritual death, *the doctrine of grace as taught by the Catholic church and by many of the born-again groups is true so far as it goes, when taught from their viewpoint. You are born in original sin, and in this condition your works will never save you.*

Nevertheless, any group is wrong—whether they call themselves Christian or not—if they say they believe that Jesus Christ atoned for original sin and for our individual sins, and yet claim that works are not necessary for full salvation. Please do not consider it sacrilegious if I paraphrase the same thoughts in the style of the words of the Lord as revealed to the prophet Mormon pertaining to infant baptism:

It is solemn mockery before God that you should say Jesus Christ had power only to provide the resurrection from physical death and that he did not have power to atone for the fall of Adam and Eve, for he did. Thus the curse of Adam is taken from all men and women in him, that it hath no power over them. All God's children can be alive in Christ and be sanctified from their individual sins if they accept and live the first principles and ordinances of the gospel. He that saith that the works of faith, repentance, baptism of water, and the reception of the Holy Ghost are not necessary to the full salvation of mankind does not understand the gospel of Jesus Christ as taught in the holy scriptures. Such deny the mercies of Christ and set at naught the atonement of him and the power of his redemption. Wo unto such persons, for if they do not do the things required, they are in danger of spiritual death, which is hell (see Moroni 8:8–9, 12, 19–21).

In case you wonder why I emphasized the last part of the earlier statement or why I paraphrased Moroni 8 the way I did, let me quote Elder Bruce R. McConkie who discussed the relationship between grace and works in these terms:

"Now, let us reason together on this matter of being saved without the need to do the works of righteousness. Did you ever wonder why our missionaries convert one of a city and two of a family while the preachers of this doctrine of salvation by grace alone gain millions of converts?

"Does it seem strange to you that we wear out our lives in bringing one soul unto Christ, that we may have joy with him in the kingdom of the Father, while our evangelist colleagues cannot even count their converts, so great is their number?

"Why are those who come to hear the message of the Restoration numbered in the hundreds *and* thousands, rather than in the hundreds *of* thousands?

"May I suggest that the difference is between the strait and narrow way, which few find, and the broad way, 'that leadeth to destruction, and many there be which go in thereat' (Matthew 7:13–14). . . .

"As we are aware, since the Fall all men have become carnal, sensual, and devilish by nature; they have become worldly; and their inclination is to live after the manner of the flesh and satisfy their lusts and appetites.

"Accordingly, anytime men can devise a system of worship that will let them continue to live after the manner of the world, to live in their carnal and fallen state, and at the same time one which will satisfy their innate and instinctive desires to worship, such, to them, is a marvelous achievement."[15]

Then, after defining what he calls the "true doctrine of salvation by grace," including definitions of salvation, the plan of salvation, and the grace of God, Elder McConkie continues:

"Truly, there is no way to overstate the goodness and grandeurs and glories of the grace of God which bringeth salvation. Such wondrous love, such unending mercy, such infinite compassion and condescension—all these can come only from the Eternal God who lives in eternal life and who desires all of his children to live as he lives and be inheritors of eternal life.

"Knowing these things, as did Paul and our fellow apostles of old, let us put ourselves in their position. What words shall we choose, to offer to the world the blessings of a freely given atoning sacrifice?

"On the one hand we are preaching to Jews who, in their lost and fallen state, have rejected their Messiah and who believe they are saved by the works and performances of the Mosaic law.

"On the other hand, we are preaching to pagans—Romans, Greeks, those in every nation—who know nothing whatever about the Messianic word, or of the need for a Redeemer, or of the working out of the infinite and eternal atonement. . . .

"Can either the Jews or the pagans be left to assume that the works they do will save them? Or must they forget their little groveling acts of petty worship, gain faith in Christ, and rely on the cleansing power of his blood for salvation?

"They must be taught faith in the Lord Jesus Christ and to forsake their traditions and performances. Surely we must tell them they cannot be saved by the works they are doing, for man cannot save himself. Instead they must turn to Christ and rely on his merits and mercy and grace."[16]

In order to understand the teachings of Paul in the New Testament on the relationship of grace and works, let us do as Elder McConkie has suggested and put ourselves in the place of Paul.

Paul fully understood that the members of his Jewish audiences believed in and emphasized the importance of works. Their master teachers, the rabbis, over the centuries had formalized the laws of God in the scriptures into hundreds of laws based on the rabbis' interpretations. The Jews had become obsessed with what they could and could not do in nearly every conceivable situation. Their lives were oriented to what they should do in their dress and grooming, what they should eat, how they should worship, what they should do (and should not do) on the Sabbath day, and so on. In fact, in their religious beliefs they had emphasized the doing so much that they overlooked the need for someone with greater power than they who could give them the privilege of living forever and the opportunity of receiving forgiveness through repentance of their sins.

Because Paul knew how much the Jews emphasized the doing, he emphasized grace—the absolutely essential element. Thus, in the formula for achieving full salvation, he emphatically taught and wrote about grace in order to compensate for the Jewish emphasis on doing.

I have not found any prophet of the Church in this dispensation who has found it necessary to minimize the writings of Paul concerning grace. Perhaps some persons have felt that Paul stressed grace too much, but evidently he felt it necessary for the people he was teaching. Concerning Paul's teachings, President Joseph Fielding Smith observed: "[The people whom Paul was teaching thought] they could be saved by some power that was within them, or by observing the law of

Moses—he pointed out to them the fact that if it were not for the mission of Jesus Christ, if it were not for this great atoning sacrifice, they could not be redeemed. And therefore it was by the grace of God that they are saved, not by any work on their part, for they were absolutely helpless. Paul was absolutely right.

"... [But Paul also] taught in other scripture, that it is our duty, of necessity, to labor, to strive in diligence, and faith, keeping the commandments of the Lord, if we would obtain that inheritance which is promised to the faithful. . . .

"So it is easy to understand that we must accept the mission of Jesus Christ. We must believe that it is through his grace that we are saved, that he performed for us that labor which we were unable to perform for ourselves, and did for us those things which were essential to our salvation, which were beyond our power; and also that we are under the commandment and the necessity of performing the labors that are required of us as set forth in the commandments known as the gospel of Jesus Christ."[17]

Let me now call an additional witness concerning Paul's writings. Brother Gerald N. Lund has written: "There is no need to go to extraordinary lengths to apologize for Paul, or try to explain away his statements on salvation by grace. We *are* saved by grace—saved by Christ's love from physical and spiritual death; saved by Christ's love from Adam's fall and our own; saved from sin and transgression by the grace or gifts of God. The atoning power of God unto salvation is a freely available gift from him—but our works of righteousness are essential to bring the gift into power in our lives. Sin brings alienation from God. The more we sin, the greater the alienation and the more difficult it becomes to effectively tap the power of God, which alone is sufficient to save us from our sins."[18]

Paul was so successful in emphasizing the importance of grace that the creeds of the predominant Christian churches have also stressed it until they verily have come to believe it is the only necessary component for full salvation. Thus, generation after generation of Christians have come and gone from this earth thinking that the grace of God (and of Jesus Christ) is all that is necessary.

When this doctrine of grace alone is combined with the doctrine of election—that God decides who is to receive his grace and who is not—we get the damning doctrine of predestination, which, if examined and analyzed carefully, indicates that even if it is felt that works might be necessary, they are accomplished only because God wills it. Such actions do not come from the will, or the agency, of man. As a result, in the terminology of the largest of the Christian churches today, we hear the terms "election to grace" for some and "election to salvation" for a very favored few.

These teachings of apostate Catholicism have now been largely adopted by apostate Protestantism—truly a case of the blind leading the blind. The challenge faced by our missionaries today is how to reconvert an apostate Christianity, which stresses only grace. Our approach has largely been to emphasize the other essential ingredient for full salvation—works. We have done this so much that many of our Christian friends have honestly concluded that we don't believe in the grace of God at all and, therefore, neither we nor our Church are truly Christian. Perhaps the time has come for us to start emphasizing again our belief in the grace of God and of his Christ; the new subtitle of the Book of Mormon, "Another Testament of Jesus Christ," is a good beginning.

Conclusion

The best definition or explanation of grace I was able to find in my research comes from the dictionary in the Latter-day Saint edition of the King James Bible:

"A word that occurs frequently in the New Testament, especially in the writings of Paul. The main idea of the word is divine means of help or strength, given through the bounteous mercy and love of Jesus Christ.

"It is through the grace of the Lord Jesus, made possible by his atoning sacrifice, that mankind will be raised in immortality. . . . It is likewise through the grace of the Lord that individuals, through faith in the atonement of Jesus Christ and repentance of their sins, receive strength and assistance to do good works. . . . This grace is an enabling power that allows men and women to lay hold on eternal life and exaltation after they have expended their own best efforts.

"Divine grace is needed by every soul in consequence of the fall of Adam and also because of man's weaknesses and shortcomings. However, grace cannot suffice without total effort on the part of the recipient. . . . It is truly the grace of Jesus Christ that makes salvation possible."[19]

Again we plead with our Christian friends: read all the scriptures. Don't read and ponder only the verses you want to believe, those that do not require repentance of your sins. Read all the references pertaining to each topic, placing plus marks between the scriptures. After you have listed all the scriptures, place an equals sign; then list honestly in your own words, all the components of the equation. If you will do this, even if you read prayerfully and carefully only the New Testament, you will come to understand the true relationship between grace and works. But if you continue to select only those scriptures you want to believe and ignore others that give additional insights on the same subject, you prove anew the statement by one of Shakespeare's characters, that even "the devil can cite Scripture for his purpose."[20]

If we could just get Christians to read and believe one short verse from that second testament of Jesus Christ called the Book of Mormon, the whole Christian world would come to an instant understanding of the relationship between grace and works. As Nephi explained so beautifully and succinctly:

"For we labor diligently to write, to persuade our children, and also our brethren, to believe in Christ, and to be reconciled to God; for we know that it is by grace that we are saved, after all we can do" (2 Nephi 25:23).

Notes

From an address delivered at the CES Symposium on the New Testament, Brigham Young University, Provo, Utah, 15–17 August 1984.

1. See Mark E. Petersen, in Conference Report, April 1982, 18–22; see also Mark E. Petersen, "'We Believe in Being Honest,'" *Ensign,* May 1982, 14–16.
2. See Gerald N. Lund, "Salvation: By Grace or by Works?" *Ensign,* April 1981, 17–23.
3. Bruce R. McConkie, "What Think Ye of Salvation by Grace?" in *Brigham Young University 1983–84 Fireside and Devotional Speeches* (Provo, Utah: University Publications, 1984), 44–50.
4. Ibid., 44.
5. Ibid., 45.
6. Ibid., 44.
7. *Webster's New International Dictionary of the English Language,* ed. Philip Babcock Gove, 3d ed. (Springfield, Mass.: G. & C. Merriam Co., 1993), "relationship."
8. Ibid., "relation."
9. Ibid., "grace."
10. James Strong, "Hebrew and Chaldee Dictionary," in *Strong's Exhaustive Concordance* (New York: Abingdon Press, 1894), "chanan" (no. 2603).
11. Ibid., "Greek Dictionary of the New Testament," in *Strong's,* "chairo" (no. 5463) and "charis" (no. 5485).
12. Bible Dictionary, "Fall of Adam," 670.
13. McConkie, "What Think Ye of Salvation by Grace?" 47.
14. Lund, "Salvation: By Grace or by Works?" 22–23; emphasis in original.
15. McConkie, "What Think Ye of Salvation by Grace?" 46; emphasis in original.
16. Ibid., 47–48.
17. *Doctrines of Salvation,* 2:310–11.
18. Lund, "Salvation: By Grace or by Works?" 23; emphasis in original.
19. Bible Dictionary, "grace," 697.
20. William Shakespeare, *The Merchant of Venice,* 1.3.99.

Chapter 2 4

THE FIRST PRINCIPLES OF THE GOSPEL: FAITH IN JESUS CHRIST AND REPENTANCE

In the Church of Jesus Christ of Latter-day Saints, "We believe that the first principles and ordinances of the Gospel are: first, Faith in the Lord Jesus Christ; second, Repentance; third, Baptism by immersion for the remission of sins; fourth, Laying on of hands for the gift of the Holy Ghost" (Articles of Faith 1:4).

Perhaps we should first define some of these terms. The dictionary defines a principle as a fundamental truth, or a primary or basic law. An ordinance is defined as a prescribed practice or usage—an outward manifestation or symbol of a principle. In the true Church of Christ, an ordinance must always be performed by one who is *ordained*—or in other words, an ordinance requires the action of the priesthood. An ordinance, of course, is also a principle because it is based on fundamental truth, but a principle is not always an ordinance because not all principles require the action of the priesthood. Why is faith in Jesus Christ referred to as the first principle of the gospel? What unique powers or attributes does true faith have that would make it the prerequisite to all other principles of the gospel?

Faith denotes action. As James said in the New Testament: "Faith, if it hath not works, is dead, being alone. Yea, a man may say, Thou hast faith, and I have works: show me thy faith without thy works, and I will show thee my faith by my works" (James 2:17–18). Faith is a motivating power—it is the motivating principle that impels men to resolve and to act.

Although I am convinced that faith in Jesus Christ is rightfully the first principle of the gospel, I believe in practice another element usually precedes faith. That element is hope. We usually desire or hope for a thing before we have the faith in it that causes us to do something about it. The two best scriptural definitions of faith both refer to hope as an element of faith. Paul's much-quoted definition of faith is recorded in Hebrews 11:1: "Now faith is the substance of things hoped for, the evidence of things not seen."

Another definition of faith is given by the prophet Alma in the Book of Mormon as follows: "Faith is not to have a perfect knowledge of things: therefore if ye have faith, ye hope for things which are not seen, which are true" (Alma 32:21). Later in his sermon, Alma suggests how we can transform hope into faith. He states: "Now, as I said concerning faith—that it was not a perfect knowledge—even so it is with my words. Ye cannot know of their surety at first, unto perfection, any more than faith is a perfect knowledge. But behold, if ye will awake and arouse your faculties, even to an experiment upon my words, and exercise a particle of faith, yea, even if ye can no more than desire to believe, let this desire work in you, even until ye believe in a manner that ye can give place for a portion of my words" (Alma 32:26–27). We frequently gain faith by first hoping—or desiring—to believe.

One of the most difficult concepts to master concerning faith is its relationship to belief and knowledge. The late James E. Talmage has written concerning this problem: "The terms faith and belief are sometimes regarded as synonyms; nevertheless each of them has a specific meaning in our language, although in earlier usage there was little distinction between them, and therefore the words are used interchangeably in many scriptural passages. Belief . . . may consist in a merely intellectual assent, while faith implies such confidence and conviction as will impel to action. . . . Belief is in a sense passive, an agreement or acceptance only; faith is active and positive, embracing such reliance and confidence as will lead to works. Faith in Christ comprises belief in Him, combined with trust in Him. One cannot have faith without belief; yet he may believe and still lack faith. Faith is vivified, vitalized, living belief. . . . Neither belief nor its superior, actual knowledge, is efficient to save; for neither of these is faith."[1]

Both Elder Talmage and Alma indicate that faith is not knowledge, although faith plus the action it motivates may lead to the acquisition of knowledge.

These statements should make it clear why faith precedes repentance as a principle of the gospel. I don't believe any of us would repent of our sins if we did not have hope in a better way of life and if we did not have the faith to attempt to realize that hope.

Let us turn, then, to the second principle of the gospel—repentance.

Unfortunately, when most of us hear the word repentance we think it is something that applies only to the other person. This is not true. I'm sure all of us are in need of repentance.

Repentance has always been an important theme in the gospel of Jesus Christ. In fact, one of the distinguishing features of a prophet of God is that he always cries repentance unto the people.

In the book of Moses in the Pearl of Great Price, we find that repentance was taught even in the day of Adam and his family: "And the Lord God called upon men by the Holy Ghost everywhere and commanded them that they should repent; and as many as believed in the Son, and repented of their sins, should be saved; and as many as believed not and repented not, should be damned; and the words went forth out of the mouth of God in a firm decree; wherefore they must be fulfilled" (Moses 5:14–15).

John the Baptist prepared the people for the coming of Christ by preaching, "Repent ye, for the kingdom of heaven is at hand" (Matthew 3:2). The Savior also preached repentance when he was upon the earth. According to Mark, the first statement made by Christ after formally beginning his ministry was: "The time is fulfilled, and the kingdom of God is at hand; repent ye, and believe the gospel" (Mark 1:15). In Luke 13:3 the Savior said, "Except ye repent, ye shall all likewise perish."

The words of Peter on the day of Pentecost are as applicable to all mankind as they were to those whom he addressed. When they asked, "Men and brethren, what shall we do? Then Peter said unto them, Repent, and be baptized every one of you in the name of Jesus Christ for the remission of sins, and ye shall receive the gift of the Holy Ghost" (Acts 3:37–38).

If repentance has been preached by all the prophets, it must be very important. But why, one might ask, is it necessary to repent?

One answer to this question is that repentance of our sins is the only way we can regain the presence of God. The scriptures tell us that no unclean or sinful thing can dwell in God's presence; thus we must repent of our sins and receive a remission of them if we are to enter into the presence of God.

Another answer to the necessity of repentance is that repentance is the principle upon which all progress is based. Essentially repentance is forsaking a wrong thing or way for a right or better thing or way. That is the only method by which progress is made.

Along this line, it is interesting to note that modern science employs the principle of repentance. At first, this statement might appear to be strange or even paradoxical, for most of us have become accustomed to thinking of repentance only in terms of religion. However, this principle has applications in other areas as well. The whole structure of modern science is based on the idea of finding the best way of doing things. When one procedure or method proves to be unsatisfactory, another procedure or method is tried until a better way is found. Then the faulty or inferior way is discontinued, and the improved or superior way is adopted. This is a clear application in science of the principle of repentance.

In the gospel, of course, we are not left to the gropings of trial and error to find the right way. That way has been clearly marked by the teachings of the prophets and the scriptures.

When we learn of the better way, however, how do we proceed to forsake our old way and adopt the new? Or, expressed differently, how can we repent of our sins?

When most of us think of repentance of sin, we probably think of the times we have stopped doing things that we shouldn't do. However, this is only one type of repentance. In the scriptures, God has given us two types of commandments. One of these begins with the injunction "Thou shalt not." For example, we are warned "Thou shalt not kill," "Thou shalt not steal," etc. Whenever we break one of these commandments, we are committing an act we should not commit; these sins are referred to as sins of *commission*. In order to repent of a sin of commission, we must stop doing the wrong thing.

However, God has also given us another type of commandment. In essence, he is saying "Thou shalt" do thus and so—for example, "Thou shalt" be baptized by water and by the spirit, "Thou shalt" pay an honest tithe, etc. Whenever we omit doing those things we have been commanded to do, we are guilty of a sin of *omission*. In order to repent of a sin of omission, we must start doing the thing that is right.

Before we can repent of either of these types of sin, however, we must first recognize that we have been doing something wrong. Then we must have a feeling of remorse or sorrow for our sinful action, which in turn will help us resolve to do better. Then we must refrain from the breaking of the commandment. If the sin is of such a nature that we have deprived someone of something, we must make restitution insofar as we are able to do so.

These steps have been referred to as the five R's of repentance: Recognition, Remorse, Resolution, Refraining, and Restitution. Notice that true repentance involves a change in both attitude and action. It is not enough to be sorry for a wrong deed; we must change our behavior and refrain from future error if we would truly repent. As modern scripture so clearly states: "By this ye may know if a man repenteth of his sins—behold, he will confess them and forsake them" (D&C 58:43).

One of the most difficult things for most of us to do concerning faith and repentance is to begin the action that produces them. They both require action by us. No one else can exercise faith for us; neither can another person repent for us. We must do these things ourselves.

It is my sincere hope that we might all follow the admonition of the prophets—that we might develop our powers of faith and that we might not procrastinate the day of our repentance.

Notes

From an address delivered over KSL Radio, Salt Lake City, Utah, 15 December 1957.

1. James E. Talmage, *Articles of Faith* (Salt Lake City: Deseret Book Co., 1988), 87–88, 89.

Chapter 25

THE FUNCTIONS AND POWERS OF THE HOLY GHOST

Since it was organized on April 6, 1830, The Church of Jesus Christ of Latter-day Saints—the so-called Mormon Church—has been considered a unique organization in the world both by its own members and those not of its faith. This unique status comes partly from its claim of being the only true restored Church of Christ on the earth, and partly from some of its teachings. In the past 127 years, hundreds of sermons have been given and dozens of books have been written attempting to point out the major differences between this Church and other Christian churches. On one occasion, the founder of the Church in this dispensation—Joseph Smith—made this distinction in a single sentence. This brief chapter will consider a few of the implications of this sentence by Joseph Smith.

In the course of an 1839 conversation with United States President Martin Van Buren, Joseph Smith was asked how his religion differed from the other religions of the day. Joseph Smith answered very simply and briefly, "We have the Holy Ghost."

In order to understand the import of Joseph Smith's statement, one must know something of the thoughts and teachings of the Prophet concerning the Holy Ghost. In the writings of Joseph Smith we find this statement: "I have always declared God to be a distinct personage, Jesus Christ a separate and distinct personage from God the Father, and that the Holy Ghost was a distinct personage and a Spirit: and these three constitute three distinct personages and three Gods."[1]

In modern scripture written by the Prophet Joseph Smith, we find this verse: "The Father has a body of flesh and bones as tangible as man's; the Son also; but the Holy Ghost has not a body of flesh and bones, but is a personage of Spirit. Were it not so, the Holy Ghost could not dwell in us" (D&C 130:22).

Joseph Smith taught that as a personage of Spirit, the Holy Ghost is able to dwell in the actual presence of God, and yet is also able to come to earth to visit and give counsel and instructions to man. Thus the Holy Ghost is a mediator between man and God, or as the Savior put it, the Holy Ghost is a comforter. In this role as a comforter, the Holy Ghost performs many functions. Through the Holy Ghost we gain a testimony concerning the other members of the Godhead. In his first letter to the Corinthian Saints, Paul stated, "No man can say that Jesus is the Lord, but by the Holy Ghost" (1 Corinthians 12:3). And in John 15:26 the Savior is recorded as having said, "When the Comforter is come, . . . he shall testify of me."

A further function of the Holy Ghost is to reveal knowledge unto man. Recall the statement of the Savior in John 16:13: "When he, the Spirit of truth, is come, he will guide you into all truth." Earlier in his ministry, the Savior said to his apostles, "The Comforter, which is the Holy Ghost, whom the Father will send in my name, he shall teach you all things, and bring all things to your remembrance, whatsoever I have said unto you" (John 14:26).

In these functions and in many other functions, the power of the Holy Ghost can and does come to man. However, as a pure and sinless member of the Godhead, the Holy Ghost can dwell within only those individuals who have accepted the atoning sacrifice of the Savior and who have followed the Savior's admonition to be baptized of water for the remission of sins. It is this "gift of the Holy Ghost," or the right to the permanent companionship of the Holy Ghost, that is unique to The Church of Jesus Christ of Latter-day Saints and to which Joseph Smith made reference in his conversation with President Van Buren.

But, one might ask, why is the right to have the Holy Ghost as a permanent companion so important to man. Once again the answer appears to be simple and brief, yet entails a great deal of the gospel. The companionship of the Holy Ghost is necessary for any person so that he can be sanctified from his sins and return to the presence of God.

Perhaps you recall the conversation the Savior had with the Pharisee ruler, Nicodemus, as recorded in the third chapter of John. Nicodemus acknowledged the Savior as "a teacher come from God." Jesus said unto him, "Verily, verily, I say unto thee, Except a man be born again, he cannot see the kingdom of God." Nicodemus, a grown man, did not understand the nature of this rebirth, and so he asked, "How can a man be born when he is old? Can he enter the second time into his mother's womb, and be born?" The Savior's answer is again clear and definite: "Verily, verily, I say unto thee, Except a man be born of water and of the Spirit, he cannot enter into the kingdom of God" (John 3:2–5).

We see that two baptisms—one of water and the other of the Holy Ghost—are necessary before we can enter the kingdom of God. The purposes of these two, separate baptisms are made quite clear in the scriptures. In Acts 2:38 Peter states, "Repent, and be baptized every one of you in the name of Jesus Christ for the remission of sins, and ye shall receive the gift of the Holy Ghost." The purpose of baptism by water is for the remission of sins. Baptism, which should be performed after repentance, is to be followed by the gift of the Holy Ghost. The purpose of the baptism of the Holy Ghost is made equally clear. In Romans 15:16 Paul talks of "being sanctified by the Holy Ghost," and in 1 Corinthians 6:11 he tells the baptized members of the Church, "Ye are washed . . . ye are sanctified."

Synonyms of the word *sanctified* in the scriptures are *sinless, purified,* and *cleansed.* Thus the purpose of baptism of the Holy Ghost is to sanctify, purify, or cleanse us from our sins after we have been baptized of water so that we can become sinless once again. Without this cleansing action of the Holy Ghost, we cannot regain the presence of God. The scriptures are clear that no evil, wicked, or unclean person can enter into his presence.

Although the Savior's teachings on these matters are quite clear in the New Testament, perhaps his clearest statements are found in the Book of Mormon. After the Savior had been crucified in the Old World and resurrected from the dead, he came to the New World and appeared as a resurrected being to the people who were living here. The Savior taught these people the principles and ordinances of the gospel. He put particular stress on the ordinances of baptism of water and baptism of the Holy Ghost. Concerning baptism of water, the Savior stated: "Whoso repenteth of his sins and desireth to be baptized in my name, on this wise shall ye baptize . . . ye shall go down and stand in the water, and in my name shall ye baptize them. And these are the words which ye shall say, calling them by name, saying: Having authority given me of Jesus Christ, I baptize you in the name of the Father, and of the Son, and of the Holy Ghost. Amen. And then shall ye immerse them in the water, and come forth again out of the water." The purpose of this baptism of water, according to the Savior, is so that the people "shall be visited with fire and with the Holy Ghost, and shall receive a remission of their sins" (3 Nephi 12:2).

Later during his ministry among the people in the Americas, the Savior gave his disciples power that they might confer the gift of the Holy Ghost by the laying on of hands. The teachings of the Savior on these matters might be summarized somewhat as follows: No evil, wicked, or unclean person can regain the presence of God. All people, after they arrive at the age of accountability, become sinful as they commit sin. This results in their being thrust spiritually out of God's presence or, as the scriptures put it, they become spiritually dead, or dead to things pertaining to the Spirit.

In order to be born again to a spiritual life, people must have faith in the atonement of Jesus Christ, repent of their sins, and be baptized in water for the remission of their sins. Then—and not until then—can they be baptized with the Holy Ghost and be sanctified from their sins. This gift of the Holy Ghost is given only by the laying on of hands by those who have the proper authority, and it is given only to those who have been previously baptized of water. The first principles and ordinances of the gospel are: "first, Faith in the Lord Jesus Christ; second, Repentance; third, Baptism by immersion for the remission of sins; fourth, Laying on of hands for the gift of the Holy Ghost" (Articles of Faith 1:4). All four steps are necessary in order for people to be cleansed or sanctified from their sins and to be found worthy to regain the presence of God. Therefore, the Savior meant exactly what he said to Nicodemus: "Except a man be born of water and of the spirit, he cannot enter into the kingdom of God."

I conclude with a direct statement of the Savior that summarizes his teachings. This statement is contained in the last sermon the Savior delivered to the Nephites in the days immediately after his resurrection. In answer to a question from his disciples regarding the name of his Church, the Savior said: "Whatsoever ye shall do, ye shall do it in my name; therefore ye shall call the church in my name; and ye shall call upon the Father in my name that he will bless the church for my sake. And how be it my church save it be called in my name? For if a church be called in Moses' name then it be Moses' church; or if it be called in the name of a man then it be the church of a man; but if it be called in my name then it is my church, *if it so be that they are built upon my gospel*" (3 Nephi 27:7–8; emphasis added).

The Savior then gave a beautiful description of his gospel. He indicated that the Father sent him to earth to be lifted up on the cross so that he could draw all people unto him. He said everyone would be resurrected and judged of their works, and he emphasized the importance of repentance. Then, in a brief paragraph, he summarizes the gospel and the need for it in our lives. Concerning the kingdom of God, he stated:

"And no unclean thing can enter into his kingdom; therefore nothing entereth into his rest save it be those who have washed their garments in my blood, because of their faith, and the repentance of all their sins, and their faithfulness unto the end. Now this is the commandment: Repent, all ye ends of the earth, and come unto me and be baptized in my name, that ye may be sanctified by the reception of the Holy

Ghost, that ye may stand spotless before me at the last day. Verily, verily, I say unto you, this is my gospel" (3 Nephi 27:19–21).

Notes

From a radio address delivered over KSL Radio, Salt Lake City, Utah, 27 October 1957.

1. *History of the Church,* 6:474.

Chapter 26

TEMPLE ORDINANCES FOR THE LIVING AND THE DEAD

A few years ago as a graduate student at Indiana University I had the opportunity of interviewing twenty-seven Christian ministers concerning their beliefs on various principles and doctrines of the gospel. Among the 150 questions I asked these ministers was this one: "Do you believe in baptism for the dead?" The ministers, without exception, replied, "No." Immediately most of them would say, "You must be a Mormon, or a member of the Church of Jesus Christ of Latter-day Saints." I assured the ministers I was.

Several beliefs or practices have made The Church of Jesus Christ of Latter-day Saints unique among the churches of Christianity. One of these is its belief in the Word of Wisdom, which prohibits the use of alcoholic beverages, tobacco, coffee, and tea. Another is the principle of tithing—each member is expected to pay one-tenth of his income to the Church as a tithe. And still another is the observance of a day of fasting: One day each month is set aside for members to abstain from two consecutive meals. The cost of these meals is then donated to help take care of the poor and needy.

To those who have studied the doctrines of the Church, however, the feature that makes it most singular or unique—or to use a scriptural term, most *peculiar*—is perhaps the ordinance work performed in the temples.

The meaning of and reasons behind this temple work are not understood by many who are not of our faith. Temples are sacred places to Latter-day Saints. They are not built for general religious meetings but are reserved for sacred priesthood ordinances—some of which must be performed only in a temple.

Up to the present time (December, 1957), the Church has ten temples used for ordinance work. They are located in Utah at Salt Lake City, Logan, Manti, and

St. George; at Mesa, Arizona; Idaho Falls, Idaho; Los Angeles, California; Cardston, Alberta, Canada; Laie, Hawaii; and Berne, Switzerland. New temples are under construction in London and New Zealand.

Once a temple is dedicated, only members of the Church who have received certificates of worthiness from their bishops and stake presidents are allowed to enter these sacred edifices.

What do Latter-day Saints do in their temples? Perhaps I can briefly outline our major beliefs and practices concerning temple work.

In the first place, we believe the Church possesses the same priesthood that was possessed by Elijah and was later given to Peter by the Savior. Recall that the Lord said to Peter, "And I will give unto thee the keys of the kingdom of heaven; and whatsoever thou shalt bind on earth shall be bound in heaven: and whatsoever thou shalt loose on earth shall be loosed in heaven." (Matthew 16:19).

This authority to "seal on earth that it might be sealed in heaven" was restored in this dispensation by Elijah to Joseph Smith in 1836. This event was in fulfillment of the words of Malachi, which appear as the last verses in the Old Testament: "Behold, I will send you Elijah the Prophet before the coming of the great and dreadful day of the Lord: And he shall turn the heart of the fathers to the children, and the heart of the children to their fathers, lest I come and smite the earth with a curse" (Malachi 4:5–6). This sealing power of the priesthood restored by Elijah is manifest in many of the ordinances performed in the temple. For example, Latter-day Saints who receive temple marriages are "sealed" for time and all eternity. We believe that marriage is intended to be eternal—not "until death do us part."

Perhaps the most unique thing about our temple ordinances, however, is that they can be performed for the dead (those who have lived on the earth during earlier periods) as well as for the living (those living on the earth now). Such ordinances as baptism, the reception of the gift of the Holy Ghost, and temple marriage are performed in our temples for the dead and the living. The ordinances for the dead are performed by proxy—a person living on this earth stands as a proxy and receives these ordinances "for and in behalf" of the deceased person. This work is often referred to as vicarious work for the dead.

The doctrine of vicarious work is not a new concept in the gospel. Indeed, the atonement of Jesus Christ is an example of vicarious work. Jesus Christ atoned for the original sin of Adam, doing something for and in behalf of Adam that Adam could not do for himself. Jesus Christ also brought to pass the resurrection of all mankind, doing something for and in behalf of all mankind that all of us together could not do for ourselves. Both of these acts by the Savior were made possible because of the doctrine of vicarious work. He stood as proxy for Adam and for all of us and performed acts that were necessary for our salvation but that we could not perform for ourselves.

But, one might ask, "Why do you perform these vicarious ordinances in the temple for people who are already dead?" We believe that the gospel pertains to the dead as well as the living. These ordinances are required of all people before they can inherit the blessings available to them. For example, the Savior very clearly taught: "Except a man be born of water and of the Spirit, he cannot enter into the kingdom of God" (John 3:5). If the Savior really meant what he said—and I sincerely believe he did—then everyone must be baptized before they can return to God's presence. This law applies to the dead as well as to the living.

Nowhere in scripture is a distinction made between the living and the dead so far as obedience to the principles and ordinances of the gospel is concerned. The New Testament clearly teaches that the doctrine of ordinance work for the dead is as much a part of the gospel as the doctrine of ordinance work for the living. Let me refer briefly to several scriptures in the New Testament that teach this doctrine.

While the Savior was on the earth he taught of his impending visit to those who were dead. The book of John records him as saying: "Verily, verily I say unto you, the hour is coming, and now is, when the dead shall hear the voice of the Son of God and they that hear shall live. . . . Marvel not at this: for the hour is coming, in the which all that are in the graves shall hear his voice" (John 5:25, 28). In his first epistle, Peter tells us that the spirit of Christ went to the spirit world to preach to the dead during the three days the body of the Savior was in the tomb. Then Peter mentions why Christ visited these spirits: "For this cause was the gospel preached also to them that are dead, that they might be judged according to men in the flesh, but live according to God in the spirit" (1 Peter 3:18–20; 1 Peter 4:6). Peter states clearly that the Savior taught the gospel to those who are dead.

But of what does the gospel of Christ consist? It consists of faith, repentance, baptism by immersion for the remission of sins, and the laying on of hands for the gift of the Holy Ghost. Does it sound reasonable that Christ would preach faith and repentance to these spirits unless they could exercise these principles? I believe most of us would say, "No." Does it sound reasonable that Christ would preach the necessity of baptism by water and the reception of the gift of the Holy Ghost to these spirits unless these ordinances could be performed for them? Again, the answer is no. But how could these disembodied spirits—who were not as yet resurrected with their bodies—be baptized in water and receive the laying on of hands? The answer is that provision was made whereby this work could be done for them vicariously—in exactly the same manner that we could not bring to pass our own resurrection, and so Christ did it for us vicariously.

Paul was well acquainted with the doctrine of vicarious work as it pertained to baptism for the dead. I am certain Paul had this doctrine in mind when he wrote to the Saints at Corinth: "If in this life only we have hope in Christ, we are of all men most miserable" (1 Corinthians 15:9). In this same letter, Paul uses the doctrine of vicarious work as proof of the resurrection of Christ. In attempting to convince the Corinthian saints of the actuality of the resurrection of all mankind through Christ, Paul asks: "Else what shall they do which are baptized for the dead if the dead rise not at all? why are they then baptized for the dead?" (1 Corinthians 15:29). These words are clear and definite. Baptism for the dead was performed in the days of Paul, and the fact that Paul refers to this practice without explanation or argument indicates that this doctrine was understood among the people to whom the letter was addressed.

This doctrine substantiates the teaching of Christ that the ordinances are absolutely necessary, but it also indicates that God is not unjust, nor partial, nor a respecter of persons. If a person did not have the opportunity to accept the gospel while he lived on the earth, he will be given that opportunity in the spirit world after his death and before his resurrection. Thus temple work for the dead in the temples has its counterpart in the spirit world where the missionary labor, instituted by Christ, is still in progress.

This doctrine also removes one of the most serious charges leveled against Christianity—the condemnation to eternal damnation and punishment those hundreds of millions of persons who lived on the earth before the time of Christ or who have lived since the time of Christ but did not have the opportunity or disposition to be baptized.

The following story illustrates the fallacy of this position. A missionary of one of the well-known Christian churches once went to China, where ancestor worship is quite common. He succeeded in converting a young man to Christianity, but before the young man was willing to be baptized, he asked the missionary: "What will happen to my ancestors? You have taught me that baptism is necessary to go to heaven. My ancestors were never baptized because they never even heard of the name Jesus Christ. What will happen to them?" The Christian missionary replied: "They cannot go to heaven, for baptism is necessary to enter there. Thus they must endure eternal damnation." The young Chinese replied: "If this is the teaching of Christianity, then I refuse to be baptized. Your God is very unfair and unjust. I will remain as I am, even if it means that I will go to hell with my ancestors."

The glorious truth of the restored gospel of Christ is that all is not lost for those who have died without the saving ordinances of the gospel. They will be taught the gospel in the spirit world, and if they accept it and exercise the necessary faith and repentance, the ordinance work will be performed in their behalf in the temples and will be as valid as though they had done the work themselves.

Despite the Biblical teachings on baptism for the dead, so far as I know this doctrine is practiced only by The Church of Jesus Christ of Latter-day Saints. It is part of the fullness of the gospel of Christ that has been restored in this dispensation.

Note

From an address delivered over KSL Radio, Salt Lake City, Utah, 29 December 1957.

Chapter 27

SPIRITUAL AND TEMPORAL DEATH

I believe it was Benjamin Franklin who said there are two certainties in this existence: death and taxes. Although it might be possible to live in a time or place where we would not have to pay taxes, we cannot live in a time or place on this earth where we would not have to die. Every mortal person who has ever lived or who will ever live on this earth must die.

Despite the universality of death, however, the topic of death is not discussed very frequently. In fact, not only do we tend to avoid the subject, but when we do talk about death or about a person who has died, we substitute those terms with such euphemisms as "he passed away," "the deceased," "the departed," or "the late person." I don't think this great fear and apprehension about death is warranted; I have therefore chosen it as the topic of this discussion.

The scriptures refer to two types of death: temporal death and spiritual death. The term *spiritual death* does not refer to the death of the spirit; rather, it refers to a death, or separation, from things referring to the spirit. If you are spiritually dead, you are in a state of spiritual alienation from God—you are dead as to things pertaining to righteousness. Two types of spiritual death are referred to in the scriptures: the first spiritual death, which is, or at least can be, temporary alienation or banishment from the presence of God; and the second spiritual death, which is permanent.

God apparently had the first spiritual death in mind when he gave this commandment to Adam and Eve in the Garden of Eden, as it is recorded in a modern scripture, the Pearl of Great Price: "And I, the Lord God, commanded the man, saying: Of every tree of the garden thou mayest freely eat, but of the tree of the knowledge of good and evil, thou shalt not eat of it, nevertheless, thou mayest choose for thyself, for it is given unto thee; but, remember that I forbid it, for in the day thou eatest thereof, thou shalt surely die" (Moses 3:16–17).

When Adam and Eve transgressed this commandment, they suffered the penalty of the broken law, which was spiritual death—that is, they were spiritually alienated from God and in this case were also physically cast out of his presence. In a similar manner, all of us have suffered this first spiritual death: whenever we commit sin or break one of the commandments of God, we alienate ourselves from God and become spiritually dead. Neither God nor his emissary the Holy Ghost can dwell in sinful or unclean tabernacles.

The only way we can then become spiritually alive again is to stop sinning and to repent—and to become sanctified and pure again. The Savior referred to this process as "being born again" (1 Peter 1:23). This concept of being reborn has confused many people, as it did Nicodemus in the days of Christ. The story in the third chapter of John records that the Pharisee Nicodemus "came to Jesus by night, and said unto him, Rabbi, we know that thou art a teacher come from God: for no man can do these miracles that thou doest, except God be with him. Jesus answered and said unto him, Verily, verily, I say unto thee, Except a man be born again, he cannot see the kingdom of God. Nicodemus saith unto him, How can a man be born when he is old. Can he enter the second time into his mother's womb, and be born? Jesus answered, Verily, verily, I say unto thee, Except a man be born of water and of the spirit, he cannot enter into the kingdom of God. That which is born of the flesh is flesh; and that which is born of the Spirit is spirit" (John 3:2–6).

There is hope for us if we have suffered the first spiritual death, for we can be spiritually reborn if we have faith in Jesus Christ, if we repent of our sins and then are "born of water and of the Spirit" or, in other words, if we are baptized in water and receive the gift of the Holy Ghost.

There is, however, apparently little if any hope for those who suffer the second spiritual death, which takes place at the final judgment, after the resurrection. Alma, one of the prophets of the Book of Mormon, describes this death as follows: "Then cometh a death, even a second death, which is a spiritual death; then is a time that whosoever dieth in his sins, as to a temporal death, shall also die a spiritual death; yea, he shall die as to things pertaining unto righteousness. Then is the time when their torments shall be as a lake of fire and brimstone. . . . Then . . . they shall be as though there had been no redemption made; for they cannot be redeemed according to God's justice; and they cannot die, seeing there is no more corruption" (Alma 12:16–18).

The people who suffer this second spiritual death are referred to as "sons of perdition" (D&C 76:32) because they have willfully decided to follow after Perdition, or Satan, after understanding and being partakers of the gospel plan of salvation, which was made possible through the atonement of Jesus Christ. Thus they deny the power of Jesus Christ to bring about the atonement, and inasmuch as repentance and mercy are based on the atonement of Jesus Christ, they deny the very power upon which repentance is based. Their sin is unpardonable or unforgivable because they cannot repent of it.

In the Doctrine and Covenants the Lord has defined the state of sons of perdition as follows: "Thus saith the Lord concerning all those who know my power, and have been made partakers thereof, and suffered themselves through the power of the devil to be overcome, and to deny the truth and defy my power—They are they who are the sons of perdition, of whom I say it had been better for them never to have been born; for they are vessels of wrath, doomed to suffer the wrath of God, and with the devil and his angels in eternity; concerning whom I have said there is no forgiveness in this world nor in the world to come—Having denied the Holy Spirit after having received it, and having denied the Only Begotten Son of the Father, having crucified him unto themselves and put him to an open shame. These are they who shall go away into the lake of fire and brimstone, with the devil and his angels—And the only ones on whom the second death shall have any power; yea, verily, the only ones who shall not be redeemed" (D&C 76:31–38). From this description of the second spiritual death, it is to be hoped that this death will come upon relatively few people.

The other type of death mentioned in the scriptures—temporal, or physical, death—comes upon everyone without exception. To comprehend the real significance of this temporal death, we must understand our true position and nature in this mortal life. We are now made up of two separate and essential things. One of these is a physical, natural body, the body of flesh and bones and blood and sinew that we can see with our eyes and feel with our hands. We can use the adjectives *physical* and *natural* to refer to this body because it is physical and it is composed of the natural elements of this earth.

We also are composed of another type of body—a spiritual body, or, as the scriptures sometimes call it, a "spirit." It is this "spirit" that gives life to the physical body. The spirit lived and had an existence before this earth was ever created. The Lord revealed to Joseph Smith that the "ego" or the "intelligence" of men—the part of our being which gives us life, which enables us to think, which makes us what we are and different from every other person—has always existed. It operates on a self-existent principle and can neither be created nor destroyed. At one stage of our development, however, this ego or intelligence of ours was clothed by a spirit body by an act of procreation on the part of God. Thus we rightfully began to refer to God as our Father—because he was literally the father of our spirit body. When we came to this earth, however, we were also provided with a physical body by an act of procreation on the part of our earthly father and mother. Our spirit was placed in this body to give life to it; we then became what the scriptures call a "living soul" (Genesis 2:7). At the time of our birth on this earth, there was also a death, for our spirit was separated from the persons and things it had known and experienced in the premortal existence.

Our spirit is thus capable of life and existence outside of our physical body. Our physical body, however, cannot live without our spirit. When our spirit leaves (or is *separated* from) the body, the body dies. That is exactly what temporal death is—the *separation* of the body and the spirit, or the *separation* of the physical body and the spiritual body. As James stated in his epistle in the New Testament, "The body without the spirit is dead" (James 2:26). The term *death,* however, refers *only* to the physical body, for the spirit continues to live when it leaves the body. Thus, at temporal death, there is also a rebirth, for, although the physical body dies, the spiritual body is reborn to the life it knew before it came to tabernacle in the flesh. Fortunately, the separation of the body and the spirit is only temporary, and that is why we call this state temporal death. Although all of us must go through the experience of having our spirits leave our bodies—which is death—we will also have the wonderful experience of having our spirits reenter and possess these bodies again—which is the resurrection. The power of resurrection was given to us through the gift of Jesus Christ in the atonement.

In conclusion, I would like to read two quotations from the prophets. The first of these is from Amulek in the Book of Mormon. Although Amulek lived nearly one hundred years before Christ was born, he clearly understood the purpose of the life and mission of the Savior: "Now, there is a death which is called a temporal death, and the death of Christ shall loose the bands of this temporal death. The spirit and the body shall be reunited again. . . . Now this restoration shall come to all, both old and young, both bond and free, both male and female, both the wicked and the righteous. . . . I have spoken unto you concerning the death of the mortal body, and also concerning the resurrection of the mortal body. I say unto you that this mortal body is raised to an immortal body, that is from death . . . unto life" (Alma 11:42–45).

The second quotation is from Paul's first epistle to the saints at Corinth: "For this corruptible must put on incorruption, and this mortal must put on immortality.

So when this corruptible shall have put on incorruption, and this mortal shall have put on immortality, then shall be brought to pass the saying that is written, Death is swallowed up in victory. O death, where is thy sting? O grave, where is thy victory?" (1 Corinthians 15:53–55).

Note

From an address delivered over KSL Radio, Salt Lake City, 5 January 1958.

Chapter 2 8

THE FINAL FRONTIER: THE SPIRIT

The title of this discussion is "The Final Frontier: The Spirit." To help us all understand how I will use the words in this title, I will begin with a few definitions from *Webster's Third New International Dictionary, Unabridged.*

Final
1. "pertaining to time sequence."
2. "relating to the purpose or ultimate end in view."
3. "relating to or occurring at the end or conclusion; last; concluding; terminating."

My first inclination was to use the term *last frontier* rather than *final frontier*, but the word *last* didn't seem as conclusive as the word *final*.

Frontier
"an area (as of thought or investigation) that constitutes the most advanced or unexploited field or line of inquiry with respect to a particular subject; the farthermost limits of knowledge or achievement."

Spirit
1. "the breath of life: the animating or vital principle giving life to physical organisms."
2. "a supernatural, incorporeal, rational being or personality."
3. "the active essence of the Deity serving as an invisible and life-giving or inspiring power in motion; one manifestation of the divine nature."

4. "the immaterial intelligent or sentient part of a person: the vital principle in man coming as a gift from God and providing one's personality with its inward structure, dynamic drive, and creative response to the demands it encounters in the process of becoming."

There are twenty-five definitions of *spirit* in the unabridged dictionary. I chose those that had the closest meanings to our discussion. Other words I considered as the final word of the title were *ego, intelligence,* and *mind.* However, I finally decided on the word *spirit* after reviewing scriptural references to these four words.

For example, the word *ego* is not used a single time in any of the standard works of the Church.

The words *intelligence* and *intelligences* are used only once in the Bible (Daniel 11:30) and thirteen times in the Doctrine and Covenants and Pearl of Great Price.

Although the word *mind* is used frequently in both the Bible and modern scriptures, it often is used with varying meanings, as indicated by the twenty-three different Hebrew and Greek words translated as *mind* in the King James Version.

The words *spirit* and *spirits* are found many times in the scriptures—over 250 times in the Old Testament, 280 times in the New Testament, 294 times in the Book of Mormon, 198 times in the Doctrine and Covenants, and 31 times in the Pearl of Great Price. The Old Testament words translated as *spirit* come from two basic Hebrew and Chaldee roots: *ruwach* (roo'akh) and *n'shamah* (nesh-aw-mah). The Greek word usually translated as *spirit* in the New Testament is *pneuma* (pnyoo'mah). The basic meanings of these root words are "rational soul," "vital principle," and "mental disposition."

When I analyzed the 523 references to *spirit* in modern scriptures, I concluded the word is used in at least four major senses:

1. As unorganized matter, or as pure intelligence (D&C 131:7).
2. As organized matter, or as organized intelligence; in this state it might also be called a "personage of spirit" as it includes a spiritual body which is the offspring of Deity (Abraham 3:22–23).
3. As emanating power from God through the influence of the Holy Ghost (D&C 76:12, 18).
4. As Holy Spirit or Holy Ghost, who does not have "a body of flesh and bones, but is a personage of Spirit. Were it not so, the Holy Ghost could not dwell in us" (D&C 130:22).

In this discussion, I will primarily be using the word *spirit* in the sense of "organized intelligence" or "personage of spirit." This is the state of the spirit that now animates each of us as part of mankind; thus I might also refer to it as "man's spirit." However, in some quotations from the scriptures and the Brethren, the term might be used in some of the other senses. Note these selected usages from the various scriptures:

Old Testament
"... the God of the spirits of all flesh" (Numbers 16:22; 27:16).
There is "a spirit in man: and the inspiration of the Almighty giveth them understanding" (Job 32:8). Note that both *ruwach* (translated as "spirit") and *n'shamah* (translated as "inspiration") appear in this one verse.
"He ... that ruleth his spirit [is better] than he that taketh a city" (Proverbs 16:32).

New Testament
"... the spirit indeed is willing, but the flesh is weak" (Matthew 26:41).
"... and her spirit came again" (Luke 8:55, speaking of the Savior's restoring of life to the daughter of Jairus, "a ruler of the synagogue").
"... into thy hands I commend my spirit" (Luke 23:46).
They thought "they had seen a spirit [but] ... a spirit hath not flesh and bones" (Luke 24:37, 39).

Book of Mormon
"And while I was thus struggling in the spirit, behold, the voice of the Lord came into my mind again" (Enos 1:10).
"The spirit and the body shall be reunited again in its perfect form; both limb and joint shall be restored to its proper frame, even as we now are at this time" (Alma 11:43).
"Behold, this body, which ye now behold, is the body of my spirit; and man have I created after the body of my spirit; and even as I appear unto thee to be in the spirit will I appear unto my people in the flesh" (Ether 3:16).

Doctrine and Covenants
"Which suffering caused myself, even God, the greatest of all, to tremble because of pain, and to bleed at every pore, and to suffer both body and spirit" (D&C 19:18).

"And the spirit and the body are the soul of man. And the resurrection from the dead is the redemption of the soul" (D&C 88:15–16).

Pearl of Great Price
"Now the Lord had shown unto me, Abraham, the intelligences that were organized before the world was. . . . And God saw these souls that they were good, and he stood . . . among those that were spirits" (Abraham 3:22–23).

"And the Gods formed man from the dust of the ground, and took his spirit (that is, the man's spirit), and put it into him; and breathed into his nostrils the breath of life, and man became a living soul. And the Gods planted a garden, eastward in Eden, and there they put the man whose spirit they had put into the body which they had formed" (Abraham 5:7–8).

EXPLANATION OF THE WORD *SPIRIT*

After reviewing these dictionary and scriptural uses of the word *spirit,* we can see why we need to explain as clearly as possible how the word will be used in this discussion. Maybe the meaning can be described better than it can be defined:
1. It is the life-giving force of our existence.
2. It is that part of our being with which we do our thinking.
3. It is our "will" or "power-to-make-decisions" capability.
4. It is the part of us that distinguishes each of us from every other person who has ever lived on this earth, who is now living on this earth, or who will ever live on this earth. There are no *identical twins* so far as *personages of spirit* are concerned (see Abraham 3:18–19)!

With these descriptions, perhaps you can see why I believe a full understanding of the *spirit* will be the *final frontier.* Because everything eventually can be conceived or understood only through the spirit, the spirit itself will be the last to be fully understood. The creation is not greater than the power or force that created it. The thing thought of cannot be greater than the thinker.

I hope none of you expected me to tell you precisely what the spirit is, exactly how it functions, or what its full capabilities really are. Frankly, I have never been able to figure out a relatively simple problem, such as which came first, the chicken or the egg. I will not attempt any new or profound definitions or explanations of this mysterious, but real, life-giving force called the *spirit.* Statements from recent Church leaders confirm the futility of trying to go beyond what God has revealed about our pre-earthly existence and this power called *spirit*. The First Presidency wrote in 1912: "The First Presidency have nothing to advance concerning pre-existing states but that which is contained in the revelations to the Church. The written standards of scripture show that all people who come to this earth and are born in mortality had a pre-existent, spiritual personality as the sons or daughters of the Eternal Father.... A spirit born of God is an immortal being."[1]

President Joseph Fielding Smith observed: "Some of our writers have endeavored to explain what an intelligence is, but to do so is futile, for we have never been given any insight into this matter beyond what the Lord has fragmentarily revealed. We know, however, that there is something called intelligence which always existed. It is the real eternal part of man, which was not created or made. This intelligence combined with the spirit constitutes a spiritual identity or individual. The spirit of man, then, is a combination of the intelligence and the spirit which is an entity begotten of God."[2]

Simply because we cannot fully define or explain the spirit does not mean we should not discuss it and analyze some of its properties and characteristics. Perhaps two brief examples would help demonstrate why we should discuss this power even though we cannot fully define it.

First, an example related to the creation: scientists and religionists disagree violently, even among themselves, as to how and when the earth was created. Certainly they cannot all be right in their theories and interpretations because they differ so widely—and they might all be wrong. I have been intrigued by the following statement, which indicates the full knowledge of the creation will not be on the earth until the Savior restores it at the time of his second coming. "In that day when the Lord shall come, he shall reveal all things . . . hidden things which no man knew, things of the earth, by which it was made, and the purpose and the end thereof" (D&C 101:32–33).

Even though we do not understand the manner of the creation of the earth and its elements, does that mean we should not study what we can concerning these subjects and utilize the elements of the earth to improve the quality of life on the earth? I don't think so.

Second, an example related to electricity: I do not know of any scientist who claims he can fully define electricity or even completely explain how the power of electricity is transmitted from one place to another. Surely, this lack of ability to define the power or to explain all of its manifestations must not keep us from learning what we can about electricity and from using it to heat, cool, clean, and light our homes; to cook, preserve, and freeze our foods; to power our machines and our communications and transportation systems. We would be foolish if we did not study or use electricity simply because we do not understand it fully.

This belief prompts me to examine and analyze some of the characteristics, attributes, functions, and powers of man's spirit. In doing this, I will use multiple witnesses, as recommended by the Lord: "in the mouth of two or three witnesses shall every truth be established" (2 Corinthians 13:1; see also Deuteronomy 17:6).

Characteristics, Attributes, Functions, and Powers of Man's Spirit

When I started to list the characteristics, attributes, functions, and powers of man's spirit, I realized how much of this information comes from modern scriptures and prophets. The ideas presented today probably would not be understood or accepted by any group except Latter-day Saints. Yet these principles were taught to Adam and Eve shortly after they were driven from the Garden of Eden. They, in turn, taught them to their descendants.

My initial list contained more than a score of items, but I have combined some and deleted others to concentrate on only six.

1. *Man's spirit has always existed and will always exist. It operates on a self-existent principle and can be neither created nor destroyed.*

The Lord has taught the eternal nature of the spirit or intelligence as follows: "Man was also in the beginning with God. Intelligence, or the light of truth, was not created or made, neither indeed can be. All truth is independent in that sphere in which God has placed it, to act for itself, as all intelligence also; otherwise there is no existence" (D&C 93:29–30).

"These . . . spirits . . . have no beginning; they existed before, they shall have no end, they shall exist after, for they are . . . eternal" (Abraham 3:18).

As the writer of Proverbs 8 declared: "I was . . . from everlasting, from the beginning, or ever the earth was" (Proverbs 8:23).

The Prophet Joseph Smith defined this power, or essence, or entity by saying: "The mind [spirit] or the intelligence which man possesses is co-equal with God himself. . . . I am dwelling on the immortality of the spirit of man. Is it logical to say that the intelligence of spirits is immortal, and yet that it had a beginning? The intelligence of spirits had no beginning, neither will it have an end. That is good logic. That which has a beginning may have an end. There never was a time when there were not spirits; for they are co-equal [coeternal] with our Father in heaven. . . .

"Intelligence is eternal and exists upon a self-existent principle. It is a spirit from age to age, and there is no creation about it."[3]

"The spirit of man is not a created being; it existed from eternity, and will exist to eternity."[4]

"Spirit is a substance; . . . it is material, but . . . it is more pure, elastic and refined matter than the body; . . . it existed before the body, can exist in the body; and will exist separate from the body, when the body will be mouldering in the dust; and will in the resurrection, be again united with it."[5]

2. *The spirit can remember everything it has learned.*

This characteristic might come as a surprise to those of us who have difficulty remembering our Social Security and home telephone numbers. Nevertheless, the ability of the spirit to remember everything it has learned is now accepted by many. The Institute of Advanced Thinking has written the following concerning the memory:

"The function of memory in your life is not only quite remarkable, it is vitally necessary to your survival as a human being. It is your memory that stores up your past experiences, enabling you to function swiftly and automatically without 'taking thought' or starting from the beginning in everything you do; . . . if it were not for memory, everything you take for granted—such as remembering your own name as well as the names of your friends and relatives, the street where you live, your telephone number, where you work, driving your car, what you had for dinner—all would require the necessity of being 're-learned' or keeping endless written and taped records for constant referral.

"There are literally thousands of important 'little' items of information and concepts in the daily routine of the average person which require remembering and automatic responses. Even the performance of the simplest activities you do—walking, talking, eating, reading, shopping, and so on and ad infinitum—are all part of your earlier conditioning and as part of your memory storehouse of 'how to' information, permits you to perform countless tasks automatically and naturally without actual concentration or conscious thought."[6]

Mark Van Doren has observed: "Memory performs the impossible for man; holds together past and present, gives continuity and dignity to human life. This is the companion, this is the tutor, the poet, the library, with which you travel."[7]

However, we must recognize that our spirits presently are operating under the limitations of the "veil of forgetfulness" that is part of our mortal probation. Many things we knew in our pre-earthly life are withheld from us. As Paul observed: "Now we see through a glass, darkly; . . . now I know in part" (1 Corinthians 13:12).

Also, our spirits may not be able to recall everything we have learned since our births into mortality because they are limited by our imperfect, mortal, physical bodies. Yet the information is still "stored" and available for recall and use. I am using computer terms to describe this tremendous capability of our spirits, but the wonders of the computer are insignificant compared to the capabilities of our spirits in storing and recalling information. Again, the creation can never be greater than the creator, nor the thing thought of greater than the thinker!

Regarding our ability to remember, President Joseph F. Smith wrote: "In reality a man cannot forget anything[.] He may have a lapse of memory; he may not be able to recall at the moment a thing that he knows, or words that he has spoken; he may not have the power at his will to call up these events and words; but let God Almighty touch the mainspring of the memory, and awaken recollection, and you will find then that you have not even forgotten a single idle word that you have spoken!"[8]

Think of the implications of this characteristic of the spirit! Should it help us decide what movies to attend, what TV shows to watch, what books or magazines to read? Those who wrongly claim that viewing pornographic materials or shows depicting violence and depravity is not harmful do not understand the capability of the spirit to remember everything it has seen, heard, or felt.

3. *Man's spirit has the capability of "direct, on-line" communication with an omniscient (all-knowing) Being.*

When we were born on this earth, an all-wise, all-knowing Father in Heaven placed over our minds a "veil of forgetfulness" so we could be tested in this mortal existence. However, our Heavenly Father also provided communication systems that (1) enable him to maintain contact with us during this mortal probation and (2) enable us to communicate with him.

Our Heavenly Father can keep in touch with us by revelation, including the more quite forms of inspiration. When our spirits are in tune with the Spirit of our Heavenly Father, we can receive knowledge directly from him through the power of the Holy Ghost. This is how the Lord reveals his mind and will to his prophets. "And whatsoever they shall speak when moved upon by the Holy Ghost shall be scripture, shall be the will of the Lord, shall be the mind of the Lord, shall be the word of the Lord, shall be the voice of the Lord, and the power of God unto salvation" (D&C 68:4).

The means our Heavenly Father provides for us to keep in touch with him is called prayer. The Savior indicated that if we "ask . . . seek, and . . . knock" (Matthew 7:7) in faith for that which is right, it shall be revealed unto us, and "by the power of the Holy Ghost ye may know the truth of all things" (Moroni 10:5). Notice this promise in a modern scripture:

"Assuredly as the Lord liveth, who is your God and your Redeemer, even so surely shall you receive a knowledge of whatsoever things you shall ask in faith, with an honest heart, believing that you shall receive . . . Yea, behold, I will tell you in your mind and in your heart, by the Holy Ghost, . . .

"Now, behold, this is the spirit of revelation; . . . Whatsoever you shall ask me to tell you by that means, that will I grant unto you, and you shall have knowledge concerning it" (D&C 8:1–3, 9).

4. *Through its direct on-line communication link with an omniscient Being, our spirit also has access to the thoughts of other spirits.*

Educators and social scientists have barely scratched the surface of the concept of extrasensory perception and, in the main, they do not understand its principles. However, the scriptures and prophets have taught clearly that the Holy Spirit can reveal to our spirits the portion of the mind of God that enables us to detect the thoughts and motives of others. Note these pertinent statements from the scriptures:

The words of Alma: "Zeezrom, . . . thou hast not lied unto men only but thou hast lied unto God; for behold, he knows all thy thoughts, and thou seest that thy thoughts are made known unto us by his Spirit; . . .

"Now when Alma had spoken these words, Zeezrom began to tremble more exceedingly, for he was convinced more and more of the power of God; and he was also convinced that Alma and Amulek had a knowledge of him, for he was convinced that they knew the thoughts and intents of his heart; for power was given unto them that they might know of these things according to the spirit of prophecy" (Alma 12:3, 7).

Please note, however, that our access to the thoughts and intents of others is made possible only through the power of God's Spirit. This protection of privacy is also mentioned in regard to the Urim and Thummim: "no man can look in them except he be commanded, lest he should look for that he ought not" (Mosiah 8:13).

The Lord in the Doctrine and Covenants: "Open ye your ears and hearken to the voice of the Lord your God, . . . [who] is a discerner of the thoughts and intents of the heart" (D&C 33:1).

"And then shall the . . . angel sound his trump, and reveal the secret acts of men, and the thoughts and intents of their hearts" (D&C 88:109).

"Behold, thou knowest that thou hast inquired of me and I did enlighten thy mind; and now I tell thee these things that thou mayest know that thou hast been enlightened by the Spirit of truth; yea, I tell thee, that thou mayest know that there is none else save God that knowest thy thoughts and the intents of thy heart" (D&C 6:15–16).

5. *The spirit of a mortal man or woman is infinitely more important than the mortal physical body. However, the physical body is very important as it serves as a home for the spirit.*

One of the great truths restored in this dispensation is the fact we all have dual natures. We have a physical body that has tremendous capabilities. Through the physical senses we can see, hear, talk, touch, smell, and feel. However, the scriptures and our experience teach us that the physical body has no power or life in and of itself. It is the spirit that "quickeneth" and giveth life, as recorded in John 6:63. The spirit commands the fingers to move and they move; the spirit commands the feet to walk and they walk; the spirit assists the eyes to see. Temporal death demonstrates this fact. When the physical body is separated from the spirit—its life-giving force—the physical body has no life in and of itself. As James 2:26 records, "the body without the spirit is dead."

The Lord has promised that eventually the spirit and the body will be reunited in a resurrection, never to be separated again. At that time, no discussion of the relative importance of the two major aspects of our being will be necessary because they will "no more be twain, but will be one." However, in this mortal life, when the spirit and the physical body can be separated, we can see clearly that the spirit is infinitely more important than the mortal physical body.

Notice these words of the Savior: "Fear not them which kill the body, but are not able to kill the soul: but rather fear him which is able to destroy both soul and body in hell" (Matthew 10:28).

"What shall it profit a man, if he shall gain the whole world, and lose his own soul? Or what shall a man give in exchange for his soul?" (Mark 8:36–37).

Note also these words from Joseph Smith: "I do not regard my own life. I am ready to be offered a sacrifice for this people; for what can our enemies do? Only kill the body, and their power is then at an end. Stand firm, my friends; never flinch. Do not seek to save your lives, for he that is afraid to die for the truth, will lose eternal life. Hold out to the end, and we shall be resurrected and become like Gods, and reign in celestial kingdoms, principalities, and eternal dominions."[9]

When our physical bodies house our spirits they are extremely important. As indicated by Paul, the physical body serves as the "temple" of our spirit and also of the Spirit of God: "Know ye not that ye are the temple of God, and that the Spirit of God dwelleth in you? . . . the temple of God is holy, which temple ye are" (1 Corinthians 3:16–17).

"Therefore glorify God in your body, and in your spirit, which are God's" (1 Corinthians 6:20).

President Harold B. Lee emphasized the importance of knowing the relationship between the spirit and the body. At the end of a talk on this subject, he said: "I trust that I might have [said] something to stimulate some sober thinking as to who you are and from whence you came; and, in so doing, that I may have stirred up within your soul the determination to begin now to show an increased self-respect and reverence for the temple of God, your human body, wherein dwells a heavenly spirit. I would charge you to . . . begin today to live closer to those ideals which will make your life happier and more fruitful because of an awakened realization of who you are."[10]

6. *Man's spirit is not limited by either time or space.*

Because of physical laws, our physical bodies can be in only one place at one time. Although the spirit is restricted within the physical body so far as location is concerned, it is not restricted in thought and memory so far as time and space are concerned. As William Henry Davies, the British poet (1871–1940), stated: "No matter where the body is, the mind is free to go elsewhere." When this attribute of the spirit is combined with the characteristics mentioned earlier (such as the capability of "direct, on-line communication" with God) and when we remember that all things past, present, and future are continually before the Lord (D&C 130:7), it is evident that man's spirit has the potential, through the Holy Spirit, to know at one time all things past, present, and future. As Alma stated, "the Spirit knoweth all things" (Alma 7:13).

Jacob adds his supporting testimony: "The Spirit speaketh the truth and lieth not. Wherefore, it speaketh of things as they really are, and of things as they really will be; wherefore, these things are manifested unto us plainly, for the salvation of our souls" (Jacob 4:13).

After Nephi tells of his experience of being caught up by the Spirit and seeing the happenings on the earth until the winding up scenes, he observed, "By the Spirit are all things made known unto the prophets, which shall come upon the children of men according to the flesh" (1 Nephi 22:2).

The Role of Our Spirit in Helping Us Achieve the Purposes of Our Mortal Probation

Another way to analyze and appreciate the characteristics and potential of the spirit is to review the vital role it plays in accomplishing the purposes of this mortal probation and in achieving our potential. We will discuss six areas.

1. *A major purpose of this mortal probation is to give our spirits the opportunity to learn to control physical matter, including our physical bodies.*

All of us lived as personages of spirit in the presence of our Heavenly Father before we were born on this earth. In this condition we were capable of tremendous accomplishments. We had spiritual bodies with spiritual eyes, hands, and feet. We could obey spiritual laws and enjoy the blessings predicated upon such obedience. However, a whole world of blessings based upon obedience to physical laws was denied to us. As part of our progress, our Heavenly Father called us into a Grand Council. There he proposed that a physical world be created, that physical bodies be created for each of us, and that our spiritual bodies be placed in the physical bodies. We would then become "living souls"—a combination of spirit body and physical body. Our Heavenly Father also proposed that when we were born into this world, we would have a "veil of forgetfulness" placed over our minds.

Brigham Young explained why the veil is necessary. "It has also been decreed by the Almighty that spirits, upon taking bodies, shall forget all they had known previously, or they could not have a day of trial— . . . in darkness and temptation, in unbelief and wickedness, to prove themselves worthy of eternal existence."[11]

This mortal, physical existence is a probationary state where we learn through the exercise of our spirit to keep all the commandments of our Heavenly Father, both spiritual and physical. Note the following statements from the prophets of this dispensation concerning this subject:

Joseph F. Smith: "Man is a dual being, composed of the spirit which gives life, force, intelligence and capacity to man, and the body which is the tenement of the spirit and is suited to its form, adapted to its necessities, and acts in harmony with and to its utmost capacity yields obedience to the will of the spirit. The two combined constitute the soul. The body is dependent upon the spirit, and the spirit during its natural occupancy of the body is subject to the laws which apply to and govern it in the mortal state."[12]

"We have come to sojourn in the flesh, to obtain tabernacles for our immortal spirits."[13]

John Taylor: "Another object that we came here for and took bodies was to propagate our species. For if it is for our benefit to come here, it is also for the benefit of others. Hence the first commandment given to man was to 'Be fruitful and multiply, and replenish the earth' (Genesis 1:28)."[14]

Brigham Young: "If man could have been made perfect, in his double capacity of body and spirit, without passing through the ordeals of mortality, there would have been no necessity of our coming into this state of trial and suffering. Could the Lord have glorified his children in spirit, without a body like his own, he no doubt would have done so."[15]

This concept of the physical body serving as a temple for the spirit illustrates the importance of commandments such as the Word of Wisdom, which appears to pertain primarily to the physical body but which is comprised of spiritual, eternal laws. The Lord has declared: "I say unto you that all things unto me are spiritual, and not at any time have I given unto you a law which was temporal" (D&C 29:34).

Some have felt that the Church has placed too much emphasis on the principles contained in the Word of Wisdom; but these laws are good tests to see whether our spirits are proving themselves able and worthy to control our physical bodies. We came to earth to allow our spirits to control physical matter, but addiction to alcohol, tobacco, and other drugs allows physical matter to control our spirits. The spirit, not the physical body, becomes addicted—and this is contrary to the purpose for which we came upon the earth.

2. *Another major purpose of mortality is to discipline our spirits and our physical bodies to willingly and voluntarily desire to keep all the commandments of our Heavenly Father.*

The invaluable gift of free agency is directly associated with the power of man's spirit; this "decision-making" power of our being was with us in the pre-earthly existence and was exercised in the Grand Council. It will continue with us forever. Obviously, if we have no spirit (mind, intelligence), we have no agency. And if we have no agency, we have no freedom of choice or even opportunity of choice.

The vital principle of agency proved to be a major cause of the great war in heaven, when "Satan . . . sought to destroy the agency of man" (Moses 4:3). Fortunately, those of us here today, together with all who have lived or will yet live on this earth, had enough confidence in ourselves, and enough faith in the plan of our Heavenly Father and in the promised atonement of Jesus Christ, to use our "decision-making" power to support our Heavenly Father's plan of progression and eternal life. This plan depends upon our freedom or right of choice, our power to make decisions, and the exercise of our "will."

Certainly a major reason for our mortal probation, with its "veil of forgetfulness," is to see whether our spirits will use their inherent "decision-making" powers to choose to do right.

Notice this pertinent statement in the council of the Gods, made even before the foundations of the earth were laid: "And there stood one among them that was like unto God, and he said unto those who were with him: We will go down, for there is space there, and we will take of these materials, and we will make an earth whereon these may dwell; and we will prove them herewith, to see if they will do all things whatsoever the Lord their God shall command them; and they who keep their first estate shall be added upon; and they who keep not their first estate shall not have glory in the same kingdom with those who keep their first estate; and they who keep their second estate shall have glory added upon their heads for ever and ever" (Abraham 3:24–26).

The terms "first estate" and "second estate" obviously refer to our spirits, not to our physical bodies.

3. *When the spirit leaves the physical body at the time of temporal death, it continues to exist and operate on spiritual principles, and it continues to be "tried and tested." The "second estate" begins with physical birth but it does not end with physical death; rather, it ends with the resurrection and final judgment.*

Notice the clear words of Alma on this subject: "Now, concerning the state of the soul between death and the resurrection—Behold, it has been made known unto me by an angel, that the spirits of all men, as soon as they are departed from this mortal body, yea, the spirits of all men, whether they be good or evil, are taken home to that God who gave them life. And then shall it come to pass, that the spirits of those who are righteous are received into a state of happiness, which is called paradise, a state of rest, a state of peace, where they shall rest from all their troubles and from all care, and sorrow" (Alma 40:11–12).

Joseph Smith taught: "The spirits of the just are . . . blessed in their departure to the world of spirits. Enveloped in flaming fire, they are not far from us, and know and understand our thoughts, feelings, and motions, and are often pained therewith."[16]

Concerning the scripture in Alma, Brigham Young explained: "It reads that the spirit goes to God who gave it. Let me render this Scripture a little plainer; when the spirits leave their bodies they are in the presence of our Father and God, they are prepared then to see, hear and understand spiritual things. But where is the spirit world? It is incorporated within this celestial system. Can you see it with your natural eyes? No. Can you see spirits in this room? No. Suppose the Lord should touch your eyes that you might see, could you then see the spirits? Yes, as plainly as you now see bodies, as did the servant of Elijah. If the Lord would permit it, and it was His will that it should be done, you could see the spirits that have departed from this world, as plainly as you now see bodies with our natural eyes. . . .

"The spirit world . . . is on this earth that was organized for the people that have lived and that do and will live upon it. No other people can have it, and we can have no other kingdom until we are prepared to inhabit this eternally."[17]

These and similar teachings by the prophets indicate the difference between the "pre-earthly" spirit world and the "postmortal" spirit world. In the post-earthly spirit world, the spirit continues to be tested and proven until the "veil of forgetfulness" is removed through righteousness or until the spirit and the physical body are reunited through the resurrection.

4. Our spirits will be given power to join eternally with our physical bodies.

Joseph F. Smith taught: "What is the body without the spirit? It is lifeless clay. What is it that affects this lifeless clay? It is the spirit, it is the immortal part, the eternal being, that existed before it came here, that exists within us, and that will continue to exist, and that by and by will redeem these tabernacles and bring them forth out of the graves."[18]

John Taylor said: "In the resurrection, both body and spirit will finally be reunited. . . . The body is not perfect without the spirit, nor the spirit without the body; it takes the two to make a perfect man, for the spirit requires a tabernacle, to give it power to develop itself and to exalt it in the scale of intelligence, both in time and eternity."[19]

The degree of righteousness achieved by the spirit in this mortal life and in the postmortal spirit world will determine the degree of glory to which the body will be resurrected by the power of that spirit.

The Lord has declared: "For notwithstanding they die, they also shall rise again. . . . They who are of a celestial spirit shall receive the same body . . . , and your glory shall be that glory by which your bodies are quickened" (D&C 88:27–28).

Note these words of Joseph F. Smith, the sixth President of the Church in this dispensation: "When we come forth out of the grave, . . . our spirits shall enter into [our bodies] again, and they shall become living souls. . . . And then those who have . . . been subject and obedient to the celestial law will . . . be quickened by the celestial glory. And those who have . . . been subject and obedient to the terrestrial law will . . . be quickened by the terrestrial glory. And those who have . . . been subject and obedient to the telestial law, will . . . be quickened by a telestial glory."[20]

President Spencer W. Kimball taught: "There will be a literal resurrection, when this live and conscious spirit will return to the earth to take up its reconstructed and resurrected body . . . and the soul, composed of the resurrected body and the eternal spirit, . . . will come before the great judge to receive its final assignment for the eternity."[21]

Only after the resurrection can we achieve a fulness of joy as taught in this scripture: "For man is spirit. The elements are eternal, and spirit and element, inseparably connected, receive a fulness of joy" (D&C 93:33).

5. Because the spirit comprises the "will" and "decision-making" ability of our being, we will be judged by every desire, inclination, and thought of the spirit. Thus, we will be judged by our words, actions, and thoughts.

The relationship of the spirit to the final judgment provides a good opportunity to review in some detail the two major areas we have been discussing: (1) the various characteristics of the spirit and (2) the different ways the spirit helps us achieve the purposes of our mortal, physical existence.

The Savior taught: "A good man out of the good treasure of the heart bringeth forth good things: and an evil man out of the evil treasure bringeth forth evil things. But I say unto you, That every idle word that men shall speak, they shall give account thereof in the day of judgment" (Matthew 12:35–37).

King Benjamin said: "If ye do not watch yourselves, and your thoughts, and your words, and your deeds, and observe the commandments of God . . . even unto the end of your lives, ye must perish. And now, O man, remember, and perish not" (Mosiah 4:30).

Alma added this testimony: "Our words will condemn us, yea, all our works will condemn us; we shall not be found spotless; and our thoughts will also condemn us" (Alma 12:14).

John Taylor spoke extensively on this subject: "We may succeed in hiding our affairs from men; but it is written that for every word and every secret thought we shall have to give an account in the day when accounts have to be rendered before God, when hypocrisy and fraud of any kind will not avail us; for by our words and by our works we shall be justified, or by them we shall be condemned."[22]

"Now, this is . . . remarkable. . . . Look at the millions of human beings that inhabit this earth, and that have inhabited it from the creation up to the present time. . . . Then, if we could discover the thoughts and reflections of these numerous millions of human beings, . . . it is so vast and complicated . . . it seems as if it would be almost a thing impossible for God . . . to comprehend the whole, and judge of the whole correctly. How shall this be done? My understanding of the thing is, that God has made each man a register within himself, and each man can read his own register, so far as he enjoys his perfect faculties. . . .

" . . . Now, if you are in possession of a spirit or intellectuality of that kind, whereby you are enabled to read your own acts, do you not think that that being who has placed that spirit and that intelligence within you holds the keys of that intelligence, and can read it whenever he pleases? Is not that philosophical, reasonable, and scriptural? I think it is. . . . Well, then, upon this principle we can readily perceive how the Lord will bring into judgment the actions of men when he shall call them forth at the last day. . . .

"... then the secret thoughts of all men are revealed before Him with whom we have to do; we cannot hide them; it would be in vain for a man to say then, I did not do so-and-so; the command would be, Unravel and read the record which he has made of himself, and let it testify in relation to these things, and all could gaze upon it. If a man has acted fraudulently against his neighbor—has committed . . . adultery, or anything else, and wants to cover it up, that record will stare him in the face, he tells the story himself, and bears witness against himself. It is written that Jesus will judge not after the sight of the eye, or after the hearing of the ear, but with righteousness shall he judge the poor, and reprove with equity the meek of the earth. It is not because somebody has seen things, or heard anything by which a man will be judged and condemned, but it is because that record that is written by the man himself in the tablets of his own mind—that record that cannot lie—will in that day be unfolded before God and angels, and those who shall sit as judges."[23]

"If I had time to enter into this subject alone I could show you upon scientific principles that man himself is a self-registering machine, his eyes, his ears, his nose, the touch, the taste, and all the various senses of the body, are so many media whereby man lays up for himself a record which perhaps nobody else is acquainted with but himself; and when the time comes for that record to be unfolded all men that have eyes to see, and ears to hear, will be able to read all things as God himself reads them and comprehends them, and all things, we are told, are naked and open before him with whom we have to do."[24]

Brigham Young said: "Each and every intelligent being will be judged according to the deeds done in the body, according to his works, faith, desires, and honesty or dishonesty before God; every *trait* of his character will receive its just merit or demerit, and he will be judged according to the law of heaven."[25]

In concluding our discussion of being judged by our words, actions, and thoughts, we should note the promise of the Lord: "He who has repented of his sins, the same is forgiven, and I, the Lord, remember them no more" (D&C 58:42).

Those bad thoughts, words, and actions that might have condemned us but of which we have fully repented will be erased from our record *so far as judgment is concerned.* God will remember them no more, and other persons may not know them. *But* this does not mean *we* cannot remember them and use that memory in helping us to avoid a repetition of the same mistakes.

6. *When our thoughts, words, and actions are totally consistent with the teachings of our Heavenly Father, we will become "like him." Our goal and our potential is to "become as God is."*

Jesus commanded when he lived on the earth: "Be ye therefore perfect, even as your Father which is in heaven is perfect" (Matthew 5:48.) After his resurrection, Jesus added another example to his commandment: "I would that ye should be perfect even as I, or your Father who is in heaven is perfect" (3 Nephi 12:48).

Lorenzo Snow coined this axiom:

"As man now is, God once was:
"As God now is, man may be."[26]

Note some of the other teachings of President Snow and others of the prophets on this vital subject:

Lorenzo Snow: "We believe that we are the offspring of our Father in heaven ... There is the nature of deity in the composition of our spiritual organization; in our spiritual birth our Father transmitted to us the capabilities, powers and faculties which he himself possessed, as much so as the child ... possesses, although in an undeveloped state, the faculties, powers and susceptibilities of its parent."[27]

"He has given us faculties and powers that are capable of enlargement until His fulness is reached which He has promised—until we shall sit upon thrones, governing and controlling our posterity from eternity to eternity, and increasing eternally."[28]

Brigham Young: "Man is made an agent to himself before his God; he is organized for the express purpose that he may become like his master.... [W]hen we have been proved in our present capacity, and been faithful with all things He puts into our possession ... [we will become] capable of creating worlds on worlds, and becoming Gods."[29]

John Taylor: "Man ... is a God in embryo and will live and progress throughout the eternal ages, if obedient to the laws of the Godhead, as the Gods progress throughout the eternal ages."[30]

Relationship of the Characteristics and Attributes of Man's Spirit to Education and Learning

By way of a brief review, it might be helpful to place the characteristics of man's spirit against the background of education and learning. For instance, all of the academic offerings and many of the service functions of a university are related directly to the characteristics of the *spirit,* or the *intellect,* or *mind.* Indeed, if the mind is not capable of understanding a subject and of organizing facts related to it, then no academic department is organized for that subject. This is true with all the departments from Accounting through Zoology.

Education also continues after our formal training, such as we receive at a university, throughout mortal life and all eternity. Again, a pertinent scripture: "Whatever principle of intelligence we attain unto in this life, it will rise with us in the resurrection. And if a person gains more knowledge and intelligence in this life through his diligence and obedience than another, he will have so much the advantage in the world to come" (D&C 130:18–19).

Whether we're involved in formal training or not, all study eventually becomes independent and individual. The ideal educational process has been defined as a teacher on one end of a log and a student on the other. The key element in this equation is the student rather than the human teacher. Unless something has been learned, nothing has been taught.

One of the greatest teachers is the Holy Spirit, but unless we are receptive to its influence we will not be edified. Indeed, we learn of eternal things almost in direct proportion to our ability to receive the influence of the Spirit. It was not a human teacher who taught the boy Jesus the things he expounded in the temple, causing the learned ones of his day to be "astonished at his understanding and answers" (Luke 2:47), nor was it a human teacher that enabled the Savior to continue "from grace to grace, until he received a fulness" (D&C 93:13). To help us take advantage of the blessings and powers of the Spirit as a teacher, the Lord has commanded us to teach by that Spirit: "And if ye receive not the Spirit ye shall not teach" (D&C 42:14).

During my tenure at Brigham Young University I had particular interest in educational experiences that involve other cultures, peoples, and places. I believe if we are actively participating in the learning process, we are more likely to *internalize* such learning so it will affect our behavior.

I think most would agree that one of the best ways to learn about other peoples and cultures is to visit or, even better, to live among such people. This is the value of travel and of travel study programs. The increasing costs of travel and living abroad might cause some to forego this type of educational opportunity. But I would like to offer another perspective on this.

When we buy a ticket to visit another country we are being charged only to provide space for the physical body; in this sense, the mind or spirit goes free of charge. Because our spirit is not bound by time or space, once it has traveled to a certain location with the body, it can return to that place time and time and time again—without purchasing additional tickets or going through the bother of procuring visas, obtaining shots, and making other preparations.

This month I had a telephone call from a sister who went to Israel with a group I directed in 1975. She said, "Brother Ludlow, that experience has influenced almost everything I have thought and done since our trip. Virtually every time I read a newspaper or a magazine or listen to a news report, and certainly every time I attend Church, participate in the sacrament, or read the scriptures, I relive some of my experiences in the Holy Land." When viewed from this perspective, perhaps study abroad and travel study will, in the long run, be among the least expensive methods of obtaining a meaningful education.

Brigham Young provided some interesting thoughts on the future potential of such travel programs. Speaking of the postmortal spirit world, he said: "The brightness and glory [of the spirit world] . . . is inexpressible. It is not encumbered. . . . [The spirits] move with ease and like lightning. If we want to visit Jerusalem, or this, that, or the other place—and I presume we will be permitted if we desire—there we are, looking at its streets. If we want to behold Jerusalem as it was in the days of the Savior; or if we want to see the Garden of Eden as it was when created, there we are, and we see it as it existed spiritually, for it was created first spiritually and then temporally, and spiritually it still remains. And when there we may behold the earth as at the dawn of creation, or we may visit any city we please that exists upon its surface. If we wish to understand how they are living [elsewhere], we are there; in fact, we are like the light of the morning. . . .

" . . . In the spirit world we are free . . . [to] enjoy life, glory, and intelligence; and we have the Father to speak to us, Jesus to speak to us, and angels to speak to us, and we shall enjoy the society of the just and the pure."[31]

Summary and Conclusion

I am grateful for this opportunity to develop some ideas on the important subject of our *spirit*. I realize we have barely scratched the surface. I also realize that even if we spent days or weeks discussing the topic, there would be more that we would *not* know about the spirit than we *would* know. Concerning this subject, I feel somewhat the same as Brigham Young felt about a study of the gospel in general when he said: "Could we live to the age of Methuselah . . . and spend our lives in searching after the principles of eternal life, we would find . . . that we had been but children . . . just commencing to learn the things which pertains to the eternities of the Gods."[32]

Certainly in this lifetime we will never learn everything about the spirit; it will indeed be one of the *final frontiers* of knowledge. However, I hope some additional pieces of the jigsaw puzzle of understanding the spirit have fallen into place for you through this paper; I know this experience has been beneficial to me. I emerge from my study with a greater appreciation—and I believe with a greater understanding—of the inherent worth of each of us.

Our spirits *are* eternal; they will be part of us forever and ever and ever. We should learn what we can of their characteristics, attributes, functions, and powers so they can help us achieve true joy and happiness.

We *are* the sons and daughters of our Heavenly Father, and have inherited the potential to become as he is. This is the "eternal life" promised to the faithful, which is "the greatest of all the gifts of God" (1 Nephi 15:36; see also D&C 6:13; 14:7).

We *are* brothers and sisters to each other and to all mankind. I hope this knowledge—and the realization of the tremendous influence we have on each other—will help us feel better about ourselves and our potential, will help us to be more thoughtful and kind and considerate to each other, and will inspire and motivate us to become better day by day.

With the memory of Christmas and what it represents still with us, with the time of making new resolutions still upon us, and with the sobering realities of the briefness of mortal life impressed upon us in recent catastrophes at home and abroad, I pray that each of us may resolve this day to exercise our spirits in "new beginnings" of worthy living.

Notes

From the Second Annual Harman Lecture, Brigham Young University, Division of Continuing Education, 7 January 1985.

1. *Gospel Doctrine,* 12.
2. Joseph Fielding Smith, *The Progress of Man* (Salt Lake City: The Genealogical Society of Utah, 1940), 11.
3. *Teachings of the Prophet Joseph Smith,* 353–54.
4. *History of the Church,* 3:387.
5. Ibid., 4:575.
6. Institute of Advanced Thinking, *Instant Memory: The Automatic Memory System* (California: The Institute of Advanced Thinking, 1972), 3.
7. Ibid.
8. Joseph F. Smith, "A Sermon of Purity," *Improvement Era,* 6 (May 1903): 503–4.
9. *History of the Church,* 6:500.

10. Harold B. Lee, "Understanding Who We Are Brings Self-Respect," *Ensign*, January 1974, 6.
11. Brigham Young, in *Journal of Discourses*, 6:333.
12. Joseph F. Smith, in *Journal of Discourses*, 23:169.
13. Joseph F. Smith, in *Journal of Discourses*, 19:259.
14. John Taylor, "Extract from a work by Elder John Taylor about to be published in France," *Millennial Star*, 13 (15 March 1851): 81.
15. Brigham Young, in *Journal of Discourses*, 11:43.
16. *History of the Church*, 6:52.
17. Brigham Young, in *Journal of Discourses*, 3:368, 372.
18. Joseph F. Smith, in *Journal of Discourses*, 25:250.
19. John Taylor, *The Government of God* (Liverpool, England: S. W. Richards, 1852), 27, 32.
20. *Gospel Doctrine*, 450–51.
21. *Teachings of Spencer W. Kimball*, 46.
22. John Taylor, in *Journal of Discourses*, 24:232.
23. John Taylor, in *Journal of Discourses*, 11:77–79.
24. John Taylor, in *Journal of Discourses*, 26:31.
25. Brigham Young, in *Journal of Discourses*, 8:154; emphasis in original.
26. Lorenzo Snow, in Eliza R. Snow, *Biography and Family Record of Lorenzo Snow* (Salt Lake City: Deseret News Press, 1884), 467.
27. Lorenzo Snow, in *Journal of Discourses*, 14:300, 302.
28. Lorenzo Snow, *Teachings of Lorenzo Snow*, comp. Clyde J. Williams (Salt Lake City: Bookcraft, 1984), 3.
29. Brigham Young, in *Journal of Discourses*, 3:93.
30. John Taylor, in *Journal of Discourses*, 23:65.
31. Brigham Young, in *Journal of Discourses*, 14:231.
32. Brigham Young, in *Journal of Discourses*, 3:202–3.

Chapter 29

THE POSTMORTAL SPIRITUAL EXISTENCE

The subject of our postmortal existence has interested me a great deal over the past several years while I have researched all the major topics associated with the plan of progression and eternal life that our Heavenly Father has prepared for us. As I have read, studied, and pondered the subject as to what might happen immediately after our physical mortal experience on this earth, I have been surprised and amazed as to what has been revealed on this subject. The Lord has given us information through revelations to prophets in ancient times as recorded in scripture and through revelations to prophets today in the dispensation of the fulness of times.

I am convinced that we as Latter-day Saints have more information and testimonies concerning this matter than anyone else. We not only have the Bible and the literature readily available to the world, but we have the modern scriptures and the words of the living prophets concerning this subject.

However, I am equally convinced that many of us have not considered and thought about this subject as much as we might. After all, we all have family, friends, and other loved ones who have already entered into the realm of that great experience. And all of us, without exception, will enter that realm ourselves.

PREPARING FOR THE POSTMORTAL EXISTENCE

In the past forty years or so I have had the opportunity of leading over seventy tours for the BYU Travel Study Department, primarily to the Near East and Middle

East, and to Central America and South America. I have noted that virtually without exception, participants who make the most preparations for the tour gain the greatest benefit from the experience.

I suspect that somewhat in the same manner, those who study, learn, and prepare for the next phase of our eternal existence will be able to benefit more, at least initially, from the opportunities available to us there. Indeed, the Lord has revealed through the Prophet Joseph Smith: "Whatever principle of intelligence we attain unto in this life, it will rise with us in the resurrection. And if a person gains more knowledge and intelligence in this life through his diligence and obedience than another, he will have so much the advantage in the world to come" (D&C 130:18–19).

The title of this chapter suggests that we also had a premortal spiritual existence, which we did. Also, *pre*mortal and *post*mortal suggest that we must now be living between the two, in a mortal existence, which, of course, we are.

To better understand some of the features and characteristics of the postmortal spiritual existence developed later in this chapter, I will briefly review (1) a few of the major features of what we know concerning our premortal spiritual existence and (2) a few salient facts pertaining to the state of existence we are now in as spiritual, physical, mortal beings.

THE PREMORTAL EXISTENCE

I would like to begin at the very beginning of time concerning these subjects, but if I understand the teachings of the scriptures and the prophets correctly concerning our premortal existence, there never really was a "time" beginning.

Numerous scriptural references on this subject are listed in the Topical Guide under such entries as "Man, a Spirit Child of Heavenly Father" and "Man, Antemortal Existence of" and in the index published with the Book of Mormon under such titles as "Premortal Existence" and "Spirit World." However, for this review of our *pre*mortal existence, I will rely primarily upon four brief statements by prophets of this dispensation.

The Prophet Joseph Smith stated: "The mind [spirit] or the intelligence which man possesses is co-equal with God himself. . . . The intelligence of spirits had no beginning, neither will it have an end. . . . There never was a time when there were not spirits; for they are co-equal [co-eternal] with our Father in heaven. . . . Intelligence is eternal and exists upon a self-existent principle. It is a spirit from age to age, and there is no creation about it."[1]

The Prophet Joseph Smith also said: "Spirit is a substance; . . . it is material, but . . . it is more pure, elastic and refined matter than the body; . . . it existed before the body, can exist in the body; and will exist separate from the body, when the body will be mouldering in the dust; and will in the resurrection, be again united with it."[2]

The First Presidency said in 1909: "The doctrine of the pre-existence . . . shows that man, as a spirit, was begotten and born of heavenly parents, and reared to maturity in the eternal mansions of the Father, prior to coming upon the earth in a temporal body to undergo an experience in mortality."[3]

President Joseph F. Smith said: "The written standards of scripture show that all people who come to this earth and are born in mortality had a pre-existent, spiritual personality as the sons or daughters of the Eternal Father. . . . A spirit born of God is an immortal being."[4]

The scriptures and prophets sometimes refer to this premortal existence as our *first estate* (see Jude 1:6). In this first estate, all of us lived as personages of spirit in the presence of our Heavenly Father before we were born on this earth. In this condition we were capable of tremendous accomplishments. We had spirit bodies with spirit eyes, hands, feet, and so on. We could obey spiritual laws and enjoy the blessings predicated upon obedience to such laws.

However, a whole world of blessings based upon obedience to physical laws was denied us. In order to give us an opportunity to progress as much as possible, our Heavenly Father proposed that a physical world be created, that physical bodies be provided for primal parents, and that each of us in due time be given the privilege of having our spirit bodies placed in physical bodies.

Our Heavenly Father also proposed that when we were born into this world a "veil of forgetfulness" be placed over our minds so we could learn to walk by faith. President Brigham Young explained why the "veil of forgetfulness" is necessary: "It has also been decreed by the Almighty that spirits, upon taking bodies, shall forget all they had known previously, or they could not have a day of trial— . . . in darkness and temptation, in unbelief and wickedness, to prove themselves worthy of eternal existence."[5]

OUR PRESENT PHYSICAL MORTAL EXISTENCE

We already know a great deal about the spiritual, physical, mortal existence in which we now live. Again, major scriptures pertaining to this topic are available in the Topical Guide under the titles of "Probation, Probationary" and "Test, Try,

Prove," and in the index under the entries "Commandments of God" and "Mortal, Mortality."

We will limit our review to only two statements pertaining to our current probationary state, in which we may learn through the exercise of our spirits to keep all the commandments of our Heavenly Father, both spiritual and physical.

President Joseph F. Smith said: "Man is a dual being, composed of the spirit which gives life, force, intelligence and capacity to man, and the body which is the tenement of the spirit. . . . The two combined constitute the soul. The body is dependent upon the spirit, and the spirit during its natural occupancy of the body is subject to the laws which apply to and govern it in the mortal state."[6]

President Young said: "If man could have been made perfect, in his double capacity of body and spirit, without passing through the ordeals of mortality, there would have been no necessity of our coming into this state of trial and suffering. Could the Lord have glorified his children in spirit, without a body like his own, he no doubt would have done so."[7]

The scriptures and the prophets of this dispensation have referred to our present condition—a combination of spirit body and physical mortal body—as being part of our *second estate*. This estate began when our spirit body and physical mortal body came together initially, and it ends at the resurrection when our spirit body and our immortal physical body come together, never to be separated again. Our second estate does *not* end with our physical temporal death; it ends with our resurrection. Therefore, our next major phase of existence—the postmortal spiritual existence—is part of our second estate.

THE POSTMORTAL SPIRITUAL EXISTENCE

Let us now examine what has been revealed concerning the postmortal spiritual existence. I will list related revelations in the following order: (1) revelations pertaining to the *state* or *condition* of the spirit, (2) revelations pertaining to the *place* or *location* of the postmortal spirit world, and (3) revelations pertaining to other major *features* or *characteristics* of the postmortal spiritual existence.

State or Condition

Perhaps the foremost scriptural authority on the subject of the *state* or *condition* of the spirit in the postmortal spirit world is Alma the Younger, who attributes his information on this subject to "an angel" sent from God:

"Now, concerning the *state* of the soul between death and the resurrection—

Behold, it has been made known unto me by an angel, that the spirits of all men, as soon as they are departed from this mortal body, yea, the spirits of all men, whether they be good or evil, are taken home to that God who gave them life.

"And then shall it come to pass, that the sprits of those who are righteous are received into a *state* of happiness, which is called paradise, a *state* of rest, a *state* of peace, where they shall rest from all their troubles and from all care, and sorrow.

"And then it shall come to pass, that the sprits of the wicked . . . shall be cast out into outer darkness . . . and this because of their own iniquity, being led captive by the will of the devil.

"Now this is the *state* of the souls of the wicked, yea, in darkness, and a *state* of awful, fearful looking for the fiery indignation of the wrath of God upon them; thus they remain in this *state,* as well as the righteous in paradise, until the time of their resurrection" (Alma 40:11–14; emphasis added).

Note that in this entire quotation Alma is talking only of the *state* or *condition* of the soul between death and the resurrection; he is not talking of the *place* or the *location* of the postmortal spirit world.

The *state* or *condition* of our spirit bodies in the postmortal existence will be essentially the same as when our spirits were in the presence of our Heavenly Father before our birth on earth. At the time of temporal physical death, the spirit body will be separated from the physical mortal body and will be free of all physical ailments, pains, and sufferings.

Place or Location

Alma said that when temporal physical death occurs, "the spirits of all men, as soon as they are departed from this mortal body, yea, the spirits of all men, whether they be good or evil, are taken home to that God who gave them life" (Alma 40:11). President Young has clarified Alma's words:

"It reads that the spirit goes to God who gave it. Let me render this Scripture a little plainer; when the spirits leave their bodies they are in the presence of our Father and God, [in the sense that] they are prepared then to see, hear and understand spiritual things. But where is the spirit world? It is incorporated within this celestial system. Can you see it with your natural eyes? No. Can you see spirits in this room? No. Suppose the Lord should touch your eyes that you might see, could you then see the spirits? Yes, as plainly as you now see bodies, as did the servant of Elijah. If the Lord would permit it, and it was His will that it should be done, you could see the spirits that have departed from this world, as plainly as you now see bodies with your natural eyes. . . . The spirit world . . . is on this earth."[8]

He also taught: "When you lay down this tabernacle, where are you going? Into the spiritual world.... Where is the spirit world? It is right here. Do the good and evil spirits go together? Yes, they do. Do they both inhabit one kingdom? Yes, they do. Do they go to the sun? No. Do they go beyond the boundaries of this organized earth? No, they do not."[9]

In a supporting statement regarding the *place* or *location* of the postmortal spiritual world, Elder Parley P. Pratt wrote: "The [postmortal] spirit world is not the heaven where Jesus Christ, [and] his Father, ... dwell.... As to its location, it is here on the very planet where we were born; or, in other words, the earth."[10]

The account of the resurrected Jesus Christ in the New Testament also verifies that the *location* of the postmortal spirit world is not in the presence of God. Remember that after his resurrection—and after his experiences in the postmortal spirit world—Jesus Christ reported to Mary Magdalene, "I am not yet ascended to my Father" (John 20:17).

Now that we have established the essentials of the state of the spirit in the postmortal spirit world and the location of the postmortal spirit world, let's examine seven major *features* or *characteristics* of the postmortal spirit world.

Characteristics of the Postmortal Spirit World

1. *"Death" essentially has to do with "separation."*

At the time of our temporal physical death, the spirit is separated from the physical body and from the physical world it has known while in the physical body. However, the spirit continues to exist as real and lively as before; in fact, it is reborn in the presence of those spirits it came to know during its physical mortal experience. In a sense, then, so far as the spirit is concerned the time of death (that is, separation from the physical body) is also a time of rebirth (reuniting with those we have known on the earth who have gone before).

2. *Agency—the power and opportunity to choose—is directly associated with the spirit.*

This decision-making power was with us in the pre-earthly existence, and we exercised it in the Grand Council in Heaven. The vital principle of agency proved to be a major cause of the great war in heaven, when "Satan ... sought to destroy the agency of man" (Moses 4:3). Fortunately, we and all who have lived or will yet live on this earth had enough confidence in ourselves, and enough faith in the plan of our Heavenly Father and in the promised atonement of Jesus Christ, to use our decision-making power to support our Heavenly Father's plan of progression and eternal life. This plan depends upon our freedom or right of choice, upon our power to make decisions, upon the exercise of our will. This power will continue with us forever. Obviously, if we have no spirit (mind, intelligence), we have no agency. And if we have no agency, we have no freedom of choice and no true opportunity of moral choice.

Certainly a major reason for our probation and its "veil of forgetfulness" is to see whether our spirits will use their inherent decision-making powers to choose to do right. Notice this pertinent conversation in the council of the Gods even before the foundations of the earth were laid:

"And there stood one among them that was like unto God, and he said unto those who were with him: We will go down, for there is space there, and we will take of these materials, and we will make an earth whereon these may dwell; And we will prove them herewith, to see if they will do all things whatsoever the Lord their God shall command them;

"And they who keep their first estate shall be added upon; and they who keep not their first estate shall not have glory in the same kingdom with those who keep their first estate; and they who keep their second estate shall have glory added upon their heads for ever and ever" (Abraham 3:24–26).

Remember, the postmortal spiritual existence is part of our second estate and remains a time of testing and proving. It is evident that agency will continue to play an important part of that realm, and will undoubtedly do so throughout all the eternities to come.

3. *The "veil of forgetfulness" that came over our spirit at our birth will continue until it is removed by the power of the Spirit, either in this life or in the life to come.*

It is important to note that this veil will not automatically be removed at the time of our temporal death. Remember, this veil was a condition of our second estate. It is associated with our time of trial, testing, and proving, and it will continue into the postmortal spiritual existence unless we have removed it by our faithfulness before that time.

4. *The scriptures and the teachings of the prophets indicate that the spirit is able to take with it from this physical mortal experience into the postmortal spiritual existence (1) everything it has acquired by the power of the Spirit through the use of its agency and (2) everything it has been given by the gift and power of God.*

It is intriguing to realize that the spirit has the potential to remember everything it has ever experienced, seen, heard, done, or thought. Regarding the ability of the spirit to remember, President Joseph F. Smith has written: "In reality a man cannot forget anything[.] He may have a lapse of memory; he may not be able to recall at the moment a thing that he knows, or words that he has spoken; he may not have the power at his will to call up these events and words; but let God Almighty touch the mainspring of the memory, and awaken recollection, and you will find then that you have not even forgotten a single idle word that you have spoken!"[11]

Also, it is important to know we can continue to receive knowledge in the hereafter directly from our Heavenly Father through the power of the Holy Ghost and on the same principles that we can obtain knowledge in this life. The Savior's counsel to ask, seek, and knock (see Matthew 7:7) in faith and the promise that we will have revealed unto us "by the power of the Holy Ghost" (Moroni 10:5) "whatsoever [we] ask that is right" (Mosiah 4:21) are as applicable there as they are here. Notice this promise in a modern scripture: "Assuredly as the Lord liveth, who is your God and your Redeemer, even so surely shall you receive a knowledge of whatsoever things you shall ask in faith. . . . Now, behold this is the spirit of revelation. . . . Whatsoever you shall ask me to tell you by that means, that will I grant unto you, and you shall have knowledge concerning it" (D&C 8:1, 3, 9).

Alma stated, "the Spirit knoweth all things" (Alma 7:13). Jacob adds his supporting testimony: "The Spirit speaketh the truth and lieth not. Wherefore, it speaketh of things as they really are, and of things as they really will be; wherefore, these things are manifested unto us plainly, for the salvation of our souls" (Jacob 4:13).

In regard to what the spirit might have acquired in this life by the power and Spirit of God, notice the completeness and exactness of the following scripture: "All covenants, contracts, bonds, obligations, oaths, vows, performances, connections, associations, or expectations, that are not made and entered into and sealed by the Holy Spirit of promise . . . are of no efficacy, virtue, or force in and after the resurrection from the dead; for all contracts that are not made unto this end have an end when men are dead" (D&C 132:7). This, of course, refers also to the marriage covenant, as is made clear later in that section.

5. *The spirit will be freed of some of the restraints of time and space associated with the physical mortal existence.*

In the postmortal spiritual existence, the spirit will continue to be governed by spiritual laws, much as it was when it existed in the presence of our Heavenly Father before birth into a physical mortal body. However, the spirit will be free from some restraints related to the time and space usually associated with this mortal existence.

President Brigham Young explains: "The brightness and glory [of the postmortal spirit world] . . . is inexpressible. It is not encumbered. . . . [The spirits] move with ease and like lightning. If we want to visit Jerusalem, or this, that, or the other place—and I presume we will be permitted if we desire—there we are, looking at its streets. If we want to behold Jerusalem as it was in the days of the Savior; or if we want to see the Garden of Eden as it was when created, there we are, and we see it as it existed spiritually, for it was created first spiritually and then temporally, and spiritually it still remains."[12]

Because of physical laws, our physical bodies can be in only one place at one time. Although the spirit is restricted within the physical body so far as location is concerned, it is not so restricted in the postmortal spirit world. When this attribute of the spirit is combined with the knowledge that all things past, present, and future are continually before the Lord (see D&C 130:7), it is evident that man's spirit has the potential, through the Holy Spirit, to know all things past, present, and future.

6. *The spirit will continue to learn and communicate things pertaining to the spirit, as allowed and permitted by God.*

Two vital questions have been asked by many concerning our possible contact with those who have gone before us into the postmortal spiritual existence: (1) Are those who have already gone through the experience of temporal physical death able to communicate with us here in our physical mortal existence? (2) Can we communicate with those in the postmortal spirit world?

The answer to both questions is *yes, if we are permitted to do so*. Remember, in addition to being physical and mortal at the present time, we are also spiritual. Indeed, it is our spirit that gives life to our physical body as indicated in the scriptures. "The spirit giveth life" (2 Corinthians 3:6), and the things of the spirit are known only "by the power of the Spirit" (D&C 76:12).

Note some of the teachings of the Brethren concerning the possibility of communication between those who are in the postmortal existence and those who are still in the physical mortal realm.

Joseph Smith taught: "The spirits of the just are . . . blessed in their departure to the world of spirits. . . . [T]hey are not far from us, and know and understand our thoughts, feelings, and motions, and are often pained therewith."[13]

President Joseph F. Smith said: "Our fathers and mothers, brothers, sisters and friends who have passed away from this earth . . . may have a mission given them to visit their relatives and friends upon the earth again, bringing . . . messages of love, of warning, of reproof and instruction to those whom they had learned to love in the flesh."[14]

In a First Presidency message, he added: "If we can see, by the enlightening influence of the Spirit of God . . . , beyond the veil that separates us from the spirit world, surely those who have passed beyond, can see more clearly through the veil back here to us than it is possible for us to see to them from our sphere of action. I believe we move and have our being in the presence of heavenly messengers and of heavenly beings. . . . If this is the case with us in our finite condition, . . . how much more certain it is and reasonable and consistent to believe that those who have been faithful, who have gone beyond . . . can see us better than we can see them; that they know us better than we know them. . . . We live in their presence, they see us, they are solicitous for our welfare, they love us now more than ever."[15]

Elder Charles A. Callis added: "We believe that there is consciousness of the spirit in the life hereafter, between death and the resurrection. . . . Death does not congeal the lips of those who go before us; they are not far from us and they help us more than we know."[16]

7. The spirit takes with it into the postmortal spiritual world the same dispositions and tendencies it has acquired here.

Some persons have wondered whether there is a sudden radical change in the feeling of a person at the time of physical death, particularly concerning such things as the basic principles and ordinances of the gospel. Such people think, "Surely when the spirit of the departed person realizes there is life after death, that person will immediately accept the idea of a resurrection, of a final judgment, and so on." That such is not the case is made clear by the scriptures and by modern prophets:

"That same spirit which doth possess your bodies at the time that ye go out of this life, that same spirit will have power to possess your body in that eternal world" (Alma 34:34).

Elder Heber C. Kimball said: "The separation of body and spirit makes no difference in the moral and intellectual condition of the spirit[.] When a person, who has always been good and faithful to his God, lays down his body in the dust, his spirit will remain the same in the spirit world. . . . When the spirit leaves the body the body becomes lifeless. The spirit has not changed one single particle of itself by leaving the body."[17]

Remember that so far as knowledge is concerned, the spirit takes with it only what it has acquired during the time of its physical mortal existence. Remember also that the spirit still has agency in the world to come, and that the world to come continues to be a time of testing and proving, and that missionary work will be one of the major activities in the postmortal spiritual existence.

How can we best understand and comprehend these things? Perhaps it would help if we remember first of all that all spirit is matter, and that all matter operates according to divine law. The spirit in our physical body is able to comprehend physical things (*see* things, *hear* things, *feel* things, and so on) because these things operate on the same laws of frequency as our physical bodies. But there are countless things that exist on frequencies that our spirits are not able to comprehend while in our present physical bodies.

When the spirit leaves the physical mortal body, it can then comprehend some of these things when they become real to the spirit, meaning that they operate on the same frequency that the spirit can interpret. I suspect that many of us have had difficulty understanding the concept that the earth is really the place of the postmortal spirit world because we are now living on the same earth, and we normally are not aware of spirits around us. That is, we normally cannot *see* or *hear* them.

Of course, the fact that we currently cannot either see or hear those who have gone before does not mean they do not exist; they simply exist in a condition, on a frequency, or according to laws that we cannot normally perceive. However, if our sight, hearing, or other senses could be modified to include their spheres of existence, we could then comprehend, see, and hear them.

Seeing

President Young said, "Can you see spirits in this room? No. Suppose the Lord should touch your eyes that you might see, could you then see the spirits? Yes, as plainly as you now see bodies."[18]

We cannot see them with our natural eyes because they are operating on a different frequency than our eyes can normally see. This subject of sight so intrigued me that I decided to go to the standard encyclopedias, including the *Encyclopedia Britannica,* the *Encyclopedia Americana,* and three encyclopedias of physics, to learn what I could about the subject. But I searched in vain for any article under an entry titled "sight." One brief entry simply stated, "See *eye* and *light.*" Of course, that's what sight is—the effect of light on the eye.

I then reviewed what they had to say about the eye. The encyclopedias all had long and interesting discussions on the eye. One of them began, "Although virtually all animals are responsive to light, visual organs are as varied as the animals that possess them."

The encyclopedia then explained the structure of the human eye using drawings and words. The characteristics of the human eye were then compared with other physical eyes. Concerning the eyes of bees, for example, the article noted:

"The visible spectrum for the bee does not extend as far into the red region as it does for man, but it reaches to 300 nanometers in the near ultraviolet portion. Moreover, for bees, as for many insects, near ultraviolet is a distinct color, and many flowers have patterns of ultraviolet reflectance (so-called nectar guides) that are invisible to man but are important visual clues to the insect."[19]

But, the article continued, "so far as can be determined, all the eyes of all the humans, animals, fish, fowls, insects, and other physical organisms known to exist comprehend only a very small range of the electromagnetic energy known as 'light.'"

I eagerly read the articles in the encyclopedias on light. The following statements are direct quotes from these sources:

"*Light* is radiant electromagnetic energy that can be detected by the human eye. Visible light is only one very small part of a vast spectrum of electromagnetic radiation."[20]

"Which encompasses radio waves and infrared radiation at wavelengths longer than light, and ultraviolet, x-ray, gamma ray, and cosmic-ray radiation at progressively shorter wavelengths."[21]

"The frequency of light waves is . . . almost a billion times higher, their wavelength a billion times shorter, than the waves of standard radio broadcast bands. . . . The eye is a detector [of light] with a relatively long response time. Photoelectric cells can react more than a million times faster."[22]

"The electromagnetic spectrum is a broad band of radiant energy which extends over a range of wavelengths running from trillionths of inches to hundreds of miles; wavelengths of visible light are measured in hundreds of thousandths of an inch."[23]

These statements were enough to convince me that the human physical eye, as marvelous and miraculous as it is, comprehends only a very small fraction of the light and electromagnetic energy that is available.

So much for the limited things we can *see*. How about what we can *hear?*

Hearing

The articles pertaining to hearing (listed primarily under the titles "sound" and "ear") were also interesting and challenging. Concerning our present very limited capacity to hear, I found the following statement under "Sound" in the *Encyclopedia Americana:*

"Hearing Ranges. The ear of an adult human can hear sounds at frequencies ranging from 15 hertz (oscillations or cycles per second) to 15,000 hertz, and children can hear sounds at frequencies up to 20,000 hertz. (A child has a hearing range of more than 10 octaves, which is considerably more than the 7.5-octave playing range of the piano.) Sounds at frequencies lower than 15 hertz (infrasonic frequencies) and higher than 20,000 hertz (ultrasonic frequencies) also exist, although such frequencies are not audible to man. Small creatures such as birds, bats, and insects regularly produce ultrasonic pulses. Even the dog has a range of sound perception that reaches into higher frequencies than man can hear. Some dog whistles produce ultrasonic vibrations to which a dog will answer, although a man will hear nothing."[24]

Again, our present physical sound-receiving capabilities—including our ears, as marvelous and miraculous as they are—can hear only a fraction of the sounds that actually exist.

Possible Analogies

Frequencies used by the media in radio and television offer a good analogy to help us understand more about the different frequencies involved in sight and sound that might exist in the postmortal spirit world.

Sights: There are sights, including images of persons, present in the very air between you and this book you are reading. These scenes and facial images are as real on the frequencies on which they exist as is the image of your face as your look at someone else. This can be proven by scientific means, available to, and at least partially understood, by all of us.

Take, for example, a small battery-operated television set. It is not a video recorder. It does not simply play back something that has already been recorded. Rather, a small television set receives light waves on very high and ultra-high frequencies that our eyes cannot normally interpret, and it changes those light waves into frequencies we can see.

It should now be easier to understand the meaning of President Young's statement: "Can you see spirits in this room? No. Suppose the Lord should touch your eyes that you might see, could you then see the spirits? Yes, as plainly as you now see bodies."[25]

Sounds: There are sounds of voices in the room in which you are sitting that are not currently audible to your ears, yet they really exist. If the listening capabilities of your ears could be modified to listen on the frequencies on which these inaudible sounds exist—or if these inaudible sounds could be changed to a frequency that your ears could interpret—you could hear them as clearly as you hear your own voice. This also can be proven by scientific means.

Take, for example, a small portable radio operated by a battery. It is not an audio tape recorder. It does not simply play back something that has already been recorded. A small radio intercepts sound waves in the air around us, operating on frequencies that our human ears normally cannot interpret. It then converts these sound waves to frequencies our ears can hear.

Concerning our ability, or lack thereof, to hear all the sounds around us, may I paraphrase President Brigham Young? "Can you hear spirits in this room? No. Suppose the Lord should modify your hearing capacity that you might hear on the same frequency that they exist, could you then hear the spirits? Yes, as plainly as you now hear each other."

SUMMARY

I have scarcely scratched the surface of what we will eventually know about the next major phase of our eternal existence—the postmortal spiritual world. Our current limited knowledge is only natural in a phase of existence during which we learn to walk by faith, receive "line upon line, precept upon precept, here a little and there a little" (2 Nephi 28:30), and remove the "veil of forgetfulness" by coming to a knowledge of the power of the Spirit and of more and more gospel truths.

We come to this knowledge by reading and pondering pertinent scriptures; by searching the truths revealed to the prophets, seers, and revelators of this dispensation; and by receiving personal revelation through the power of the Holy Ghost.

May we do more in preparation for the next major phase of our eternal existence. If we are wise, we will spend more time on those things we can take with us—family relationships, knowledge, the ability to obey our Heavenly Father's commandments and serve our fellowman—rather than on things we must leave behind, such as worldly possessions. I hope we will not fear death but rather prepare with confidence and faith to meet it. As Jacob explained, death is part of "the merciful plan of the great Creator" (2 Nephi 9:6).

If we learn more about our postmortal existence and prepare for its coming, perhaps an additional promise of the Lord will be fulfilled for us: "Blessed are those who hearken unto my precepts, and lend an ear unto my counsel, for they shall learn wisdom; for unto him that receiveth I will give more" (2 Nephi 28:30).

Notes

Excerpts from a talk given at BYU Campus Education Week, 17 August 1998.

1. *Teachings of the Prophet Joseph Smith,* 353–54.
2. *History of the Church,* 4:575.
3. Joseph F. Smith, John R. Winder, and Anthon H. Lund, in *Messages of the First Presidency,* 4:205.
4. *Gospel Doctrine,* 12.
5. Brigham Young, in *Journal of Discourses,* 6:333.
6. Joseph F. Smith, in *Journal of Discourses,* 23:169.
7. Brigham Young, in *Journal of Discourses,* 11:43.
8. Ibid., 3:368, 372.
9. Ibid., 3:369.

10. Parley P. Pratt, *Key to the Science of Theology* (Salt Lake City: Deseret Book Co., 1965), 126.
11. Joseph F. Smith, "A Sermon on Purity," *Improvement Era*, 6 (May 1903): 503–4.
12. Brigham Young, in *Journal of Discourses*, 14:231.
13. *History of the Church*, 6:52.
14. Joseph F. Smith, in *Journal of Discourses*, 22:351.
15. Joseph F. Smith, in *Messages of the First Presidency*, 5:6–7.
16. Charles A. Callis, in Conference Report, October 1939, 20.
17. Heber C. Kimball, in *Journal of Discourses*, 3:108.
18. Brigham Young, in *Journal of Discourses*, 3:368.
19. *Encyclopedia Americana*, 30 vols. (Danbury, Conn.: Grolier, Inc., 1997), "Eye."
20. *Encyclopedia Americana*, "Light."
21. *Encyclopedia of Physics*, ed. Rita G. Lerner and George L. Trigg, 2d ed. (New York: VCH, 1991), "Light."
22. *Encyclopedia of Physics*, ed. Robert M. Besancon (New York: Van Nostrand Reinhold Co., 1985), "Light."
23. *McGraw-Hill Encyclopedia of Physics*, ed. Sybil P. Parker, 2d ed. (New York: McGraw Hill, 1993), "Light."
24. *Encyclopedia Americana*, "Sound."
25. Brigham Young, in *Journal of Discourses*, 3:368.

Chapter 30

THE THREE HEAVENS, OR THE THREE DEGREES OF GLORY

The idea is quite generally taught in Christianity that at the time of resurrection a person is assigned either to heaven, a place in the presence of God, or to hell, a place in the presence of the devil. According to this belief there is no other alternative: If a person is not worthy of the presence of God, he is thrust into the presence of the devil.

The doctrine of one heaven and one hell means that all who go to heaven share and share alike in the blessings and that all who fail to go to heaven are sent to hell, where they share and share alike in the miseries. This teaching does not seem to be consistent with the other teachings of the gospel, which indicate that a man reaps what he sows. Also, such a doctrine does not encourage people to do the very best they can—after all, if they are reasonably good, they will still get into heaven and enjoy all the blessings enjoyed by the most valiant, righteous, and faithful. In a similar way, if people are more wicked than the average, they sometimes feel they might as well do all the bad they can, because they are doomed to damnation anyway.

Also the doctrine of one heaven and one hell is not consistent with the character of a merciful God who claims he is not a respecter of persons and yet is a rewarder of all good. Certainly God is a God of justice as well as a God of mercy; therefore, if a person willfully and knowingly breaks the commandments of God and refuses to repent of them, he must be cast out. No evil, wicked, or unclean thing can dwell in God's presence.

But what of the multitudes of people who are willing to accept some of the teachings of Christ and yet are unwilling to obey all the commandments necessary to get back into the presence of God? Is there no hope for them? Is there no place provided for people who are unworthy of the direct presence of God and yet who are not wicked enough to justify condemnation with Satan? I believe there is such a place, and I further believe this doctrine, which is called the doctrine of a plurality of heavens, is taught in the gospel of Christ.

The New Testament contains statements by Christ and his apostles that clearly indicate there are different orders of heaven, or degrees of glory. In the book of John the Savior said: "Let not your heart be troubled: ye believe in God, believe also in me. In my Father's house are many mansions: if it were not so, I would have told you. I go to prepare a place for you. And if I go and prepare a place for you, I will come again, and receive you unto myself; that where I am, there ye may be also" (John 14:1–3).

The whole doctrine of being judged of our works at the final judgment and of receiving rewards or punishments according to our deeds indicates there must be different levels of rewards and punishments, for certainly there is great variety in the number and quality of works performed by different people. John the Revelator mentions this judgment in his book of Revelation: "And I saw the dead, small and great, stand before God; and the books were opened: and another book was opened, which is the book of life and the dead were judged out of those things which were written in the books, according to their works" (Revelation 20:12).

Paul also understood and taught the doctrine of various heavens, or degrees of glory. In fact, in his second letter to the saints at Corinth, he states that he knew a man who was "caught up to the third heaven" (2 Corinthians 12:2). Naturally, if there is a "third" heaven, there must also be a first and a second. In 1 Corinthians 15, Paul identifies three degrees of glory and gives names to two of these heavens. In speaking of the order of resurrected bodies, he states: "There are also celestial bodies, and bodies terrestrial: but the glory of the celestial is one, and the glory of the terrestrial is another. There is one glory of the sun, and another glory of the moon, and another glory of the stars: for one star differeth from another star in glory. *So also is the resurrection of the dead*" (1 Corinthians 15:40–42; emphasis added). Thus Paul indicates that the highest heaven, whose glory is like the sun, is called the celestial. The second heaven, whose glory is like the moon, is the terrestrial. The lowest order of heaven, whose glory is like the stars, is not named by Paul.

The clearest and most comprehensive statement in all scripture on the three heavens, or degrees of glory, comes from modern scripture, the Doctrine and Covenants. This book contains the testimony of Joseph Smith and Sidney Rigdon, who, on 16 February 1832, were shown these heavens in vision and who recorded their experience.

Concerning the celestial glory, they said: "And again we bear record—for we saw and heard, and this is the testimony of the gospel of Christ concerning them who shall come forth in the resurrection of the just—They are they who received the testimony of Jesus and believed on His name and were baptized after the manner of His Burial, being buried in the water in His name.... That... they might be washed and cleansed from all their sins, and receive the Holy Spirit by laying on of the hands of him who is ordained and sealed unto this power; And who overcome by faith, and are sealed by the Holy Spirit of promise, which the Father sheds forth upon those who are just and true. They are they who are the church of the Firstborn.... They are they into whose hands the Father has given all things.... These shall dwell in the presence of God and His Christ forever and ever" (D&C 76:50–55). "These are they who are just men made perfect through Jesus the mediator of the new covenant, who wrought out this perfect atonement through the shedding of his own blood. These are they whose bodies are celestial, whose glory is that of the sun, even the glory of God, the highest of all, whose glory the sun of the firmament is written of as being typical" (D&C 62:69–70).

To obtain the celestial heaven, or the kingdom of glory where God dwells, one must be baptized of water, receive the gift of the Holy Ghost by the laying on of hands of one who has authority, and fully repent of all one's sins. Only then will one be worthy to enter into the presence of God.

Those who are unwilling to accept the fulness of the obligations of the gospel but who still repent of their sins and acknowledge the atonement of Christ enter into the second heaven, or degree—the terrestrial. This heaven is described as follows: "And again, we saw the terrestrial world.... These are they... whose glory differs from that of the church of the Firstborn who have received the fulness of the Father, even as that of the moon differs from the sun in the firmament. Behold, these are they who died without law; And also they who are the spirits of men kept in prison, whom the Son visited and preached the gospel unto them, that they might be judged according to men in the flesh; Who received not the testimony of Jesus in the flesh, but afterwards received it. These are they who are honorable men of the earth, who were blinded by the craftiness of men. These are they who receive of his glory, but not of his fulness. These are they who receive of the presence of the Son, but not of the fulness of the Father.... And now this is the end of the vision which we saw of the terrestrial, that the Lord commanded us to write while we were yet in the Spirit" (D&C 76:71–77, 80).

The lowest order of heaven, the telestial, will be occupied by people who are not willing to accept the full obligations of the gospel either in this life or in the life to come, yet they acknowledge and recognize Christ as the Savior and Redeemer. These people are not worthy of the presence of either the Father or the Son, but they likewise are not so wicked nor rebellious that they should be cast entirely out of heaven. Therefore, they enter into the lowest degree of glory, which is described as follows: "And again, we saw the glory of the telestial, which glory is that of the lesser, even as the glory of the stars differs from that of the glory of the moon in the firmament. These are they who received not the gospel of Christ, neither the testimony of Jesus. These are they who deny not the Holy Spirit. . . . These are they who shall not be redeemed from the devil until the last resurrection, until the Lord, even Christ the Lamb, shall have finished His work. . . . And they shall be servants of the Most High; but where God and Christ dwell, they cannot come, worlds without end" (D&C 76:81–83, 85, 112).

Those who inherit the telestial kingdom are required to repent and suffer fully for all their sins before their redemption comes, but eventually they are redeemed. Thus, everyone who inherits a kingdom of glory will be redeemed through the atonement of Christ.

In addition to the three degrees of glory, there is at least one kingdom that is not a kingdom of glory. This kingdom is inhabited by the devil and his followers and by all those who become sons of perdition in this life. The Lord has revealed that the occupants of this kingdom are the only ones on whom the second spiritual death shall have power—that is, they shall not be redeemed. Their condition is described in the scriptures as follows: "And he who cannot abide the law of a telestial kingdom cannot abide a telestial glory; therefore, he is not meet for a kingdom of glory. Therefore, he must abide a kingdom which is not a kingdom of glory. . . . And they . . . shall . . . be quickened; nevertheless, they shall return again to their own place to enjoy that which they are willing to receive, because they were not willing to enjoy that which they might have received" (D&C 88:24, 32). "They shall go away into everlasting punishment, which is endless punishment, which is eternal punishment, to reign with the devil and his angels in eternity" (D&C 76:44).

What glorious principles of truth! The hell that is outer darkness, which is as a lake of fire and brimstone to be endured eternally, is not a place where approximately 50 percent of the human race are destined to go; rather, it pertains only to those relatively few who are so rebellious and wicked that they become sons of perdition. Every other person will eventually repent of his sins and enter the heaven, or degree of glory, to which he is entitled. In the justice and mercy of God, however, only those who are willing to accept and keep the first principles and ordinances of the gospel are worthy to enter into the actual presence of God, which is the celestial heaven.

These are the teachings of the scriptures. So far as I know, however, this doctrine is now taught by only one church—The Church of Jesus Christ of Latter-day Saints. It is part of the fulness of the gospel, which has been restored in this dispensation.

Note

From an address delivered over KSL Radio, Salt Lake City, 19 January 1958.

Chapter 31

ETERNAL LIFE OR EXALTATION WITHIN THE CELESTIAL KINGDOM

In this discussion I will consider a doctrine of the gospel that pertains to our eternal happiness because it is concerned with the type of life we might enjoy in the eternities to come after the resurrection. This topic might be introduced by two very brief scriptures. The first of these is a statement by the Savior recorded in the New Testament: "This is life eternal, that they might know thee, the only true God, and Jesus Christ whom thou has sent" (John 17:3). The second scripture is a statement by God and is recorded in the Pearl of Great Price: "This is my work and my glory—the bring to pass the immortality and eternal life of man" (Moses 1:39).

These two scriptures indicate that eternal life is the great gift of God and that we obtain this gift only as we learn to know God and to understand the mission of his Son, Jesus Christ.

But what is eternal life? It is not the mere promise of immortality or the power to live forever but is something in addition to immortality. Notice again the words of God: "This is my work and my glory—to bring to pass the immortality *and* eternal life of man." The immortality of man has now been realized through the resurrection of Christ; all of us will be resurrected from the dead. But the other aspect of God's work, the eternal life of man, depends primarily upon man himself and has not yet been fully achieved.

Perhaps we can best determine what eternal life is by examining some of its synonyms in the scriptures. For example, the word "exaltation" is a scriptural term frequently used to denote the end goal of life. Also, in some cases the word "salvation" or the idea of "being saved" is used. But when we receive eternal life, *to what* are we being exalted and *from what* are we being saved?

These questions can be answered by referring to the three heavens or degrees of glory. Recall that these are identified in the scriptures: first, the celestial—the highest heaven where God dwells, which is as the glory of the sun; second, the terrestrial—which is as the glory of the moon; and third, the telestial—which is as the glory of the stars. Recall that certain conditions prevail in all of these heavens. For example, each of these heavens is a place of purposeful activity—we do not spend the eternities playing harps. Also, we retain our individual entity in heaven; we continue to be thinking personalities—to be ourselves, different from everyone else. Thus we are able to enjoy the friendship and companionship of others. We also will have our bodies after the resurrection, just as the Savior had his body after his resurrection. Of course, our resurrected bodies will not be subject to death or to the pains or diseases of mortality. As Paul states, our bodies will be immortal and incorruptible.

However, different conditions also exist within each of the heavens. For example, Paul states that resurrected bodies are of different orders; some are of the celestial order, others of the terrestrial, and still others of the telestial (1 Corinthians 15:40–42). Our resurrected bodies will be suited to the heaven we obtain, which in turn depends upon our degree of worthiness.

If a person attains any of the three degrees of glory, however, he achieves a degree of salvation, for he is "saved" from the permanent effects of temporal death through the resurrection and is also "saved" from the eternal influences of the devil. But in order to obtain a *fulness* of salvation, or an exaltation, one must obtain the highest heaven where God dwells—the celestial—and then must be exalted *within* that kingdom. Such a person receives the gift of eternal life. Thus eternal life might be defined as life in the presence of God and also as "the type of life that God lives." This means that a person who has eternal life becomes as God is.

In order for a person to inherit eternal life, however, he must keep not only the first principles and ordinances of the gospel, which are prerequisites to the celestial kingdom, but also the higher ordinances of the gospel, including temple marriage for time and all eternity. A man cannot obtain eternal life by himself; he must have the companionship of a wife. If a man and his wife receive these higher ordinances and remain faithful to the covenants they make, they are entitled to the gift of eternal life, which includes the right of eternal increase—the power and right to have children after the resurrection. This right and power will be given only to those who fulfill all the requirements. Notice the clarity of God's word on this subject: "In the celestial glory there are three heavens or degrees; And in order to obtain the highest, a man must enter into this order of the priesthood (meaning the new and everlasting covenant of marriage); And if he does not, he cannot obtain it. He may enter into the other, but that is the end of his kingdom; he cannot have an increase" (D&C 131:1–4).

An erroneous concept has crept into Christianity that men and women do not live together as husbands and wives after death—that there are no family groups or family relationships after the resurrection. This is not the teaching of the gospel of Christ. In the second chapter of Genesis, God said it is not good that man should be alone (Genesis 2:18), and later he instituted marriage between Adam and Eve. It is evident that this marriage was to last forever, for Adam and Eve were not even subject to death at the time they were joined together as husband and wife by the Lord. There was no clause saying, "I pronounce you husband and wife *until death do you part*" in this marriage or in any other marriage performed by the sealing power of God. The Savior made it clear that marriage is meant to be eternal when he said: "Have ye not read, that he which made them at the beginning made them male and female, and said, For this cause shall a man leave father and mother, and shall cleave to his wife; and they twain shall be one flesh? Wherefore they are no more twain, but one flesh. What therefore God hath joined together, let not man put asunder" (Matthew 19:4–6).

Earlier the Savior said to Peter, "And I will give unto thee the keys of the kingdom of heaven: and whatsoever thou shalt bind on earth shall be bound in heaven: and whatsoever thou shalt loose on earth shall be loosed in heaven" (Matthew 16:19).

This sealing power—given to Peter by the Christ and restored in this dispensation to Joseph Smith by the prophet Elijah—enables a man and woman to be married or sealed together as husband and wife not only for this life but for time and all eternity. As the Savior said, "They are no more twain, but one flesh" (Matthew 19:6).

Paul taught this same doctrine in his first letter to the saints at Corinth when he said, "Neither is the man without the woman, neither the woman without the man, in the Lord" (1 Corinthians 11:11).

But, one might ask, if the gospel teaches that a husband and wife can continue to live as a married couple after the resurrection, why is the belief so common in Christianity that there are no marriage relationships in heaven? This false idea has come from a misinterpretation of a statement by the Savior in the New Testament. The Sadducees—who did not even believe in a resurrection—came to the Savior in an attempt to trick him, saying, "Master, Moses said, If a man die, having no children, his brother shall marry his wife, and raise up seed unto his brother. Now there were with us seven brethren: and the first, when he had married a wife, deceased, and having no issue, left his wife unto his brother: Likewise the second also, and the third, unto the seventh. And last of all the woman died also. Therefore in the resurrection whose wife shall she be of the seven? . . . Jesus answered and said unto them. Ye do err, not knowing the scriptures, nor the power of God. For in the resurrection they neither marry, nor are given in marriage, but are as the angels of God in heaven" (Matthew 22:24–30).

This answer has often been construed to mean there are no marriage *relationships* in heaven. However, a careful reading of these verses indicates the Savior is merely saying that marriage cannot be *performed* in heaven; it is an earthly ordinance and must be performed *on* earth. There are no marriages in heaven.

An explanation by the Savior in a modern scripture helps to make this distinction clear. He states: "Therefore, if a man marry him a wife in the world, and he marry her not by me nor by my word, and he covenant with her so long as he is in the world and she with him, their covenant and marriage are not of force when they are dead, and when they are out of the world; therefore, they are not bound by any law when they are out of the world. Therefore, when they are out of the world they neither marry nor are given in marriage" (D&C 132:15–16).

However, the Savior also makes it clear that the marriage of those who are "sealed" by the power of the priesthood and who remain faithful will be in effect in heaven for time and all eternity. He continues: "And again, verily I say unto you, if a man marry a wife by my word, which is my law, and by the new and everlasting covenant, and it is sealed unto them by the Holy Spirit of promise, by him who is anointed, unto whom I have appointed this power and the keys of this priesthood . . . it shall be . . . of full force when they are out of the world; and they shall pass . . . to their exaltation and glory in all things, as hath been sealed upon their heads, which glory shall be a fulness and a continuation of the seeds forever and ever" (D&C 132:19).

The wonderful message of the restored gospel of Christ is that we not only live after death but that we can live in the presence of God and become as God is. This means that we can live together with our husband or wife and can receive the gift of eternal increase or the "continuation of the seeds." These blessings are predicated upon our faithfulness and obedience to the higher ordinances of the gospel, which are performed only by priesthood power in the temples of God. These ordinances can be performed either for the living or, by proxy, for and in behalf of the dead who did not have the opportunity to learn of these truths during mortality.

Thus can the great gift of eternal life be realized by man. No wonder God said that this was his work and his *glory*.

In conclusion, I turn to a statement by the resurrected Christ that he gave to Joseph Smith in 1843: "Verily, verily, I say unto you, except ye abide my law ye cannot attain to this glory. For strait is the gate, and narrow the way that leadeth unto the exaltation and continuation of the lives, and few there be that find it, because ye receive me not in the world neither do ye know me. But if ye receive me in the world, then shall ye know me, and shall receive your exaltation; that where I am ye shall be also. This is eternal lives—to know the only wise and true God, and Jesus Christ, whom he hath sent. I am He. Receive ye, therefore, my law" (D&C 132:21–24).

Note

From an address delivered over KSL Radio, Salt Lake City, Utah, 26 January 1958.

Chapter 32

OUR DIVINE DESTINY—
A THIRD DIMENSION VIEW

FOUR BACKGROUND INCIDENTS

I would like to refer to four incidents or experiences that will provide background for the ideas I would like to present in this chapter regarding our divine destiny.

The first of these is an experience Jedediah Morgan Grant had while serving a mission for the Church in the Southern States from 1837–38. Brother Grant, with his knowledge of the scriptures, soon earned a degree of notoriety because of the debates he had participated in with several Protestant ministers. Finally, a Baptist minister decided he would try to put Brother Grant in his place, challenging him to debate. He knew that Brother Grant was not an ordained minister in the regular sense of the word, and that he was not even a presiding elder in the Church. The minister evidently felt Brother Grant was not trained for the ministry; therefore, he thought he could surely best him in the debate.

As the debate started, this rather pompous individual stood up and introduced himself somewhat as follows: "I am Reverend Baldwin, and I stand at the head of my church in southwest Virginia. Mr. Grant, who stands at the head of your church in southwest Virginia?"

Brother Grant stood up and said, "Jesus Christ, sir," and then sat down.[1]

The second incident occurred on November 29, 1839, when the Prophet Joseph Smith had an interview with President Martin Van Buren. During that interview, President Van Buren asked the Prophet, "What is there about your Church that makes it different from all of the other Christian churches?" Joseph Smith answered that we differ "in mode of baptism, and the gift of the Holy Ghost by the laying on of hands."[2]

The third incident occurred in March 1842 when Mr. John Wentworth, editor of the *Chicago Democrat,* asked the Prophet Joseph Smith if he would write a statement concerning the basic beliefs of The Church of Jesus Christ of Latter-day Saints. Joseph Smith agreed to do this on the condition that his statement would not be edited and would be published in its entirety. This letter, which we refer to in Church history as the "Wentworth Letter," marks one of the high points of the literary efforts of the Prophet. In fact, the last thirteen paragraphs of that letter have been canonized; they appear as the Articles of Faith in the Pearl of Great Price.[3]

In answer to the question, "Why The Church of Jesus Christ of Latter-day Saints?" the Prophet answered, in substance, in these words, "This Church was restored to prepare a people to be worthy to live with Christ when he comes."

The fourth and last incident occurred with the publication of a guest editorial by Brigham Young University President Ernest L. Wilkinson in the *Provo Daily Herald.* In the editorial, President Wilkinson indicated that he was asked by a student, "What is the most important accomplishment of your eighteen years as president of BYU?" He answered, "If I had to name the one single most important development with the greatest impact and influence, I would have to choose the establishment on campus of the wards and stakes of The Church of Jesus Christ of Latter-day Saints."

In his next sentence President Wilkinson said he guessed that many people would be surprised at his answer. I am sure some of them thought he would mention something about the tremendous buildings that have been erected on campus, or the large increase in number of students and faculty. But I am convinced that the verdict of history and of eternity will prove that President Wilkinson was right. The most important thing that happened during the first eighteen years of his tenure was the organization of wards and stakes by President David O. McKay and other Church leaders.

Our Divine Destiny

I should explain how I am going to use the words "our divine destiny" in this chapter. First, I will use the pronoun "our" to refer not only to the Church but also to members of the Church, individually and collectively.

Second, the Church is "divine" because Jesus Christ is its head—not only in southwest Virginia but on the whole earth and in heaven as well. We members of the Church are also "divine" because we are of divine parentage. We are sons and daughters of our Heavenly Father; in this relationship, Jesus Christ is our elder brother. If we follow the teachings of the Church, we can receive our "divine" inheritance, to which we are all heirs if we are faithful to the principles and ordinances we espouse.

Of course, the divine "destiny" of the Church, as the kingdom of God on earth, is to someday become one with the kingdom of God in heaven. It is with this union in mind that the Savior counseled us to pray, "Thy kingdom come. Thy will be done in earth, as it is in heaven" (Matthew 6:10). I will use the term "divine destiny" in relationship to individual members of the Church to indicate that we and our families can achieve exaltation in the celestial kingdom. I believe that our divine destiny is intertwined with the divine destiny of the Church. We cannot achieve our divine destiny without the Church, and the Church cannot achieve its divine destiny without us.

A Third Dimension View

In photography you can take certain elements or parts of a picture and put them on two separate transparencies. Put the two transparencies together, and sometimes a new dimension—referred to as a third dimension—becomes evident. In a third-dimensional picture, there appear to be more elements than in any of the original pictures.

I would like to examine some of the basic doctrines of the Church and then (1) attempt to look at them through the viewpoint of our Heavenly Father and his efforts to bring about our eternal life and (2) attempt to look at them from the viewpoint of Lucifer, who is trying to thwart our efforts to achieve our divine destiny. If we can see these doctrines in a new relationship and visualize ourselves in relation to these doctrines, we will be able to achieve a new perspective, a third-dimensional outlook.

I am going to list seven reasons why we came to earth. Obviously, I could list more reasons; there is nothing sacred about the number seven. The seven reasons are:

1. To obtain a physical body capable of procreation and to use these powers righteously.

2. To exercise our moral agency.

3. To learn to subject the physical to the spiritual through the use of our moral agency.

4. To come to a knowledge of God "in and of ourselves."

5. To learn to walk by faith and to follow the teachings of the Church.

6. To help prepare ourselves and our families to be worthy to regain the presence of God and to be exalted.

7. To help prepare the earth and all mankind for a more glorious future—for the millennial reign of Jesus Christ upon the earth.

Gospel Principles: God's View and Lucifer's View

Let us look at each of these reasons through the transparency of the principles of the gospel as espoused by God, and then see what Lucifer is trying to do to keep us from achieving our divine destiny in these particular areas.

Man's Power of Procreation

We came to earth to obtain a physical body capable of procreation and to learn to use this power righteously. God instituted marriage; marriage, therefore, is ordained of God. As we are told in the Doctrine and Covenants, "Whoso forbiddeth to marry is not ordained of God, for marriage is ordained of God unto man" (D&C 49:15). God built into our physical bodies the miraculous power of increase, but we don't receive that power until we reach an age (puberty) in which we are able to exercise judgment in the use of it. He has given us direction and counsel as to how this power should be used, and he has reserved its use for the marriage relationship. Finally, he has commanded married couples to multiply so that they might have "joy and rejoicing" in their posterity.

On the other hand, let us see what Lucifer has to say about this particular area. This might be clearer if I could do a bit of role playing and put myself in the place of Lucifer. If I were Lucifer, knowing what I know about the plan of God concerning man's power to procreate, I think I would do everything I could do to prostitute those powers. I would forbid marriage if this would do any good, and if I could get churches to forbid marriage so much the better. I would advocate celibacy and, if I could, get large groups of people, particularly religious leaders, to practice celibacy, I could make marriage appear to be a second-rate institution. I would do everything that I could do, if I were Lucifer, to weaken the marriage vows. I would advocate easy divorce; I would advocate free love; I would emphasize every way I could through the news media and television that marriage really is not important. I would inspire people to write movie scripts and television scripts that mock marriage and flaunt immorality. In short, I would do everything I could to weaken the marriage vow.

I would also do everything I could to promote promiscuity and prostitution, and I would emphasize a "new morality," which is really the old immorality. I would also belittle the power of reproduction, and I would have people refer to it as a mere animal instinct. If all these efforts failed, I would do everything I could to discourage married couples from having children, even if I had to influence someone to invent a pill that would prevent conception. If I had to, I would influence legislators, parliamentarians, and other government leaders to legalize abortion. Then I would influence celebrities—entertainers, athletes, news commentators, and others—to say that it is a shame for any family to have more than two children.

When you take the teachings of our Heavenly Father on the one hand and the teachings of Lucifer on the other hand, and then put them together, you can sometimes see the issue in a new relationship. For example, the basic question today concerning population growth is not whether the earth can take care of this increased population. After all, doesn't God have the power, inasmuch as he created the earth, to even create another earth if necessary? Doesn't he have power to bless this earth so that it could produce spontaneously and abundantly? You see, that is not the question. The question is very simply this: "Will we or will we not obey God's command to multiply so that we can have joy and rejoicing in our posterity?"

Moral Agency

We came to earth to exercise our agency. To enable us to do so, the Lord, first of all, gave us law. We have to have law in order to exercise agency; that is, we have to have the opportunity of choice. Second, he gave us freedom of choice. He said to Adam and Eve in the Garden of Eden, "Of every tree of the garden thou mayest freely eat, But of the tree of the knowledge of good and evil, thou shalt not eat of it, nevertheless, thou mayest choose for thyself" (Moses 3:16–17). So he gave them their agency. Of course God realizes that when he gives us law he also gives us two possible consequences. We can obey the law, which results in a blessing, which in turn results in happiness or joy; or we can disobey the law, which results in punishment, which in turn results in misery. But if we want to have the one possibility (joy), we must have the other possibility (misery). Therefore, our Heavenly Father is trying to guarantee us opportunity of choice as well as freedom of choice. To accomplish this, among other things, he raised up men to establish a Constitution. He has raised up countries that will protect citizens in certain inalienable rights.

Now let us see how Lucifer looks at agency by playing his role. If I were Lucifer, I would not give people choice. I would advocate a dictatorship, and if I were not successful in that, I would do everything I could to get people to delegate their agency to some superpower or government, either through a welfare state, socialism, a guaranteed annual-wage-forever plan, or something of this type. If I were Lucifer, I would do everything I could to destroy the exercise of agency on this earth. I would destroy law and order; I would bring the police into ill-repute, if I could. Above all else, I would hamper and, if possible, destroy the judicial system of every country on earth because this is the system that has been given the responsibility for upholding law and order. In particular, I would set my sights on America, and I would do everything I could to destroy her bastion of moral agency and free enterprise.

Once again, when you put the two transparencies together and see the issue in a new dimension, you find that what Lucifer really wants to do is what is so obviously being done in the world today. Among other things, he is trying to tell people: "Look, it doesn't make any difference what you do; rationalize your sins. Wickedness does not result in unhappiness." The Book of Mormon prophet Alma exposed this lie when he said, "Wickedness never was happiness" (Alma 41:10). Let us read what Samuel the Lamanite said about this principle in speaking to apostate Nephites: "Your destruction is made sure; yea, for ye have sought all the days of your lives for that which ye could not obtain; and ye have sought for happiness in doing iniquity, which thing is contrary to the nature of that righteousness which is in our great and Eternal Head" (Helaman 13:38).

Nevertheless, people in the last days will say: "[God] will justify in committing a little sin; yea, lie a little, take the advantage of one because of his words, dig a pit for thy neighbor; there is no harm in this; and do all these things, for tomorrow we die; and if it so be that we are guilty, God will beat us with a few stripes, and at last we shall be saved in the kingdom of God. . . . And thus the devil cheateth their souls, and leadeth them away carefully down to hell" (2 Nephi 28:8, 21).

If I were Lucifer, I would try to get people, particularly Latter-day Saints, to rationalize away their sins. The story is told that on one occasion, a brother in the Church told Brigham Young that he knew that Joseph Smith was a fallen prophet. Brigham Young said, "How do you know that Joseph Smith is a fallen prophet?" The man said, "Because Joseph Smith once taught, and I heard it from his own lips, that if a man commits adultery he will lose the spirit and deny the faith, and I have committed adultery and I have not lost the spirit, and I have not denied the faith; therefore I know that Joseph Smith is a fallen prophet."[4] Such an incident is a good example of rationalizing away one's sins.

Subject the Physical to the Spiritual

We came to this earth to learn to subject the physical to the spiritual through the use of our agency. The Lord has given us certain principles on this. For example, in Matthew he says, "And fear not them which kill the body, but are not able to kill the soul: but rather fear him which is able to destroy both soul and body in hell" (Matthew 10:28). And in Mark he adds, "For what shall it profit a man, if he shall gain the whole world, and lose his own soul?" (Mark 8:36).

In other words, our spirits are more important than the physical elements of the earth, and we came here so that our spirits could learn to control matter. In fact, God gave us dominion over the earth and a command to subdue the earth. He also gave us the law of consecration and the law of stewardship whereby we might learn to do this.

How does Lucifer try to thwart or defeat us in this? To me this is the real issue involved in the Word of Wisdom. You see, one thing that is wrong with smoking, drinking, and the other harmful things mentioned in the Word of Wisdom is that their use is entirely contrary to the purposes of our coming here. The use of addictive substances puts the physical above the spiritual. If I were Lucifer, I would do everything I could do to get people to smoke. Tobacco would be all right, but marijuana would be better. I would also try to get people to use heroin and other drugs, including alcohol, because by doing so they would be subjecting their spirits to the physical. If you don't think these things addict or influence the spirit, just sit in an airplane next to a heavy smoker and watch his hands shake during the flight.

If I were Lucifer, I would do everything I could to tell people to "eat, drink, and be merry, for tomorrow [they] die" (2 Nephi 28:7), and I would tell them that God has no right dictating what they may or can eat and drink.

I would also tell them that they are entitled to a living and that other people owe them a living. I would tell them, "You have certain rights, and if someone has something you need or want, go ahead and take it."

If you want to do some reading that will quickly sober you, pick up a newspaper and read the articles about crime, including murder, rape, robbery, assault, and drug abuse. Lucifer is doing quite well in this world in getting people to emphasize the physical over the spiritual and, therefore, keeping them from achieving their divine destiny.

A Knowledge of God "In and of Ourselves"

We were born on earth to come to a knowledge of God "in and of ourselves." The Savior said, "And this is life eternal, that they might know thee the only true God, and Jesus Christ, whom thou hast sent" (John 17:3).

God has sent prophets to us to teach the gospel. God has also given us scriptures. In these scriptures he has put the essentials of the gospel, including some great principles that will help us to solve our problems. He has commanded and encouraged us to read the scriptures: "Search the scriptures . . . they are they which testify of me" (John 5:39).

Furthermore, he has promised us additional scriptures if we will read and live up to what we have. He said: "I will give unto the children of men line upon line, precept upon precept, here a little and there a little; . . . for unto him that receiveth I will give more; and from them that shall say, We have enough, from them shall be taken away even that which they have" (2 Nephi 28:30).

If I were Lucifer, I would do everything I could to belittle the words of the prophets; in fact, I would even deny the power of prophecy. And I would inspire the scholars of the earth to criticize the Bible by saying that the prophetic elements of the Bible could not have occurred because no one can know about anything before it happens. Soon thereafter I could influence people to consider the Bible simply as sort of a book of myths. If I were Lucifer, I would do everything I could to keep people from reading the scriptures. If you don't think Lucifer has been quite successful in this, read the results of a survey by Dr. George Gallup, director of the American Institute of Public Opinion, which he conducted concerning the religious literacy of people in the United States.

I offer here the results of one question Dr. Gallup included in his questionnaire: "Will you tell me the names of any of the first four books of the New Testament of the Bible, that is, the Four Gospels?" In a select group of people (all of whom were twenty-one years of age and over, and all of whom were high school graduates and above), he found out that 35 percent of the people could name all four of the books, 4 percent could name three of the books, 4 percent could name two of the books, and 4 percent could name one of the books. In other words, he found that 47 percent of the people could name one or more of the books, while 53 percent of the people in the United States, twenty-one years of age and over, could not even name one of the four Gospels of Jesus Christ![5]

If I were Lucifer, I would do everything I could do to keep people from reading the scriptures, and I would especially try to keep Latter-day Saints from reading the Book of Mormon and the Doctrine and Covenants. And if they insisted on reading them, I would encourage them to read them as history and to ignore the great teaching principles contained therein. After all, some of them might apply these principles in their lives. If I were Lucifer, I would prefer to have the scriptures destroyed, but if I couldn't do that, I would have them altered or taken away.

To Walk by Faith and to Follow Christ's Teachings

We came to earth to learn to walk by faith and to follow the teachings of Christ. We are told to pray—to ask, to seek, to knock. We are told that certain signs will follow them that believe. Our Heavenly Father has established the true church to help us fellowship each other and to live the truth. Our Heavenly Father wants us to have freedom of religion so we can exercise our agency and worship as we want so long as doing so does not impinge on the freedoms of others to do the same.

Lucifer does the opposite. He tries to keep us from praying. He belittles faith and emphasizes knowledge and reason. If I were Lucifer, I would work particularly among college students by saying, "Belittle faith, enthrone knowledge and reason, and ask for signs." I wouldn't tolerate freedom of religion.

Preparation for Exaltation

We came to earth to help prepare individual members of the Church and their families to become worthy to be exalted in the presence of God. The gospel is relatively simple. I am afraid those of us who teach religion make it much too complex. The Savior defined the gospel in one verse of scripture:

"Now this is the commandment: Repent, all ye ends of the earth, and come unto me and be baptized in my name, that ye may be sanctified by the reception of the Holy Ghost, that ye may stand spotless before me at the last day. Verily, verily, I say unto you, this is my gospel" (3 Nephi 27:20–21).

Notice the phrase "that ye may be sanctified by the reception of the Holy Ghost." Now do you understand what Joseph Smith meant when he told President Martin Van Buren, "We have the Holy Ghost"? If we have the Holy Ghost, we have the power to give the Holy Ghost. If we have the power to give the Holy Ghost, we have the true priesthood of God. If we have the true priesthood of God, we are the true church upon the earth.

The gift of the Holy Ghost is necessary in order for us to achieve our individual destiny. The statement of the Savior in 3 Nephi 27 indicates that God is a holy person and that no sinful person can enter his presence. In fact, the Savior said, "No unclean thing can enter into his kingdom" (3 Nephi 27:19). The question, then, is how can a sinful person become sinless so that he can qualify for God's presence? The answer is that he must become sinless through the cleansing power of the Holy Ghost. This power is a gift of the Holy Ghost and is given only by the laying on of hands by one who has authority (or priesthood) of God. This "baptism of the Holy Ghost" is received only after the baptism of water, which is for the remission of sins. However, a remission of sins is achieved only through repentance, and a person repents only if he has faith in the atonement of Jesus Christ. Thus, I have listed in reverse order the basic principles and ordinances of the gospel. As we usually list them, we state that a person must have faith in the Lord Jesus Christ, repent, be baptized by immersion for the remission of sins, and then receive the gift of the Holy Ghost by the laying on of hands. Receiving the gift of the Holy Ghost is a necessary prerequisite for the celestial kingdom once a person has committed a sin.

If I were Lucifer, I would do everything I could to get people not to believe in the Holy Ghost, even if I had to tell them to deny the power of the Holy Ghost and to convince them that the Holy Ghost is not separate from the spirit of God the Father. In fact, if I were Lucifer, I would say: "There are no saving ordinances so far as the gospel is concerned. If you want to be baptized, that is fine, but baptism is simply a symbol; it is not necessary. If you want to be baptized, then anyone can baptize you." Many Protestant churches believe in the priesthood of all believers; they believe that anyone who believes in Christ has as much priesthood as any other believer. The predominant Christian church in the world today, meanwhile, doesn't even require priesthood authority in order to baptize. Anyone can baptize a person into this church. If I were Lucifer, I would make sure that people didn't believe in the saving ordinances and principles of the gospel of Jesus Christ.

Preparation for the Millennial Reign

We came to earth to help prepare the earth and all mankind for a more glorious future—the millennial reign of Jesus Christ upon the earth. How is God helping us prepare for the Millennium? First of all, he has given us the Holy Ghost so we can improve our personal worthiness. He has also given us such programs as family home evening, during which we can be taught the gospel. Second, we see in priesthood correlation today an attempt by our Heavenly Father to prepare qualified and experienced leadership so that within the Church we can develop our own system of government. Thus, if other governments fall (federal governments, state governments, municipal governments), we can still govern ourselves.

Once you see priesthood correlation in the perspective of training qualified and worthy priesthood leaders, then all of a sudden home teaching, priesthood quorum leadership, ward bishoprics, ward priesthood executive committees, stake presidencies and high councils, stake councils, and regional meetings all come a little bit more into focus. This Church was restored to prepare a people to be worthy to live with Jesus Christ when he comes.

If I were Lucifer, I would attack people's preparation for the Millennium from two main points. I would tell them not to believe in the Second Coming or the Millennium. Lucifer has succeeded in this area very well. Well over two-thirds of the people on earth aren't even Christian; they don't look forward to the Second Coming, much less believe in it. And of those who are Christian, an overwhelming majority of them don't believe in a millennial reign here on the earth—they don't believe in the Millennium.

According to a book published by the Catholic Church: "The Catholic Church has never considered the Millennium as an article of faith or held that it was taught by the Scriptures or Apostolic tradition. There is no trace of Millenarianism [the teachings of a millennium] in the Gospels or the Epistles. The resurrection of the just and the unjust, the general Judgment and the end of the world are mentioned as happening in close succession, leaving no possible room for the mythical reign of Christ for one thousand years."[6]

If I were Lucifer, I would do everything I could to prevent people from believing in the Millennium, but if some strange, independent, separate group insisted on doing so, I would do as much as I could to prevent them from preparing themselves to be worthy to be with Christ.

When we put together these two transparencies of what is happening in these last days, don't things come into focus a little bit? And yet, I wonder why we have so much difficulty getting the priesthood members of the Church to carry out their home teaching responsibilities. Why are we having so much difficulty with this important "weld" program, this program that brings the authority of the Church into contact with the home? If I were Lucifer, I would strike quickly at the home teaching program. I wouldn't want to connect the homes of the Church to the power and authority of the Church.

In preparation for the millennial reign, two great world capitals will be established: one here in America and one in Israel. Lucifer knows this. He has read the scriptures; in fact, he probably knows them better than we do. Now do you understand a little better why the Saints were driven out of Missouri, which is the area designated by the Lord as one of these world capitals? Now do you see what was really behind the extermination order of Governor Boggs? When you remember the scriptural promise that the descendants of Judah are to gather back to Israel before the Second Coming of Christ, do you understand a little better why a dictator was devilishly inspired to kill over six million Jewish people in the gas chambers of Germany, thus preventing them from returning to Israel? According to the scriptures, Judah must return, Jerusalem must be rebuilt, the temple in Jerusalem must be built, and the temple in Jackson County, Missouri, must be built—all before

Jesus Christ returns to earth to rule as King of kings and Lord of lords. If I were Lucifer, I would do everything I could to destroy America and Israel so that these two great world capitals could not be established.

May we be worthy of the great responsibility the Lord has placed upon us, that we might individually achieve our eternal destiny. Only in this way can we save ourselves and be the means by which this Church can achieve its divine destiny of having the kingdom of this earth and the kingdom of heaven become one, with Jesus Christ as the rightful head of the Church.

Notes

From an address given to the Brigham Young University student body, 17 March 1970.

1. See Andrew Jenson, *Latter-day Saint Biographical Encyclopedia,* 4 vols. (Salt Lake City: Andrew Jenson History Co., 1901), 1:58.
2. *History of the Church,* 4:42.
3. The entirety of "The Wentworth Letter" can be found in *History of the Church,* 4:535–41.
4. See John Taylor, in *Journal of Discourses,* 1:372–73.
5. See Leo Rosten, ed., *Religions in America* (New York: Simon and Schuster, 1963), 327.
6. Bertrand L. Conway, *The Question Box* (New York: Paulist Press, 1929), 380.

Prophets of God

Chapter 33

JOHN, THE BELOVED APOSTLE

I have always been very interested in the apostle John the Beloved. I am convinced that he is one of the great ones who have lived on earth.

We should not confuse John the Beloved with John the Baptist. John the Baptist, the son of Zacharias, was the forerunner of Christ. He was the one who baptized Christ. He was the one who was beheaded by Herod. He was the one who appeared as a resurrected being on May 15, 1829, and restored the Aaronic Priesthood to Joseph Smith and Oliver Cowdery.

The man I am referring to has several titles: John the Beloved, John the Revelator, John the Apostle, John the brother of James, and John the son of Zebedee.

BACKGROUND OF JOHN THE BELOVED

The first time we meet him is in his hometown on the Sea of Tiberias, the Sea of Galilee (see Matthew 4). When the Savior walked around the shore of the sea, he saw Simon and his brother Andrew casting a net. He called to them and said, "Follow me, and I will make you fishers of men" (Matthew 4:19). Then he saw another boat where the sons of Zebedee, James and John, were mending their nets, and he also called them forth into the ministry. "And they immediately left the ship and their father, and followed him" (Matthew 4:22).

I find it intriguing to note how faithful they are the first time we meet them, leaving not only their former life and profession but perhaps even leaving their parents in order to follow this man whom they came to know as the Messiah. Later these four mean were called to the apostleship (see Matthew 10).

Evidently James was the elder brother because he is usually listed first, although John is listed at times before James. In Matthew 10, we read about the calling of the apostles and the charge the Savior gave to them. After the Savior called the Twelve Apostles, he gave them a commandment:

"Go not into the way of the Gentiles, and into any city of the Samaritans enter ye not: But go rather to the lost sheep of the house of Israel. And as ye go, preach, saying, The kingdom of heaven is at hand.

"Heal the sick, cleanse the lepers, raise the dead, cast out devils: freely ye have received, freely give. . . . And into whatsoever city or town ye shall enter, enquire who in it is worthy; and there abide till ye go thence. And when ye come into an house, salute it. And if the house be worthy, let your peace come upon it: but if it be not worthy, let your peace return to you. And whosoever shall not receive you, nor hear your words, when ye depart out of that house or city, shake off the dust of your feet. Verily I say unto you, It shall be more tolerable for the land of Sodom and Gomorrah in the day of judgment, than for that city.

"Behold, I send you forth as sheep in the midst of wolves: be ye therefore wise as serpents, and harmless as doves. But beware of men: for they will deliver you up to the councils, and they will scourge you in their synagogues; and ye shall be brought before governors and kings for my sake, for a testimony against them and the Gentiles. But when they deliver you up, take no thought how or what ye shall speak: for it shall be given you in that same hour what ye shall speak. For it is not ye that speak, but the Spirit of your Father which speaketh in you. . . .

"And ye shall be hated of all men for my name's sake: but he that endureth to the end shall be saved. But when they persecute you in this city, flee ye into another" (Matthew 10:5–8, 11–20, 22–23).

The city of Ephesus was visited not only by John the Beloved but also by the great apostle Paul. If these brethren followed the admonitions the Savior gave to them, I suspect they dusted their feet of Ephesus, for this great city, in which at one time one of the seven wonders of the world was located, became desolate ruins. Physically, it is more tolerable almost for Sodom and Gomorrah than for the people John taught at Ephesus.

The Uniqueness of John the Beloved

We, as Latter-day Saints, should know more about the apostle John than any other people on the face of the earth. We know everything the Bible records about him, but we know much more about him. The Book of Mormon and the Doctrine and Covenants make several references to John, and many modern prophets have testified concerning this great man. He is unique among men who have been called to be apostles, though he shares with them certain responsibilities.

He was called among the original Twelve Apostles. He was called to be with Peter and James on the Mount of Transfiguration. He was also called with Peter and James to be present in the Garden of Gethsemane when part of the great miracle of the Atonement took place.

At least one thing in regard to John the Beloved, however, was not shared with the other apostles. When the Savior was on the cross, he selected John to take care of his mother, Mary:

"Now there stood by the cross of Jesus his mother, and his mother's sister, Mary the wife of Cleophas, and Mary Magdalene. When Jesus therefore saw his mother, and the disciple standing by, whom he loved, he saith unto his mother, Woman, behold thy son! Then saith he to the disciple, Behold thy mother! And from that hour that disciple took her unto his own home" (John 19:25–27).

That alone would make John the Beloved unique among men. Of all men on the earth at that time, the Savior selected him to take custody of his mother. From then on the lives of John and Mary were entwined. According to tradition, Mary was buried in Patmos. The scriptures indicate that Mary was placed in John's custody, but they do not indicate that she was ever in the area of Patmos.

We know that Mary was about eighteen or so when she gave birth to Christ; therefore, she would have been in her early fifties at the time of the crucifixion. We also know that John was in Patmos after Paul; if Mary had still been alive, she would have been in her eighties at the time John was in Patmos. Interesting enough, there are two burial places of Mary in Jerusalem: one, the Church of the Dormition, near the Church of the Last Supper; the other, the Tomb or the Sepulchre of Mary near the Garden of Gethsemane. There are also two places in Asia Minor where Mary is supposedly buried. Obviously, not all of these locations can be correct; in fact, they might all well be wrong. We simply do not know where she was buried.

I don't think we could point to any location in Patmos today and say that Paul stood here or that John stood here. But they were both in that city, and they may well have walked down its broad streets. A church built over a grotto in Patmos is believed to be where John wrote the book of Revelation. Although we are not sure this is the exact spot, we are sure he wrote the book while he was on the island. In the first chapter of Revelation we read the following: "I John, who also am your brother, and companion in tribulation, and in the kingdom and patience of Jesus Christ, was in the isle that is called Patmos, for the word of God, and for the testimony of Jesus Christ. I was in the Spirit on the Lord's day, and heard behind me a great voice, as of a trumpet" (Revelation 1:9–10).

It is the Savior who used the term "beloved" in referring to this apostle as "John, my beloved" (3 Nephi 28:6). I think the Savior used "beloved" not only because he loved John but because he was loved by John. John was the apostle who leaned on the Savior's breast at the time of the Feast of the Passover. In the gospel of John, we find the Savior's great sermon of love. In fact, John equates the gospel of Jesus Christ with the word *love*. After the Savior had announced that one of the Twelve would betray him, John, in what I suspect was a somewhat trembling voice, asked, "Lord, who is it?" (John 13:25).

John had the same spirit as Brigham Young and J. Reuben Clark Jr., who in some of their great discourses cautioned the Latter-day Saints not to challenge Lucifer by saying they would never deny the Church or the Savior. We can imagine the little drama during the Feast of the Passover when the Savior announced that one of the Twelve would deny him. First of all, it seems logical that everyone would say to himself, "Well, it must be someone else." Then, finally, they might ask themselves, "Is it possible that it could be me? I don't think so. I hope not. But could it be me?" It was John who put word to the question, "Lord, who is it?"

It was also John who gave us the great intercessory prayer found in only one place in the New Testament. In John 17, we read this great prayer recorded in its fulness, or near fulness:

"These words spake Jesus, and lifted up his eyes to heaven, and said, Father, the hour is come; glorify thy Son, that thy Son also may glorify thee: As thou hast given him power over all flesh, that he should give eternal life to as many as thou hast given him. And this is life eternal, that they might know thee the only true God, and Jesus Christ, whom thou hast sent. I have glorified thee on the earth: I have finished the work which thou gavest me to do. And now, O Father, glorify thou me with thine own self with the glory which I had with thee before the world was" (John 17:1–5).

THE GOSPEL WRITTEN BY JOHN, CHAPTER 21

Then we come to the last chapter of the book of John—one of the most confusing chapters in all scripture to scriptorians and those who write scriptural commentaries. Remember that Peter and the other apostles had returned to the Sea of Galilee after the resurrection of Christ. The Savior had already appeared to them twice in Jerusalem. On the day of his resurrection, he appeared to ten of them—Thomas not being there and Judas already having committed suicide. A week later he appeared to the eleven, including Thomas. Then the apostles returned to the Sea of Galilee, and we read that they were together—Simon Peter, Thomas and Nathaniel, the sons of Zebedee, and two other disciples.

"Simon Peter saith unto them, I go a fishing. They say unto him, We also go with thee. They went forth, and entered into a ship immediately; and that night they caught nothing" (John 21:3).

Then the Savior appeared on the shores at sunrise and asked them whether they had caught any fish. When they answered no, he said, "Cast the net on the right side of the ship, and ye shall find." They did so and caught a "multitude of fishes" (John 21:6). Then John recognized the Savior.

"Therefore that disciple whom Jesus loved saith unto Peter, It is the Lord. Now when Simon Peter heard that it was the Lord, he girt his fisher's coat unto him, . . . and did cast himself into the sea" (John 21:7).

The other disciples also came to shore. Then occurred an interesting dialogue wherein the Savior, knowing that Peter earlier had denied him three times, gave him three opportunities to reaffirm his confidence and faith.

"Simon, son of Jonas, lovest thou me more than these?" Three times Peter replied, "Yea, Lord." I hope none of us is guilty of misinterpreting that scripture. I have heard some ministers indicate that on that occasion the Savior was seeing how faithful Peter was in relation to the other apostles. I do not believe that—that would be entirely foreign to the personality and character of the Savior.

When the Savior asked Peter, "Simon, son of Jonas, lovest thou me more than these?" the antecedent of *these* is not the other apostles. He is not saying, "Do you, Peter, love me more than James, John, and the other apostles love me?" What he is saying is something like this: "Now, Peter, when I called you to the apostleship, you were a fisher of men. You followed me for three years, and you have done very well. But now you've gone back to your old ways again. You're doing the same things you did before I called you. Do you love me more than you love these things? If you do, then come follow me. Feed my sheep and take care of the flock." So the Savior is not trying to test Peter against the other apostles. He is testing Peter against himself: "Do you love me more than you love these things?"

Then come the confusing verses:

"Then Peter, turning about, seeth the disciple whom Jesus loved following.... Peter seeing him saith to Jesus, Lord, and what shall this man do? Jesus saith unto him, If I will that he tarry till I come, what is that to thee? follow thou me. Then went this saying abroad among the brethren, that that disciple should not die: yet Jesus said not unto him, He shall not die; but, If I will that he tarry till I come, what is that to thee? This is the disciple which testifieth of these things, and wrote these things: and we know that his testimony is true" (John 21:20–24).

Of course, the person who is bearing that testimony is John the Beloved himself. Now the question the scholars have asked is, "What did John mean when he wrote, 'If I will that he tarry till I come, what is that to thee?'"

This question was also on the mind of the Prophet Joseph Smith on one occasion. As he translated the Book of Mormon, he came to the visit of the resurrected Jesus Christ to the Nephites. When the disciples met with the Savior just before he left them, the Savior asked this question:

"What is it that ye desire of me, after that I am gone to the Father? And they all spake, save it were three, saying: We desire that after we have lived unto the age of man, that our ministry, wherein thou hast called us, may have an end, that we may speedily come unto thee in thy kingdom. And he said unto them: Blessed are ye because ye desired this thing of me; therefore, after that ye are seventy and two years old ye shall come unto me in my kingdom; and with me ye shall find rest.

"And when he had spoken unto them, he turned himself unto the three, and said unto them: What will ye that I should do unto you, when I am gone unto the Father? And they sorrowed in their hearts, for they durst not speak unto him the thing which they desired.

"And he said unto them: Behold, I know your thoughts, and ye have desired the thing which *John, my beloved,* who was with me in my ministry, before that I was lifted up by the Jews, *desired of me.* Therefore, more blessed are ye, for ye shall never taste of death; but ye shall live to behold all the doings of the Father unto the children of men, even until all things shall be fulfilled according to the will of the Father, when I shall come in my glory with the powers of heaven" (3 Nephi 28:1–7; emphasis added).

When Joseph Smith read and translated this account, he evidently asked himself, "Well, what is meant here when these three Nephite disciples desired the same thing which John, the beloved disciple of Christ, desired?" Therefore, he went before the Lord and asked him what this was all about. In an interesting foreword to one of the sections of the Doctrine and Covenants, we read: "Revelation given to Joseph Smith the Prophet and Oliver Cowdery, at Harmony, Pennsylvania, April 1829, when they inquired through the Urim and Thummim as to whether John, the beloved disciple, tarried in the flesh or had died. The revelation is the translated version of the record made on parchment by John and hidden up by himself" (D&C 7, section heading).

If we as Latter-day Saints really believe this, we are not going to put the Doctrine and Covenants down immediately. In Doctrine and Covenants 7 we can read the first-person account of what John actually wrote concerning events on the shore of the Sea of Tiberias when the resurrected Christ appeared to the apostles. According to John's writings on that parchment:

"The Lord said unto me: John, my beloved, what desirest thou? For if you shall ask what you will, it shall be granted unto you. And I said unto him: Lord, give unto me power over death, that I may live and bring souls unto thee.

"And the Lord said unto me: Verily, verily, I say unto thee, because thou desirest this thou shalt tarry until I come in my glory, and shalt prophesy before nations, kindreds, tongues and people. And for this cause the Lord said unto Peter: If I will that he tarry till I come, what is that to thee? For he desired of me that he might bring souls unto me, but thou desiredst that thou mightest speedily come unto me in my kingdom.

"I say unto thee, Peter, this was a good desire; but my beloved has desired that he might do more, or a greater work yet among men than what he has before done. Yea, he has undertaken a greater work; therefore I will make him as flaming fire and a ministering angel; he shall minister for those who shall be heirs of salvation who dwell on the earth.

"And I will make thee to minister for him and for thy brother James; and unto you three I will give this power and the keys of this ministry until I come. Verily I say unto you, ye shall both have according to your desires, for ye both joy in that which ye have desired" (D&C 7).

All of a sudden, we as Latter-day Saints know more about the translation of John, or the transfiguration of John, than any other people upon the face of the earth. Evidently, before the Savior left his apostles on the eastern continent, he called them together and said, "Ask of me what you will and I shall grant it unto you."

Bold, impetuous Peter spoke up first and said, "I want to live out my life speedily on the earth, and then I want to come unto thee."

So the Savior said, "All right, Peter, you have made the request and it shall be given unto you. Now, John, my beloved, what do you desire of me?"

John said, "I would that I might tarry upon the earth, that I might bring souls unto you until you come in your power."

And the Savior said, "All right, John, I will grant that unto you."

Then Peter said in effect, "Me too. I want what John asked for."

But the Savior had to remind Peter, "I asked you what you wanted. You had your first say. You asked, and what you asked for was very good. I have granted it unto you. Therefore, it shall be done unto you as you have asked. But John has asked for this other thing, and I have given it unto him. He also will receive what he asked."

I hope we read that scripture carefully. I have heard more than one teacher claim that the Savior said that John had asked to do a greater work than Peter was to do. That is not what the scripture says at all. The comparison here is not between the work of Peter and the work of John. The comparison is between the work John previously did with what he was going to subsequently do. Read the scripture again:

"And for this cause the Lord said unto Peter: If I will that he tarry till I come, what is that to thee? For he desired of me that he might bring souls unto me, but thou desiredst that thou mightest speedily come unto me in my kingdom.

"I say unto thee, Peter, this was a good desire; but my beloved has desired that he might do more, or a greater work [and most of us turn off our minds right then and think that he is going to compare the work of John with the work of Peter] yet among men *than what he has before done.*

"Yea, he has undertaken a greater work [than what he has before done]" (D&C 7:4–6; emphasis added).

The Savior is not comparing the work of John and Peter here. Who knows how important the work of Peter may actually have been?

The Work of John after the Resurrection of Jesus Christ

On the Isle of Patmos there is a church where guides say John the Beloved was buried. They claim that the reason this church was built was that the bones of John the Beloved were discovered there. We as Latter-day Saints know two things about that place—first, we know that it is not where John the Beloved was buried because he has not yet been buried; second, we know his bones were not discovered there because John the Beloved has not yet died.

As far as we know, John was at Ephesus, and it was from there that he was placed in exile. Domitian was the Roman emperor at that time, and he did not like what John was preaching. But rather than cause an insurrection by killing him (or trying to do so), Domitian exiled him to the Isle of Patmos. John did not stay there long, however, because when Domitian died, the next emperor forgave all those who had been placed in exile. As far as we know, John then left and went other places.

According to what we know, John the Revelator is now working among the lost tribes of Israel. I find that rather intriguing. In the 1820s the Three Nephites appeared quite regularly to the Prophet Joseph Smith, but we do not read very much about John the Revelator. He has appeared on occasion but not as frequently as the Three Nephites. For example, John the Revelator appeared with Peter and James to restore the Melchizedek Priesthood. As far as we know, Peter and James were resurrected beings. John was a translated being—he was not resurrected. All three men had physical hands that they placed on top of Joseph Smith's head when they conferred upon him the Melchizedek Priesthood. They also restored blessings in addition to the Melchizedek Priesthood.

In Doctrine and Covenants 128, the Prophet Joseph Smith reviews some of the great events that have happened during this dispensation. Among other things, he writes:

"And again, what do we hear? . . . The voice of Peter, James, and John in the wilderness between Harmony, Susquehanna county, and Colesville, Broome county, on the Susquehanna river, declaring themselves as possessing the keys of the kingdom, and of the dispensation of the fulness of times!" (v. 20).

Although we do not know the exact date of this great appearance, we know that it occurred after May 15, 1829, because John the Baptist declared that he was restoring only the Aaronic Priesthood and that the Melchizedek Priesthood was yet to be restored by Peter, James, and John. We also know that this restoration took place before April 6, 1830, the day the Church was organized. The keys of the kingdom and of the gospel of the dispensation of the fulness of times had to be restored before the Church could be organized. Therefore, during that time period, John visited Joseph Smith and his companions to help restore those keys.

We know of one other appearance of John the Beloved, as recorded in Church records. Joseph Smith was leading the Zion's Camp march. When the men entered

Missouri, Joseph Smith left the company and walked down the road a ways in company with another person and visited for some time with him. When Joseph returned to the company, the other brethren were interested in who this man was. Joseph Smith announced that he had been visiting with John, the beloved apostle.

But Joseph did not see John the Beloved very much, and so he finally went to the Lord and asked why. In response, we have another revelation to the Prophet Joseph Smith indicating that John the Beloved was then among the lost tribes of Israel and that he was working to prepare them to become worthy to return after their long dispersion. Therefore, it has become the accepted doctrine and teaching of the Church that John the Beloved is now with the lost tribes of Israel helping them to prepare to return and to receive their blessings under Ephraim.

Some of the Writings of John

So the record of John—the life record of John—is still an open book. But we do not have all the writings of John. Hundreds of years before John was even born on this earth, the great prophet Nephi saw him in vision. In his vision, Nephi saw the Lamb of God come down to earth, and he saw Twelve Apostles follow the Lamb of God. An angel then said to him:

"Look! And I looked and beheld a man, and he was dressed in a white robe. And the angel said unto me: Behold one of the twelve apostles of the Lamb. Behold, he shall see and write the remainder of these things; yea, and also many things which have been. And he shall also write concerning the end of the world.

"Wherefore, the things which he shall write are just and true; and behold they are written in the book which thou beheld proceeding out of the mouth of the Jew; and at the time they proceeded out of the mouth of the Jew, or, at the time the book proceeded out of the mouth of the Jew, the things which were written were plain and pure, and most precious and easy to the understanding of all men.

"And behold, the things which this apostle of the Lamb shall write are many things which thou hast seen; and behold, the remainder shalt thou see. But the things which thou shalt see hereafter thou shalt not write; for the Lord God hath ordained the apostle of the Lamb of God that he should write them.

"And also others who have been, to them hath he shown all things, and they have written them; and they are sealed up to come forth in their purity, according to the truth which is in the Lamb, in the own due time of the Lord, unto the house of Israel.

"And I, Nephi, heard and bear record, that *the name of the apostle of the Lamb was John,* according to the word of the angel. And behold, I, Nephi, am forbidden that I should write the remainder of the things which I saw and heard; wherefore the things which I have written sufficeth me; and I have written but a small part of the things which I saw" (1 Nephi 14:18–28; emphasis added).

Notice that the angel said to Nephi that he was going to see everything John the Revelator would write down. Nephi wrote only a small part, and yet we have in the writings of Nephi almost as much as we have in the book of Revelation. But some teachers claim that the book of Revelation contains the writings of John referred to in this scripture. Although Revelation may include a greatly abridged version of the writings of John, these are not the writings of John referred to in this scripture, as the Lord himself declared later.

Isn't it interesting that this great apostle, John the Beloved, was seen in vision over 500 years before he was born on this earth and described in the same manner that the Christ himself was described:

"I looked and beheld a man, and he was dressed in a white robe. And the angel said unto me: Behold one of the twelve apostles of the Lamb. . . . And I, Nephi, heard and bear record, that the name of the apostle of the Lamb was John, according to the word of the angel" (1 Nephi 14:19–20, 27).

This means that over five hundred years before John the Beloved was born, he had already been foreordained to write this great record of his that would contain an account of the creation of the world to the end thereof. That's why I say that when we talk about this man we are talking about one of the great ones.

In Doctrine and Covenants 27 the resurrected Jesus Christ, in instituting the sacrament in this dispensation, indicates that when he comes in his power and glory, he is going to partake of the sacrament with certain of the great leaders on this earth, including John, his beloved disciple (v. 12).

In speaking of the resurrection in Doctrine and Covenants 76, the resurrected Christ quotes the words of John. Isn't that interesting? Who knows more about the resurrection than Jesus Christ? And yet when he explains the resurrection to the Prophet Joseph Smith, he uses the words of John the Revelator.

According to its section heading, Doctrine and Covenants 77 is a "revelation given to Joseph Smith the Prophet, at Hiram, Ohio, March 1832." The revelation is an "explanation of the Revelation of St. John" and answers the following questions:

"What is the sea of glass spoken of by John, 4th chapter, and 6th verse of the Revelation?"

"What are we to understand by the four beasts, spoken of in the same verse?"

"Are the four beasts limited to individual beasts, or do they represent classes or orders?"

"What are we to understand by the eyes and wings, which the beasts had?"

Latter-day Saints not only know more about John the Beloved than any other people, but we know more about his writing. We can take all the Bible commentaries concerning the writings of John the Beloved in the book of Revelation and throw them out the window, for we have the Doctrine and Covenants and the Book of Mormon, which contain inspired commentary as to what John was really teaching.

The Savior tells us about the great writings of John in these words: "And John saw and bore record of the fulness of my glory, and the fulness of John's record is hereafter to be revealed. [Jesus Christ is speaking May 6, 1833.] And he bore record, saying: I saw his glory, that he was in the beginning, before the world was; therefore, in the beginning the Word was, for he was the Word, even the messenger of salvation—The light and the Redeemer of the world; the Spirit of truth, who came into the world, because the world was made by him, and in him was the life of men and the light of the world and the light of men. The worlds were made by him; men were made by him; all things were made by him, and through him, and of him. And I, John, bear record that I beheld his glory, as the glory of the Only Begotten of the Father, full of grace and truth" (D&C 93:2–11).

John then bears testimony that the Savior progressed from "grace to grace" (D&C 93:13) until "he received a fulness of the glory of the Father" (D&C 93:16). After the Savior concludes quoting John to the Prophet Joseph Smith, he adds, "And it shall come to pass, that if you are faithful you shall receive the fulness of the record of John" (D&C 93:18).

We do not have yet in the scriptures of the Church the fulness of the records of John. Nephi saw that many of the writings of John were going to be taken away—the plain and precious things (probably much of what we now have in Doctrine and Covenants 77) that must at one time have been in the New Testament. But they were taken out when they proceeded through the hands of the great and abominable church referred to in the record.

The great prophet Ether had at his disposal the long history of his people, and he had an account of the great vision of the brother of Jared. In Ether we read something about that vision when the Savior says:

"Come unto me, O ye house of Israel, and it shall be made manifest unto you how great things the Father hath laid up for you, from the foundation of the world; and it hath not come unto you, because of unbelief.

"Behold, when ye shall rend that veil of unbelief which doth cause you to remain in your awful state of wickedness, and hardness of heart, and blindness of mind, then shall the great and marvelous things which have been hid up from the foundation of the world from you—yea, when ye shall call upon the Father in my name, with a broken heart and a contrite spirit, then shall ye know that the Father hath remembered the covenant which he made unto your fathers, O house of Israel.

"And then shall my revelations which I have caused to be written by my servant John be unfolded in the eyes of all the people. Remember, when ye see these things, ye shall know that the time is at hand that they shall be made manifest in very deed. Therefore, when ye shall receive this record ye may know that the work of the Father has commenced upon all the face of the land.

"Therefore, repent all ye ends of the earth, and come unto me, and believe in my gospel, and be baptized in my name; for he that believeth and is baptized shall be saved; but he that believeth not shall be damned; and signs shall follow them that believe in my name.

"And blessed is he that is found faithful unto my name at the last day, for he shall be lifted up to dwell in the kingdom prepared for him from the foundation of the world. And behold it is I that hath spoken it. Amen" (Ether 4:14–19).

If we relate that scripture to Doctrine and Covenants 93 and to 1 Nephi 14, we see that the great apostle John the Beloved, also known as John the Revelator because of the great revelation he had on the Isle of Patmos, wrote a record of the history of this earth from before the creation of the earth to the very end thereof. That record is written but is yet to come forth.

John's Mission Still Being Performed

We are not sure exactly how long John lived on the Isle of Patmos. But while he was there, he saw the vision that he recorded in the book of Revelation. I have always been intrigued by the promise that was made to John: "The Lord said unto me: Verily, verily, I say unto thee, because thou desirest this thou shalt tarry until I come in my glory, and shalt prophesy before nations, kindreds, tongues and people" (D&C 7:3).

Because of the great vision John the Revelator had on the Isle of Patmos, he has been selected as a unique representative of Christ on this earth and undoubtedly has been or will be called to represent him before nations, kindreds, tongues, and people, as was prophesied.

I guess Latter-day Saints know more about translated beings than anyone else.

There is one power or gift that translated beings have that we should not overlook. People often refer to the apostasy of the priesthood on the earth, but there has never been an apostasy of the priesthood on the earth. There has never been a single instance in the history of this earth since the fall of Adam to our day that the priesthood power has not been here on the earth. We can trace the priesthood from Adam to the time of Christ, and we as Latter-day Saints can trace it from the time of Christ to our day because of John the Beloved. There was an apostasy of the Church and there was a great apostasy from the Church, but there has never been an apostasy of the priesthood because of the power and authority held by John. I hope that some day in the Church we might have a special *Ensign* devoted to this man. I think his teachings best exemplify the teachings of Christ. Perhaps that is why the Savior referred to him as his beloved—the Savior loved him, and he loved the Savior.

SOME OF THE TEACHINGS OF JOHN THE BELOVED

I end this chapter with some selected readings from the writings of this great man:

"That which was from the beginning, which we have heard, which we have seen with our eyes, which we have looked upon, and our hands have handled, of the Word of life; . . . That which we have seen and heard declare we unto you, that ye also may have fellowship with us: and truly our fellowship is with the Father, and with his Son Jesus Christ. And these things write we unto you, that your joy may be full" (1 John 1:1, 3–4).

"My little children, these things write I unto you, that ye sin not. And if any man sin, we have an advocate with the Father, Jesus Christ the righteous: And he is the propitiation for our sins: and not for ours only, but also for the sins of the whole world.

"And hereby we do know that we know him, if we keep his commandments. He that saith, I know him, and keepeth not his commandments, is a liar, and the truth is not in him. But whoso keepeth his word, in him verily is the love of God perfected: hereby know we that we are in him. He that saith he abideth in him ought himself also so to walk, even as he walked.

"Brethren, I write no new commandment unto you, but an old commandment which ye had from the beginning. The old commandment is the word which ye have heard from the beginning. . . .

"And now, little children, abide in him; that, when he shall appear, we may have confidence, and not be ashamed before him at his coming. If ye know that he is righteous, ye know that every one that doeth righteousness is born of him" (1 John 2:1–7, 28–29).

"Behold, what manner of love the Father hath bestowed upon us, that we should be called the sons of God: therefore the world knoweth us not, because it knew him not.

"Beloved, now are we the sons of God, and it doth not yet appear what we shall be: but we know that, when he shall appear, we shall be like him; for we shall see him as he is. And every man that hath this hope in him purifieth himself, even as he is pure. . . .

"Hereby perceive we the love of God, because he laid down his life for us: and we ought to lay down our lives for the brethren. But whoso hath this world's good, and seeth his brother have need, and shutteth up his bowels of compassion from him, how dwelleth the love of God in him?" (1 John 3:1–3, 16–17).

"Beloved, let us love one another: for love is of God; and every one that loveth is born of God, and knoweth God. He that loveth not knoweth not God; for God is love. In this was manifested the love of God toward us, because that God sent his only begotten Son into the world, that we might live through him. Herein is love, not that we loved God, but that he loved us, and sent his Son to be the propitiation for our sins. Beloved, if God so loved us, we ought also to love one another. . . . If a man say, I love God, and hateth his brother, he is a liar: for he that loveth not his brother whom he hath seen, how can he love God whom he hath not seen? And this commandment have we from him, That he who loveth God love his brother also" (1 John 4:7–11, 20–21).

"These things have I written unto you that believe on the name of the Son of God; that ye may know that ye have eternal life, and that ye may believe on the name of the Son of God.

"And this is the confidence that we have in him, that, if we ask any thing according to his will, he heareth us: And if we know that he hear us, whatsoever we ask, we know that we have the petitions that we desired of him. . . .

"And we know that the Son of God is come, and hath given us an understanding, that we may know him that is true, and we are in him that is true, even in his Son Jesus Christ. This is the true God, and eternal life" (1 John 5:13–15, 20).

"Whosoever transgresseth, and abideth not in the doctrine of Christ, hath not God. He that abideth in the doctrine of Christ, he hath both the Father and the Son. If there come any unto you, and bring not this doctrine, receive him not into your house, neither bid him God speed: For he that biddeth him God speed is partaker of his evil deeds" (2 John 1:9–11).

"I have no greater joy than to hear that my children walk in truth" (3 John 1:4).

The ancient apostle John the Beloved referred to all the Saints as his "beloved children." I think if he were here today he would again refer to us as his beloved children, and that he would "have no greater joy than to hear that [his] children walk in truth."

Note

Excerpts from a talk prepared for a Mediterranean cruise sponsored by the BYU Travel Study department in the latter part of the 1970s.

Chapter 34

PAUL—THE MAN AND THE MESSAGE

I introduce this chapter by briefly discussing a subject *on* which I know very little, but *in* which I have a great deal of interest: laser beams. Perhaps one reason I am so interested in laser beams is that this whole field of science has been developed in my lifetime. In fact, the first laser was built in 1960, and since then I have read of many remarkable things that can be done with lasers.

Lasers have revolutionized several fields of science and medicine. They are used to "spot weld" detached or torn retinas, to excise malignant tumors, to cut through thick steel beams at the rate of fifteen inches per minute, to drill holes in ruby watch jewels, to resize holes in worn wire-drawing diamond dies, and to determine long distances accurately (for example, measurements of the earth-moon separation have been made to an accuracy of six inches). Lasers may prove to be useful in predicting earthquakes, since a change in earth surface strain as small as one part in ten billion can now be detected.

In communications, high frequency light waves from lasers provide one hundred thousand times the bandwidth that is present in the microwave frequency range. In the military, ruby-laser tank range finders are operational, and "smart bombs" have been developed that direct a laser infrared beam at targets, allowing bombs with infrared sensors to home in on the reflected infrared light. Research is being done secretly on the ability of high-powered continuous-wave lasers to disable aircraft or missiles in mid-flight.

What enables the laser to perform these feats? In simple language, the laser changes incoherent light into coherent light.

In preparation for this brief reference on laser beams, I reviewed an eight-page article in the *Encyclopedia Americana* and a three-page article in the *Encyclopedia Britannica*. From these readings, I offer two abridged statements:

"The word LASER is an acronym derived from *l*ight *a*mplification by *s*timulated *e*mission of *r*adiation. A LASER is a device that produces an intense beam of light of a very pure single color. This light beam may be intense enough to vaporize the hardest and most heat-resistant materials."[1]

"*Fundamental principles:* Atoms and molecules exist at low and high energy levels. Those at low levels can be excited to higher levels, usually by heat, and after reaching the higher levels they give off light when they return to a lower level. In ordinary light sources the many excited atoms or molecules emit light independently and in many different colors (wavelengths). If, however, during the brief instant that an atom is excited, light of a certain wavelength impinges on it, the atom can be stimulated to emit radiation that is in phase (in step) with the wave that stimulated it. The new emission thus augments or amplifies the passing wave; if the phenomenon can be multiplied sufficiently, the resulting beam, made up of wholly coherent light (i.e., light of a single frequency or color in which all the components are in step with each other) will be tremendously powerful."[2]

POSSIBLE APPLICATIONS OF "LASER BEAM" PRINCIPLES IN TEACHING

I am convinced that there is strength and power in the unity of teaching and living spiritual truths, just as there is strength and power in the unity or coherence of physical light. Isn't faith, in a sense, the concentration of one's spiritual power into a coherent whole? The Savior said: "If ye have faith as a grain of mustard seed, ye shall say unto this mountain, Remove hence to yonder place; and it shall remove; and nothing shall be impossible unto you" (Matthew 17:20).

Moroni quoted Christ as follows: "If ye will have faith in me ye shall have power to do whatsoever thing is expedient in me" (Moroni 7:33).

Also, isn't faith an exercise of the spirit, and hasn't the word *light* been used by the Lord to define both *Spirit* and *truth*?

Notice these teachings of the Lord:

"And I now give unto you a commandment to beware concerning yourselves, to give diligent heed to the words of eternal life. For you shall live by every word that proceedeth forth from the mouth of God. For the word of the Lord is truth, and whatsoever is truth is light, and whatsoever is light is Spirit, even the Spirit of Jesus

Christ. And the Spirit giveth light to every man that cometh into the world; and the Spirit enlighteneth every man through the world, that hearkeneth to the voice of the Spirit. And every one that hearkeneth to the voice of the Spirit cometh unto God, even the Father" (D&C 84:43–47).

"The Spirit may be given to every man to profit withal" (D&C 46:16).

"The holy scriptures are given of me for your instruction; and the power of my Spirit quickeneth all things" (D&C 33:16).

"And again, the . . . teachers of this church shall teach the principles of my gospel . . . as they shall be directed by the Spirit. And the Spirit shall be given unto you by the prayer of faith; and if ye receive not the Spirit ye shall not teach. And all this ye shall observe to do as I have commanded concerning your teaching, until the fulness of my scriptures is given" (D&C 42:12–15).

Concerning this subject, Paul has testified: "And my speech and my preaching was not with enticing *[persuasive]* words of man's wisdom, but in demonstration of the Spirit and of power" (1 Corinthians 2:4).

This power principle concerning spiritual matters is similar to the "laser beam" principle with physical matter: we should concentrate all our efforts to be one with God's Spirit—or to obtain the companionship of God's Spirit. Then all things will be possible to us.

We need to obtain the Spirit in order to teach by the power of the Spirit; we need to teach by the power of the Spirit in order for our children and our students to learn by that same power. I am convinced that the light of Christ in each of us can be reflected in the hearts and minds of those we teach.

Now let's read from the scriptures a few references that might indicate another "homing" technique used by God in the realm of the Spirit:

"For behold, my brethren, it is given unto you to judge, that ye may know good from evil; and the way to judge is as plain, that ye may know with a perfect knowledge, as the daylight is from the dark night. For behold, the Spirit of Christ is given to every man, that he may know good from evil; wherefore, I show unto you the way to judge; for every thing which inviteth to do good, and to persuade to believe in Christ, is sent forth by the power and gift of Christ; wherefore ye may know with a perfect knowledge it is of God. . . . And now, my brethren, seeing that ye know the light by which ye may judge, which light is the light of Christ, see that ye do not judge wrongfully; for with that same judgment which ye judge ye shall also be judged" (Mormon, in Moroni 7:15–16, 18).

The Lord obviously knows much more about light—including physical light—and how to use it than we know. Note for example the following wording from the account of Joseph Smith concerning the first visit of the angel Moroni: "Not only was his robe exceedingly white, but his whole person was glorious beyond description, and his countenance truly like lightning. The room was exceedingly light, but not so very bright as immediately around his person. When I first looked upon him, I was afraid; but the fear soon left me. . . .

"While he was conversing with me about the plates, the vision was opened to my mind that I could see the place where the plates were deposited, and that so clearly and distinctly that I knew the place again when I visited it.

"After this communication, I saw the light in the room begin to gather immediately around the person of him who had been speaking to me, and it continued to do so until the room was again left dark, except just around him; when, instantly I saw, as it were, a conduit open right up into heaven, and he ascended till he entirely disappeared, and the room was left as it had been before this heavenly light had made its appearance" (Joseph Smith—History 1:32, 42–43).

Use of One "Laser Beam" Principle with Israel Tour Groups

I now relate that principle to the ending of a trip I took to Israel, where I directed two consecutive tours. Upon completion of the tours, we made our way to the airport early one morning so that we could be there by 5 A.M. to get through strict Israeli security, obtain boarding passes, and go through passport control.

As we traveled from Jerusalem to the International Airport at Tel Aviv in the darkness of 4 A.M., I sat in the guide seat at the front of the bus, and over the microphone I invited the tour members to review with me *in their minds* with a concentration of thought some of the major places we had visited in Israel during the previous ten days. I then said—with a substantial pause between each item—such words or terms as: *Sea of Galilee, Capernaum, Mount of Beatitudes, Lazarus' tomb in Bethany, Shepherds' Field in Bethlehem, room of the Last Supper, Garden of Gethsemane,* and *Garden Tomb.* I could almost feel the spirit and strength of our collective coherent thoughts as we concentrated and pondered over our experiences in these various places. Because of the freshness of our visits there, I felt confident that we all visualized essentially the same thing as we remembered these places.

I would never have engaged in that activity with that group of tour members just a few weeks earlier. I am confident our thoughts would not have been coherent if I had said the word "Bethlehem" fourteen days earlier; the particular vision of each group member would have varied greatly from the image of the other members. There is power in "thinking together" on a particular subject.

Paul, the Man

Now, as you read this chapter, think deeply about the topic. As you read the words *Paul, the man,* what impressions come to your mind?

Individual impressions vary widely. Undoubtedly, when you think of a "man" you think of various characteristics and attributes, such as height, weight, color of hair and eyes, manner of speech, personal traits such as strength, kindness, and so on. Do you think of Paul as being tall, or short, or about average? Did he have brown hair? Or was it black, blond, or red? Was he dark complexioned or fair? Did he have a deep resonant voice—or more of a shrill whine? Do you think of Paul as being a fanatic, a religious zealot, or a devoted and dedicated servant?

Let's review what we can learn from the scriptures and the teachings of the prophets concerning "Paul—The Man and the Message." The Prophet Joseph Smith gave the following description of the Apostle Paul on January 5, 1841, at the organization of a school of instruction: "He is about five feet high; very dark hair; dark complexion; dark skin; large Roman nose; sharp face; small black eyes, penetrating as eternity; round shoulders; a whining voice, except when elevated, and then it almost resembled the roaring of a lion. He was a good orator, active and diligent, always employing himself in doing good to his fellow man."[3]

Do you now have a different image of "Paul, the man" than you had only a few minutes earlier? What else do we know of the Apostle Paul?

In addition to giving us the above description of Paul, Joseph Smith has listed some of Paul's characteristics and attributes as follows: "Though he once, according to his own word, persecuted the Church of God and wasted it, yet after embracing the faith, his labors were unceasing to spread the glorious news: and like a faithful soldier, when called to give his life in the cause which he had espoused, he laid it down, as he says, with an assurance of an eternal crown. Follow the labors of this Apostle from the time of his conversion to the time of his death, and you will have a fair sample of industry and patience in promulgating the Gospel of Christ. Derided, whipped, and stoned, the moment he escaped the hands of his persecutors he as zealously as ever proclaimed the doctrine of the Savior. And all may know that he did not embrace the faith for honor in this life, nor for the gain of earthly goods. What, then, could have induced him to undergo all this toil? It was, as he said, that he might obtain the crown of righteousness from the hand of God. No one, we presume, will doubt the faithfulness of Paul to the end. None will say that he did not keep the faith, that he did not fight the good fight, that he did not preach and persuade to the last."[4]

Most of the information we have of Paul comes from the New Testament, although he is mentioned also in the Doctrine and Covenants (18:9; 76:99; 127:2; 128:13, 15–16.) Note the following information as provided in the Bible Dictionary of the LDS edition of the Bible under the title "Paul": "He was known in early life as Saul; his Latin name Paul is first mentioned at the beginning of his gentile ministry (Acts 13:9). He belonged to Tarsus, in Cilicia (Acts 9:11); was a Pharisee and a pupil of Gamaliel (Acts 22:3); was active in the persecution of Christians (Acts 8:3; 26:10; Gal. 1:13; Philip. 3:6); and took part in the martyrdom of Stephen (Acts 7:58; 8:1). He started for Damascus for the purpose of further persecution (Acts 9:1) and on the road saw a vision of the Lord Jesus, which changed the whole current of his life (Acts 9:4–19; 22:7; 26:14; Gal. 1:15–16). After his baptism by Ananias (Acts 9:18), he retired into Arabia (Gal. 1:17), and then returned to Damascus, where he preached (Acts 9:19–25; 2 Cor. 11:32; Gal. 1:17–18). Being compelled to flee, about three years after his conversion he went to Jerusalem, where he stayed 15 days, Barnabas introducing him to Peter and James (Acts 9:26–30; Gal. 1:18–19). Being in danger, he retired to Tarsus (Acts 9:29–30) and there remained six or seven years, preaching in Syria and Cilicia (Gal. 1:21–24). He was then brought by Barnabas to Antioch (Acts 11:26), and after one year paid a visit to Jerusalem (Acts 11:29–30). After two more years' work in Antioch, he started with Barnabas and Mark on his first missionary journey (Acts 13:1–14:26). Then came another visit to Jerusalem with Barnabas to attend a conference with the other apostles (Acts 15:1–33; Gal. 2:1–10), after which they returned to Antioch (Acts 15:35). He then started on his second missionary journey (Acts 15:36–18:22), which lasted about three years, and ended with a visit to Jerusalem. After a short stay in Antioch, Paul began his third journey, which occupied about 3 1/2 years (Acts 18:23–21:15). On his return to Jerusalem he was arrested and sent to Caesarea (Acts 21:17–23:35), where he remained a prisoner for two years (Acts 24:1–26:32), and was then sent for trial to Rome, suffering shipwreck on the way (Acts 27:1–28:10). He remained in Rome two years (Acts 28:30) and was then released. He then appears to have visited Asia, Macedonia, Crete, and perhaps Spain. At the end of about four years he was again taken a prisoner to Rome, and suffered martyrdom, probably in the spring of A.D. 65."[5]

Reviewing the Bible Dictionary Entry "Paul" Sentence by Sentence

When you begin teaching about Paul either in class or at home, have your students or children review the article from the Bible Dictionary under the title "Paul." It then becomes "their" resource! Then you might want to provide additional background on each of the fifteen sentences of the article that are quoted here. Let's try this, sentence by sentence. (Note: The following key applies to these examples: BD=Bible Dictionary; GAZ=Gazetteer; LTJA=*The Life and Teachings of Jesus and His Apostles;* NTSTO=*New Testament Seminary Teacher Outline.*)

1. *"He was known in early life as Saul; his Latin name Paul is first mentioned at the beginning of his gentile ministry (Acts 13:9)."*

"Saul"
BD, "Saul," 769.
LTJA, "Who Was Saul?" 245–46.
NTSTO, "Saul's Conversion," 267–68.

"Paul"
BD, "Paul," 742–43.
LTJA, "Biography of Paul," 238–39, with a note indicating that additional biographical material on Paul is included in other sections.
NTSTO, "Paul's Preparation," 269.

2. *"He belonged to Tarsus, in Cilicia (Acts 9:11); was a Pharisee and a pupil of Gamaliel (Acts 22:3); was active in the persecution of Christians (Acts 8:3; 26:10; Gal. 1:13; Philip. 3:6); and took part in the martyrdom of Stephen (Acts 7:58; 8:1)."*

"Tarsus"
BD, 780. "Capital of Cilicia, Paul's city. . . . It was a place of considerable importance (Paul calls it 'no mean city'), containing a university celebrated for its school of philosophy and literature. It was situated on an important highway leading from Antioch . . . toward the cities of the Roman province of Asia."
GAZ, 825, on eight maps.

"Pharisees"
BD, 750. "A religious party among the Jews. The name denotes separatists. They prided themselves on their strict observance of the law, and on the care with which they avoided contact with things gentile. Their belief included the doctrine of immortality and resurrection of the body and the existence of angels and spirits.

They upheld the authority of oral tradition as of equal value with the written law. The tendency of their teaching was to reduce religion to the observance of a multiplicity of ceremonial rules, and to encourage self-sufficiency and spiritual pride."

"Gamaliel"

BD, 677. "A Pharisee, a doctor of the law, held in honor with all the people (Acts 5:34). He was a celebrated Jewish teacher who belonged to the more liberal school. His influence carried great weight in the Sanhedrin (Acts 5:35–40)."

"Stephen"

BD, 777. "One of the seven, 'a man full of faith and of the Holy Spirit' (Acts 6:5); . . . [he] proclaimed that the law of Moses was fulfilled in Christ and ought not to be continued in the Church. In this thing he foreshadowed the great work of Paul. . . . Paul was present when this speech was made [Stephen's speech before the Sanhedrin] (Acts 8:1; 22:20), and was probably influenced by it, though at the moment he was a consenting party to his death. A few years later he went on with the work that Stephen had introduced to him."

3. *"He started for Damascus for the purpose of further persecution (Acts 9:1) and on the road saw a vision of the Lord Jesus, which changed the whole current of his life (Acts 9:4–19; 22:7; 26:14; Gal. 1:15–16.)"*

"Damascus"

BD, 652. "An ancient city of Syria. . . . In New Testament times it was . . . part of the dominions of Aretas, an Arabian prince subject to the Roman emperor."

GAZ, 819, on fifteen maps.

LTJA, 257–58, "What Was the Importance of Damascus?"

"Paul's Vision"

LTJA, 258, "What Are Two Important Lessons We Can Learn from the Accounts of Paul's Conversion?"

LTJA, 258, "It Is Hard for Thee to Kick Against the Pricks."

LTJA, 258, "What Blinded Saul on the Road to Damascus?"

LTJA, 258, "Why Was It Necessary for Paul, Who Saw a Vision, to Submit to Baptism?"

LTJA, 259, "What New Problems Did Paul Face Following the Conversation?"

4. *"After his baptism by Ananias (Acts 9:18), he retired into Arabia (Gal. 1:17), and then returned to Damascus, where he preached (Acts 9:19–25; 2 Cor. 11: 32; Gal. 1:17–18)."*

"Ananias"
BD, 608 (three different ones). "(2) A Christian disciple at Damascus who baptized Paul (Acts 9:10–18; 22:12)."

"Arabia"
BD, 612 (including help on "Arabians").
GAZ, 817, on three maps.

5. *"Being compelled to flee, about three years after his conversion he went to Jerusalem, where he stayed 15 days, Barnabas introducing him to Peter and James (Acts 9:26–30; Gal. 1:18–19)."*

"Jerusalem"
BD, 712. "Formerly Salem (Gen. 14:18; Ps. 76:2), a Jebusite city until it was captured by David (2 Sam. 5:6ff.)."
GAZ, 822, on twenty maps.

"Barnabas"
BD, 619. "*Son of consolation.* A name given to Joseph, a Levite of Cyprus, who sold his possessions and gave the proceeds to the apostles (Acts 4:36–37); was of service to Saul after his conversion (9:27); was sent by the apostles to Antioch, where he worked with Saul (11:22–30; 12:25); with Paul on missionary journey (chs. 13–14); and at Jerusalem, (ch. 15); they parted (15:39). . . . Though not one of the twelve, he was regarded as an apostle (Acts 14:4, 14)."
LTJA, "Who Was Barnabas?" 259.

"Peter"
BD, 749. "*Rock.* Brother of Andrew (John 1:40) son of Jonah (Matt. 16:17); also known as Simeon (Acts 15:14; 2 Pet. 1:1) or Simon; . . . Peter was one of the greatest of men. . . . Peter was the chief apostle of his day. . . . In the latter days Peter, with James and John, came from heaven and literally conferred the Melchizedek Priesthood and the keys thereof upon Joseph Smith and Oliver Cowdery."

"James"
BD, 709. "An English form of the Hebrew name Jacob. . . . (1) Son of Zebedee. . . . He was beheaded by Herod (Acts 12:2)."

6. *"Being in danger, he retired to Tarsus (Acts 9:29–30) and there remained six or seven years, preaching in Syria and Cilicia (Gal. 1:21–24)."*

"Syria"
BD, 778. "Originally known as Aram (or 'the highlands'), a general name for the country north and northeast of Palestine."
GAZ, 825, on twelve maps.

7. *"He was then brought by Barnabas to Antioch (Acts 11:26), and after one year paid a visit to Jerusalem (Acts 11:29–30)."*

"Antioch"

BD, 609. "In New Testament times the third city in the Roman Empire. It was the chief meeting point of East and West. . . . During Paul's life it was a center of gentile Christianity (Acts 6:5; 11:19–30; 13:1; 14:26; 15:22–35; 18:22; Gal. 2:11)."

GAZ, 817, on six maps.

8. *"After two more years' work in Antioch, he started with Barnabas and Mark on his first missionary journey (Acts 13:1—14:26)."*

"Mark"

BD, 728. "Also called John; son of Mary, who had a house of considerable size in Jerusalem (Acts 12:12); cousin (or nephew) of Barnabas (Col. 4:10); accompanied Paul and Barnabas from Jerusalem (Acts 12:25). . . . Tradition states that after Peter's death, Mark visited Egypt, founded the Church of Alexandria, and died by martyrdom."

LTJA, "Who Was John Mark?" 253.

"Paul's First Missionary Journey"

GAZ, map 19.

LTJA, "What Is the Primary Significance of Paul's First Missionary Journey?" 263.

"Paul the Missionary," 270–71.

NTSTO, "Paul's First Missionary Journey," 271.

9. *"Then came another visit to Jerusalem with Barnabas to attend a conference with the other apostles (Acts 15:1–33; Gal. 2:1–20), after which they returned to Antioch (Acts 15:35)."*

BD. All the major terms have already been examined in the first eight sentences.

10. *"He then started on his second missionary journey (Acts 15:36–18:22), which lasted about three years, and ended with a visit to Jerusalem."*

"Paul's Second Missionary Journey"

GAZ, 20.

LTJA, "What Are the Significant Elements of Paul's Second Missionary Journey?" 265.

NTSTO, "Paul's Second Missionary Journey," 273–74.

11. *"After a short stay in Antioch, Paul began his third journey, which occupied about 3 1/2 years (Acts 18:23—21:15)."*

"Paul's Third Missionary Journey"
GAZ, map 21.
LTJA, "Background to Paul's Third Missionary Journey," 281.
NTSTO, "Paul's Third Missionary Journey," 277–78.

12. *"On his return to Jerusalem he was arrested and sent to Caesarea (Acts 21:17–23:35), where he remained a prisoner for two years (Acts 24:1–26:32), and was then sent for trial to Rome, suffering shipwreck on the way (Acts 27:1–28:10)."*

"Caesarea"
BD, 628. "An important seaport town of Palestine, on the main road from Tyre to Egypt. . . . The official residence of Festus, Felix, and other Roman procurators of Judaea (Acts 23:23, 33; 25:1–13)." Philip, Cornelius, and Herod Agrippa all taught, lived, or died here. "Caesarea is also frequently mentioned in connection with Paul's journeys (Acts 9:30; 18:22; 21:8, 16; 23:23, 33; 25:1, 4, 6, 13)."

GAZ, 819, on nine maps.

"Rome"
BD, 764. The capital of the ancient world. See "Roman Empire."
GAZ, 824, "Rome," on two maps.
"Paul's Journey to Rome," map 22.
NTSTO, "Paul's Imprisonment and Defense," 279–80. "A Shipwrecked Journey to Rome," 283–84.

13. *"He remained in Rome two years (Acts 28:30) and was then released."*

14. *"He then appears to have visited Asia, Macedonia, Crete, and perhaps Spain."*

"Asia"
BD, 615. In the New Testament, Asia "denotes the Roman province that included the western parts of what is now called Asia Minor, . . . Ephesus being the capital."

GAZ, 818, under "Asia, Roman province," on four maps.

"Macedonia"
BD, 727. "South of what are now called the Balkan Mountains . . . a Roman Province under the government of a proconsul, who lived at Thessalonica."

GAZ, 823, on five maps.

"Crete"
BD, 651.
GAZ, 819, and on seven maps.

"Spain"
Paul's reference to a possible visit to Spain is in Romans 15:24.

15. *At the end of about four years he was again taken a prisoner to Rome, and suffered martyrdom, probably in the spring of* A.D. *65.*

Paul, the Message

Paul's teachings in his various epistles span the whole range of beliefs, doctrines, practices, and principles of organization needed by new members of new branches of the Church widely scattered from each other. How can one major message be selected and separated from all the others?

I decided to make this selection initially by participating in a word association activity with myself (noting the first thing that came to mind when I thought of a certain word or phrase). I then thought: "The major message of Paul."

The responding thought was strikingly clear and definite: "Jesus Christ is the Son of God."

After a few minutes, I repeated the activity. My mental response was a reinforcement and expansion of my first thought: "Jesus Christ is the Son of God, the long-awaited message of Jewish hope and expectation."

I then quickly read through the epistles of Paul, and this major message seemed to leap out from almost every page. In fact, in twelve of Paul's fourteen epistles, he declares within the first three verses of each epistle that Jesus Christ is the Son of God! I list only a few examples of Paul's teachings here:

Jesus Christ Is the Messiah

Paul introduced himself in the first verse of his first epistle as contained in our present New Testament as follows: "Paul, a servant of Jesus Christ, called to be an apostle, separated unto the gospel of God, (Which he had promised afore by his prophets in the holy scriptures,) Concerning his Son Jesus Christ our Lord, which was made of the seed of David according to the flesh; And declared to be the Son of God with power, according to the spirit of holiness, by the resurrection from the dead: . . .

"For I am not ashamed of the gospel of Christ: for it is the power of God unto salvation to every one that believeth; to the Jew first, and also to the Greek" (Romans 1:1–4, 16).

Also, in the beginning of his letter to the Colossians, Paul identified Jesus Christ as the Son of God and then stated: "In whom we have redemption through his blood, even the forgiveness of sins: Who is the image of the invisible God, the firstborn of every creature: For by him were all things created, that are in heaven, and that are in earth, visible and invisible, whether they be thrones, or dominions, or principalities, or powers: all things were created by him, and for him: And he is before all things, and by him all things consist" (Colossians 1:14–17).

The Resurrection of Jesus Christ—and of All of Us

In compiling a list of Paul's quotations on Jesus Christ as the Messiah, I became aware of the frequency of another teaching of Paul: Just as Jesus Christ was resurrected from the dead, so will all of us be resurrected. Space will permit only a few of Paul's statements on this subject:

Paul taught concerning the resurrection (and thus of the proof of the divinity of Jesus Christ):

"Christ died for our sins . . . he was buried, and . . . rose again the third day . . . he was seen of Cephas [Peter], then of the twelve. After that . . . of above five hundred at once . . . of James: then of all the apostles. And last of all *he was seen of me also.* . . .

"If Christ be not raised, your faith is vain; ye are yet in your sins. . . . If in this life only we have hope in Christ, we are of all men most miserable [Greek: to be pitied]. But now is Christ risen from the dead, and become the firstfruits of them that slept.

"For since by man came death, by man came also the resurrection of the dead. For as in Adam all die, even so in Christ shall all be made alive" (1 Corinthians 15:3–8, 17, 19–22).

Paul also wrote to the Hebrews concerning the universal nature of Christ's resurrection:

"But we see Jesus . . . that he by the grace of God should taste death for every man. For it became him, for whom are all things, and by whom are all things, in bringing many sons unto glory, to make the captain of their salvation perfect through sufferings. For both he that sanctifieth and they who are sanctified are all of one: for which cause he is not ashamed to call them brethren, . . .

"Forasmuch then as the children are partakers of flesh and blood, he also himself likewise took part of the same; that through death he might destroy him that had the power of death, that is, the devil; And deliver them who through fear of death were all their lifetime subject to bondage" (Hebrews 2:9–11, 14–15).

"Christ died for us" (Romans 5:8).

"For since by man came death, by man came also the resurrection of the dead.

For as in Adam all die, even so in Christ shall all be made alive" (1 Corinthians 15:21–22).

It soon became evident to me why Paul emphasized that "Jesus Christ is the Son of God, the Messiah" and that "Jesus Christ was resurrected from the dead, and that we will all be resurrected." The second topic or message establishes and reinforces the first:

1. *"The resurrection of Jesus Christ is proof that he is the Son of God, that he is the Messiah."*

2. *"The fact that we will all be resurrected from the dead proves that we can follow Jesus Christ in all things, and can become even as he is."*

Before reviewing some of the other major teachings of the Apostle Paul, let me digress long enough to share some ideas I discovered while researching another topic.

The "Grandest Principle" of the Gospel

In *The Contributor* magazine for August 1895, I found a letter prepared by the editors of a ward newspaper. In this letter the editors invited readers to respond to the following question: "What, in your opinion, constitutes the greatest principle, or the most attractive feature of the Gospel?" The responses included the following:

S. W. Jenkinson thought that the grandest principle was the principle of progression: "For what are we striving but eternal life, and what is eternal life but eternal progression? . . . Is not progression the underlying principle of all?"

Joseph F. Smith responded: "The principle of exaltation to a fullness of power and glory in the presence of God. This may constitute the most attractive feature to all such as desire through obedience, humility and righteousness to fulfill their high and glorious destiny."

B. H. Roberts suggested: "The grandest principle of the Gospel, its most attractive feature, is that which teaches that man may become like God. It is the sun into which the scattered rays of the Gospel meet. . . . Hence it is an idea that we may say is the parent of all the virtues."

Orson F. Whitney added: "Eternal progress is to me the grandest doctrine of Mormonism."

Thomas Hull, after listing most of the teachings of the gospel, concluded: "I cannot and dare not particularize, but can simply exclaim, 'how glorious is the work, and how boundless the love of our God!'"[6]

A Possible List of the "Ten Grandest Principles of the Gospel"

I was so impressed with the ideas from this article that I decided to prepare my own list of "ten grandest principles of the gospel." After I list my ten principles, I will tie them in to "Paul, the Message."

1. The characteristics, attributes, personality traits, and relationship of God the Father and Jesus Christ, the Son.

2. The relationship of the Father and the Son to man; the literal fatherhood of God and, thus, the brotherhood and sisterhood of us all; Jesus Christ as the Savior and Redeemer of all mankind.

3. The reality of both a pre-earthly and a postmortal existence, including the resurrection of all mankind and the different degrees of glory.

4. The potential destiny of man—the plan of eternal progression, including eternal marriage and the possibility of eventual godhood or eternal life.

5. The basic principles and ordinances of the gospel of Jesus Christ, including the basic eternal laws upon which they are based: justice, mercy, and so on.

6. The necessity of an organization for carrying out the gospel—the kingdom of God in heaven and on earth; the importance of unity among the members of this organization.

7. The relationship of laws to blessings and righteousness (and to sin and punishment); the nature of an "opposition in all things."

8. The eternal and universal nature of the gospel—for all who have lived, now live, or will live upon the earth; missionary work necessary to spread the gospel; apostasy to be avoided; restoration may be necessary.

9. The vital necessity of agency; the importance of total devotion to the things we know to be true and choose to follow, and to testifying of them.

10. Love, charity, and the pure love of Christ—the importance of exemplifying these traits.

Paul's Contributions to the "Grandest Principles"

Now let us consider some of Paul's contributions to each of these areas:

1. *The characteristics, attributes, personality traits, and relationship of God the Father and Jesus Christ, the Son.*

Paul clearly taught that the Father and the Son are separate from each other: "God, who at sundry times and in divers manners spake in time past unto the fathers by the prophets, Hath in these last days spoken unto us by his Son, whom he hath appointed heir of all things, by whom also he made the worlds; Who being the brightness of his glory, and the express image of his person, and upholding all things by the word of his power, when he had by himself purged our sins, sat down on the right hand of the Majesty on high" (Hebrews 1:1–3).

Notice also the following salutation that Paul uses at the beginning of eleven of his epistles (Galatians 1:3; 1 Corinthians 1:3; 2 Corinthians 1:2; Ephesians 1:2; Philippians 1:2; Colossians 1:2; 1 Thessalonians 1:1; 2 Thessalonians 2:2; 1 Timothy 1:2; 2 Timothy 1:2; Philemon 1:3.): "Grace be to you and peace from God our Father, and from the Lord Jesus Christ. Blessed be God, even the Father of our Lord Jesus Christ" (2 Corinthians 1:2–3).

In the epistle to the Galatians this salutation is expanded to read: "Grace be to you and peace from God the Father, and from our Lord Jesus Christ, Who gave himself for our sins, that he might deliver us from this present evil world, according to the will of God and our Father" (Galatians 1:3–4).

Paul ties in the Saints with God the Father and Jesus Christ, the Son, in his first epistle to the Thessalonians: "Now God himself and our Father, and our Lord Jesus Christ, direct our way unto you. And the Lord make you to increase and abound in love one toward another, and toward all men, even as we do toward you: To the end he may stablish your hearts unblameable in holiness before God, even our Father, at the coming of our Lord Jesus Christ with all his saints" (1 Thessalonians 3:11–13).

2. *The relationship of the Father and the Son to man; the literal fatherhood of God and, thus, the brotherhood and sisterhood of us all; Jesus Christ as the Savior and Redeemer of all mankind.*

We have already discussed some of Paul's teachings indicating that he fully believed Jesus Christ was the Savior and Redeemer of mankind. Paul taught that salvation was made possible through the atonement of Jesus Christ, not through the legalism of the ceremonial law. (See Romans 4:16; JST, Romans 4:16; Romans 3:23–30; and the entire epistles to the Galatians and Colossians.)

3. *The reality of both a pre-earthly and a postmortal existence, including the resurrection of all mankind and the different degrees of glory.*

Paul taught concerning the principle of pre-earthly existence: "He hath chosen us in him before the foundation of the world, that we should be holy and without blame before him in love" (Ephesians 1:4).

Paul taught that we are all the spirit children of God: "The Spirit itself beareth witness with our spirit, that we are the children of God" (Romans 8:16).

Paul taught concerning the three major degrees of glory: "There are also celestial bodies, and bodies terrestrial. . . . There is one glory of the sun, and another glory of the moon, and another glory of the stars. . . . So also is the resurrection of the dead" (1 Corinthians 15:40–42; see also JST, 1 Corinthians).

4. *The potential destiny of man—the plan of eternal progression, including eternal marriage and the possibility of eventual godhood or eternal life.*

Paul taught that Christ could and did become like God the Father, and that we can become like Christ: "Christ Jesus: Who, being in the form of God, thought it not robbery to be equal with God. . . . Wherefore God also hath highly exalted him. . . . Wherefore, my beloved . . . work out your own salvation with fear and trembling. . . . That ye may be blameless and harmless, the sons of God" (Philippians 2:5–6, 9, 12, 15).

Paul taught concerning the importance of marriage, or of the relationship of the family to the Church and to Christ and our Heavenly Father: "But I would have you know, that the head of every man is Christ; and the head of the woman is the man; and the head of Christ is God. . . . Neither is the man without the woman, neither the woman without the man, in the Lord" (1 Corinthians 11:3, 11).

"Let every man have his own wife, and let every woman have her own husband. Let the husband render unto the wife due benevolence: and likewise also the wife unto the husband" (1 Corinthians 7:2–3).

"Husbands, love your wives, even as Christ also loved the church, and gave himself for it. . . . For this cause shall a man leave his father and mother, and shall be joined unto his wife, and they two shall be one flesh" (Ephesians 5:25, 31).

Paul also indicated that it is wrong to forbid to marry: "Now the Spirit speaketh expressly, that in the latter times some shall depart from the faith, giving heed to seducing spirits, and doctrines of devils; Speaking lies in hypocrisy; having their conscience seared with a hot iron; Forbidding to marry, and commanding to abstain from meats, which God hath created to be received with thanksgiving of them which believe and know the truth" (1 Timothy 4:1–3).

5. *The basic principles and ordinances of the gospel of Jesus Christ, including the basic eternal laws upon which they are based: justice, mercy, and so on.*

Paul taught with clarity and emphasized the principle of faith: "Now faith is the substance [Greek: assurance] of things hoped for, the evidence of things not seen" (Hebrews 11:1). (See the entire epistle to the Hebrews, especially chapter 11, and Romans 4:1–13.)

Paul taught concerning the sacrament of the Lord's Supper: "The Lord Jesus the same night in which he was betrayed took bread: And when he had given thanks, he brake it, and said, Take, eat: this is my body, which is broken for you: this do in remembrance of me. After the same manner also he took the cup . . . saying, This cup is the new testament in my blood: this do ye, as oft as ye drink it, in remembrance of me. For as often as ye eat this bread, and drink this cup, ye do shew [Greek: proclaim, announce] the Lord's death till he come" (1 Corinthians 11:23–26).

Paul taught of the gifts of the Spirit that should be enjoyed by the Saints. (See 1 Corinthians 11:2–14:40.)

Paul taught concerning the healing of the sick by the power of the Spirit, and of casting out devils: "And God wrought special miracles by the hands of Paul: So that from his body were brought unto the sick handkerchiefs or aprons, and the diseases departed from them, and the evil spirits went out of them" (Acts 19:11–12).

Then we read how the seven sons of Scerva, a Jew and chief of the priests, tried to cast out a devil: "And the evil spirit answered and said, Jesus I know, and Paul I know, but who are ye? . . . And this was known to all the Jews and Greeks also dwelling at Ephesus; fear fell on them all, and the name of the Lord Jesus was magnified. . . . So mightily grew the word of God and prevailed" (Acts 19:15, 17, 20).

Paul taught of the grace of God, and of the relationship of grace to faith and to works: "By grace are ye saved through faith; and that not of yourselves: it is the gift of God: Not of works, lest any man should boast" (Ephesians 2:8–9).

Paul wrote to Timothy concerning confession, penance, humility, contriteness, grace, and mercy: "[I] . . . was before a blasphemer, and a persecutor, and injurious: but I obtained mercy, because I did it ignorantly in unbelief. And the grace of our Lord was exceeding abundant. . . . Christ Jesus came into the world to save sinners; of whom I am chief. Howbeit for this cause I obtained mercy, that in me first Jesus Christ might shew forth all longsuffering, for a pattern to them which should hereafter believe on him to life everlasting" (1 Timothy 1:13–16).

The word *grace* appears 130 times in the New Testament; of these, 107 are from the writings of Paul. Paul preached largely to a people who believed that they were saved through their works. Therefore, he emphasized the saving power of grace. Of course, other apostles also taught the principle of grace, including Peter: "But we believe that through the grace of the Lord Jesus Christ we shall be saved" (Acts 15:11).

Perhaps the most widely quoted statements of Paul on grace are as follows: "Knowing that a man is not justified by the works of the law, but by the faith of Jesus Christ, even we have believed in Jesus Christ, that we might be justified by the faith of Christ, and not by the works of the law: for by the works of the law shall no flesh be justified" (Galatians 2:16).

"But God, who is rich in mercy, for his great love wherewith he loved us, Even when we were dead in sins, hath quickened us together with Christ, (by grace ye are saved;) And hath raised us up together, and made us sit together in heavenly places in Christ Jesus: That in the ages to come he might shew the exceeding riches of his grace in his kindness toward us through Christ Jesus. For by grace are ye saved through faith; and that not of yourselves: it is the gift of God: Not of works, lest any man should boast. For we are his workmanship, created in Christ Jesus unto good works, which God hath before ordained that we should walk in them" (Ephesians 2:4–10).

Paul was evidently so successful in stressing the importance of grace that today members of some Christian groups believe that *only* grace is necessary. Our missionaries stress *works* when they teach such people.

Of course, both grace *and* works are necessary. As recorded in 2 Nephi 25:30: "It is by grace that we are saved, after all we can do."

6. *The necessity of an organization for carrying out the gospel—the kingdom of God in heaven and on earth; the importance of unity among the members of this organization.*

Paul taught concerning the offices in the Church and of the possibility of becoming perfect: "And he gave some, apostles; and some, prophets; and some, evangelists; and some, pastors and teachers; For the perfecting of the saints, for the work of the ministry, for the edifying of the body of Christ: Till we all come in the unity of the faith, and of the knowledge of the Son of God, unto a perfect man, unto the measure of the stature of the fulness of Christ" (Ephesians 4:11–13).

Paul wrote concerning the organization of the Church and the family spirit of members of the Church: "Now therefore ye are no more strangers and foreigners, but fellow citizens with the saints, and of the household of God; And are built upon the foundation of the apostles and prophets, Jesus Christ himself being the chief corner stone; In whom all the building fitly framed together groweth unto an holy temple in the Lord. In whom ye also are builded together for an habitation of God through the Spirit" (Ephesians 2:19–22).

Paul wrote concerning the importance of unity in the Church and among members of the Church: "I beseech you . . . by the name of our Lord Jesus Christ, that ye all speak the same thing, and that there be no divisions [Greek: factions, schisms] among you: but that ye be perfectly joined together in the same mind and in the same judgment" (1 Corinthians 1:10).

"Keep the unity of the Spirit in the bond of peace. There is one body, and one Spirit . . . One Lord, one faith, one baptism, One God and Father of all" (Ephesians 4:3–6).

Paul taught that divisions in the Church should be avoided, as should petty grievances and the apostasy of individuals or groups: "[Let] there be no divisions among you; but that ye be perfectly joined together in the same mind and in the same judgment. . . . [Let there be no] contentions among you. . . . Now this I say, that every one of you saith, I am of Paul; and I of Apollos; and I of Cephas; and I of Christ. Is Christ divided? was Paul crucified for you? or were ye baptized in the name of Paul?" (1 Corinthians 1:10–13).

Paul cautioned against unnecessary lawsuits and against going to civil courts for every matter: "Dare any of you, having a matter against another, go to law before the unjust, and not before the saints? Do ye not know that the saints shall judge the world? and if the world shall be judged by you, are ye unworthy to judge the smallest matters? Know ye not that we shall judge angels? how much more things that pertain to this life?" (1 Corinthians 6:1–3).

Paul taught that vengeance is contrary to the spirit of the gospel: "Recompense to no man evil for evil. Provide things honest in the sight of all men. If it be possible, as much as lieth in you, live peaceably with all men. Dearly beloved, avenge not yourselves, but rather give place unto wrath: for it is written, Vengeance is mine; I will repay, saith the Lord. Therefore if thine enemy hunger, feed him; if he thirst, give him drink: for in so doing thou shalt heap coals of fire on his head. Be not overcome of evil, but overcome evil with good" (Romans 12:17–21).

7. *The relationship of laws to blessings and righteousness (and to sin and punishment); the nature of an "opposition in all things."*

Paul taught concerning the many sins of sexual impurity: "Know ye not that the unrighteous shall not inherit the kingdom of God? Be not deceived: neither fornicators [Greek: sexually immoral persons, male prostitutes], nor idolaters, nor adulterers, . . . nor abusers of themselves with mankind [Greek: male homosexuals] . . . shall inherit the kingdom of God. . . . Know ye not that your body is the temple of the Holy Ghost which is in you, which ye have of God, and ye are not your own? For ye are bought with a price: therefore glorify God in your body, and in your spirit, which are God's" (1 Corinthians 6:9–10, 19–20).

Paul also clearly taught of the existence of the devil, and of the devil's opposition to the things of God. He counseled and warned: "Satan himself is transformed into an angel of light. Therefore, it is no great thing if his ministers also be transformed as the ministers of righteousness; whose end shall be according to their works" (2 Corinthians 11:14–15).

8. *The eternal and universal nature of the gospel—for all who have lived, now live, or will live upon the earth; missionary work necessary to spread the gospel; apostasy to be avoided; restoration may be necessary.*

Paul emphasized the universal nature of the gospel. It is not limited to the Jew only, nor to the Gentile only, nor alone to the Roman, Greek, master, or slave. (See 1 Corinthians 12:12–20; Ephesians 2:1–3:21.)

Paul taught the importance of missionary work: "Even so hath the Lord ordained that they which preach the gospel should live of the gospel. . . . For though I preach the gospel, I have nothing to glory of: for necessity is laid upon me; yea, woe is unto me, if I preach not the gospel! For if I do this thing willingly, I have a reward. . . . What is my reward then? Verily that, when I preach the gospel, I may make the gospel of Christ without charge . . . yet have I made myself servant unto all, that I might gain the more . . . that I might by all means save some" (1 Corinthians 9:14, 16–19, 22).

Paul taught concerning baptism for the dead: "Else what shall they do which are baptized for the dead, if the dead rise not at all? why are they then baptized for the dead?" (1 Corinthians 15:29).

Paul foresaw, witnessed, and warned against the impending apostasy. (See Galatians 1:6–8; 3:1; 1 Timothy 4:1–3; 2 Timothy 3:1–8; 4:3–4.)

Paul taught concerning the restoration in the last days: "That in the dispensation of the fulness of times he might gather together in one all things in Christ, both which are in heaven, and which are on earth; even in him" (Ephesians 1:10).

9. *The vital necessity of agency; the importance of total devotion to the things we know to be true and choose to follow, including testifying of them.*

Paul taught of putting on the whole armor of God (see Ephesians 6:10–18), and of the importance of example: "Take heed lest by any means this liberty of yours become a stumblingblock to them that are weak. . . . Wherefore, if meat make my brother to offend [Greek: cause my brother to stumble, falter], I will eat no flesh while the world standeth, lest I make my brother to offend" (1 Corinthians 8:9, 13).

Paul taught of courage, bravery, devotion, and commitment: "If after the manner of men I have fought with beasts at Ephesus, what advantageth it me, if the dead rise not?" (1 Corinthians 15:32).

"But I will tarry at Ephesus until Pentecost. For a great door and effectual is opened unto me, and there are many adversaries. . . . Watch ye, stand fast in the faith, quit you [Greek: behave] like men, be strong" (1 Corinthians 16:8–9, 13).

In connection with the mobs aroused by Demetrius the silversmith ("Our craft is in danger"), the people cried in the theater for about two hours ("Great is Diana of the Ephesians"). Then we read: "And when Paul would have entered in unto the people, the disciples suffered him not" (Acts 19:27–28, 30, 34).

Paul taught concerning the futility of man's unaided learning or of unreasonable emphasis on knowledge alone or of the acquirement of degrees: "For Christ sent me . . . to preach the gospel: not with wisdom of words. . . . For it is written, I will destroy the wisdom of the wise, and will bring to nothing the understanding of the prudent.... Hath not God made foolish the wisdom of this world?... the Jews require a sign, and the Greeks seek after wisdom. But we preach Christ crucified.... The foolishness of God is wiser than men.... God hath chosen the foolish things of the world to confound the wise; and God hath chosen the weak things of the world to confound the things which are mighty" (1 Corinthians 1:17, 19–20, 22–23, 25, 27).

Paul taught the importance of boldly bearing testimony: "[Pray] for me, that utterance may be given unto me, that I may open my mouth boldly, to make known the mystery of the gospel, For which I am an ambassador... that therein I may speak boldly, as I ought to speak" (Ephesians 6:19–20).

10. *Love, charity, and the pure love of Christ—the importance of exemplifying these traits.*

Paul taught that charity (the pure love of Christ) is basic to everything else. (See 1 Corinthians 13 and Articles of Faith 1:13.) Note Paul's words to the Philippians: "Whatsoever things are true, whatsoever things are honest, whatsoever things are just, whatsoever things are pure, whatsoever things are lovely, whatsoever things are of good report, if there be any virtue, and if there be any praise, think on these things" (Philippians 4:8).

Paul taught concerning the ending of mortal life and of the final judgment: "I am now ready to be offered, and the time of my departure is at hand. I have fought a good fight, I have finished my course, I have kept the faith: Henceforth there is laid up for me a crown of righteousness, which the Lord, the righteous judge, shall give me at that day: and not to me only, but unto all them also that love his appearing" (2 Timothy 4:6–8).

Contributions of the Joseph Smith Translation to Understanding Paul's Epistles

The Joseph Smith Translation makes changes in 340 verses in the 100 chapters of the 14 epistles of Paul. The essential changes in 162 of these 340 verses are included in the footnotes of the LDS edition of the Bible. Some of them are listed here:

Romans

In sixteen chapters, changes in 114 verses; LDS Bible includes fifty-six of these: 1:5–6, 17, 18; 3:1–2, 5–8, 24; 4:2–5, 16; 6:7, 14; 7:5–27; 8:8, 9, 10, 29–30, 31; 9:3, 7; 13:1, 6–7; 14:15; 16:10, 11, 16.

1:18 (KJV) "For the wrath of God is revealed from heaven against all ungodliness and unrighteousness of men, who hold the truth in unrighteousness."

1:18 (JST) "For the wrath of God is revealed from heaven against all ungodliness and unrighteousness of men; who love not the truth, but remain in unrighteousness."

3:5 (KJV) "But if our unrighteousness commend the righteousness of God, what shall we say? Is God unrighteous who taketh vengeance? (I speak as a man)."

3:5 (JST) "But if we remain in our unrighteousness and commend the righteousness of God, how dare we say, God is unrighteous who taketh vengeance? (I speak as a man who fears God,)" (compare KJV, Romans 7:14–25 to JST, Romans 7:14–27).

1 Corinthians

In sixteen chapters, changes in seventy-two verses; LDS Bible includes thirty-five of these: 1:24, 26; 2:11; 3:15; 4:4; 5:4; 6:12; 7:1, 2, 5, 9, 26, 29–33, 38; 8:4; 10:11, 23, 24; 11:20; 14:2, 4, 13, 14, 19, 27, 34, 35; 15:31, 40; 16:20.

2:11 (KJV) "For what man knoweth the things of a man, save the spirit of man which is in him? even so the things of God knoweth no man, but the Spirit of God."

2:11 (JST) "For what man knoweth the things of a man, save the spirit of man which is in him? even so the things of God knoweth no man, except he has the Spirit of God."

4:4 (KJV) "For I know nothing by myself; yet am I not hereby justified: but he that judgeth me is the Lord."

4:4 (JST) "For though I know nothing against myself; yet I am not hereby justified; but he who judgeth me is the Lord."

6:12 (KJV) "All things are lawful unto me, but all things are not expedient: all things are lawful for me, but I will not be brought under the power of any."

6:12 (JST) "All these things are not lawful unto me, and all these things are not expedient. All things are not lawful for me, therefore I will not be brought under the power of any."

7:1 (KJV) "Now concerning the things whereof ye wrote unto me: It is good for a man not to touch a woman."

7:2 "Nevertheless, to avoid fornication, let every man have his own wife, and let every woman have her own husband."

7:1 (JST) "Now concerning the things whereof ye wrote unto me, saying, It is good for a man not to touch a woman."

7:2 "Nevertheless, I say, to avoid fornication, let every man have his own wife, and let every woman have her own husband."

7:28 (KJV) "But and if thou marry, thou hast not sinned; and if a virgin marry, she hath not sinned. Nevertheless such shall have trouble in the flesh: but I spare you."

7:29 "But this I say, brethren, the time is short: it remaineth, that both they that have wives be as though they had none."

7:32 "But I would have you without carefulness. He that is unmarried careth for the things that belong to the Lord, how he may please the Lord:"

7:33 "But he that is married careth for the things that are of the world, how he may please his wife."

7:28 (JST) "But if thou marry, thou hast not sinned; and if a virgin marry, she hath not sinned. Nevertheless, such shall have trouble in the flesh. For I spare you not."

7:29 *"But I speak unto you who are called unto the ministry.* For this I say, brethren, the time that remaineth is but short, that ye shall be sent forth unto the ministry. Even they who have wives, shall be as though they had none; for ye are called and chosen to do the Lord's work" (emphasis added).

7:32 "But I would, brethren, that ye magnify your calling. I would have you without carefulness. For he who is unmarried, careth for the things that belong to the Lord, how he may please the Lord; therefore he prevaileth."

7:33 "But he who is married, careth for the things that are of the world, how he may please his wife; therefore there is a difference, for he is hindered."

10:23 (KJV) "All things are lawful for me, but all things are not expedient: all things are lawful for me, but all things edify not."

10:24 "Let no man seek his own, but every man another's wealth."

10:23 (JST) "All things are not lawful for me, for all things are not expedient; all things are not lawful, for all things edify not."

10:24 "Let not man seek therefore his own, but every man another's good."

11:20 (KJV) "When ye come together therefore into one place, this is not to eat the Lord's supper."

11:20 (JST) "When ye come together into one place, is it not to eat the Lord's supper?"

14:33 (KJV) "For God is not the author of confusion, but of peace, as in all churches of the saints."

14:34 "Let your women keep silence in the churches: for it is not permitted unto them to speak; but they are commanded to be under obedience, as also saith the law."

14:35 "And if they will learn any thing, let them ask their husbands at home: for it is a shame for women to speak in the church."

14:33 (JST) "For God is not the author of confusion, but of peace, as in all churches of the saints."

14:34 "Let your women keep silence in the churches; for it is not permitted unto them to rule: but to be under obedience, as also saith the law."

14:35 "And if they will learn any thing, let them ask their husbands at home; for it is a shame for women to rule in the church."

15:31 (KJV) "I protest by your rejoicing which I have in Christ Jesus our Lord, I die daily."

15:31 (JST) "I protest unto you the resurrection of the dead; and this is my rejoicing which I have in Christ Jesus our Lord daily, though I die."

15:40 (KJV) "There are also celestial bodies, and bodies terrestrial: but the glory of the celestial is one, and the glory of the terrestrial is another."

15:40 (JST) "Also celestial bodies, and bodies terrestial, and bodies telestial; but the glory of the celestial, one; and the terrestial another; and the telestial, another."

2 Corinthians

In thirteen chapters, changes in nineteen verses; LDS Bible includes six of these: 5:13, 16; 6:1; 11:23, 29; 13:12.

5:13 (KJV) "For whether we be beside ourselves, it is to God: or whether we be sober, it is for your cause."

5:13 (JST) "For we bear record that we are not beside ourselves; for whether we glory, it is to God, or whether we be sober, it is for your sakes."

13:12 (KJV) "Greet one another with an holy kiss."

13:12 (JST) "Greet one another with a holy salutation."

Galatians

In six chapters, changes in twelve verses; LDS Bible includes five of these: 1:10; 2:4; 3:19–20, 24.

3:18 (KJV) "For if the inheritance be of the law, it is no more of promise: but God gave it to Abraham by promise."

3:19 "Wherefore then serveth the law? It was added because of transgressions, till the seed should come to whom the promise was made; and it was ordained by angels in the hand of a mediator."

3:20 "Now a mediator is not a mediator of one, but God is one."

3:18 (JST) "For if the inheritance is of the law, then it is no more of promise; but God gave it to Abraham by promise."

3:19 "Wherefore then, the law was added because of transgressions, till the seed should come to whom the promise was made in the law given to Moses, who was ordained by the hand of angels to be a mediator of this first covenant, (the law)."

3:20 "Now this mediator was not a mediator of the new covenant; but there is one mediator of the new covenant, who is Christ, as it is written in the law concerning the promises made to Abraham and his seed. Now Christ is the mediator of life; for this is the promise which God made unto Abraham."

Ephesians

In six chapters, changes in thirteen verses; LDS Bible includes one of these: 4:26.

4:26 (KJV) "Be ye angry, and sin not: let not the sun go down upon your wrath."

4:26 (JST) "Can ye be angry, and not sin? let not the sun go down upon your wrath."

Philippians

In four chapters, changes in fourteen verses; LDS Bible includes four of these: 1:28; 3:11, 19; 4:6.

3:11 (KJV) "If by any means I might attain unto the resurrection of the dead."

3:11 (JST) "If by any means I might attain unto the resurrection of the just."

Colossians

In four chapters, changes in six verses; LDS Bible includes four of these: 1:6; 2:2, 21–22.

2:21 (KJV) "(Touch not; taste not, handle not;"

2:22 "Which all are to perish with the using;) after the commandments and doctrines of men?"

2:23 "Which things have indeed a shew of wisdom in will worship, and humility, and neglecting of the body; not in any honour to the satisfying of the flesh."

2:21 (JST) "Which are after the doctrines and commandments of men, who teach you to touch not, taste not, handle not; all those things which are to perish with the using?"

2:22 "Which things have indeed a show of wisdom in will worship, and humility, and neglecting the body as to the satisfying the flesh, not in any honor to God."

1 Thessalonians

In five chapters, changes in six verses; LDS Bible includes four of these: 1:1; 4:15, 17; 5:26.

2 Thessalonians

In three chapters, changes in seven verses; LDS Bible includes five of these: 1:1; 2:2, 3, 7–9.

2:7 (KJV) "For the mystery of iniquity doth already work: only he who now letteth will let, until he be taken out of the way."

2:8 "And then shall that Wicked be revealed, whom the Lord shall consume with the spirit of his mouth, and shall destroy with the brightness of his coming:"

2:9 "Even him, whose coming is after the working of Satan with all power and signs and lying wonders."

2:7 (JST) "For the mystery of iniquity doth already work, and he it is who now worketh, and Christ suffereth him to work, until the time is fulfilled that he shall be taken out of the way."

2:8 "And then shall that wicked one be revealed, whom the Lord shall consume with the spirit of his mouth, and shall destroy with the brightness of his coming."

2:9 "Yea, the Lord, even Jesus, whose coming is not until after there cometh a falling away, by the working of Satan with all power, and signs and lying wonders."

1 Timothy

In six chapters, changes in fourteen verses; LDS Bible includes seven of these: 2:4, 15; 3:15–16; 5:10; 6:15–16.

2:4 (KJV) "Who will have all men to be saved, and to come unto the knowledge of the truth."

2:4 (JST) "Who is willing to have all men to be saved, and to come unto the knowledge of the truth which is in Christ Jesus, who is the Only Begotten Son of God, and ordained to be a Mediator between God and man; who is one God, and hath power over all men."

2 Timothy

In four chapters, changes in nine verses; LDS Bible includes two of these: 3:16; 4:2.

3:16 (KJV) "All scripture is given by inspiration of God, and is profitable for doctrine, for reproof, for correction, for instruction in righteousness."

3:16 (JST) "And all Scripture given by inspiration of God, is profitable for doctrine, for reproof, for correction, for instruction in righteousness."

Titus

In three chapters, changes in two verses; LDS Bible includes both of these: 1:15; 2:11.

Philemon

In one chapter, changes in one verse; LDS Bible does not include this one.

Hebrews

In thirteen chapters, changes in fifty-one verses; LDS Bible includes thirty-one of these: 1:6–7; 4:3, 5, 12; 5:7; 6:1, 3–10; 7:3, 19–21, 25–26; 8:4; 9:15, 16, 26; 10:1, 10, 13; 11:1, 35, 40.)

4:3 (KJV) "For we which have believed do enter into rest, as he said, As I have sworn in my wrath, if they shall enter into my rest: although the works were finished from the foundation of the world."

4:3 (JST) "For we who have believed do enter into rest, as he said, As I have sworn in my wrath, If they harden their hearts they shall not enter into my rest; also, I have sworn, If they will not harden their hearts, they shall enter into my rest; although the works of God were prepared, (or finished,) from the foundation of the world."

6:1 (KJV) "Therefore leaving the principles of the doctrine of Christ, let us go on unto perfection; not laying again the foundation of repentance from dead works, and of faith toward God,"

6:2 "Of the doctrine of baptisms, and of laying on of hands, and of resurrection of the dead, and of eternal judgment."

6:3 "And this will we do, if God permit."

6:1 (JST) "Therefore not leaving the principles of the doctrine of Christ, let us go on unto perfection; not laying again the foundation of repentance from dead works, and of faith toward God."

6:2 "Of the doctrine of baptisms, of laying on of hands, and of the resurrection of the dead, and of eternal judgment."

6:3 "And we will go on unto perfection if God permit."

7:1 (KJV) "For this Melchisedec, king of Salem, priest of the most high God, who met Abraham returning from the slaughter of the kings, and blessed him;"

7:2 "To whom also Abraham gave a tenth part of all; first being by interpretation King of righteousness, and after that also King of Salem, which is, King of peace;"

7:3 "Without father, without mother, without descent, having neither beginning of days, nor end of life; but made like unto the Son of God; abideth a priest continually."

7:1 (JST) "For this Melchizedek, king of Salem, priest of the most high God, who met Abraham returning from the slaughter of the kings, and blessed him;"

7:2 "To whom also Abraham gave a tenth part of all; first being by interpretation King of righteousness, and after that also King of Salem, which is, King of peace;"

7:3 "For this Melchizedek was ordained a priest after the order of the Son of God, which order was without father, without mother, without descent, having neither beginning of days, nor end of life. And all those who are ordained unto this priesthood are made like unto the Son of God, abiding a priest continually."

8:4 (KJV) "For if he [the high priest sitting on the right hand of the Majesty in heaven] were on earth, he should not be a priest, seeing that there are priests that offer gifts according to the law."

8:4 (JST) "Therefore while he was on the earth, he offered for a sacrifice his own life for the sins of the people. Now every priest under the law, must needs offer gifts, or sacrifices, according to the law."

11:1 (KJV) "Now faith is the substance of things hoped for, the evidence of things not seen."

11:1 (JST) "Now faith is the assurance of things hope for, the evidence of things not seen."

11:40 (KJV) "God having provided some better thing for us, that they without us should not be made perfect."

11:40 (JST) "God having provided some better things for them through their sufferings, for without sufferings they could not be made perfect."

Changes Not Included in the LDS Edition of the Bible

Following are a few of the changes that were not included as footnotes in the LDS edition of the Bible:

1 Corinthians

12:30 (KJV) "Have all the gifts of healing? do all speak with tongues? do all interpret?"

12:31 "But covet earnestly the best gifts: and yet shew I unto you a more excellent way."

12:30 (JST) "Have all the gifts of healing? do all speak with tongues? do all interpret?"

12:31 "I say unto you, Nay; for I have shown unto you a more excellent way, therefore covet earnestly the best gifts."

Philippians

1:21 (KJV) "For to me to live is Christ, and to die is gain."

1:22 (JST) "For me to live, is to do the will of Christ; and to die, is my gain."

1 Timothy

6:16 (KJV) "Who only hath immortality, dwelling in the light which no man can approach unto; whom no man hath seen, nor can see."

6:16 (JST) "Whom no man hath seen, nor can see, unto whom no man can approach, only he who hath the light and the hope of immortality dwelling in him."

Hebrews

12:12 (KJV) "Wherefore lift up the hands which hang down, and the feeble knees."

12:12 (JST) "Wherefore lift up the hands which hang down, and strengthen the feeble knees."

Major Greek Contributions to the LDS Bible

The LDS edition of the Bible includes 564 footnotes offering alternative translations from the Greek ("GR") in the fourteen epistles of Paul. Some of the most important ones are listed here. Additional Greek contributions not included in the LDS Bible appear at the end of the following sections.

Romans (137 included in LDS Bible)

1:1 Paul "separated" [to be an apostle] = "set apart"

1:4 "And *declared* to be the Son of God with power, according to the spirit of holiness, by the resurrection from the dead" = "appointed, decreed, set forth"

1:13 I was "let hitherto" = "hindered, restrained, prevented"

1:21 they became "vain in their imaginations" = "corrupt in their reasonings, deliberations"

3:4, 6, 31, and so on "God forbid!" = "May it not be!"

3:19 all the world may "become guilty before God" = "become liable to God for punishment"

4:3 Abraham "believed God" = "exercised faith in Jehovah"

5:11 "atonement" = "reconciliation, restoration to favor"

5:14 "the *figure* of him that was to come" = "type, pattern"

6:5 For if we have "been planted together" in the likeness of his death = "become united with him"

8:13 "*mortify* the deeds of the body" = "put to death, subdue"

8:29, 30 "For whom he did foreknow he also did *predestinate*"[7] = "appointed beforehand, foreordained."

10:21 a "gainsaying" people = a "contradicting, opposing" people.

11:2 "Wot ye not" = "Know ye not"

11:25 "*blindness* in part is happened to Israel" = "callousness"

11:25 "For I would not, brethren, that ye should be ignorant of the *mystery*[8] = "sacred secret"

11:30, 31 "believed"[9] = "obeyed" (note the implication of this translation to Mark 9:23: "all things are possible to him that believeth")

12:4 "all members have not the same *office*" = all members have not the same "function, operation"

12:9 "Let love be *without dissimulation*" = "sincere, unfeigned, real"

12:16 "Mind not high things, but *condescend* to men of low estate" = "conform willingly with the humble"

13:4 the "minister" of God = "servant"

14:2 "who is weak, eateth *herbs*" = "vegetables"

14:17 "For the kingdom of God is not *meat* and drink" = "food"

15:9 "I will *confess* to thee among the Gentiles" = "profess openly, praise"

15:27 in "carnal" things = "material, temporal"

16:20 "The God of peace shall *bruise* Satan . . . shortly" = "break the power of, crush"

1 Corinthians (126 included in LDS Bible)

1:25 "the weakness" of God is stronger than men = "a weak thing"

1:26 not many "noble" are called = not many of "noble birth" are called

3:9 "Ye are God's *husbandry*" = "cultivated field, farm"

3:19 "For the *wisdom* of the world is foolishness with God" = "cunning, villainy"

6:9–10 "Be not deceived . . . *abusers of themselves with mankind* . . . shall [not] inherit the kingdom of God" = "male homosexuals"

7:23 "Ye are bought with a price; be not ye the *servants* of men" = "slaves"

8:13 "If meat *make my brother to offend,* I will eat no flesh while the world standeth" = "cause my brother to stumble, falter"

15:9 "I . . . am not *meet* to be called an apostle" = "adequate, sufficient, competent"

15:19 "If in this life only we have hope in Christ, we are of all men most *miserable*" = "to be pitied"

15:29 "Else what shall they do which are baptized *for* the dead" = "in behalf of, for the sake of"

16:13 "Watch ye, stand fast in the faith, *quit you like men*" = "behave like men"

2 Corinthians (twenty included in LDS Bible)

8:1 "Brethren, we *do you to wit of* the grace of God" = "we make known (or declare) to you the grace of God"

11:8 "I *robbed* other churches, taking wages of them, to do you service" = I "despoiled other churches, having taken provisions for you"

13:1 "In the mouth of two or three witnesses shall every *word* be established" = "matter"

Galatians (thirty included in LDS Bible)

2:6 "God *accepteth* no man's person" = "God does not go by a man's outward appearance"

4:20 "I *stand in doubt of* you" = I "am perplexed about" you

Ephesians (five included in LDS Bible)

4:1 "Walk worthy of the *vocation* wherewith ye are called" = "calling"

Philippians (twenty-three included in LDS Bible)

1:7 "It is *meet* for me" = "just, right"

1:8 "in the *bowels* of Jesus Christ" = "affections, compassions"

1:23 "I am *in a strait betwixt* two" = I am "hard pressed to choose" between two

2:10 That in the name of Jesus every knee should bow of *"things"* in heaven, and "things" in earth, and "things" under the earth = "those"
3:2 "beware of the concision" = "look out for those who mutilate the flesh"
3:21 "Who shall change our *vile* body" = "humble, of low estate"
4:3 "yolkfellow" = "associate"
4:6 "Be careful for nothing" = "Don't be unduly concerned about anything"

Colossians (nine included in LDS Bible)
1:12 "which hath *made us meet* to be partakers" = "qualified us"
1:22 "holy and unblameable and unreproveable in his sight" = "open to no accusation before him"
3:15 let the peace of "God" rule in your hearts = "the Christ"

1 Thessalonians (twenty-five included in LDS Bible)
1:4 (transposition) "Knowing, brethren beloved, your election of God" = "Knowing, brethren beloved of God, your election"
2:2 we were "shamefully entreated" = "insolently treated"
4:15 "we which are alive and remain unto the coming of the Lord shall not *prevent* them which are asleep" = "precede, make progress over"
5:2 "For yourselves know *perfectly* that the day of the "Lord" = "quite well," "Jehovah"

2 Thessalonians (fifteen included in LDS Bible)
2:12 "That they all might be *damned* who believed not the truth" = "brought to account, trial"

1 Timothy (fifty-seven included in LDS Bible)
3:2 A bishop then must be "apt" to teach = "qualified" to teach
3:13 "they that have used the office of deacon well *purchase to themselves a good degree*" = "earn, acquire for themselves good standing rank"
4:8 "bodily exercise profiteth *little*" = "a little while"
5:12 "having *damnation*" = "judgment, condemnation"
6:4 "doting about questions" = "obsessed with questions"; "evil surmisings" = "wicked suspicions"

2 Timothy (twenty-eight included in LDS Bible)
2:12 "if we *suffer,* we shall also reign with him" = "endure, remain constant"

2:26 that they may "recover themselves" from the snare of the devil = "come back to their proper senses"

Titus (twenty-four included in LDS Bible)
1:9 "convince the *gainsayers*" = "those who deny, contradict"
1:11 "for filthy lucre's sake" = "for the sake of dishonest gain"
1:12 "slow bellies" = "lazy gluttons"
2:14 a "peculiar people" = a "people peculiarly his own"
2:15 "Let no man *despise* thee" = "disregard"

Philemon (five included in LDS Bible)
1:14 "without thy *mind* would I do nothing" = "assent, suggestion"
1:17 receive him "as myself" = "kindly the way you would me"

Hebrews (fifty-six included in LDS Bible)
1:1 "God . . . *at sundry times and in divers manners* spake in time past" = "in many locations and various ways"
2:4 "divers miracles" = "various powerful works"
2:7 "Thou madest [man] a little lower than the *angels*" = "angels" (note: the Hebrew is "gods")
5:4 "And no man taketh this honour unto himself, but he that is called of God, as was Aaron" = "Also a man takes this honor, not of his own accord, but only when he is called by God, just as Aaron was"
10:32 after ye were "illuminated" = "enlightened"
11:17 Abraham "offered up Isaac" = "as good as offered up Isaac"
12:2 "Jesus the author and *finisher* of our faith" = "one who completes, perfects"

Summary

President Brigham Young challenged us to read and ponder the scriptures so carefully that we will become as well acquainted with the major characters and their teachings as we are with the members of our households.

"Do you read the Scriptures, my brethren and sisters, as though you were writing them a thousand, two thousand, or five thousand years ago? Do you read them as though you stood in the place of the men who wrote them? If you do not feel thus, it is your privilege to do so, that you may be as familiar with the spirit and meaning of the written word of God as you are with your daily walk and conversation, or as you are with your workmen or with your households."[10]

Paul is the dominant character in Acts 13 through 28, and he wrote the fourteen epistles that follow the book of Acts. These final chapters in Acts and these fourteen epistles occupy 150 pages in our current edition of the New Testament, over one-third of the total.

Read and study Paul until you feel you know him. Then you will be able to inspire and challenge others to do the same. I have felt Paul's presence at special times as I have stood in the places he visited: Damascus, on the street called Straight; Jerusalem, near St. Stephen's gate and where the Sanhedrin met; Caesarea, where Paul was imprisoned for months; Ephesus, in the great amphitheater; Athens, on Mars Hill; Corinth, at the agora; Rome, at various traditional sites.

I have never felt Paul's influence more strongly, however, than when I have read and studied his words. I close this chapter with words of tribute to Paul from Robert J. Matthews: "[Paul's] records that have come to us display a great love for the Savior. And no one of that day has given us a more extensive discussion of the mission of Jesus Christ in fulfilling the law of Moses and in being the savior of all nations and peoples. Paul is most eloquent when writing of the Savior's grace, mercy, and love for mankind.

"Paul was indeed a chosen vessel, a special man for a particular need, at a particular time, and in a particular place. Yet, with all his varied talents and education, the things that made him most useful to the Lord were his total, unwavering devotion and testimony. Without these, all his other skills would have been ineffective or, as in his early years, used for the wrong purposes.

"Paul was the right man in the right place at the right time. This was not a coincidence but the result of divine foreknowledge and selection—Jesus appointed him as a special witness, not only for the time of his own mortality, but also to leave an example and a written record for all future generations."[11]

Notes

Excerpts from an address delivered in the mid-1970s on a Mediterranean cruise sponsored by the BYU Travel Study department and from a lecture at the CES Symposium on the New Testament, 15 August 1988.

1. *Encyclopedia Americana,* 30 vols. (New York: Americana Corp., 1975), "LASER."
2. *Encyclopedia Britannica,* 24 vols. (Chicago: Encyclopedia Britannica, 1966), "LASER."
3. *Teachings of the Prophet Joseph Smith,* 180.
4. Ibid., 63–64.
5. Bible Dictionary, "Paul," 742–43.

6. In "The Grandest Principle of the Gospel," *The Contributor,* 16 (August 1895): 610.
7. The translators of the King James Bible use the word *predestinate* twice (Romans 8:29, 30) and the word *predestinated* twice (Ephesians 1:5, 11). Note that all four uses of these words are in the translations of Paul's writings.

    One definition of *predestinate* in *Webster's Third New International Dictionary, Unabridged* is "destined, fates, or determined beforehand." The same volume lists as the first definition of *predestination*: "the act of predestinating or the state of being predestinated." A second definition is: "the theological doctrine that all events throughout eternity have been *foreordained* by divine decree or purpose." The word "predestine" is defined as "to destine, decree, determine, appoint or settle beforehand." Note that in both the Greek and the English the word *foreordain* can be used in place of the word *predestinate*.
8. Paul invites the Colossian Saints to come to an understanding "of the mystery of God, and of Christ who is of God, even the Father. In whom are hid all the treasures of wisdom and knowledge" (JST, Colossians 2:2–3).

    "Howbeit we speak wisdom among them that are perfect: yet not the wisdom of this world, nor of the princes of this world, that come to nought: But we speak the wisdom of God in a mystery, even the hidden wisdom, which God ordained before the world unto his glory. . . . But as it is written, Eye hath not seen, nor ear heard, neither have entered into the heart of man, the things which God hath prepared for them that love him" (1 Corinthians 2:6–7, 9; quoting Isaiah 64:4).
9. Joseph Smith said concerning various translations of the Bible: "Our latitude and longitude can be determined in the original Hebrew with far greater accuracy than in the English Version" (*Teachings of the Prophet Joseph Smith,* 290). I think this is also true of the Greek language. For example, I note in *Strong's Exhaustive Concordance of the Bible* eight different words in the Greek New Testament translated as "believe" in the English King James Bible. The word *believe* in the English Bible does not always mean the same thing.
10. *Discourses of Brigham Young,* 128.
11. Robert J. Matthews, "Saul of Tarsus: Chosen for a Special Need," *Ensign,* September 1987, 63.

Chapter 35

JOSEPH SMITH, THE PROPHET

It may seem strange to begin a tribute to Joseph Smith Jr. by emphasizing what he is *not,* but many biographies and articles about him have tended toward one extreme or the other. Those who have spoken of the "good" of Joseph Smith have appeared in the eyes of some critics to have virtually deified him. On the other hand, other critics feel that those who have spoken of the "bad" of Joseph Smith have depicted him as a tool of the devil or even worse.

When the angel Moroni appeared to Joseph Smith on September 21, 1823, he told the seventeen-year-old youth that his "name should be had for good and evil among all nations, kindreds, and tongues, or that it should be both good and evil spoken of among all people" (Joseph Smith—History 1:33). This statement has been fulfilled, as is quickly evident when the various publications about Joseph Smith are examined closely.

At the beginning of this tribute it might be well to point out that Joseph Smith is *not* Deity; nor is the opposite extreme, that Joseph Smith was a tool of the devil, even a possibility so far as this author is concerned.

JOSEPH SMITH IS NOT JESUS CHRIST

Latter-day Saints have never claimed that Joseph Smith is a member of the Godhead. He is not Jesus Christ. He is not the Firstborn Son of God in the spirit (see D&C 93:21). He is not the Only Begotten Son of God in the flesh. These sacred titles belong uniquely and forever to Jesus Christ, the divine Son of God.[1]

Latter-day Saints do not worship Joseph Smith, as is indicated in this statement by President Gordon B. Hinckley: "We do not worship the Prophet. We worship God our Eternal Father, and the risen Lord Jesus Christ. But we acknowledge him [Joseph Smith], we proclaim him, we respect him, we reverence him as an instrument in the hands of the Almighty in restoring to the earth the ancient truths of the divine gospel, together with the priesthood through which the authority of God is exercised in the affairs of his church and for the blessing of his people."[2]

Elder Neal A. Maxwell suggested that the word *venerate* might be appropriate for Joseph Smith: "The Prophet Joseph Smith, of course, was not a perfect man. There has been only one such—Jesus Christ. But Joseph Smith was a special witness for Jesus Christ. . . . We do not, as some occasionally charge, worship Joseph Smith, nor place him on a par with Jesus. But we do venerate him, remembering, hopefully that *the highest and best form of veneration is emulation*."[3]

Dr. Richard L. Bushman wrote that Joseph Smith never indicated anything other than that he was a servant of Jesus Christ: "We never have to apologize for the place of Jesus Christ in Latter-day Saint theology. He heads the Church. He reveals His will to the Prophet. We depend upon Jesus Christ as the very rock and foundation of our lives and personal salvation, and look to Him as a model in every possible way. We worship no man; it is God we worship, and we worship Him through the Savior. Who would be more disappointed than Joseph Smith if ever these convictions faded in the hearts of the Latter-day Saints?

"At the same time, we honor Joseph Smith, and with good cause."[4]

As powerful and as great as Joseph Smith was and is in the eyes of members of the Church, it is well to remember that his greatness was and is derived from his devoted discipleship to the Lord and Savior of us all, Jesus Christ. Joseph Smith is great precisely because he was one chosen of God and of Jesus Christ to serve under them for the blessing of mankind. Perhaps the greatest tribute that could be given to Joseph Smith is that he had such great faith and he lived such a worthy life that he was able during his lifetime to call upon the powers of heaven and receive answers; he was able to commune directly with Jesus Christ and with angels and representatives sent from the presence of God. Joseph Smith's greatness is derived directly from his faithful discipleship to the members of the Godhead.

Circumstances, Attributes, and Characteristics of Joseph Smith

The following circumstances, attributes, and characteristics explain the greatness of Joseph Smith:

1. He was foreordained in the premortal existence to head the dispensation of the fulness of times.

2. He set an example of obedience to God and of love for his fellowman.

3. He was entrusted with the priesthood power and authority necessary to reestablish and build up the kingdom of God on the earth.

4. He became a great prophet, seer, and revelator of the Lord.

5. He survived the tests of ridicule and persecution.

6. He has been assured of eternal life through his great faith and worthy life.

Each of these will be considered in this chapter, with brief tributes from those who knew Joseph Smith personally or who have become acquainted with him through a careful study of his life.

Foreordained to Head the Dispensation of the Fulness of Times

Praise to the man who communed with Jehovah! . . .
Blessed to open the last dispensation, . . .
Ever and ever the keys he will hold.[5]

Because of his great faith and because he lived a worthy life that enabled him to commune with Jehovah, Joseph Smith was able to fulfill his foreordained calling. Concerning the foreordination of Joseph Smith, President Ezra Taft Benson stated:

"Joseph was truly foreordained to his great mission.

"To get a vision of the magnitude of the prophet's earthly mission we must view it in the light of eternity. He was among 'the noble and great ones' whom Abraham described as follows:

"'Now the Lord had shown unto me, Abraham, the intelligences that were organized before the world was; and among all these there were many of the noble and great ones;

"'And God saw these souls that they were good, and he stood in the midst of them, and he said: These I will make my rulers; for he stood among those that were spirits, and he saw that they were good; and he said unto me: Abraham, thou art one of them; thou wast chosen before thou wast born' (Abraham 3:22–23).

"So it was with Joseph Smith. He too was there. He too sat in council with the noble and great ones. Occupying a prominent place of honor and distinction, he unquestionably helped in the planning and execution of the great work of the Lord to 'bring to pass the immortality and eternal life of man,' the salvation of all our Father's children (Moses 1:39). His mission had had and was to have, impact on all who had come to earth; all who then dwelt on earth and the millions yet unborn.

"The Prophet Joseph Smith made this eternal fact clear in the words: 'Every man who has a calling to minister to the inhabitants of the world was ordained to that very purpose in the Grand Council of heaven before this world was. I suppose that I was ordained to this very office in that Grand Council. It is the testimony that I want that I am God's servant, and this people His people.'"[6]

Brigham Young also testified concerning the foreordination of the Prophet Joseph Smith: "It was decreed in the counsels of eternity, long before the foundations of the earth were laid, that he [Joseph Smith] should be the man, in the last dispensation of this world, to bring forth the word of God to the people, and receive the fulness of the keys and power of the Priesthood of the Son of God. . . . [Joseph Smith] was foreordained in eternity to preside over this last dispensation."[7]

Elder Neal A. Maxwell wrote of this special calling of Joseph Smith:

"Indeed, on the scale of impact, what has been written in the scriptures is unfoldingly true:

"'Joseph Smith, the Prophet and Seer of the Lord, has done more, save Jesus only, for the salvation of men in this world, than any other man that ever lived in it' (D&C 135:3).

"It should not surprise us that it should be so, since he began the dispensation in which most of the people who ever lived will live, a dispensation in which there would be an explosion of knowledge and truth, as well as of people."[8]

An Example of Obedience to God and Love for Fellowman

Because of his great faith and because he lived a worthy life that enabled him to commune with Jehovah, Joseph Smith learned early in life to be obedient to the commandments of God, and he demonstrated love for his fellowmen. Dr. Richard L. Bushman wrote of the obedience of Joseph Smith: "Joseph commented that 'as my life consisted of activity and unyielding exertions, I made this one rule: When the Lord commands do it.'"[9]

Brother Jerry Roundy also noted this attribute of Joseph Smith: "It is hard to study the life of the Prophet Joseph Smith without remembering that he learned to serve the Lord fully, at all times, and at all costs."[10]

Two statements by Joseph Smith allude to his feelings of concern and love for his fellowman:

"Sectarian priests cry out concerning me, and ask, 'Why is it this babbler gains so many followers, and retains them?' I answer, It is because I possess the principle of love."[11]

"Love is one of the chief characteristics of Deity, and ought to be manifested by those who aspire to be the sons of God. A man filled with the love of God, is not content with blessing his family alone, but 'ranges through the whole world, anxious to bless the whole human race.'"[12]

Entrusted with Priesthood Power and Authority to Build Up the Kingdom of God on the Earth

> *Great is his glory and endless his priesthood.*
> *Ever and ever the keys he will hold.*
> *Faithful and true, he will enter his kingdom,*
> *Crowned in the midst of the prophets of old.*[13]

Because of his great faith and because he lived a worthy life that enabled him to commune with Jehovah, Joseph Smith had priesthood power and authority bestowed upon him that enabled him to reestablish the kingdom of God upon the earth.

Elder Gordon B. Hinckley noted this important mission of Joseph Smith and quoted the words of William W. Phelps concerning these powers: "One is led to marvel at the energies of the man. The breadth of his vision, the intensity of his activity are explained only by his great sense of mission and the inspiration of heaven which quickened his understanding. He was a man possessed by a sense of destiny—and that destiny was nothing less than the building of the Kingdom of God in the earth."[14]

Brother Robert J. Matthews mentioned some of the heavenly messengers who restored priesthood keys and authority to Joseph Smith: "The story of the restoration of the gospel is truly one of the most stimulating of all time. Many personalities from beyond the veil visited Joseph Smith as the gospel's restoration unfolded—among them were persons whose mortal lives are discussed in the Old Testament, including, said President John Taylor, 'Abraham, Isaac, Jacob, Noah, Adam, Seth, Enoch, and Jesus and the Father, and the apostles that lived on this continent as well as those who lived on the Asiatic continent. He seemed to be as familiar with these people as we are with one another.' The Doctrine and Covenants has references to visits also by Moses, Elias, Elijah, and of 'divers angels, from Michael or Adam down to the present time.'"[15]

A Great Prophet, Seer, and Revelator

> *Praise to the man who communed with Jehovah!*
> *Jesus anointed that Prophet and Seer.*[16]

Because of his great faith and because he lived a worthy life that enabled him to commune with Jehovah, Joseph Smith was called of God to be His prophet, seer, and revelator. Although in the minds of some, the terms *prophet, seer,* and *revelator* might seem to be synonymous, Ammon makes a distinction between the terms in his discussion with King Limhi: "And Ammon said that a seer is a revelator and a prophet also; and a gift which is greater can no man have, except he should possess the power of God, which no man can; yet a man may have great power given him from God. But a seer can know of things which are past, and also of things which are to come, and by them shall all things be revealed, or, rather, shall secret things be made manifest, and hidden things shall come to light, and things which are not known shall be made known by them, and also things shall be made known by them which otherwise could not be known" (Mosiah 8:16–17).

President Howard W. Hunter explained the calling of a prophet and begins by quoting Elder Widtsoe: "Dr. John A. Widtsoe defines a prophet as a teacher—one who expounds truth. 'He teaches the body of truth, the gospel, revealed by the Lord to man; and under inspiration explains it to the understanding of the people.' The word 'prophet' is often used to designate one who receives revelation and direction from the Lord. Many have thought that a prophet is essentially a foreteller of future events and happenings, but this is only one of the many functions of a prophet. He is a spokesman for the Lord."[17]

President Harold B. Lee quoted the Prophet Joseph Smith concerning the calling of a prophet: "The Prophet Joseph Smith explained something about the refining process through which he went. He said, 'A Prophet is not always a Prophet. He is a Prophet only when he's acting as such.' This is an illuminating statement and doubtless holds good in the cases of most ancient men of God. Very likely the ancient Prophet received his polishing in much the same way that Joseph Smith said he was polished."[18]

Hyrum Smith left this testimony of his brother's calling as a prophet: "There were prophets before, but Joseph has the spirit and power of all the prophets."[19]

Joseph Smith's calling as a seer was foretold by his ancestor Joseph who was sold into Egypt:

"Wherefore, Joseph [who was sold into Egypt] truly saw our day. And he obtained a promise of the Lord, that out of the fruit of his loins the Lord God would raise up a righteous branch unto the house of Israel. . . .

"For Joseph truly testified, saying: A seer shall the Lord my God raise up, who shall be a choice seer unto the fruit of my loins. Yea, Joseph truly said: Thus saith the Lord unto me: A choice seer will I raise up out of the fruit of thy loins; and he shall be esteemed highly among the fruit of thy loins. And unto him will I give commandment that he shall do a work for the fruit of thy loins, his brethren, which shall be of great worth unto them, even to the bringing of them to the knowledge of the covenants which I have made with thy fathers. And I will give unto him a commandment that he shall do none other work, save the work which I shall command him. And I will make him great in mine eyes; for he shall do my work. And he shall be great like unto Moses" (2 Nephi 3:5–9).

President Marion G. Romney testified that Joseph Smith was that "choice seer": "Joseph Smith was this great seer. Next to the Savior Himself there has, in my judgment, never been a greater seer on the earth."[20]

President Gordon B. Hinckley indicated that the seership of Joseph Smith enabled him to prepare himself and the kingdom of God for the future: "Joseph Smith, the prophet of God . . . was indeed a mighty seer, who saw this day and greater days yet to come as the work of the Lord moves over the earth."[21]

Joseph Smith, the prophet and seer, was also a revelator of God's truths. The Lord promised Joseph Smith: "God shall give unto you knowledge by his Holy Spirit, yea, by the unspeakable gift of the Holy Ghost, that has not been revealed since the world was until now" (D&C 121:26).

President Howard W. Hunter explained the role of a revelator: "A revelator makes known something presently unknown or which has been known previously by man and taken from his memory. Always the revelation deals with truth, and always it comes with the divine stamp of approval. Revelation is received in various ways, but it always presupposes that the revelator has so lived and conducted himself as to be in tune or harmony with the divine spirit of revelation, the spirit of truth, and therefore capable of receiving divine messages."[22]

Survived Tests of Ridicule and Persecution

Because of his great faith and because he lived a worthy life that enabled him to commune with Jehovah, Joseph Smith was able to endure and overcome the tests of ridicule and persecution. Jesus Christ, the Savior of all mankind, suffered persecution above all others, which led to His eventual crucifixion. Few others who have lived upon the earth have approached the ridicule and persecution heaped upon the Master, but Joseph Smith was one whose persecution also led to martyrdom.

President Hugh B. Brown reflected on the possible reasons for the persecution of Joseph Smith:

"I've often wondered why those early American Christians persecuted Joseph Smith as they did. Many of the mobs that came against him were led by professed ministers of the gospel of Jesus Christ. Now why did they persecute him? Did he come to them and say, 'There is no Christ'? Did he say to them, 'I am the Christ'?

He said none of these things. He said, 'Jesus of Nazareth is the Christ, the Son of God and His is the only Name under heaven whereby men must be saved.' That was his declaration. . . .

"I again ask why they persecute a man when he comes to them, professed Christians, and tells them that the one whom they claim to believe in is, in fact, the Christ? What they couldn't tolerate was his—to them—blasphemous statement, 'I have seen Him and I have heard Him.' Why should it be thought a thing incredible to any one who believes the Holy Bible that a man could see and hear and talk with God? Did not all the prophets make that claim?"[23]

Historian Dean Jessee also wrote about the scorn and antagonism heaped upon Joseph Smith:

"Even though Joseph Smith was warned by a heavenly messenger at an early age that his name would be known for both good and evil among all nations, he was not quite prepared for the intensity of the scorn that was heaped upon him. It was a source of 'serious reflection' to him that one so obscure as he was, whose circumstances made him of 'no consequence in the world,' should attract such bitter opposition.

"But so it was. Few historical figures have confronted more antagonism during their lives than did Joseph Smith. Practically everything written about him in the public print of his time was colored by a spirit of malice. Yet much of this writing was contradictory in detail, though it may have agreed in tone. On the other hand, those contemporaries who knew him best wrote sympathetic and praiseworthy accounts of his life. Such widespread disagreement makes the Prophet an intriguing subject for historians' scrutiny. But the careful examination of original sources has to a great extent resolved the puzzles, shedding helpful light on the Prophet and his critics."[24]

SUMMARY TRIBUTES TO JOSEPH SMITH

Praise to the man who communed with Jehovah! . . .
Kings shall extol him, and nations revere.[25]

In 1892 Dr. Andrew White, United States foreign minister to Russia, called on Count Leo Tolstoy. In the course of their conversation Dr. Tolstoy said, "Dr. White, I wish you would tell me about your American religion."

Explaining that America had many religions and that each American was free to belong to the church of his choice, Dr. White said, "We have no state church in America."

"I know all of this, but I want to know about the *American* religion," Count Tolstoy said. "The Church to which I refer originated in America, and is commonly known as the Mormon Church. What can you tell me of the teachings of the Mormons?"

Dr. White admitted that he knew little of the Church, to which Count Tolstoy replied, "Dr. White, I am greatly surprised and disappointed that a man of your great learning and position should be so ignorant on this important subject. The Mormon people teach the American religion; their principles teach the people not only of Heaven and its attendant glories, but how to live so that their social and economic relations with each other are placed on a sound basis. If the people follow the teachings of this Church, nothing can stop their progress—it will be limitless. There have been great movements started in the past but they have died or been modified before they reach maturity. If Mormonism is able to endure, unmodified, until it reaches the third and fourth generation, it is destined to become the greatest power the world has ever known."[26]

Brigham Young speaks of Joseph Smith's transcendent spiritual power in these words: "When I first heard him preach, he brought heaven and earth together; and all the priests of the day could not tell me anything correct about heaven, hell, God, angels, or devils: they were as blind as Egyptian darkness. When I saw Joseph Smith, he took heaven, figuratively speaking, . . . and opened up, in plainness and simplicity, the things of God; and that is the beauty of his mission."[27] "I feel like shouting hallelujah, all the time, when I think that I ever knew Joseph Smith, the Prophet whom the Lord raised up and ordained, and to whom He gave keys and power to build up the kingdom of God on earth."[28]

Perhaps the most widely quoted tribute to Joseph Smith is the one prepared by Elder John Taylor, who subsequently served as the third President of the Church in this dispensation: "Joseph Smith, the Prophet and Seer of the Lord, has done more, save Jesus only, for the salvation of men in this world, than any other man that ever lived in it. . . . He lived great, and he died great in the eyes of God and his people; and like most of the Lord's anointed in ancient times, has sealed his mission and his works with his own blood" (D&C 135:3).

John Taylor also testified: "I was with him living, and with him when he died. . . . I have seen him under all these various circumstances, and I testify before God, angels and men that he was a good, honorable, virtuous man—and that his doctrines were good, scriptural, and wholesome—that his precepts were such as became a man of God—that his private and public character was unimpeachable—that he lived and died as a man of God, and a gentleman."[29]

Notes

From an essay prepared for the book *The Prophet Joseph,* edited by Larry C. Porter and Susan Easton Black (Salt Lake City: Deseret Book Co., 1988).

1. Hundreds of other terms and titles that apply to Jesus Christ would not be used by thoughtful Latter-day Saints to refer to Joseph Smith, including the following: "Beloved Son of God" (Matthew 3:17), "Great I Am" (Exodus 3:14; D&C 29:1), "Alpha and Omega, the beginning and the ending, the first and the last" (Revelation 1:8, 11), "Jehovah" (Exodus 6:3; Psalms 83:18), "Redeemer" (Job 19:25), "Savior" (Matthew 1:21), "Lamb of God" (John 1:29), "Messiah" (Daniel 9:25–26), "King of Zion, the Rock of Heaven" (Moses 7:53), "God, Lord God, God of Abraham, Isaac, and Jacob" (Exodus 3:15), "Good and Great and True Shepherd" (John 10:11–14; Hebrews 13:20; Helaman 15:13), "Captain of Man's Salvation" (Hebrews 2:10), "Founder and Prince of Peace" (Mosiah 15:18; Isaiah 9:6), "Head and Chief Corner Stone" (Psalm 118:22; Ephesians 2:20), "Resurrection and the Life" (John 11:25), "First Born and First Begotten of the Dead" (Colossians 1:18; Revelation 1:5), "the First Fruits of them that slept" (1 Corinthians 15:20; 2 Nephi 2:8–9), "Father of Heaven" (1 Nephi 22:9) and "of Earth" (Helaman 14:12), and "King of kings, and Lord of lords" (1 Timothy 6:15; Revelation 17:14).
2. Gordon B. Hinckley, "Joseph the Seer," *Ensign,* May 1977, 65.
3. Neal A. Maxwell, "The Prophet Joseph Smith: Spiritual Statesman," Annual Joseph Smith Memorial Sermons, Logan, Utah, 19 January 1975, 12.
4. Richard L. Bushman, "The Teaching of Joseph Smith," Annual Joseph Smith Memorial Sermons, Logan, Utah, 18 January 1976, 1.
5. "Praise to the Man," in *Hymns of The Church of Jesus Christ of Latter-day Saints* (Salt Lake City: The Church of Jesus Christ of Latter-day Saints, 1985), no. 27.
6. Ezra Taft Benson, "Joseph Smith—Man of Destiny," Annual Joseph Smith Memorial Sermons, Logan, Utah, 3 December 1967, 3. See also *History of the Church,* 6:364.
7. Brigham Young, in *Journal of Discourses,* 7:289–90.
8. Neal A. Maxwell, "The Prophet Joseph Smith: Spiritual Statesman," 13.
9. Richard L. Bushman, "The Teaching of Joseph Smith," 10.
10. Jerry C. Roundy, "The Greatness of Joseph Smith and His Remarkable Visions," *New Era,* December 1973, 12.
11. *Teachings of the Prophet Joseph Smith,* 313.
12. Ibid., 174.
13. "Praise to the Man," in *Hymns,* no. 27.
14. Gordon B. Hinckley, "Joseph Smith from the Perspective of 150 Years," Annual Joseph Smith Memorial Sermons, Logan, Utah, 3 February 1980, 8.
15. Robert J. Matthews, "Modern Revelation, Window to the Old Testament," *Ensign,* October 1973, 23; see also Brigham Young, in *Journal of Discourses,* 21:94; and D&C 128:21.
16. "Praise to the Man," in *Hymns,* no. 27.
17. Howard W. Hunter, "Joseph—the Seer," Annual Joseph Smith Memorial Sermons, Logan, Utah, 15 December 1960, 7; see also John A. Widtsoe, *Evidences and Reconciliations* (Salt Lake City: Bookcraft, 1943), 204.
18. Harold B. Lee, "Joseph Smith—His Mission Divine," Annual Joseph Smith Memorial Sermons, Logan, Utah, 4 December 1955, 132.
19. *History of the Church,* 6:346.
20. Marion G. Romney, "Joseph Smith the Seer, and Truth," Annual Joseph Smith Memorial Sermons, Logan, Utah, 15 January 1978, 3.

21. Hinckley, "Joseph the Seer," 65.
22. Hunter, "Joseph—the Seer," 8–9.
23. Hugh B. Brown, "Joseph among the Prophets," Annual Joseph Smith Memorial Sermons, Logan, Utah, 7 December 1958, 175–76.
24. Dean C. Jessee, "Joseph Smith's Reputation," *Ensign,* September 1979, 57; see also *History of the Church,* 1:7, 11.
25. "Praise to the Man," in *Hymns,* no. 27.
26. Thomas J. Yates, "Count Tolstoi and the 'American Religion,'" *Improvement Era,* 42 (February 1939): 94.
27. Brigham Young, in *Journal of Discourses,* 5:332.
28. Ibid., 3:51.
29. B. H. Roberts, *Comprehensive History of the Church,* 6 vols. (Salt Lake City: Deseret News Press, 1930), 2:353.

The House of Israel

Chapter 36

JOSEPH SMITH'S CONTRIBUTIONS TO AN UNDERSTANDING OF ISRAEL

BACKGROUND OF JOSEPH SMITH

I am convinced that Joseph Smith knew more about Israel than any other person of his century. A major branch of Jewish people refers to Theodor Herzl as the father of political Zionism—the person who inspired a branch of the house of Israel to gather back to Jerusalem. But over nineteen years before Theodor Herzl was even born, the Prophet Joseph Smith sent an apostle of the restored Church to the Holy Land to dedicate the land for the return of Judah. Yes, I am convinced without any shadow of a doubt that the Prophet Joseph Smith knew more about Israel than any man of his century.

I doubt there were any miraculous signs in the heavens that occurred on December 23, 1805, when Joseph Smith was born. Perhaps it is appropriate that there would be no special indication of the significance of the birth of this man. It seems to me that only at the birth of the Savior, the Creator of the world, should the heavens rejoice, a special star appear, and a day and a night and a day of light be given to the house of Israel. In heaven, however, I suspect that there were notes taken of the significance of Joseph Smith's birth. I am convinced that the Prophet had been preparing for millennia to come to earth to fulfill his great foreordained calling as the prophet of the dispensation of the fulness of times.

Some 3,400 years before Joseph Smith was born upon the earth, Jehovah himself referred to the coming of this prophet of the last dispensation. When Lehi was giving a patriarchal blessing to his son Joseph, he explained why he named his son Joseph by saying essentially, "I have named you this because I am a descendant of Joseph who was carried captive into Egypt" (see 2 Nephi 3:1–4). Lehi also told his son Joseph that Joseph of old truly saw our day; then he records a dialogue that Joseph had with Jehovah:

"Yea, Joseph truly said: Thus saith the Lord unto me: A choice seer will I raise up out of the fruit of thy loins; and he shall be esteemed highly among the fruit of thy loins. And unto him will I give commandment that he shall do a work for the fruit of thy loins, his brethren, which shall be of great worth unto them, even to the bringing of them to the knowledge of the covenants which I have made with thy fathers.

"And I will give unto him a commandment that he shall do none other work, save the work which I shall command him. And I will make him great in mine eyes; for he shall do my work. . . .

"But a seer will I raise up out of the fruit of thy loins; and unto him will I give power to bring forth my word unto the seed of thy loins—and not to the bringing forth my word only, saith the Lord, but to the convincing them of my word, which shall have already gone forth among them.

"Wherefore, the fruit of thy loins shall write; and the fruit of the loins of Judah shall write; and that which shall be written by the fruit of thy loins, and also that which shall be written by the fruit of the loins of Judah, shall grow together, unto the confounding of false doctrines and laying down of contentions, and establishing peace among the fruit of thy loins, and bringing them to the knowledge of their fathers in the latter days, and also to the knowledge of my covenants, saith the Lord.

"And out of weakness he shall be made strong, in that day when my work shall commence among all my people, unto the restoring thee, O house of Israel, saith the Lord" (2 Nephi 3:7–8, 11–13).

I think that is a rather remarkable statement to be made concerning the Prophet Joseph Smith long before he was born, especially when you remember that the pre-earthly Jehovah is saying these words. Then Joseph who was sold into Egypt concluded with these prophetic words:

"Behold that seer will the Lord bless; and they that seek to destroy him shall be confounded; for this promise, which I have obtained of the Lord, of the fruit of my loins, shall be fulfilled. Behold, I am sure of the fulfilling of this promise; And his name shall be called after me; and it shall be after the name of his father. And he shall be like unto me; for the thing, which the Lord shall bring forth by his hand, by the power of the Lord shall bring my people unto salvation" (2 Nephi 3:14–15).

I do not believe that Brigham Young exaggerated when he made this statement concerning the Prophet Joseph Smith: "It was decreed in the councils of eternity, long before the foundations of the earth were laid, that [Joseph Smith] should be the man, in the last dispensation of this world, to bring forth the word of God to the people, and receive the fulness of the keys and power of the Priesthood of the Son of God. The Lord had his eye upon him, and upon his father, and upon his father's father, and upon their progenitors clear back to Abraham, and from Abraham to the flood, from the flood to Enoch, and from Enoch to Adam. He has watched that family and that blood as it has circulated from its fountain to the birth of that man. [Joseph Smith] was foreordained in eternity to preside over this last dispensation."[1]

I have also been intrigued that others, some not even of our faith, have also been impressed with the life and mission of the Prophet Joseph Smith. Josiah Quincy, mayor of Boston and a contemporary of the Prophet Joseph Smith, after he had visited Nauvoo and visited with the Prophet, wrote in his book of recollections concerning that visit: "It is by no means improbable that some future textbook for the use of generations yet unborn, will contain a question something like this: What historical American of the nineteenth century has exerted the most powerful influence upon the destinies of his countrymen? And it is by no means impossible that the answer to that interrogatory may be thus written: Joseph Smith, the Mormon Prophet."[2]

In addition to this statement of Josiah Quincy, a Russian sociologist who visited the United States after World War II also praised Joseph Smith. An account of his visit reads as follows: "As he boarded a ship at the pier in New York to return to his native land, newspaper correspondents crowded about him and among other questions asked, 'Who do you consider the greatest Americans?' They were astounded at his answer. He said, 'You have only had one great American—Joseph Smith, the Mormon Prophet. He is the only man in your culture who has given to the world ideas which if followed will revolutionize the human race.'"[3]

I do not know what kind of definition others would want to apply to the question, "Who is the greatest American?" It seems to me, however, that the greatest American of all time would be that person who has had the greatest impact on the largest number of people over the longest period of time. Some Americans have had tremendous impact on large numbers of people for a relatively short period of time, but when those persons have died, their influence has died with them. Some

Americans have had great influence on small numbers of people over long periods of time. But if we look at the significance and importance of American leaders from the viewpoint of eternity, there has not been or ever will be an American citizen who will have a greater influence on a larger number of people over a longer period of time than the Prophet Joseph Smith. Therefore, I think Mr. Quincy and the Russian sociologist may well be right—that in time we will find that Joseph Smith is the greatest of all American citizens.

Sources of Joseph Smith's Understanding of Israel

We do not know how much the Prophet Joseph Smith knew about the gospel or about the house of Israel before the spring of 1820. In fact, the account we have of the First Vision in the Pearl of Great Price really does not help us very much. Joseph Smith tells us something about what the Savior said to him on that occasion concerning churches—that he should join none of them. The Savior said, "They draw near to me with their lips, but their hearts are far from me" (Joseph Smith—History 1:19). Inasmuch as that answered the essential question the Prophet Joseph Smith had on that occasion, that is the only answer we are given. I am sure the Prophet must have been given some other help concerning his foreordained destiny, but he tells us little concerning that episode. However, what he did say was significant, and the fact that he had this experience was most significant.

For a few moments (how long we do not know), Joseph Smith was privileged to see into eternity and to visit with the Father and the Son. Those who know the power of revelation and vision know that in five minutes a man gazing into heaven can learn more about heaven than a man who only wonders about it can learn in hundreds or thousands of years. Undoubtedly during that vision or subsequent visions the Prophet Joseph Smith was allowed to see not only the great history and destiny of Israel in the last days but also his role in that destiny. Probably, in regard to knowledge of Israel, Joseph Smith grew as did the Savior anciently as recorded in D&C 93:13, wherein we learn that the Lord grew "from grace to grace, until he received a fulness" (see also Luke 2:52).

Visits of the Angel Moroni

Another major event, however, tells us a great deal more about what Joseph Smith understood concerning Israel. On September 21, 1823, after the Prophet had retired to his bed, he tells of the appearance of the angel Moroni to him. We have an account of this in the Pearl of Great Price, and it is interesting to note that after indicating something about the Book of Mormon, Moroni then gave further information to the Prophet Joseph Smith. The Prophet tells about it in these words: "After telling me these things, he commenced quoting the prophecies of the Old Testament. He first quoted part of the third chapter of Malachi; and he quoted also the fourth or last chapter of the same prophecy, though with a little variation from the way it reads in our Bibles" (Joseph Smith—History 1:36).

Joseph Smith gives us some of the changes made by the angel Moroni concerning the prophecies of Malachi. Then the Prophet continued, "In addition to these, he quoted the eleventh chapter of Isaiah, saying that it was about to be fulfilled" (Joseph Smith—History 1:40). Now that is a rather remarkable statement in and of itself—particularly if you review the contents of the eleventh chapter of Isaiah. This chapter has probably generated more controversy than all of the other chapters of Isaiah concerning the gathering of Israel. In this chapter Isaiah prophesied: "And it shall come to pass in that day, that the Lord shall set his hand again the second time to recover the remnant of his people. . . . And he shall set up an ensign for the nations, and shall assemble the outcasts of Israel, and gather together the dispersed of Judah from the four corners of the earth. The envy also of Ephraim shall depart, and the adversaries of Judah shall be cut off: Ephraim shall not envy Judah, and Judah shall not vex Ephraim" (Isaiah 11:11–13).

Most theologians and biblical scholars maintain that this prophecy was fulfilled at the time the Babylonian captivity of ancient Israel was completed. At one time the people of "blood Israel" lived in "land Israel," and they were part of "covenant Israel" because they had entered into covenants with Heavenly Father. But after living under judges for about 300 years, they divided into two kingdoms—about 1,095 years B.C.E (before the Common Era or before the time of Christ). For about 120 years they had kings as part of the United Kingdom—Saul, David, and Solomon—but upon the death of Solomon they could not agree on who the new king should be, and they divided into two kingdoms. The northern kingdom consisted of about ten of the tribes, headed by Josephites—Ephraim particularly, with headquarters at Shechem in Samaria. The southern kingdom took upon itself the name of the Kingdom of Judah, and was headed by descendants of Judah, with headquarters in Jerusalem. In 722 B.C. Assyria came out of the north, captured the northern kingdom, and took many of the people captive into Assyria. The next year these people fled north out of Assyria and were never mentioned again in the Bible. Because about ten tribes were represented in that dispersion and because they were lost from the Bible, we still refer to them as the ten lost tribes.

Subsequently, our Heavenly Father inspired others of the house of Israel to leave the land of Israel—Lehi and his colony, Ishmael and his family, Zoram, and Mulek and his colony. Thus, the house of Israel started to be dispersed among the nations of the earth. Lehi and his colony specifically left because the Lord had warned that the Babylonians were going to destroy the city of Jerusalem and take the people of Judah into captivity. Surely enough, in the eleventh year of the reign of Zedekiah, king of Judah, Nebuchadnezzar and his Babylonian armies marched against Jerusalem, destroyed the city, and took many of the people as captives back into Babylonia. They remained there for about 70 years. Then Cyrus, king of Persia, conquered Babylonia and allowed the Jewish people to return to their land. They returned and, under their prophets, rebuilt their temple and lived there for over 500 years. But they were never an independent kingdom again, living under five major powers during that period of time.

Finally, when the Savior was born among them, they were a province in the Roman Empire. But he prophesied that even that status would soon cease. In the year 68 C.E., thirty-five years after the crucifixion of Christ and sixty-eight years after his birth—when Nero was emperor of Rome, and Titus and Vespasian were his great military leaders—the tenth and twelfth legions of Rome marched against Israel, destroyed the city of Jerusalem, tore down the temple so that not one stone remained upon another, slaughtered hundreds of thousands of people, and took many others captive, scattering them throughout the Roman Empire. Thus, "blood Israel" and "land Israel" were almost completely severed from each other. Within about one hundred years, the people had gone into apostasy, and "covenant Israel" was essentially banished from the earth, except for the remnant here in America that we read about in the Book of Mormon.

Now let us go back and read the words of Isaiah: "And it shall come to pass in that day, that the Lord shall set his hand again the second time to recover the remnant of his people" (Isaiah 11:11). We, as Latter-day Saints, say that scripture refers to the latter days, but scholars and theologians have tended to say that it refers to the return from Babylonian captivity in about 537 B.C. But verse 13 indicates that "the envy also of Ephraim shall depart, and the adversaries of Judah shall be cut off: Ephraim shall not envy Judah, and Judah shall not vex Ephraim." This is rather interesting because scholars, in interpreting this passage of scripture as they do, have no explanation for the reference to Ephraim, who was not around at the time. The tribe of Joseph had either been dispersed or scattered by that time.

The angel Moroni told the Prophet Joseph Smith that the eleventh chapter of Isaiah "was about to be fulfilled," confirming that this prophecy was not fulfilled at the time of the Assyrians or Babylonians. It is being fulfilled in our lifetimes. Therefore, at that moment Joseph Smith, if he understood and comprehended the significance and the extent of that statement, probably knew more and understood more about Israel than anyone else on the earth during his time. But the angel Moroni said much more than that. The Prophet continues: "He quoted also the third chapter of Acts, twenty-second and twenty-third verses, precisely as they stand in our New Testament. He said that that prophet was Christ; but the day had not yet come when 'they who would not hear his voice should be cut off from among the people,' but soon would come" (Joseph Smith—History 1:40).

You see what an opportunity it would be to have an angel sent from God to tell you what the scriptures really mean, so that you are no longer left to wonder or speculate.

"He also quoted the second chapter of Joel, from the twenty-eighth verse to the last. He also said that this was not yet fulfilled, but was soon to be. And he further stated that the fulness of the Gentiles was soon to come in. He quoted many other passages of scripture, and offered many explanations which cannot be mentioned here" (Joseph Smith—History 1:41).

WENTWORTH LETTER

In 1835 when the Prophet Joseph Smith wrote the account we have in the Pearl of Great Price, he said he could not tell us more about the appearance of the angel Moroni at that time. However, seven years later in 1842, an editor in Chicago by the name of John Wentworth asked the Prophet to write a statement for his newspaper on the history of the Church. In response, Joseph Smith wrote what is referred to in Church history as the Wentworth Letter. In that letter he felt freer, evidently, to tell more about the appearance of the angel Moroni in 1823. In his diary, Joseph Smith wrote: *"March 1, 1842.*—At the request of Mr. John Wentworth, Editor and Proprietor of the *Chicago Democrat,* I have written the following sketch of the rise, progress, persecution, and faith of the Latter-day Saints."

Then he tells about the First Vision and other events. He wrote the following concerning the appearance of Moroni:

"On the evening on the 21st of September, A.D. 1823, while I was praying unto God, and endeavoring to exercise faith in the precious promises of Scripture, on a sudden a light like that of day, only of a far purer and more glorious appearance and brightness, burst into the room, indeed the first sight was as though the house was filled with consuming fire; the appearance produced a shock that affected the whole body; in a moment a personage stood before me surrounded with a glory yet greater than that with which I was already surrounded. This messenger proclaimed himself to be an angel of God, sent to bring the joyful tidings that the covenant which God made with ancient Israel was at hand to be fulfilled, that the preparatory work for the second coming of the Messiah was speedily to commence; that the time was at hand for the Gospel in all its fullness to be preached in power, unto all nations that a people might be prepared for the Millennial reign. I was informed that I was chosen to be an instrument in the hands of God to bring about some of His purposes in this glorious dispensation.

"I was also informed concerning the aboriginal inhabitants of this country and shown who they were, and from whence they came."[4]

I submit that after that experience on September 21, 1823, the Prophet Joseph Smith understood more about Israel than any other person who was then living upon the earth, and he had as his tutor an angel who came directly from the presence of God to deliver that understanding to him.

I think another interesting account and date in the lifetime of the Prophet would be that of May 15, 1829, when the Aaronic Priesthood was restored to the earth. In ordaining Joseph Smith and Oliver Cowdery, John the Baptist said that the power of the Aaronic Priesthood would not be taken from the earth until the sons of Levi "do offer again an offering unto the Lord in righteousness" (D&C 13). The account of that appearance refers to prophecy—the fact that some of these things have been prophesied.

Explanation of Prophecy

The relevance, solidity, and importance of prophecy cannot be overstated. There are four absolute prerequisites to prophecy. First of all, the foreknowledge of our Heavenly Father. Unless Heavenly Father knows what is going to happen, how can he tell us what is going to happen? Our scriptures clearly indicate that God does know what is going to happen. In the Book of Mormon we read, "He [God] knoweth all things, and there is not anything save he knows it" (2 Nephi 9:20). The Book of Mormon also states, "All things have been done in the wisdom of him who knoweth all things" (2 Nephi 2:24). But notice this profound statement in the Doctrine and Covenants, "All things . . . past, present, and future, . . . are continually before the Lord" (130:7). So the first prerequisite of prophecy is the foreknowledge of God.

The second prerequisite is the principle of revelation—to have a worthy spokesman upon the earth. Even though our Heavenly Father may know what is going to happen in the future, if there is no means or power by which he can reveal his mind to man, we cannot have revelation or prophecy. And if there is no person on the earth who is willing and worthy to receive the mind and will of our Heavenly Father, we cannot have prophecy. But the scriptures indicate that there is a principle of revelation and that there have been times when there have been worthy prophets upon the earth. Amos said, "Surely the Lord God will do nothing, but he revealeth his secret unto his servants the prophets" (Amos 3:7). In the Book of Mormon we read, "For by the Spirit are all things made known unto the prophets" (1 Nephi 22:2). Then, of course, we Latter-day Saints have the Articles of Faith: "We believe in the gift of tongues, prophecy, revelation" (7), and "We believe all that God has revealed, all that He does now reveal, and we believe that He will yet reveal many great and important things pertaining to the Kingdom of God" (9).

The third prerequisite of prophecy is that prophecy be not of private interpretation. In fact, Peter wrote in his second epistle: "Knowing this first, that no prophecy of the scripture is of any private interpretation. For the prophecy came not in old time by the will of man: but holy men of God spake as they were moved by the Holy Ghost" (2 Peter 1:20–21).

The fourth requirement comes from the law of witnesses: "In the mouth of two or three witnesses shall every word be established" (2 Corinthians 13:1).

Explanation of History

I would prefer to read the words of prophets as to what is going to happen than to read the words of historians as to what has happened. In other words, I would always take the words of the prophets over those of the historians. The *Encyclopedia Britannica* defines history as a recording of events that have happened; if that is the definition of history, then I will stand by the statement that prophecy is more sure than history. If we apply a more specific and a more narrow definition to history—that history is the actual event that happened—that is something else. In a sense, perhaps nothing could be more certain than that which has happened.

But let us look at some things we call history. Let us consider the American Revolutionary War for a moment. What do we know about the Revolutionary War? Absolutely nothing except for those things a teacher, parent, peer, or author has told us. And that "someone" has given us his interpretation of what happened. If you do not think it is important to know whose interpretation you are reading, then read some books in the local library on the American Revolutionary War written by British authors. When I was at Columbia University, I had to pass some doctoral exams on history, and for the first time I read some history books about the American Civil War written from what one of my friends from South Carolina referred to as "an unprejudiced Southern viewpoint."

History is *always* of private interpretation. Prophecy is *never* of private interpretation. Prophecy is given by the influence of God through the Holy Ghost to worthy men, and the only way it can be interpreted is by the influence of the Holy Ghost upon them (see 2 Peter 1:20–21). I am not trying to belittle history. I respect historians. So far as I know, they are honest, sincere people; therefore, when I say that the historian cannot be completely objective, I am not saying so in a derogatory sense. But historians cannot be completely objective. The historian is always prejudiced—he always makes prejudgments. He decides what he is going to tell you, what he is not going to tell you, what he is going to put in a chapter, and what he is going to put in a sentence. The historian is a different person than he would be if he had not learned about a particular event; therefore, the event has had an influence on him. The historian can never be completely objective because he always speaks from a prejudiced viewpoint. Perhaps that is why we do not have a good history of the Church. Who could write it? Certainly not a member of the Church because he is prejudiced—he has made some prejudgments. But certainly a nonmember of the Church could not write an objective history of the Church either because he is also prejudiced—he has made some prejudgments. So I have never been able to figure out who could write an objective history.

I do not believe a prophet can be completely objective either. But a prophet can be more objective than a historian, even if both are trying to be honest and sincere. The prophet can be more objective than the historian for this major reason: He is not a product of the event because the event has not yet happened. Therefore, I would rather take prophecy over history any day.

Prophecies in the Book of Mormon

I now refer to some specific prophecies of the Prophet Joseph Smith concerning prophecy and Israel. When we read prophecy, we are reading history in the future. Just as prophecy is sort of history in reverse, the prophecies I am going to refer to constitute the future history of the house of Israel, although references about it will be in the present.

In March 1830 the Book of Mormon was published. Its preface indicates that one purpose of the book is to show "unto the remnant of the House of Israel what great things the Lord hath done for their fathers; and that they may know the covenants of the Lord, that they are not cast off forever—And also to the convincing of the Jew and Gentile that Jesus is the Christ, the Eternal God, manifesting himself unto all nations."

We have to assume that after 1830 Joseph Smith knew everything pertaining to the house of Israel that was in the Book of Mormon because under the power and influence of the Holy Ghost he translated that sacred record. I submit that those who know what is taught in the Book of Mormon concerning the great destiny of Israel in the last dispensation know more about Israel than 99 percent of the people who live on this earth.

When I was preparing material on this subject, I went to all the statements in the scriptures concerning Israel. These scriptures indicate three aspects to the gathering of Israel, just as there were three aspects to the scattering—the lost tribes, the dispersed of Israel, and Judah. Some peoples of the world understand one of these aspects, but I honestly do not know anyone except the Latter-day Saints who understand all three of these aspects. All of these deal with Israel, and we have to assume that during his lifetime Joseph Smith knew of all of these statements concerning Israel.

The Book of Mormon makes hundreds, perhaps thousands, of references to Israel. I refer to only a few of them to indicate the scope of the understanding of the Prophet Joseph Smith concerning the gathering of Israel:

"Nevertheless, when that day cometh, saith the prophet, that they no more turn aside their hearts against the Holy One of Israel, then will he remember the covenants which he made to their fathers. Yea, then will he remember the isles of the sea; yea, and all the people who are of the house of Israel, will I gather in, saith the Lord, according to the words of the prophet Zenos, from the four quarters of the earth. Yea, and all the earth shall see the salvation of the Lord, saith the prophet; every nation, kindred, tongue and people shall be blessed" (1 Nephi 19:15–17).

In a second reference to Israel, Nephi prophesies, "And the Lord will set his hand again the second time to restore his people from their lost and fallen state" (2 Nephi 25:17).

The first time these people were restored, according to the scholars, would have been when they were brought out of Egypt; the second time was when they were brought out of Babylonia. But Latter-day Saints say no. When the prophecies were made, the people of Israel were already in the land of Israel, so the first time after that period would have been when they came out of Babylonia, and the second time would be in the last days. Therefore, it is important in reading prophecy to put it in the proper perspective with history. Now let us finish the second scriptural reference:

"And the Lord will set his hand again the second time to restore his people from their lost and fallen state. Wherefore, he will proceed to do a marvelous work and a wonder among the children of men. Wherefore, he shall bring forth his words unto them . . . for the purpose of convincing them of the true Messiah, who was rejected by them; and unto the convincing of them that they need not look forward any more for a Messiah to come . . . for there is save one Messiah spoken of by the prophets, and that Messiah is he who should be rejected of the Jews" (2 Nephi 25:17–18).

A third reference tells us: "And it shall come to pass that the Jews which are scattered also shall begin to believe in Christ; and they shall begin to gather in upon the face of the land; . . . The Lord God shall commence his work among all nations, kindreds, tongues, and people, to bring about the restoration of his people upon the earth" (2 Nephi 30:7–8).

After Mormon had abridged the records to the book of 3 Nephi and had seen how all the prophecies of the prophets had been fulfilled for hundreds of years, he could not help but reminisce concerning the implications. Although the following remarkable quotation is from 3 Nephi, the author of these words was the prophet Mormon:

"Surely he hath blessed the house of Jacob, and hath been merciful unto the seed of Joseph. And insomuch as the children of Lehi have kept his commandments he hath blessed them and prospered them according to his word. Yea, and surely shall he again bring a remnant of the seed of Joseph to the knowledge of the Lord their God. And as surely as the Lord liveth, will he gather in from the four quarters of the earth all the remnant of the seed of Jacob, who are scattered abroad upon all the face of the earth.

"And as he hath covenanted with all the house of Jacob, even so shall the covenant wherewith he hath covenanted with the house of Jacob be fulfilled in his own due time, unto the restoring all the house of Jacob unto the knowledge of the covenant that he hath covenanted with them. And then shall they know their Redeemer, who is Jesus Christ, the Son of God; and then shall they be gathered in from the four quarters of the earth unto their own lands, from whence they have been dispersed; yea, as the Lord liveth so shall it be. Amen" (3 Nephi 5:21–26).

If the Prophet Joseph Smith had done no more than read and understand the

Book of Mormon, by the time he got to 3 Nephi, chapter 5, he would have known more about Israel in the last days than any of his contemporaries. A few chapters later, we have these profound and prophetic words of the Savior himself:

"And then will I gather them in from the four quarters of the earth; and then will I fulfil the covenant which the Father hath made unto all the people of the house of Israel" (3 Nephi 16:5).

"The Father . . . sent me to bless you . . . this because ye are the children of the covenant—

. . . then fulfilleth the Father the covenant which he made with Abraham, saying: In thy seed shall all the kindreds of the earth be blessed— . . .

"And I will remember the covenant which I have made with my people; and I have covenanted with them that I would gather them together in mine own due time, that I would give unto them again the land of their fathers for their inheritance, which is the land of Jerusalem, which is the promised land unto them forever, saith the Father.

"And it shall come to pass that the time cometh, when the fulness of my gospel shall be preached unto them; And they shall believe in me, that I am Jesus Christ, the Son of God, and shall pray unto the Father in my name" (3 Nephi 20:26–27, 29–31).

In 1830 a quotation published in the Book of Mormon from the resurrected Jesus Christ said, in effect, that in time the blood of Judah would be gathered back to the land of Jerusalem. The Book of Mormon also contains a prophecy stating: "The time cometh, when the fulness of my gospel shall be preached unto them; And they shall believe in me, that I am Jesus Christ, the Son of God, and shall pray unto the Father in my name" (3 Nephi 20:30–31).

We all know of the fulfillment of the first part of that prophecy. In November 1947 the General Assembly of the United Nations decided that on May 15, 1948, the modern state of Israel would be established. I have often wondered if there was any connection between that date and the date the Aaronic Priesthood was restored: May 15, 1829. The restoration of this priesthood was the beginning of the restoration of power on the earth to gather Israel together again in this dispensation.

It is going to be very interesting to see how the second part of the prophecy is going to be fulfilled: "the fulness of my gospel shall be preached unto them." Many Latter-day Saints ask, "When are we going to open a mission in Israel? When are we going to send missionaries there?" To date, the modern country of Israel now has a law prohibiting proselytizing by missionaries, and The Church of Jesus Christ of Latter-day Saints abides by that law. Note that the law does not prohibit missionaries *per se;* rather, it prohibits the *proselytizing* of persons, or the attempt to have them change their religious beliefs. Thus, other Christian groups presently have "missionaries" in Israel running schools, orphanages, hospitals, and other facilities. Also, since 1968 Brigham Young University, an official arm of our Church, has had students and faculty in Israel participating in semester-abroad programs, has received permission and built the Brigham Young University Jerusalem Center for Near Eastern Studies, and has sponsored many tours of Israel. However, all of the participants in all of these programs are required by BYU to sign a statement agreeing not to proselytize others while they are in Israel; otherwise, they will be released from their respective program and returned home immediately.

Again, it will be interesting to see how the prophecy will be fulfilled: "the time cometh, when the fulness of [the] gospel shall be preached unto them."

The very day the Church was organized, April 6, 1830, a revelation was given to the Prophet Joseph Smith in which the Lord said: "For thus saith the Lord God: Him [Joseph Smith] have I inspired to move the cause of Zion in mighty power for good, and his diligence I know, and his prayers I have heard. Yea, his weeping for Zion I have seen, and I will cause that he shall mourn for her no longer; for his days of rejoicing are come unto the remission of his sins, and the manifestations of my blessings upon his works" (D&C 21:7–8).

Seaton Letter

Shortly thereafter the Prophet Joseph Smith wrote a letter to N. E. Seaton, the editor of a newspaper in Rochester, New York. Joseph Smith commented in the letter that it was written "by commandment of God."[5] Here are some of the statements Joseph Smith made to Mr. Seaton:

"Trusting in that God who has said that these things are hid from the wise and prudent and revealed unto babes, I step forth into the field to tell you what the Lord is doing, and what you must do. . . . The time has at last arrived when the God of Abraham, of Isaac, and of Jacob, has set His hand again the second time to recover the remnants of his people, . . . and establish that covenant with them, which was promised when their sins should be taken away"[6] (see Isaiah 11; Romans 11:25–27; Jeremiah 31:31–33).

This next point is very important. Many students of the Bible may be surprised at this, and some who teach the Bible may have to change their teaching a little bit.

Notice the next words of the Prophet Joseph Smith: "This covenant has never been established with the house of Israel, nor with the house of Judah, for it requires two parties to make a covenant, and those two parties must be agreed, or no covenant can be made. Christ, in the days of His flesh, proposed to make a covenant with them, but they rejected Him and His proposals, . . . and no covenant was made with them at that time."[7]

Even in some of my teaching I have talked about the covenant the Lord made with the Jewish people. Actually, the covenant he made was with Abraham, and by the time we get to the time of Christ, at least 400 years had passed since the people had apostatized and rejected the covenant. Therefore, the covenant was taken away from them. The Prophet Joseph Smith continues:

"Thus after this chosen family had rejected Christ . . . the Gentiles received the covenant, and were grafted in from whence the chosen family were broken off: but the Gentiles have not continued in the goodness of God, but have departed from the faith that was once delivered to the Saints, and have broken the covenant in which their fathers were established. . . .

"And now what remains to be done . . . ? I will proceed to tell you what the Lord requires of all people, high and low, rich and poor, male and female, ministers and people, professors of religion and non-professors, in order that they may enjoy the Holy Spirit of God to a fulness. . . . Repent of all your sins, and be baptized in water for the remission of them, in the name of the Father, and of the Son, and of the Holy Ghost, and receive the ordinance of the laying on of the hands of him who is ordained and sealed unto this power. . . .

"The Book of Mormon is a record of the forefathers of our western tribes of Indians . . . [who] are descendants from that Joseph which was sold into Egypt, and that the land of America is a promised land unto them, . . . with the requisitions of the new covenant. . . . The city of Zion spoken of by David, in the one hundred and second Psalm, will be built upon the land of America. . . . But Judah shall obtain deliverance at Jerusalem. . . . The Good Shepherd will . . . lead them out from all nations where they have been scattered in a cloudy and dark day, to Zion, and to Jerusalem."[8]

We see that the Prophet Joseph Smith fully understood there were to be two major gatherings in the last days: (1) the gathering of the dispersed of Israel to become part of "covenant Israel" (the Church) and to gather here to Zion and (2) a gathering of Judah back to the land of Jerusalem. Both groups have been given the responsibility of preparing temples in their holy cities so that the Lord, whose right it is to rule upon the earth, can come and rule as King of kings and Lord of lords.

He will then have two great capital cities—one in Jerusalem, Israel, from which the word of the Lord will go forth and from whence Christ will rule as Lord of lords, and one in Jackson County, Missouri, in Zion, from which the law will go forth and from whence he will rule as King of kings.

Letter to the Elders of the Church

In September 1835, Joseph Smith wrote a letter to the elders of the Church in which he said:

"I received, by a heavenly vision, a commandment in June following, to take my journey to the western boundaries of the State of Missouri, and there designate the very spot which was to be the central place for the commencement of the gathering together of those who embrace the fullness of the everlasting Gospel. Accordingly I undertook the journey, with certain ones of my brethren, and after a long and tedious journey, suffering many privations and hardships, arrived in Jackson County, Missouri, and after viewing the country, seeking diligently at the hand of God, He manifested Himself unto us, and designated, to me and others, the very spot upon which He designed to commence the work of the gathering, and the upbuilding of an 'holy city,' which should be called Zion— . . .

" . . . Now we learn from the Book of Mormon the very identical continent and spot of land upon which the New Jerusalem is to stand, and it must be caught up according to the vision of John upon the isle of Patmos.

"Now many will feel disposed to say, that this New Jerusalem spoken of, is the Jerusalem that was built by the Jews on the eastern continent. But you will see, from Revelation xxi: 2, there was a New Jerusalem coming down from God out of heaven, adorned as a bride for her husband; that after this, the Revelator was caught away in the Spirit, to a great and high mountain, and saw the great and holy city descending out of heaven from God. Now there are two cities spoken of here. . . . There is a New Jerusalem to be established on this continent, and also Jerusalem shall be rebuilt on the eastern continent."[9]

These concepts are not even understood today by more than one out of a thousand. Again, Joseph Smith was far ahead of his times in his understanding of Israel.

Discussion with the High Council

In January 1836 the Prophet spoke to the high council in Kirtland as follows:

"One of the most important points in the faith of the Church of the Latter-day Saints, through the fullness of the everlasting Gospel, is the gathering of Israel (of whom the Lamanites constitute a part) that happy time when Jacob shall go up to the house of the Lord, to worship Him in spirit and in truth, to live in holiness; when the Lord will restore His judges as at first . . . ; when it shall no longer be said, . . . the Lord lives that brought up the children of Israel from the land of the north, and from all the lands whither He has driven them. That day is one, all important to all men. . . .

"In speaking of the gathering, we mean to be understood as speaking of it according to scripture, the gathering of the elect of the Lord out of every nation on earth, and bringing them to the place of the Lord of Hosts, when the city of righteousness shall be built, and where the people shall be of one heart and one mind, . . . where even upon the bells of the horses shall be written *'Holiness to the Lord.'*

"The Book of Mormon has made known who Israel is, upon this continent."[10]

In section 110 of the Doctrine and Covenants, we find a record of some of the great events that are occurring in this dispensation. On April 3, 1836, shortly after the dedication of the Kirtland Temple, when Joseph Smith and Oliver Cowdery had retired to one end of the temple, a glorious vision burst upon them and the Savior appeared to them and accepted the temple. Moses, as a resurrected being, also appeared to them and restored the keys of the gathering of Israel from the four corners of the earth. Elias appeared to them and restored the keys of the gospel of the dispensation of Abraham. Elijah appeared to them and restored the keys of turning the hearts of the fathers to the children, and the hearts of the children to the fathers, and the sealing powers of the priesthood. Another purpose of the calling of Elijah is made clear in Doctrine and Covenants: "And again, the hearts of the Jews unto the prophets, and the prophets unto the Jews; lest I come and smite the whole earth with a curse" (D&C 98:17).

Thus, the great gathering of the dispersed of Israel began. No formal missions were established in the Church before 1836 because Joseph Smith did not have the keys for the gathering of Israel until after April 3, 1836. The first mission in this dispensation was established in July 1837, and it was established in the British Isles because the Lord told Joseph Smith that that land was rich with the blood of Israel. Within two years the Prophet sent nine of the apostles to England, and within a short time, during the period of the exodus of members of the Church from Nauvoo, there were more members of the Church in the British Isles than in the United States. Literally, that land was rich with the blood of Israel.

It is interesting to remember that it was the Romans who scattered the Israelites in about A.D. 68–71. If we examine a map of the Roman Empire of the first century

A.D., we see that the farthermost part of the Roman Empire from Jerusalem was the British Isles. The Romans wanted to scatter these people as far away from Jerusalem as they could so that they could not rise up in rebellion and try to get back to Jerusalem. Evidently many of the blood of Israel were scattered to the British Isles at that time.

Shortly after Joseph Smith received the keys to gather Israel again, he called Orson Hyde and John Page to go to the Holy Land and dedicate that land for the return of Judah. In a letter the Prophet wrote to them on May 14, 1840, he said: "I am happy in being informed by your letter that your mission swells 'larger and larger.' It is a great and important mission, and one that is worthy those intelligences who surround the throne of Jehovah to be engaged in. Although it appears great at present, yet you have but just begun to realize the greatness, the extent and glory of the same. If there is anything calculated to interest the mind of the Saints, to awaken in them the finest sensibilities, and arouse them to enterprise and exertion, surely it is the great and precious promises made by our heavenly Father to the children of Abraham; and those engaged in seeking the outcasts of Israel, and the dispersed of Judah, cannot fail to enjoy the Spirit of the Lord and have the choicest blessings of heaven rest upon them in copious effusion.

"Brethren, you are in the pathway to eternal fame, and immortal glory; and inasmuch as you feel interested for the covenant people of the Lord, the God of their fathers shall bless you. Do not be discouraged on account of the greatness of the work; only be humble and faithful, and then you can say, 'What art thou, O great mountain! before Zerubbabel shalt thou be brought down.' He who scattered Israel has promised to gather them; therefore inasmuch as you are to be instrumental in this great work, He will endow you with power, wisdom, might and intelligence, and every qualification necessary; while your minds will expand wider and wider, until you can circumscribe the earth and the heavens, reach forth into eternity, and contemplate the mighty acts of Jehovah in all their variety and glory."[11]

Despite that divine calling, Hiram Page did not make it to Jerusalem. It was left to Orson Hyde, therefore, to dedicate that land for the return of Judah, which he did in October 1841.

Theodor Herzl, the great father of political Zionism, was born in 1860. Nineteen years earlier, an apostle of our Church had already dedicated that land for the return of Judah. If Orson Hyde had had 20–20 spiritual vision and could have perceived every Jewish person in those lands, according to the historians, he could not have seen more than 5,000. Yet during the lifetime of many Latter-day Saints born since 1948, those people have been gathering back by thousands, tens of thousands, hundreds of thousands, and even millions. Over 10 million of "blood Israel" have gathered as part of "covenant Israel," while six million of "blood Israel" have gathered back to "land Israel." Now all that remains to be done is to bring the two of them together; then the great millennial reign of Christ can begin upon the earth.

Times and Seasons Editorial

The May 2, 1842, editorial in the *Times and Seasons* reads: "The building up of Zion is a cause that has interested the people of God in every age; it is a theme upon which prophets, priests and kings have dwelt with peculiar delight; they have looked forward with joyful anticipation to the day in which we live; and fired with heavenly and joyful anticipations they have sung and written and prophesied of this our day; but they died without the sight; we are the favored people that God has made choice of to bring about the Latter-day glory; it is left for us to see, participate in and help to roll forward the Latter-day glory, 'the dispensation of the fulness of times, when God will gather together all things that are in heaven, and all things that are upon the earth,' 'even in one,' when the Saints of God will be gathered in one from every nation, and kindred, and people, and tongue, when the Jews will be gathered together into one."[12]

One of the last great public discourses of the Prophet Joseph Smith on the subject of Israel was at the April conference in 1843. In two or three sentences he sketched out the prophetic future of the return of Judah: "Judah must return, Jerusalem must be rebuilt, and the temple, and water come out from under the temple, and the waters of the Dead Sea be healed. It will take some time to rebuild the walls of the city and the temple, &c.; and all this must be done before the Son of Man will make His appearance."[13]

Teachings from the Doctrine and Covenants

Some sections of the Doctrine and Covenants also pertain to this subject:
"And Israel shall be saved in mine own due time; and by the keys which I have given shall they be led, and no more be confounded at all" (D&C 35:25).
"And this I have told you concerning Jerusalem; and when that day shall come, shall a remnant be scattered among all nations; But they shall be gathered again; but they shall remain until the times of the Gentiles be fulfilled. . . . And then shall

the Jews look upon me and say: What are these wounds in thine hands and in thy feet?" (D&C 45:24–25, 51).

"Q. What is to be understood by the two witnesses, in the eleventh chapter of Revelation?

"A. They are two prophets that are to be raised up to the Jewish nation in the last days, at the time of the restoration, and to prophesy to the Jews after they are gathered and have built the city of Jerusalem in the land of their fathers" (D&C 77:15).

"And again, the hearts of the Jews unto the prophets, and the prophets unto the Jews; lest I come and smite the whole earth with a curse, and all flesh be consumed before me" (D&C 98:17).

"And let them who be of Judah flee unto Jerusalem, unto the mountains of the Lord's house. . . . And they also of the tribe of Judah, after their pain, shall be sanctified in holiness before the Lord, to dwell in his presence day and night, forever and ever" (D&C 133:13, 35).

"And the land of Jerusalem and the land of Zion shall be turned back into their own place, and the earth shall be like as it was in the days before it was divided" (D&C 133:24).

Proclamation of 1845

I now refer to some statements that many people have not thought to ascribe to the Prophet Joseph Smith because they were not published until after his death. These statements are from a letter called "Proclamation of the Twelve Apostles of The Church of Jesus Christ of Latter-day Saints to all the Kings of the World, to the President of the United States of America, to the Governors of the Several States, and to the Rulers and People of All Nations." But, as indicated in *Messages of the First Presidency,* it is believed that "this proclamation could be the one that Joseph Smith was commanded in a revelation given January 19, 1841 to issue (D&C 124:1–11). The similarity between the wording of D&C 124:3 and the heading of this Proclamation seems too close not to have a connection."[14] Therefore, even though this message was not issued until April 6, 1845, many Latter-day Saint scholars subscribe to the possibility that the Prophet Joseph Smith wrote this epistle. I quote only fragments of this epistle:

"Know Ye:—

"That the kingdom of God has come: as has been predicted by ancient prophets, and prayed for in all ages. . . .

"Being established in these last days for the restoration of all things spoken of by the prophets since the world began; and in order to prepare the way for the coming of the Son of Man. . . .

"In order to meet this great event there must needs be a preparation.

"Therefore we send unto you with authority from on high, and command you all to repent and humble yourselves as little children, before the majesty of the Holy One; and come unto Jesus with a broken heart and a contrite spirit; and be baptized in his name, for the remission of sins . . . and you shall receive the gift of the Holy Spirit. . . .

"We testify that the foregoing doctrine is the doctrine or gospel of Jesus Christ. . . .

"We also bear testimony that the *'Indians'* (so called) of North and South America are a remnant of the tribes of Israel; as is now made manifest by the discovery and revelation of their ancient oracles and records.

"And that they are about to be gathered, civilized, and made *one nation* in this glorious land.

"They will also come to the knowledge of their forefathers, and of the fulness of the gospel; and they will embrace it, and become a righteous branch of the house of Israel.

"And we further testify that the Lord has appointed a holy city and temple to be built on this continent. . . .

"And we further testify, that the Jews among all nations are hereby commanded, in the name of the Messiah, to prepare, to return to Jerusalem in Palestine; and to rebuild that city and temple unto the Lord:

"And also to organize and establish their own political government, under their own rulers, judges, and governors in that country.

"For be it known unto them that *we* now hold the keys of the priesthood and kingdom which is soon to be restored unto them. . . .

"There is also another consideration of vast importance to all the rulers and people of the world, in regard to this matter. It is this: As this work progresses in its onward course, and becomes more and more an object of political and religious interest and excitement, no king, ruler, or subject, no community or individual, will stand *neutral.* All will at length be influenced by one spirit or the other; and will take sides either for or against the kingdom of God, and the fulfilment of the prophets, in the great restoration and return of his long dispersed covenant people. . . .

"To such an extreme will this great division finally extend, that the nations of the old world will combine to oppose these things by military force. They will send a great army to Palestine, against the Jews; and they will besiege their city, and will reduce the inhabitants of Jerusalem to the greatest extreme of distress and misery.

"Then will commence a struggle in which the fate of nations and empires will be suspended on a single battle.

"In this battle the governors and people of Judah distinguish themselves for their bravery and warlike achievements. The weak among them will be like David, and the strong among them will be like God: or like the angel of the Lord.

"In that day the Lord will pour upon the inhabitants of Jerusalem the spirit of grace and supplication, and they shall look upon the Messiah whom they have pierced.

"For lo! he will descend from heaven, as the defender of the Jews: and to complete their victory. His feet will stand in that day upon the Mount of Olives, which shall cleave in sunder at his presence, and remove one half to the north, and the other to the south; thus forming a great valley where the mountain now stands. . . .

"In that day all who are in the siege, both against Judea and against Jerusalem, shall be cut in pieces; though all the people of the earth should be gathered together against it. . . .

"The Jews as a nation become holy from that day forward; and their city and sanctuary becomes holy. There also the Messiah establishes his throne, and seat of government.

"Jerusalem then becomes the seat of empire, and the great centre and capital of the old world. . . .

"While these great events are rolling on the wheels of time, and being fulfilled in the old world, the Western Continent will present a scene of grandeur, greatness, and glory, far surpassing the scene just described.

"The Lord will make her . . . who was cast afar off, a strong nation; and will reign over *them* in Mount Zion from that time forth and for ever.

"Or, in other words, He will assemble the Natives, the remnants of Joseph in America; and make of them a great, and strong, and powerful nation: and he will civilize and enlighten them, and will establish a holy city, and temple, and seat of government among them, which shall be called Zion.

"And there shall be his tabernacle, his sanctuary, his throne, and seat of government for the whole continent of North and South America for ever.

"In short, it will be to the western hemisphere what Jerusalem will be to the eastern. . . .

"The despised and degraded son of the forest, who has wandered in dejection and sorrow, and suffered reproach, shall then drop his disguise, and stand forth in manly dignity, and exclaim to the Gentiles who have envied and sold him: *'I am Joseph: does my father yet live?'* Or, in other words: I am a descendant of that Joseph who was sold into Egypt. You have hated *me,* and sold *me,* and thought *I* was dead. But lo! I live, and am heir to the inheritance, titles, honors, priesthood, sceptre, crown, throne, and eternal life and dignity of my fathers, who live for evermore. . . .

"Americans! This mighty and strange work has been commenced in your midst, and must roll on in fulfilment.

"You are now invited, and earnestly intreated, to investigate it thoroughly, and to aid and participate in its accomplishment. . . .

"The Lord has spoken, and who can disannul it? He has uttered his voice, and who can gainsay it? He has stretched out his arm, and who can turn it back? . . .

"We say, then, in life or in death, in bonds or free, that the great God has spoken in this age.—*And we know it.*

"He has given us the Holy Priesthood and Apostleship, and the keys of the kingdom of God, to bring about the restoration of all things as promised by the holy prophets of old.—*And we know it.*

"He has revealed the origin and the Records of the aboriginal tribes of America, and their future destiny.—*And we know it.*

"He has revealed the fulness of the gospel, with its gifts, blessings, and ordinances.—*And we know it.*

"He has commanded *us* to bear witness of it, first to the Gentiles, and then to the remnants of Israel and the Jews.—*And we know it.*

"He has commanded us to gather together his Saints on this Continent, and build up holy cities and sanctuaries.—*And we know it.*

"He has said, that the Gentiles should come into the same gospel and covenant; and be numbered with the house of Israel; and be a blessed people upon this good land for ever, if they would repent and embrace it.—*And we know it.*

"He has also said that, if they do not repent, and come to the knowledge of the truth, and cease to fight against Zion, and also put away all murder, lying, pride, priestcraft, whoredom, and secret abomination, they shall soon perish from the earth, and be cast down to hell.—*And we know it.*

"He has said, that the time is at hand for the Jews to be gathered to Jerusalem.—*And we know it.*

"He has said, that the Ten Tribes of Israel should also be revealed in the North country, together with their oracles and records, preparatory to their return, and to their union with Judah, no more to be separated.—*And we know it.*

"He has said, that when these preparations were made, both in this country and in Jerusalem, and the gospel in all its fulness preached to all nations for a witness and testimony, He will come, and all the Saints with him, to reign on the earth one thousand years.—*And we know it.*

"He has said that he will not come in his glory and destroy the wicked, till these warnings were given and these preparations were made for his reception.—*And we know it.* . . .

"But be ye sure of this, that whether we live or die, the words of the testimony of this proclamation which we now send unto you, shall all be fulfilled.

"Heaven and earth shall pass away, but not one jot or tittle of his revealed word shall fail to be fulfilled."[15]

In light of the above insightful observations, whether by the Prophet Joseph Smith himself or by those tutored by him, I ask: How can any honest, sincere person read these words and study the life of the Prophet Joseph Smith and not conclude that he did indeed understand Israel better than any man of his century?

Concluding Testimonies

Joseph Smith and his associate Sidney Rigdon have given the world the following testimony of Jesus Christ:

"After the many testimonies which have been given of him, this is the testimony, last of all, which we give of him: That he lives! For we saw him, even on the right hand of God; and we heard the voice bearing record that he is the Only Begotten of the Father" (D&C 76:22–23).

If I were to paraphrase that scripture and apply it to the Prophet Joseph Smith, I would say: This is the testimony, last of all, that I give of him, That he is indeed the prophet of God chosen to lead the gathering of Israel in the last days, in the dispensation of the fulness of times; that he was indeed foreordained to be born of the house of Israel to help restore Israel to her rightful place in the last days; and that he, Joseph Smith the Prophet, has been faithful to his foreordained calling.

Notes

From an address delivered at the Annual Joseph Smith Memorial Sermons, Logan, Utah, 16 January 1977.

1. Brigham Young, in *Journal of Discourses,* 7:289–90.
2. Josiah Quincy, *Figures of the Past from the Leaves of Old Journals* (Boston: Little, Brown, and Company, 1926), 376–400.
3. Quoted in William E. Berrett, "Joseph Smith, Symbol of Greatness," address at Brigham Young University, Provo, Utah, 13 June 1960.

4. *History of the Church,* 4:535, 536–37.
5. Ibid., 1:326.
6. Ibid., 1:313.
7. Ibid.
8. Ibid., 1:313–15.
9. Ibid., 2:254, 261–62.
10. *Teachings of the Prophet Joseph Smith,* 92–93; emphasis in original.
11. Ibid., 163.
12. Ibid., 231.
13. *History of the Church,* 5:337.
14. *Messages of the First Presidency,* 1:252.
15. Ibid., 1:252–54, 257–61, 263–64; emphasis in original.

Chapter 37

OF THE HOUSE OF ISRAEL

The question is raised hundreds of times each year throughout the Church: Are Church members literal descendants of Israel, as most patriarchal blessings state? Or are we Gentiles and belong to the house of Israel only by adoption?

The answer is important, for the literal seed of Abraham are the natural heirs to the remarkable promises given anciently to Abraham, Isaac, and Jacob.

Most members of the Church understand the principles of heirship and adoption, but they often misunderstand the meaning of some key terms in the scriptures. Terms like *literal descendants of Abraham by birth, tribe of Israel, house of Israel, lineage,* and *Gentiles* are sometimes confused, and some terms have a range of meanings, referring to different ideas in different contexts.

Let's review these terms, then, and examine what the prophets, both ancient and modern, have said about the topic.

WHO IS A LITERAL DESCENDANT OF ABRAHAM BY BIRTH?

In the scriptures, a literal descendant of Abraham is often referred to by the word *Hebrew,* a word derived from the same root as *Eber* (Genesis 10:21). The first time the word is used in the Bible (in Genesis 14:13) it refers to Abraham himself. In Genesis 39:14 it refers to Joseph, a great-grandson of Abraham. Rather consistently throughout the remainder of the scriptures, *Hebrew* is used to refer to those who are direct, literal descendants of Abraham.

The descendants of Abraham (Hebrews) include anyone whose lineage goes back to any of the sons born to Abraham and his three wives. These wives and their sons, listed in the order of the wives' marriages to Abraham, are as follows: from Sarah—Isaac; from Hagar—Ishmael; from Keturah—Zimran, Jokshan, Medan, Midian, Ishbak, and Shuah.

Please note that the descendants of Abraham include many, many more peoples than those who are descended from Isaac, the son who is discussed most in the Bible. Entire nations are directly descended from Abraham, including citizens of the numerous Arab countries and those from multitudinous groups who have intermarried into other cultures and races.

WHO BELONGS TO A "TRIBE OF ISRAEL" OR TO THE "HOUSE OF ISRAEL"?

Isaac, the son of Abraham and Sarah, had a son called Jacob, whose name was subsequently changed to Israel. Jacob had four wives, by whom he had twelve sons: from Leah—Reuben, Simeon, Levi, Judah, Issachar, and Zebulun; from Rachel—Joseph and Benjamin; from Bilhah—Dan and Naphtali; from Zilpah—Gad and Asher. The descendants of these twelve sons have been divided into separate family tribes, each carrying the name of the son of Israel through whom they were born: Reuben, Simeon, and so forth. Collectively, the descendants of the tribes of Israel are known as the house of Israel and are called Israelites. Obviously, all *Israelites* (descendants of Jacob) are *Hebrews* (descendants of Abraham), but not all *Hebrews* are *Israelites*.

Additional family names are used for some groups in the house of Israel. The descendants of Judah (the fourth-born son of Jacob), for example, are known as Jews, and the descendants of Ephraim (a son of Joseph) are called Ephraimites (see Judges 12:4–6).

In summary, then, the literal descendants of Abraham (Hebrews) include the descendants of Jacob (Israelites), Judah (Jews), and Ephraim (Ephraimites), all of whom are mentioned extensively in the scriptures. However, the descendants of Abraham also include many additional peoples who would be included in the Lord's promise to Abraham: "I will multiply thee, and thy seed after thee, like unto these [stars]; and if thou canst count the number of sands, so shall be the number of thy seeds" (Abraham 3:14).

Who Is a "Gentile"?

The basic meaning of the word *Gentile* is "foreign," "other," or "non." Thus, to a Hebrew, a Gentile is a non-Hebrew; to an Israelite, a Gentile is a non-Israelite; and to a Jew, a Gentile is a non-Jew. In this sense, some Latter-day Saints have referred to those who are not members of the Church as Gentiles, even though the nonmembers might be Jews!

The word Gentile might also be used in several different ways to refer to family, religious, political, or even geographical relationships. For example, a person might be considered an Israelite in a family or blood sense, but might be called a Gentile in a political or geographical sense because he or she lives in a land or nation that is primarily Gentile, or non-Israelitish.

What Does the Term *Lineage* Mean As It Pertains to Patriarchal Blessings?

The basic meaning of *lineage* is "descent in a line from a common progenitor." Thus, in a patriarchal blessing, lineage is being declared (from Abraham, or Israel, or Ephraim, etc.) when terms indicating direct descent are used, such as "son of," "daughter of," "seed of," "blood of," "descendant of," or "from the loins of."

Concerning the responsibility of the patriarch to declare such lineage, the First Presidency of Heber J. Grant, J. Reuben Clark Jr., and David O. McKay announced, "Patriarchal blessings contemplate inspired declaration of the lineage of the recipient."[1]

Patriarchs have also been counseled: "A vital part of every patriarchal blessing is the declaration of lineage. . . . The patriarch should be responsive to the whisperings of the Spirit as he identifies lineage and the special promises and blessings attendant thereto. . . . The declaration of lineage is to come by the promptings of the Holy Ghost. This inspiration can come to the patriarch regardless of the race or nationality of the person receiving the blessing."[2]

In view of the foregoing statements, we can see that the lineages declared in patriarchal blessings are almost always statements of actual blood lines; they are not simply tribal identifications by assignment.

In light of these definitions and explanations, let's examine some statements from the scriptures and from prophets of this dispensation that relate to the question of adoption and lineage, which in turn relates to the gathering of Israel in the latter days.

REFERENCES FROM THE SCRIPTURES

Many scriptures address the question of lineage directly (which is indicative of its importance), but only a relatively few selected ones can be listed here. Those marked with an asterisk are particularly important:

Genesis: 12:1–3*; 13:14–17; 15:1–6; 17:1–8; 21:12–13; 22:15–18; 25:1–2; 26:1–5*; 28:1–4; 32:27–28; 35:9–12*; 48:1–20 (JST, 48:5–11); 49:1–28 (JST, 50:24–38).

Deuteronomy: 32:8*; 33:13–17.

Isaiah: 5:26–30; 11:10–16*; 14:1–3; 27:6, 12–13; 49:8–16; 52:1–12; 60:1–22; 61:1–11; 66:5–13.

Jeremiah: 3:14–18; 16:14–21; 23:5–8*; 31:chapter heading (LDS edition).

Daniel: 2:44–45.

Amos: 9:8–9.*

Micah: 5:7–8.*

Zechariah: 8:1–23; 10:1–12.*

Romans: 11:13–36.

Galatians: 3:6–29 (vv. 8–9*).

Ephesians: 1:10.

1 Nephi: 22:1–28.

2 Nephi: 6:5–18; 9:1–3; 30:1–8.

Jacob: 5:1–77; 6:1–4.

Helaman: 15:1–17.

3 Nephi: 15:4–10; 16:1–20 (vv. 7, 13*); 20:10–46; 21:1–29 (vv. 2, 6, 26–29*); 29:1–9; 30:1–2.

Mormon: 7:10.

Doctrine and Covenants: 45:24–25; 58:45; 86:8–9*; 90:8–11*; 96:7; 109:57–67 (vv. 57–58, 60, 67*); 110:11–12; 113:7–8; 132:30.

Abraham: 2:8–11*; 3:14.

Joseph Smith—Matthew: 1:26–31*.

Joseph Smith—History: 1:41.

Space will permit only brief quotations from three of these scriptures (italics added for emphasis):

Abraham 2:9–11: "Thou shalt be a blessing *unto thy seed* after thee, that in their hands they shall bear this ministry and Priesthood unto all nations; and I will bless them through thy name; for *as many as receive this Gospel shall be called after thy name, and shall be accounted thy seed,* and shall rise up and bless thee, as their father; . . . and in thy seed after thee (that is to say, the literal seed, or the seed of the body) shall all the families of the earth be blessed, even with the blessings of the Gospel, which are the blessings of salvation, even of life eternal."

Doctrine and Covenants 86:8–9: "Therefore, thus saith the Lord unto you, with whom the priesthood hath continued *through the lineage of your fathers—for ye are lawful heirs,* according to the flesh, and have been hid from the world with Christ in God."

Doctrine and Covenants 109:57–58, 60, 67: "That all the ends of the earth may know that we, thy servants, have heard thy voice, and that thou hast sent us; that from among all these, *thy servants, the sons of Jacob, may gather out the righteous.* . . . Now these words, O Lord, we have spoken before thee, concerning the revelations and commandments which thou hast given *unto us, who are identified with the Gentiles.* . . . And may all the scattered remnants of Israel, who have been driven to the ends of the earth, come to a knowledge of the truth, believe in the Messiah, and be redeemed from oppression, and rejoice before thee."

Statements from Church Leaders

Several leaders of the Church in this dispensation have discussed various aspects of the topic of heirship and adoption. (Italics have been added for emphasis.)

Are Most Members of the Church Literal Descendants of Abraham by Birth?

President Joseph Fielding Smith made it clear that a majority of the members of the Church today are descendants of Israel and thus of Abraham: "The Lord said he would scatter Israel among the Gentile nations, and by doing so he would bless the Gentile nations with the blood of Abraham. Today we are preaching the gospel in the world and we are gathering out, according to the revelations given to Isaiah, Jeremiah, and other prophets, the scattered sheep of the house of Israel. These scattered sheep are coming forth mixed with Gentile blood from their Gentile forefathers. Under all the circumstances it is very possible that *the majority, almost without exception, of those who come into the Church in this dispensation have the blood of two or more of the tribes of Israel* as well as the blood of the Gentiles."[3]

On another occasion President Joseph Fielding Smith emphatically stated: "The great majority of those who become members of the Church are literal descendants of Abraham through Ephraim, son of Joseph."[4]

While identifying the Lamanites as some of the children of Abraham, President Spencer W. Kimball wrote: "The Lamanite is a chosen child of God, but he is not the only chosen one. There are many other good people including the Anglos, the French, the German, and the English, who are also of Ephraim and Manasseh. They, with the Lamanites, are also chosen people, and they are a remnant of Jacob. The Lamanite is not wholly and exclusively the remnant of the Jacob which the Book of Mormon talks about. *We are all of Israel!* We are of Abraham and Isaac and Jacob and Joseph through Ephraim and Manasseh. We are *all of us* remnants of Jacob."[5]

Concerning the subject of the gathering of Israel, President Brigham Young stated: "The set time is come for God to gather Israel, and for His work to commence upon the face of the whole earth, and the Elders who have arisen in this Church and Kingdom are actually of Israel. Take the Elders who are now in this house, and *you can scarcely find one out of a hundred [who is not] of the house of Israel.* . . .

"Will we go to the Gentile nations to preach the Gospel? Yes, and gather out the Israelites, wherever they are mixed among the nations of the earth. . . . Ephraim has become mixed with all the nations of the earth, and it is Ephraim that is gathering together. . . .

" . . . If there are any of the other tribes of Israel mixed with the Gentiles we are also searching for them. . . . We want the blood of Jacob, and that of his father Isaac and Abraham, which runs in the veins of the people. . . .

" . . . It is the house of Israel we are after, and we care not whether they come from the east, the west, the north, or the south; from China, Russia, England, California, North or South America, or some other locality. . . . The Book of Mormon came to Ephraim, for Joseph Smith was a pure Ephraimite, and the Book of Mormon was revealed to him."[6]

Is It Possible for the Same Person to Be an Israelite by Birth and Yet Be Considered a Gentile?

Although President Young identified Joseph Smith as a "pure Ephraimite" in the above quotation, so far as the Prophet's family or blood lines were concerned, Brigham Young and others have recognized that (1) Joseph Smith was from a

Gentile nation and (2) some of Joseph Smith's progenitors may have come from bloodlines other than that of Ephraim.[7]

President Joseph Fielding Smith also provided insight on how the term Gentile could apply to Joseph Smith even though he was a descendant of Jacob (Israel) through Joseph, the father of Ephraim: "In this Dispensation of the Fulness of Times, the gospel came first to the Gentiles and then is to go to the Jews. However, *the Gentiles who receive the gospel are in the greater part, Gentiles who have the blood of Israel in their veins.* There is a very significant statement in the words of Moroni as recorded on the title page of the Book of Mormon that it was: '. . . To come forth . . . by way of the Gentile. . . .'

"How did the Book of Mormon come forth? By the hand of Joseph Smith. Yet we read in the Book of Mormon [see 2 Nephi 3:7–15] that Joseph Smith is the descendant of Joseph who was sold into Egypt by his brethren, nevertheless he came by 'way of the Gentile,' according to Moroni's prediction."[8]

Thus, Joseph Smith was of the house of Israel so far as his family or blood lines were concerned, but he came from a Gentile nation and thus might also be considered a Gentile in the political or geographical sense.

How Can a Gentile by Birth Be "Adopted" into the House Of Israel?

In considering the principle of adoption, the Brethren consistently refer to the significant allegory of the tame and wild olive tree contained in Jacob 5. It is instructive to read and ponder that chapter in company with the following quotations pertaining to those who might be of Gentile blood who have been baptized into the Church:

Brigham Young: "If any of the Gentiles will believe, we will lay our hands upon them that they may receive the Holy Ghost, and *the Lord will make them of the house of Israel.* They will be broken off from the wild olive tree, and be grafted into the good and tame olive tree, and will partake of its sap and fatness. . . . It is so with the House of Israel and the Gentile nations; if the Gentiles are grafted into the good olive tree they will partake of its root and fatness."[9]

Joseph Fielding Smith: *"Every person who embraces the gospel becomes of the house of Israel.* In other words, they become members of the chosen lineage, or Abraham's children through Isaac and Jacob unto whom the promises were made. The great majority of those who become members of the Church are literal descendants of Abraham through Ephraim, son of Joseph. Those who are not literal descendants of Abraham and Israel must become such, and when they are baptized and confirmed they are grafted into the tree and are entitled to all the rights and privileges as heirs."[10]

The clear teaching of the prophets is that few persons not of the blood of Abraham have become members of the Church in this dispensation; the terms "adopted into the house of Israel" or "assigned to a tribe of Israel" pertain only to those relatively few members.

It is important to remind ourselves that the blessings of eternity are guaranteed for all who are faithful to the gospel of Jesus Christ, regardless of their lineage. Furthermore, those blessings are withheld from anyone who is disobedient and unfaithful, again regardless of ancestry. As Nephi stated: "Behold, the Lord esteemeth all flesh in one; he that is righteous is favored of God" (1 Nephi 17:35). And Paul reminds us, "They are not all Israel, which are of Israel" (Romans 9:6).

What Special Responsibilities Are Held by Ephraimites in This Dispensation?

President Joseph Fielding Smith and others have made it abundantly clear that the descendants of Ephraim hold the presiding keys to carry forth the work of the Restoration and of the gathering of Israel in the last days. He said:

"The members of the Church, most of us of the tribe of Ephraim, are of the remnant of Jacob. We know it to be the fact that the Lord called upon the descendants of Ephraim to commence his work in the earth in these last days. We know further that he has said that he set Ephraim, according to the promises of his birthright, at the head. Ephraim receives the 'richer blessings,' these blessings being those of presidency or direction. The keys are with Ephraim. It is Ephraim who is to be endowed with power to bless and give to the other tribes, including the Lamanites, their blessings. All the other tribes of Jacob, including the Lamanites, are to be crowned with glory in Zion by the hands of Ephraim. . . .

"That the remnants of Joseph, found among the descendants of Lehi, will have part in this great work is certainly consistent, and the great work of this restoration, the building of the temple and the City of Zion, or New Jerusalem, will fall to the lot of the descendants of Joseph, but it is Ephraim who will stand at the head and direct the work."[11]

From what the prophets have said, then, most members of the Church come from Gentile nations, but they have some Israelite ancestors in their lineage. Therefore, they are not "assigned to" or "adopted into" the house of Israel. They are legal heirs of the covenant, and the lineage proclaimed in their patriarchal blessings identifies the blood line that ties them back to Abraham.

Notes

From *Ensign,* January 1991, 51–55.

1. *Messages of the First Presidency,* 6:194.
2. *Information and Suggestions for Patriarchs* (Salt Lake City: The Church of Jesus Christ of Latter-day Saints, n.d.), 4; quoted by permission.
3. Joseph Fielding Smith, *Answers to Gospel Questions,* 5 vols. (Salt Lake City: Deseret Book Co., 1957–66), 3:63; emphasis added.
4. Joseph Fielding Smith, "How One May Become of the House of Israel," *Improvement Era,* 26 (October 1923): 1149.
5. *Teachings of Spencer W. Kimball,* 600–601; some of the emphasis shown can be found in the original.
6. *Journal of Discourses,* 2:268–69; emphasis added.
7. See *Journal of Discourses,* 2:268.
8. Smith, *Answers to Gospel Questions,* 4:39; emphasis added.
9. *Journal of Discourses,* 2:269; emphasis added.
10. *Doctrines of Salvation,* 3:246; emphasis added.
11. *Doctrines of Salvation,* 2:250–51; italics in original removed.

Chapter 38

THE DESTINY OF THE HOUSE OF ISRAEL

Following a habit developed in high school and college when I participated in debate tournaments, I have gone to the dictionary and to concordances of the scriptures to make certain I understand the full ramifications of the terms *destiny* and *house of Israel.*

DESTINY

Webster's Third New International Dictionary of the English Language, Unabridged helped me with the word *destiny.* It contains five different definitions of the word, the basic meaning of which is "that to which any person or thing is destined." Some of the definitions and explanations of the word *destiny* are as follows:

"*1a* predetermined state: condition foreordained by divine will or by human will: unavoidable lot.

"*1b* culminating condition or end indicated as probable, inevitable, or having been reached.

"*2a* the predetermined course of events often conceived as a resistless power or agency: the foreordained future whether in general or of an individual.

"*2b* continuing activity and functional behavior that tend to determine eventual status especially as to progress or decadence—usually used in plural.

"*3* a real or imaginary power or agency conceived as predetermining the course of events and choice of alternatives."

When I looked up the meaning of the basic word *destiny,* I was surprised to note that it comes from the Latin and the French *"de + -stinare;* akin to *stare* to stand." Its fundamental meaning is "to direct and impel inescapably on a fixed course."

I say *surprised,* for I remembered a similar experience some years ago when I was in Perth, Australia, and heard that the Brethren had announced that henceforth the Book of Mormon would have a subtitle: "Another Testament of Jesus Christ." I went to the national library in Perth to look up the word *testament.* There, in the largest dictionary of the English language that I could find, I noted that the word *testament* came into English from the Latin and the French from "a prehistoric Italic compound whose first and second constituents respectively are akin to Latin *tres* three and to Latin *stare* to stand."

I had never before associated the word *destiny* with the word *testament,* yet as indicated, both come from the same basic root, *stare,* meaning "to stand." By the time I had concluded pondering on the possible meanings of the word *destiny,* I realized that a discussion of the destiny of the house of Israel would cover much more than the prophetic future of the *house of Israel*—a term many would associate with the word *destiny.* I also need to include something of the historical past and of present conditions associated with the house of Israel.

House of Israel

My attention then centered on the other major term in the title of this discussion: *house of Israel.* This time I used two sources: *The Exhaustive Concordance of the Bible,* by James Strong, and *An Exhaustive Concordance of the Book of Mormon, Doctrine and Covenants, and Pearl of Great Price,* compiled by R. Gary Shapiro.

The Exhaustive Concordance of the Bible, according to its subtitle, shows "every word of the text of the common English Version of the canonical books, and every occurrence of each word in regular order."[1] According to a reference in another book, "Dr. James Strong's *Exhaustive Concordance* of the King James translation was first issued in 1894 after a hundred men had worked on it for thirty years."[2]

An Exhaustive Concordance of the Book of Mormon, Doctrine and Covenants, and Pearl of Great Price, according to its preface, "lists alphabetically all words exactly as they appear in the sacred text," and offers this note: "with the use of today's computer technology . . . the work was completed in four years."[3]

According to the concordances, the term "House of Israel" appears in the scriptures 280 times. In the Old Testament, it occurs 146 times: Exodus—2 (16:31; 40:38); Leviticus—5 (10:6; 17:3, 8, 10; 22:18); Numbers—1 (20:29); Joshua—1 (21:45); Ruth—1 (4:11); 1 Samuel—2 (7:2, 3); 2 Samuel—5 (1:12; 6:5, 15; 12:8; 16:3); 1 Kings—2 (12:21; 20:31); Psalms—3 (98:3; 115:12; 135:19); Isaiah—4 (5:7; 14:2; 46:3; 63:7); Jeremiah—20 (2:4, 26; 3:18, 20; 5:11, 15; 9:26; 10:1; 11:10, 17; 13:11; 18:6 [twice]; 23:8; 31:27, 31, 33; 33:14, 17; 48:13); Ezekiel—83 (3:1, 4, 5, 7 [twice], 17; 4:3, 4, 5; 5:4; 6:11; 8:6, 10, 11, 12; 9:9; 11:5, 15; 12:6, 9, 10, 24, 27; 13:5, 9; 14:4, 5, 6, 7, 11; 17:2; 18:6, 15, 25, 29 [twice], 30, 31; 20:13, 27, 30, 31, 39, 40, 44; 22:18; 24:21; 28:24, 25; 29:6, 16, 21; 33:7, 10, 11, 20; 34:30; 35:15; 36:10, 17, 21, 22 [twice], 32, 37; 37:11, 16; 39:12, 22, 23, 25, 29; 40:4; 43:7, 10; 44:6 [twice], 12, 22; 45:6, 8, 17 [twice]); Hosea—5 (1:4, 6; 5:1; 6:10; 11:12); Amos—8 (5:1, 3, 4, 25; 6:1, 14; 7:10; 9:9); Micah—3 (1:5; 3:1, 9); Zechariah—1 (8:13).

In the New Testament, it occurs six times: Matthew—2 (10:6; 15:24); Acts—2 (2:36; 7:42); Hebrews—2 (8:8, 10).

In the Book of Mormon, it occurs 122 times: Title Page—2 (first paragraph; second paragraph); 1 Nephi—39 (10:12, 14 [twice]; 11:35; 12:9; 13:23 [twice], 33, 34; 14:2 [twice], 5, 8, 17, 26; 15:12 [three times], 14, 16, 17, 18, 20; 19:10, 11, 16, 19, 24 [twice]; 21:1 [twice], 12, 15; 22:3, 6, 7, 9, 11, 14); 2 Nephi—23 (3:5, 9, 13, 24; 6:5 [three times]; 7:2, 4; 9:1, 53; 10:18, 22; 15:7; 24:2; 25:4; 28:2; 29:1, 2, 12, 14 [twice]; 33:13); Jacob—5 (5:1, 2, 3; 6:1, 4); 3 Nephi—36 (10:4, 5 [twice], 6, 7; 15:15; 16:5, 7, 8 [twice], 9 [twice], 11, 12 [twice], 13, 14, 15 [twice]; 17:14; 20:10, 12, 21, 25, 27; 21:1, 4, 6, 7, 20, 23; 23:2; 29:3, 8, 9; 30:2); Mormon—11 (3:17; 4:12; 5:10, 11, 14, 20; 7:1, 2; 8:21 [twice]; 9:37); Ether—5 (4:14, 15; 13:5 [twice], 10); Moroni—1 (10:31).

In the Doctrine and Covenants, it occurs six times: 14:10; 18:6; 29:12; 39:11; 42:39; 138:25. The term does not appear in the Pearl of Great Price.

By comparison, all other major terms referring to the greater house of Israel—"tribes of Israel," "tribes of the children of Israel," and "tribes of the house of Israel"—are used a total of only seventy times in the scriptures.

The other major terms are used sixty times in the Old Testament: Genesis—2 (49:16, 28); Exodus—3 (24:4; 28:21; 39:14); Numbers—4 (31:4; 32:28; 36:3, 9); Deuteronomy—2 (29:21; 33:5); Joshua—9 (3:12; 4:5, 8; 12:7; 14:1; 19:51; 21:1; 22:14; 24:1); Judges—7 (18:1; 20:2, 10, 12; 21:5, 8, 15); 1 Samuel—4 (2:28; 9:21; 10:20; 15:17); 2 Samuel—7 (5:1; 7:7; 15:2, 10; 19:9; 20:14; 24:2); 1 Kings—3 (8:16; 11:32; 14:21); 2 Kings—1 (21:7); 1 Chronicles—3 (27:16, 22; 29:6);

2 Chronicles—4 (6:5; 11:16; 12:13; 33:7); Ezra—1 (6:17); Psalms—1 (78:55); Ezekiel—7 (37:19; 47:13, 21, 22; 48:19, 29, 31); Hosea—1 (5:9); Zechariah—1 (9:1).

They are used four times in the New Testament: Matthew—1 (19:28); Luke—1 (22:30); Revelation—2 (7:4; 21:12).

They are used eight times in the Book of Mormon: "Tribes of Israel"—6 (1 Nephi 12:9; 2 Nephi 29:13 [twice]; 3 Nephi 17:4; 28:29; Mormon 3:18); "Tribes of the house of Israel"—2 (2 Nephi 29:12; 3 Nephi 15:15).

"Tribes of Israel" is used five times in the Doctrine and Covenants: 77:9 [twice], 11, 14; 133:34. "Ten Tribes" appears once in the Pearl of Great Price: Articles of Faith 1:10.

Truth

The Book of Mormon offers this definition of truth: "The Spirit speaketh the truth and lieth not. Wherefore, it speaketh of things as they really are, and of things as they really will be" (Jacob 4:13). The Doctrine and Covenants provides a more complete definition: "And truth is knowledge of things as they are, and as they were, and as they are to come" (D&C 93:24).

Let us examine some of the "truths" pertaining to the house of Israel, primarily those in the Bible and the Book of Mormon and those that have been clarified in the teachings of the Prophet Joseph Smith and of later prophets, seers, and revelators.

In presenting these statements I am well aware of the admonition of Peter: "Knowing this first, that no prophecy of the scripture is of any private interpretation. For the prophecy came not in old time by the will of man: but holy men of God spake as they were moved by the Holy Ghost" (2 Peter 1:20–21).

I am also aware that the Lord has declared in several places that in the mouth of two or three witnesses every word and truth shall be established: "At the mouth of two witnesses, or at the mouth of three witnesses, shall the matter be established" (Deuteronomy 19:15). "In the mouth of two or three witnesses shall every word be established" (2 Corinthians 13:1). "Know ye not that the testimony of two nations is a witness unto you that I am God?" (2 Nephi 29:8). "In the mouth of two or three witnesses shall every word be established" (D&C 6:28).

In fact, the Lord declared that at least three scriptural witnesses would testify of his work:

"For behold, I shall speak unto the Jews and they shall write it; and I shall also speak unto the Nephites and they shall write it; and I shall also speak unto the other tribes of the house of Israel, which I have led away, and they shall write it; and I shall also speak unto all nations of the earth and they shall write it. . . .

"And it shall come to pass that my people, which are of the house of Israel, shall be gathered home unto the lands of their possessions; and my word also shall be gathered in one. And I will show unto them that fight against my word and against my people, who are of the house of Israel, that I am God, and that I covenanted with Abraham that I would remember his seed forever" (2 Nephi 29:12, 14).

The Truths of the House of Israel "as They Were" and "as They Are"

We rely primarily on the teachings of the Old Testament concerning the origin and early history of the house of Israel. The first time the word *Israel* appears in the Old Testament (and, I assume, the first time it is used upon the earth) is in connection with the man otherwise known as Jacob—the son of Isaac and the grandson of Abraham.

A messenger of God told Jacob, "Thy name shall be called no more Jacob, but Israel: for as a prince hast thou power with God and with men, and hast prevailed" (Genesis 32:28). Later, "God said unto him, Thy name is Jacob: thy name shall not be called any more Jacob, but Israel shall be thy name: and he called his name Israel" (Genesis 35:10).

Israel becomes the family title of the family of Jacob. This family also becomes known collectively as the *house of Israel*. Because Jacob (or Israel) had twelve sons, his descendants are known as the *twelve tribes of Israel*, the *tribes of Israel*, or *Israelites*.

Usually the term *house of Israel* in the Old Testament can be read as though it were worded *family of Israel* or *descendants of Israel*, or even as *house of Jacob* or *descendants of Jacob*. For example, in Isaiah's writing we see the term *house of Israel* used four times, while the term *house of Jacob* is used nine times, both terms clearly referring to the descendants of Jacob.

However, during the Old Testament period of the divided kingdom, the term *house of Israel* is used occasionally as though it were worded *kingdom of Israel*— usually used in conjunction with the terms *house of Judah* or *kingdom of Judah*. The Lord announces in Jeremiah 5:11 that "the house of Israel and the house of Judah have dealt very treacherously against me," and in Jeremiah 11:10 that "the house of Israel and the house of Judah have broken my covenant which I made with their fathers."

In the Book of Mormon, however, the term *house of Israel* is used consistently to refer to the *family* or the *descendants* of Israel (Jacob). The term *house of Jacob* also appears fifteen times in the Book of Mormon, usually in reference to the descendants of Lehi as a "remnant" of the house of Jacob. The term *house of Judah* does not appear a single time in the Book of Mormon. This would be consistent with the fact that the period of the divided kingdom had ended in 722 B.C. with the capture of the kingdom of Israel by the Assyrians, 122 years before the opening of the Book of Mormon.

The family designation for the descendants of Judah—*Jew*—is also used extensively in both the Bible and the Book of Mormon. It first appears as a plural (*Jews*) in 2 Kings 16:6 and in the Book of Mormon in 1 Nephi 1:2. The words *Jew* and *Jews* appear 403 times in the scriptures: 92 times in the Old Testament, 197 times in the New Testament, 89 times in the Book of Mormon, 22 times in the Doctrine and Covenants, and 3 times in the Pearl of Great Price.

The faithful members of Lehi's descendants knew a great deal about the origin and early history of the house of Israel. In discussing the plates of brass obtained from Laban, Nephi notes that "they did contain the five books of Moses, which gave an account of the creation of the world, . . . and also a record of the Jews from the beginning, even down to the commencement of the reign of Zedekiah, king of Judah" (1 Nephi 5:11–12).

Evidently by the time of Lehi, the meaning of the word *Jew* had been expanded to include those who were citizens of the kingdom of Judah, as well as those who were literal descendants of Judah, the fourth son of Jacob.

As Nephi says, "I have charity for the Jew—I say Jew, because I mean them from whence I came" (2 Nephi 33:8). "And the things which shall be written out of the book shall be of great worth unto the children of men, and especially unto our seed, which is a remnant of the house of Israel" (2 Nephi 28:2).

It is my firm conviction that when the Prophet Joseph Smith was martyred on June 27, 1844, he understood more about the destiny of the house of Israel—including its origin, history, and prophesied future—than any person then living upon the earth, with the possible exceptions of translated beings such as John the Beloved, the three Nephite disciples, and other "holy men" of God "that [we] know not of" (D&C 49:8).

The remainder of this chapter will consist primarily of the writings and teachings of the Prophet Joseph Smith concerning the destiny of the house of Israel as revealed in his (1) visions and visitations of divine persons and messengers, (2) translation of the Book of Mormon, (3) inspired translation of the Bible, (4) revelations on the subject, including those in the Doctrine and Covenants, (5) revealing of truths in the books of Abraham and Moses in the Pearl of Great Price, and (6) other diverse and sundry manners.

For purposes of ready identification, each item has been given its own subhead—but the order in which they are given is not meant to suggest that the events have happened or will happen in the same sequence as listed here:

Israel's Number Foreordained

Joseph Smith knew that the number of the house of Israel had been foreordained from before the foundations of the earth.

1. "And hath made of one blood all nations of men for to dwell on all the face of the earth, and hath determined the times before appointed, and the bounds of their habitation" (Acts 17:26).

2. "When the most High divided to the nations their inheritance, when he separated the sons of Adam, he set the bounds of the people according to the number of the children of Israel" (Deuteronomy 32:8).

God's Special Promises

Joseph Smith knew that God, who cannot and does not lie, has throughout the centuries made special promises to individuals, groups, and nations of people, predicated on their obedience to certain laws and principles. These *covenants* are binding upon the Lord:

1. "I, the Lord, am bound when ye do what I say; but when ye do not what I say, ye have no promise" (D&C 82:10).

2. "The grass withereth, the flower fadeth: but the word of our God shall stand for ever" (Isaiah 40:8).

A Covenant People

Joseph Smith knew that God had entered into sacred covenants with our father Abraham and that these promises had been reaffirmed through Isaac and through Jacob and his descendants. Therefore, the people of the house of Israel are a covenant people.

1. "And the Lord said, Shall I hide from Abraham that thing which I do; Seeing that Abraham shall surely become a great and mighty nation, and all the nations of the earth shall be blessed in him?" (Genesis 18:17–18).

2. "For thou art an holy people unto the Lord thy God: the Lord thy God hath chosen thee to be a special people unto himself, above all people that are upon the face of the earth" (Deuteronomy 7:6).

Promised Lands

Joseph Smith knew that God's covenant with ancient Israel, then living in the land of Israel, provided that they would remain in their promised lands so long as they were obedient to their part of the covenant. An example of these promises (given through Moses and Joshua) is found in Deuteronomy 28:1–14:

1. "The Lord thy God will set thee on high above all nations of the earth" (v. 1).
2. "Blessed shalt thou be in the city, . . . and in the field" (v. 3).
3. "Blessed shall be the fruit of thy body, and the fruit of thy ground, and the fruit of thy cattle" (v. 4).
4. "Blessed shall be thy basket and thy store" (v. 5).
5. "Blessed shalt thou be when thou comest in, and . . . goest out" (v. 6).
6. "The Lord shall cause thine enemies that rise up against thee to be smitten before thy face: they shall come out against thee one way, and flee before thee seven ways" (v. 7).
7. "The Lord shall command the blessing upon thee in thy storehouses, and in all that thou settest thine hand unto; . . . The Lord shall establish thee an holy people unto himself, . . . [and] shall make thee plenteous in goods, in the fruit of thy body, . . . thy cattle, [and] thy ground (vv. 8–11).
8. "The Lord shall open unto thee his good treasure, the heaven to give the rain unto thy land, . . . and thou shalt lend unto many nations, and thou shalt not borrow" (v. 12).
9. "And the Lord shall make thee the head, and not the tail; and thou shalt be above only, and thou shalt not be beneath" (v. 13).
10. "And thou shalt not go aside from any of the words which I command thee this day, to the right hand, or to the left, to go after other gods to serve them" (v. 14).

Israel's Captivity

Joseph Smith knew that when the people of the ancient house of Israel were disobedient to their promises, they were taken captive: the kingdom of Israel by the Assyrians 722 years before the prophesied birth of the Messiah, and the kingdom of Judah by the Babylonians approximately 600 B.C. These dispersions and other calamities (warned of by Moses and Joshua) would come upon them because of their disobedience, as recorded in Deuteronomy 28:15–67:

1. "Thy sons and thy daughters shall be given unto another people, and thine eyes shall look, and fail with longing for them all the day long: and there shall be no might in thine hand. The fruit of thy land, and all thy labours, shall a nation which thou knowest not eat up; and thou shalt be only oppressed and crushed. . . . The Lord shall bring thee, and thy king which thou shalt set over thee, unto a nation which neither thou nor thy fathers have known; and there shalt thou serve other gods, wood and stone. And thou shalt become an astonishment, a proverb, and a byword, among all nations whither the Lord shall lead thee. . . . Thou shalt beget sons and daughters, but . . . they shall go into captivity. . . . And ye shall be left few in number, whereas ye were as the stars of heaven for multitude; because thou wouldest not obey the voice of the Lord thy God. . . . And the Lord shall scatter thee among all people, from the one end of the earth even unto the other. . . . And among these nations shalt thou find no ease, neither shall the sole of thy foot have rest: but the Lord shall give thee there a trembling heart, and failing of eyes, and sorrow of mind: And thy life shall hang in doubt before thee; and thou shalt fear day and night, and shalt have none assurance of thy life: In the morning thou shalt say, Would God it were even! and at even thou shalt say, Would God it were morning! for the fear of thine heart wherewith thou shalt fear, and for the sight of thine eyes which thou shalt see" (vv. 32–33, 36–37, 41, 62, 64–67).

2. "Cursed shalt thou be in the city, and . . . in the field" (v. 16).

3. "Cursed shall be the fruit of thy body [and] land [and] flocks" (v. 18).

4. "Cursed shall be thy basket and thy store" (v. 17).

5. "Cursed shalt thou be when thou comest in, and . . . goest out" (v. 19).

6. "The Lord shall cause thee to be smitten before thine enemies: thou shalt go out one way against them, and flee seven ways before them" (v. 25).

7. "The Lord shall send upon thee cursing, vexation, and rebuke, in all that thou settest thine hand . . . to do" (v. 20).

8. "The Lord shall smite thee with a consumption, and with a fever, and with an inflammation, and with an extreme burning, and with the sword, and with blasting, and with mildew; and they shall pursue thee until thou perish. And thy heaven that is over thy head shall be brass, and the earth that is under thee shall be iron. The Lord shall make the rain of thy land powder and dust: from heaven shall it come down upon thee, until thou be destroyed" (vv. 22–24).

9. "And thou shalt grope at noonday, as the blind gropeth in darkness, and thou

shalt not prosper in thy ways: and thou shalt be only oppressed and spoiled evermore, and no man shall save thee" (v. 29).

10. "The Lord shall bring thee . . . unto a nation . . . and there shalt thou serve other gods, wood and stone" (v. 36). "And the Lord shall scatter thee . . . and there thou shalt serve other gods, . . . even wood and stone" (v. 64).

The Olive Tree

Joseph Smith knew that the house of Israel would be likened to an olive tree, as explained in the allegory of Zenos in the fifth chapter of Jacob, and that many branches of the house of Israel would be scattered throughout the earth, even to the nethermost parts of the vineyard.

1. "Yea, even my father spake . . . concerning the house of Israel, that they should be compared like unto an olive-tree, whose branches should be broken off and should be scattered upon all the face of the earth" (1 Nephi 10:12).

2. "For behold, thus saith the Lord, I will liken thee, O house of Israel, like unto a tame olive-tree, which a man took and nourished in his vineyard; and it grew, and waxed old, and began to decay" (Jacob 5:3).

Judah's Captivity and Return

Joseph Smith knew that when another major portion of the house of Israel (then known as the kingdom of Judah) was disobedient, those people would be taken into captivity by the Babylonians, but that after a time they would be allowed to return to their promised lands of inheritance in the land of Israel before the Messiah's appearance to them.

1. "Now in the first year of Cyrus king of Persia, that the word of the Lord spoken by the mouth of Jeremiah might be accomplished, the Lord stirred up the spirit of Cyrus king of Persia, that he made a proclamation throughout all his kingdom, and put it also in writing, saying, Thus saith Cyrus king of Persia, All the kingdoms of the earth hath the Lord God of heaven given me; and he hath charged me to build him an house in Jerusalem, which is in Judah. Who is there among you of all his people? The Lord his God be with him, and let him go up" (2 Chronicles 36:22–23; see also Ezra 1:1–6).

2. "Now in the first year of Cyrus king of Persia, that the word of the Lord by the mouth of Jeremiah might be fulfilled, the Lord stirred up the spirit of Cyrus king of Persia, that he made a proclamation throughout all his kingdom, and put it also in writing, saying, Thus saith Cyrus king of Persia, The Lord God of heaven hath given me all the kingdoms of the earth; and he hath charged me to build him

an house at Jerusalem, which is in Judah. Who is there among you of all his people? his God be with him, and let him go up to Jerusalem, which is in Judah, and build the house of the Lord God of Israel, (he is the God,) which is in Jerusalem. And whosoever remaineth in any place where he sojourneth, let the men of his place help him with silver, and with gold, and with goods, and with beasts, beside the freewill offering for the house of God that is in Jerusalem.

"Then rose up the chief of the fathers of Judah and Benjamin, and the priests, and the Levites, with all them whose spirit God had raised, to go up to build the house of the Lord which is in Jerusalem. And all they that were about them strengthened their hands with vessels of silver, with gold, with goods, and with beasts, and with precious things, beside all that was willingly offered" (Ezra 1:1–6; see also 2 Chronicles 36:22–23).

3. "Now these are the children of the province that went up out of the captivity, of those which had been carried away, whom Nebuchadnezzar the king of Babylon had carried away unto Babylon, and came again unto Jerusalem and Judah, every one unto his city" (Ezra 2:1).

The Scattering to America

Joseph Smith knew that one of the major branches of the house of Israel to be scattered consisted of the descendants of Lehi, Zoram, Ishmael, Zarahemla, and Mulek, who were led to their promised lands of inheritance in the lands of the everlasting hills, which were shaped as the great wings of a bird, even the lands of North America and South America.

1. "The blessings of thy father have prevailed above the blessings of my progenitors unto the utmost bound of the everlasting hills: they shall be on the head of Joseph, and on the crown of the head of him that was separate from his brethren" (Genesis 49:26).

2. "Woe to the land shadowing with wings, which is beyond the rivers of Ethiopia: . . . All ye inhabitants of the world, and dwellers on the earth, see ye, when he lifteth up an ensign on the mountains; and when he bloweth a trumpet, hear ye" (Isaiah 18:1, 3).

The Descendants of Lehi

Joseph Smith knew that the descendants of Lehi in the Book of Mormon were descendants of Jacob (Israel) through the loins of Joseph.

1. "My father, Lehi, . . . found upon the plates of brass a genealogy of his

fathers; wherefore he knew that he was a descendant of Joseph; yea, even that Joseph who was the son of Jacob, who was sold into Egypt" (1 Nephi 5:14).

2. "Behold, I say unto you, that the house of Israel was compared unto an olive-tree, by the Spirit of the Lord which was in our father; and behold are we not broken off from the house of Israel, and are we not a branch of the house of Israel?" (1 Nephi 15:12)

3. "And now, the words which I shall read are they which Isaiah spake concerning all the house of Israel; wherefore, they may be likened unto you, for ye are of the house of Israel. And there are many things which have been spoken by Isaiah which may be likened unto you, because ye are of the house of Israel" (2 Nephi 6:5).

Covenants in the Scriptures

Joseph Smith knew that the scriptures—both the Bible and the Book of Mormon—contained many of the covenants with the house of Israel.

1. "Moreover, thou son of man, take thee one stick, and write upon it, For Judah, and for the children of Israel his companions: then take another stick, and write upon it, For Joseph, the stick of Ephraim, and for all the house of Israel his companions" (Ezekiel 37:16).

2. "For the fulness of mine intent is that I may persuade men to come unto the God of Abraham, and the God of Isaac, and the God of Jacob, and be saved" (1 Nephi 6:4).

3. "And he said: Behold it proceedeth out of the mouth of a Jew. And I, Nephi, beheld it; and he said unto me: The book that thou beholdest is a record of the Jews, which contains the covenants of the Lord, which he hath made unto the house of Israel; and it also containeth many of the prophecies of the holy prophets; and it is a record like unto the engravings which are upon the plates of brass, save there are not so many; nevertheless, they contain the covenants of the Lord, which he hath made unto the house of Israel" (1 Nephi 13:23).

4. "And behold, they shall go unto the unbelieving of the Jews; and for this intent shall they go—that they may be persuaded that Jesus is the Christ, the Son of the living God; that the Father may bring about, through his most Beloved, his great and eternal purpose, in restoring the Jews, or all the house of Israel, to the land of their inheritance, which the Lord their God hath given them, unto the fulfilling of his covenant" (Mormon 5:14).

The Law of Moses

Joseph Smith knew that the law of Moses was given to the house of Israel in ancient times to prepare them for the coming of Jesus Christ.

1. "Behold, my soul delighteth in proving unto my people the truth of the coming of Christ; for, for this end hath the law of Moses been given; and all things which have been given of God from the beginning of the world, unto man, are the typifying of him" (2 Nephi 11:4).

2. "And, notwithstanding we believe in Christ, we keep the law of Moses, and look forward with steadfastness unto Christ, until the law shall be fulfilled. For, for this end was the law given; wherefore the law hath become dead unto us, and we are made alive in Christ because of our faith; yet we keep the law because of the commandments. And we talk of Christ, we rejoice in Christ, we preach of Christ, we prophesy of Christ, and we write according to our prophecies, that our children may know to what source they may look for a remission of their sins" (2 Nephi 25:24–26).

A Purpose of the Book of Mormon

Joseph Smith knew that one of the major purposes for the writing and coming forth of the Book of Mormon was to convince the Gentiles and the house of Israel that Jesus Christ is the Son of God.

1. On the title page of the Book of Mormon we read: "It is an abridgment of the record of the people of Nephi, and also of the Lamanites—Written to the Lamanites, who are a remnant of the house of Israel; and also to Jew and Gentile—Written by way of commandment, and also by the spirit of prophecy and of revelation— . . . Which is to show unto the remnant of the House of Israel what great things the Lord hath done for their fathers; and that they may know the covenants of the Lord, that they are not cast off forever—And also to the convincing of the Jew and Gentile that Jesus is the Christ, the Eternal God, manifesting himself unto all nations."

2. "And now, my beloved brethren, and also Jew, and all ye ends of the earth, hearken unto these words and believe in Christ; and if ye believe not in these words believe in Christ. And if ye shall believe in Christ ye will believe in these words, for they are the words of Christ, and he hath given them unto me" (2 Nephi 33:10).

Jehovah, the God of Israel

Joseph Smith knew that the God who made these promises to ancient covenant Israel was Jehovah, who later came to earth as the promised Messiah.

1. "And I appeared unto Abraham, unto Isaac, and unto Jacob, by the name of God Almighty, but by my name JEHOVAH was I not known to them" (Exodus 6:3).

"And I appeared unto Abraham, unto Isaac, and unto Jacob. I am the Lord

God Almighty; the Lord JEHOVAH. And was not my name known unto them?" (Exodus 6:3, JST).

2. "That men may know that thou, whose name alone is JEHOVAH, art the most high over all the earth" (Psalm 83:18).

3. "Behold, God is my salvation; I will trust, and not be afraid: for the Lord JEHOVAH is my strength and my song; he also is become my salvation" (Isaiah 12:2).

4. "Trust ye in the Lord for ever: for in the Lord JEHOVAH is everlasting strength" (Isaiah 26:4).

Jehovah and Jesus Christ

Joseph Smith knew that at least a portion of the people of the house of Israel anciently knew that Jehovah in the Old Testament was the very same personage who later became known by the name-title of Jesus Christ in the New Testament. Even many years before the physical birth of the Messiah upon the earth, at least favored groups within the house of Israel knew that:

1. The angel Gabriel would announce the coming birth of the Messiah to a virgin living in Nazareth who was the foreordained mother of the Son of God, even a virgin who was fairer than any other virgin. Nephi wrote in his vision, "I beheld the city of Nazareth; and in the city of Nazareth I beheld a virgin . . . most beautiful and fair above all other virgins." And the angel declared to Nephi, "The virgin whom thou seest is the mother of the Son of God, after the manner of the flesh" (1 Nephi 11:13, 15, 18).

2. The name of his mother would be Mary (Mosiah 3:8; Alma 7:10).

3. He would be born in Bethlehem in the inheritance of Judah (Micah 5:2).

4. A new star would announce his birth (Helaman 14:5; 3 Nephi 1:21).

5. The Messiah would be born six hundred years after the beginning of the reign of Zedekiah, king of Judah. Nephi wrote that his father left Jerusalem "in the . . . first year of the reign of Zedekiah, king of Judah" (1 Nephi 1:4), and that "even six hundred years from the time that my father left Jerusalem, a prophet would the Lord God raise up among the Jews—even a Messiah, or, in other words, a Savior of the world. . . . or this Redeemer of the world" (1 Nephi 10:4–5). In 2 Nephi 25:19 he adds the confirming witness: "For according to the words of the prophets, the Messiah cometh in six hundred years from the time that my father left Jerusalem; and according to the words of the prophets, and also the word of the angel of God, his name shall be Jesus Christ, the Son of God." Nephi also testified that "the Son of God was the Messiah who should come" (1 Nephi 10:17).

6. The Messiah would come forth out of Egypt (Hosea 11:1) to dwell in the inheritance lands of Zebulon and Naphtali (Isaiah 9:1–2), where those who were sitting in darkness would see a great light.

7. He would make a triumphal entry into Jerusalem seated on the foal of an ass (Zechariah 9:9; Matthew 21:6–11).

8. His name-titles would include "the Christ" (Matthew 16:16), the "Messiah" (1 Nephi 10:4), "Immanuel" (Isaiah 7:14), "the Son of the Highest" (Luke 1:32), "the Son of Man" (Moses 6:57), "the Son of David" (Matthew 1:1), "the Only Begotten of the Father . . . in the flesh" (2 Nephi 25:12), "the Lamb of God . . . the Son of the Eternal Father" (1 Nephi 11:21), "the messenger of the covenant" (Malachi 3:1), the "Savior" and "Redeemer" (Mormon 3:14; Isaiah 41:14), and "Wonderful, Counsellor, The mighty God, The everlasting Father, The Prince of Peace" (Isaiah 9:6).

9. At the time of his death a special sign should be given to those of the house of Israel, yea, "three days of darkness . . . should be a sign given of his death unto those who should inhabit the isles of the sea, more especially given unto those who are of the house of Israel" (1 Nephi 19:10). Then, continued the prophet Zenos, "And as for those who are at Jerusalem, . . . they shall be scourged by all people, because they crucify the God of Israel, and turn their hearts aside, rejecting signs and wonders, and the power and glory of the God of Israel. And because they turn their hearts aside, . . . and have despised the Holy One of Israel, they shall wander in the flesh, and perish, and become a hiss and a byword, and be hated among all nations" (1 Nephi 19:13–14).

The Rejection of Christ

Despite all these prophecies, Joseph Smith knew that the Jews—a major portion of the house of Israel among whom the Messiah would live—would reject Jesus Christ, and their leaders would agree to his death.

1. As Jacob (the son of Lehi) prophesied hundreds of years before the birth of the Messiah, the Jews would be a "stiffnecked people" who would despise "the words of plainness" and would seek "for things that they could not understand. Wherefore, because of their blindness, which blindness came by looking beyond the mark," they would "reject the stone upon which they might build and have safe foundation" (Jacob 4:14–15).

2. Jacob also revealed that the Messiah would be born among the Jews, since it was needful that his life should be taken and since no other people would take the life of their Creator: "It must needs be expedient that Christ—for in the last night

the angel spake unto me that this should be his name—should come among the Jews, among those who are the more wicked part of the world; and they shall crucify him—for thus it behooveth our God, and there is none other nation on earth that would crucify their God" (2 Nephi 10:3).

The Crucifixion of Christ

Joseph Smith knew that when the Messiah came to the earth, he would live in the lands of his ancestors among his kindred "friends," but that he would be rejected of them and even be crucified in their midst.

1. "When the day cometh that the Only Begotten of the Father, yea, even the Father of heaven and of earth, shall manifest himself unto them in the flesh, behold, they will reject him, because of their iniquities, and the hardness of their hearts, and the stiffness of their necks" (2 Nephi 25:12).

2. "Nevertheless, the Lord has shown unto me that they should return again. And he also has shown unto me that the Lord God, the Holy One of Israel, should manifest himself unto them in the flesh; and after he should manifest himself they should scourge him and crucify him, according to the words of the angel who spake it unto me" (2 Nephi 6:9).

3. "And lo, he cometh unto his own, that salvation might come unto the children of men even through faith on his name; and even after all this they shall consider him a man, and say that he hath a devil, and shall scourge him, and shall crucify him" (Mosiah 3:9).

The Resurrected Lord Appears to the Branches of Israel

Joseph Smith knew that after Jesus Christ was resurrected from the dead, he would not only appear to representatives of the Jews in the land of Israel but also to other branches of the house of Israel, including those in the Americas and even to the lost tribes of Israel. The resurrected Jesus Christ spoke to the righteous Lehites in the Americas who survived the destruction associated with his crucifixion:

1. "And verily I say unto you, that ye are they of whom I said: Other sheep I have which are not of this fold; them also I must bring, and they shall hear my voice; and there shall be one fold, and one shepherd. But behold, ye have both heard my voice, and seen me; and ye are my sheep, and ye are numbered among those whom the Father hath given me" (3 Nephi 15:21, 24).

2. "And verily, verily, I say unto you that I have other sheep, which are not of this land, neither of the land of Jerusalem, neither in any parts of that land round about whither I have been to minister. For they of whom I speak are they who have

not as yet heard my voice; neither have I at any time manifested myself unto them. But I have received a commandment of the Father that I shall go unto them, and that they shall hear my voice, and shall be numbered among my sheep, that there may be one fold and one shepherd; therefore I go to show myself unto them" (3 Nephi 16:1–3).

3. "But now I go unto the Father, and also to show myself unto the lost tribes of Israel, for they are not lost unto the Father, for he knoweth whither he hath taken them" (3 Nephi 17:4).

The Scattering of the Jews after Christ

Joseph Smith knew that, as a result of their rejection of Jesus Christ and subsequent disobedience and rebellion, the descendants of the kingdom of Judah, then known as Jews, would be separated again from the lands of their inheritance and would be sifted like corn among the nations of the earth. This scattering was accomplished by the Romans in the first century following the birth of the Messiah.

1. "For behold, the Lord has shown me that those who were at Jerusalem, from whence we came, have been slain and carried away captive" (2 Nephi 6:8).

2. "But because of priestcrafts and iniquities, they at Jerusalem will stiffen their necks against him, that he be crucified. Wherefore, because of their iniquities, destructions, famines, pestilences, and bloodshed shall come upon them; and they who shall not be destroyed shall be scattered among all nations" (2 Nephi 10:5–6).

3. "And behold it shall come to pass that after the Messiah hath risen from the dead, and hath manifested himself unto his people, unto as many as will believe on his name, behold, Jerusalem shall be destroyed again; for wo unto them that fight against God and the people of his church. Wherefore, the Jews shall be scattered among all nations; yea, and also Babylon shall be destroyed; wherefore, the Jews shall be scattered by other nations" (2 Nephi 25:14–15).

4. "For, lo, I will command, and I will sift the house of Israel among all nations, like as corn is sifted in a sieve, yet shall not the least grain fall upon the earth" (Amos 9:9).

5. "And again: Hearken, O ye house of Israel, all ye that are broken off and are driven out because of the wickedness of the pastors of my people; yea, all ye that are broken off, that are scattered abroad, who are of my people, O house of Israel. Listen, O isles, unto me, and hearken ye people from far" (1 Nephi 21:1; compare Isaiah 49:1).

6. "Wherefore, the things of which I have read are things pertaining to things both temporal and spiritual; for it appears that the house of Israel, sooner or later,

will be scattered upon all the face of the earth, and also among all nations" (1 Nephi 22:3).

Apostasy by the Chosen People

Joseph Smith knew that there would be an apostasy from the covenants of God by the chosen people, followed by a period of darkness known as the Dark Ages, during which there would be a dearth of spiritual truth upon the earth and the heavens would be even as brass.

1. "Behold, the days come, saith the Lord God, that I will send a famine in the land, not a famine of bread, nor a thirst for water, but of hearing the words of the Lord: And they shall wander from sea to sea, and from the north even to the east, they shall run to and fro to seek the word of the Lord, and shall not find it" (Amos 8:11–12).

2. "Thus saith the Lord . . . Therefore night shall be unto you, that ye shall not have a vision; and it shall be dark unto you, that ye shall not divine; and the sun shall go down over the prophets, and the day shall be dark over them. Then shall the seers be ashamed, and the diviners confounded: yea, they shall all cover their lips; for there is no answer of God" (Micah 3:5–7).

3. "For the time will come when they will not endure sound doctrine; but after their own lusts shall they heap to themselves teachers, having itching ears; and they shall turn away their ears from the truth, and shall be turned unto fables" (2 Timothy 4:3–4).

A Time of Restoration

Joseph Smith knew, for the prophets of the Old Testament and the apostles of the New Testament had so declared, that a time of restitution or restoration would occur, when the iron ceiling of heaven would be shattered and the rock of revelation coming directly from the "Rock of Israel" (2 Samuel 23:3) would again return to the earth.

1. "And he shall send Jesus Christ, which before was preached unto you: Whom the heaven must receive until the times of restitution of all things, which God hath spoken by the mouth of all his holy prophets since the world began" (Acts 3:20–21).

2. "Having made known unto us the mystery of his will, according to his good pleasure which he hath purposed in himself: That in the dispensation of the fulness of times he might gather together in one all things in Christ, both which are in heaven, and which are on earth; even in him" (Ephesians 1:9–10).

3. "Wherefore the Lord said, Forasmuch as this people draw near me with their mouth, and with their lips do honour me, but have removed their heart far from me, and their fear toward me is taught by the precept of men: Therefore, behold, I will proceed to do a marvellous work among this people, even a marvellous work and a wonder: for the wisdom of their wise men shall perish, and the understanding of their prudent men shall be hid" (Isaiah 29:13–14).

A Restoration of Covenants

Joseph Smith knew that, as part of this restoration or restitution in the latter days, the covenants of the Lord would once again be made available to the various scattered segments of the house of Israel.

1. "Wherefore, our father hath not spoken of our seed alone, but also of all the house of Israel, pointing to the covenant which should be fulfilled in the latter days; which covenant the Lord made to our father Abraham, saying: In thy seed shall all the kindreds of the earth be blessed" (1 Nephi 15:18).

2. "Wherefore, the Lord God will proceed to make bare his arm in the eyes of all the nations, in bringing about his covenants and his gospel unto those who are of the house of Israel. Wherefore, he will bring them again out of captivity, and they shall be gathered together to the lands of their inheritance; and they shall be brought out of obscurity and out of darkness; and they shall know that the Lord is their Savior and their Redeemer, the Mighty One of Israel" (1 Nephi 22:11–12).

3. "But behold, there shall be many—at that day when I shall proceed to do a marvelous work among them, that I may remember my covenants which I have made unto the children of men, that I may set my hand again the second time to recover my people, which are of the house of Israel; And also, that I may remember the promises which I have made unto thee, Nephi, and also unto thy father, that I would remember your seed; and that the words of your seed should proceed forth out of my mouth unto your seed; and my words shall hiss forth unto the ends of the earth, for a standard unto my people, which are of the house of Israel" (2 Nephi 29:1–2).

4. "And as surely as the Lord liveth, will he gather in from the four quarters of the earth all the remnant of the seed of Jacob, who are scattered abroad upon all the face of the earth. And as he hath covenanted with all the house of Jacob, even so shall the covenant wherewith he hath covenanted with the house of Jacob be fulfilled in his own due time, unto the restoring all the house of Jacob unto the knowledge of the covenant that he hath covenanted with them. And then shall they know their Redeemer, who is Jesus Christ, the Son of God; and then shall they be

gathered in from the four quarters of the earth unto their own lands, from whence they have been dispersed; yea, as the Lord liveth so shall it be. Amen" (3 Nephi 5:24–26).

A Portion of Lehi's Descendants Accept the Gospel

Joseph Smith knew that in the last days at least a portion of the descendants of Lehi, known as a remnant of the Jews, would accept the gospel and become part of covenant Israel once again.

1. "Wherefore, Joseph truly saw our day. And he obtained a promise of the Lord, that out of the fruit of his loins the Lord God would raise up a righteous branch unto the house of Israel; not the Messiah, but a branch which was to be broken off, nevertheless, to be remembered in the covenants of the Lord that the Messiah should be made manifest unto them in the latter days, in the spirit of power, unto the bringing of them out of darkness unto light—yea, out of hidden darkness and out of captivity unto freedom" (2 Nephi 3:5).

2. "And behold how great the covenants of the Lord, and how great his condescensions unto the children of men; and because of his greatness, and his grace and mercy, he has promised unto us that our seed shall not utterly be destroyed, according to the flesh, but that he would preserve them; and in future generations they shall become a righteous branch unto the house of Israel" (2 Nephi 9:53).

3. "And after the house of Israel should be scattered they should be gathered together again; or, in fine, after the Gentiles had received the fulness of the Gospel, the natural branches of the olive-tree, or the remnants of the house of Israel, should be grafted in, or come to the knowledge of the true Messiah, their Lord and their Redeemer" (1 Nephi 10:14).

4. "And at that day shall the remnant of our seed know that they are of the house of Israel, and that they are the covenant people of the Lord; and then shall they know and come to the knowledge of their forefathers, and also to the knowledge of the gospel of their Redeemer, which was ministered unto their fathers by him; wherefore, they shall come to the knowledge of their Redeemer and the very points of his doctrine, that they may know how to come unto him and be saved. . . . Yea; they shall be remembered again among the house of Israel; they shall be grafted in, being a natural branch of the olive-tree, into the true olive-tree" (1 Nephi 15:14, 16).

5. "For behold, the Lord God has led away from time to time from the house of Israel, according to his will and pleasure. And now behold, the Lord remembereth

all them who have been broken off, wherefore he remembereth us also" (2 Nephi 10:22).

6. "For it is wisdom in the Father that they should be established in this land, and be set up as a free people by the power of the Father, that these things might come forth from them unto a remnant of your seed, that the covenant of the Father may be fulfilled which he hath covenanted with his people, O house of Israel" (3 Nephi 21:4).

7. "But behold, it shall come to pass that they shall be driven and scattered by the Gentiles; and after they have been driven and scattered by the Gentiles, behold, then will the Lord remember the covenant which he made unto Abraham and unto all the house of Israel" (Mormon 5:20).

The Jews Return to Their Land

Joseph Smith knew that after many generations the portion of the house of Israel then known as the house of Judah (the Jews) would return again the second time to the lands of their inheritance.

1. "And after they have been scattered, and the Lord God hath scourged them by other nations for the space of many generations, yea, even down from generation to generation until they shall be persuaded to believe in Christ, the Son of God, and the atonement, which is infinite for all mankind—and when that day shall come that they shall believe in Christ, and worship the Father in his name, with pure hearts and clean hands, and look not forward any more for another Messiah, then, at that time, the day will come that it must needs be expedient that they should believe these things" (2 Nephi 25:16).

2. "Yea, then will he remember the isles of the sea; yea, and all the people who are of the house of Israel, will I gather in, saith the Lord, according to the words of the prophet Zenos, from the four quarters of the earth" (1 Nephi 19:16).

3. "And now, my beloved brethren, I have read these things [Isaiah 50–52:2] that ye might know concerning the covenants of the Lord that he has covenanted with all the house of Israel—That he has spoken unto the Jews by the mouth of his holy prophets, even from the beginning down, from generation to generation, until the time comes that they shall be restored to the true church and fold of God; when they shall be gathered home to the lands of their inheritance, and shall be established in all their lands of promise" (2 Nephi 9:1–2).

4. "But behold, thus saith the Lord God: When the day cometh that they [descendants of those at Jerusalem at the time of the crucifixion] shall believe in me, that I am Christ, then have I covenanted with their fathers that they shall be

restored in the flesh, upon the earth, unto the lands of their inheritance. And it shall come to pass that they shall be gathered in from their long dispersion, from the isles of the sea, and from the four parts of the earth; and the nations of the Gentiles shall be great in the eyes of me, saith God, in carrying them forth to the lands of their inheritance" (2 Nephi 10:7–8).

5. "In those days the house of Judah shall walk with the house of Israel, and they shall come together out of the land of the north to the land that I have given for an inheritance unto your fathers" (Jeremiah 3:18).

6. "Therefore, behold, the days come, saith the Lord, that they shall no more say, The Lord liveth, which brought up the children of Israel out of the land of Egypt; But, The Lord liveth, which brought up and which led the seed of the house of Israel out of the north country, and from all countries whither I had driven them; and they shall dwell in their own land" (Jeremiah 23:7–8).

7. "And he shall set up an ensign for the nations, and shall assemble the outcasts of Israel, and gather together the dispersed of Judah from the four corners of the earth" (Isaiah 11:12).

8. "He [Moroni] quoted the eleventh chapter of Isaiah, saying that it was about to be fulfilled" (Joseph Smith—History 1:40).

9. "Thus saith the Lord God; When I shall have gathered the house of Israel from the people among whom they are scattered, and shall be sanctified in them in the sight of the heathen, then shall they dwell in their land that I have given to my servant Jacob" (Ezekiel 28:25).

10. "And I will multiply men upon you, all the house of Israel, even all of it: and the cities shall be inhabited, and the wastes shall be builded" (Ezekiel 36:10).

11. "And many nations shall be joined to the Lord in that day, and shall be my people: and I will dwell in the midst of thee, and thou shalt know that the Lord of hosts hath sent me unto thee. And the Lord shall inherit Judah his portion in the holy land, and shall choose Jerusalem again" (Zechariah 2:11–12).

Enemies Seek to Destroy the Jews

Joseph Smith knew that at the time of the second return of the Jews to their promised land, major powers and forces on the earth would seek their destruction and try to prevent their return. However, the Lord would preserve them as a people, and would enable them to reclaim their lands.

1. "The Messiah will set himself again the second time to recover them; wherefore, he will manifest himself unto them in power and great glory, unto the destruction of their enemies" (2 Nephi 6:14).

2. "And every nation which shall war against thee, O house of Israel, shall be turned one against another, and they shall fall into the pit which they digged to ensnare the people of the Lord. And all that fight against Zion shall be destroyed" (1 Nephi 22:14).

3. "For the Lord will have mercy on Jacob, and will yet choose Israel, and set them in their own land; and the strangers shall be joined with them, and they shall cleave to the house of Jacob. And the people shall take them and bring them to their place; yea, from far unto the ends of the earth; and they shall return to their lands of promise. And the house of Israel shall possess them . . . and they shall take them captives unto whom they were captives; and they shall rule over their oppressors" (2 Nephi 24:1–2; see also Isaiah 14:1–2).

4. "For the Lord will have mercy on Jacob, and will yet choose Israel, and set them in their own land: and the strangers shall be joined with them, and they shall cleave to the house of Jacob. And the people shall take them, and bring them to their place: and the house of Israel shall possess them in the land of the Lord for servants and handmaids: and they shall take them captives, whose captives they were; and they shall rule over their oppressors" (Isaiah 14:1–2; see also 2 Nephi 24:1–2).

5. "Behold, they shall surely gather together against thee, not by me; whosoever shall gather together against thee shall fall for thy sake. . . . No weapon that is formed against thee shall prosper" (3 Nephi 22:15, 17).

6. "Behold, I will make Jerusalem a cup of trembling unto all the people round about, when they shall be in the siege both against Judah and against Jerusalem. And in that day will I make Jerusalem a burdensome stone for all people: all that burden themselves with it shall be cut in pieces, though all the people of the earth be gathered together against it. . . . In that day will I make the governors of Judah like an hearth of fire among the wood, and like a torch of fire in a sheaf; and they shall devour all the people round about, on the right hand and on the left: and Jerusalem shall be inhabited again in her own place, even in Jerusalem. The Lord also shall save the tents of Judah first, that the glory of the house of David and the glory of the inhabitants of Jerusalem do not magnify themselves against Judah. In that day shall the Lord defend the inhabitants of Jerusalem; and he that is feeble among them at that day shall be as David; and the house of David shall be as God, as the angel of the Lord before them. And it shall come to pass in that day, that I will seek to destroy all the nations that come against Jerusalem" (Zechariah 12:2–3, 6–9).

Israel Will Have a Second Chance to Become God's Covenant People

Joseph Smith knew that, although the Jews had rejected the covenants of the gospel at the first coming of the Messiah, in the last days they would have another chance to become a covenant people of the Lord, together with other branches of the house of Israel.

1. "I spake unto them concerning the restoration of the Jews in the latter days. And I did rehearse unto them the words of Isaiah, who spake concerning the restoration of the Jews, or of the house of Israel" (1 Nephi 15:19–20).

2. "The time has at last arrived," said the Prophet Joseph Smith, "when the God of Abraham, of Isaac, and of Jacob, has set His hand again the second time to recover the remnants of his people, . . . and establish that covenant with them, which was promised when their sins should be taken away. See Isaiah xi, Romans xi: 25, 26, and 27, and also Jeremiah xxxi: 31, 32, and 33. This covenant has never been established with the house of Israel, nor with the house of Judah, for it requires two parties to make a covenant, and those two parties must be agreed, or no covenant can be made.

"Christ, in the days of His flesh, proposed to make a covenant with them, but they rejected Him and His proposals, and in consequence thereof, they were broken off, and no covenant was made with them at that time. But their unbelief has not rendered the promise of God of none effect: no, for there was another day . . . [when] His people, Israel, should be a willing people;—and He would write His law in their hearts, and print it in their thoughts; their sins and their iniquities He would remember no more.

"Thus after this chosen family had rejected Christ and His proposals, the heralds of salvation said to them, 'Lo, we turn unto the Gentiles;' and the Gentiles received the covenant, and were grafted in from whence the chosen family were broken off: but the Gentiles have not continued in the goodness of God, but have departed from the faith that was once delivered to the Saints, and have broken the covenant in which their fathers were established (See Isaiah xxiv: 5); and have become high-minded, and have not feared; therefore, but few of them will be gathered with the chosen family. . . .

"And now what remains to be done, under circumstances like these? I will proceed to tell you what the Lord requires of all people, high and low, rich and poor, male and female, ministers and people, professors of religion and non-professors, in order that they may enjoy the Holy Spirit of God to a fulness and escape the judgments of God, which are almost ready to burst upon the nations of the earth. Repent of all your sins, and be baptized in water for the remission of them, in the name of the Father, and of the Son, and of the Holy Ghost, and receive the ordinance of the laying on of the hands of him who is ordained and sealed unto this power, that ye may receive the Holy Spirit of God; and this is according to the Holy Scriptures."[4]

3. "But behold, thus saith the Lord God: When the day cometh that they shall believe in me, that I am Christ, then have I covenanted with their fathers that they shall be restored in the flesh, upon the earth, unto the lands of their inheritance" (2 Nephi 10:7).

4. "And how merciful is our God unto us, for he remembereth the house of Israel, both roots and branches; and he stretches forth his hands unto them all the day long; and they are a stiffnecked and a gainsaying people; but as many as will not harden their hearts shall be saved in the kingdom of God" (Jacob 6:4).

5. "And then will I gather them in from the four quarters of the earth; and then will I fulfill the covenant which the Father hath made unto all the people of the house of Israel" (3 Nephi 16:5).

6. "And when these things come to pass that thy seed shall begin to know these things—it shall be a sign unto them, that they may know that the work of the Father hath already commenced unto the fulfilling of the covenant which he hath made unto the people who are of the house of Israel" (3 Nephi 21:7).

7. "And ye need not imagine in your hearts that the words which have been spoken are vain, for behold, the Lord will remember his covenant which he hath made unto his people of the house of Israel. . . . Yea, and ye need not any longer hiss, nor spurn, nor make game of the Jews, nor any of the remnant of the house of Israel; for behold, the Lord remembereth his covenant unto them, and he will do unto them according to that which he hath sworn. Therefore ye need not suppose that ye can turn the right hand of the Lord unto the left, that he may not execute judgment unto the fulfilling of the covenant which he hath made unto the house of Israel" (3 Nephi 29:3, 8–9).

8. "And awake, and arise from the dust, O Jerusalem; yea, and put on thy beautiful garments, O daughter of Zion; and strengthen thy stakes and enlarge thy borders forever, that thou mayest no more be confounded, that the covenants of the Eternal Father which he hath made unto thee, O house of Israel, may be fulfilled" (Moroni 10:31).

9. "At the same time, saith the Lord, will I be the God of all the families of Israel, and they shall be my people. . . . Behold, the days come, saith the Lord, that I will make a new covenant with the house of Israel, and with the house of Judah: . . . But this shall be the covenant that I will make with the house of Israel; After those days, saith the Lord, I will put my law in their inward parts, and write it in

their hearts; and will be their God, and they shall be my people" (Jeremiah 31:1, 31, 33).

10. "Thus shall they know that I the Lord their God am with them, and that they, even the house of Israel, are my people, saith the Lord God" (Ezekiel 34:30).

11. "Trusting in that God who has said that these things are hid from the wise and prudent and revealed unto babes," said the Prophet Joseph Smith, "I step forth into the field to tell you what the Lord is doing, and what you must do. . . .

"The time has at last arrived when the God of Abraham, of Isaac, and of Jacob has set His hand again the second time to recover the remnants of his people, . . . and establish that covenant with them, which was promised when their sins should be taken away. See Isaiah xi, Romans xi: 25, 26, and 27, and also Jeremiah xxxi: 31, 32, and 33."[5]

Joseph Smith Would Be an Instrument in the Restoration

Joseph Smith knew that he would be an instrument in the hands of the Lord in helping to restore ancient and yet new and everlasting covenants, including the ordinances of baptism by immersion for the remission of sins and the laying on of hands for the gift of the Holy Ghost.

1. "Behold, the days come, saith the Lord, when I will make a new covenant with the house of Israel and with the house of Judah: Not according to the covenant that I made with their fathers in the day when I took them by the hand to lead them out of the land of Egypt; because they continued not in my covenant, and I regarded them not, saith the Lord. For this is the covenant that I will make with the house of Israel after those days, saith the Lord; I will put my laws into their mind, and write them in their hearts: and I will be to them a God, and they shall be to me a people" (Hebrews 8:8–10).

2. "For thus saith the Lord God: Him [Joseph Smith] have I inspired to move the cause of Zion in mighty power for good, and his diligence I know, and his prayers I have heard. Yea, his weeping for Zion I have seen, and I will cause that he shall mourn for her no longer; for his days of rejoicing are come unto the remission of his sins, and the manifestations of my blessings upon his works" (D&C 21:7–8).

3. "On the evening of the 21st of September, A.D. 1823, while I was praying unto God, and endeavoring to exercise faith in the precious promises of Scripture," said the Prophet Joseph Smith, "on a sudden a light like that of day, only of a far purer and more glorious appearance and brightness, burst into the room, indeed the first sight was as though the house was filled with consuming fire; the appearance

produced a shock that affected the whole body; in a moment a personage stood before me surrounded with a glory yet greater than that with which I was already surrounded. This messenger proclaimed himself to be an angel of God, sent to bring the joyful tidings that the covenant which God made with ancient Israel was at hand to be fulfilled, that the preparatory work for the second coming of the Messiah was speedily to commence; that the time was at hand for the Gospel in all its fullness to be preached in power, unto all nations that a people might be prepared for the Millennial reign. I was informed that I was chosen to be an instrument in the hands of God to bring about some of His purposes in this glorious dispensation.

"I was also informed concerning the aboriginal inhabitants of this country and shown who they were, and from whence they came."[6]

4. "And there shall rise up one mighty among them, who shall do much good, both in word and in deed, being an instrument in the hands of God, with exceeding faith, to work mighty wonders, and do that thing which is great in the sight of God, unto the bringing to pass much restoration unto the house of Israel, and unto the seed of thy brethren" (2 Nephi 3:24).

5. "It was decreed in the councils of eternity, long before the foundations of the earth were laid, that [Joseph Smith] should be the man, in the last dispensation of this world, to bring forth the word of God to the people, and receive the fulness of the keys and power of the Priesthood of the Son of God," said President Brigham Young. "The Lord had his eye upon him, and upon his father, and upon his father's father, and upon their progenitors clear back to Abraham, and from Abraham to the flood, from the flood to Enoch, and from Enoch to Adam. He has watched that family and that blood as it has circulated from its fountain to the birth of that man. [Joseph Smith] was foreordained in eternity to preside over this last dispensation."[7]

Joseph Smith Received Priesthood Keys

Joseph Smith and his associate Oliver Cowdery received from John the Baptist and later from Peter, James, and John the keys of the priesthood necessary to establish the kingdom of God upon the earth and to administer the earlier covenants and ordinances of the gospel.

"Upon you my fellow servants, in the name of Messiah I confer the Priesthood of Aaron, which holds the keys of the ministering of angels, and of the gospel of repentance, and of baptism by immersion for the remission of sins; and this shall never be taken again from the earth, until the sons of Levi do offer again an offering unto the Lord in righteousness" (D&C 13).

Joseph Smith Received Keys to Fulfill God's Promises to Israel

Joseph Smith and Oliver Cowdery received from Moses, Elias, and Elijah those keys of the priesthood necessary to fulfill the promises of the Lord to the descendants of his ancient covenant people. These appearances were in fulfillment of prophecies in Malachi 4:4–6, 3 Nephi 24 and 25, D&C 133:64, and Joseph Smith—History 1:36–39.

1. "Behold, I will send you Elijah the prophet before the coming of the great and dreadful day of the Lord: And he shall turn the heart of the fathers to the children, and the heart of the children to their fathers, lest I come and smite the earth with a curse" (Malachi 4:5–6).

2. "Behold, I will reveal unto you the Priesthood, by the hand of Elijah the prophet, before the coming of the great and dreadful day of the Lord. And he shall plant in the hearts of the children the promises made to the fathers, and the hearts of the children shall turn to their fathers. If it were not so, the whole earth would be utterly wasted at his coming" (D&C 2:1–3).

3. "After this vision closed, the heavens were again opened unto us; and Moses appeared before us, and committed unto us the keys of the gathering of Israel from the four parts of the earth, and the leading of the ten tribes from the land of the north. After this, Elias appeared, and committed the dispensation of the gospel of Abraham, saying that in us and our seed all generations after us should be blessed. After this vision had closed, another great and glorious vision burst upon us; for Elijah the prophet, who was taken to heaven without tasting death, stood before us, and said: Behold, the time has fully come, which was spoken of by the mouth of Malachi—testifying that he [Elijah] should be sent, before the great and dreadful day of the Lord come—To turn the hearts of the fathers to the children, and the children to the fathers, lest the whole earth be smitten with a curse—Therefore, the keys of this dispensation are committed into your hands; and by this ye may know that the great and dreadful day of the Lord is near, even at the doors" (D&C 110:11–16).

Joseph Smith Exercised Priesthood Keys in Behalf of God's Kingdom

Under the inspiration of the Lord, Joseph Smith exercised these keys in behalf of the kingdom of God upon the earth.

1. "Daniel answered in the presence of the king, . . . There is a God in heaven that revealeth secrets, and maketh known to the king Nebuchadnezzar what shall be in the latter days. Thy dream, and the visions of thy head upon thy bed, are these; As for thee, O king, thy thoughts came into thy mind upon thy bed, what

should come to pass hereafter: and he that revealeth secrets maketh known to thee what shall come to pass. . . . Thou sawest till that a stone was cut out without hands, which smote the image upon his feet that were of iron and clay, and brake them to pieces. Then was the iron, the clay, the brass, the silver, and the gold, broken to pieces together, and became like the chaff of the summer threshingfloors; and the wind carried them away, that no place was found for them: and the stone that smote the image became a great mountain, and filled the whole earth" (Daniel 2:27–29, 34–35).

2. "And in the days of these kings shall the God of heaven set up a kingdom, which shall never be destroyed: and the kingdom shall not be left to other people, but it shall break in pieces and consume all these kingdoms, and it shall stand for ever" (Daniel 2:44).

A Mission to the Blood of Israel

In 1837 the first formally organized mission of the Church was established in the British Isles, the exact region into which many of the blood of Israel had been scattered by the Romans. The hearts of the prophets of the dispensation of the fulness of times started to be turned toward the Jews and toward all the descendants of the house of Israel.

"Therefore, . . . seek diligently to turn the hearts of the children to their fathers, and the hearts of the fathers to the children; And again, the hearts of the Jews unto the prophets, and the prophets unto the Jews; lest I come and smite the whole earth with a curse, and all flesh be consumed before me" (D&C 98:16–17).

Dedicating the Land of Israel

In 1841 Joseph Smith set apart two apostles, Orson Hyde and John E. Page, to go to the ancient covenant land of Israel and dedicate that land for the return of the Jews.

1. "I am happy in being informed by your letter that your mission swells 'larger and larger,'" the Prophet wrote concerning the importance of their mission. "It is a great and important mission, and one that is worthy those intelligences who surround the throne of Jehovah to be engaged in. Although it appears great at present, yet you have but just begun to realize the greatness, the extent and glory of the same. If there is anything calculated to interest the mind of the Saints, to awaken in them the finest sensibilities, and arouse them to enterprise and exertion, surely it is the great and precious promises made by our heavenly Father to the children of Abraham; and those engaged in seeking the outcasts of Israel, and the dispersed of

Judah, cannot fail to enjoy the Spirit of the Lord and have the choicest blessings of heaven rest upon them in copious effusions.

"Brethren, you are in the pathway to eternal fame, and immortal glory; and inasmuch as you feel interested for the covenant people of the Lord, the God of their fathers shall bless you. Do not be discouraged on account of the greatness of the work; only be humble and faithful. . . . He who scattered Israel has promised to gather them; therefore inasmuch as you are to be instrumental in this great work, He will endow you with power, wisdom, might and intelligence, and every qualification necessary; while your minds will expand wider and wider, until you can circumscribe the earth and the heavens, reach forth into eternity, and contemplate the mighty acts of Jehovah in all their variety and glory."[8]

2. "[I] dedicate and consecrate this land unto Thee, for the gathering together of Judah's scattered remnants, according to the predictions of the Holy Prophets," Orson Hyde said in his dedicatory prayer. " . . . Incline them to gather in upon this land according to Thy word. Let them come like clouds and like doves to their windows. Let the large ships of the nations bring them from the distant isles; and let kings become their nursing fathers, and queens with motherly fondness wipe the tear of sorrow from their eyes."[9]

Temple Work Begins

By 1846 the temple in Nauvoo, Illinois, had been completed to a point where sacred sections could be dedicated wherein sacred covenants could be administered. Truly, the blood of Israel started to be gathered again into covenant Israel. The hearts of the fathers turned toward the children, and the hearts of the children toward the fathers. Joseph Smith said:

"The Bible says, 'I will send you Elijah the Prophet before the coming of the great and dreadful day of the Lord; and he shall turn the heart of the fathers to the children, and the heart of the children to the fathers, lest I come and smite the earth with a curse' (Malachi 4:4–6).

"Now, the word *turn* here should be translated *bind*, or seal. But what is the object of this important mission? or how is it to be fulfilled? The keys are to be delivered, the spirit of Elijah is to come, the Gospel to be established, the Saints of God gathered, Zion built up, and the Saints to come up as saviors on Mount Zion."[10]

The Nation of Israel Established

By 1948 an independent nation called Israel had been established under the auspices of the United Nations (which included membership of most of the major countries on the earth), and the blood of a special section of the house of Israel returned with fervor to the lands of ancient covenant Israel.

1. "And it shall come to pass that my people, which are of the house of Israel, shall be gathered home unto the lands of their possessions; and my word also shall be gathered in one. And I will show unto them that fight against my word and against my people, who are of the house of Israel, that I am God, and that I covenanted with Abraham that I would remember his seed forever" (2 Nephi 29:14).

2. "And it shall come to pass that the Jews which are scattered also shall begin to believe in Christ; and they shall begin to gather in upon the face of the land; and as many as shall believe in Christ shall also become a delightsome people. And it shall come to pass that the Lord God shall commence his work among all nations, kindreds, tongues, and people, to bring about the restoration of his people upon the earth" (2 Nephi 30:7–8).

3. "And I will make them one nation in the land upon the mountains of Israel; and one king shall be king to them all: and they shall be no more two nations, neither shall they be divided into two kingdoms any more at all" (Ezekiel 37:22).

The Truths of the House of Israel "As They Will Be"

What of the future?

Most of the concepts discussed to this point have been concerned with the origin and history of the house of Israel, but what of the prophesied destiny of the house of Israel? The things I list now will be just as certain and definite as the items listed as part of the present and historical past. As the Lord said through Isaiah, "Remember the former things of old: for I am God, and there is none else; I am God, and there is none like me, Declaring the end from the beginning, and from ancient times the things that are not yet done, saying, My counsel shall stand, and I will do all my pleasure" (Isaiah 46:9–10).

Nations Will War against Judah

The descendants of Judah of the house of Israel will continue to return to their lands of inheritance. This endeavor will continue to so excite and concern other nations that they will fight against Judah:

1. "Behold, the day of the Lord cometh, and thy spoil shall be divided in the

midst of thee. For I will gather all nations against Jerusalem to battle; and the city shall be taken, and the houses rifled, and the women ravished; and half of the city shall go forth into captivity, and the residue of the people shall not be cut off from the city" (Zechariah 14:1–2).

2. "And in that day shall be heard of wars and rumors of wars, and the whole earth shall be in commotion, and men's hearts shall fail them, and they shall say that Christ delayeth his coming until the end of the earth. And the love of men shall wax cold, and iniquity shall abound" (D&C 45:26–27).

3. Wilford Woodruff: "O house of Judah, . . . it is true that after you return and gather your nation home, and rebuild your City and Temple, that the Gentiles may gather together their armies to go against you to battle, to take you a prey and to take you as a spoil, which they will do, for the words of your prophets must be fulfilled."[11]

Missionary and Temple Work around the Earth

The descendants of Ephraim (and of Joseph) will continue to carry the "good news" of the gospel throughout the earth, and will build holy houses to the Lord where conditions and need merit.

1. "Send forth the elders of my church unto the nations which are afar off; unto the islands of the sea; send forth unto foreign lands; call upon all nations, first upon the Gentiles, and then upon the Jews" (D&C 133:8).

2. "And if thou do this, I have prepared thee for a greater work. Thou shalt preach the fulness of my gospel, which I have sent forth in these last days, the covenant which I have sent forth to recover my people, which are of the house of Israel" (D&C 39:11).

3. "And this gospel of the kingdom shall be preached in all the world for a witness unto all nations; and then shall the end come" (Matthew 24:14).

4. "Wherefore, I must bring forth the fulness of my gospel from the Gentiles unto the house of Israel" (D&C 14:10).

5. "And they shall be filled with songs of everlasting joy. Behold, this is the blessing of the everlasting God upon the tribes of Israel, and the richer blessing upon the head of Ephraim and his fellows. And they also of the tribe of Judah, after their pain, shall be sanctified in holiness before the Lord, to dwell in his presence day and night, forever and ever" (D&C 133:33–35).

6. Joseph Smith Jr.: "In speaking of the gathering, we mean to be understood as speaking of it according to scripture, the gathering of the elect of the Lord out of every nation on earth, and bringing them to the place of the Lord of Hosts, when

the city of righteousness shall be built, and where the people shall be of one heart and one mind, . . . where even upon the bells of the horses shall be written '*Holiness to the Lord.*'

"The Book of Mormon has made known who Israel is, upon this continent."[12]

The Gospel Taken to Israel

Eventually—and this is clearly in the future—the message of the fulness of the gospel of Jesus Christ will be taken to the blood of the house of Israel living in the land of Israel.

1. We read these prophetic words of the resurrected Jesus Christ himself: "And I will remember the covenant which I have made with my people; and I have covenanted with them that I would gather them together in mine own due time, that I would give unto them again the land of their fathers for their inheritance, which is the land of Jerusalem, which is the promised land unto them forever, saith the Father. And it shall come to pass that the time cometh, when the fulness of my gospel shall be preached unto them; And they shall believe in me, that I am Jesus Christ, the Son of God, and shall pray unto the Father in my name. Then shall their watchmen lift up their voice, and with the voice together shall they sing; for they shall see eye to eye. Then will the Father gather them together again, and give unto them Jerusalem for the land of their inheritance. Then shall they break forth into joy—Sing together, ye waste places of Jerusalem; for the Father hath comforted his people, he hath redeemed Jerusalem. The Father hath made bare his holy arm in the eyes of all the nations; and all the ends of the earth shall see the salvation of the Father; and the Father and I are one" (3 Nephi 20:29–35).

2. "Now these things are written unto the remnant of the house of Jacob; and they are written after this manner, because it is known of God that wickedness will not bring them forth unto them; and they are to be hid up unto the Lord that they may come forth in his own due time. And this is the commandment which I have received; and behold, they shall come forth according to the commandment of the Lord, when he shall see fit, in his wisdom. And behold, they [the writings in the Book of Mormon] shall go unto the unbelieving of the Jews; and for this intent shall they go—that they may be persuaded that Jesus is the Christ, the Son of the living God; that the Father may bring about, through his most Beloved, his great and eternal purpose, in restoring the Jews, or all the house of Israel, to the land of their inheritance, which the Lord their God hath given them, unto the fulfilling of his covenant" (Mormon 5:12–14).

3. "Come unto me, O ye house of Israel, and it shall be made manifest unto

you how great things the Father hath laid up for you, from the foundation of the world; and it hath not come unto you, because of unbelief. Behold, when ye shall rend that veil of unbelief which doth cause you to remain in your awful state of wickedness, and hardness of heart, and blindness of mind, then shall the great and marvelous things which have been hid up from the foundation of the world from you—yea, when ye shall call upon the Father in my name, with a broken heart and a contrite spirit, then shall ye know that the Father hath remembered the covenant which he made unto your fathers, O house of Israel" (Ether 4:14–15).

4. Wilford Woodruff: "When the Gentiles reject the Gospel it will be taken from them, and go to the house of Israel, to that long suffering people that are now scattered abroad through all the nations upon the earth, and they will re-build Jerusalem their ancient city, and make it more glorious than at the beginning, and they will have a leader in Israel with them, a man that is full of the power of God and the gift of the Holy Ghost; but they are held now from this work, only because the fulness of the Gentiles has not yet come in."[13]

The Two Prophets in Jerusalem

As part of this preaching of the gospel of Jesus Christ to the blood of Israel in Judah, two prophets will be sent to Jerusalem.

1. "For it [the court which is without the temple] is given unto the Gentiles: and the holy city shall they tread under foot forty and two months. And I will give power unto my two witnesses, and they shall prophesy a thousand two hundred and threescore days, clothed in sackcloth. . . . These have power to shut heaven, that it rain not in the days of their prophecy: and have power over waters to turn them to blood, and to smite the earth with all plagues, as often as they will. And when they shall have finished their testimony, the beast that ascendeth out of the bottomless pit shall make war against them, and shall overcome them, and kill them. And their dead bodies shall lie in the street of the great city, which spiritually is called Sodom and Egypt, where also our Lord was crucified. And they of the people and kindreds and tongues and nations shall see their dead bodies three days and an half, and shall not suffer their dead bodies to be put in graves. And they that dwell upon the earth shall rejoice over them, and make merry, and shall send gifts one to another; because these two prophets tormented them that dwelt on the earth. And after three days and an half the Spirit of life from God entered into them, and they stood upon their feet; and great fear fell upon them which saw them. And they heard a great voice from heaven saying unto them, Come up hither. And they ascended up to heaven in a cloud; and their enemies beheld them" (Revelation 11:2–3, 6–12).

2. "Q. What is to be understood by the two witnesses, in the eleventh chapter of Revelation?

"A. They are two prophets that are to be raised up to the Jewish nation in the last days, at the time of the restoration, and to prophesy to the Jews after they are gathered and have built the city of Jerusalem in the land of their fathers" (D&C 77:15).

3. LeGrand Richards: "No doubt these prophets will be called and ordained and sent by the First Presidency of The Church of Jesus Christ of Latter-day Saints, for the Lord's house is a house of order, and true prophets are never self sent—they must be called and sent of God."[14]

A Temple in Jerusalem

As part of the preparation and sanctifying of the land, a temple will be built in Jerusalem.

1. "Thus saith the Lord of hosts; Behold, I will save my people from the east country, and from the west country; And I will bring them, and they shall dwell in the midst of Jerusalem: and they shall be my people, and I will be their God, in truth and in righteousness. Thus saith the Lord of hosts; Let your hands be strong, ye that hear in these days these words by the mouth of the prophets, which were in the day that the foundation of the house of the Lord of hosts was laid, that the temple might be built" (Zechariah 8:7–9).

2. "For it is ordained that in Zion, and in her stakes, and in Jerusalem, those places which I have appointed for refuge, shall be the places for your baptisms for your dead. And again, verily I say unto you, how shall your washings be acceptable unto me, except ye perform them in a house which you have built to my name?" (D&C 124:36–37).

3. Joseph Smith Jr.: "What was the object of gathering the Jews, or the people of God in any age of the world? The main object was to build unto the Lord a house whereby He could reveal unto His people the ordinances of His house and the glories of His kingdom, and teach the people the way of salvation; for there are certain ordinances and principles that, when they are taught and practiced, must be done in a place or house built for that purpose."[15]

4. Joseph Smith Jr.: "It was the design of the councils of heaven before the world was, that the principles and laws of the priesthood should be predicated upon the gathering of the people in every age of the world. Jesus did everything to gather the people, and they would not be gathered, and He therefore poured out curses upon them. Ordinances instituted in the heavens before the foundation of the world,

in the priesthood, for the salvation of men, are not to be altered or changed. All must be saved on the same principles.

"It is for the same purpose that God gathers together His people in the last days, to build unto the Lord a house to prepare them for the ordinances and endowments, washings and anointings, etc. One of the ordinances of the house of the Lord is baptism for the dead. God decreed before the foundation of the world that that ordinance should be administered in a font prepared for that purpose in the house of the Lord."[16]

Water Will Flow from the Temple

Water will issue forth from under the temple (house of the Lord) and flow into the Dead Sea; its waters will be healed and will contain "the fish of the great sea."

1. "Afterward he [the Lord] brought me again unto the door of the house; and, behold, waters issued out from under the threshold of the house eastward: for the forefront of the house stood toward the east, and the waters came down from under from the right side of the house, at the south side of the altar.

"Then brought he me out of the way of the gate northward, and led me about the way without unto the utter gate by the way that looketh eastward; and, behold, there ran out waters on the right side. And when the man that had the line in his hand went forth eastward, he measured a thousand cubits, and he brought me through the waters; the waters were to the ankles.

"Again he measured a thousand, and brought me through the waters; the waters were to the knees. Again he measured a thousand, and brought me through; the waters were to the loins. Afterward he measured a thousand; and it was a river that I could not pass over: for the waters were risen, waters to swim in, a river that could not be passed over.

"And he said unto me, Son of man, hast thou seen this? Then he brought me, and caused me to return to the brink of the river. Now when I had returned, behold, at the bank of the river were very many trees on the one side and on the other.

"Then said he unto me, These waters issue out toward the east country, and go down into the desert, and go into the sea: which being brought forth into the sea, the waters shall be healed. And it shall come to pass, that every thing that liveth, which moveth, whithersoever the rivers shall come, shall live: and there shall be a very great multitude of fish, because these waters shall come thither: for they shall be healed; and every thing shall live whither the river cometh.

"And it shall come to pass, that the fishers shall stand upon it from En-gedi even unto En-eglaim; they shall be a place to spread forth nets; their fish shall be according to their kinds, as the fish of the great sea, exceeding many. But the miry places thereof and the marishes thereof shall not be healed; they shall be given to salt.

"And by the river upon the bank thereof, on this side and on that side, shall grow all trees for meat, whose leaf shall not fade, neither shall the fruit thereof be consumed: it shall bring forth new fruit according to his months, because their waters they issued out of the sanctuary: and the fruit thereof shall be for meat, and the leaf thereof for medicine" (Ezekiel 47:1–12).

2. Joseph Smith Jr.: "Judah must return, Jerusalem must be rebuilt, and the temple, and water come out from under the temple, and the waters of the Dead Sea be healed. It will take some time to rebuild the walls of the city and the temple, &c.; and all this must be done before the Son of Man will make His appearance."[17]

A King Named David

A leader named David, a descendant of the loins of ancient David, will become a king, a shepherd, and a prince in Israel. This leader is mentioned in Jeremiah 23:38; 30:3–9; Ezekiel 34:23–24, 28; 37:24–25; Isaiah 55:3–4; Hosea 3:4–5; Zechariah 3:8–9; 6:11–13.

1. "Thus saith the Lord God; Behold, I will take the children of Israel from among the heathen, whither they be gone, and will gather them on every side, and bring them into their own land: And I will make them one nation in the land upon the mountains of Israel; and one king shall be king to them all: and they shall be no more two nations, neither shall they be divided into two kingdoms any more at all: Neither shall they defile themselves any more with their idols, nor with their detestable things, nor with any of their transgressions: but I will save them out of all their dwellingplaces, wherein they have sinned, and will cleanse them: so shall they be my people, and I will be their God. And David my servant shall be king over them; and they all shall have one shepherd: they shall also walk in my judgments, and observe my statutes, and do them. And they shall dwell in the land that I have given unto Jacob my servant, wherein your fathers have dwelt; and they shall dwell therein, even they, and their children, and their children's children for ever: and my servant David shall be their prince for ever" (Ezekiel 37:21–25).

2. Joseph Smith Jr.: "The throne and kingdom of David is to be taken from him and given to another by the name of David in the last days, raised up out of his lineage."[18]

3. Said Elder Orson Hyde in his dedicatory prayer: "Let them know that it is

Thy good pleasure to restore the kingdom unto Israel—raise up Jerusalem as its capital, and constitute her people a distinct nation and government, with David Thy servant, even a descendant from the loins of ancient David to be their king."[19]

The Messiah Will Appear to Those in Israel

And then, as a confirming sign to the blood of Israel living in the land of Israel, their Messiah will appear to them, declaring that he is indeed the Messiah, even Jesus Christ, the Son of God, and a "nation" (the descendants of the house of Israel then living in Israel) will "be born at once" (converted to the Lord and to his gospel).

1. "Who hath heard such a thing? who hath seen such things? Shall the earth be made to bring forth in one day? or shall a nation be born at once? for as soon as Zion travailed, she brought forth her children" (Isaiah 66:8).

2. "And I will pour upon the house of David, and upon the inhabitants of Jerusalem, the spirit of grace and of supplications: and they shall look upon me whom they have pierced, and they shall mourn for him, as one mourneth for his only son, and shall be in bitterness for him, as one that is in bitterness for his firstborn" (Zechariah 12:10).

3. "And one shall say unto him, What are these wounds in thine hands? Then he shall answer, Those with which I was wounded in the house of my friends" (Zechariah 13:6).

4. "And then shall the Jews look upon me and say: What are these wounds in thine hands and in thy feet? Then shall they know that I am the Lord; for I will say unto them: These wounds are the wounds with which I was wounded in the house of my friends. I am he who was lifted up. I am Jesus that was crucified. I am the Son of God. And then shall they weep because of their iniquities; then shall they lament because they persecuted their king" (D&C 45:51–53).

Christ Will Lead the Armies of Israel

Jesus Christ will then lead the armies of Israel to victory over the combined armies of the nations of the earth.

1. "Then shall the Lord go forth, and fight against those nations, as when he fought in the day of battle. . . . And the Lord shall be king over all the earth: in that day shall there be one Lord, and his name one" (Zechariah 14:3, 9).

2. Wilford Woodruff: "The Jews have got to gather to their own land in unbelief. . . . [A]nd when they have done this and rebuilt their city, the Gentiles, in

fulfillment of the words of Ezekiel, Jeremiah and other prophets, will go up against Jerusalem to battle and to take a spoil and a prey; and then when they have taken one-half of Jerusalem captive and distressed the Jews for the last time on the earth, their Great Deliverer, Shiloh, will come."[20]

The Two World Capitals

Then comes the completion of the destiny of the house of Israel leading up to the great millennial reign of Jesus Christ upon the earth as King of kings and Lord of lords. In preparation for this great day, two world capitals must be prepared as prophesied—one in "Zion" and one in Jerusalem.

1. "And it shall come to pass in the last days, that the mountain of the Lord's house shall be established in the top of the mountains, and shall be exalted above the hills; and all nations shall flow unto it. And many people shall go and say, Come ye, and let us go up to the mountain of the Lord, to the house of the God of Jacob; and he will teach us of his ways, and we will walk in his paths: for out of Zion shall go forth the law, and the word of the Lord from Jerusalem" (Isaiah 2:2–3).

2. "Wherefore, prepare ye for the coming of the Bridegroom; go ye, go ye out to meet him. For behold, he shall stand upon the mount of Olivet, and upon the mighty ocean, even the great deep, and upon the islands of the sea, and upon the land of Zion. And he shall utter his voice out of Zion, and he shall speak from Jerusalem, and his voice shall be heard among all people" (D&C 133:19–21).

3. "And they shall assist my people, the remnant of Jacob, and also as many of the house of Israel as shall come, that they may build a city, which shall be called the New Jerusalem" (3 Nephi 21:23).

4. "And he spake also concerning the house of Israel, and the Jerusalem from whence Lehi should come—after it should be destroyed it should be built up again, a holy city unto the Lord; wherefore, it could not be a new Jerusalem for it had been in a time of old; but it should be built up again, and become a holy city of the Lord; and it should be built unto the house of Israel" (Ether 13:5).

5. "And then cometh the New Jerusalem; and blessed are they who dwell therein, for it is they whose garments are white through the blood of the Lamb; and they are they who are numbered among the remnant of the seed of Joseph, who were of the house of Israel" (Ether 13:10).

6. Joseph Smith Jr.: "The Book of Mormon is a record of the forefathers of our western tribes of Indians; . . . [who] are descendents from that Joseph who was sold into Egypt. . . . [T]he land of America is a promised land unto them, and unto it all the tribes of Israel will come, with as many of the Gentiles as shall comply with

the requisitions of the new covenant. . . . The city of Zion spoken of by David, in the one hundred and second Psalm, will be built upon the land of America. . . . But Judah shall obtain deliverance at Jerusalem. . . . These are testimonies that the Good Shepherd will put forth His own sheep, and lead them out from all nations where they have been scattered in a cloudy and dark day, to Zion, and to Jerusalem."[21]

7. Joseph Smith Jr.: "I received, by a heavenly vision, a commandment in June following, to take my journey to the western boundaries of the State of Missouri, and there designate the very spot which was to be the central place for the commencement of the gathering together of those who embrace the fullness of the everlasting Gospel. Accordingly I undertook the journey, with certain ones of my brethren, and after a long and tedious journey, suffering many privations and hardships, arrived in Jackson County, Missouri, and after viewing the country, seeking diligently at the hand of God, He manifested Himself unto us, and . . . designed to commence the work of the gathering, and the upbuilding of an 'holy city,' which should be called Zion— . . .

"Now we learn from the Book of Mormon the very identical continent and spot of land upon which the New Jerusalem is to stand, and it must be caught up according to the vision of John upon the isle of Patmos.

" . . . Now many will feel disposed to say, that this New Jerusalem spoken of, is the Jerusalem that was built by the Jews on the eastern continent. But you will see, from Revelations xxi: 2, there was a New Jerusalem coming down from God out of heaven, adorned as a bride for her husband; that after this, the Revelator was caught away in the Spirit, to a great and high mountain, and saw the great and holy city descending out of heaven from God. *Now there are two cities spoken of here. . . . [T]here is a New Jerusalem to be established on this continent, and also Jerusalem shall be rebuilt on the eastern continent.*"[22]

8. Joseph Fielding Smith: "Jerusalem of old, after the Jews have been cleansed and sanctified from all their sin, shall become a holy city where the Lord shall dwell and from whence he shall send forth his word unto all people. Likewise, on this continent, the city of Zion, New Jerusalem—shall be built, and from it the law of God shall also go forth [D&C 45:66–67; 84:2]. There will be no conflict, for each city shall be headquarters for the Redeemer of the world, and from each he shall send forth his proclamations as occasion may require. Jerusalem shall be the gathering place of Judah and his fellows of the house of Israel, and Zion shall be the gathering place of Ephraim and his fellows, upon whose heads shall be conferred 'the richer blessings'" (see D&C 133:34).[23]

The Messiah and His Apostles Will Judge Israel

Eventually the resurrected Messiah and his apostles will judge "the whole house of Israel" (D&C 29:12).

1. "For I command all men, both in the east and in the west, and in the north, and in the south, and in the islands of the sea, that they shall write the words which I speak unto them; for out of the books which shall be written I will judge the world, every man according to their works, according to that which is written" (2 Nephi 29:11).

2. "I saw in the night visions, and, behold, one like the Son of man came with the clouds of heaven, and came to the Ancient of days, and they brought him near before him. And there was given him dominion, and glory, and a kingdom, that all people, nations, and languages, should serve him: his dominion is an everlasting dominion, which shall not pass away, and his kingdom that which shall not be destroyed" (Daniel 7:13–14).

SUMMARY

Reflecting upon these teachings, President Wilford Woodruff stated:

"The Lord has decreed that the Jews should be gathered from all the Gentile nations where they have been driven, into their own land, in fulfillment of the words of Moses their law-giver. And this is the will of your great Elohim, O house of Judah, and whenever you shall be called upon to perform this work, the God of Israel will help you. *You have a great future and destiny before you and you cannot avoid fulfilling it;* you are the royal chosen seed, and the God of your father's house has kept you distinct as a nation. . . . You may not wait until you believe on Jesus of Nazareth, but when you meet with Shiloh your king, you will know him; *your destiny is marked out, you cannot avoid it.* . . . [O house of Judah,] it is true that after you return and gather your nation home, and rebuild your City and Temple, that the Gentiles may gather together their armies to go against you to battle, to take you a prey and to take you as a spoil, which they will do, for the words of your prophets must be fulfilled; but when this affliction comes, the living God, that led Moses through the wilderness, will deliver you, and your Shiloh will come and stand in your midst and will fight your battles; and you will know him, and the afflictions of the Jews will be at an end, while the destruction of the Gentiles will be so great that it will take the whole house of Israel who are gathered about Jerusalem, seven months to bury the dead of their enemies, and the weapons of war will last them seven years for fuel, so that they need not go to any forest for wood. *These are tremendous sayings*—who can bear them? *Nevertheless they are true,* and will be fulfilled, according to the sayings of Ezekiel, Zechariah, and other prophets. Though the heavens and the earth pass away, not one jot or tittle will fall unfulfilled."[24]

Feeling the spirit of this great work of the last days, the prophet Joseph Smith exclaimed: "The building up of Zion is a cause that has interested the people of God in every age; it is a theme upon which prophets, priests and kings have dwelt with peculiar delight; they have looked forward with joyful anticipation to the day in which we live; and fired with heavenly and joyful anticipations they have sung and written and prophesied of this our day; but they died without the sight; we are the favored people that God has made choice of to bring about the Latter-day glory; it is left for us to see, participate in and help to roll forward the Latter-day glory, 'the dispensation of the fullness of times, when God will gather together all things that are in heaven, and all things that are upon the earth,' 'even in one,' when the Saints of God will be gathered in one from every nation, and kindred, and people, and tongue, when the Jews will be gathered together into one, the wicked will also be gathered together to be destroyed, as spoken of by the prophets; the Spirit of God will also dwell with His people, and be withdrawn from the rest of the nations, and all things whether in heaven or on earth will be in one, even in Christ. The heavenly Priesthood will unite with the earthly, to bring about those great purposes; and whilst we are thus united in the one common cause, to roll forth the kingdom of God, the heavenly Priesthood are not idle spectators, the Spirit of God will be showered down from above, and it will dwell in our midst. The blessings of the Most High will rest upon our tabernacles, and our name will be handed down to future ages; our children will rise up and call us blessed; and generations yet unborn will dwell with peculiar delight upon the scenes that we have passed through, the privations that we have endured; the untiring zeal that we have manifested; the all but insurmountable difficulties that we have overcome in laying the foundation of a work that brought about the glory and blessing which they will realize; a work that God and angels have contemplated with delight for generations past; that fired the souls of the ancient patriarchs and prophets; a work that is destined to bring about the destruction of the powers of darkness, the renovation of the earth, the glory of God, and the salvation of the human family."[25]

"Brethren," the Prophet added a short time later, "shall we not go on in so great a cause? Go forward and not backward. Courage, brethren; and on, on to the victory!" (D&C 128:22).

That we may do our small part in the cause of teaching and advancing this great work is the prayer that I would ask for each of us.

Notes

From *Nurturing Faith through the Book of Mormon: The 24th Annual Sidney B. Sperry Symposium* (Salt Lake City: Deseret Book Co., 1995), 25–88.

1. James Strong, *The Exhaustive Concordance of the Bible* (Nashville: Abingdon, 1894).
2. *An Exhaustive Concordance of the Book of Mormon, Doctrine and Covenants, and Pearl of Great Price,* comp. Gary R. Shapiro (Salt Lake City: Hawkes Publishing, 1977), iv.
3. *An Exhaustive Concordance of the Book of Mormon, Doctrine and Covenants, and Pearl of Great Price,* iii, iv.
4. *History of the Church,* 1:313–14.
5. Ibid., 1:313.
6. Ibid., 4:536–37.
7. Brigham Young, in *Journal of Discourses,* 7:289–90.
8. *Teachings of the Prophet Joseph Smith,* 163.
9. *Temples of the Most High,* comp. N. B. Lundwall, 2d ed. (Salt Lake City: Bookcraft, 1996), 256–57.
10. *Teachings of the Prophet Joseph Smith,* 330.
11. Matthias F. Cowley, *Wilford Woodruff: History of His Life and Labors* (Salt Lake City: Bookcraft, 1964), 509.
12. *Teachings of the Prophet Joseph Smith,* 93; emphasis in original.
13. Wilford Woodruff, in *Journal of Discourses,* 2:200.
14. LeGrand Richards, *Israel! Do You Know?* (Salt Lake City: Deseret Book Co., 1990), 197.
15. *History of the Church,* 5:423.
16. *Teachings of the Prophet Joseph Smith,* 308.
17. *History of the Church,* 5:337.
18. Ibid., 6:253.
19. Ibid., 4:457.
20. Wilford Woodruff, in *Journal of Discourses,* 15:277–78.
21. *History of the Church,* 1:315.
22. Ibid., 2:254, 261–62; emphasis added.
23. Joseph Fielding Smith, "Zion and Jerusalem," *Improvement Era,* 22 (July 1919): 815–16.
24. Cowley, *Wilford Woodruff,* 509–10; emphasis added.
25. *History of the Church,* 4:609–10.

Scripture Index

This index does not include entries from the following sections of the book:
  A list of Messianic Psalms and Psalms quoted in the New Testament, p. 54
  A list of major messages for our time from the Book of Mormon, pp. 126–28
  "Significant Topics—and Related Sections in the Doctrine and Covenants," pp. 150–52
  "Bible Dictionary References as Possible Bible Footnotes," pp. 159–78
  A listing of scriptures pertaining to Jesus Christ, pp. 208–9
  The summary lists found under "Contributions of the Joseph Smith Translation to Understanding Paul's Epistles," pp. 472–80
  "Major Greek Contributions to the LDS Bible," pp. 480–84
  A list of scriptures pertaining to lineage, p. 529
  A list of scriptures pertaining to the house of Israel, pp. 537–38.

OLD TESTAMENT

GENESIS
1, pp. 38, 45
1:1, pp. 38, 45, 282
1:28, pp. 46, 313, 385
1–2, p. 46
1–3, p. 210
2:7, pp. 323, 372
2:8, p. 323
2:18, p. 418
3:3, p. 314
3:15, p. 219
3:23, p. 313
5, p. 30
6:13, p. 45
6:13–22, p. 217
9, p. 44
9:4–6, p. 44
10:21, p. 526
11:8, p. 192
14, pp. 44, 46
14:13, p. 526
14:18, p. 459
15, 19, p. 44
17, pp. 44–46
18:14, p. 46
18:17–18, p. 541
18:25, p. 231
21, p. 44
25, 29, p. 30
32:28, p. 539
35:10, p. 539
39:14, p. 526
48, pp. 44, 46
49:10, p. 217
49:24, p. 218
49:26, p. 545
50, pp. 44, 46

EXODUS
3:6, 15–16, p. 217
3:13, p. 214
3:14, pp. 213, 214, 496
3:15, pp. 216, 496
6:3, pp. 46, 496, 547, 548
23:19, p. 34
34:1–2, p. 46

LEVITICUS
19:2, p. 47

NUMBERS
16, p. 307
16:22, pp. 281, 376
21:9, p. 47
24:17, pp. 47, 217
27:16, p. 376
27:22, p. 47

DEUTERONOMY
4–11, p. 48
6:9, p. 35
7:6, p. 542
10:12, p. 48
11:9, 14–15, p. 26
11:20, p. 35
17:6, pp. 123, 379
19:15, pp. 88, 103, 203
24:1–2, p. 78
28:1–14, p. 542
28:15–67, p. 543
29–34, p. 48
32:8, pp. 307, 541

JOSHUA
24:14–15, p. 48

JUDGES
2, p. 49
6:13, p. 49
12:4–6, p. 527

RUTH
1:16, p. 49

1 SAMUEL
2:2, p. 217

2:10, p. 298
8:7, p. 50

2 SAMUEL
5:6, p. 459
7:13, p. 206
14:14, p. 287
22:2, p. 50
23:3, pp. 217, 552

1 KINGS
17, 18, 19, p. 50
18:21, p. 50

2 KINGS
1–7, p. 51
6:16, p. 51
6:17, p. 288
13:13–21, p. 51
16:6, p. 540
17, p. 51
24–25, p. 51

1 CHRONICLES
5:1–2, p. 51
17:1–15, p. 51
29:29, p. 51

2 CHRONICLES
15:9–10, p. 51
36:22–23, pp. 544, 545

EZRA
1:1–6, pp. 544, 545
2:1, p. 545
9:9, p. 52

NEHEMIAH
8:8–9, p. 52
9:6, p. 52

ESTHER
2:7, p. 53

JOB
19:25, pp. 206, 496
19:25–27, p. 53
32:8, p. 376
38:4, 7, p. 307
38:7, pp. 251, 312

PSALMS
8:4–5, p. 327
8:5, p. 93
18:2, p. 217
19:9, p. 298

22:16, p. 206
24:10, p. 230
47:7, p. 229
76:2, p. 459
83:18, pp. 496, 548
85, p. 210
85:11, p. 210
89:3, 4, p. 137
89:4, p. 206
110:4, p. 230
118:22, pp. 218, 496
132:17, pp. 206, 218

PROVERBS
8, p. 379
8:23, p. 379
16:32, p. 376
29:26, p. 298

ECCLESIASTES
3:17, p. 231
11–12, p. 55
12:7, pp. 55, 307
12:12, p. 298
12:14, pp. 231, 297

ISAIAH
1:4, p. 224
2:2–3, p. 573
2:3, p. 230
2:5, p. 223
7:14, pp. 205, 207, 216, 549
8:14, p. 218
9:1–2, pp. 205, 220, 549
9:2, p. 223
9:6, pp. 56, 207, 216, 220, 232, 496, 549
9:7, p. 206
11, pp. 505, 507, 514, 558, 560
11:1, pp. 206, 217
11:11, 13, p. 506
11:11–13, p. 505
11:12, p. 556
12:2, pp. 207, 548
12:2–3, p. 216
14:1–2, p. 557
14:12–13, p. 323
18:1, 3, p. 545
25:8, pp. 206, 226
26:4, p. 548
26:19, p. 206

28:10, p. 191
29:13–14, p. 553
40:8, p. 541
40:11, p. 222
41:14, p. 549
42:5–7, p. 205
43:14–15, pp. 207, 233
43:25, p. 300
44:6, pp. 207, 234
46:9–10, p. 565
49:1, p. 551
49:26, pp. 207, 234
50:6, p. 206
50–52:2, p. 555
53:4–6, 12, p. 206
53:4, 7, p. 226
53:9, pp. 206, 226
54, p. 55
54:5, pp. 206, 216
55:3–4, p. 571
60:16, p. 217
60:19, p. 223
64:4, p. 486
66:8, pp. 229, 572

JEREMIAH
1, pp. 56, 57
1:4–5, pp. 56, 307
1:21, p. 57
2, p. 51
2:1–11, p. 57
3, p. 57
3:18, p. 556
3:42–44, p. 57
4, 5, p. 57
5:11, p. 539
10:10, p. 229
11:10, p. 539
16, p. 56
16:14–16, p. 57
23–25, p. 56
23:5, pp. 206, 231
23:6, p. 220
23:7–8, p. 556
23:38, p. 571
30–33, p. 56
30:3–9, p. 571
31:1, p. 560
31:31, 32, 33, pp. 514, 558, 560
31:34, p. 300
33:15, pp. 206, 218
50, p. 56

LAMENTATIONS
5:21, p. 57

EZEKIEL
11, 20, 34–39, 47–48, p. 58
14:14, p. 53
28:25, p. 556
34:23–24, 28, p. 571
34:30, p. 560
36:10, p. 556
37, p. 210
37:12, p. 206
37:15–19, pp. 58, 192
37:16, p. 546
37:16–19, p. 112
37:21–25, p. 571
37:22, p. 565
47:1–12, p. 571

DANIEL
1:3, p. 58
2:27–29, 34–35, 44, p. 563
2:34, p. 58
7:9–14, p. 229
7:13–14, p. 575
7:14, p. 230
9:2, p. 58
9:25–26, pp. 225, 496
11:30, p. 375
12:10, p. 59

HOSEA
1:10, p. 59
2:23, p. 59
3:4–5, p. 571
6:6, p. 59
10:8, p. 59
11:1, pp. 59, 206, 219, 549
13:14, pp. 59, 206

JOEL
2:28–32, pp. 60, 507
3, p. 60

AMOS
3:7, pp. 60, 154, 210, 509
8:11, p. 60
8:11–12, p. 552
9, p. 60
9:9, p. 551

MICAH
3:5–7, p. 552
5:2, pp. 61, 205, 218, 548
6:8, p. 61

NAHUM
1:3, p. 61

HABAKKUK
2:20, p. 62

ZEPHANIAH
3:9, p. 62

HAGGAI
2:7, 9, p. 62

ZECHARIAH
2–3, p. 62
2:11–12, p. 556
3:8–9, p. 571
6:11–13, p. 571
8–14, p. 62
8:7–9, p. 569
9:9, pp. 62, 206, 549
11:12–13, p. 206
12:2–3, 6–9, p. 557
12:10, pp. 98, 206, 572
13:6, pp. 206, 229, 572
14:1–2, p. 566
14:3, 9, p. 572
14:4, p. 229

MALACHI
1:14, p. 229
3:1, pp. 218, 549
3–4, pp. 63, 505
4:5–6, pp. 365, 562, 564
4:6, p. 63

NEW TESTAMENT

MATTHEW
1:1, pp. 217, 218, 549
1:21, pp. 226, 496
1:23, p. 242
2:4, p. 68
2:6, pp. 68, 218
2:15, pp. 59, 219
2:23, p. 220
3:2, p. 356
3:17, pp. 213, 234, 496
3:46 (JST), p. 234
4, p. 435
4:1–2, p. 70
4:13–16, p. 220
4:19, pp. 223, 435
4:22, p. 435
4:23, p. 221
5:1–6, p. 76
5:1–8 (JST), p. 77
5:31–32, p. 77
5:48, pp. 345, 391
6, p. 77
6:9, p. 342
6:10, pp. 230, 423
6:25, p. 77
6:33, p. 260
7:7, pp. 183, 381, 403
7:13–14, p. 349
7:14, p. 231
7:21, 24, 26, p. 345
7:23, p. 79
7:33 (JST), p. 79
8:2–4, 27, p. 221
9:12, 24–26, p. 221
10, p. 436
10:5–8, 11–20, 22–23, p. 436
10:28, pp. 383, 427
10:34 (JST), p. 260
12:8, 32, p. 233
12:35–37, p. 389
12:36, p. 297
12:39–40, p. 61
13:3–6, p. 79
13:3–9, p. 220
13:5 (JST), p. 79
13:24–30, p. 145
14:15–21, 25–27, p. 221
15:24, p. 194
15:32–38, p. 221
16:13, 27, p. 233
16:16, pp. 82, 232, 234, 549
16:17, p. 459
16:18, p. 154
16:19, pp. 365, 418
16:28, p. 79
17:5, p. 234
17:20, p. 452
18:16, p. 203
19:3–9, p. 78
19:4–6, p. 418
19:17, p. 221
21:6–11, p. 549
21:6–17, p. 239
21:8–9, p. 237
21:11, p. 220
21:12, 13, p. 239
21:18–20, p. 238
21:23–46, p. 240
22:1–14, p. 240
22:16, p. 69
22:17–21, 28, 30–32, 36, p. 241
22:21, pp. 237, 244
22:24–30, p. 419
22:37–39, 42–46, p. 242
23:33, p. 242
23:38, p. 239
24, pp. 80, 242
24:1, p. 80
24:2, p. 242
24:14, p. 566
24:28, 34, p. 80
25:1–13, p. 145
25:21, p. 15
25:34–40, 46, p. 258
26:22–25 (JST), p. 315
26:26, p. 41
26:39, p. 255
26:41, p. 376
26:63, 65–66, p. 244
27:11, 37, p. 218
27:25, p. 245
27:45–46, p. 255
27:46, p. 246
27:50, p. 80
27:52–53, pp. 248, 267
27:54 (JST), p. 80
28:5–7, p. 247
28:6, p. 226

MARK
1:15, pp. 345, 356
1:24, p. 224
1:34, p. 221
2:28, p. 220
4:25, p. 70
5:7, pp. 232, 234
6:3, pp. 219, 220
6:25, p. 71
8:36, p. 427
8:36–37, p. 383
9:43–48, p. 80
10:2–12, p. 78
10:17, p. 220
11:11, p. 238
11:11, 15, p. 239
12:9, p. 222
12:28, p. 241
13, p. 242
13:20–24 (JST), p. 81
14:14–15, p. 243
14:22–24, p. 81
14:61, p. 219
14:62, p. 244
15:2, p. 218
15:33–34, p. 255
16:16, p. 345
16:17–18, p. 179

LUKE
1:26–27, 30–32, 35, p. 218
1:30–33, p. 253
1:32, pp. 219, 549
1:41, p. 81
2:7–14, p. 254
2:19, p. 13
2:21–23, p. 81
2:25, p. 217
2:26, p. 225
2:32, p. 223
2:47, p. 392
2:49, pp. 71, 220
2:52, pp. 82, 504
4:34, 41, p. 234
6:27–28, p. 82
6:46, p. 345
8:21, p. 345
8:24, p. 221
8:55, p. 376

9:20, p. 225
9:35, p. 234
10:31–33, p. 82
11:2, p. 308
11:52, p. 82
13:3, p. 356
16:18, p. 78
17:21, p. 82
19:45, 47–48, p. 239
20:39–40, p. 241
21, p. 242
22:32, pp. 82, 243
22:44, p. 83
22:52, p. 244
22:66, p. 69
23:2, 3, p. 244
23:5, 16, 18, 21, 34, p. 245
23:43, pp. 246, 289
23:44, 56, p. 246
23:46, pp. 246, 255, 376
24:3, p. 220
24:37, 39, p. 376
24:37–39, p. 306
24:39, pp. 83, 87, 226

JOHN
1:1, p. 83
1:1, 14, p. 219
1:1–5 (JST), p. 219
1:9, p. 223
1:14, 18, p. 218
1:19 (JST), p. 233
1:29, pp. 215, 226, 496
1:34, 49, p. 234
1:40, p. 459
1:41, pp. 225, 234
2:7–9, p. 221
2:16, p. 239
3:2, p. 221
3:2–5, p. 360
3:2–6, p. 370
3:3, p. 221
3:3–5, p. 345
3:5, pp. 296, 331, 366
3:13–14, p. 233
3:14–17, p. 47
3:16, pp. 218, 257, 260
4:7, 9–11, 13–14, p. 223
4:10–14, p. 222
4:42, p. 234

4:44, p. 220
5:1–9, p. 221
5:22, pp. 231, 298
5:25, 28, pp. 83, 366
5:25–28, p. 247
5:26, p. 287
5:29, pp. 145, 268
5:31, p. 83
5:32 (JST), p. 83
5:36, p. 232
5:39, pp. 7, 26, 204, 428
6:31, 32–33, 35, 48–51, p. 222
6:38–40, p. 250
6:63, p. 383
6:69, p. 234
7:16, p. 232
7:16–17, p. 194
7:17, p. 345
8:11, 28, p. 221
8:16, pp. 231, 298
8:31–32, p. 318
8:56, p. 84
9:1–3, p. 308
9:1–7, p. 221
9:39, p. 231
10:11, 15, p. 221
10:11–14, p. 496
10:7, 14–16, p. 222
10:16, pp. 84, 193
10:17–18, p. 266
10:30, p. 232
11:8–53, p. 221
11:25, pp. 226, 232, 496
11:26, p. 287
12:19, 27, 29, 35–36, p. 238
12:27, p. 244
13:15, p. 224
13:25, p. 438
13:34, p. 243
14:1–3, p. 412
14:2, pp. 271, 295
14:6, pp. 216, 224
14:26, pp. 84, 243, 360
15:1, 5, p. 243
15:1–2, p. 222
15:13, pp. 225, 260
15:26, p. 360
16:13, p. 360

17, p. 438
17:1–3, p. 243
17:1–5, p. 438
17:3, pp. 7, 250, 319, 416, 427
18:36, pp. 237, 244
19:12, 21–22, p. 245
19:25–27, p. 437
19:30, pp. 246, 255
19:30–31, p. 84
20:1, p. 247
20:17, pp. 84, 308, 401
20:31, p. 248
21, p. 145
21:3, 6, 7, p. 439
21:15–17, p. 258
21:20–24, pp. 80, 440

ACTS
1:11, p. 229
2:37–38, pp. 186, 345
2:38, p. 361
3:14, p. 231
3:20–21, pp. 84, 552
3:21, p. 228
3:22–23, p. 507
3:37–38, p. 356
4:11, p. 218
4:27, p. 219
4:36–37, p. 459
5:34–40, p. 458
6:5, pp. 458, 460
7:52, p. 231
7:58, pp. 456, 457
8:1, pp. 456, 457, 458
8:3, pp. 456, 457
9:1, 4–25, pp. 456, 458
9:10–18, p. 459
9:11, pp. 456, 457
9:26–30, pp. 456, 459
9:27, p. 459
9:30, p. 461
10:36, p. 220
10:42, p. 231
11:19–30, p. 460
11:22–30, p. 459
11:26, 29–30, pp. 456, 460
12:2, p. 459
12:12, p. 460
12:25, pp. 459, 460
13:1, p. 460
13:1–14:26, p. 456

13:9, pp. 456, 457
13:48, p. 85
13–14, p. 459
13–28, p. 485
14:4, 14, p. 459
14:26, p. 460
15, p. 459
15:1–33, pp. 456, 460
15:11, pp. 338, 468
15:14, 39, p. 459
15:22–35, p. 460
15:35, pp. 456, 460
15:36–18:22, pp. 456, 460
16:30–33, p. 345
17:26, pp. 307, 541
18:22, pp. 460, 461
18:23, p. 460
18:23–21:15, p. 456
19:11–12, 15, 17, 20, p. 468
19:27–28, 30, 34, p. 471
20:35, pp. 85, 260
21: 8, 16, p. 461
21:17–23:35, pp. 456, 461
22:3, pp. 456, 457
22:7, pp. 456, 458
22:12, p. 459
22:20, p. 458
23:23, 33, p. 461
24:1–26:32, pp. 456, 461
25:1–13, p. 461
26:10, pp. 456, 457
26:14, pp. 456, 458
27:1–28:10, pp. 456, 461
28:30, pp. 456, 461

ROMANS
1:1–4, 16, p. 462
2:2, p. 298
2:15, p. 231
3:23–24, 27–28, p. 338
3:23–30, p. 466
3:25, p. 97
3:28, p. 346
4:1–13, p. 467
4:2–5, 13–16, p. 339
4:16 (JST), p. 466
4:16, p. 466

5:8, p. 463
5:11, p. 85
6:23, p. 318
7:15–17 (JST), p. 85
7:15–19, p. 85
8:14–17, p. 232
8:16, pp. 85, 281, 307, 466
8:16–17, p. 301
8:29, 30, p. 486
8:29–30, p. 86
9:6, p. 533
9:29, p. 68
10:9–10, p. 346
11:25, 26, 27, p. 558
11:5–6, p. 339
11:6, p. 336
11:21, 24, p. 86
11:25, 26, 27, p. 560
11:25–27, p. 514
11:26, pp. 218, 229
12:17–21, p. 470
14:10, p. 297
15:12, p. 217
15:16, p. 361
15:24, p. 461

1 CORINTHIANS
1:3, p. 466
1:10, p. 469
1:10–13, p. 470
2:4, p. 453
2:6–7, 9, p. 486
2:11, pp. 86, 183
3:11, p. 224
3:16–17, p. 383
6:1–3, p. 470
6:9–10, 19–20, p. 470
6:11, p. 361
6:14, pp. 265, 292
6:20, p. 384
7:2–3, p. 467
7:14, p. 145
8:6, p. 215
8:9, 13, p. 471
9:14, 16–19, 22, p. 471
10:23–24, p. 86
11:2–14:40, p. 468
11:3, 11, p. 467
11:11, p. 418
11:23–26, p. 468
12:3, p. 360
12:12–20, p. 471

13:12, pp. 330, 380
14:34–35, p. 86
15, p. 412
15:3–8, 17, 19–22, p. 463
15:9, p. 367
15:19–23, p. 267
15:20, pp. 226, 292, 496
15:21–22, p. 464
15:22, pp. 225, 226, 264, 286, 291
15:29, pp. 87, 343, 367, 471
15:32, p. 471
15:40–42, pp. 87, 412, 417, 466
15:47, p. 220
15:50, p. 87
15:53–55, p. 373
15:55, p. 226
16:8–9, 13, p. 471

2 CORINTHIANS
1:2–3, p. 466
3:6, p. 404
3:17, p. 320
4:4, p. 219
5:21, p. 223
11:14, p. 87
11:14–15, p. 470
12:2, pp. 88, 412
13:1, pp. 88, 103, 179, 191, 203, 379, 509

GALATIANS
1:3–4, p. 466
1:4, p. 224
1:6–8, p. 471
1:13, pp. 456, 457
1:15–16, 17, pp. 456, 458
1:17–18, pp. 88, 456, 458
1:18–19, 21–24, pp. 456, 459
2:1–10, p. 456
2:1–20, p. 460
2:16, pp. 339, 346, 468
3:1, p. 471
3:6–8, p. 88
5:1, p. 318
5:4, p. 340
6:7, p. 318

EPHESIANS
1:2, 4, p. 466
1:4–5, p. 88
1:5, 11, pp. 86, 486
1:7, p. 226
1:9–10, p. 552
1:10, pp. 89, 228, 471
2:1–3:21, p. 471
2:4–10, pp. 340, 469
2:8–9, pp. 336, 468
2:10, p. 336
2:14, p. 220
2:19–21, p. 89
2:19–22, p. 469
2:20, pp. 218, 496
4:3–6, p. 469
4:5–8, p. 340
4:11–13, pp. 89, 469
4:26, p. 89
5:2, p. 226
5:23, p. 224
5:25, 31, p. 467
6:10–18, p. 471

PHILIPPIANS
1:2, p. 466
2:5–6, 9, 12, 15, p. 467
2:10–11, p. 230
3:6, pp. 456, 457
3:11, p. 89
4:7, p. 220
4:8, p. 89

COLOSSIANS
1:2, p. 466
1:14–16, p. 90
1:14–17, p. 463
1:15, pp. 251, 308
1:18, pp. 224, 226, 496
1:27, p. 217
2:2–3 (JST), p. 486
4:10, p. 460

1 THESSALONIANS
3:11–13, p. 466
4:13–18, p. 90
4:14, p. 226
5:1–6, p. 91

2 THESSALONIANS
2:2, p. 466
2:7–9, p. 91

1 TIMOTHY
1:2, p. 466
1:13–16, p. 468
1:15, pp. 224, 225
2:5, pp. 216, 225
2:13–14, p. 91
3:2, 12, p. 92
4:1–3, p. 467
6:15, pp. 230, 496

2 TIMOTHY
2:8, pp. 92, 226
3:1–8, p. 471
3:16, p. 92
4:3–4, pp. 471, 552
4:8, p. 231

TITUS
1:15, p. 92
2:14, pp. 92, 224, 225

PHILEMON
1:3, p. 466
1:6, p. 93

HEBREWS
1, p. 93
1:1–3, p. 466
1:2, pp. 215, 232
1:3, pp. 217, 219, 232
1:6–7, p. 93
2:6–7, p. 93
2:7, p. 68
2:9, pp. 226, 230
2:9–11, 14–15, p. 463
2:10, pp. 221, 224, 496
2:17, p. 230
2:18, p. 223
3:1, p. 230
5:4, p. 93
5:6, p. 230
5:8, p. 223
5:8–9, p. 318
5:8–10, p. 93
5:9, p. 221
6:1, p. 94
6:13–20, p. 137
6:20, p. 226
7:1–3, p. 94
7:3 (JST), p. 94
7:24, p. 215
7:25, pp. 221, 225
7:26, p. 224
8:2, p. 218

8:6, p. 225
8:8–10, p. 560
8:12, p. 94
9:12, p. 225
9:14, p. 226
9:15 (JST), p. 225
9:15, p. 216
10:14, p. 226
10:17, p. 300
11, p. 467
11:1, pp. 132, 355, 467
11:5, 24–26, p. 94
12:2, p. 215
12:9, pp. 95, 307
12:24, p. 216
13:8, pp. 154, 215
13:12, p. 225
13:20, pp. 221, 496

JAMES
1:5, p. 4
1:5–6, p. 95
1:6, pp. 183, 254
2:1, p. 220
2:14, 17, 19, 20, 24, 26, p. 95
2:14–19, p. 341
2:14–20, p. 340
2:14–21 (JST), p. 95
2:17–18, p. 354
2:17–26, p. 346

2:26, pp. 372, 383
4:17, pp. 318, 346
5:11, p. 53
5:14–15, p. 95

1 PETER
1:19, p. 226
1:20, p. 214
1:23, p. 370
2:4, p. 218
2:9, p. 96
2:21, p. 224
3:18–19, p. 246
3:18–20, pp. 96, 145, 366
3:19, p. 289
3:22, p. 215
3–4, p. 343
4:6, pp. 96, 145, 246
4:16, p. 289

2 PETER
1:16–19, p. 96
1:20–21, pp. 97, 205, 341, 509, 510
1:21, p. 142
2:4, p. 323
3:3–4, 8, p. 97
3:3–13 (JST), p. 97

1 JOHN
1:1, p. 219

1:1, 3–4, p. 448
1:7, p. 225
2:1, p. 216
2:1–2, p. 97
2:1–7, 28–29, p. 449
2:2, p. 226
3:1–3, 16–17, p. 449
4:7–11, 20–21, p. 449
4:9, p. 218
4:10, 12, p. 97
5:6, p. 183
5:13–15, 20, p. 449
5:18, p. 97
5:20, p. 221

2 JOHN
1:9, p. 97
1:9–11, p. 450

3 JOHN
1:4, pp. 98, 450

JUDE
1:6, pp. 98, 281, 398
1:9, p. 98
6, p. 323

REVELATION
1:5, p. 496
1:7, p. 98
1:8, p. 216
1:8, 11, pp. 214, 496
1:9–10, p. 438

1:10, p. 99
1:18, pp. 99, 231
3:7, p. 218
3:12, p. 99
3:14, p. 214
4:6, 10, p. 99
5:1, p. 100
5:5, p. 217
5:12, p. 226
7:1, 2, 4, p. 100
7:14, p. 226
8:6, p. 100
9:1, p. 100
10:2, 8–11, p. 100
11, p. 520
11:2–3, 6–12, p. 568
11:3, 6, 8–12, p. 101
12, p. 101
12:7–9, pp. 101, 323
14:6–7, p. 101
15:3, p. 230
17:14, pp. 230, 496
19:7–9, p. 217
19:10, p. 101
19:13, p. 219
20:5–6, 7, p. 102
20:12, p. 412
22:7, 8–9, 13, 18–19, 20, p. 102
22:14, p. 346
22:16, pp. 217, 218

BOOK OF MORMON

1 NEPHI
1:2, p. 540
1:4, pp. 51, 548
2:5, 6, 9, 14, p. 128
2:10, p. 254
3:7, pp. 11, 132
3:12, p. 128
3:12, 24, p. 112
4:15–16, p. 13
4:16, 24, 38, p. 112
5:10, 11, 14, p. 112
5:11–12, p. 540
5:14, p. 546
6:3, 5, p. 113
6:4, p. 546
9:1–6, p. 128
9:2, 4, p. 113

10:4, p. 549
10:4–5, p. 548
10:4–6, p. 224
10:10, p. 226
10:12, p. 544
10:14, p. 554
10:17, p. 548
10:20, p. 297
10–16, p. 128
11, p. 116
11:13, 15, 18, p. 548
11:14–24, 31–33, p. 256
11:21, p. 549
11:32, p. 232
12:18, p. 232
13:20, p. 112

13:23, p. 546
13:25–29, p. 69
14, p. 447
14:18–28, p. 445
14:30, p. 131
15:12, p. 546
15:14, 16, p. 554
15:15, pp. 222, 232
15:18, p. 553
15:19–20, p. 558
15:36, p. 394
16:29, p. 131
17: 3, p. 131
17:17, p. 11
17:25–29, p. 12
17:35, p. 533
17:41, p. 47

17:50–51, p. 132
17:51, p. 12
19:2, p. 188
19:2–6, p. 113
19:10, p. 549
19:12, p. 221
19:13–14, p. 549
19:14, p. 224
19:15–17, p. 511
19:16, p. 555
19:22–23, p. 132
19:23–24, p. 108
21:1, p. 551
21:7, p. 224
22:2, pp. 384, 509
22:3, p. 552
22:9, pp. 231, 496

22:11–12, p. 553
22:12, p. 216
22:14, p. 557
22:21, p. 298
22:25, p. 221

2 NEPHI
1:5, p. 220
1:10, p. 218
2:6, 10, p. 224
2:11, p. 329
2:11, 14–16, 26–27, p. 312
2:22–23, p. 324
2:23–25, p. 329
2:24, p. 508
2:25, p. 325
2:27–28, p. 216
3:1–4, p. 502
3:5, p. 554
3:5–9, p. 493
3:7–8, 11–13, p. 502
3:7–15, p. 532
3:14–15, p. 503
3:24, p. 561
4:2, p. 9
4:11, p. 121
4:14, 15, p. 113
4:15–16, p. 132
6, p. 116
6:5, p. 546
6:8, p. 551
6:9, p. 550
6:14, p. 556
9:1–2, p. 555
9:5, p. 215
9:6, pp. 286, 409
9:6, 8–9, p. 262
9:7, p. 265
9:9, p. 315
9:12, p. 226
9:15, pp. 231, 297
9:20, p. 508
9:39, p. 224
9:41, p. 231
9:46, p. 220
9:53, p. 554
10, p. 116
10:3, p. 550
10:5–6, p. 551
10:7, p. 559
10:7–8, p. 556
10:14, p. 223

10:22, p. 555
11:2–3, p. 187
11:3, pp. 115, 182
11:4, p. 547
11:8, p. 132
22:2, p. 220
24:1–2, p. 557
24:12–14, p. 281
25, 26, p. 116
25:3–23, p. 189
25:12, pp. 549, 550
25:14–15, p. 551
25:16, p. 555
25:17, p. 511
25:17–18, p. 512
25:19, p. 548
25:20, pp. 225, 231
25:20–26, p. 111
25:23, p. 353
25:23, 26, p. 188
25:24–26, p. 547
25:30, p. 469
26:16–24, p. 189
27:23, p. 221
27:34, p. 224
28:2, p. 540
28:7, p. 427
28:8, p. 316
28:8, 21, p. 426
28:29–30, p. 3
28:30, pp. 5, 21, 189, 409, 428
29:1–2, p. 553
29:12, p. 575
29:12–14, p. 181
29:14, p. 565
30:7–8, pp. 512, 565
32:1, p. 13
33:8, p. 540
33:10, pp. 181, 182, 547
33:10–11, p. 18, 111
33:14, p. 18
33:10–15, p. 118
33:11, p. 231
33:14–15, pp. 18, 211

JACOB
1:2–3, 4, p. 113
1:17–19, p. 188
2:10, p. 216
4, p. 116
4:4, p. 188

4:4, 13–16, p. 189
4:13, pp. 384, 403
4:14, p. 237
4:14–15, p. 549
5, pp. 86, 532, 544
5:3, p. 544
5:75, p. 222
6:4, p. 559
6:11–13, p. 118
7:22, p. 231

ENOS
1:10, p. 376

OMNI
1:9, 10–11, p. 114

MOSIAH
1:4, p. 112
1:7, p. 18
2:17, 20–24, p. 259
2:19, p. 230
3:8, p. 548
3:9, p. 550
3:12, 21, p. 220
4:21, p. 403
4:30, pp. 231, 389
5:7, p. 232
8:13, p. 382
8:16–17, p. 492
13:28, p. 262
15:4, p. 232
15:18, pp. 220, 496
25:2, p. 121

ALMA
5:44, p. 225
5:50, p. 230
5:57, p. 222
7:10, p. 548
7:13, pp. 384, 403
10:3, p. 51
11:42, p. 226
11:42–45, pp. 269, 372
11:43, p. 376
11:43–44, p. 269
11:43–45, p. 293
11:44, pp. 225, 264, 291
12:3, 7, p. 382
12:14, pp. 231, 389
12:14–15, p. 297
12:16–18, p. 370

12:24, pp. 285, 328
17:2, pp. 29, 108, 204
22:14, p. 226
29, p. 20
30, pp. 127, 130
30:17, p. 316
30:44, p. 215
32:21, pp. 132, 355
32:26–27, p. 355
33:18–22, p. 47
34:9, p. 253
34:10, 12, 14, p. 227
34:12, p. 265
34:34, p. 405
40:11, pp. 288, 400
40:11–12, p. 387
40:11–14, p. 400
40:12, 13–14, p. 289
40:23, pp. 269, 293
41:4, pp. 269, 293
41:10, p. 426
42:1–2, p. 333
42:13–15, 23–26, p. 334

HELAMAN
6:10, p. 121
8:21, p. 121
10:2–4, p. 13
13:25, p. 267
13:38, pp. 232, 426
14:5, p. 548
14:12, pp. 231, 496
14:30–31, p. 318
15:13, pp. 221, 496

3 NEPHI
5, p. 513
5:21–26, p. 512
5:24–26, p. 554
9:13–17, p. 247
9:15, pp. 231, 233, 257
10:18, p. 109
11:27, 32, 35–36, p. 180
11:27, 32, 36, p. 233
11:27–36, p. 213
11:32, pp. 98, 180
11:35, p. 180
12:1–6, p. 77
12:2, p. 361
12:48, pp. 224, 301, 391

15:4–5, p. 216
15:5, p. 217
15:13–24, p. 84
15:21, 24, p. 550
16:1–3, pp. 84, 551
16:5, pp. 513, 559
16:6–12, p. 132
17:3, p. 13
17:4, p. 551
17:15, p. 12
18:7, p. 41
18:24, p. 223
20:26–27, 29–31, p. 513
20:29–35, p. 567
20:30–31, p. 514
21:4, p. 555
21:7, p. 559
21:23, p. 573
22:15, 17, p. 557
23:1, p. 56
23:1–3, p. 55
23:7–14, p. 117
23:9–13, p. 268
23:11, p. 248
24–25, p. 63
26:6–12, p. 117
26:7, p. 113
26:12, p. 188
26:15, p. 221
27, p. 429

27:7–8, p. 362
27:8, p. 224
27:13–22, p. 186
27:19, p. 429
27:19–21, pp. 187, 363
27:19–27, p. 296
27:20–21, p. 429
27:21, 27, p. 224
28:1–7, p. 440
28:6, p. 438
28:17, 36–40, p. 287
28:26, p. 116
29:3, 8–9, p. 559
30:1, p. 188

4 NEPHI
1:17, 35, 36, 38–39, p. 120

MORMON
1:5, p. 189
1:15, pp. 115, 187
1–7, p. 114
3:14, p. 549
3:20, 21–22, p. 119
5:9–13, p. 188
5:12–14, p. 567
5:14, p. 546
5:20, p. 555
7:5, p. 226
7:5, 8–9, p. 188

7:8–9, pp. 123, 181, 211
7:9, p. 182
8–9, pp. 114, 115, 116
8:1, p. 188
8:11, p. 116
8:25–35, p. 189
8:34–35, pp. 116, 132
8:35, p. 10
9:6, p. 226
1:5, p. 189

ETHER
1:1–4, p. 197
1:2, p. 111
1:3–4, pp. 124, 212
2:12, p. 320
3:9–16, p. 187
3:16, p. 376
4:5, p. 114
4:12, p. 223
4:14–15, p. 568
4:14–19, p. 447
5:2–4, p. 182
5:4, p. 184
8:20, p. 188
9:22, p. 232
12:6, p. 130
12:22–23, 38–39, p. 115
12:39, p. 187

13:5, 10, p. 573
13:13, p. 188

MORONI
1, p. 116
1:1, p. 121
7:15–16, 18, p. 453
7:16–18, p. 317
7:33, p. 452
7–9, p. 114
8, p. 349
8:3, pp. 219, 224
8:8, p. 227
8:8–9, 12, 19–21, pp. 348, 349
8:19–21, p. 227
9:23, p. 121
10, p. 129
10:1–4, p. 196
10:1–5, p. 197
10:3, pp. 18, 108, 211
10:3–5, pp. 124, 132, 184
10:4, p. 123
10:4–5, p. 194
10:5, pp. 382, 403
10:24, 27, 29, p. 119
10:24–34, p. 189
10:27, 32–33, p. 188
10:31, p. 559
10:34, pp. 231, 232

DOCTRINE AND COVENANTS

1:6, p. 136
1:30, pp. 224, 228
2:1–3, p. 562
3:9–10, p. 146
5:11–15, p. 182
6:13, p. 394
6:15–16, p. 383
6:21, p. 223
7, pp. 80, 441
7:3, p. 447
7:4–6, p. 442
8:1, 3, 9, p. 403
8:1–3, p. 146
8:1–3, 9, p. 382
8:1–4, p. 290
8:1–5, p. 145
11:21, p. 19
13, pp. 508, 561
14:7, pp. 231, 301, 394

14:10, p. 566
17:6, pp. 15, 111
18:9, p. 456
19:4, p. 232
19:16, 18, p. 83
19:16–19, p. 255
19:16–20, p. 224
19:18, p. 376
20:9, p. 186
21:3, p. 228
21:7–8, pp. 514, 560
23:1–6, p. 146
27:1, p. 98
27:12, p. 445
29:1, pp. 213, 496
29:5, p. 216
29:12, p. 575
29:24–25, p. 265
29:34, p. 386

29:39, p. 318
30:1–2, p. 146
33:1, p. 382
33:16, p. 453
35:25, p. 519
38:1–3, p. 214
38:3, p. 215
39:7–8, p. 146
39:11, p. 566
42:12–15, p. 453
42:14, p. 392
42:29, p. 258
42:44, p. 95
42:46–47, p. 287
45:24–25, 51, p. 520
45:26–27, p. 566
45:48–53, p. 229
45:51–53, pp. 98, 572
45:66–67, p. 574

46:16, p. 453
49:8, p. 540
49:15, p. 424
50:13–14, 17, p. 146
50:43, p. 233
58:22, p. 230
58:26–27, p. 260
58:27–28, p. 318
58:42, p. 390
58:43, p. 357
59:5–6, p. 258
62:69–70, p. 413
63:49, p. 286
64:8–10, 32–33, p. 146
66:9, p. 95
68:4, pp. 107, 108, 190, 198, 381
76, pp. 99, 189, 271, 445

76:12, p. 404
76:12, 18, p. 375
76:16–17, p. 268
76:22–23, p. 524
76:23, p. 218
76:31–32, 34–37, p. 271
76:31–38, p. 371
76:31–39, p. 295
76:32, p. 371
76:44, p. 414
76:50–55, p. 413
76:50–60, p. 294
76:51–52, 64–65, p. 271
76:64–65, p. 269
76:69, p. 216
76:71–77, 80, p. 413
76:71–79, p. 294
76:72–75, 79, p. 271
76:73, p. 289
76:81–83, 85, 112, p. 414
76:81–88, 98–112, p. 294
76:82–85, 103, p. 271
76:99, p. 456
76:112, p. 296
76, p. 87
77, pp. 99, 445, 446
77:1–4, p. 99
77:2, p. 289

77:5–14, p. 100
77:15, pp. 101, 520, 569
82:10, pp. 332, 541
84:2, p. 574
84:43–47, p. 453
84:56, p. 108
84:57, p. 21
84:85, p. 20
86:8–9, p. 530
88:2–4, 15–31, pp. 272, 295
88:7–9, p. 215
88:15, p. 329
88:15–16, p. 377
88:17–18, 25–26, p. 265
88: 22–32, p. 87
88:24, 32, p. 414
88:27–28, p. 388
88:34, 37–39, p. 331
88:109, p. 382
93, p. 447
93:2–11, p. 446
93:4, pp. 219, 232
93:8, p. 218
93:11–17, p. 234
93:13, pp. 392, 446, 504
93:13–14, p. 189
93:16, 18, p. 446
93:17, p. 232

93:19, 27, p. 189
93:21, pp. 213, 487
93:21–22, p. 308
93:29–30, p. 379
93:33, p. 389
98:8, p. 316
98:16–17, p. 563
98:17, pp. 517, 520
101:32–33, p. 378
101:80, p. 320
105:19, p. 283
107:3, p. 215
107:53, p. 229
107:54, p. 98
109:57–58, 60, 67, p. 530
110:10–15, p. 229
110:11–16, p. 562
110:15, p. 63
115:3–4, p. 228
116:1, p. 229
121:10, p. 53
121:26, p. 493
124, p. 189
124:1–11, p. 520
124:36–37, p. 569
127:2, p. 456
128:13, 15–16, p. 456
128:20, pp. 87, 443
128:21, pp. 98, 496
128:22, pp. 230, 576
128:23, p. 230

130:7, pp. 384, 404, 508
130:18–19, pp. 392, 397
130:20, 21, p. 332
130:22, pp. 359, 375
131, p. 189
131:1–4, p. 418
131:7, p. 375
132, p. 189
132:7, p. 403
132:8, p. 331
132:15–16, 19, p. 419
132:20, p. 301
132:21–24, p. 420
132:24, 55, p. 301
133:8, p. 566
133:13, 35, p. 520
133:19–21, p. 573
133:24, p. 520
133:33–35, p. 566
133:34, p. 574
133:64, p. 562
135:3, pp. 490, 495
135:6, p. 14
137, p. 138
137:9, p. 298
137:10, p. 296
138, pp. 83, 138, 247
138:7–10, p. 96
138:16, 36, p. 289
138:28–29, 57, p. 289

PEARL OF GREAT PRICE

MOSES
1:1, p. 45
1:38–39, p. 301
1:39, pp. 213, 281, 326, 344, 416, 489
2:27, p. 253
3:5, pp. 282, 323
3:16–17, pp. 324, 370, 425
3:17, pp. 253, 314
4:1, p. 313
4:1, 3–4, p. 252
4:2, pp. 214, 251
4:3, pp. 313, 386, 401
4:10–11, p. 325
5:6, p. 26
5:10–11, p. 325

5:14–15, p. 356
5:15, 59, p. 215
5:16, p. 217
6:57, pp. 231, 233, 298, 549
6:59, p. 286
7:32, p. 317
7:38, 57, p. 289
7:53, pp. 230, 496
7:53–54, p. 217
7:61, p. 140
7:62, pp. 140, 210

ABRAHAM
2:7–8, p. 217
2:9–11, p. 530
3:4, p. 97
3:14, p. 527

3:18, p. 379
3:18–19, p. 377
3:21–23, p. 280
3:22, pp. 280, 281
3:22–23, pp. 375, 377, 489
3:24–26, pp. 387, 402
3:25, p. 283
3:25–26, p. 330
3:26, p. 98
3:27, p. 218
4:1, p. 282
4–5, p. 46
5:7–8, p. 377
5:13, p. 314

JOSEPH SMITH—MATTHEW
1:23, p. 242

JOSEPH SMITH—HISTORY
1:4, p. 128
1:17, pp. 228, 235
1:19, pp. 228, 504
1:30–54, 59, 67, p. 182
1:32, 42–43, p. 454
1:33, p. 487
1:36, p. 505
1:36–39, p. 562
1:40, pp. 505, 507, 556
1:41, pp. 60, 507

ARTICLES OF FAITH
1:4, pp. 354, 362
1:8, p. 27
1:10, pp. 99, 230
1:13, p. 90

Subject Index

Aaronic Priesthood, 435, 508, 513, 561–62
Abbreviations, in LDS edition of Bible, 38
Abinadom, 114, 115
Abortion, 425
Abraham: family of, 31; practiced polygamy, 32; knew of Jesus Christ, 84; Jesus appeared to, 217; on noble and great ones, 489–90; covenant of, 515; literal descendants of, 526–27, 530–31
Abraham, Book of (Pearl of Great Price), 46, 97, 98, 530
Absalom, 50
Accountability, 316
Acts of the Apostles, book of: contains Christ's forty-day ministry, 74; selections from the, 84–85; Moroni quoted the, 507
Adam: "save the Lord commanded me," 26; and Eve, 91–92; angels taught, 215, 333–34, 379; fall of, 224, 285–86, 322, 325, 328, 352; as the Ancient of Days, 229, 323; and agency, 252–53, 425; Lucifer tempted, 314; in the Garden of Eden, 322–26, 329; was taught repentance, 356; Christ stood proxy for, 366; death of, 369–70; marriage of, 418. *See also* Michael
Adam-ondi-Ahman, 229
Adonijah, 50
Adoption, into Israel, 532–33
Adultery, 77–78
Adversity, 283–84
Agency: and principles of righteousness, 26; Satan sought to deny, 252, 312–13, 316, 386, 401; was taught to Adam and Eve, 253; gift of, 257; and the resurrection, 272–73, 293; and moral agency, 281, 309, 310, 314; and premortal life, 282, 309–12; and mortal probation, 284–85, 328, 425–26; and death, 287; and the spirit world, 291; in the Garden of Eden, 313–14; and the atonement, 314–16; efforts to limit, 316–18; scriptural references to, 318–19; is necessary for gospel to flourish, 319–20; and the Spirit, 386, 401–2; Paul's teachings about, 471
Alma: on justice and mercy, 333; on faith, 355; on death, 370; on thoughts, 382; on spirit world, 387, 399–400; on the Spirit, 403; "wickedness never was happiness," 426
Amaleki, 114, 115
Amalekites, 122
Amalickiahites, 122
Amaron, 114, 115
America, 109, 121, 247, 319–20, 361, 426, 506, 545, 550
American Institute of Public Opinion, 4, 428
Amlicites, 122
Ammon, on seers, 492
Ammonihahites, 122
Ammonites, 122
Amos, book of, 60–61; on prophets, 210
Amulek: on the atonement, 227, 265; on the resurrection, 269; on death, 372

Amulonites, 122
Ananias, 459
Anarchy, 316
Ancient of Days, 229, 323
Andrew, 234, 435
Angels, 87, 93, 116, 254, 256, 310, 399–400
Animals, resurrection of, 265, 291–92
Anti-Mormons, 130, 336–37
Anti-Nephi-Lehies, 122
Antioch, 460
Apocalypse. *See* Revelation of St. John the Divine
Apostasy, 471, 552
Apostles, 435–36, 439–40, 517
Appendix, in the LDS edition of the Bible, 40–41
Arabia, 459
Arabs, 32, 527
Articles of Faith, 153, 190, 422
Asher, 527
Asia, 461
Assyria, 505, 507, 542
Atonement. *See* Jesus Christ, atonement of
Australia, 536

Babylon, 506, 507, 542, 544, 545
Baldwin, Reverend, 421
Ballard, Melvin J.: on celestial bodies, 272, 296; on degrees of glory, 296
Bank (analogy), 333
Baptism, 234, 331, 344–45, 348, 360–61, 366; for the dead, 87, 189, 343, 364, 367, 471
Baptists, 421
Barabbas, 245
Barnabas, 459
Barton, Bruce: *The Book Nobody Knows*, 28
Bath-sheba, 50
Beatitudes, 76–77
Belief, 355
Benjamin (Nephite king): on service, 259; on our thoughts, 389
Benjamin (son of Jacob), 527, 545
Benson, Ezra Taft: on condemnation of Church, 21, 108; on the New Testament, 103; on daily scripture reading, 108; on the Book of Mormon, 129, 210; on the Doctrine and Covenants, 139–40, 141; on the atonement, 261; on noble and great ones, 489–90
Bethany, 236, 238, 239, 243, 247
Bethlehem, 219
Bible: in modern Israel, 4, 21; statements of leaders about the, 26–28; lost books of the, 51; excuses for not reading the, 107; Book of Mormon witnesses for the, 123–24; and the Book of Mormon, 180–82, 188, 191–95, 204; as a witness, 180–82; contains every doctrine, 203–4; Moroni's promise concerning, 211; scholarly criticism of the, 428. *See also* New Testament; Old Testament
Bible (Joseph Smith Translation): and the LDS edition of the Bible, 36, 43–44, 69–71; and the King James Version, 37; and the book of Genesis, 46; and book of Exodus, 46–47; and the Song of Solomon, 55; and the gospel titles, 74; the beatitudes in the, 77; clarifies Matthew, 79, 80; clarifies Mark, 80, 81; clarifies Luke, 82; clarifies John, 83, 84; clarifies Acts, 85; clarifies Romans, 85, 472–73; clarifies Corinthians, 86, 473–75, 480; clarifies Ephesians, 89, 476; clarifies Thessalonians, 90–91, 477; clarifies Timothy, 92, 477–78, 480; clarifies Titus, 92, 478; clarifies Hebrews, 93, 94, 478–79, 480; clarifies epistle of John, 97; clarifies Paul's epistles, 472–80; clarifies Galatians, 475–76; clarifies Philippians, 476, 480; clarifies Colossians, 476–77
Bible (King James Version): strength of the, 22, 36–37; Joseph Smith's use of the, 37; why use the, 66–67
Bible (LDS edition): why use the, 35–44, 67; title and contents pages of the, 37; abbreviations in the, 38; footnotes in the, 38–39, 67–71; cross-references in the, 39, 71; chapter headings in the, 39–40; Topical Guide in the, 40–41; appendix in the, 40–44, 72–73; Bible Dictionary in

the, 41–43; Joseph Smith Translation in the, 43–44; gazetteer and maps in the, 44, 72–73; "GR" footnotes in the, 67–68; "HEB" footnotes in the, 68; "IE" footnotes in the, 68–69; "JST" footnotes in the, 69–71; "OR" footnotes in the, 71

Bible, meaning of term, 25

Bible Dictionary: as the sealed portion of the Bible, 22; on dietary restrictions, 34; on Biblical symbols, 35; description of the, 41–43; on Moses, 45; on book of Leviticus, 47; on book of Numbers, 47; on Book of Joshua, 48; on First and Second Kings, 50; on books of Chronicles, 51; on feasts, 53; on Book of Psalms, 54; on Ecclesiastes, 54–55; on book of Lamentations, 57; on book of Hosea, 59; New Testament entries in the, 71–72; on the Gospels, 74; on the Pauline Epistles, 75; on the General Epistles, 75–76; on the book of Revelation, 76; on the Stick of Ephraim, 123; Old Testament references in the, 159–71; New Testament references in the, 171–78; reference to Jesus Christ in the, 205–7; on the resurrection, 262; on Paul, 456, 457–62

Bilhah, 527

Birth control, 425

Birthright, law of, 32

Bishops, qualifications of, 92

Blacks, and the priesthood, 336

Blessings, 470

Body, physical: and the spirit, 18–19, 323, 399, 405–6; in the resurrection, 269–70, 272, 293, 296, 388; and mortal probation, 283–84, 385–86, 424; and death, 371, 372, 387, 401

Boggs, Lilburn W., 431

Book of Abraham, 46, 97, 98, 530

Book of Commandments, A, 135–36

Book of Daniel, 58–59

Book of Esther, 52–53

Book of Ether, 111–12

Book of Job, 53

Book of Joshua, 48

Book of Judges, 48–49

Book of Mormon: rejection of the, 4, 21; is incomplete, 8; study of the, 15–16, 131–33; reading the, 18, 141–43; excuses for not reading the, 107–8; "is and is not" of the, 109–10; author of the, 110–11; plates of the, 111–14; engravers of the, 114–19, 142–43, 187–89, 211; prophets of the, 119–20; peoples of the, 120–22; purposes of the, 122–27; as a witness, 123–24, 179, 180–82; do's of studying the, 128–29; archaeology and geography of the, 129; don'ts of studying the, 129–31; changes in the, 130; pronunciation of names in the, 130; parable on critics of the, 130–31; and the Doctrine and Covenants, 138, 139–43; and the Bible, 180–82, 188, 191–95, 204; witnesses to the, 182–83; as a modern scripture, 191–95; receiving a testimony of the, 196–99; on spirits, 376; prophecies about Israel in the, 510–14; was translated into Hebrew, 514; subtitle of the, 536; on truth, 538; on the House of Israel, 540; is to convince Israel, 547

Book of Nehemiah, 52

Book of the Prophet Ezekiel, 57–58, 191–92

Book of the Prophet Isaiah, 55–56

Book of the Prophet Jeremiah, 56–57

Book of Psalms, 53–54

Book of Ruth, 49

Boynton, John F., 144

Brass plates of Laban. *See* Plates of brass

Brigham Young University, 347, 392, 396, 422

British Isles, 517–18, 563

Brown, Hugh B., on persecution of Joseph Smith, 493–94

Bushman, Richard L., on Joseph Smith, 488, 490

Bywater, George G., on the grandest principle, 147

Caesar, 241, 244, 245

Caesarea, 461

Caiaphas, 244

Cain, 217
Callings, 257
Callis, Charles A., on the spirit world, 289, 405
Calvary, 224–25
Canaan, 48
Cannon, George Q.: on the Bible, 63; on the New Testament, 103; on continuous revelation, 155–56; on degrees of glory, 272, 295
Capitalization, in the Bible, 49
Catholic Church, 74, 77–78, 319, 347, 348, 352, 431
Celestial glory, 271, 294, 296, 300, 301, 413, 417
Celestial marriage. *See* Marriage, celestial
Chain reference systems, 41
Chapter headings, in Bible, 39–40
Charity, 472
Chastity, 470
Chemish, 114, 115
Chicago Democrat, 422, 507
Children: resurrection of, 270, 293; baptism of, 348
China, 367
Choice. *See* Agency
Christianity, 4, 21
Christmas, 249, 260, 394
Chronicles, First and Second books of, 51–52
Church of the Dormition, 437
Church of Jesus Christ, 227–28; condemnation of, 21, 108
Church of the Last Supper, 437
Church magazines, 23
Church News, 335
Churches, Protestant, 319, 336, 337, 421, 430
Circumcision, 82
Civil War, 510
Clark, J. Reuben, Jr.: on the Joseph Smith Translation, 36; on the King James Version, 66–67; on not challenging Satan, 438; on patriarchal blessings, 528
Cleophas, 437

Color coding, of the scriptures, 13, 38–39, 44, 68, 71, 128
Colossians. *See* Epistle of Paul the Apostle to the Colossians
Columbia University, 510
Columbus, 193
Communism, 316
Constitution (U.S.), 320
Contributor, 146, 464
Corianton, 333, 334
Corinthians. *See* First Epistle of Paul the Apostle to the Corinthians; Second Epistle of Paul the Apostle to the Corinthians
Council in heaven, 281, 282, 310–12, 322–23, 324, 327–28, 385, 386–87, 401–2, 489
Courage, 471
Covenants, 137, 254–55, 515, 546, 553–54
Cowdery, Oliver, 136, 183, 435, 441, 508, 517, 561, 562
Creation, 215, 282–83, 378
Crete, 461
Cross-references, in the scriptures, 39, 71, 145
Cultures, 392–93
Cyrus of Persia, 52, 506, 544–45

Damascus, 458
Dan, 527
Daniel, 562–63
Daniel, Book of, 58–59
Dark Ages, 552
David (Bible king): genealogy of, 49; in Second Book of Samuel, 50; and Nathan, 51; and Jesus Christ, 218, 237; united kingdom under, 505; new leader named for, 571–72
Davies, William Henry, 384
Dead Sea, 570, 571
Dead Sea Scrolls, 53, 88
Death: spiritual, 253, 287, 314, 343, 369–71; physical, 285–88, 314, 324, 343, 348, 371–73, 383, 400, 401, 405
Degrees of glory, 87, 270–72, 294–97, 411–15, 416–17, 466

Destiny: of man, 422–32; definition of, 535–36; of Israel, 536–38
Deuteronomy, 47–48, 78–79
Devil. *See* Satan
Dictatorships, 316, 426
Dietary restrictions (Biblical), 33–34
Divine destiny. *See* Destiny, of man
Divine investiture of authority, 231
Divorce, 77–79
Doctrine, meaning of term, 137
Doctrine and Covenants: is incomplete, 8–9; on condemnation of Church, 21; and the epistle of Peter, 96; description of the, 134–35; sections added to the, 135; and *A Book of Commandments,* 135–36, 137; preface of the, 136, 139; significance of title of the, 136–37; earlier editions of the, 137–38; and other scriptures, 138–39; and the Book of Mormon, 139–43; reasons for reading the, 141–43; was written in English, 143; witnesses to the, 143–44; aids to study of the, 143–46; teachings of the, 146–52; and doctrinal differences, 148; Topical Guide entries for the, 149–50; significant topics of the, 150–52; on spirits, 376–77; teachings about Israel in the, 519–20, 530; on truth, 538
Doctrine and Covenants Commentary (Smith and Sjodahl), 136–37
Domitian, 443
Dowry, concept of, 33
Dress and grooming standards (Bible), 34

Earth: creation of the, 215, 282–83, 378; resurrection of the, 265; spirit world is on the, 289, 400
Ecclesiastes, 54–55
Eden, Garden of, 313–14, 322–26, 329
Education, 391–93, 427–28, 471–72
Election, 242
Electricity, 378–79
Elias, 228, 517
Elijah, 50–51, 63, 94, 228–29, 365, 418, 517, 562, 564
Elisha, 51

Emmaus, 248
Enoch, 94, 217
Enos, 114, 115
Ensign, 23, 448
Ephesians. *See* Epistle of Paul the Apostle to the Ephesians
Ephesus, 436, 443
Ephraim: stick of, 112, 192; in the northern kingdom, 505; descendants of, 527, 533, 566
Epistle of Paul the Apostle to the Colossians, 90, 476–77, 483
Epistle of Paul the Apostle to the Ephesians, 89, 476, 482
Epistle of Paul the Apostle to the Galatians, 88, 475–76, 482
Epistle of Paul the Apostle to the Hebrews, 93–95, 478–79, 480, 484
Epistle of Paul the Apostle to the Philippians, 89–90, 476, 480, 482–83
Epistle of Paul the Apostle to the Romans, 85–86, 472–73, 480–81
Epistle of Paul to Philemon, 93, 478, 484
Epistle of Paul to Titus, 92–93, 478, 484
Equal Rights Amendment, 336
Esther, Book of, 52–53
Eternal life, 300–302, 416–20
Eternal progression, 302
Ether, 446–47
Ether, Book of, 111–12
Evans, Richard L., on freedom, 319–20
Eve: and Adam, 91–92; angels taught, 215, 333–34, 379; fall of, 224, 285–86, 325, 328; and agency, 252–53, 425; Lucifer tempted, 314; in the Garden of Eden, 322–26, 329; death of, 369–70; marriage of, 418
Evil spirits, 234, 468
Exaltation, 300–302, 416–20, 429–30
Example, 490–91
Exhaustive Concordance of the Bible, The (Strong), 37, 337, 536
Exodus, 46–47
Extrasensory perception, 382

Eyring, Henry B., on daily scripture study, 19–20
Ezekiel, book of. *See* Book of the Prophet Ezekiel
Ezias, 112, 120
Ezra, book of, 52

Faith, 11, 310, 312, 330, 346, 354–55, 370, 429, 452, 467, 491
Fall, of man, 91–92, 215, 224, 252–53, 285–86, 322, 324, 325, 328, 352
Far West Record, 136
Fasting, 364
Father in Heaven: oneness of Christ with, 233; our relationship to, 250–51, 394; goal of, 281, 416; communication with, 381–82
Feasts and festivals (Bible), 35, 53
Featherstone, Vaughn J., on living the scriptures, 12
Fig tree, blighting of, 238–39
Final judgment. *See* Judgment
First Book of Chronicles, 51–52
First Epistle General of John, 97
First Epistle General of Peter, 96
First Epistle of Paul the Apostle to the Corinthians, 86–87, 473–75, 480, 481–82
First Epistle of Paul the Apostle to the Thessalonians, 90–91, 477, 483
First Epistle of Paul the Apostle to Timothy, 91–92, 477, 480, 483
First estate. *See* Premortal life
First Presidency: on the Bible, 27, 104; on premortal life, 280, 281, 378, 398; on the spirit world, 404–5
First resurrection. *See* Resurrection, first general
Footnotes: in LDS edition of the Bible, 38–39, 67–71, 480–84; in the Doctrine and Covenants, 138
Foreordination, 213, 214, 215, 250–52, 281, 445, 489–90, 501, 541, 561
Forgiveness, 299
Franklin, Benjamin, on death and taxes, 369
Free agency. *See* Agency
Freedom. *See* Agency

Gabriel, 218, 253, 548
Gad, 527
Gadianton robbers, 122
Galatians. *See* Epistle of Paul the Apostle to the Galatians
Galilee, 245
Gallup, George M., New Testament survey of, 4–5, 428
Gamaliel, 458
Garden of Eden, 313–14, 322–26, 329
Garden of Gethsemane. *See* Gethsemane
Gazetteer (Bible), 44
Genealogy, 289
General Epistle of James, 95–96
General Epistle of Jude, 98
Genesis, 45–46
Gentiles, 74, 528, 531–33, 547, 555, 568
Germany, 431
Gethsemane, 224, 243–44, 255, 262, 315, 437
Gift(s): of the Spirit, 95–96; of Jesus Christ, 249–57, 266; that we give to Christ, 257–60
Godhead, 179–80, 180–82, 233, 359. *See also* Father in Heaven; Holy Ghost; Jesus Christ
Godhood, 301–2, 391
Golgotha, 245, 315
Gospel: in the Book of Mormon, 186–90; provides the living water, 222–23; Church built upon, 224; freedom necessary for, 319; universal nature of, 470–71
Gospel According to St. John: selections from the, 83–84; last chapter of the, 439–41
Gospel According to St. Luke, selections from the, 81–83
Gospel According to St. Mark, selections from the, 80–81
Gospel According to St. Matthew, selections from the, 76–80
Gospels (New Testament), 73–74, 76–84, 439–41
Governments, 316, 317, 425
Grace and works, 335–37; definition of

terms, 337–38; basic scriptures about, 338–41; questions about, 342; answers about, 342–43; and salvation, 344–46; ideas about, 346–52; Paul's teachings about, 468–69
Grandest principle, 147, 464, 465–72
Grant, Heber J.: on living the scriptures, 11; on patriarchal blessings, 528
Grant, Jedediah Morgan, 421
Great Council. *See* Council in heaven
Greek footnotes, in LDS edition of the Bible, 38, 67–68, 480–84
Greeks, 74

Habakkuk, book of, 62
Hadassah, 53
Hagar, 527
Haggai, book of, 62
"Harmony of the Gospels" (chart), 72
Harmony, Pennsylvania, 441
Harris, Martin, 183
Healings, 95–96, 468
Hearing, 407–8, 408–9
Heavenly Father. *See* Father in Heaven
Hebrew footnotes, in LDS edition of the Bible, 38, 68
Hebrews, epistle to the. *See* Epistle of Paul the Apostle to the Hebrews
Hebrews (family of), 30–32, 526–27
Hell, 411, 414
Herod, 245
Herodians, 240–41
Herzl, Theodor, 501, 518
Hinckley, Gordon B.: on reading the Book of Mormon, 18; in scripture video, 23; on the Bible, 104; on daily scripture reading, 108; on the resurrection, 273–74; on not worshipping prophets, 488; Joseph Smith's mission, 491
Hiram, Ohio, 136
History, 509–10
History of the Church, 9, 136
Holy Ghost: and daily scripture study, 19; and understanding the Doctrine and Covenants, 146; testifies of scriptures, 183–85; and receiving a testimony, 198; oneness of Christ with the, 233; Jesus promised the, 243; functions and powers of the, 359–63; gift of the, 360, 361, 362, 429; and the mind and will of the Lord, 381–82, 403; is the greatest teacher, 392; and preparation for exaltation, 429–30; and the declaration of lineage, 528
Holy Spirit of promise, 403
Hope, 354–55
Hosea, book of, 59
Hull, Thomas, on the grandest principle, 147, 464
Hunter, Howard W.: on scripture study, 18; on prophets, 492; on revelators, 493
Hyde, Orson, 144, 518, 563, 571
Hypocrisy, 242

Idioms (Bible), 38–39, 68–69
Immorality, 470
Immortality, 301, 416, 417, 425
Indiana University, 364
Indians. *See* Native Americans
Inheritance, law of, 32
Inspired Version of the Bible. *See* Bible (Joseph Smith Translation)
Institute of Advanced Thinking, 380
Intelligences, premortal, 280–81, 306, 327, 371, 375, 379–80, 397. *See also* Spirits
Isaac, 527
Isaiah: on Jesus Christ, 56, 219–20; "line upon line," 191; used several titles for Jesus, 216; "born at once," 229; on the war in heaven, 323; was quoted by Moroni, 505, 556; on the gathering, 506
Isaiah, book of, 55–56
Ishbak, 527
Ishmael, 506, 527, 545
Israel: and the Bible, 4; as a family, 30–32; customs and practices of ancient, 33–35, 128–29; Jesus is God of, 46–47, 216, 217–18, 547–48; conquered Canaan, 48; kings over, 49–50; gathering of, 56, 515–16; Messiah will appear to, 57; Amos prophesied of, 60–61; will be converted, 229; experience in modern, 393; tours of modern, 454–55; Moroni on,

504–7; Joseph Smith's understanding of, 504–24; Wentworth letter on, 507–8; Book of Mormon prophecies about, 510–14; modern state of, 513, 518–19, 564–65; missionary work in modern, 513–14; Seaton letter about, 514–16; covenant of, 515, 546; letter to the elders about, 516; keys to the gathering of, 517; in the British Isles, 517–18, 563; dedication of, 518, 563–64; *Times and Seasons* editorial on, 519; Doctrine and Covenants teachings about, 519–20; Proclamation of 1845 on, 520–24; war against, 521–22, 565–66; and Abraham's literal descendants, 526–27; who belongs to tribe of, 527; scriptural references to, 529–30; leaders' statements about, 530–33; adoption into, 532–33; mission to the blood of, 536; scriptural references to destiny of, 536–38; truths of, 539–41; foreordination of, 541; God's special promises to, 541; as a covenant people, 541–42, 558–60; promised lands to, 542; captivity of, 542–44; and Judah, 544–45; scattered in America, 545; and descendants of Lehi, 545–46; and the Law of Moses, 546–47; Book of Mormon is to convince, 547; Jesus appeared to branches of, 550–51; apostasy of, 552; and the Restoration, 552–53; will have a second chance, 558–60; gospel to be taken to, 567–68; two prophets to, 568–69; Christ will lead armies of, 572–73; capitals of, 573–74

Issachar, 527

Jackson County, Missouri, 136, 431
Jacob (son of Isaac): family of, 31; on spirits, 384; became Israel, 527, 539
Jacob (son of Lehi): as an engraver, 114, 115, 116, 117, 118, 142–43, 187–88; was tutored by angels, 116; on Jesus Christ, 142; on the Jews, 237; on the resurrection, 261–62; on the infinite atonement, 265; on death, 409
Jacobites, 121

James: "If any of you lack wisdom," 4, 95, 183; restored priesthood keys, 228, 561; on the Mount of Transfiguration, 234; resurrected body of, 268; on faith, 354; on the body and spirit, 372; called by Jesus, 435; was John's brother, 436; and Paul, 459
James, epistle of, 95–96
Jaredites, 121, 122, 192–93
Jarom, 114, 115
Jehovah, 46–47, 216–17
Jenkinson, S.W., on the grandest principle, 464
Jeremiah (Bible prophet), 193; on premortal life, 307; on the House of Israel, 539–40
Jeremiah, book of, 56–57
Jeremiah, Lamentations of, 57
Jerusalem: Lehi left, 112; Mulek left, 121, 193; Jesus entered, 236–38, 247; temple in, 431, 545, 569–70; tour of modern, 454; and Paul, 459; and the Kingdom of Judah, 505; Romans destroyed, 506, 518; Judah to gather to, 513, 515, 519; two prophets in, 568–69
Jessee, Dean, on persecution of Joseph Smith, 494
Jesus Christ: on searching the scriptures, 7; Old Testament is a witness of, 26, 205–7, 207–10, 216–17; is the God of the Old Testament, 46–47, 216, 217–18, 547–49; quoted Deuteronomy, 48; genealogy of, 49; resurrection of, 53, 99, 226, 247–48, 251, 261–74, 306, 329, 463–64; quoted Isaiah, 55; second coming of, 79–80, 98, 102, 125–26, 229, 268, 431; believed in spirits, 83; Abraham knew of, 84; atonement of, 85, 186–87, 216, 224, 227, 254–57, 261–62, 264–65, 314–16, 333, 343, 346, 347, 401, 430; as the cornerstone, 89; Book of Mormon testifies of, 109, 110–11, 117–18, 122–23, 186–90; as author of the Book of Mormon, 110, 142; testifies of the Father, 179–80; on the Godhead, 180; defined *gospel,* 186; on receiving the fulness, 189; scriptures

testify of, 204–5; Jews rejected, 205, 237; Old Testament titles of, 206–7, 216; is our elder brother, 213; is the foreordained Savior, 213–14, 250–52, 281; is Alpha and Omega, 214; is the Great I AM, 214; is the author of salvation, 215; is the Creator, 215; is our advocate, 216; titles of, 217–18, 220, 549; is the Only Begotten, 218, 308, 328; is the Holy Child of Bethlehem, 219; is the Word of God, 219; is the prophet of Nazareth, 219–20; is Lord of the Earth, 220; is the Prince of Peace, 220–21; is the God of Miracles, 221; is the Healing Physician, 221; is the Good Shepherd, 221–22; is Lord of the Vineyard, 222; is the Bread of Life, 222; provides the living waters, 222–23; is the Life, Light, and Truth, 223; is the Perfect Exemplar, 223–24; is the head of His Church, 224; is the Anointed One of the New Testament, 225; is the Lamb of God, 226; is head of latter-day church, 227–28; is King of Kings, 230; is Lord of Lords, 230; is the Righteous Judge, 231, 298, 575; is the Father, 231–32; is the Son of God, 232, 234–35; is a distinct personage, 233; is the Son of Man, 233; testifies of Himself, 233–34; last week of, 236–48; enters Jerusalem on a donkey, 236–38; blights the fig tree, 238–39; cleanses the temple, 239, 240; is questioned, 240–42; goes to the Mount of Olives, 242; at the Last Supper, 243; in Gethsemane, 243–44, 255, 262; before Pilate, 244–45; before Herod, 245; crucifixion of, 245–46, 255, 550; burial of, 246; visits the spirit world, 246–47, 401; appears to the Nephites, 248; gave the greatest gift, 249–57; birth of, 253–54; our gift to, 257–60; on degrees of glory, 271, 295; had power over death, 286–87; on spiritual death, 287; joint-heirs with, 301; on premortal life, 307–8; on repentance, 356; on the Holy Ghost, 360, 392; "in my name," 362; vicarious work of, 365–66; "being born again," 370; "both soul and body," 383; "every idle word," 389; on eternal life, 416; on marriage, 419; millennial reign of, 430–32; called apostles, 435; on John, 438; and Peter, 439–40; on faith, 452; on light, 452–53; was major message of Paul, 462–64; on Israel, 513; appeared to branches of Israel, 550–51; will appear to Israel, 572; will lead armies of Israel, 572–73

Jews: rejected New Testament, 4, 21, 549–50; deserted Old Testament, 28; as Judah's family, 30–32; and the Promised Land, 32; Matthew wrote to the, 74; rejected Jesus Christ, 205, 237; Jesus Christ is the Anointed One of the, 225; Christ will appear to the, 229; killing of the, 431; gathering of the, 520; are descendants of Judah, 540; scattering of the, 551–52; to return to their land, 555–56; enemies seek to destroy the, 556–57

Job (Bible figure): on the resurrection, 53; on premortal life, 307, 312

Job, Book of. *See* Book of Job

Joel, book of, 60, 507

John: wrote to the Saints, 74; and the Book of Revelation, 76; translation of, 79–80, 94, 441–42, 447–48; on other sheep, 193; on "the word," 219; restored priesthood keys, 228, 561; on the Mount of Transfiguration, 234; on the resurrection, 247; on Christ's last week, 248; on premortal life, 307–8; on baptism, 331; on the dead, 366; on Nicodemus, 370; on degrees of glory, 412; background of, 435–36; uniqueness of, 437–38; on Christ's resurrection, 442–44; some of the writings of, 444–47; foreordination of, 445; continuing mission of, 447–48; teachings of, 448–50

John, epistles of. *See* First Epistle General of John; Second Epistle General of John; Third Epistle General of John

John, gospel of. *See* Gospel According to St. John
John the Baptist, 81, 228, 234, 356, 435, 508
Johnson, Luke S., 144
Johnson, Lyman E., 144
Jokshan, 527
Jonah, book of, 61
Joseph (Bible prophet): book of, 9; as birthright son, 51; stick of, 58, 112; prophesied of Joseph Smith, 492–93, 502–3; Lehi was a descendant of, 502, 546; Indians are descendants of, 515, 573; and the tribes of Israel, 527
Joseph of Arimathaea, 246
Josephites, 121
Joseph Smith Translation. *See* Bible (Joseph Smith Translation)
Joshua, Book of, 48
Judah: captivity and return of, 50, 519, 544–45; stick of, 58, 192; son of Leah, 527; descendants of, 540; war against, 565–66
Judas Iscariot, 243, 244, 439
Jude, on the war in heaven, 323
Jude, Epistle of, 98
Judges, Book of, 48–49
Judgment: and reading the scriptures, 14–15, 17–18, 25; Book of Mormon convinces of the, 125; resurrection as, 273; final, 293, 370, 389–91; Catholic view of, 431; and the light of Christ, 453; Paul on the, 472; and Jesus Christ as judge, 575
Justice, 216, 231, 311, 331–34
Justification, 335–36, 346

Keturah, 527
Keys, priesthood, 228–29, 517, 561, 562–63
Kimball, Heber C., 144; on the spirit world, 405
Kimball, Spencer W.: on scripture study, 3, 5–6, 15, 153; on knowing the patriarchs and prophets, 26; on the Bible, 64, 104; on continuous revelation, 154; on the resurrection, 266, 292, 388; on mourning, 286; on degrees of glory, 296–97; on judgment, 298, 299; on Lamanites, 531

Kingdom of God, 469–70
King James Version. *See* Bible (King James Version)
Kings, First and Second books of, 50–51
Kirtland, Ohio, 143
Kirtland Temple, 63, 134, 228–29, 517
Knowledge. *See* Education

Lamanites, 120, 122, 125, 193, 531, 547. *See also* Native Americans
Lamentations of Jeremiah, 57
Laser beams, 451–55
Latter days, 227–28
Law(s), 331–32; of birthright, 32; of primogeniture, 32
Lawsuits, 470
Lazarus, 236
Leah, 527
Learning. *See* Education
Lectures on Faith, 137, 138
Lee, Harold B.: on scripture study, 18; on the scriptures, 153; on spirit and body, 384
Lehi: was of Manasseh, 51; was contemporary of Jeremiah, 56; and the Book of Mormon, 109; knew Egyptian, 112; as engraver, 113; on agency, 311–12; on the Fall, 324; on opposition, 329; on Joseph Smith, 502; left land of Israel, 506; descendants of, 545–46, 554–55
Lemuelites, 121
Levi, 527
Levites, 545
Leviticus, 47
Lewis, T.B., on the grandest principle, 147
Light, 407, 451–54
Lincoln, Abraham, on the Bible, 26–27
Lineage, meaning of term, 528–29
Lost Books, of the Bible, 51
Lost Tribes. *See* Ten Tribes
Love, 490–91
Lucifer. *See* Satan
Luke: wrote to the Greeks, 74; on the birth of Christ, 218, 253–54
Luke, gospel of, 81–83
Lund, Gerald N.: "Salvation: By Grace or by Works," 335; on grace, 351

Macedonia, 461
Magazines, Church, 23
Malachi, 365; book of, 63, 505, 562
Manasseh, 51
Manuals, 14, 20
Maps (Bible), 44
Mark: wrote to the Gentiles, 74; on repentance, 356; on the soul, 427; and Paul, 460
Mark, gospel of, 80–81
Marriage, celestial, 296, 365, 417–19, 424–25, 467
Marsh, Thomas B., 144
Martha, 236
Mary (mother of Jesus), 13, 237, 253, 266, 437, 548
Mary (sister of Martha), 236
Mary (wife of Cleophas), 437
Mary Magdalene, 247, 248, 401, 437
Matthew: wrote to the Jews, 74; on Christ's entry into Jerusalem, 236–37, 238; on the resurrection, 248; on the soul, 427
Matthew, gospel of, 76–80
Matthews, Robert J.: on Paul, 485; on authority of Joseph Smith, 491
Maxwell, Neal A.: on venerating Joseph Smith, 488; on calling of Joseph Smith, 490
McConkie, Bruce R.: on withholding of scriptures, 8; in scripture video, 23, 24; on King James Version, 36; on the Topical Guide, 41; on the Joseph Smith Translation, 70–71; on the four gospels, 74; on the New Testament, 104–5; on importance of scriptures, 152–53; on future revelation, 156, 157; on the atonement, 261; on the resurrection, 265, 268; on degrees of glory, 273; on mortal probation, 284; on death, 286; on exaltation, 300; on the "Eternal Spring," 302; "What Think Ye of Salvation by Grace?" 335; on salvation by grace, 335–36, 344–45; on grace and works, 349–50
McKay, David O.: organized BYU wards, 422; on patriarchal blessings, 528

McKenzie, David, on the grandest principle, 147
McLellin, William E., 144
Medan, 527
Mediation and Atonement (Taylor), 265
Melchizedek, 94, 230
Melchizedek Priesthood, 443
Memory, 10, 299, 380–81, 402–3
Mercy, 231, 311, 371
Micah, book of, 61
Michael, 98, 281, 282, 323. *See also* Adam
Midian, 527
Millennium, 430–32
Miracles, 221
Missionary work, 471, 513–14, 566–67
Missouri, 431, 443–44, 516, 574
Monson, Thomas S., 23
Moral agency. *See* Agency
Mormon: abridged plates, 110, 113, 189; as an engraver, 115, 116, 117, 142–43, 187–88, 211; caution of, 118–19; is not author of Book of Mormon, 141–42; on the Bible, 181; testified of Jesus Christ, 188; on the atonement, 227; on repentance, 347–48; on Israel, 512–13
Moroni: speaks to our day, 10; quoted Joel, 60; delivered the plates of Mormon, 113–14; as an engraver, 115, 116, 117, 142–43, 187–89; warning of, 119; on the Bible and the Book of Mormon, 123–24; on the Bible, 124, 211; is not author of Book of Mormon, 142; promise of, 184, 196, 198, 211; testified of Jesus Christ, 188–89; resurrected body of, 268; on faith, 452; light of, 454; on Joseph Smith, 487; on Israel, 504–7; quoted Isaiah, 505, 556
Mortal probation, 282–85, 327–30, 384–91, 398–99, 423–32
Moses (Bible prophet): as *the* Prophet, 48; on divorce, 78–79; was translated, 94; asked God His name, 214; Jesus appeared to, 217; restored priesthood keys, 228; "Thou shalt love the Lord," 241–42; on premortal life, 307

Moses, book of (Pearl of Great Price), 45, 356
Moses, Fifth Book of, Called Deuteronomy, 47–48, 78–79
Moses, First Book of, Called Genesis, 45–46
Moses, Fourth Book of, Called Numbers, 47
Moses, law of, 546–47
Moses, Second Book of, Called Exodus, 46–47
Moses, Third Book of, Called Leviticus, 47
Mount of Olives, 238, 242, 243
Mount of Transfiguration, 234, 437
Mourning, 286
Moyle, Henry D., on guarding our agency, 317
Mulek, 121, 193, 506, 545

Nahum, book of, 61
Naisbitt, Henry W., on the grandest principle, 147
Naomi, 49
Naphtali, 219–20, 527, 549
Nathan, 50, 51
Nathaniel, 234
Native Americans, 193, 521, 573. *See also* Lamanites
Nauvoo, Illinois, 503, 517
Nauvoo Temple, 564
Nazareth, 219–20, 237
Nebuchadnezzar, 57, 506, 562
Nehemiah, Book of, 52
Nephi: on Joseph of Egypt, 9; as an example of faith, 11; likened the scriptures, 11–12, 132; pondered, 13; farewell of, 17–18; on the Bible, 69; testified of Jesus Christ, 110–11, 188; as engraver, 113, 114, 115, 116, 118, 142–43, 187–88, 211; on the Book of Mormon, 181; testified of the Old Testament, 211; had vision of Christ's life, 256, 548; on spirits, 384; had vision of John, 445, 446; "esteemeth all flesh in one," 533; on the Jews, 540
Nephites, 55, 120, 122, 193, 247, 362
Nero, 506
Neum, 112, 120
New Jerusalem, 230, 516, 573–74

New Testament: rejection of the, 4, 21; taking away of the, 4–5; Old Testament quotations in the, 43, 72; Deuteronomy quoted in the, 47–48; why use King James Version of the, 66–67; "GR" footnotes in the, 67–68; LDS edition of the, 67–73; "HEB" footnotes in the, 68; "IE" footnotes in the, 68–69; "JST" footnotes in the, 69–71; cross-references in the, 71; "OR" footnotes in the, 71; and the Bible Dictionary, 71–72; maps in the, 72–73; Gospels in the, 73–74; Pauline Epistles in the, 75; General Epistles in the, 75–76; Matthew selections from the, 76–80; Mark selections from the, 80–81; Luke selections from the, 81–83; John selections from the, 83–84; Acts selections from the, 84–85; Romans selections from the, 85–86; Corinthians selections from the, 86–88; Galatians selections from the, 88; Ephesians selections from the, 88–89; Philippians selections from the, 89–90; Colossians selections from the, 90; Thessalonians selections from the, 90–91; Timothy selections from the, 91–92; Titus selections from the, 92–93; Hebrews selections from the, 93–95; James selections from the, 95–96; Peter selections from the, 96–97; epistles of John selections from the, 97–98; Jude selections from the, 98; book of Revelation selections from the, 98–103; testimonies of the, 103–5; and the Doctrine and Covenants, 138; Bible Dictionary references to the, 171–78; Jesus Christ is the Anointed One of the, 225; on work for the dead, 366; on spirits, 376; on degrees of glory, 412; on Paul, 456; on the Restoration, 552. *See also individual books*
Nibley, Hugh, parable by, 130–31
Nicodemus, 360, 370
Noah, 217
Noble and great ones, 488–90
Numbers, book of, 47

Obadiah, book of, 61
Obedience, 332, 346, 490–91
Old Testament: as a witness of Jesus Christ, 26, 203–10; reasons to read the, 26–28; statements of leaders about the, 26–28; excuses for not reading the, 28; how to understand the, 29; do's and don'ts of studying the, 29–30; pronunciation of names in the, 29–30; as a history of families, 30–32; background to the, 30–35; customs and practices in the, 32–35; LDS edition of the, 35–44; New Testament quotations from the, 43, 72; books of the, 44–63; Jesus Christ is God (Jehovah) of the, 46–47, 216, 217–18, 547–48; capitalization in the, 49; testimonies pertaining to the, 63–65; and the Doctrine and Covenants, 138; Bible Dictionary references to the, 159–71; testifies of Jesus Christ, 205–7; titles of Jesus Christ in the, 206–7; teaches the gospel of Jesus Christ, 207–10; witness for other scriptures, 210–12; Jesus is the Anointed One of the, 216; on spirits, 376; was quoted by Moroni, 505; House of Israel in the, 539–40; on the Restoration, 552. *See also individual books*
Olive tree allegory, 532, 544, 554
Omni, 114, 115
Ordinances, 257, 354, 364–68
Original sin, 343
Outer darkness, 414

Packer, Boyd K.: in scripture video, 23; on importance of scriptures, 152; on death, 285
Page, Hiram, 518
Page, John E., 563
Paradise, 289
Passover, 243, 245, 438
Patmos, 437–38, 442–43, 447, 516
Patriarchal blessings, 526, 528–29
Patriarchal order, 32
Patten, David W., 144
Paul: and baptism for the dead, 87, 367, 471; on witnesses, 191; on premortal life, 307; "through a glass darkly," 330, 380; on justification, 346; on grace, 350–51, 468–69; on the Holy Ghost, 360; on sanctification, 361; on death, 372–73; on degrees of glory, 412, 417; on immortality, 417; visited Ephesus, 436; on power of the Spirit, 453; physical description of, 455; characteristics of, 455–56; vision of, 458; missionary journeys of, 460–61; message of, 462–64; on the resurrection, 463–64; on the Father and the Son, 465–66; on faith, 467; on marriage, 467; on sacrament, 467–68; on healing of the sick, 468; on the kingdom of God, 469–70; on unity, 469–70; on lawsuits, 470; on Satan, 470; on sexual impurity, 470; on vengeance, 470; on universal gospel, 470–71; on agency, 471; on the apostasy, 471; on courage, 471; on missionary work, 471; on knowledge, 471–72; on charity, 472; on judgment, 472; on testimony, 472; on Israel, 533
Pauline Epistles, 75, 472–80. *See also individual epistles*
Peace, 220–21
Pearl of Great Price: is incomplete, 9; book of Moses in the, 45; book of Abraham in the, 46; and the Doctrine and Covenants, 138; on spirits, 376–77
Pentateuch, 45
Perdition, sons of, 264, 370–71, 414
Persecution, 493–94
Persia, 52, 506, 544
Perth, Australia, 536
Peter: testimony of, 82–83; on prophecy, 142, 538; on Jesus Christ, 186–87; restored priesthood keys, 228, 561; on the Mount of Transfiguration, 234; testified of Christ, 234; on Christ in the spirit world, 246–47; resurrected body of, 268; on the war in heaven, 323; on repentance, 356; on baptism, 361; priesthood of, 365; on the dead, 366; loved Jesus, 439–40; and Paul, 459

Peter, epistles of. *See* First Epistle General of Peter; Second Epistle General of Peter
Petersen, Mark E., "We Believe in Being Honest," 335
Pharisees, 238, 241–42, 243, 360, 370, 457–58
Phelps, William W., 136, 143; on Joseph Smith's mission, 491
Philemon. *See* Epistle of Paul to Philemon
Philippians. *See* Epistle of Paul the Apostle to the Philippians
Photography, 423
Physical body. *See* Body, physical
Pilate, 244
Pinegar, Rex D., on likening the scriptures, 145
Plan of progression: and premortal life, 88, 179, 189, 213–14, 224, 232, 250–52, 279–82, 305–8, 309–12, 322–26, 397–98, 466; and the spirit world, 246–47, 288–91, 387–88, 393, 399–409; and death, 253, 285–88, 369–73; and mortal probation, 282–85, 323–432, 327–30, 384–91, 398–99; and the resurrection, 291–93, 291–94; and degrees of glory, 294–97, 466; and the final judgment, 297–300; and exaltation, 300–302; and the Garden of Eden, 322–26; and justice and mercy, 331–34. *See also* Agency; Jesus Christ, atonement of; Jesus Christ, resurrection of
Plants, resurrection of, 265
Plates. *See* Book of Mormon, plates of the
Plates of brass, 56, 112–13, 120, 540
Political institutions, 317
Polygamy, 32–33, 336
Pondering, 13, 197–98
Pontius Pilate, 244
Postmortal world. *See* Spirit world
Powerhouse (analogy), 346
Pratt, Orson, 137, 144
Pratt, Parley P., 144; on the Book of Mormon, 116–17; on the spirit world, 289, 290, 401
Prayer, 381–82, 429

Predestination, 88, 287–88
Premortal life, 279–82, 305–8, 322–26, 397–98; in Paul's teachings, 88; Joseph Smith's teachings about, 189; Jesus Christ in, 213–14, 224, 232, 250–52; Paul's teachings about, 466. *See also* Veil, of forgetfulness
Priesthood: false, 91; power of the, 93; restoration of keys of the, 228–29; and Jesus Christ, 230; and blacks, 336; ordinances require, 354; of Peter, 365; and temple ordinances, 419; restoration of the Aaronic, 435, 508, 513; restoration of the Melchizedek, 443; of Joseph Smith, 491; keys of the, 561–63
Primogeniture, law of, 32
Prison, spirit, 289–90
Proclamation, of 1845, 520–24
Procreation, 322–23, 372, 424–25
Promised land, 32, 542
Pronunciation, of scripture names, 29–30, 130
Prophecy, 508–9
Prophets, 310–11, 488, 492
Protestant churches, 319, 336, 337, 421, 430
Proverbs, book of, 54
Provo Daily Herald, 422
Psalms, 53–54
Punishment, 332, 414
Purification procedures (Biblical), 34
Purim, feast of, 53

Quincy, Josiah, on Joseph Smith, 503
Qumran, 53

Rachel, 527
Radio (analogy), 408
Rationalization, 426
Reagan, Ronald: on the Bible, 27
Remembering. *See* Memory
Repentance, 299–300, 346, 355–58, 361, 362, 370, 371, 429–30
Restitution, 84–85, 357
Restoration, 552–54, 560–61
Resurrection: and blood, 87; Paul's teachings about, 89; of Jesus Christ, 99, 247–48;

Jesus Christ is first fruits of, 226; and the atonement, 261–63; questions about, 263–64; answers to questions about, 264–74; of animals and plants, 265, 291–92; first general, 267–68, 268–69, 292–93; second general, 268–69, 292–93; and degrees of glory, 270–72, 295; infinite, 287; and immortality, 301, 416, 417; and mortal probation, 329; and the physical body, 383–84; Paul's message of the, 463–64
Reuben, 51, 527
Revelation: continuous, 153–55, 191; in the future, 156–57
Revelation of St. John the Divine, 76, 98–103, 438, 520, 569
Revelators, 493
Revolutionary War, 509–10
Reynolds, George, on the grandest principle, 147
Rigdon, Sidney, 99, 412, 524
Roberts, B.H., on the grandest principle, 464
Rochester, New York, 514
Romans. *See* Epistle of Paul the Apostle to the Romans
Rome, 461, 506, 517–18, 551, 563
Romney, Marion G.: on the Bible, 104; on the Book of Mormon, 108; on eternal life, 301; on guarding our agency, 317; on Joseph Smith, 493
Roundy, Jerry, on obedience of Joseph Smith, 490
Russians, 503
Ruth, Book of, 49

Sabbath observance, 34, 84, 341
Sacrament, 225, 243, 467–68
Sadducees, 241, 418
Salvation, 335–36, 417
Samaritans, 82, 234
Samuel, First and Second, 49–50
Samuel the Lamanite, 248, 267, 426
Sanctification, 361, 370, 429
Sanhedrin, 244, 245
Sarah, 527
Satan: as an angel of light, 87; sought to destroy agency, 252, 312–13, 316, 328, 386, 401, 426; tempted Adam and Eve, 253; in council in heaven, 281; was cast out of heaven, 314; tried to thwart Christ, 315; and the war in heaven, 323; in the Garden of Eden, 324–25; and the sons of perdition, 414; tries to thwart our destiny, 423; and procreation, 424–25; and the Word of Wisdom, 427; denies power of prophecy, 428; belittles faith, 429; denies the Holy Ghost, 430; attacks millennial preparation, 430–31; challenging, 438; Paul taught existence of, 470
Saul (Bible king), 50, 505
Saul of Tarsus. *See* Paul
Scerva, 468
Scriptures: study of the, 3, 6–7, 9–16, 18, 19–20, 21–22, 108, 204; receiving additional, 3–4, 5, 21, 109, 156, 157, 191; withholding of the, 8; are incomplete, 8–9; living the, 10–13, 132; pondering the, 13, 197–98; marking the, 13–14, 38–39, 44, 68, 69, 71, 128, 145; Church program for study of the, 14, 20–21, 22–23; teaching the, 14; and final judgment, 14–15, 17–18, 25; as a guide, 17; various editions of the, 22; LDS editions of the, 23–24, 35–44; importance of the, 152–53; and the law of witnesses, 180–82, 191, 538–39; Holy Ghost testifies of the, 183–85; testify of Jesus Christ, 204–5; Old Testament witnesses for other, 210–12; are declared irrelevant today, 316–17. *See also individual scriptures*
Sea of Galilee, 435, 439
Sea of Tiberias, 248, 435
Sealing power, 365, 418
Seaton, N.E., 514
Second Book of Chronicles, 51–52
Second Coming. *See* Jesus Christ, second coming of
Second Epistle General of John, 97–98
Second Epistle General of Peter, 96–97

Second Epistle of Paul the Apostle to the Corinthians, 87–88, 475, 482
Second Epistle of Paul the Apostle to the Thessalonians, 91, 477, 483
Second Epistle of Paul the Apostle to Timothy, 92, 478, 483–84
Second estate. *See* Mortal probation
Second resurrection. *See* Resurrection, second general
Seeing, 406–7
Seers, 492–93
Semites, 30–32
Sermon on the Mount, 76–77
Service, 258–60
Seven seals (symbol), 100
Shakespeare, William, "a poor player," 330
Shechem, Samaria, 505
Shem, 31
Shuah, 527
Shunary, Jonathan, 514
Sight, 408
Simeon, 527
Simon of Cyrene, 245
Sins, 357
Smith, George Albert, on celestial glory, 296
Smith, Hyrum, on Joseph Smith, 492
Smith, Hyrum M., on the resurrection, 264, 291
Smith, Joseph: and the New Testament, 4, 103; and the Book of Mormon, 15, 110, 113–14, 141, 182; on the Bible, 27; used the King James Version, 37; on the Song of Solomon, 55; Joel quoted to, 60; on the resurrection, 87, 269, 293, 383; on the book of Revelation, 99; was "in the spirit," 99; and the Doctrine and Covenants, 134, 142–43; on the preface to the Doctrine and Covenants, 136; first vision of, 179, 228, 235, 336; and premortal life, 189, 306; on premortal intelligences, 280, 371, 379–80, 397; on obtaining a body, 283; on mourning, 286; on Godhood, 302; on agency, 309–10; on Michael, 323; on the Godhead, 359; and Martin Van Buren, 359, 360, 421–22, 429; on the Holy Ghost, 359–60, 421–22, 429; authority restored to, 365, 418, 491, 508, 517, 561–63; on the spirit world, 387, 404; on spirit, 398; receives vision of degrees of glory, 412–13; and the Wentworth letter, 422, 507–8; received Aaronic Priesthood, 435; asked about John's condition, 441; Three Nephites appeared to, 443; led Zion's Camp, 443–44; and Moroni, 454, 487, 507–8, 560–61; on Paul, 455–56; is not Jesus Christ, 487–88; attributes of, 488–89; foreordination of, 489–90, 501–3, 524, 561; as an example of obedience and love, 490–91; as prophet, seer and revelator, 491–93; persecution of, 493–94; tributes to, 494–96; background of, 501–4; taught by Moroni about Israel, 504–7; and the Seaton letter, 514–16; and the Letter to the Elders, 516; High Council discussion of, 516–19; given keys to gathering, 517; and the Proclamation of 1845, 520–24; testified of Jesus Christ, 524; as a pure Ephraimite, 531–32; teachings about Israel by, 540–75; as an instrument in the Restoration, 560–61; on Zion, 576
Smith, Joseph F.: scriptures belonging to, 24; "Vision of the Redemption of the Dead," 83, 96, 247; on the New Testament, 104; on the Doctrine and Covenants, 137–38; on the resurrection, 264, 266, 270, 291, 292, 293; on the resurrection of children, 270, 293; on degrees of glory, 272; on premortal life, 280, 281, 398; on obtaining a body, 283; on man's dual nature, 283–84, 385, 399; on death, 285; on the spirit world, 288–89; on degrees of glory, 295; on judgment, 297; on memory, 299, 381, 402–3; on spirits, 388, 404; on the grandest principle, 464
Smith, Joseph Fielding: on reading the scriptures, 6; on withholding of scriptures, 8; on the Doctrine and Covenants, 8–9, 134, 139–40; on Jesus as Jehovah, 47; on

future revelation, 156; on the resurrection, 265, 292, 293; on the resurrection of children, 270, 293; on premortal intelligences, 280–81, 378; on mortal probation, 284; on the doctrine of translation, 287; on eternal life, 301; on descendants of Abraham, 530–31; on Gentiles, 532; on adoption into Israel, 532–33; on Ephraimites, 533; on Zion, 574
Smith, William, 144
Smoking, 427
Snow, Lorenzo: on trials, 283; on Godhood, 301, 302, 391
Socialism, 316
Solomon, 50, 505
Song of Solomon, 55
Southern States Mission, 421
Sower, parable of the, 79
Spain, 461–62
Spirit prison, 289–90
Spirits, 280–81, 283–84, 287, 306, 327, 371, 374–94. *See also* Intelligences, premortal
Spiritual death. *See* Death, spiritual
Spirit world, 232, 246–47, 288–91, 387–88, 393, 396–97, 399–409
Stephen, 458
Strong, James: *The Exhaustive Concordance of the Bible,* 37, 337, 536
Symbols (Biblical), 34–35
Syria, 459–60

Talmage, James E.: on blighting of the fig tree, 239; on degrees of glory, 271, 295; on the resurrection, 272–73; on trials, 284; on faith and belief, 355
Tanner, N. Eldon, 144
Tarsus, 457
Taylor, John: on the resurrection, 87, 265–66, 269, 291, 292, 293, 388; on continuous revelation, 155; on obtaining a body, 283, 284, 385; on judgment, 298–99; on Godhood, 302, 391; on agency, 319; on our words, 389–90; on Joseph Smith, 495–96
Teaching, 14, 452–54
Tel Aviv, Jerusalem, 454

Telestial glory, 271, 294, 413–14, 417
Television (analogy), 408
Temple marriage. *See* Marriage, celestial
Temple: Christ cleanses the, 239, 240; ordinances of the, 257, 289–90, 364–68, 419, 564, 566–67; in Jerusalem, 569–71
Temporal death. *See* Death, physical
Ten Tribes, 84, 99, 193–94, 443, 505–6
Terrestrial glory, 271, 294, 413, 417
Testimony, 360, 472
Thessalonians, 90–91, 477, 483
Third Epistle General of John, 98
Thomas, 248, 439
Thoughts, 381–83, 389–91
Three degrees of glory. *See* Degrees of glory
Three Nephites, 94, 116, 440–41, 443
Times and Seasons, 519
Timothy, 91–92, 477–78, 480, 483–84
Tithing, 364
Titus (Roman military leader), 506
Titus, book of. *See* Epistle of Paul to Titus
Tobacco, 427
Tolstoy, Leo, 494–95
Topical Guide (Bible), 14, 22, 34, 35; explanation of the, 40–41; Doctrine and Covenants entries in the, 149–50; reference to Jesus Christ in the, 205–7; references to resurrection in the, 262, 291; references to premortal life in the, 270, 397; references to mortal probation in the, 282; references to death in the, 285; references to spirit world in the, 288; references to degrees of glory in the, 294; references to judgment in the, 297; references to eternal life in the, 300
Torah, 4, 21, 45
Translation, doctrine of, 79–80, 94, 287, 441–42, 447–48
Tree of knowledge, 314
Tree of life, 256
Trials, 283–84, 329
Truth, 538–39

United Nations, 513
Unity, 469–70
Uriah, 50

Urim and Thummim, 382
Uzzah, 50

Van Buren, Martin, 359, 360, 421–22, 429
Van Doren, Mark, on memory, 380
Veil, of forgetfulness, 179, 284, 290, 310, 328, 380, 381, 385, 386, 388, 398, 402, 409
Vengeance, 470
Vespasian, 506
Vicarious work, 365–67
Video, on the scriptures, 23
"Vision of the Redemption of the Dead," 83, 96, 247

War in heaven, 281, 323, 328, 386
Washing, of feet, 243
Wentworth, John, 422, 507
White, Andrew, 494–95
Whitmer, David, 183
Whitmer, John, 136
Whitney, Orson F.: on death, 285; on the grandest principle, 464
Widtsoe, John A.: on the Doctrine and Covenants, 142; on prophets, 492
Wilkinson, Ernest L., 347, 422
Witnesses: principle of, 88; Book of Mormon as part of system of, 123–24, 179; to the Doctrine and Covenants, 143–44; scriptures as, 180–82, 191, 210–12, 538–39; of the Book of Mormon, 182–83; of the resurrection, 248; of the atonement, 262
Wives, in the Old Testament, 33
Women: in the Book of Mormon, 128; and the priesthood, 336
Woodruff, Wilford: on the Bible, 27; on the Doctrine and Covenants, 134; on continuous revelation, 155; on degrees of glory, 272, 295; on celestial glory, 296; on eternal progression, 302; on destiny of Israel, 575–76
Word of Wisdom, 317–18, 364, 386, 427
Works. *See* Grace and works

Young, Brigham: on the Bible, 27–28, 29, 59, 203–4, 205, 212; on the New Testament, 103–4; on the Book of Mormon, 124–25, 181, 212; on living the scriptures, 132, 484–85; as a witness to the Doctrine and Covenants, 144; on the resurrection, 266, 267; on obtaining a body, 283; on trials, 283, 284; on veil of forgetfulness, 284, 385, 398; on death, 285; on the spirit world, 288, 289–90, 387–88, 393, 400, 401, 403–4; on judgment, 298, 390; on Godhood, 302, 391; on eternal life, 302–3; on body and spirit, 385–86; on eternal learning, 393–94; on man's dual nature, 399; on spirits, 406, 408, 409; on rationalizing, 426; on not challenging Satan, 438; on Joseph Smith's foreordination, 490, 503, 561; on Joseph Smith's spiritual power, 495; on the gathering of Israel, 531; on Joseph Smith as a pure Ephraimite, 531; on adoption into Israel, 532

Zacharias, 435
Zadok, 57
Zarahemla, 545; people of, 121, 122
Zebulon, 549
Zebulum, 527
Zebulun, 219–20
Zechariah, book of, 62–63, 229, 237
Zedekiah, 51, 121, 193, 506, 548
Zeezrom, 382
Zenock, 112, 120
Zenos, 112, 120; allegory of, 544
Zephaniah, book of, 62
Zilpah, 527
Zimran, 527
Zion, 230, 515, 519, 564, 573–74
Zionism, 501, 518
Zion's Camp, 443–44
Zoram, 506, 545